Contemporary Theatre, Film and Television

ISSN 0749-064X

Contemporary Theatre, Film and Television

A Biographical Guide Featuring Performers, Directors, Writers, Producers, Designers, Managers, Choreographers, Technicians, Composers, Executives, Dancers, and Critics in the United States, Canada, Great Britain and the World

Thomas Riggs, Editor

Volume 111

GALE
CENGAGE Learning

Detroit • New York • San Francisco • New Haven, Conn • Waterville, Maine • London

Contents

Preface

Provides Broad, Single-Source Coverage in the Entertainment Field

Contemporary Theatre, Film and Television (*CTFT*) is a biographical reference series designed to provide students, educators, researchers, librarians, and general readers with information on a wide range of entertainment figures. Unlike single-volume reference works that focus on a limited number of artists or on a specific segment of the entertainment field, *CTFT* is an ongoing publication that includes entries on individuals active in the theatre, film, and television industries. Before the publication of *CTFT*, information-seekers had no choice but to consult several different sources in order to locate the in-depth biographical and credit data that makes *CTFT*'s one-stop coverage the most comprehensive available about the lives and work of performing arts professionals.

Scope

CTFT covers not only performers, directors, writers, and producers, but also behind-the-scenes specialists such as designers, managers, choreographers, technicians, composers, executives, dancers, and critics from the United States, Canada, Great Britain, and the world. With 197 entries in *CTFT 111*, the series now provides biographies on approximately 28,827 people involved in all aspects of theatre, film, and television.

CTFT gives primary emphasis to people who are currently active. New entries are prepared on major stars as well as those who are just beginning to win acclaim for their work. *CTFT* also includes entries on personalities who have died but whose work commands lasting interest.

Compilation Methods

CTFT editors identify candidates for inclusion in the series by consulting biographical dictionaries, industry directories, entertainment annuals, trade and general interest periodicals, newspapers, and online databases. Additionally, the editors of *CTFT* maintain regular contact with industry advisors and professionals who routinely suggest new candidates for inclusion in the series. Entries are compiled from published biographical sources which are believed to be reliable, but have not been verified for this edition by the listee or their agents.

Revised Entries

To ensure *CTFT*'s timeliness and comprehensiveness, entries from previous volumes, as well as from Gale's *Who's Who in the Theatre*, are updated for individuals who have been active enough to require revision of their earlier biographies. Such individuals will merit revised entries as often as there is substantial new information to provide. Obituary notices for deceased entertainment personalities already listed in *CTFT* are also published.

Accessible Format Makes Data Easy to Locate

CTFT entries, modeled after those in Gale's highly regarded *Contemporary Authors* series, are written in a clear, readable style designed to help users focus quickly on specific facts. The following is a summary of the information found in *CTFT* sketches:

- *ENTRY HEADING:* the form of the name by which the listee is best known.

- *PERSONAL:* full or original name; dates and places of birth and death; family data; colleges attended, degrees earned, and professional training; political and religious affiliations when known; avocational interests.

- *ADDRESSES:* home, office, agent, publicist and/or manager addresses.

- *CAREER:* tagline indicating principal areas of entertainment work; resume of career positions and other vocational achievements; military service.

- *MEMBER:* memberships and offices held in professional, union, civic, and social organizations.

- *AWARDS, HONORS:* theatre, film, and television awards and nominations; literary and civic awards; honorary degrees.

- *CREDITS:* comprehensive title-by-title listings of theatre, film, and television appearance and work credits, including roles and production data as well as debut and genre information.

- *RECORDINGS:* album, single song, video, and taped reading releases; recording labels and dates when available.

- *WRITINGS:* title-by-title listing of plays, screenplays, scripts, and musical compositions along with production information; books, including autobiographies, and other publications.

- *ADAPTATIONS:* a list of films, plays, and other media which have been adapted from the listee's work.

- *OTHER SOURCES:* books, periodicals, and internet sites where interviews or feature stories can be found.

Access Thousands of Entries Using *CTFT*'s Cumulative Index

Each volume of *CTFT* contains a cumulative index to the entire series. As an added feature, this index also includes references to all seventeen editions of *Who's Who in the Theatre* and to the four-volume compilation *Who Was Who in the Theatre.*

Available in Electronic Format

Online. Recent volumes of *CTFT* are available online as part of the Gale Biographies (GALBIO) database accessible through LEXIS-NEXIS. For more information, contact LEXIS-NEXIS, P.O. Box 933, Dayton, OH 45401-0933; phone (937) 865-6800, toll-free: 800-543-6862.

Suggestions Are Welcome

Contemporary Theatre, Film and Television is intended to serve as a useful reference tool for a wide audience, so comments about any aspect of this work are encouraged. Suggestions of entertainment professionals to include in future volumes are also welcome. Send comments and suggestions to: The Editor, *Contemporary Theatre, Film and Television,* Gale, 27500 Drake Rd., Farmington Hills, MI 48331-3535; or call toll-free at 1-800-877-GALE.

Contemporary Theatre, Film and Television

ADEFARASIN, Remi 1948–

PERSONAL

Born in 1948, in London, England.

Addresses: *Agent*—Casarotto Marsh Ltd., Waverly House, 7–12 Noel St., London W1F 7GQ, England.

Career: Cinematographer.

Member: British Society of Cinematographers.

Awards, Honors: Television Award nomination, best film cameraman, British Academy of Film and Television Arts, 1989, for *Christabel;* Television Award nomination, best film/video photography (fiction), British Academy of Film and Television Arts, 1993, for *Screen Two;* Academy Award nomination, best cinematography, American Society of Cinematographers nomination, outstanding achievement in cinematography in theatrical release, Film Award, best cinematography, British Academy of Film and Television Arts, Best Cinematography Award, British Society of Cinematographers, Chicago Film Critics Association Award nomination, best cinematography, Chlotrudis Award nomination, best cinematography, Golden Frog Award, Camerimage, 1999, all for *Elizabeth;* Golden Frog Award nomination, Camerimage, 2000, for *Onegin;* Emmy Award nomination, outstanding cinematography for a miniseries or a movie, 2002, for *Band of Brothers;* Emmy Award nomination, outstanding cinematography for a miniseries or movie, 2010, for *The Pacific.*

CREDITS

Film Cinematographer:
Truly Madly Deeply, 1990.
The Hummingbird Tree, BBC Enterprises, 1992.
Captives, Miramax, 1994.
Midnight Movie, 1994.
(Second unit) *The English Patient,* Miramax, 1995.
Hollow Reed (also known as *Believe Me*), Cinepix, 1996.
Sliding Doors, Miramax, 1998.
Elizabeth (also known as *Elizabeth: The Virgin Queen*), Gramercy, 1998.
Onegin, Samuel Goldwyn Films, 1999.
The House of Mirth, Sony Pictures Classics, 2000.
About a Boy, Universal, 2002.
Unconditional Love, New Line Cinema, 2002.
The One and Only, Pathe, 2002.
Johnny English, Universal, 2003.
The Haunted Mansion (also known as *Disney's "The Haunted Mansion"*), Buena Vista, 2003.
In Good Company, Universal, 2004.
Match Point, DreamWorks, 2005.
Scoop, Focus Features, 2006.
Amazing Grace, Samuel Goldwyn Films, 2006.
Elizabeth: The Golden Age (also known as *Elizabeth: Golden Age*), Universal, 2007.
Fred Claus, Warner Bros., 2007.
Cemetery Junction, Sony, 2010.
Little Fockers (also known as *Meet the Parents: Little Fockers*), Universal, 2010.

Film Work; Other:
Camera operator, *Match Point,* 2005.

Film Appearances:
Himself, *Cinematographer Style* (documentary), 2006.

Television Assistant Camera; Series:
The Borderers, BBC, 1968.
Roads to Freedom, BBC, 1970.
(Uncredited) *Five–Minute Films,* 1982.

Television Cinematographer; Series:
The British Greats, 1980.
Jury, BBC, 1983.

Screenplay, Granada Television, 1986–92.
Screen Two, BBC, 1988–92.
Chef!, BBC, 1993.
The Fast Show (also known as *Brilliant!*), BBC, 1994.
Cold Lazarus, 1996.

Television Assistant Camera; Miniseries:
The Runaway Summer, 1971.
Moll Flanders, PBS, 1975.

Television Camera Operator; Miniseries:
Fish, 1973.

Television Cinematographer; Miniseries:
(Great Britain) *The Files on Jill Hatch,* PBS, 1983.
The December Rose, BBC and PBS, 1986.
Christabel, BBC2 and PBS, 1988.
Summer's Lease, PBS, 1989.
Sleepers, PBS, 1991.
Goodbye Cruel World, BBC, 1992.
The Buccaneers, PBS, 1995.
Into the Fire, BBC, 1996.
Arabian Nights, ABC, 2000.
Band of Bothers, HBO, 2001.
(Blue unit) *Band of Bothers,* HBO, 2001.
The Pacific, HBO, 2010.

Television Lighting Cameraman; Miniseries:
Summer's Lease, PBS, 1989.

Television Assistant Camera; Movies:
Daft as a Brush, 1975.
(Uncredited) *The Evacuees,* BBC, 1975.
Arnhem: The Story of an Escape, BBC, 1976.
(Uncredited) *Rogue Male,* 1976.

Television Cinematographer; Movies:
The Case of the Frightened Lady, BBC, 1983.
Amy, 1984.
Four Days in July, BBC, 1985.
Shoot for the Sun, 1986.
Love After Lunch, BBC, 1987.
Dream Baby, BBC, 1989, PBS, 1992.
Great Moments in Aviation (also known as *Shades of Fear*), BBC, 1993.
The Wedding Gift, BBC, 1993.
Emma (also known as *Jane Austen's "Emma"*), Arts and Entertainment, 1996.
The Ebb-Tide, Arts and Entertainment, 1998.
The Human Bomb, The Movie Channel, 1998.

Television Assistant Camera; Specials:
Three Men in a Boat, BBC, 1975.

Television Photography; Specials:
The Machine That Changed the World (documentary), PBS, 1992.

Television Cinematography; Specials:
"The Wild Side," *Rock & Roll* (documentary), 1995.

Television Assistant Camera; Episodic:
"Happy," *The Wednesday Play,* BBC, 1969.
"An Imaginative Woman," *Wessex Tales,* BBC2, 1973.
"The Vineyard," *Dial M for Murder,* 1974.
"Robinson Crusoe," *BBC Play for Murder,* BBC, 1974.
"The Cheviot, the Stag and the Black, Black Oil," *Play for Today,* BBC1, 1974.
"Sunset Across the Bay," *Play for Today,* BBC1, 1975.
"Play Things," *BBC2 Playhouse,* BBC2, 1976.
"The Price of Coal: Part 1," *Play for Today,* BBC1, 1977.

Television Film Cameraman; Episodic:
"Hey Diddle Diddle," *Hi-de-Hi!,* BBC, 1980.
"Terminus: Parts 2, 3 & 4," *Doctor Who,* BBC, 1983.
"The King's Demons: Parts 1 & 2," *Doctor Who,* BBC, 1983.

Television Camera Operator; Episodic:
"Mike Leigh Making Plays," *Arena,* BBC, 1982.

Television Cinematographer; Episodic:
"Grown-Ups," *BBC2 Playhouse,* BBC2, 1980.
"The Guest," *BBC2 Playhouse,* BBC2, 1982.
"Home Sweet Home," *Play for Today,* BBC1, 1982.
"Stan's Last Game," *Play for Today,* BBC1, 1983.
"Under the Hammer," *Play for Today,* BBC1, 1984.
"Thanks for Everything," *Bergerac,* BBC1, 1987.
"News Hounds," *Screen One,* BBC, 1990.
"The Lost Language of Cranes," *Great Performances,* PBS, 1991.
"Wide-Eyed and Legless," *Screen One,* BBC, 1993.
"Money for Nothing," *Screen One,* BBC, 1993.

ALBERTINI, Ellen R.
   See DOW, Ellen Albertini

ALDREDGE, Theoni V. 1922–2011

PERSONAL

Full name, Theoni Athanasiou Vachliotis Aldredge; born August 22, 1922 (some sources say 1932), in Salonica, Greece; died January 21, 2011, in Stamford, CT.

Costume designer. The creator of thousands of costumes for Broadway plays and musicals and Hollywood films during a span of more than half a century, Aldredge won three Antoinette Perry Awards for her work on the musicals *Annie, Barnum* and *La Cage aux Folles* and a 1975 Academy Award for *The Great Gatsby,* starring Robert Redford and Mia Farrow. She designed her first costumes in 1950, and her handiwork for Tennesee Williams's 1959 *Sweet Bird of Youth* brought her the admiration she needed to find steady work on Broadway. Aldredge won her first of fifteen Tony nominations for *The Devil's Advocate* in 1961. She designed costumes for Lauren Bacall, Richard Burton, and Elizabeth Taylor, among others.

Aldredge began a partnership with stage producer Joseph Papp, founder of the New York Shakespeare Festival. Beginning as a volunteer, she became Papp's resident designer, working on eighty productions, representing the full canon of the festival, over a twenty-year span. In 1962 she worked on *I Can Get It for You Wholesale,* Barbra Streisand's Broadway debut. Edward Albee's *Who's Afraid of Virginia Woolf?* employed her skills during the same year. She began collaborating with musical producer Michael Bennett in 1975, first designing costumes for *A Chorus Line. Dreamgirls* followed in 1980, *42nd Street* in 1981, *La Cage Aux Folles* in 1983, and *Annie* in 1997. Her creations for musicals produced her most widespread fame. After her success with *The Great Gatsby* in 1974, she worked on many other films, including *Ghostbusters, Moonstruck,* and *Addams Family Values.* Aldredge's hundreds of credits include productions in ballet, television, opera, Las Vegas stage shows, and exercise videos, and she created everything from Elizabethan period costumes to contemporary street fashion. She was inducted into the Theatre Hall of Fame in 1990 and won the Costume Designers Guild lifetime award in 2000.

PERIODICALS

Guardian, January 27, 2011.
Scotsman, January 24, 2011.
Wrap, January 21, 2011.

ALTMAN, Mark A.
(Mark Altman)

PERSONAL

Married; wife's name, Naomi.

Addresses: *Office*—Maltman Entertainment, 9854 National Blvd., Suite 196, Los Angeles, CA 90034.

Career: Screenwriter, producer, and actor. Mindfire Entertainment, chief executive officer for ten years; Maltman Entertainment (a production company), Los Angeles, CA, chief executive officer. *Cinefantastique Magazine,* publisher and editorial director; also former entertainment writer; wrote numerous books for DC Comic and Malibu Comics.

Awards, Honors: AFI Fest Award (with Robert Meyer Burnett), best new writer, 1998, for *Free Enterprise.*

CREDITS

Film Appearances:
(As Mark Altman) Cousin Ira, *Free Enterprise,* Anchor Bay Entertainment, 1998.
Himself, *Where No Fan Has Gone Before: The Making of "Free Enterprise"* (documentary), Pioneer Entertainment, 1999.
Hazmat recovery team member, *The Specials,* Fluid Entertainment, 2000.
(Uncredited) Himself, *Festival in Cannes,* Paramount Classics, 2001.
(As Mark Altman) Himself, *Behind the House: Anatomy of the Zombie Movement* (short documentary), Artisan Entertainment, 2004.
(As Mark Altman) Bystander, *The Thirst,* Anchor Bay Entertainment, 2006.
(As Mark Altman) Dr. Altman, *Room 6,* Anchor Bay Entertainment, 2006.
Jailhouse Rock: The Stunts of "All Souls Day," 2006.
Himself, *Raising the Undead: The Making of "All Souls Day"* (short documentary), Anchor Bay Entertainment, 2006.
Himself, *Faces of Death: The Make–Up Effects of "All Souls Day"* (short documentary), Anchor Bay Entertainment, 2006.
Himself, *CFQ: Cafe Fantastique* (short film), 2006.
Himself, *Reinventing the House: Making a Bloody Sequel* (short documentary), 2006.
Hospital from Hell (short documentary), Anchor Bay Entertainment, 2006.
"The Darkroom" Exposed (short documentary), 2007.

Film Work:
Producer, *Free Enterprise,* Anchor Bay Entertainment, 1998.
Producer, *Where No Fan Has Gone Before: The Making of "Free Fnterprise"* (documentary), Pioneer Entertainment, 1999.
Producer, *The Specials,* Fluid Entertainment, 2000.
Executive producer, *House of the Dead,* Mill Creek Entertainment, 2003.
Producer, *All Souls Day: Dia e los Muertos* (also known as *Dia de los muertos* and *West of the Dead*), IDT Entertainment, 2005.

Producer, *The Darkroom* (also known as *Darkroom*), Anchor Bay Entertainment, 2006.

Executive producer, *CFQ: Cafe Fantastique* (short film), 2006.

Producer and second unit director, *The Thirst*, Anchor Bay Entertainment, 2006.

Producer, *DOA: Dead or Alive* (also known as *DOA*), Dimension Films, 2006.

Producer, *Room 6*, Anchor Bay Entertainment, 2006.

Executive producer, *Caught on Tape*, Fluid Entertainment, 2010.

Television Appearances; Movies:

AMS interrogator, *House of the Dead 2* (also known as *House of the Dead 2: All Guts, No Glory, House of the Dead II*, and *House of the Dead II: Dead Aim*), Sci–Fi Channel, 2005.

Television Appearances; Episodic:

Himself (editor of *Sci–Fi Universe*), "Leonard Nimoy: Spock and Beyond," *Biography*, Arts and Entertainment, 1996.

Television Work; Series:

Coproducer, *Castle*, ABC, 2009.

Television Work; Movies:

Producer, *House of the Dead 2* (also known as *House of the Dead 2: All Guts, No Glory, House of the Dead II*, and *House of the Dead II: Dead Aim*), Sci–Fi Channel, 2005.

Producer and second unit director, *Dead & Deader*, 2006.

WRITINGS

Screenplays:

Free Enterprise, 1998.

(As Mark Altman) *House of the Dead*, Mill Creek Entertainment, 2003.

All Souls Day: Dia de los muertos (also known as *Dia de los muertos* and *West of the Dead*), IDT Entertainment, 2005.

The Darkroom (also known as *Darkroom*), Anchor Bay Entertainment, 2006.

The Thirst, Anchor Bay Entertainment, 2006.

Room 6, Anchor Bay Entertainment, 2006.

Film Stories:

(As Mark Altman) *House of the Dead*, Mill Creek Entertainment, 2003.

Television Movies:

Dead & Deader, 2006.

Television Movie Stories:

House of the Dead 2 (also known as *House of the Dead 2: All Guts, No Glory, House of the Dead II*, and *House of the Dead II: Dead Aim*), Sci–Fi Channel, 2005.

Nonfiction Books:

Twin Peaks: Behind the Scenes, Pioneer Books, 1991.

Also wrote *Captains' Logs; Trek Navigator,* Little Brown & Company.

ALVARADO, Trini 1967–

PERSONAL

Full name, Trinidad Alvarado; born January 10, 1967, in New York, NY; daughter of Domingo (a flamenco singer) and Sylvia (a flamenco dancer) Alvarado; married Robert McNeill (an actor). *Education:* Attended Professional Children's School, New York City; attended Fordham University.

Addresses: *Agent*—Allison Levy, Innovative Artists, 235 Park Ave. S., 10th Floor, New York, NY 10003.

Career: Actress. Performed as a flamenco dancer in her parents' dance troupe beginning at age seven.

Awards, Honors: Young Artist Award nomination, best juvenile actress in a motion picture, 1980, for *Rich Kids;* ALMA Award nomination, outstanding actress in a feature film in a crossover role, American Latin Media Arts Awards, National Council of La Raza, 1999, for *Paulie.*

CREDITS

Film Appearances:

Franny Phillips, *Rich Kids*, United Artists, 1979.

Pamela "Pammy" Pearl, *Times Square*, Associated Film Distribution, 1980.

Irene Soffel, *Mrs. Soffel*, Metro–Goldwyn–Mayer, 1984.

Molly Garber, *Sweet Lorraine*, Angelika, 1987.

May "Mooch" Stark, *Satisfaction* (also known as *Girls of Summer*), Twentieth Century–Fox, 1988.

Lisa Titus, *The Chair* (also known as *Hot Seat*), Imperial Entertainment, 1989.

Lorraine, *American Blue Note* (also known as *Fakebook*), Panorama Entertainment, 1989.

Jenny Claire, *Stella*, Buena Vista, 1990.

Miss Elinor Hartley, *American Friends,* 1991, Castle Hill, 1993.
Helen Woodford–Ruth, *The Babe,* Universal, 1992.
Meg March, *Little Women,* Columbia, 1994.
Teresa Perez, *The Perez Family,* Samuel Goldwyn, 1995.
Dr. Lucy Lynskey, *The Frighteners* (also known as *Robert Zemeckis Presents: "The Frighteners"*), Universal, 1996.
Adult Marie Alweather, *Paulie,* DreamWorks, 1998.
Theresa, *Little Children,* New Line Cinema, 2006.
Sylvia, *The Good Guy,* Roadside Attractions, 2009.
Sarah Davis, *All Good Things,* Wild Bunch Benelux, 2010.

Television Appearances; Movies:
Teresa, *Dreams Don't Die,* ABC, 1982.
Lisa Castello, *Jacobo Timerman: Prisoner without a Name, Cell without a Number* (also known as *Prisoner without a Name, Cell without a Number*), NBC, 1983.
Anna Rogna, *Frank Nitti: The Enforcer* (also known as *Nitti*), ABC, 1988.
Beth, *The Christmas Tree,* ABC, 1996.
Denise Cope, *The Last Dance,* CBS, 2000.
Bitter Winter, 2001.

Television Appearances; Specials:
(Uncredited) Jump rope girl, "The Magic Pony Ride," *Unicorn Tales,* NBC, 1977.
Goldilocks, "Big Apple Birthday," *Unicorn Tales,* NBC, 1978.
Dena McKain, "A Movie Star's Daughter," *ABC Afterschool Specials,* ABC, 1979.
Alicia Marin, "Starstruck," *ABC Afterschool Specials,* ABC, 1981.
Gail Brock, "Private Contentment," *American Playhouse,* PBS, 1982.
The Making of "Mrs. Soffel," 1984.
Younger Elinor Blair, "Sensibility and Sense," *American Playhouse,* PBS, 1990.

Television Appearances; Episodic:
Mindy, "Winning," *Kate & Allie,* CBS, 1986.
Sarah Avery, "The Big Vacation," *Kay O'Brien,* CBS, 1986.
Laurie Kincaid, "Sleepless Dream," *Spenser: For Hire,* ABC, 1987.
Behind the Scenes, E! Entertainment Television, 1996.
Maggie Shaye, "Ritual," *Law & Order: Special Victims Unit* (also known as *Law & Order: SVU* and *Special Victims Unit*), NBC, 2004.
Sandra Saramago, "Three Boys and a Gun," *The Jury,* Fox, 2004.
Samantha Loeb (some sources cite Jessica Loeb), "In Which We Meet Mr. Jones," *Fringe,* Fox, 2008.
Samantha Loeb (some sources cite Jessica Loeb), "Bound," *Fringe,* Fox, 2009.

Television Appearances; Pilots:
Elizabeth "Betsey" Wood, *The Human Factor,* CBS, 1992.

Stage Appearances:
Becca (musical), 1976.
Melinda, *Runaways* (musical), New York Shakespeare Festival, Martinson Hall, Public Theatre, New York City, 1978.
Anne Frank, *Yours, Anne* (musical), Playhouse 91, New York City, 1985.
Maggie, *Maggie Magalita,* Lamb's Theatre, New York City, 1986.
Godspell (musical), Lamb's Theatre, 1988.

Also appeared in productions of *I Love You, I Love You Not, The Magic Show,* and *Reds.*

Radio Appearances:
The Frighteners, WFSB, 1996.

RECORDINGS

Videos:
The Making of "The Frighteners," 1998.

Albums:
(Background vocalist) Soul Asylum, *Let Your Dim Light Shine,* Columbia, 1995.

OTHER SOURCES

Periodicals:
Detroit News, July 13, 1996.
Maclean's, June 6, 1994.
People Weekly, February 26, 1990, p. 58.

ANDREWS, Giuseppe 1979–
　　(Joey Andrews)

PERSONAL

Original name, Joey Andrews; born April 25, 1979, in Key Largo, FL.

Addresses: *Contact*—c/o Barbara Cameron Associates, 8369 Sausalito Ave., Suite A, West Hills, CA 91304; Michael Slessinger and Associates, 8730 Sunset Blvd.,

Ste. 270, West Hollywood, CA 90069. *Agent*—Abrams Artists Agency, 9200 Sunset Blvd., Suite 1130, Los Angeles, CA 90069.

Career: Actor, director, cinematographer, producer and writer. Appeared in television commercials for Dr. Pepper, 1999, and Public Broadcasting Service, 2000.

CREDITS

Film Appearances:
(As Joey Andrews) Luke, *Getting It Right,* MCEG, 1989.
(As Joey Andrews) Roughneck leader, *Prehysteria! 2,* Moonbeam, 1994.
(As Joey Andrews) Ash, *Unstrung Heroes,* Buena Vista, 1995.
(As Joey Andrews) Young Sandman, *Sleepstalker* (also known as *Sleepstalker: The Sandman's Last Rites*), Prism, 1995.
(As Joey Andrews) Johnny Thomas, *Invisible Mom,* 1995.
Troy Casse, *Independence Day* (also known as *ID4*), Twentieth Century–Fox, 1996.
Howard, *Pleasantville,* New Line Cinema, 1998.
Jason, *American History X,* New Line Cinema, 1998.
Tough guy Trevor, *The Other Sister,* Buena Vista, 1999.
Coney Island, *Touch Me in the Morning,* 1999.
Denominator, *Never Been Kissed,* Twentieth Century–Fox, 1999.
Lex, *Detroit Rock City,* New Line Cinema, 1999.
Willy, *Local Boys,* First Look Pictures Releasing, 2002.
Deputy Winston, *Cabin Fever,* Lions Gate Films, 2002.
Guy going crazy, *Dribble,* Troma Team Video, 2004.
Tater Tots, 2004.
Randall, *Neo Ned,* Vivendi Entertainment, 2005.
Bill Jensen, *Tweek City,* Madacy Entertainment, 2005.
Harper Alexander, *2001 Maniacs,* Lions Gate Films, 2005.
Period Piece, Troma Team Video, 2006.
Ped, *Ants,* Troma Team Video, 2006.
Wiggly, Troma Team Video, 2006.
The Laundry Room, Troma Team Video, 2006.
Garbanzo Gas, Troma Team Video, 2007.
Zig, *Homo Erectus* (also known as *National Lampoon's "The Stoned Age"*), National Lampoon, 2007.
Stock boy, *The Go–Getter,* Peace Arch Releasing, 2007.
Cat Piss, 2007.
Young male addict, *Careless,* Image, 2007.
Willie, *Look,* Anchor Bay Entertainment, 2007.
Schoof, 2008.
Deputy Winston, *Cabin Fever 2: Spring Fever,* Eagle, 2009.

Film Director:
Touch Me in the Morning, 1999.
In Our Garden, 2002.
Trailer Town, Troma Team Video, 2003.

Dribble, Troma Team Video, 2004.
Tater Tots, 2004.
Who Flung Poo?, Troma Team Video, 2004.
Grandpa, 2005.
Wiggly, Troma Team Video, 2006.
The Laundry Room, Troma Team Video, 2006.
Ants, Troma Team Video, 2006.
Period Piece, Troma Team Video, 2006.
Jacuzzi Roosm, 2006.
Garbanzo Gas, 2007.
Cat Piss, 2007.
Schoof, 2008.

Film Producer:
In Our Garden, 2002.
Trailer Town, 2003.
Dribble, Troma Team Video, 2004.
Tater Tots, 2004.
Wiggly, Troma Team Video, 2006.
The Laundry Room, Troma Team Video, 2006.
Ants, Troma Team Video, 2006.
Garbanzo Gas, 2007.
Cat Piss, 2007.
Schoof, 2008.

Film Editor:
Touch Me in the Morning, 1999.
In Our Garden, 2002.
Trailer Town, Troma Team Video, 2003.
Dribble, Troma Team Video, 2004.
Tater Tots, 2004.
Wiggly, Troma Team Video, 2006.
The Laundry Room, Troma Team Video, 2006.
Ants, Troma Team Video, 2006.
Garbanzo Gas, 2007.
Cat Piss, 2007.
Schoof, 2008.

Film Cinematographer:
Touch Me in the Morning, 1999.
In Our Garden, 2002.
Trailer Town, Troma Team Video, 2003.
Dribble, Troma Team Video, 2004.
Tater Tots, 2004.
Who Flung Poo?, Troma Team Video, 2004.
Grandpa, 2005.
Jacuzzi Rooms, 2006.
Period Piece, Troma Team Video, 2006.
Garbanzo Gas, 2007.
Cat Piss, 2007.
Schoof, 2008.

Television Appearances; Series:
Miles Novacech, *Nick Freno: Licensed Teacher,* The WB, 1997–98.

Germ, a recurring role, *Two Guys, a Girl and a Pizza Place* (also known as *Two Guys and a Girl*), ABC, 1999–2001.

Television Appearances; Movies:
(As Joey Andrews) Kyle, *12:01,* Fox, 1993.
(As Joey Andrews) Doug, also known as Never the Shifter, *White Dwarf,* Fox, 1995.
Joey, *David and Lisa* (also known as *Oprah Winfrey Presents: David and Lisa*), ABC, 1998.
Dave, *Student Affairs,* 1999.

Television Appearances; Episodic:
(As Joey Andrews) Cowboy, "Things That Go Bang in the Night," *Beverly Hills, 90210,* Fox, 1994.
"Nomads," *That's Life,* ABC, 2001.
Bobby Mendoza, "Chapter Thirty–Nine," *Boston Public,* Fox, 2002.
Mike, "Mudlarking," *The Minor Accomplishments of Jackie Woodman,* Independent Film Channel, 2006.
Mike Ackerman, "Pounded," *The Minor Accomplishments of Jackie Woodman,* Independent Film Channel, 2006.
Mike, "Tumor Has It," *The Minor Accomplishments of Jackie Woodman,* Independent Film Channel, 2006.
Joe, "Let It Bleed," *CSI: Crime Scene Investigation* (also known as *CSI: Las Vegas* and *C.S.I.*), CBS, 2008.

RECORDINGS

Music Videos:
Appeared in "Perfect," 1998, and "1979," both by Smashing Pumpkins.

Videos:
Miscellaneous Shit: Behind the Scenes of "Detroit Rock City," 1999.
Inside the Asylum: The Making of "2001 Maniacs," Lions Gate Films, 2006.

WRITINGS

Screenplays:
Touch Me in the Morning, 1999.
In Our Garden, 2002.
Trailer Town, Troma Team Video, 2003.
Dribble, Troma Team Video, 2004.
Tater Tots, 2004.
Who Flung Poo?, Troma Team Video, 2004.
Grandpa, 2005.
Wiggly, Troma Team Video, 2006.
The Laundry Room, Troma Team Video, 2006.
Ants, Troma Team Video, 2006.

Period Piece, Troma Team Video, 2006.
Garbanzo Gas, 2007.
Cat Piss, 2007.
Schoof, 2008.

Film Score:
*Touch Me in the Morning,*1999.
In Our Garden, 2002.
Trailer Town, Troma Team Video, 2003.
Grandpa, 2005.
Wiggly, 2006.
The Laundry Room, Troma Team Video, 2006.
Ants, 2006.
Period Piece, Troma Team Video, 2006.
Jacuzzi Rooms, 2006.
Garbanzo Gas, 2007.
Cat Piss, 2007.
Schoof, 2008.

Film Music:
Songwriter, "Surf Bum," *Local Boys,* 2002.
Songwriter, "I Don't Want to Be a Caveman Anymore," "Ishbo's Love," *Homo Erectus,* National Lampoon, 2007.

ANNIS, Francesca 1944(?)–

PERSONAL

Born May 14, 1944 (some sources say 1946), in London, England; daughter of Anthony (an actor and director) and Mariquita Annis; companion of Patrick Wiseman (a photographer), beginning c. 1974 (relationship ended c. 1994); companion of Ralph Fiennes (an actor), beginning c. 1995; children: (with Wiseman) Charlotte, Taran, Andreas.

Addresses: *Contact*—c/o 2 Vicarage Ct., Flat 2, London WE 8RJ, England.

Career: Actress. Royal Shakespeare Company, member of company, 1975–78.

Awards, Honors: Television Award nomination, best actress, British Academy of Film and Television Arts, 1974, for *A Pin to See the Peepshow;* Television Award nomination, best actress, British Academy of Film and Television Arts, 1976, for *Madame Bovary;* Television Awards, both best television actress, British Academy of Film and Television Arts, 1978, for *Lillie* and *The Comedy of Errors;* Television Award nomination, best actress, British Academy of Film and Television Arts, 1998, for *Reckless;* Television Award nomination, best actress, British Academy of Film and Television Arts, 1999, for *Reckless: The Movie;* Television Award nomination, best actress, British Academy of Film and Television Arts, 2000, for *Wives and Daughters;* Outer Critics Circle Award nomination, for *Hamlet.*

CREDITS

Television Appearances; Series:
Angela Berridge, *Between the Lines* (also known as *Inside the Line*), 1992.

Television Appearances; Miniseries:
Estella, *Great Expectations,* 1967.
Emma Bovary (title role), *Madame Bovary,* BBC, then broadcast as a segment of *Masterpiece Theatre,* PBS, 1976.
Lillie Langtry, *Edward the King* (also known as *Edward the Seventh* and *The Royal Victorians*), 1979.
Lillie Langtry (title role), *Lillie,* London Weekend Television, then broadcast as a segment of *Masterpiece Theatre,* PBS, 1979.
Tuppence Beresford, "Partners in Crime" (also known as "Agatha Christie's Partners in Crime"), *Mystery!,* PBS, 1984.
Tuppence Beresford, *Partners in Crime* (Series II), PBS, 1986.
Prudence "Tuppence" Cowley, "The Secret Adversary" (also known as "Agatha Christie's 'The Secret Adversary'" and "Partners in Crime: The Secret Adversary"), *Mystery!,* PBS, 1987.
Lily Amberville, *I'll Take Manhattan,* 1987.
Paula Croxley, *Inside Story,* 1988.
Jacqueline Kennedy, *The Richest Man in the World: The Story of Aristotle Onassis* (also known as *Onassis: The Richest Man in the World, Ari: The Private Life of Aristotle Onassis,* and *Onassis*), ABC, 1988.
Katharine O'Shea, *Parnell & the Englishwoman,* 1990, then broadcast as a segment of *Masterpiece Theatre,* PBS, 1991.
Anna Fairley, *Reckless,* PBS, 1997.
Claire Gibson, *Wives and Daughters,* PBS and BBC America, 1999.
Lady Ludlow, *Return to Cranford,* PBS, 2009.

Television Appearances; Movies:
Mabel Hubbard, *Alexander Graham Bell,* 1965.
Luciana, *The Comedy of Errors,* 1978.
Lady Frances Derwent, *Why Didn't They Ask Evans?,* 1980.
Galina, *Coming Out of the Ice,* CBS, 1982.
Tuppence Cowley, *The Secret Adversary,* 1983.
Catherine Frode, *The Maze,* 1985.
Jacqueline Kennedy, *Onassis: The Richest Man in the World,* 1988.
Katya Princip, *The Gravy Train Goes East,* 1991.
Elizabeth Collier, *Absolute Hell,* 1991.

Leila, *Weep No More, My Lady* (also known as *Pleure pas ma belle*), syndicated, 1992.
Sophie, *Doomsday Gun,* HBO, 1994.
David's mother, *A Haunting Harmony,* 1993.
Sally Hall, *Headhunters,* 1994.
Bonnie Fielding, *Dalziel and Pascoe: An Autumn Shroud,* Arts and Entertainment, 1996.
Celia Harcourt, *Deadly Summer,* 1997.
Anna Fairley, *Reckless: The Movie* (also known as *Reckless: The Sequel*), 1998.
Ellen Richmond, *Deceit,* BBC America, 2000.
Elizabeth Collier, *Absolute Hell,* Thirteen, 2000.
Margrethe Bohr, *Copenhagen,* PBS, 2002.
Lady Selina Hazy, *Marple: At Pertram's Hotel* (also known as *Miss Marple: At Bertram's Hotel*), ITV, 2007.

Television Appearances; Specials:
Girls in Uniform (also known as *Play of the Month: Girls in Uniform*), 1967.
The Wood Demon (also known as *Play of the Month: The Wood Demon*), 1974.
Kate, *Stronger than the Sun* (also known as *Play for Today: Stronger than the Sun*), 1977.
Luciana, *The Comedy of Errors,* Arts and Entertainment, 1978.
Lady Frances Derwent, *Why Didn't They Ask Evans?,* syndicated, 1981.
Tuppence Beresford, *Partners in Crime, Series I,* PBS, 1984.
Tuppence Beresford, *Partners in Crime, Series II,* PBS, 1985.
Backstage at Masterpiece Theatre: A 20th Anniversary Special, PBS, 1991.

Television Appearances; Episodic:
"The Wind and the Sun," *BBC Sunday–Night Play,* 1960.
Jenny Bates, *Harpers West One,* 1961.
Ethel Rice, "High Wire," *Ghost Squad,* 1961.
Carla, "Children of the Sun," *ITV Television Playhouse,* ITV, 1961.
Liz, "A Free Weekend," *ITV Television Playhouse,* ITV, 1962.
Mariella, "Visit to Spain," *Sir Francis Drake,* 1962.
Marge Hamilton, "The Gentle Assassin," *ITV Play of the Week,* 1962.
Sally, "Drama '63: 54 Minute Affair," *Drama 61–67,* 1963.
Ann, "Blackbird," *Suspense,* 1963.
Ann, "The Mate Market," *Comedy Playhouse,* 1964.
Fiona Senlac, "A Present from Father," *Dr. Finlays' Casebook,* 1964.
Amy Racey, "Old Soldiers," *Armchair Theatre,* 1964.
Mary, "Wild Goose Chase," *The Human Jungle,* 1964.
Sheila Sutherland, "That's Two of Us Sorry," *Secret Agent* (also known as *Danger Man*), CBS, 1965.

Judy, "No Marks for Servility," *Secret Agent* (also known as *Danger Man*), CBS, 1965.

Frances harding, "Four Hundred Years' Thick," *Our Man at St. Mark's,* 1965.

Christine Burrows, "An Aspidistra in Babylon," *ITV Play of the Week,* ITV, 1965.

Catherine, "View from the Bridge," *ITV Play of the Week,* ITV, 1966.

Maria, "Locate and Destroy," *The Saint,* 1966.

Jenny, "Cause for Alarm," *No Hiding Place,* 1967.

Anne, "Women," *The Golden Age,* 1967.

Manuela von Meinhardis, "Girls in Uniform," *BBC Play of the Month,* BBC, 1967.

Helen, "Home Sweet Honeycombe," *Theatre 625,* 1968.

Jill, "The Explorer," *ITV Playhouse,* ITV, 1968.

"The Family Is a Vicious Circle," *ITV Saturday Night Theatre,* 1970.

Antigone, "Antigone: Part 1 & 2," *Heritage,* 1971.

The Tonight Show Starring Johnny Carson, 1971.

Roxane, "The Chinese Prime Minister," *ITV Playhouse,* ITV, 1971.

Julia Almond, *A Pin to See the Peepshow,* 1973.

Nicole Zachary, "Death of an Old–Fashioned Girl," *Great Mysteries,* 1973.

Tracy Conway, "Sign It Death," *Thriller,* ABC, 1974.

Call My Bluff, 1974.

Helen, "The Wood Demon," *BBC Play of the Month,* BBC, 1974.

Lily Langtry, "Dearest Prince," *Edward the Seventh* (also known as *Edward the King*), 1975.

Kate Crowley, "Stronger Than the Sun," *Play for Today,* 1977.

Catherine Frode, "The Maze," *Shades of Darkness,* 1984.

Penelope St. Clair, "Deja Vu: Parts 1 & 2," *Magnum, P.I.,* CBS, 1985.

Aspel & Company, 1991.

Katya Princip, *The Gravy Train Goes East,* 1991.

Entertainment UK, 1992.

Bonnie Fielding, "An Autumn Shroud," *Dalziel and Pascoe,* 1996.

Sharon Bannister, "A Slight Case of Murder," *Tales from the Crypt,* 1996.

Hyacinth Gibson, *Wives and Daughters,* 1999.

Lady Clare Wellesley, "A Pair of Ragged Claws," *Jericho,* ITV, 2005.

Lady Ingram, *Jane Eyre,* 2006.

Television Appearances; Other:

A Pin to See the Peepshow, 1973.

The Ragazza, 1978.

Also appeared in *Love Story; The Human Jungle.*

Film Appearances:

Sylvia, *The Cat Gang,* Realist/CFF, 1959.

Young Jacobites, 1959.

(Uncredited) *No Kidding* (also known as *Beware of Children*), 1960.

Wanda, *His and Hers,* Sabre/Eros, 1961.

Phyl, *West 11,* Associated British/Warner Bros./Pathe, 1963.

Title role, *The Eyes of Annie Jones,* Twentieth Century–Fox, 1963.

Eiras, *Cleopatra,* Twentieth Century–Fox, 1963.

Jean, *Saturday Night Out,* Compton Cameo, 1964.

June, *Crooks in Cloisters,* Associated British/Warner Bros./Pathe, 1964.

Sheila Upward, *Murder Most Foul* (also known as *Agatha Christie's "Murder Most Foul"*), Metro–Goldwyn–Mayer, 1964.

Gwen, *Flipper's New Adventure* (also known as *Flipper and the Pirates*), Metro–Goldwyn–Mayer, 1964.

Jean Parker, *Run with the Wind,* GEFD, 1966.

Sally Feathers, *The Pleasure Girls* (also known as *Die Goldpuppen*), Times Films, 1966.

Arabella Dainton, *The Walking Stick,* Metro–Goldwyn–Mayer, 1970.

Uptight girl, *The Sky Pirate,* Filmmakers Distribution Center, 1970.

Lady Macbeth, *Macbeth,* Columbia, 1971.

Delphi/Diane, *Penny Gold,* 1973.

Lyssa, Widow of the Web, *Krull* (also known as *Dragons of Krull, Dungeons and Dragons, The Dungeons of Krull,* and *Krull: Invaders of the Black Fortress*), Columbia, 1983.

Lady Jessica, *Dune,* Dino De Laurentiis/Universal, 1984.

Dubarry, *El rio de oro* (also known as *The Golden River*), Tesauro/Incine S.A./Federal, 1986.

Mrs. Wellington, *Under the Cherry Moon,* Warner Bros., 1986.

Voice of Juliet, *Romeo–Juliet,* 1990.

Sally Hall, *Headhunters,* 1992.

Edward the King, 1997.

Harriet, *Milk,* Arrow Releasing, 1999.

Val Dryden, *The Debt Collector,* 1999.

(Uncredited) Katiusha, *Onegin,* Samuel Goldwyn Films, 1999.

Countess, *The Libertine,* The Weinstein Company, 2004.

Tracy Conway, *Thriller: The Restoration,* Granada International, 2005.

Lily Walker, *Revolver,* 2005.

Valerie, *Shifty,* Metrodome, 2008.

Stage Appearances:

The Passion Flower Hotel (musical), Prince of Wales Theatre, London, 1965.

Ophelia, *Hamlet,* Lunt–Fontanne Theatre, New York City, 1969.

Isabella, *Measure for Measure,* Royal Shakespeare Company, Stratford–upon–Avon, England, 1974.

Juliet, *Romeo and Juliet,* Royal Shakespeare Company, Stratford–upon–Avon, 1976.

Cressida, *Troilus and Cressida,* Royal Shakespeare Company, Stratford–upon–Avon, 1976.

Miranda, *The Tempest,* Royal Shakespeare Company, Stratford–upon–Avon, 1976.

Luciana, *The Comedy of Errors* (musical), Royal Shakespeare Company, Stratford–upon–Avon, 1976.

Juliet, *Romeo and Juliet,* Royal Shakespeare Company, Aldwych Theatre, London, 1977.

Cressida, *Troilus and Cressida,* Royal Shakespeare Company, Aldwych Theatre, 1977.

Natalya, *A Month in the Country,* National Theatre, London, 1981.

Masha, *Three Sisters,* Albery Theatre, London, 1987.

Melitta, *Mrs. Klein,* National Theatre, 1988.

Rebekka West, *Rosmersholm,* Young Vic Theatre, London, 1992.

Mrs. Erlynne, *Lady Windermere's Fan,* Birmingham Repertory Theatre, Albery Theatre, 1994.

Gertrude, *Hamlet,* Belasco Theatre, New York City, 1995.

Mrs. Alving, *Ghosts,* Comedy Theatre, London, 2001.

Florence Lancaster, *The Vortex,* Donmar Warehouse, London, 2002.

George Dillon, Comedy Theatre, 2005.

Amanda Wingfield, *The Glass Menagerie,* Gafe Theatre, Dublin, Ireland, 2008.

Also appeared in *The Heretic.*

RECORDINGS

Videos:
Lady Jessica, *Deleted "Dune,"* Universal Studios Home Video, 2006.

ARSENIO
   See HALL, Arsenio

ATHENS, J. D.
   See LAWTON, J. F.

B

BADISH, Kenneth M.
(Ken Badish)

PERSONAL

Addresses: *Office*—Active Entertainment, 209 Garfield St., Lafayette, LA 70501.

Career: Producer, writer, and executive. Home Box Office, acquisition executive, prior to 1981; The Movie Store (also known as TMS Pictures/Moviestore Entertainment), founder and principal, 1981–93; Active Entertainment, Lafayette, LA, founder and president.

CREDITS

Television Executive Producer; Movies:
Conflict of Interest, HBO, 1992.
Kraken: Tentacles of the Deep, Sci–Fi Channel, 2006.
Headless Horseman, Sci–Fi Channel, 2007.
Ghouls, Sci–Fi Channel, 2008.
Flu Bird Horror (also known as *Flu Birds*), Sci–Fi Channel, 2008.
Wolvesbayne, Syfy, 2009.
The Dunwich Horror (also known as *H. P. Lovecraft's "The Dunwich Horror"*), Syfy, 2009.
House of Bones, Syfy, 2010.
Quantum Apocalypse (also known as *Judgment Day*), Comcast–on–Demand, 2010.
Monsterwolf, Syfy, 2010.
Swamp Shark, Syfy, 2011.

Television Producer; Movies:
(As Ken Badish) *Automatic,* HBO, 1995.
(As Ken Badish) *Alien Lockdown* (also known as *PredatorMan*), Sci–Fi Channel, 2004.

MorphMan (also known as *Larva*), Sci–Fi Channel, 2005.
(As Ken Badish) *Mansquito* (also known as *Mosquito Man*), Sci–Fi Channel, 2005.
(As Ken Badish) *The Snake King* (also known as *Snakeman*), Sci–Fi Channel, 2005.
SharkMan (also known as *Hammerhead* and *Hammerhead: Shark Frenzy*), Sci–Fi Channel, 2005.
The Black Hole, Sci–Fi Channel, 2006.
(As Ken Badish) *Gryphon* (also known as *Attack of the Gryphon* and *Dungeon & Gryphon*), Sci–Fi Channel, 2007.
(As Ken Badish) *Showdown at Area 51,* Sci–Fi Channel, 2007.

Film Producer:
Ernest Goes to Africa, Ventura Distribution, 1997.
Ernest in the Army, Ventura Distribution, 1998.
The All New Adventures of Laurel & Hardy in "For Love or Mummy," Mummy Productions, 1999.
Pirates of the Plain, Promark Entertainment Group, 1999.
Chrome Angels (also known as *Cyborg Conquest*), IPA Asia Pacific, 2009.
Executive producer, *Maskerade,* Active Entertainment, 2010.

RECORDINGS

Videos:
Creating "Larva," First Look International, 2005.
Exploring the Black Hole, Platinum Disc, 2006.

WRITINGS

Television Movies:
(As Ken Badish) *Gryphon* (also known as *Attack of the Gryphon* and *Dungeon & Gryphon;* also based on story by Badish), Sci–Fi Channel, 2007.

ADAPTATIONS

Several of the television movies produced by Badish were also based on stories by Badish, including *Alien Lockdown, MorphMan, Mansquito, The Snake King, SharkMan, The Black Hole,* and *Ghouls.*

BAKER, Amanda 1979–

PERSONAL

Full name, Laura Amanda Baker; born December 22, 1979, in Mount Pleasant, SC. *Education:* University of South Carolina, B.S., business marketing; trained at Shari Shaw Studios and WestEnd Acting Studios, both Los Angeles; studied with various instructors. *Avocational Interests:* Outdoor activities, including hiking.

Addresses: *Agent*—Silver Massetti & Szatmary (also known as SMS Talent, Inc.), 8730 West Sunset Blvd., Suite 440, West Hollywood, CA 90069; (commercials) CESD Talent Agency, 10635 Santa Monica Blvd., Los Angeles, CA 90025. *Manager*—Ric Beddingfield, The Beddingfield Company, 13600 Ventura Blvd., Suite B, Sherman Oaks, CA 91423–5046.

Career: Actress. Appeared in industrial films and commercials. Sold Out (band), former lead singer. Volunteer with organizations; supporter of charities, including the American Cancer Society, Big Brothers Big Sisters, and the Susan G. Komen Breast Cancer Foundation.

Member: Zeta Tau Alpha.

CREDITS

Television Appearances; Series:
Callah O'Connell, *Palmetto Pointe,* i: Independent Television, 2005.
Jolene Crowell, *General Hospital: Night Shift,* SOAPnet, 2007.
Arabella "Babe" Carey Chandler, *All My Children* (also known as *All My Children: The Summer of Seduction* and *La force du destin*), ABC, 2007–2009.

Television Appearances; Movies:
Girl in marsh, *The Dead Will Tell* (also known as *Dead Man Calling*), CBS, 2004.
Gina, *Locusts* (also known as *Locusts: Day of Destruction*), CBS, 2005.

Betsy, *Hello Sister, Goodbye Life!* (also known as *Hello Sister, Goodbye Life* and *Same as It Never Was*), ABC Family, 2006.

Television Appearances; Episodic:
Charlotte, "Near Wild Heaven," *One Tree Hill* (also known as *Ravens, Filoi gia panta, Les freres Scott, Tunteet pelissae,* and *Tuti gimi*), The WB, 2004.
Wardrobe girl, "Episode 11," *Surface* (also known as *Fathom, A Melyseg fantomja,* and *Surface—Unheimliche Tiefe*), NBC, 2006.
Melanie, "Safety First," *Campus Ladies,* Oxygen, 2007.
Jolene Crowell, *General Hospital* (also known as *Hopital central* and *Hospital general*), ABC, multiple episodes, 2007.
Meghan, "Flirting," *Rules of Engagement,* CBS, 2010.

Television Appearances; Pilots:
Callah O'Connell, *Palmetto Pointe,* i: Independent Television, 2005.

Film Appearances:
Waitress, *The Other Side,* Bishop Studios/Wonder Studios, 2006.
Lizzy Allen, *Lizzie* (also known as *Lizzie: The Movie*), Dark Morgue Pictures/Empire Films/Sheerface Productions/Shadowcast Pictures, c. 2010.

Appeared as Ms. Anne Ryan in *Bells,* Guerilla Films; and as Brooke, *Blue,* Slide Films.

Stage Appearances:
Appeared as Annie, *Evan's Story,* as Ruth, *The Hero,* and as Martha, *The Touch,* all Seacoast Auditorium; and appeared as Amanda, *Cabaret,* Black Box Auditorium. Appeared in church plays; also appeared as various characters, *Improv Showcase,* American Cinema. Participated in her high school's show choir.

WRITINGS

Writings for the Stage:
Contributed to *Improv Showcase,* American Cinema.

OTHER SOURCES

Electronic:
Amanda Baker, http://www.officialamandabaker.com, August 4, 2010.

BAKER, Roy Ward 1916–2010
(Roy Baker)

PERSONAL

Full name, Roy Horace Baker; born December 19, 1916, in London, England; died October 5, 2010, in

London, England. Director. Known for his understated precision and his concern with grounding even his improbable film narratives in reality, Baker is best remembered for his 1958 *Night to Remember,* a documentary-style feature film about the Titanic disaster. After beginning his career in the British film industry as an errand boy, he worked his way quickly up to assistant director to Alfred Hitchcock in his 1938 thriller *The Lady Vanishes.* Baker made documentaries and educational films for British troops during World War II. Novelist and screenwriter Eric Ambler, one of his superior officers, admired his work and in 1947 asked him to direct his feature-length script of the psychological melodrama *The October Man,* which featured prolific British actor John Mills. Mills also starred in Baker's 1950 *Morning Departure* and many other films during a fifteen-year collaboration.

The director moved to Hollywood in 1952 and worked with Marilyn Monroe on one of her first leading roles in *Don't Bother to Knock.* In 1953 he made the grim thriller *Inferno,* the first three-dimensional film. He returned to Britain in 1958 to work with Ambler on *A Night to Remember.* Continuing to direct well-regarded films, his efforts included *The One That Got Away* in 1957 and *Quatermass and the Pit* in 1968. In the 1960s and 1970s, he won the admiration of horror movie fans for a series of movies that included the 1970 film *The Vampire Lovers* and *The Vault of Horror* in 1973. During his later career he primarily directed for television, overseeing several episodes of the 1960s Cold War spy fiction series *The Avengers* and directing Roger Moore in the spy thriller series *The Saint.*

PERIODICALS

Los Angeles Times, October 8, 2010.
New York Times, October 8, 2010.
Washington Post, October 7, 2010.

BEASLEY, John 1943–

PERSONAL

Born June 26, 1943, in Omaha, NE; married, 1965; wife's name, Judith; children: Tyrone (an actor), Michael (an actor).

Addresses: *Agent*—Adam Lazarus, Bauman, Redanty, and Shaul Agency, 5757 Wilshire Blvd., Suite 473, Los Angeles, CA 90036. *Manager*—Don Spradlin, Essential Talent Management, 6565 Sunset Blvd., Suite 415, Los Angeles, CA 90028.

Career: Actor. John Beasley Theatre and Workshop, Omaha, NE, founder, 2002; West Omaha Films, partner. Union Pacific Railroad, worked as a clerk for seven years; also former bill collector and longshoreman. Founder of John Beasley Foundation, Atlanta, GA; active with youth athletic programs and charity fundraisers.

Awards, Honors: Honorary D.H.L., University of Nebraska at Omaha, 2005; Mary Riepma Ross Award, Great Plains Film Festival.

CREDITS

Film Appearances:
Henchman, *Rapid Fire,* 1989.
Ernie, *V. I. Warshawski* (also known as *V. I. Warshaw-ski, Detective in High Heels*), Buena Vista, 1991.
Mr. Hall, *The Mighty Ducks* (also known as *Champions* and *The Mighty Ducks Are the Champions*), Buena Vista, 1992.
Cook, *Untamed Heart,* Metro–Goldwyn–Mayer, 1993.
Coach Warren, *Rudy,* TriStar, 1993.
Roberts, *Little Big League,* Warner Bros., 1994.
Garbage collector, *Losing Isaiah,* Paramount, 1995.
Second skipper, *The Cure* (also known as *My Friend Forever*), Universal, 1995.
Brother C. Charles Blackwell, *The Apostle,* October Films, 1997.
Baker, *Overnight Delivery,* New Line Cinema, 1998.
Nehemiah Jackson, *Crazy in Alabama,* Columbia, 1999.
Colonel Donald Slesinger, *The General's Daughter* (also known as *The General's Daughter: Elizabeth Campbell*), Paramount, 1999.
The Living Witness (also known as *Wanted*), Riverside Productions, 1999.
Detective Mike Smythe, *Lost Souls,* New Line Cinema, 2000.
Albert Hawkins, *The Gift,* Paramount, 2000.
Reverend James, *The Operator,* Black Wolf Productions, 2001.
Cleofas, *The Journeyman,* THINKFilm, 2001.
General Lasseter, *The Sum of All Fears* (also known as *Total Fears*), Paramount, 2002.
Chris Vaughn, Sr., *Walking Tall,* Metro–Goldwyn–Mayer, 2004.
Judge of 125 Family Court, *Daddy's Little Girls* (also known as *Tyler Perry's "Daddy's Little Girls"*), Lions Gate Films, 2007.
Mr. Tate, *For Love of Amy,* 2009.

Television Appearances; Series:
Irv Harper, *Everwood,* The WB, 2002–2006.

Television Appearances; Movies:
Bo, *Lucky Day,* ABC, 1991.
Greg Emory, *To Sir with Love 2,* CBS, 1996.

Traces of Insanity (also known as *Shattered Mind*), 1998.

Jonah Summer, *Freedom Song,* TNT, 2000.

Nathaniel Myles, *The Moving of Sophia Myles,* CBS, 2000.

Mr. Banks, *Disappearing Acts,* HBO, 2000.

Peter Boscow, *Chasing a Dream,* Hallmark Channel, 2009.

Television Appearances; Pilots:

Ogden, *EZ Streets,* CBS, 1996.

Secretary Robert Edwards, *A.T.F.,* ABC, 1999.

Irv Harper, *Everwood,* The WB, 2002.

Television Appearances; Miniseries:

Mr. Coleman, *Laurel Avenue,* HBO, 1993.

Gus, *The Lost Room,* Sci–Fi Channel, 2006.

Television Appearances; Episodic:

Mr. Willie, "Open for Business," *Brewster Place,* ABC, 1990.

Mr. Willie, "Spring Fever," *Brewster Place,* ABC, 1990.

Mr. Willie, "Whatever Happened to Patience Jones?," *Brewster Place,* ABC, 1990.

Mr. Willie, "Bernice Sands Comes Home," *Brewster Place,* ABC, 1990.

"Railroaded," *The Untouchables,* 1993.

Davison's lawyer, "What Do You Want ... a Signed Confession?," *Missing Persons,* 1994.

Captain Haines, "A Minor Miracle," *Early Edition,* CBS, 1998.

Captain Haines, "The Quality of Mercy," *Early Edition,* CBS, 1998.

Ed Thomas, "Bloodlines: Parts 1 & 2," *The Pretender,* NBC, 1998.

James Edward Hollis, "Darwin's Eye," *Millennium,* Fox, 1999.

James Edward Hollis, "Via Dolorosa," *Millennium,* Fox, 1999.

James Edward Hollis, "Goodbye to All That," *Millennium,* Fox, 1999.

Charles Moore, "Crate n' Burial," *CSI: Crime Scene Investigation* (also known as *C.S.I.* and *CSI: Las Vegas*), CBS, 2000.

Judge Henry Bromell, "Dog Days," *Judging Amy,* CBS, 2000.

Charles Moore, "Evaluation Day," *CSI: Crime Scene Investigation* (also known as *C.S.I.* and *CSI: Las Vegas*), CBS, 2001.

Judge Henry Bromell, "Shock and Awe," *Judging Amy,* CBS, 2003.

Judge Henry Bromell, "Kilt Trip," *Judging Amy,* CBS, 2003.

Daryl Hardy, "Suspicion," *NCIS: Naval Criminal Investigative Service* (also known as *Navy NCIS: Naval Criminal Investigative Service* and *NCIS*), CBS, 2007.

Detective Walter McKay, "The Chicken and the Leg," *Boston Legal,* ABC, 2007.

Henry Dawson, "Backfire," *CSI: Miami,* CBS, 2010.

Stage Appearances:

Troy Maxon, *Fences,* John F. Kennedy Center for the Performing Arts, Washington, DC, 2008.

Appeared as Turbo in *Jitney,* Alliance Theatre, Atlanta, GA; also appeared in productions of *The Boys Next Door,* Mixed Blood Theatre, Minneapolis, MN; *Death of a Salesman; Driving Miss Daisy,* Chicago, IL; *Othello; A Streetcar Named Desire;* and *Two Trains Running,* Goodman Theatre, Chicago.

RECORDINGS

Videos:
The Journey of "The Apostle," 1998.

BEDI, Kabir 1946–
  (Kabeer Bedi)

PERSONAL

Born January 16, 1946, in Lahore, India (now Pakistan); some sources cite birthplace as Bombay (now Mumbai), India; son of Baba Phyare Lal (an author and psychic healer) and Freda Marie (maiden name, Houlston; later became a well known Buddhist nun) Bedi; married Protima Gupta (a model and actress), October 14, 1968 (divorced, 1978); married Susan Humphreys (a fashion designer), February 1, 1979 (divorced); married Nikki Vijayakar Moolgaoker (an actress and television personality), 1993 (divorced, 2004); children: (first marriage) Pooja (an actress and talk show host), Siddharth (deceased); (second marriage) Adam (an actor). *Education:* Delhi University, B.A. (with honors), 1967.

Career: Actor. Appeared in television commercials and magazine ads. All India Radio, Delhi, announcer, c. 1964; Oberoi Hotel, worked as disc jockey, 1960s; worked in advertising in Bombay, India, including work as a model for cigarette ads, 1968; Lintas, film and radio chief, 1968; S. H. Bensons, film and radio chief, 1968; Dimension 70 (film and commercial production company), owner, 1970; stage actor, 1971.

Awards, Honors: Several awards for documentary films and commercials, c. 1970; Maschera d'Argento, 1999; Abby Award, distinctive achievement in the Indian advertising industry, 2003; Ischia Award, lifetime achievement, Ischia Global Film and Music Festival, 2003; Capri Award, lifetime achievement, Capri–Hollywood Film Festival, 2003; Asian Jewel Award, lifetime achievement, 2005; Pegaso d'Oro, lifetime achievement, Premio Internationale Flaiano, 2007.

CREDITS

Film Appearances:
Seema, 1971.
Mahesh Jetley, *Hulchul,* 1971.
Sazaa, 1972.
Suraj, *Rakhi Aur Hathkadi,* 1972.
Roopa/Pandit Tulsiram, *Kuchhe Dhaage,* 1973.
Jhumru, *Yauwan,* 1973.
Maa Bahen Aur Biwi, 1974.
Manzilein Aur Bhi Hain (also known as *Miles to Go*), 1974.
Diwana/Ravikant Vyas, *Ishq Ishq Ishq* (also known as *Love, Love, Love*), Eros International, 1974.
Anari, 1975.
The Bandit (originally titled *Daaku*), 1975.
Faulad Singh, *Harfan Maulaa,* 1976.
Uday, *Nagin,* Shankar Movies, 1976.
Title role, *Il corsaro nero* (also known as *The Black Corsair* and *The Black Pirate*), American International Pictures, 1976.
Durga Prasad "D. P." *Bullet,* 1976.
Daku Aur Mahatma, 1977.
Uday, *Vishwasghaat* (also known as *The Betrayal*), 1977.
Malik, *Ashanti* (also known as *Ashanti, Land of No Mercy*), Warner Bros., 1979.
Kishan/Badal, *Aakhri Kasam,* 1979.
Samrat Suryadev, *Yuvraaj,* 1979.
The succubus, *Satan's Mistress* (also known as *Dark Eyes, Demon Rage,* and *Fury of the Succubus*), Motion Picture Marketing, 1982.
Artist, *Girl from India,* 1982.
Gabriel Bagradian, *40 Days of Musa Dagh,* 1982.
Gobinda, *Octopussy,* Metro–Goldwyn–Mayer, 1983.
Terrorist commander, *Terminal Entry,* United Film Distribution, 1986.
Koura, *Escuadron* (also known as *Counterforce* and *Escuadron: Counterforce*), 1987.
Akbar, *The Beast of War* (also known as *The Beast*), Columbia, 1988.
Mera Shikar, 1988.
Sanjay Verma, *Khoon Bhari Mang,* Atlantic Video, 1988.
Har Jeet, 1990.
Senior Inspector Shah Nawaz Khan, *Police Public,* 1990.
Inspector Suraj Singh, *Kurbaan,* 1991.
Yeh Aag Kab Bujhegi, 1991.
Forest Officer Vikram Singh, *Vishkanya,* 1991.
Title role, *Lambu Dada,* 1992.

Rai Bahadur Digvijay Singh, *Dil Aashna Hai* (also known as *The Heart Knows the Truth*), H.M. Creations, 1992.
(As Kabeer Bedi) Raj Pratap Singhal, *Yalgaar,* Eros International, 1992.
Thakur Ganga Singh, *Kshatriya* (also known as *Warriors*), Worldwide Entertainment Group, 1992.
Moulet, *Beyond Justice* (also known as *Desert Law*), Trimark Pictures, 1992.
Captain, *Salaami,* 1994.
Rajan, *Kismat,* 1995.
Police inspector, *Aatank Hi Aatank,* 1995.
Tahar Id Bran, *Mashamal—ritorno al deserto,* 1998.
Brigadier Bedi, *Kohram,* 1999.
Mahendra Pratap Rana, *Kranti,* Eastern Film Corporation, 2002.
Mr. Varma, *Maine Dil Tujhko Diya,* 2002.
Yeti, *Anita and Me,* Icon Film Distribution, 2002.
Chote Pathan, *Talaash: The Hunt Begins ...,* Chiragdeep International, 2003.
Mr. Zakaria, *The Hero: Love Story of a Spy* (also known as *The Hero*), Video Sound, 2003.
Ved Pujan, *Rudraksh,* Karma Entertainment, 2003.
Raj Mallya, *Kismat,* Video Sound, 2004.
Tolstoj, *A/R andata+ritorno,* 01 Distribuzione, 2004.
General Amarjeet Bakshi, *Main Hoon Na,* Eros Entertainment, 2004.
Shah Jahan as an old man, *Taj Mahal: An Eternal Love Story,* Mashreq Communications/Trilogy Entertainment Group, 2005.
Anjali's father, *Rewafaa,* EuroVideo, 2006.
Mo, *Take 3 Girls,* Inspired Movies, 2006.
Rakesh Khullar, *Hello? Kuan Hai!,* Swahti Films and Entertainment, 2006.
Himself, *Halla Bol,* Indian Films/Pyramid Saimira Group/Sunrise Pictures, 2008.
Captain Jagat Malhotra, *Blue,* Shree Ashtavinayak Cine Vision, 2009.
Bob, *Kites* (also released as *Brett Ratner Presents Kites: The Remix*), Icon Film Distribution, 2010.

Television Appearances; Miniseries:
Title role, *Sandokan,* 1976.
Mohammad, *On Wings of Eagles,* NBC, 1986.
Kammamuri, *I Misteri della giungla nera* (also known as *The Mysteries of the Dark Jungle*), 1991.
Moulay Beni–Zair, *Il principe del deserto* (also known as *Lion of the Desert*), 1991.
Chandragupta, *The Maharaja's Daughter,* 1994.
Abdul, *OP Center* (also known as *Tom Clancy's "OP Center"*), NBC, 1995.
Sandokan, *Il ritorno di Sandokan* (also known as *The Return of Sandokan*), 1996.
Napoleon Duarte, *Noi siamo angeli* (also known as *We Are Angels*), 1997.
Sandokan, *Il figlio de Sandokan* (also known as *The Son of Sandokan*), 1998.

Friar Sand, *The Lost Empire* (also known as *The Lost Empire: The Legend of the Monkey King* and *The Monkey King*), NBC, 2001.

Television Appearances; Movies:

Sandokan, *La tigre e ancora viva: Sandokan alla riscossa!*, 1977.

Prince Taj, *The Thief of Baghdad*, 1978.

Dr. Charles Malik, *Eleanor, First Lady of the World*, CBS, 1982.

Khatib Nasif, *Hostage Flight*, NBC, 1985.

Koura, *Counterforce*, syndicated, 1991.

Kabir, *Lie Down with Lions* (also known as *Red Eagle*), Lifetime, 1994.

Khamis bin Abdullah, *Forbidden Territory: Stanley's Search for Livingstone*, ABC, 1997.

Television Appearances; Series:

Farouk Ahmed, a recurring role, *Dynasty*, ABC, 1982, 1986.

Lord Rama, *General Hospital*, ABC, 1983.

Colonel Carlos Demitri, *One Life to Live*, ABC, 1986.

Prince Omar Rashid, a recurring role, *The Bold and the Beautiful* (also known as *Belleza y poder*), CBS, 1994, 2005.

Emir Ibrahim, *Vivere*, 2006.

Kabir, *Un medico in famiglia*, 2007.

Also presenter of the children's program *Mirror of India/Mirror of the World*, DDTV, c. 1960s.

Television Appearances; Episodic:

Kroll, "Mr. Smith Rescues Bobo," *Mr. Smith*, NBC, 1983.

Kruger, "The Java Tiger," *The Master* (also known as *Master Ninja*), NBC, 1984.

Ahmed Kamal, "Mirage," *Riptide*, NBC, 1984.

Vascone, "Knight Sting," *Knight Rider*, NBC, 1985.

Leo Zukoff, "The Beautiful and the Dead: Parts 1 & 2," *Hunter*, NBC, 1986.

Dousseau, "The Second Finest Man Who Ever Lived," *Stingray*, NBC, 1987.

Birmanyi/Bill, "Here's Why Cosmetics Should Come in Unbreakable Bottles," *The Days and Nights of Molly Dodd*, NBC, 1987.

Birmanyi/Bill, "Here's Why There Are Instances When Vegetables Aren't Necessarily Good for You," *The Days and Nights of Molly Dodd*, NBC, 1987.

Birmanyi/Bill, "Here's Another Bedtime Story," *The Days and Nights of Molly Dodd*, NBC, 1987.

Dr. Sanjay Resta, "Silent Partners," *Buck James*, 1987.

Vikram Singh (some sources cite Vikram Akbar), "Curse of the Daanau," *Murder, She Wrote*, CBS, 1988.

Malcolm, "Legend of the Lost Art," *Magnum, P.I.*, CBS, 1988.

Kamir, "The Wrath of Kali," *Highlander* (also known as *Highlander: The Series*), syndicated, 1995.

Aristotle Drago, "The Blonde Woman," *Team Knight Rider*, syndicated, 1998.

Himself, *The Heaven and Earth Show*, BBC, 2005.

(In archive footage) Sandokan, *La imagen de tu vida*, 2006.

Domenica in, 2007.

Asia Today, 2007.

Miss Italia nel mondo, 2007.

Porta a porta, 2009.

Also appeared in *L'isola dei famosi 2*.

Television Appearances; Specials:

Presenter, *49th Manikchand Filmfare Awards*, 2003.

L'isola dei famosi–Le Olimpiadi, 2006.

Adolfo Celi, un uomo per due culture, LA7, 2006.

55th Idea Filmfare Awards, 2010.

Television Appearances; Pilots:

Gar the Draikian, *The Archer: Fugitive from the Empire* (also known as *The Archer and the Sorceress* and *Fugitive from the Empire*), NBC, 1981.

Stage Appearances:

Lead role, *Tughlaq*, 1971.

The Far Pavilions, Shaftesbury Theatre, London, 2005.

RECORDINGS

Videos:

James Bond in India, 1983.

Inside "Octopussy," 2000.

Voice, *Bond Rescues Octopussy Storyboard Sequence*, Metro–Goldwyn–Mayer Home Entertainment, 2006.

(In archive footage) *The Taxi Chase Storyboard Sequence*, Metro–Goldwyn–Mayer Home Entertainment, 2006.

Sollima & die piraten—der schwarze korsar, 2008, Koch Media, 2010.

WRITINGS

Author of fiction and magazine articles.

OTHER SOURCES

Periodicals:

Stage, September 5, 2005.

Electronic:

Kabir Bedi Official Site, http://www.kabir-bedi.com, August 16, 2010.

BERGER, Howard

PERSONAL

Born in Los Angeles, CA; father, a film editor; mother, a teacher; children: Kelsey, Travis, Jacob.

Addresses: *Office*—KNB EFX Group, Inc., 7535 Woodman Pl., Van Nuys, CA 91405.

Career: Special effects makeup artist, special effects makeup designer, special effects makeup supervisor, puppeteer, and actor. KNB EFX Group, Inc., Van Nuys, CA, cofounder and principal, 1988—.

Awards, Honors: CableACE Award nomination (with others), make–up, 1994, for *Body Bags;* CableACE Award nomination (with others), make–up, 1995, for *State of Emergency;* Saturn Award (with others), best make–up, Academy of Science Fiction, Fantasy, and Horror Films, 1999, for *Vampire$;* Best Make–Up (with others), Sitges–Catalonian International Film Festival, 2002, for *Cabin Fever;* Golden Satellite Award nomination (with Gregory Nicotero), best visual effects, International Press Academy, Phoenix Film Critics Society Award nomination (with Nicotero), best visual effects, 2004, both for *Kill Bill: Vol. 1;* Academy Award (with Tami Lane), best achievement in makeup, Film Award (with Nicotero and Nikki Gooley), best makeup/hair, British Academy of Film and Television Arts, Saturn Award (with Nicotero and Gooley), best make–up, Academy of Science Fiction, Fantasy, and Horror Films, 2006, all for *The Chronicles of Narnia: The Lion, the Witch and the Wardrobe;* Saturn Award nomination (with Nicotero), best make–up, Academy of Science Fiction, Fantasy, and Horror Films, 2006, for *Sin City;* Saturn Award nomination (with Nicotero), best make–up, Academy of Science Fiction, Fantasy, and Horror Films, 2006, for *Land of the Dead;* Time–Machine Honorary Award, Sitges–Catalonian International Film Festival, 2006; Saturn Award nomination (with others), best make–up, Academy of Science Fiction, Fantasy, and Horror Films, 2007, for *The Hills Have Eyes;* Saturn Award nomination (with others), best make–up, Academy of Science Fiction, Fantasy, and Horror Films, 2008, for *Planet Terror;* Saturn Award nomination (with Nicotero), best make–up, Academy of Science Fiction, Fantasy & Horror Films, 2010, for *The Book of Eli;* Saturn Award nomination (with Nicotero), best make–up, Academy of Science Fiction, Fantasy, and Horror Films, 2010, for *Drag Me To Hell.*

CREDITS

Film Work:
Additional ghoulie operator, *Ghoulies,* Empire Pictures, 1985.

Special makeup effects, *Day of the Dead* (also known as *George A. Romero's "Day of the Dead"*), United Film Distribution Company, 1985.

Additional special makeup effects, *Invasion U.S.A.,* Cannon, 1985.

Makeup imageries, *Trancers,* Empire Entertainment Company, 1985.

Makeup effects artist, *Night of the Creeps,* TriStar, 1986.

Fabricator, *Troll,* Empire Pictures, 1986.

Creature effects crew, *Invaders from Mars,* Cannon, 1986.

Special effects, *Creepshow 2* (also known as *Dead and Undead: Creepshow 2*), New World Pictures, 1987.

Assistant mold maker, *Harry and the Hendersons* (also known as *Bigfoot*), Universal, 1987.

Creature effects crew, *Predator,* Twentieth Century–Fox, 1987.

Special make effects unit crew, *Evil Dead II,* Rosebud Releasing Corp., 1987.

Makeup effects crew, *The Hidden,* New Line Cinema, 1987.

Art department creature effects, *Pumpkinhead,* United Artists, 1988.

Shop supervisor for Chucky construction crew and Chucky puppeteer, *Child's Play,* United Artists, 1988.

Makeup application for Freddy Krueger, *A Nightmare on Elm Street 4: The Dream Master,* New Line Cinema, 1988.

Shop supervisor, *976–EVIL,* New Line Cinema, 1988.

Special effects and special makeup effects artist for Freddy Krueger, *The Horror Show,* United Artists, 1989.

Autopsy cadaver creator, *Gross Anatomy,* Walt Disney Studios Distribution, 1989.

Special effects, *Nightwish,* 1989.

Special makeup effects artist and supervisor, *A Nightmare on Elm Street: The Dream Child* (also known as *A Nightmare on Elm Street 4: The Dream Child* and *Nightmare on Elm Street 5*), New Line Cinema, 1989.

Special makeup effects supervisor, *Halloween 5* (also known as *Halloween 5: The Revenge of Michael Myers*), Galaxy International Releasing, 1989.

Special makeup effects artist, *Intruder* (also known as *Night Crew: The Final Checkout*), Empire Pictures, 1989.

Special makeup effects artist and special makeup effects and bride effects creator, *Bride of Re–Animator,* 50th Street Films, 1990.

Creature effects for art crew, *Tremors,* Universal, 1990.

Additional makeup supervisor, *Night Angel,* Fries Entertainment, 1990.

Buffalo effects supervisor, *Dances with Wolves,* Orion, 1990.

Makeup artist, *Texas Chainsaw Massacre 3* (also known as *Leatherface: Texas Chainsaw Massacre III, Leatherface,* and *Leatherface: The Texas Chainsaw Massacre III*), New Line Cinema, 1990.

Special makeup effects supervisor, *Tales from the Darkside: The Movie* (also known as *Creepshow 3, Darkside Movie,* and *Tales from the Darkside*), Paramount, 1990.

Special makeup effects, *Sibling Rivalry,* Columbia, 1990.

Special makeup effects artist, *Misery,* Columbia, 1990.

Special makeup effects artist, *Children of the Night,* Columbia, 1991.

Special makeup effects supervisor, *The People Under the Stairs,* Universal, 1991.

Mechanical animal effects, *City Slickers,* Columbia, 1991.

Designer, *Mindwarp* (also known as *Brain Slasher*), Columbia TriStar Home Video, 1992.

Special makeup effects and special makeup effects supervisor, *Army of Darkness* (also known as *Army of Darkness: The Ultimate Experience in Medieval Horror* and *Bruce Campbell vs. Army of Darkness*), Universal, 1992.

Special makeup effects supervisor, *Dr. Giggles,* Universal, 1992.

Special makeup effects, *The Nutt House* (also known as *The Nutty Nutt*), Triboro Entertainment Group, 1992.

Effects supervisor and special makeup effects artist, *Jason Goes to Hell: The Final Friday* (also known as *Jason Goes to Hell*), New Line Cinema, 1993.

Special effects supervisor and special makeup effects artist, *Skinner,* A–Pix Entertainment, 1993.

Production coordinator, *Through an Open Window* (short film), 1993.

Special makeup effects, *Doppelganger* (also known as *Doppelanger: The Evil Within*), CBS/Fox, 1993.

Special makeup effects supervisor, *Maniac Cop 3: Badge of Silence* (also known as *MC3: Maniac Cop 3* and *Maniac Cop III: Badge of Silence*), Academy Home Entertainment, 1993.

Special makeup effects supervisor second unit, *Infested* (also known as *Ticks*), Republic Pictures Home Video, 1993.

Special makeup effects, *Ed and His Dead Mother,* IRS Media, 1993.

Special makeup effects artist, *Lookin' Italian* (also known as *Showdown*), Vision Quest Entertainment, 1994.

(Uncredited) Special makeup supervisor, *Pulp Fiction,* Miramax, 1994.

Special makeup effects, *New Nightmare* (also known as *Wes Craven's "New Nightmare"*), New Line Cinema, 1994.

Special makeup effects supervisor, *Pumpkinhead II: Blood Wings* (also known as *Pumpkinhead II*), Motion Picture Corp. of America, 1994.

Puppeteer, *Color of Night,* Walt Disney Studios Distribution, 1994.

Special effects supervisor, *Village of the Damned,* Universal, 1995.

Supervisor, *Darkman II: The Return of Durant,* MCA/Universal, 1995.

Special makeup effects supervisor, *Lord of Illusions,* United Artists, 1995.

On–set makeup effects application, *Vampire in Brooklyn* (also known as *Wes Craven's "Vampire in Brooklyn"*), Paramount, 1995.

Special makeup effects, *In the Mouth of Madness* (also known as *John Carpenter's "In the Mouth of Madness"*), New Line Cinema, 1995.

Special makeup effects supervisor, *Galaxis,* Prism Entertainment Corp., 1995.

Special makeup effects, *Lord of Illusions,* United Artists, 1995.

Animatronic crocodiles supervisor, *Eraser,* Warner Bros., 1996.

Supervisor for turboman suit, *Jingle All the Way,* Twentieth Century–Fox, 1996.

Makeup effects supervisor, *From Dusk Till Dawn,* Dimension Films, 1996.

Special makeup effects supervisor, *Scream,* Dimension Films, 1996.

Special effects consultant, *Sub Down,* New Films International, 1997.

Puppeteer, *Men in Black* (also known as *MIB*), Columbia, 1997.

Special makeup supervisor, *DNA* (also known as *Genetic Code*), Astra Cinema, 1997.

Special makeup effects supervisor, *The Night Flier,* New Line Cinema, 1997.

Animatronic creature effects and special makeup effects, *Spawn,* New Line Cinema, 1997.

Special makeup effects supervisor, *Boogie Nights,* New Line Cinema, 1997.

Special makeup effects, *Wishmaster* (also known as *Wes Craven Presents "Wishmaster"*), Imperial Entertainment, 1997.

Special makeup effects supervisor, *Scream 2,* Dimension Films, 1997.

Puppeteer, *Wild America,* Warner Bros., 1997.

Makeup effects supervisor, *Phantoms* (also known as *Dean Koontz's "Phantoms"* and *Phantom*), Dimension Films, 1998.

Special makeup effects, *Vampire$* (also known as *Vampires* and *John Carpenter's "Vampires"*), Columbia, 1998.

Supervisor, *Very Bad Things,* Polygram Filmed Entertainment, 1998.

Special makeup and creature effects, *The Faculty* (also known as *Parasite*), Dimension Films, 1998.

Creature effects supervisor, *Tale of the Mummy* (also known as *Talos the Mummy* and *Russell Mulcahy's "Tale of the Mummy"*), Dimension Films, 1998.

Makeup special effects, *The Eighteenth Angel,* 1998.

Makeup effects supervisor, *Bats,* Columbia, 1999.

Special makeup effects supervisor, *From Dusk Till Dawn 2: Texas Blood Money,* Amuse Pictures, 1999.

Special makeup effects supervisor, *The Haunting* (also known as *La maldicion*), DreamWorks, 1999.

Makeup artist and special makeup effects artist, *House on Haunted Hill,* Warner Bros., 1999.

Special makeup effects and supervisor, *From Dusk Till Dawn 3: The Hangman's Daughter* (also known as *The Hangman's Daughter*), Buena Vista Home Video, 1999.

Special makeup effects supervisor, *The Green Mile* (also known as *Stephen King's "The Green Mile"*), Warner Bros., 1999.

Special makeup and creature effects supervisor, *Little Nicky,* New Line Cinema, 2000.

Special makeup effects artist, *The Crow: Salvation,* Dimension Films, 2000.

Special makeup effects supervisor, *Picking Up the Pieces* (also known as *Virgin Hand*), WMA Independent, 2000.

Prosthetics supervisor, special makeup effects artist, and special makeup effects supervisor, *The Cell* (also known as *Lethal Cell*), New Line Cinema, 2000.

Special makeup effects supervisor, *Unbreakable,* Buena Vista, 2000.

Special effects makeup, *Hearts in Atlantis,* Warner Bros., 2001.

Puppeteer, *Rat Race,* Paramount, 2001.

Special makeup and creature effects, *Soulkeeper,* Overseas FilmGroup, 2001.

Special makeup effects supervisor, *Spy Kids,* Dimension Films, 2001.

Special makeup effects artist, *The Animal* (also known as *Animal Man*), Columbia, 2001.

Special makeup effects artist, *Mulholland Dr.* (also known as *Mulholland Drive*), Universal, 2001.

Special makeup effects artist, *Ghost of Mars* (also known as *John Carpenter's "Ghost of Mars"*), Screen Gems, 2001.

Key special makeup effects supervisor, *Thir13en Ghosts,* Warner Bros., 2001.

Special makeup effects supervisor, *Vanilla Sky,* Paramount, 2001.

Special effects makeup supervisor, *feardotcom,* Warner Bros., 2002.

Supervisor for special makeup and animatronic effects, *The Salton Sea,* Warner Bros., 2002.

Supervisor, *Murder by Numbers* (also known as *Murd3r 8y Num8ers*), Warner Bros., 2002.

Special effects makeup supervisor, *Bubba Ho–tep,* Vitagraph, 2002.

Special makeup effects supervisor, *Cabin Fever,* Lions Gate Films, 2002.

Special makeup effects artist, *Big Fat Liar,* Universal, 2002.

Character prosthetics supervisor, *Austin Powers in Goldmember* (also known as *Austin Powers: Goldmember*), New Line Cinema, 2002.

Special makeup effects supervisor, *Spy Kids 2: Island of Lost Dreams* (also known as *Spy Kids 2: The Island of Lost Dreams*), Dimension Films, 2002.

Special makeup effects supervisor, *Vampires: Los Muertos* (also known as *John Carpenter's "Vampires: Los Muertos"* and *John Carpenter Presents "Vampires 2: Los Muertos"*), Screen Gems, 2002.

Special makeup effects supervisor, *Kill Bill: Vol. 1* (also known as *Kill Bill, Kill Bill Part 1, Quentin Tarantino's "Kill Bill: Volume One,"* and *Kiru Biru*), Miramax, 2003.

Animatronics effects supervisor and puppeteer, *Hulk,* Universal, 2003.

Special effects director, *Ginger Snaps: Unleashed* (also known as *Ginger Snaps 2: Unleashed* and *Werewolf: Gingersnaps*), Lions Gate Films Home Entertainment, 2004.

Designer for special makeup effects and werewolf animatronics and on–set puppeteer, *Ginger Snaps Back: The Beginning* (also known as *Hellwolf: You Will Be Eaten*), 2004.

Special makeup effects, *Riding the Bullet* (also known as *Stephen King's "Riding the Bullet"*), Innovation Film Group, 2004.

Special makeup supervisor and puppeteer, *Kill Bill: Vol. 2* (also known as *Kill Bill, Kill Bill Part 2,* and *Vol. 2*), Miramax, 2004.

Special effects supervisor, *Lemony Snicket's A Series of Unfortunate Events,* Paramount, 2004.

Still photographer behind–the–scenes, *Nightmares in Foam Rubber* (short documentary; also known as *The Making of Creepshow 2*), Anchor Bay Entertainment, 2004.

Supervisor, *Employee of the Month,* DEJ Productions, 2004.

Prosthetics, *I Heart Huckabees* (also known as *I Love Huckabees*), Fox Searchlight, 2004.

Special makeup effects supervisor, *Ray,* Universal, 2004.

Additional werewolf effects creator, *Cursed* (also known as *Wes Craven's "Cursed"*), Miramax, 2005.

Special makeup effects supervisor, *Sin City* (also known as *Frank Miller's "Sin City"*), Dimension Films, 2005.

Special makeup effects artist and special makeup effects designer and creator, *The Amityville Horror,* Metro–Goldwyn–Mayer, 2005.

(Uncredited) Special makeup effects artist, *House of Wax,* Warner Bros., 2005.

Special makeup effects artist, *The Adventures of Sharkboy and Lavagirl 3–D,* Dimension Films, 2005.

Special makeup effects supervisor, *Land of the Dead* (also known as *George A. Romero's "Land of the Dead"*), Universal, 2005.

Project supervisor, *The Island,* DreamWorks, 2005.

Supervisor, *Serenity,* Universal, 2005.

On–set makeup effects artist and special makeup effects designer and creator, *Hostel,* Lions Gate Films, 2005.

Prosthetic makeup set supervisor and special makeup and creatures, *The Chronicles of Narnia: The Lion, the Witch and the Wardrobe* (also known as *The Chronicles of Narnia*), Buena Vista, 2005.

Special makeup effects designer, *The Hills Have Eyes,* Fox Searchlight, 2006.

Makeup effects supervisor, *Poseidon* (also known as *Poseidon: The IMAX Experience*), Warner Bros., 2006.

Special makeup effects artist, *Deja Vu,* Buena Vista, 2006.

On–set makeup artist and special make–up effects designer and creator, *Hostel,* Lions Gate Films, 2006.

Special makeup effects artist, *Primeval* (also known as *Kiss*), Buena Vista, 2007.

Special makeup effects designer and creator, *The Hitcher,* Rogue Pictures, 2007.

Supervisor, *The Reaping* (also known as *Reaping*), Warner Bros., 2007.

Special effects for dog puppet, *Spider–Man 3* (also known as *Spider–Man 3: The IMAX Experience*), Columbia, 2007.

Supervisor, *Underdog* (also known as *Iron–Puppy Underdog*), Buena Vista, 2007.

Special makeup effects designer, *The Hills Have Eyes II,* Fox Atomic, 2007.

Special makeup effects supervisor, *Disturbia,* Paramount, 2007.

Special makeup effects designer, *Death Proof* (also known as *Grindhouse Presents: Quentin Tarantino's "Death Proof," Grindhouse: "Death Proof," Quentin Tarantino's "Death Proof,"* and *Quentin Tarantino's "Thunder Bolt"*), Genius Products, 2007.

Special makeup effects designer and creator, *Hostel: Part II,* Lions Gate Films, 2007.

Special makeup effects show supervisor, *Transformers* (also known as *Transformers: The IMAX Experience*), Paramount, 2007.

Special makeup effects designer, *Planet Terror* (also known as *Grindhouse Presents: Robert Rodriguez's "Planet Terror"* and *Robert Rodriguez's "Planet Terror"*), 2007.

Creature designer and creature makeup effects, *The Mist* (also known as *Stephen King's "The Mist"*), Metro–Goldwyn–Mayer, 2007.

Special makeup effects artist, *The Great Debators,* Weinstein Company, 2007.

Tattoo artist, *The Bucket List,* Warner Bros., 2007.

Special makeup effects artist, and prosthetic makeup and creature supervisor, *The Chronicles of Narnia: Prince Caspian* (also known as *Prince Caspian*), Walt Disney Studios Motion Pictures, 2008.

Special makeup effects designer, *Mirrors,* Twentieth Century–Fox, 2008.

Special makeup effects designer and creator, *The Unborn,* Rogue Pictures, 2009.

Special makeup effects supervisor, *Drag Me to Hell* (also known as *Spell*), Universal, 2009.

Special makeup effects, *Inglourious Basterds,* Weinstein Company, 2009.

Special makeup effects, *Public Enemies,* Universal, 2009.

Key special makeup effects supervisor, *Shorts* (also known as *Shorts: The Adventures of the Wishing Rock*), Warner Bros., 2009.

Special makeup effects, *The Final Destination* (also known as *The Final Destination in 3–D* and *Final Dead Circuit 3–D*), Warner Bros., 2009.

Special makeup effects and animatronics, *Jennifer's Body,* Twentieth Century–Fox, 2009.

Special makeup effects artist, *This Is It* (documentary; also known as *Michael Jackson's "This Is It," Michael Jackson's "This Is It": The IMAX Experience,* and *Michael Jackson: This Is It*), Columbia, 2009.

Special effects makeup, *Splice,* Warner Bros., 2009.

Special makeup effects and prosthetics, *Edge of Darkness,* Warner Bros., 2010.

Special makeup and creature effects, *Predators,* Twentieth Century–Fox, 2010.

Special makeup effects, *Piranha* (also known as *Piranha 3D*), Dimension Films, 2010.

Special effects makeup, *The Last Exorcism,* Lions Gate Films, 2010.

Film Appearances:

Ben, *A Secret Space* (short film), 1977.

Beta Zombie, *Night of the Creeps,* TriStar, 1986.

First arty guard, *Wishmaster,* Imperial Entertainment, 1997.

Himself, *Full Tilt Boogie* (documentary), Miramax, 1997.

Himself, *The Men Behind the Army* (short documentary), Anchor Bay Entertainment, 1999.

Himself, *The Making of "Evil Dead II'* or *The Gore the Merrier* (short documentary), Anchor Bay Entertainment, 2000.

Himself, *Behind the "Scream"* (short documentary), Dimension Home Video, 2000.

Gorilla, *Planet of the Apes,* Twentieth Century–Fox, 2001.

Demon, *Soulkeeper,* Overseas FilmGroup, 2001.

Himself, *Adam Sandler Goes to Hell* (short documentary), New Line Home Video, 2001.

Himself, *Thir13en Ghosts Revealed* (short documentary), Columbia TriStar, 2002.

Himself, *Making of "Bubba Ho–tep"* (short documentary), Metro–Goldwyn–Mayer/United Artists Home Entertainment, 2004.

Himself, *Nightmares in Foam Rubber* (short documentary; also known as *The Making of Creepshow 2*), Anchor Bay Entertainment, 2004.

Himself, *Fangoria: Blood Drive II,* Koch Vision, 2005.

Stoner dude Doug, *Cemetery Gates,* 2006.

Himself, *Hostel Dissected* (documentary), Sony Pictures Home Entertainment, 2006.

Working with a Master: John McNaughton (short documentary), Anchor Bay Entertainment, 2006.

Himself, *Wigs, Teeth and Powder!: The Makeup Effects of "The Washingtonians"* (short film), Anchor Bay Entertainment, 2007.

Himself, *Down to the Bone: Anatomy of a Prequel* (documentary), New Line Home Video, 2007.

Himself, *He Who Made Monsters: The Life and Art of Jack Pierce* (short film), Universal Studios Home Video, 2008.

Voice of Rob's father and Rob's boss, *Fourth Time Around,* 2009.

Himself, *Thrill Me!: The Making of "Night of the Creeps"* (documentary), Sony Pictures Home Entertainment, 2009.

Himself, *Creating the Creeps* (short documentary), Sony Pictures, 2009.

Himself, *Fred Heads: The Ultimate Freddy Fans* (short film), 2010.

Himself, *Never Sleep Again: The Elm Street Legacy* (documentary), 1428 Films, 2010.

A Director's Playground: Vincenzo Natali on the Set of "Splice" (short documentary), 2010.

Television Work; Series:

Prosthetic effects supervisor, prosthetic effects, and supervisor, *Deadwood,* HBO, 2004–2006.

Special effects makeup, *Masters of Horror,* Showtime, 2005–2007.

Special makeup effects artist, *Fear Itself,* NBC, 2008.

Television Work; Miniseries:

Special creature effects supervisor, *Frank Herbert's "Dune,"* Sci–Fi Channel, 2000.

Special makeup effects supervisor, *Desperation* (also known as *Stephen King's "Desperation"*), ABC, 2006.

Special makeup effects artist, *The Pacific,* HBO, 2010.

Television Work; Movies:

Special makeup effects, *Body Bags* (also known as *John Carpenter Presents "Mind Games"*), Showtime, 1993.

Special makeup supervisor, *Attack of the 50 Ft. Woman,* HBO, 1993.

Supervisor, *Hercules and the Amazon Woman,* syndicated, 1994.

Special makeup effects supervisor, *Stephen King's "The Night Flier,"* HBO, 1997.

Puppeteer, *The Apartment Complex,* Showtime, 1999.

Special makeup and animatronic effects, *Spiders,* USA Network, 2000.

Special makeup and animatronic effects, *Crocodile,* USA Network, 2000.

Special makeup and creature effects, *Soulkeeper,* Sci–Fi Channel, 2001.

Animatronic effects, *Desperation* (also known as *Stephen King's "Desperation"*), ABC, 2006.

Special makeup effects, *R. L. Stine's "The Haunting Hour: Don't Think About It,"* Cartoon Network, 2007.

Television Work; Episodic:

Special effects, "Halloween Candy," *Tales from the Darkside,* syndicated, 1985.

Special makeup effects artist, "Judy, You're Not Yourself Today," *Tales from the Crypt,* HBO, 1990.

Creature special effects designer, "A Lady in Hades," *Young Hercules,* Fox, 1998.

Creature special effects designer, "Iolaus Goes Stag," *Young Hercules,* Fox, 1999.

Creature effects designer, "Home," *Cleopatra 2525,* syndicated, 2000.

Creature effects designer, "No Thanks for the Memories," *Cleopatra 2525,* syndicated, 2000.

Special effects, "Incident On and Off a Mountain Road," *Masters of Horror,* Showtime, 2005.

Special makeup effects artist, "Dreams in the Witch–House," *Masters of Horror,* Showtime, 2005.

Special makeup effects artist, "Valerie on the Stairs," *Masters of Horror,* Showtime, 2006.

Also worked as creature effects designer, *Jack of All Trades,* syndicated.

Television Appearances; Movies:

Soulkeeper, Sci–Fi Channel, 2001.

Television Appearances; Specials:

Anatomy of Horror (documentary), UPN, 1995.

Hollywood Goes to Hell, 2000.

"Scream": The E! True Hollywood Story, E! Entertainment Television, 2001.

Boogeyman II: "Masters of Horror" (documentary), Sci–Fi Channel, 2004.

Monsterama: KNB EFX, 2004.

The 78th Annual Academy Awards, ABC, 2006.

30 Even Scarier Movie Moments, Bravo, 2006.

Starz Inside: "Fantastic Flesh," Starz!, 2008.

Television Appearances; Episodic:

"The Lion, the Witch, and the Wardrobe: Part 2," *Super Short Show* (also known as *Mike's "Super Short Show"*), The Disney Channel, 2006.

RECORDINGS

Video Games:

Special makeup effects, *Maximum Surge,* Flash Entertainment, 1996.

BILCOCK, Jill 1948–

PERSONAL

Original name, Jillian Elizabeth Stevenson; born 1948, in Melbourne, Victoria, Australia; married (divorced);

married (marriage ended). *Education:* Graduated with degree in film editing from Victoria College of Arts (some sources say Swinburne College of Technology).

Career: Editor.

Awards, Honors: Australian Film Institute Award nomination, best achievement in editing, 1984, for *Strikebound;* Australian Film Institute Award nomination, best achievement in editing, 1989, for *A Cry in the Dark;* Australian Film Institute Award, best achievement in editing, 1992, Film Award nomination, best editing, British Academy of Film and Television Arts, 1993, for *Strictly Ballroom;* Australian Film Institute Award nomination, best achievement in editing, 1994, for *Muriel's Wedding;* Byron Kennedy Award, Australian Film Institute, 1995; Golden Satellite Award nomination, outstanding film editing, International Press Academy, 1997, Film Award nomination, best editing, British Academy of Film and Television Arts, 1998, for *Romeo + Juliet;* Australian Film Institute Award, best achievement in editing, 1998, for *Head On;* Film Award nomination, best editing, British Academy of Film and Television Arts, 1999, for *Elizabeth;* Australian Centenary Medal, 2001; Film Critics Circle of Australia Award nomination, best editing, 2001, for *The Dish;* Academy Award nomination, best editing, American Film Institute Film Award, AFI editor of the year, 2002, Australian Film Institute Award, best editing, Eddie Award, best edited feature film—comedy or musical, American Cinema Editors, IF Award nomination, best editing, 2001, Film Award nomination, best editing, British Academy of Film and Television Arts, Film Critics Circle of Australia Award nomination, best editing, Golden Satellite Award nomination, best film editing, International Press Academy, Phoenix Film Critics Society Award nomination, best film editing, 2002, all for *Moulin Rouge;* Phoenix Film Critics Society Award nomination, best film editing, 2003, for *Road to Perdition;* Australian Film Institute Award, best editing, Film Critics Circle of Australia Award nomination, best editing, IF Award nomination, best editing, 2003, all for *Japanese Story;* Living Legend IF Award, 2003; International Award, excellence in filmmaking, Australian Film Institute, 2007; Australian Film Institute Award nomination, best editing, IF Award nomination, best editing, 2009, both for *Blessed.*

CREDITS

Film Editor:
Strikebound, 1984.
The More Things Change ..., 1986.
Dogs in Space, Skouras Pictures, 1986.
Australian Made: The Movie, 1987.
A Cry in the Dark (also known as *Evil Angels*), Warner Bros., 1988.

Till There Was You, Sovereign Pictures, 1990.
Strictly Ballroom (also known as *Dancing Hero*), Miramax, 1992.
Say a Little Prayer, 1993.
You Seng (also known as *Temptation of a Monk*), Northern Arts Entertainment, 1993.
Erotique, Odyssey Films, 1994.
Muriel's Wedding, Miramax, 1994.
I.Q., Paramount, 1994.
How to Make an American Quilt, Universal, 1995.
Romeo + Juliet (also known as *William Shakespeare's "Romeo + Juliet"*), Twentieth Century–Fox, 1996.
Head On, Strand, 1998.
Elizabeth (also known as *Elizabeth: The Virgin Queen*), Gramercy, 1998.
The Dish, Warner Bros., 2000.
Moulin Rouge!, Twentieth Century–Fox, 2001.
Road to Perdition, DreamWorks, 2002.
Japanese Story, Samuel Goldwyn Films, 2003.
The Libertine, Weinstein Company, 2004.
Catch a Fire, Focus Features, 2006.
Elizabeth: The Golden Age, Universal, 2007.
The Young Victoria, Apparition, 2009.
Blessed, Icon Film Distribution, 2009.
Don't Be Afraid of the Dark, Miramax, 2010.

Film Work; Other:
Assistance, *Ground Zero,* Avenue Entertainment, 1988.
Associate producer and title designer, *Romeo + Juliet* (also known as *William Shakespeare's "Romeo + Juliet"*), Twentieth Century–Fox, 1996.

Television Editor; Movies:
Harry's War (short film), 1999.

BIRK, Raye 1943–

PERSONAL

Born 1943, in Flint, MI; married Candace Barrett Birk, 1966; children: Joshua.

Career: Actor. American Conservatory Theatre, San Francisco, CA, member of company, 1973–82. University of Southern California, professor of theatre.

Awards, Honors: DramaLogue awards for *The Cherry Orchard* and *A Private View.*

CREDITS

Film Appearances:
Sonny, *Best Defense,* Paramount, 1984.

First reporter, *The Adventures of Buckaroo Banzai across the 8th Dimension* (also known as *The Adventures of Buckaroo Banzai*), Twentieth Century–Fox, 1984.

The jogger, *Burglar*, Warner Bros., 1987.

Vanya, *Amazon Women on the Moon* (also known as *Cheeseburger Film Sandwich*), MCA/Universal, 1987.

Detective Bushkin, *Jake's M.O.*, 1987.

Pinsky, *Throw Momma from the Train*, Orion, 1987.

Papshmir, *The Naked Gun: From the Files of Police Squad!* (also known as *The Naked Gun*), Paramount, 1988.

Speaker on television, *Martians Go Home*, Taurus Entertainment, 1990.

Simon Tidwell, *Doc Hollywood*, Warner Bros., 1991.

Principal Kratz, *Class Act*, Warner Bros., 1992.

Hotel manager, *Josh and S.A.M.*, Columbia, 1993.

Uncle Sal, *A Song for You*, 1993.

Papshmir, *Naked Gun 33 1/3: The Final Insult*, Paramount, 1994.

Gary Dedmarch, *Illegal in Blue*, Orion, 1995.

Contractor, *The Big Squeeze* (also known as *Body of a Woman*), First Look Pictures Releasing, 1996.

Son'a doctor, *Star Trek: Insurrection* (also known as *Star Trek 9*), Paramount, 1998.

Sandy's father, *Loves Me Loves Me Not*, 1999.

Heathercliff, *Factotum* (also known as *Factotum: A Man Who Performs Many Jobs*), IFC, 2005.

Tom motel clerk, *North Country*, Warner Bros., 2005.

Postal clerk, *Sweet Land*, Paris Filmes, 2005.

Dr. Shapiro, *A Serious Man*, Focus Features, 2009.

Television Appearances; Series:

Leonard Brown, *The Popcorn Kid*, CBS, 1987.

Mr. Al Diperna, a recurring role, *The Wonder Years*, ABC, between 1988 and 1991.

Grimbach, *Under Cover*, Fox, 1991.

Atticus Dunn, *Silk Stalkings*, USA Network, 1993–95.

Dr. Phineas Phoenix, a recurring role, *Black Scorpion* (also known as *Roger Corman Presents Black Scorpion*), Sci-Fi Channel, 2001.

Television Appearances; Movies:

Gremio, *The Taming of the Shrew*, 1976.

Marley's ghost, *A Christmas Carol*, 1981.

Dowdy, *Mister Roberts*, 1984.

Harding, *Deadly Messages*, ABC, 1985.

George Larson, *The Stepford Children*, NBC, 1987.

Sam Morgan, *Perry Mason: The Case of the Lethal Lesson*, NBC, 1989.

Joseph Kilminster, *Challenger*, ABC, 1990.

Dr. Frenzel, *Aftermath: A Test of Love*, CBS, 1991.

Tim Grimbach, *Spy Games*, ABC, 1991.

Grimbach, *Under Cover*, 1991.

Travis Gaines, *Barbarians at the Gate*, HBO, 1993.

Sterling, *Caught in the Act*, NBC, 1993.

Judge Spota, *Untamed Love*, Lifetime, 1994.

Judge Bonner, *Cries from the Heart* (also known as *Touch of Truth*), CBS, 1994.

Dr. Roth, *My Brother's Keeper*, CBS, 1995.

John Davies, *After Jimmy*, CBS, 1996.

Howard Seltzer, *Columbo: A Trace of Murder*, ABC, 1997.

Justice of the peace, *My Sister's Keeper*, CBS, 2002.

Television Appearances; Pilots:

Vince Martoni, *The Earthlings*, ABC, 1984.

Detective Bushkin, *Jake's M.O.*, NBC, 1987.

Mr. Diperna, *The Wonder Years*, ABC, 1988.

Mason Lowell, *The High Life*, ABC, 1990.

Judge Brown, *Archie: To Riverdale and Back Again* (also known as *Archie: Return to Riverdale* and *Weekend Reunion*), NBC, 1990.

Mike Caton, *Picket Fences*, CBS, 1992.

Television Appearances; Episodic:

Mr. Atwater, "Target–a Cop," *Hawaii Five–0*, CBS, 1976.

Maitre d', "Red Holt Steele," *Remington Steele*, NBC, 1983.

Cecil Cosgrove, "Lofty Steele," *Remington Steele*, NBC, 1984.

Whitley McVeigh, "Happy Trails to You," *Newhart*, CBS, 1984.

Singer, "The End of Logan's Run," *Hill Street Blues*, 1984.

Martin C. Sharp, "Clipped Wings," *Blue Thunder*, 1984.

Dworkin (some sources cite Dr. Lawrence Osbourne), "Nuts about Harry," *Night Court*, NBC, 1985.

Walt Twitchell, "The Executive's Executioner," *Cheers*, NBC, 1985.

Bearded man, "Wordplay," *The Twilight Zone*, CBS, 1985.

Earl, "Requiem," *Mr. Belvedere*, ABC, 1985.

"Lost and Found in Space," *St. Elsewhere*, NBC, 1985.

"Here Comes the Bribe," *Off the Rack*, 1985.

"Table for Two," *Mary*, CBS, 1986.

Time traveler, "Lost and Found," *The Twilight Zone*, CBS, 1986.

Walt Twitchell, "Knights of the Scimitar," *Cheers*, NBC, 1986.

"Ships in the Night," *Tough Cookies*, 1986.

God number one, "A Day in the Life," *Night Court*, NBC, 1987.

Lenny Scott, "Take a Look at Me Now," *ALF*, NBC, 1987.

"City of Passion: Part 1," *Hunter*, NBC, 1987.

Wrenn, "Haven," *Star Trek: The Next Generation*, syndicated, 1987.

Mr. Evans, "Thelma's Reunion," *Amen*, 1987.

John, "Moving In," *Throb*, 1987.

Vladimir Horowitz, "I Never Played for my Father: Part 1," *Duet*, 1987.

"Tea for Tuba," *Marblehead Manor*, syndicated, 1988.

Officer Griswold, "Someone to Watch Over Me: Parts 1 & 2," *ALF*, NBC, 1988.

"Heather's Monk," *Mr. Belvedere,* ABC, 1988.

Ward, "Jung and the Restless," *Night Court,* NBC, 1988.

Judge Steven Lang, "Open Heart Perjury," *Night Court,* NBC, 1988.

Caterer, "Sophia's Wedding: Part 1," *The Golden Girls,* NBC, 1988.

Albert, "What's a Father to Do?," *Empty Nest,* NBC, 1988.

Maitre d' Bjorn, "Blast from the Past," *Eisenhower & Lutz,* 1988.

"Good Neighbor Sam," *My Sister Sam,* 1988.

Edmonton, "Fever," *Beauty and the Beast,* 1988.

Judge Steven Lang, "Izzy Ackerman or Is He Not," *L.A. Law,* NBC, 1989.

Dean Dackman, "Another Saturday Night," *Newhart,* CBS, 1989.

Riley Pringle, "I'm in Love with a Boy Named Stuart," *Coach,* ABC, 1989.

Riley Pringle, "Dauber's Blow–out," *Coach,* ABC, 1989.

Dr. Dellerton, "On the Nose," *Duet,* 1989.

Simon Le Simple, "The Clown," *Matlock,* NBC, 1989.

Judge Steven Lang, "One Rat, One Ranger," *L.A. Law,* NBC, 1989.

Riley Pringle, "If Keith Jackson Calls, I'll Be at My Therapist's," *Coach,* ABC, 1989.

Riley Pringle, "The Curley O'Brien Award," *Coach,* ABC, 1990.

Dr. Hendricks, "John's New Job: Part 1," *Dear John,* NBC, 1990.

Dr. Hendricks, "Matter of Trust: Part 1," *Dear John,* NBC, 1990.

Judge Steven Lang, "Whatever Happened to Hannah?," *L.A. Law,* NBC, 1990.

Barney, "Bad Girls," *Murphy Brown,* CBS, 1990.

"The President's Coming! The President's Coming! Parts 1 & 2," *The Golden Girls,* NBC, 1990.

Joe McNulty, "Safe at Home," *Perfect Strangers,* ABC, 1990.

Judge Steven Lang, "Armand's Hammer," *L.A. Law,* NBC, 1990.

Caterer, "There Goes the Bride: Part 2," *The Golden Girls,* NBC, 1991.

Reginald, "Daffy Dicks," *Morton & Hayes,* CBS, 1991.

Butler, "Home Buddies," *Morton & Hayes,* CBS, 1991.

Mr. Warner, "A Matter of Principal," *True Colors,* 1991.

Frank Pepitone, "A Guy Named Phantom: Parts 1 & 2," *Night Court,* NBC, 1991.

Mr. Hendricks, "Freddy's Back," *Dear John,* NBC, c. 1991.

Walt Twitchell, "A Diminished Rebecca with a Suspended Cliff," *Cheers,* NBC, 1992.

Mr. Eckworth, "Moon over Miami," *Nurses,* NBC, 1992.

Fred, "Luck Be a Taylor Tonight," *Home Improvement,* ABC, 1992.

Carlton Brunell, "Empty Rooms," *Sisters,* NBC, 1992.

Judge Steven Lang, "Silence of the Lambskins," *L.A. Law,* NBC, 1992.

Derek, *Shaky Ground,* Fox, 1992.

Earl Elliott, "Was It Good for You Too?," *Silk Stalkings,* USA Network, 1993.

Judge Talmadge, "Love and Marriage," *Empty Nest,* NBC, 1993.

Dr. Bryant, "Bedfellows," *Life Goes On,* ABC, 1993.

Judge Steven Lang, "Come Rain or Come Schein," *L.A. Law,* NBC, 1993.

Riley Pringle, "Belly of the Beast," *Coach,* ABC, 1993.

Chaplain, "The Birth of a Marriage," *Nurses,* NBC, 1993.

Prosecuting attorney, "High Treason: Part 1," *The Adventures of Brisco County, Jr.,* Fox, 1994.

Superintendent, "Belding's Prank," *Saved by the Bell: The New Class,* NBC, 1994.

Spy, "George Speaks His Mind," *The George Carlin Show,* 1994.

Ticket seller, *Wild Oats,* Fox, 1994.

Mayor, "Fast Forward," *M.A.N.T.I.S.,* Fox, 1995.

Mr. Pless, "The Face Painter," *Seinfeld,* NBC, 1995.

Judge Quinn, "Murphy's Law," *Murphy Brown,* CBS, 1995.

Tobe Alder, "The Enemy Within," *Nowhere Man,* UPN, 1995.

Dr. Jeff Eckerle, "War of the Coprophages," *The X–Files,* Fox, 1996.

Prince Restivon, "A Tale of Two Sister Cities," *Wings,* NBC, 1996.

Francis Bolt, "Red, White, or Blue," *Due South,* CBS, 1996.

Mr. Hartley, "Let the Games Begin," *ER,* NBC, 1996.

Jeweler, "A Dick on One Knee," *3rd Rock from the Sun,* NBC, 1997.

Danny, "Caroline and the Critics," *Caroline in the City,* NBC, 1997.

William Lanning, "Trial by Fire," *Baywatch,* NBC, 1997.

William, "Intersections in Real Time," *Babylon 5,* syndicated, 1997.

"The Art of Murder," *Mike Hammer, Private Eye,* syndicated, 1998.

Earl, "I Like Your Moxie," *Ned and Stacey,* Fox, 1999.

Mr. McFarlane, "Monica's Bad Day," *Touched by an Angel,* CBS, 2000.

Igor, "Whatever Happened to Tammi Tyler," *Strip Mall,* 2001.

Igor, "The Judge Is Free," *Strip Mall,* 2001.

Igor, "Hedda Bags Josh," *Strip Mall,* 2001.

Igor, "Elyce's Baby Blues," *Strip Mall,* 2001.

Walt Twitchell, "Cheerful Goodbyes," *Frasier,* NBC, 2002.

Judge Broe (four episodes), *Days of Our Lives,* NBC, 2002–2003.

Also appeared as Rick Paritte in an episode of *Tough Cookies.*

Television Appearances; Specials:

Dowdy, *Mister Roberts,* NBC, 1984.

Casting director, *Public Enemy Number 2,* Showtime, 1991.

Television Appearances; Miniseries:
Mr. Loats, *Fresno,* CBS, 1986.

Stage Appearances:
Ebenezer Scrooge, *A Christmas Carol,* American Conservatory Theatre, San Francisco, CA, annually, between 1995 and 2002.
Jacob Marley, *Christmas Carol,* Guthrie Theatre, MN, 2004.

Appeared as Nate Miller, *Ah, Wilderness!,* South Coast Repertory, Costa Mesa, CA; in *Aristocrats,* Mark Taper Forum, Los Angeles; in *The Browning Version,* American Conservatory Theatre; as Gayev, *The Cherry Orchard,* South Coast Repertory; in *Equus,* American Conservatory Theatre; in *The Good Doctor,* Pasadena Playhouse, Pasadena, CA; in *Green Card,* Mark Taper Forum; as Jack, *Home,* American Conservatory Theatre; in *Hotel Paradiso,* American Conservatory Theatre; title role, *The Imaginary Invalid,* Yale Repertory Theatre, New Haven, CT; title role, *King Lear,* Colorado Shakespeare Festival; in *Mad Forest,* Matrix Theatre Company; as Thomas More, *A Man for All Seasons,* Alliance Theatre Company, Atlanta, GA; as Sir George Crofts, *Mrs. Warren's Profession,* American Conservatory Theatre; in *Nothing Sacred,* Mark Taper Forum; in the title role, *Pantagleize,* American Conservatory Theatre; in *A Private View,* Mark Taper Forum; as Mercutio, *Romeo and Juliet;* in *Three Sisters,* American Conservatory Theatre; and in *Travesties,* American Conservatory Theatre.

Stage Director:
Angel Street, California Theatre Center, Sunnyvale Community Center Theatre, Sunnyvale, CA, 2002.

RECORDINGS

Audio Books:
Forbidden Tales of the Bible: The Harlot by the Side of the Road by Jonathan Kirsch, Audio Literature, 1998.

OTHER SOURCES

Periodicals:
Babylon 5, June, 1998, p. 43.

BISHOP, Meredith 1976–

PERSONAL

Full name, Meredith Anne Bishop; born January 15, 1976, in Los Angeles, CA.

Addresses: *Agent*—Kazarian, Spencer, Ruskin, and Associates, 11969 Ventura Blvd., 3rd Floor, Box 7409, Studio City, CA 91604. *Manager*—Ken Jacobson, Ken Jacobson Management Group, 11271 Ventura Blvd., Suite 464, Studio City, CA 91604.

Career: Actress and producer. Appeared in commercials for Geico insurance, 2004, Taco Bell restaurants, 2006, and Expedia.com travel site, 2006.

CREDITS

Television Appearances; Series:
Annie Mack, *The Secret World of Alex Mack* (also known as *Alex Mack*), Nickelodeon, 1994–97.

Television Appearances; Episodic:
Mabel at age eighteen, "Letters to Mabel," *Mad About You,* NBC, 1997.
Jenny Anderson, "The Dying Fields," *Sliders,* Sci–Fi Channel, 1998.
Denise, "The Right Thing," *Chicken Soup for the Soul,* PAX, 2000.
Lurleen, "Technical Knockup," *Nikki,* The WB, 2001.
Lurleen, "Vaya con Nikki," *Nikki,* The WB, 2001.
Samantha, "Boooz," *Felicity,* The WB, 2001.
Samantha, "Oops ... Noel Did It Again," *Felicity,* The WB, 2001.
Samantha, "Future Shock," *Felicity,* The WB, 2002.
Melissa, "My Day at the Races," *Scrubs* (also known as *Scrubs: Med School*), NBC, 2006.

Film Appearances:
Emily, *Klepto,* Showcase Entertainment, 2004.
Celeste, *Bed & Breakfast,* BB Film Productions, 2010.

Film Executive Producer:
Klepto, Showcase Entertainment, 2004.

Internet Appearances; Series:
Nina, *Speedie Date,* Strike.tv, 2008.

BJORLIN, Kamilla 1976–
    (Kamilla Bjoerlin)

PERSONAL

Some sources transliterate surname as Bjoerlin; full name, Kamilla Pariser Bjorlin; born December 31, 1976, in Lidingo (some sources transliterate name as Lidingoe), Sweden; daughter of Ulf Alexander, Sr. (a composer and conductor) and Fary (an interior decorator and painter) Bjorlin; sister of Nadia Bjorlin (an actress and singer) and Ulf Bjorlin (an actor and musician). *Education:* Attended Performing Arts Academy, Sweden, The Boston Conservatory, and other places; studied acting, comedy, and dance. *Avocational Interests:* Singing, kickboxing, tae kwon do, fencing, snow skiing, water skiing, ice skating, inline skating, hiking, mountain biking, horseback riding.

Addresses: *Agent*—Neil Bagg, Don Buchwald & Associates, 6500 Wilshire Blvd., Suite 2200, Los Angeles, CA 90048.

Career: Actress and producer. TOUCH (female performing group), choreographer, singer, and performer at various venues, 1993–97.

Member: American Federation of Television and Radio Artists, Screen Actors Guild.

CREDITS

Film Appearances:
America So Beautiful, 2001, Noor Film Festival, 2007.
Devil's Knight, MTI Home Video, 2003.
Countess Elan, *The Princess Diaries 2: Royal Engagement* (also known as *The Princess Diaries 2*), Buena Vista, 2004.
Holly, *Miss Castaway and the Island Girls* (also known as *Michael Jackson in Neverlanding Story, Miss Cast Away, Silly Movie 2,* and *Silly Movie 2.0*), Showcase Entertainment, 2004.
Mourner, *Raising Helen,* Buena Vista, 2004.
(Uncredited) Actress, *Cattle Call* (also known as *National Lampoon's "Cattle Call"* and *National Lampoon's: "To Casting"*), Lionsgate/National Lampoon Productions, 2006.
Saloon madam, *I Am Somebody: No Chance in Hell* (also known as *Chinaman's Chance*), Plus Entertainment, c. 2006.
Betty Burkin (a reporter), *Light Years Away,* By the River's Side Films, 2008.
Laura Baker, *MARy* (also known as *Bloody Mary*), GruntWorks Entertainment, 2008.
Anne, *First Dog,* First American Cinema, 2010.
Sherry Donaldson, *Valentine's Day,* Warner Bros./New Line Cinema, 2010.

Appeared in other films, including *Grave Digger* and *Last Marshall.*

Film Producer:
MARy (also known as *Bloody Mary*), GruntWorks Entertainment, 2008.

Produced other films.

Television Appearances; Movies:
Police officer, *Ghost Dog: A Detective Tail* (also known as *Dog Gone*), PAX, 2003.

Television Appearances; Episodic:
Maximum Bob, ABC, 1998.
Lilith the evil serpent, *Days of Our Lives* (also known as *Cruise of Deception: Days of Our Lives, Days, DOOL, Tropical Temptation, Tropical Temptation: Days of Our Lives, Des jours et des vies, Horton–sagaen, I gode og onde dager, Los dias de nuestras vidas, Meres agapis, Paeivien viemaeae, Vaara baesta aar, Zeit der Sehnsucht,* and *Zile din viata noastra*), NBC, 2000.
Kitchen Confidential, Fox, 2005.

Also appeared in episodes of other programs, including *Catherine Crier Live,* Court TV; *The Girl Next Door,* USA Network; *Hell's Kitchen* (also known as *Hell's Kitchen USA*), Fox; *House of Blues Tonight,* MTV; *My Crazy Life,* E! Entertainment Television; and *The Tonight Show with Jay Leno* (also known as *Jay Leno* and *Jay Leno Show*), NBC.

Television Appearances; Pilots:
Jane, *Predators* (documentary), Animal Planet, 2000.

Appeared in the pilot for *Top Model.*

Television Appearances; Other:
Host of *Live on the Net,* VH1; also appeared in *Chester French,* MTV; *The Hugh Hefner Story,* ABC; and *Judgmental,* Court TV.

Stage Appearances:
Move Over, Mrs. Markham, Lake Worth Playhouse, Lake Worth, FL, c. 1997–98.

Appeared in *Truth,* Palm Beach Playhouse; and in *Visit from Wild Man,* The Group Rep at the Lonny Chapman Theatre, North Hollywood, CA. Also appeared in productions of *A Chorus Line* (musical), *The Merry Wives of Windsor, Speed-the-Plow, Terminal Cafe,* and *True West,* all The Boston Conservatory, Boston, MA.

Radio Appearances:
Appeared in radio productions in Sweden.

OTHER SOURCES

Electronic:
KamillaBjorlin.com: The Official Website, http://www.kamillabjorlin.com, August 4, 2010.

BJORLIN, Ulf 1979–
(Ulf Bjoerlin)

PERSONAL

Some sources transliterate surname as Bjoerlin; full name, Ulf Alexander Bjorlin, Jr.; born June 8, 1979, in Lidingo (some sources transliterate name as Lidingoe), Sweden; son of Ulf Alexander, Sr. (a composer and conductor) and Fary (an interior decorator and painter) Bjorlin; brother of Nadia Bjorlin (an actress and singer) and Kamilla Bjorlin (an actress and producer). *Education:* Attended the Interlochen Summer Arts Camp, Boston University Tanglewood Music Institute, and Manhattan School of Music.

Addresses: *Agent*—Jerry Pace, Jerry Pace Agency, 4717 Van Nuys Blvd., Suite 102, Sherman Oaks, CA 91403.

Career: Actor and musician. Voice for films, radio programs, and video games. Voice artist and musician for commercials. Member of the Bjorlin Trio and performed at various venues. As a trombone player, worked with various musical artists and performed with a number of musical groups in different musical genres; also played other instruments. Music instructor for middle school and high school students.

Member: American Federation of Television and Radio Artists, Screen Actors Guild.

Awards, Honors: Florida All–State and Tri–State Festival honoree and named to first chair for his work as a musician.

CREDITS

Film Appearances:
Scott, *The Marriage Undone*, Bel Age Pictures/Bokken Films, 2002.
Marry Me (short film), RoxyRosie Productions, c. 2004.
(As Ulf Bjoerlin) Private Stern, *Alien Abduction*, The Asylum, 2005.
Walsh, *Way of the Vampire* (also known as *Bram Stoker's "Way of the Vampire," Van Helsing's "Way of the Vampire," Van Helsing vs. Dracula,* and *Way of the Vampire*), The Asylum, 2005.
Asole, *Let Some Air In* (short film), CSM Productions, 2006.
Ulf, *Transgressions* (short film), American Film Institute, 2006.
The Test Subject (short film), WopBopper Productions, c. 2008.

Witness, *Absolute Evil—Final Exit* (also known as *Absolute Evil* and *Savannah*), Peacock Films, 2009.
New tenant, *Unit 30* (short film), CSM Productions, 2010.

Also appeared in the films *Day Dream*, Warped Reality Pictures; *Intervention: Tejava*, CSM Productions; *March Madness*, Montgomery Films; and *Time*, New York University.

Film Musician:
Dropping In: The True Story of Don Wimmer, 2008, also a podcast series, 2009.
Boychik (short film), 2009.

Musician for other films, including *Deadline, The Legacy, Pedro,* and *The 7.*

Television Appearances; Documentary Specials:
Voice of Sergeant Joseph Gould, *Secret Missions of the Civil War*, History Channel, 2005.
Voice of Jean Lafitte, *Andrew Jackson*, History Channel, 2007.

Television Appearances; Episodic:
Mailroom person, *The Young and the Restless* (also known as *Y&R, The Innocent Years, Atithasa niata, Les feux de l'amour, Schatten der Leidenschaft,* and *Tunteita ja tuoksuja*), CBS, 2001 (uncredited), 2002.
Dot Com clerk, cashier, and server, *Days of Our Lives* (also known as *Cruise of Deception: Days of Our Lives, Days, DOOL, Tropical Temptation, Tropical Temptation: Days of Our Lives, Des jours et des vies, Horton–sagaen, I gode og onde dager, Los dias de nuestras vidas, Meres agapis, Paeivien vi-emaeae, Vaara baesta aar, Zeit der Sehnsucht,* and *Zile din viata noastra*), NBC, miscellaneous episodes, 2001, 2002, 2004.
David, "Spring Break Surprise," *I Didn't Know I Was Pregnant*, The Learning Channel, 2009.
ATF sniper, "Ruby Ridge," *Aftermath with William Shatner*, Biography, 2010.

Television Appearances; Pilots:
Appeared in the pilot *Shape Up or Ship Out!.*

Television Work; Series:
Mover, *Your Place or Mine?*, The Learning Channel, 2008.

Stage Musician:
Musician for the musicals *The Mystery of Edwin Drood* and *Oklahoma!*, both off–Broadway productions; and musician for the operas *Falstaff, L'elisir d'amore,* and *Rigoletto*.

Radio Appearances:
Appeared in radio programs.

Internet Musician:
Dropping In: The True Story of Don Wimmer (podcast series), 2009, released as a film, 2008.

Appeared in Internet broadcasts and in footage posted on the Internet, including musical footage and footage of The Bjorlin Trio.

RECORDINGS

Albums:
(With The Bjorlin Trio) *The Bjorlin Trio* (EP), Robo Records, 2008.

With The Bjorlin Trio, appeared in the singles "The Prayer" and "Time to Say Goodbye (Con Te Partiro)," both Robo Records, 2008. Participated in studio and session work.

Video Game Appearances:
Provided voices for video games.

BLAKE, Yvonne 1938–
(Ivonne Blake)

PERSONAL

Born 1938, in England; married Gil Carretero (a director). *Education:* Attended Manchester Regional College of Art.

Addresses: *Agent*—Marsh, Best and Associates, 9150 Wilshire Blvd., Suite 220, Beverly Hills, CA 90212.

Career: Costume designer. Worked as assistant to designers Cecil Beaton and Oliver Messel; commissioned costume designer for London Festival Ballet; also worked as assistant art director and costume coordinator in film industry.

Member: Costume Designers Guild.

Awards, Honors: Academy Award and Film Award nomination, British Academy of Film and Television Arts, both best costume design (with Antonio Castillo), 1972, for *Nicholas and Alexandra;* Film Award nominations, best costume design, British Academy of Film and Television Arts, 1974, for *Jesus Christ Superstar,* and 1975, for *The Three Musketeers;* Academy Award nomination (with Ron Talsky) and Film Award nomination, British Academy of Film and Television Arts, both best costume design, 1976, for *The Four Musketeers;* Saturn Award nomination (with Richard Bruno), best costumes, Academy of Science Fiction, Fantasy, and Horror Films, 1979, for *Superman;* Emmy Award nomination, best costume design for a miniseries or special, 1987, for *Casanova;* Goya Award, best costume design, Academia de las Artes y las Ciencias Cinematograficas de Espana, 1989, for *Remando al viento;* Goya Award nominations, best costume design, 1992, for *Don Juan en los infiernos,* and 1993, for *La reina anonima;* Goya Award, best costume design, 1995, for *Cancion de cuna;* Emmy Award nomination (with Randy Gardell), outstanding costumes for a miniseries, movie or a special, 2002, for *James Dean;* Goya Awards, best costume design, 2004, for *Carmen,* and 2005, for *The Bridge of San Luis Rey;* Satellite Award nomination, International Press Academy, and Goya Award nomination, both best costume design, 2007, for *Goya's Chosts.*

CREDITS

Film Costume Designer:
Judith (also known as *Conflict*), 1966.
The Idol, 1966.
The Spy with a Cold Nose, 1966.
Charlie Bubbles, Universal, 1967.
Assignment K, Columbia, 1968.
Duffy, Columbia, 1968.
The Best House in London, Metro–Goldwyn–Mayer, 1969.
Country Dance (also known as *Brotherly Love* and *The Same Skin*), 1970.
The Last Valley, 1970.
Puppet on a Chain, 1970.
Nicholas and Alexandra, Columbia, 1971.
Jesus Christ Superstar, Universal, 1973.
The Three Musketeers (also known as *The Three Musketeers: The Queen's Diamonds*), 1973.
The Four Musketeers (also known as *The Four Musketeers: Milady's Revenge*), Twentieth Century–Fox, 1974.
All Creatures Great and Small (also known as *All Things Great and Small*), 1974.
Ace Up My Sleeve (also known as *Crime and Passion*), 1975.
The Eagle Has Landed, 1976.
Robin and Marian, Columbia, 1976.
Cuando los maridos se iban a la guerra, 1976.
Superman (also known as *Superman: The Movie*), Warner Bros., 1978.
Escape to Athena, Associated Film Distribution, 1979.
Superman II, Warner Bros., 1980.
Green Ice, 1981.

Las aventuras de Enrique y Ana, 1981.

(As Ivonne Blake) *Bearn o la sala de las munecas* (also known as *Bearn*), 1982.

Escarabajos asesinos (also known as *Scarab*), 1982.

Finders Keepers, Warner Bros., 1984.

Flesh + Blood (also known as *The Rose and the Sword*), Orion, 1985.

(As Ivonne Blake) *Remando al viento* (also known as *Rowing in the Wind* and *Rowing with the Wind*), 1988.

The Return of the Musketeers, Universal, 1989.

Company Business, Metro–Goldwyn–Mayer, 1991.

Don Juan en los infiernos (also known as *Don Juan in Hell*), 1991.

La reina anonima (also known as *The Anonymous Queen*), 1992.

The Detective and Death (also known as *El detective y la muerte*), 1994.

Cradle Song (also known as *Cancion de cuna*), Nickel Odeon Dos, 1994.

Looking for Richard, 1996.

What Dreams May Come, PolyGram Filmed Entertainment, 1998.

Presence of Mind, 1999.

Gaudi Afternoon, First Look Home Entertainment, 2001.

The Reckoning (also known as *Morality Play*), Paramount, 2004.

Carmen, Parasol Pictures Releasing, 2004.

The Bridge of San Luis Rey, Fine Line, 2005.

Tirante el blanco (also known as *The White Knight*), Arclight Films, 2006.

Goya's Ghosts, Samuel Goldwyn, 2007.

There Be Dragons, 2010.

Film Appearances:

(Uncredited) Book person, "The Jewish Question," *Fahrenheit 451,* Universal, 1966.

Television Costume Designer; Movies:

Casanova, ABC, 1987.

Crime of the Century, HBO, 1996.

The Price of Heaven (also known as *Blessed Assurance*), CBS, 1997.

James Dean, TNT, 2001.

Television Costume Designer; Miniseries:

Harem, ABC, 1986.

The Richest Man in the World: The Story of Aristotle Onassis (also known as *Onassis: The Richest Man in the World*), ABC, 1988.

Television Appearances; Specials:

Presenter, *Premios Goya,* 1987, 2000.

Premios Goya, 2004, 2005.

Geraldine en Espana, 2006.

Television Appearances; Episodic:

"The Unsung Oscar," *Film Night,* BBC, 1972.

RECORDINGS

Videos:

Taking Flight: The Development of Superman, 2001.

Making "Superman:" Filming the Legend, 2001.

BLESSED, Brian 1936(?)–

PERSONAL

Born October 9, 1936 (some sources cite 1937), in Mexborough, Yorkshire, England; son of William (a coal miner) and Hilda (maiden name, Wall) Blessed; married Ann Bomann (divorced); married Hildegarde Zimmermann Neil (an actress), December 28, 1978; children: (first marriage) Catherine; (second marriage) Rosalind Josephine. *Education:* Trained for the stage at Bristol Old Vic Theatre School.

Addresses: *Manager*—Derek Webster, Associated International Management, Nederlander House, 7 Great Russell St., London WC1B 3NH, England.

Career: Actor and director. Royal Shakespeare Company, Stratford–upon–Avon, England, actor, 1985; voice for commercials, including Elastoplast Silver Healing Plasters, 2004, voice of driver for CocaCola radio ads, 2008, and ads for Toymaster stores. Yorkshire Wildlife Trust, president of Council for National Parks; Bowles Rocks Trust, member of board of trustees; patron of Freshfield, Kinder Mountain Rescue, Nepal Trust, and Scope. Originally worked as steeplejack, plasterer, and undertaker's assistant. *Military service:* Royal Air Force, served in parachute regiment.

CREDITS

Film Appearances:

Policeman, *The Christmas Tree,* CFF, 1966.

Sergeant, *Alf 'n' Family* (also known as *Till Death Do Us Part*), Sherpix, 1968.

Jack Baird, *Brotherly Love* (also known as *Country Dance* and *The Same Skin*), Metro–Goldwyn–Mayer, 1970.

Korski, *The Last Valley,* Cinerama, 1971.

Tathybius, *The Trojan Women,* Cinerama, 1971.

Suffolk, *Henry VIII and His Six Wives,* Metro–Goldwyn–Mayer, 1972.

Pedro, *Man of La Mancha,* United Artists, 1972.

Mark of Cornwall, *King Arthur, the Young Warlord,* 1975.

Prince Vultan, *Flash Gordon,* Universal, 1980.

Suleman Khan, *High Road to China,* Warner Bros., 1983.

Thomas Beaufort, Duke of Exeter, *Henry V,* Samuel Goldwyn, 1989.

(English–language version) Voice of Caous, *Asterix and the Big Fight* (animated; originally released in French as *Asterix et le coup du menhir;* also known as and *Asterix and the Stone's Blow*), Gaumont/Palace, 1989.

Lord Locksley, *Robin Hood: Prince of Thieves,* Warner Bros., 1991.

Pozzo, *Waiting for Godot,* 1991.

Chazov, *Back in the U.S.S.R.,* FoxVideo, 1992.

Voice of El Supremo, *Freddie as F.R.O.7* (animated; also known as *Freddie the Frog*), Miramax, 1992.

Antonio, *Much Ado about Nothing,* Samuel Goldwyn, 1993.

Major Elliot, *Chasing the Deer,* 1994.

Ghost of Hamlet's father, *Hamlet* (also known as *William Shakespeare's "Hamlet"*), Columbia, 1996.

Edward I, *The Bruce,* Cromwell Productions, 1996.

Edward the Confessor, *Macbeth,* 1997.

Voice of Boss Nass, *Star Wars: Episode I—The Phantom Menace* (also known as *The Phantom Menace* and *Star Wars I: The Phantom Menace*), 1999.

Voice of Mr. Clayton, *Tarzan* (animated), 1999.

Title role, *King Lear,* Lamancha, 1999.

Lucifer Bounder, *The Mumbo Jumbo,* Vine International, 2000.

Father Gabriel Norton, *Devil's Harvest,* Paragon Film Group, 2004.

Narrator, *Olympiad 448 BC: Olympiad of Ancient Hellas,* Arcadia Digital, 2004.

Wrestling trainer, *Alexander* (also known as *Alexander: Director's Cut* and *Alexander Revisited: The Final Cut*), Warner Bros., 2004.

Voice, *Midsummer Dream* (animated; also known as *El sueno de una noche de San Juan*), Filmes Lusomundo, 2005.

Lord Francisco del Ruiz, *Day of Wrath,* Screen Media Films, 2006.

Duke Senior and Duke Frederick, *As You Like It,* Lions Gate Films, 2006.

Aeneas Sylvius Piccolomin, *The Conclave,* Bogeydom Licensing, 2006.

Trevor Pilkington, *Back in Business,* Success Entertainment, 2007.

Voice of Boris Goudphater, *Agent Crush* (animated), Fantastic Films International, 2008.

Mr. Finney, *Re–evolution,* British Youth Academy, 2010.

Film Director:

Director of witches' scenes, *Macbeth,* 1997.

King Lear, Lamancha, 1999.

Television Appearances; Series:

Constable Fancy Smith, *Z Cars,* BBC, 1962–65.

Porthos, *The Three Musketeers,* 1966–67.

Porthos, *The Further Adventures of the Musketeers,* 1967.

Storyteller, *Jackanory,* BBC, 1971.

Mark of Cornwall, *Arthur of the Britons,* ITV, 1972–73.

William Woodcock, *Boy Dominic,* ITV, 1974.

King Richard IV, *Blackadder* (also known as *The Black Adder*), BBC, 1983.

William "Bill" Sticker, *Johnny and the Dead,* 1995.

Narrator, *Homeground,* 1997.

Voice of Sir Morris, *The Big Knights* (animated), BBC2, 1999.

Dr. Batch, *Let's Write a Story,* 2004.

Voice of Bob, *Kika & Bob* (animated), 2008.

Himself, *What Are You Like?,* BBC, 2008.

Announcer, *Let's Dance for Comic Relief,* 2009–10.

Television Appearances; Miniseries:

Reuben Starkadder, *Cold Comfort Farm,* BBC, 1968, then broadcast by *Masterpiece Theatre,* PBS, 1971.

Albert Grzymala, *Notorious Woman,* BBC, 1974, then broadcast by *Masterpiece Theatre,* PBS, 1975.

Abner, *The Story of David,* ABC, 1976.

Augustus, *I, Claudius,* BBC, 1976, then broadcast by *Masterpiece Theatre,* PBS, 1977.

Basileos, *The Aphrodite Inheritance,* BBC, 1979.

Peppone, *The Little World of Don Camillo,* BBC, 1980.

Geoffrey Lyons, *The Hound of the Baskervilles,* BBC, 1983.

Presenter, *Great Little Railways,* BBC, 1983.

Olinthus, *The Last Days of Pompeii,* ABC, 1984.

Long John Silver, *Return to Treasure Island,* 1986, then The Disney Channel, 1989.

Spiro, *My Family and Other Animals,* BBC, 1987.

General Yevlenko, *War and Remembrance,* ABC, 1988, 1989.

Sam, *The Castle of Adventure,* 1990.

Petty officer, *Lady Chatterley,* BBC, 1992.

Cluny McPherson, *Kidnapped,* The Family Channel, 1995.

Squire Western, *Henry Fielding's "Tom Jones"* (also known as *The History of Tom Jones, a Foundling*), Arts and Entertainment, 1998.

Full Mountie, 2000.

How TV Changed Britain, Channel 4, 2008.

Television Appearances; Movies:

Tom Gardner, *Barrister at Law,* BBC1, 1969.

Brian Ridware, *Whom God Hath Joined,* 1970.

Harry Shannon, *The Venturers,* 1972.

The Great Alfred, 1975.

Detective Sergeant George Briggs, "Appointment with a Killer" (also known as "A Midsummer Nightmare"), broadcast on *Thriller,* ABC, 1975.

Mentor, *Cosmic Princess* (released abroad in 1975, 1982.

Captain Teach, *The Master of Ballantrae*, CBS, 1984.
Hereward the Wake, *Blood Royal: William the Conqueror*, 1990.
General Gonse, *Prisoner of Honor*, HBO, 1991.
Chatillon, *Blood and Dust* (also known as *De terre et de sang*), 1992.
Mr. Carksdale, *Exam Conditions*, 1992.
Atticus, *MacGyver: Lost Treasure of Atlantis*, ABC, 1994.
Bestuzhev, *Catherine the Great*, Arts and Entertainment, 1995.
Mr. Scottley, *The Greatest Store in the World*, HBO, 1999.
King Henry VIII, *The Nearly Complete and Utter History of Everything*, BBC, 1999.
Max, *Winter Solstice*, 2003.
(In archive footage) Constable Fancy Smith, *Total Cops*, 2003.
Sir Gregory, *Mist: The Tale of a Sheepdog Puppy*, 2006.

Television Appearances; Specials:
Peter, "Son of Man," *Wednesday Play*, BBC, 1969.
Reg Sugden, "Double Agent," *ITV Playhouse*, ITV, 1969.
Will, "Wine of India," *Wednesday Play*, BBC, 1970.
Sergeant Kite, "The Recruiting Officer," *Play of the Month*, BBC, 1973.
Ted Gissing, "Lorna and Ted," *ITV Saturday Night Theatre*, ITV, 1973.
Tom Bowen, "Into Infinity," *NBC Special Treat*, NBC, 1975.
(Uncredited) Narrator, *A Christmas Carol*, BBC, 1977.
Host, narrator, and Johann Sebastian Bach, *The Joy of Bach*, PBS, 1980.
Night of One Hundred Stars, 1980.
David Macaulay: Castle, 1983.
Voice of Master Guillaume, *David Macaulay: Cathedral*, 1986.
Rudolf Kammerling, "Once in a Lifetime," *Great Performances*, PBS, 1988.
Voice of Ankhaf, *Pyramid* (animated; also known as *David Macaulay: Pyramid*), PBS, 1988.
Himself, *Galahad of Everest*, BBC, 1991.
Voice of General Gaius Valerius, *City* (animated; also known as *David Macaulay: Roman City*), PBS, 1994.
Old Deuteronomy, "Hey, Mr. Producer! The Musical World of Cameron Mackintosh" (also known as "Hey, Mr. Producer!"), *Great Performances*, PBS, 1998.
Narrator, *Eclipse: Herald of the Millennium*, 1999.
Night of a Thousand Shows, BBC, 2000.
Father Christmas and host, *I Love Christmas*, BBC, 2001.
Presenter, *The Laurence Olivier Awards 2002*, 2002.
(In archive footage) *Judi Dench: A BAFTA Tribute*, 2002.
(Uncredited; in archive footage) *Death on Everest*, Channel 5, 2003.
Voice of wild boar, *The Legend of the Tamworth Two*, BBC, 2004.

Sport Relief, BBC, 2004.
Happy Birthday BBC Two, BBC, 2004.
ITV West at 50, ITV West, 2005.
The Passion: Films, Faith & Fury, Channel 4, 2006.
Greatest Ever Blockbuster Movies, Channel 5, 2006.
Guest presenter, *Should I Really Give Up Flying?*, BBC, 2007.
The 50 Greatest Television Dramas, Channel 4, 2007.
We Love "The Sky at Night," BBC, 2007.
Secrets of Celebrity Stars in Their Eyes, ITV, 2007.
Togas on TV, BBC, 2007.
The Flash Gordon Story, 2008.
Blackadder's Most Cunning Moments, 2008.
(Uncredited; in archive footage) Richard IV, *Blackadder Exclusive: The Whole Rotten Saga*, 2008.
(Uncredited; in archive footage) Richard IV, *Blackadder Rides Again*, BBC, 2008.

Narrator of *The Natural World*, BBC; also appeared in *Brahms*, *Hadleigh*, *Justice*, *Public Eye*, *Son of a Man*, and *William the Conqueror*.

Television Appearances; Episodic:
Policeman, "Catspaw," *Ghost Squad*, 1963.
Mark Dayton, "The Superlative Seven," *The Avengers*, ITV, 1967.
Eddie Barnaby, "Stop It, You're Breaking My Heart," *Mogul* (also known as *The Troubleshooters*), 1968.
Sergeant Hearn, "The Morning After," *The Avengers*, ITV, 1969.
Jim Lawsey, "The Ghost Who Saved the Bank at Monte Carlo," *Randall and Hopkirk (Deceased)* (also known as *My Partner the Ghost*), 1969.
Hubert Innes, "A Clear and Easy Duty," *The Expert*, BBC, 1971.
Sir Nigel, "The Reunion," *Shirley's World*, 1971.
Tiger Lawson, "The Whole Truth?," *Justice*, ITV, 1973.
Joseph Roper, "The Last Rent Dinner," *Hadleigh*, YTV, 1973.
Reverend William Pratt, "Egg & Cress Sandwiches," *Public Eye*, ITV, 1973.
Frank Kemble, "Ringer," *The Sweeney*, ITV, 1975.
Guthrum, "King Alfred," *Churchill's People*, BBC, 1975.
Dr. Cabot Rowland, "Death's Other Dominion," *Space 1999*, syndicated, 1975.
Interviewee, "Frank Windsor," *This Is Your Life*, ITV, 1975.
Mentor, "The Metamorph," *Space 1999*, syndicated, 1976.
Brod, "Law of the Jungle," *Survivors*, BBC1, 1977.
Call My Bluff, BBC, 1977.
Vargas, "Cygnus Alpha," *Blake's 7*, BBC1, 1978.
Member of the public, "Pressure," *Z Cars*, BBC, 1978.
Detective Sergeant Jack Nolan, "Lamb to the Slaughter," *Tales of the Unexpected*, syndicated, 1979.
Thomas Myers, "Room for an Inward Light," *Leap in the Dark*, BBC, 1980.

Richard XII of Scotland, "Born to Be King," *Blackadder* (also known as *The Black Adder*), BBC, 1983.

"Brian Blessed," *This Is Your Life,* ITV, 1984.

"Warwickshire," *Treasure Hunt,* 1985.

Yrcanos, "Mindwarp," *Doctor Who,* syndicated, 1986.

"Dingley Dell," *Roland Rat, the Series,* BBC, 1986.

(Uncredited; in archive footage) Yrcanos, "The Ultimate Foe," *Doctor Who,* syndicated, 1986.

Yrcanos, "The Trial of a Time Lord: Parts 5–8, 14," *Doctor Who,* syndicated, 1986.

The Kenny Everett Television Show, BBC, 1986.

Gaston, "The Imposter," *Crossbow* (also known as *Willem Tell*), 1987.

Gaston, "The Pass," *Crossbow* (also known as *Willem Tell*), 1987.

Gaston, "Misalliance," *Crossbow* (also known as *Willem Tell*), 1987.

Lambert Sampson, "Banbury Blue," *Boon,* ITV, 1988.

A Question of Entertainment, BBC, 1988.

Blankety Blank, BBC, 1988.

Inspector Freddi Dyer, "The Last Video Show," *Minder,* ITV, 1989.

Harry Catapodis, "Black Virgin of Vladimir," *Lovejoy,* Arts and Entertainment, 1991.

Harry Catapodis, "Riding in Rollers," *Lovejoy,* Arts and Entertainment, 1991.

(In archive footage) Harry Catapodis, "Friends in High Places," *Lovejoy,* Arts and Entertainment, 1992.

Television's Greatest Hits, BBC, 1992.

Entertainment UK, 1992.

Pebble Mill at One, BBC1, 1992.

Voice of captain, "Skull and Crossbones," *Dennis the Menace,* 1998.

Cavalier, "A Cavalier Spirit," *Adam's Family Tree,* 1999.

"Pantomime Special," *Call My Bluff,* BBC, 1999.

Melinda's Big Night In, 1999.

Himself, "The Mountains of Doom," *Fun at the Funeral Parlour,* BBC, 2001.

"Z Cars," *After They Were Famous,* ITV, 2002.

Call My Bluff, BBC, 2004.

Room 101, BBC, 2004.

"Live on the Night," *Time Shift,* BBC, 2004.

"Z Cars," *Stars Reunited,* BBC, 2004.

Himself and Luciano Pavarotti, "2004 Celebrity Special," *Stars in Their Eyes,* ITV, 2004.

"I, Claudius," *Drama Connections,* BBC, 2005.

"Max Beesley," *A Taste of My Life,* BBC, 2006.

A Question of Sport, 2006.

"Lucas and Walliams' Perfect Night In," *Perfect Night In,* Channel 4, 2007.

Micky "Rebel" Becket, "Rebel, Rebel," *Doctors,* BBC, 2007.

Captain Goiter, "The Train Pirates," *The Wrong Door,* Independent Film Channel, 2008.

Captain Goiter, "Bondo," *The Wrong Door,* Independent Film Channel, 2008.

Voice of Prince Vultan, "Road to Germany," *Family Guy* (animated; also known as *Padre de familia*), Fox, 2008.

Sir Edward Fawcett, "Pastures New," *The Royal,* ITV, 2008.

"Z Cars," *Call the Cops,* BBC4, 2008.

Have I Got News for You, BBC, 2008.

All Star Mr & Mrs, ITV, 2009.

The Gadget Show, 2009, (in archive footage) 2010.

Great Uncle Walter, "I Want My Horace," *Little Princess,* 2010.

Also appeared in *Pob's Programme,* Channel 4, and *Turning Points,* BBC.

Television Talk Show Guest Appearances; Episodic:

Today with Des and Mel, ITV, 2003.

The Terry and Gaby Show, Channel 5, 2003.

Richard and Judy, Channel 4, 2003.

Saturday Brunch, 2004.

The Paul O'Grady Show, ITV, 2004, 2005.

This Morning, ITV, 2004, 2006.

Wogan Now & Then, 2006.

Loose Women, ITV, 2006, 2007, 2008.

Breakfast, BBC, 2008.

Ant & Dec's Saturday Night Takeaway, ITV, 2009.

Stage Appearances:

Edmund, *The Exorcism,* Comedy Theatre, London, 1975.

Maxim Gorky, *State of Revolution,* Royal National Theatre, Lyttelton Theatre, London, 1977.

Macbeth, Old Vic Theatre, London, 1980.

Old Deuteronomy and Bustopher Jones, *Cats* (musical), New London Theatre, London, 1981.

Lord Hastings, *Richard III,* Royal Shakespeare Company, Royal Shakespeare Theatre, Stratford–upon–Avon, England, 1984, then Theatre Royal, Newcastle–upon–Tyne, England, 1985.

Duke of Exeter, *Henry V,* Royal Shakespeare Company, Royal Shakespeare Theatre, 1984, then Theatre Royal, 1985.

Claudius, *Hamlet,* Royal Shakespeare Company, Royal Shakespeare Theatre, 1984, then Theatre Royal, 1985.

John Freeman, *Metropolis* (musical), Piccadilly Theatre, London, 1989.

An Evening with Brian Blessed (solo show), 1992–93, then 1995–96.

Mr. Darling/Captain Hook, *Peter Pan,* Yvonne Arnaud Theatre, Guildford, England, 1993–94.

Hard Times, London, 2000.

Sir Tunbelly Clumsey, *The Relapse,* Royal National Theatre, London, 2001.

Baron Bomburst, *Chitty Chitty Bang Bang* (musical), London Palladium, c. 2002.

Mr. Darling/Captain Hook, *Peter Pan,* Orchard Theatre, Dartford, England, 2003.

Narrator, *The Six Wives of Henry VIII,* Hampton Court Palace Theatre, 2009.

Also appeared as Henry II, *The Lion in Winter;* in *Incident at Vichy* and *Oedipus,* both in London; and in repertory at Nottingham, England, and Birmingham, England.

Stage Director:

The Room, Royal Shakespeare Company, Gulbenkian Studio Theatre, Newcastle–upon–Tyne, England, 1985.
The Glass Menagerie, England, 1998.

Radio Appearances; Specials:

Performed as voice of Jean Valjean, *Les Miserables,* Family Radio Theatre.

Internet Appearances; Episodic:

Guest presenter, *Have I Got News for You: The Inevitable Internet Spin–off,* BBC.com, 2008.

RECORDINGS

Videos:

(In archive footage) Vargas, *Blake's 7: The Beginning,* 1978.
Narrator, *Agincourt 1415: The Triumph of the Longbow,* 1993.
The Doctors, 30 Years of Time Travel and Beyond, 1995.
Edward the Confessor, *Macbeth: A Critical Guide,* 1997.
King Lear, *King Lear: A Critical Guide,* 1997.
Himself as a historical actor, *Battles that Changed the World: Peloponnesian Wars,* 1998.
Narrator and presenter, *The Boer War and Other Colonial Adventures,* 1999.
I Claudius: A Television Epic, 2002.
Narrator, *Alexander the Great,* Arcadia, 2006.
(In archive footage) King Yccranos, *Trials and Tribulations,* 2 Entertain Video, 2008.
(In archive footage) *Let Loose ... The Very Best of "Loose Women,"* 2008.

Video Games:

Voice of Uncle Kashumai, *Privateer 2: The Darkening,* 1996.
Voice of Clayton, *Tarzan* (also known as *Disney's "Tarzan"*), 1999.
Voice of Clayton, *Kingdom Hearts,* Square Electronic Arts, 2002.
Voice, *Extreme Skate Adventure* (also known as *Disney's "Extreme Skate Adventure"*), 2003.
Voice of the admiral, *Warhammer 40,000: Fire Warrior,* THQ, 2003.
Voice, *Rome: Total War—Alexander,* Sega of Japan, 2006.

Narrator, *Viking: Battle for Asgard,* Sega of America, 2008.

Audio Books:

Reader, *George and the Dragon, by Chris Wormell,* Red Fox, 2006.

WRITINGS

Books:

The Turquoise Mountain: Brian Blessed on Everest, Bloomsbury, 1991, Pocket Books, 1993.
The Dynamite Kid, Bloomsbury, 1992, Pocket Books, 1993.
Nothing's Impossible, Simon & Schuster, 1994.
Blessed Everest: Climb to the Summit of Mount Everest with Brian Blessed, Britain's Own Actor/Adventurer, Salamander, 1995.
Quest for the Lost World, Boxtree, 1999.

OTHER SOURCES

Television Episodes:

"Brian Blessed," *This Is Your Life,* ITV, 1984.

BLOCK, Larry 1942–
(Larry Bloch)

PERSONAL

Full name, Lawrence Joel Block; born October 30, 1942, in New York, NY; son of Harold (in the garment industry) and Sonia (a travel agent; maiden name, Kutcher) Block; married Jolly King (an actress), September 25, 1981; children: Zoe Lenna, Zachary Harold. *Education:* University of Rhode Island, B.A., 1964; trained for the stage with Wynn Handman.

Addresses: *Agent*—Gage Group, 14724 Ventura Blvd., Suite 505, Sherman Oaks, CA 91403.

Career: Actor. *Military service:* U.S. Army, Special Services, 1967–69; received Commendation Medal, 1969.

CREDITS

Stage Appearances:

(Stage debut) Mercutio's page, *Romeo and Juliet,* American Shakespeare Festival, Stratford, CT, 1965.
Coriolanus, American Shakespeare Festival, 1965.

The Taming of the Shrew, American Shakespeare Festival, 1965.

King Lear, American Shakespeare Festival, 1965.

(Broadway debut) Understudy for the roles of Malcolm Scrawdyke and Irwin Ingham, *Hail, Scrawdyke,* Booth Theatre, 1966.

Boy, *La turista,* St. Clement's Church Theatre, New York City, 1967.

Eh?, Circle in the Square, New York City, 1967.

Harry, Noon, and Night, Theatre of the Living Arts, Philadelphia, PA, 1970.

The Recruiting Officer, Theatre of the Living Arts, 1970.

Jesse, *Fingernails Blue as Flowers,* American Place Theatre, New York City, 1971–72.

Lucky, *Waiting for Godot,* St. Clement's Church Theatre, 1974.

Understudy for the roles of Johann Sebastian Fabiani and Whimsey, *Where Do We Go from Here?,* New York Shakespeare Festival, Public Theatre, New York City, 1974.

Dromio of Ephesus, *The Comedy of Errors,* New York Shakespeare Festival, Delacorte Theatre, Public Theatre, New York City, 1975.

The Last Days of British Honduras, New York Shakespeare Festival, 1976.

Manny Alter, *Coming Attractions,* Playwrights Horizons Theatre, New York City, 1980–81.

Gadshill, *Henry IV, Part One,* New York Shakespeare Festival, Delacorte Theatre, Public Theatre, 1981.

Sir Toby Belch, *Twelfth Night,* Shakespeare and Company, Lee, MA, 1981.

Leon, *The Workroom* (also known as *L'atelier*), Center Stage, Baltimore, MD, 1981.

Martin Bormann, *The Fuehrer Bunker,* American Place Theatre, 1981.

Manhattan Love Songs, Actors' Studio, New York City, 1982.

A Tantalizing, Actors Theatre of Louisville, Louisville, KY, 1983.

Benny Silverman, *The Value of Names,* Actors Theatre of Louisville, 1983, then Hartford Stage Company, Hartford, CT, 1984.

The Hotel Manager, *Souvenirs,* Cubiculo Theatre, New York City, 1984.

One-Eyed, *The Golem,* New York Shakespeare Festival, Delacorte Theatre, Public Theatre, 1984.

Sir Toby Belch, *Twelfth Night,* Tyrone Guthrie Theatre, Minneapolis, MN, 1984.

Mr. Fezziwig, *A Christmas Carol,* Tyrone Guthrie Theatre, 1984.

Randolph, *Responsible Parties,* Vineyard Theatre, New York City, 1985.

Del Bates, *The Hit Parade,* Manhattan Punch Line, New York City, 1985.

Lada I, *Largo Desolato,* New York Shakespeare Festival, LuEsther Hall, Public Theatre, New York City, 1986.

Yuri Brushnik, "Coup d'etat," *Young Playwrights Festival,* Playwrights Horizons Theatre, 1986.

Censor, *Hunting Cockroaches,* Manhattan Theatre Club Stage I, New York City, 1987.

Elliot Atlas, *The Square Root of Three,* Jewish Repertory Theatre, New York City, 1987.

Antonio, *Two Gentlemen of Verona,* New York Shakespeare Festival, Delacorte Theatre, Public Theatre, 1987.

Willis, *Moonchildren,* Second Stage Theatre Company, McGinn–Cazale Theatre, New York City, 1987.

Cecil, *The Yellow Dog Contract,* Apple Corps Theatre, New York City, 1988.

Augustin Feraillon, *A Flea in Her Ear,* Long Wharf Theatre, New Haven, CT, 1989.

Herbie, *The Loman Family Picnic,* Manhattan Theatre Club Stage II, New York City, 1989.

Deputy director, *Temptation,* New York Shakespeare Festival, Estelle R. Newman Theatre, Public Theatre, New York City, 1989.

Bernie Weiner, *Selling Off,* John Houseman Theatre, New York City, 1991.

Lord/Fisherman/Cerimon/Pandar, *Pericles,* New York Shakespeare Festival, Estelle R. Newman Theatre, Public Theatre, 1991.

Alvin, *One of the All–Time Greats,* Vineyard Theatre, 1992.

The Last Laugh, Jewish Repertory Theatre, New York City, 1992.

Angelo, *The Comedy of Errors,* New York Shakespeare Festival, Delacorte Theatre, Public Theatre, 1992.

Director/Fyodor, *The Flying Karamazov Brothers in The Brothers Karamazov,* Seattle Repertory Theatre, Seattle, WA, 1992, then Arena Stage, Washington, DC, 1993.

Leon, *The Workroom,* American Jewish Theatre, New York City, 1993.

Title role, *Shlemiel the First,* American Repertory Theatre, Cambridge, MA, 1995, then American Music Theatre Festival, Philadelphia, PA, later Lincoln Center's Serious Fun Festival, New York City, c. 1995.

Mr. Appopolous, *Wonderful Town* (musical), New York City Opera Company, New York State Theatre, New York City, 1995.

Doc, Border, Taxman, and Stylagi, *Him,* New York Shakespeare Festival, LuEsther Hall, Public Theatre, 1995.

Leporello, *Don Juan in Chicago,* Primary Stages, New York City, 1996.

Uncle Phillip's Coat (solo show), American Jewish Theatre, 1998.

Nathan, *2 ½ Jews,* Raymond J. Greenwald Theatre, New York City, 1999.

Reb Eli, *God of Vengeance,* Adams Memorial Theatre, Williamstown, MA, 2002.

Storyteller, *Evolution,* Urban Empire Company, Bleecker Street Theatre, New York City, 2002.

Voice of police officer and judge, *The Exonerated;* appeared in productions of *The Faithful Brethren of Pitt Street;* and *Festival of One Acts.*

Major Tours:
2 ½ Jews, U.S. cities, 1998–2001.
Uncle Phillip's Coat (solo show),New England cities, 2003.

Film Appearances:
Springy, *Shamus* (also known as *Passion for Danger*), Columbia, 1973.
Peterboro referee, *Slap Shot,* Universal, 1977.
Ted Peters, *Heaven Can Wait,* Paramount, 1978.
Detective Burrows, *Hardcore* (also known as *The Hardcore Life*), Columbia, 1979.
First Family, 1980.
Taxi driver, *After Hours,* Warner Bros., 1985.
Bar owner, *Cocktail,* Touchstone, 1988.
Julius Enderby, *Robots,* 1988.
Harvey, *High Stakes* (also known as *Melanie Rose*), 1989.
Routed (short film), Izar, 1989.
Barber, *Betsy's Wedding,* Buena Vista, 1990.
Defense attorney, *My Blue Heaven,* 1990.
Man in restaurant, *Big Night,* Samuel Goldwyn, 1996.
Andy, *The Electric Urn,* Groovy Boots Productions, 1997.
Dr. Butler, *Dangerous Proposition,* IFM, 1998.
Herbie, *Isn't She Great,* Universal, 2000.
Customer, *Bait* (also known as *Wild Chase*), Warner Bros., 2000.
Doorman, *Don't Say a Word* (also known as *Sound of Silence*), Twentieth Century–Fox, 2001.
Discount store manager, *Garmento* (also known as *Threads*), Spanish Moss, 2002.
Harry, *Book of Danny,* 2002.
Nigel, *Stealing Martin Lane,* G–Machine, 2005.
Chef Buddy, *Live at Five* (short film), 2005.
Mr. Faddis, *The Guitar,* Lightning Media, 2008.
Dr. Ken "Mecca" Rennet, *Triptosane,* Supernatural Productions, 2010.

Television Appearances; Series:
Mickey Potter, *The Secret Storm,* CBS, 1971.
Cal Jamison, *General Hospital,* ABC, 1978.

Television Appearances; Miniseries:
Lasie, "Roanoak," *American Playhouse,* PBS, 1986.

Television Appearances; Pilots:
Harry, *Rosetti and Ryan: Men Who Love Women,* NBC, 1977.
Private Arnold Fleck, *Space Force,* NBC, 1978.

Television Appearances; Movies:
Springy, *A Matter of Wife ... and Death,* NBC, 1976.
Barney Fayne, *The Lindbergh Kidnapping Case,* NBC, 1976.
(As Larry Bloch) Leroy Keenan, *The Last Ride of the Dalton Gang,* NBC, 1979.

Kleinfeld, *Dead Man Out* (also known as *Dead Man Walking*), HBO, 1989.

Television Appearances; Specials:
Hardcore TV, HBO, 1993.
Voices of Yaacov Baror, Judge Moshe Landau, and Gavriel Bach, *The Trial of Adolf Eichmann,* PBS, 1997.
Narrator, "The Zodiac," *Case Reopened,* The Learning Channel, 1999.
Mr. Giapetto, *Kenny the Shark,* The Discovery Channel, 2000.

Television Appearances; Episodic:
Tom, *Sesame Street* (also known as *Open Sesame, The New Sesame Street,* and *Sesame Street Unpaved*), PBS, 1971, 1972.
Gerry Erskine, "Dark Sunday," *Kojak,* CBS, 1973.
"Set Up City," *Baretta,* ABC, 1975.
Floor director, "The Adventure of the Hard–Hearted Huckster," *Ellery Queen,* NBC, 1976.
Eddie Hendrix, "Images," *M*A*S*H,* CBS, 1977.
Liquor store clerk, "Requiem for a Loser," *Delvecchio,* 1977.
Arlo Spinner, "Game, Set, Death," *Charlie's Angels,* ABC, 1978.
Cimoli, "Dear Comrade," *M*A*S*H,* CBS, 1978.
Russell Schuman, "Evaluation," *Barney Miller,* ABC, 1978.
Bartender, "The Best of Enemies," *Operation Petticoat* (also known as *Life in the Pink*), 1978.
Abel, "Death Watch," *CHiPs* (also known as *CHiPs Patrol*), NBC, 1979.
Stan Feller, *Ryan's Hope,* 1981.
FBI agent, "Heroes of the Revolution," *Miami Vice,* NBC, 1987.
Mr. Seeger, "Two Income Family," *Family Matters,* ABC, 1989.
Al Henderson, "But First a Word from Our Sponsor," *Murphy Brown,* CBS, 1990.
Feldman, "His Hour upon the Stage," *Law & Order,* NBC, 1991.
Slater, "Cruel and Unusual," *Law & Order,* NBC, 1995.
Rossmore, "Bad Blood," *New York Undercover,* Fox, 1996.
Stan, "Divorce," *Law & Order,* NBC, 1998.
Helmut Kaiser, "Officer Involved," *Third Watch,* NBC, 2000.
Podiatrist, "Foot," *The Job,* ABC, 2001.
Lonnie, "Wrath," *Law & Order: Special Victims Unit* (also known as *Law & Order: SVU* and *Special Victims Unit*), NBC, 2001.
Darryl Moffatt, "Attorney Client," *Law & Order,* NBC, 2002.
Frank Kastner, "Blink," *Law & Order: Criminal Intent* (also known as *Law & Order: CI*), NBC, 2003.

Radio Appearances; Series:
Appeared in *The Other Side,* KCRW; and *Work in Progress.*

Radio Appearances; Episodic:
Appeared in pilot episode of *National Public Radio Playhouse*, National Public Radio; "Prairie du Chien," *Earplay*, National Public Radio; and *Under the Gun*, WBAI.

RECORDINGS

Videos:
Voices, *I, Robot* (video game), 1983.

BLOUNT, Lisa 1957–2010

PERSONAL

Full name, Lisa S. Blount. Born July 1, 1957, in Fayetteville, AR; died October 27, 2010, in Little Rock, AR. Actress and producer. Blount is best known for her supporting actress role in the 1982 film drama *An Officer and a Gentleman*, for which she won a Golden Globe nomination. In 1978, as a teenager, she made her film debut in *September 30, 1955*, by writer-director James Bridges. During the next decades, she played roles in *Prince of Darkness* in 1987, *Needful Things* in 1993, and *Box of Moonlight* in 1996. She also appeared regularly in the television series *Profit*. *Great Balls of Fire!*, a 1989 film about rock-and-roll star Jerry Lee Lewis, matched her up with Dennis Quaid and Winona Ryder. After Blount's 1998 marriage to fellow Southerner Ray McKinnon, the two collaborated with Walton Goggins to start Ginny Mule Pictures in 1999 in order to make authentic Southern movies. Expanding on her talents, she began producing films, sharing an Academy Award with her husband for the 2002 short film *The Accountant*. She produced and starred in both McKinnons feature film directorial debuts, the 2004 drama *Chrystal* (acting opposite Billy Bob Thornton) and his 2007 comedy *Randy and the Mob*. Shortly before her death, Blount acted in a 2010 pilot for the cable television series *Outlaw Country*.

PERIODICALS

Los Angeles Times, October 29, 2010.
New York Times, October 29, 2010.
Washington Post, October 29, 2011.

BOLGER, Sarah 1991–

PERSONAL

Born February 28, 1991, in Dublin, Ireland; daughter of Derek (a butcher) and Monica Bolger; sister of Emma Bolger (an actress). *Education:* Trained with Dublin Youth Theatre and at Anne Kavanagh Young People's Theatre School.

Addresses: *Agent*—Hylda Queally, Creative Artists Agency, 2000 Avenue of the Stars, Los Angeles, CA 90067; Michael Symons, Hamilton Hodell Ltd., 66–68 Margaret St., 5th Floor, London W1W 8SR, England.

Career: Actress.

Awards, Honors: Washington DC Area Film Critics Association Award nomination, best supporting actress, 2003, Independent Spirit Award nomination, best supporting actress, Independent Features Project/West, Phoenix Film Critics Society Award, best youth actress in a lead or supporting role, Chicago Film Critics Association Award nomination, most promising performer, Critics Choice Award nomination, best young actor or actress, Broadcast Film Critics Association, rising star, Marco Island Film Award nomination, and Screen Actors Guild award nomination (with others), outstanding cast in a motion picture, all 2004, all for *In America*; nomination for Rising Star Award, Irish Film and Television Awards, 2009; Irish Film and Television Award nomination, best supporting actress in a film, 2009, for *The Spiderwick Chronicles*; Irish Film and Television Award, best supporting actress in a television role, 2010, for *The Tudors*.

CREDITS

Film Appearances:
Eileen Cloney, *A Love Divided*, 1999, Cinema Guild, 2001.
Christy, *In America*, Fox Searchlight, 2003.
Azura, *Premonition* (short film), 2005.
Annie, *Tara Road*, 2005, First Look International, 2007.
Sabina Pleasure, *Alex Rider: Operation Stormbreaker* (also known as *Alex Rider: Stormbreaker* and *Stormbreaker*), Metro–Goldwyn–Mayer, 2006.
Mallory Grace, *The Spiderwick Chronicles* (also released as *The Spiderwick Chronicles: The IMAX Experience*), Paramount, 2008.
Kashka, *Iron Cross*, Calibra Pictures, 2009.

Television Appearances; Series:
The World of Tosh, 2002.
Mary Tudor, *The Tudors*, Showtime, 2008–10.

Television Appearances; Movies:
Helena Fitzgerald, *A Secret Affair* (also known as *Barbara Taylor Bradford's "A Secret Affair"*), CBS, 1999.

Television Appearances; Miniseries:
Lorraine Keegan, *Stardust*, Radio Telefis Eireann, 2006.

Television Appearances; Episodic:
The View, ABC, 2003.
The Late Late Show, 2003, 2004.
Janey Quinn, *The Clinic,* Radio Telefis Eireann, 2004.
Late Night with Conan O'Brien, NBC, 2008.
Xpose, TV3, 2009, 2010.

Television Appearances; Specials:
Happy Birthday Oscar Wilde, BBC, 2004.
Los Tudor: Rodaran cabezas, 2009.

Television Appearances; Awards Presentations:
10th Annual Screen Actors Guild Awards, TNT, 2004.
The 2004 IFP/West Independent Spirit Awards, Bravo
　and Independent Film Channel, 2004.
The 6th Annual Irish Film and Television Awards, 2009.

RECORDINGS

Video Games:
Voice of Mallory Grace, *The Spiderwick Chronicles,*
　Sierra Entertainment, 2008.
Voice of Eleanor Lamb, *BioShock 2,* 2K Games, 2010.

OTHER SOURCES

Periodicals:
Teen Vogue, March, 2008.

BOLT, Anna

PERSONAL

Sister of Jeremy Bolt (a film producer).

Addresses: *Agent*—Patrick Hambleton Management.
Manager—Laina Cohn Management, 15066 Sutton St.,
Sherman Oaks, CA 91403.

Career: Actress.

CREDITS

Film Appearances:
Anna, *The Turn of the Screw,* Live Video, 1992.
Sandy, *Crimetime,* Trimark Pictures, 1996.
Misha, *Vigo* (also known as *Vigo—Passion for Life*),
　Channel Four Films, 1998.
K J, *Running Time,* 2000.

Dr. Green, *Resident Evil* (also known as *Biohazard*),
　Screen Gems, 2002.
Nurse Jones, *DOA: Dead or Alive* (also known as
　DOA), Dimension Films, 2006.
Her, *Dance for Eternity* (short film), 2008.
Louise, *War Wounds* (short film), 2010.

Television Appearances; Series:
Nell Miller, *London Bridge,* ITV, 1995.

Television Appearances; Movies:
Elizabeth Knight, *The Life and Death of Philip Knight,*
　1993.
Private Brenda Riley, *The Investigator,* 1997.
Kathryn, *The Place of the Dead,* ITV, 1997.
Death in Disguise, Arts and Entertainment, 1998.
Ly, *Cyclops,* 2001.

Television Appearances; Episodic:
Sally Lister, "First Impressions," *Casualty,* BBC1, 1994.
Nursery nurse, "Band of Gold," *Solider Soldier,* ITV,
　1994.
Dancer, "A Barbecue at Violet's," *Keeping Up Appear-
　ances,* BBC, 1995.
Kay Ross, "All for Love," *The Bill,* ITV1, 1997.
Suhami and Sylvie Gamelin, "Death in Disguise," *Mid-
　somer Murders,* ITV and Arts and Entertainment,
　1999.
Mandy Fry, "Tolerance: Parts 1 & 2," *The Bill,* ITV1,
　2001.
Maureen Harding, "A Dog's Life," *Heartbeat,* ABC,
　2002.
Susan Wingrove, "Survival of the Fittest," *Doctors,* BBC,
　2003.
Tanya Holmes, "Til Death Do Us Part," *Holby City,*
　BBC, 2003.
Sally Simmons, "Seeing Is Believing," *Down to Earth,*
　BBC, 2004.
Claire Wright, "Pride Before a Fall," *Holby City,* BBC,
　2006.

BOOK, Asher 1988–

PERSONAL

Full name, Asher Monroe Book; born September 18,
1988, in Arlington, VA. *Education:* Studied the performing arts. *Religion:* Christian. *Avocational Interests:*
Horseback riding, traveling, skiing.

Addresses: *Agent*—Paradigm, 360 North Crescent Dr.,
North Building, Beverly Hills, CA 90210. *Manager*—
Bryan Leder, Management 101, 5527 1/2 Cahuenga
Blvd., North Hollywood, CA 91601.

Career: Actor. Worked as a voice artist. Appeared in advertisements. Singer and guitarist; member of the band V Factory and performer at various venues, beginning 2006. Also a community volunteer.

Awards, Honors: *StarShine* magazine award nominations (both with V Factory), best dance song, for "Love Struck," and favorite band/group, both 2009.

CREDITS

Film Appearances:
Chris, *Come Away Home,* American Family Movies, 2004.
Chris, *Eight One Eight* (short film), 168 Hour Film Project & Festival, 2007.
Marco, *Fame,* Metro–Goldwyn–Mayer, 2009.

Film Work:
Stunt performer, *Eight One Eight* (short film), 168 Hour Film Project & Festival, 2007.

Television Appearances; Series:
Steve Williams, *Parenthood,* NBC, 2010.

Television Appearances; Movies:
Liam Harden, *Pop Rocks* (also known as *Head Rush* and *Rockstars Forever*), ABC Family, 2004.

Television Appearances; Specials:
Himself, *VH1 Divas Live,* VH1, 2009.

Appeared in other programs, including the *Macy's Thanksgiving Day Parade.*

Television Appearances; Episodic:
Voice of prince, "Dora's First Trip," *Dora the Explorer* (animated; also known as *Dora*), Nickelodeon, 2004.
Glen Davis, "School Dance," *Zoey 101* (also known as *Zoe*), Nickelodeon, 2005.
Alex Towers, "The Good Doctor," *Close to Home* (also known as *American Crime, Fiscal Chase, Juste cause,* and *Justicia cerrada*), CBS, 2006.
Wyatt Forrester, "Mother's Little Helper," *Medium* (also known as *Ghost and Crime* and *A medium*), NBC, 2007.
Himself, *CW 11 Morning News* (also known as *CW11 Morning News* and *The WB 11 Morning News*), The CW, 2009.
Himself, *Entertainment Tonight* (also known as *Entertainment This Week, E.T., ET Weekend,* and *This Week in Entertainment*), syndicated, 2009.

Himself, *The Wendy Williams Show,* Black Entertainment Television and syndicated, 2009.
Himself, *Xpose,* TV3 Television Network, 2009.
Jackson Winter, "Red Carpet Treatment," *The Mentalist* (also known as *Mentalist*), CBS, 2010.

Appeared in other programs, including *Late Night with Conan O'Brien,* NBC.

Stage Appearances; Musicals:
Applemando, *Applemando's Dream,* Borough of Manhattan Community College Tribeca Performing Arts Center, New York City, 2001.
Oliver!, North Carolina Theatre, Raleigh, NC, 2001.

Appeared as Conrad Birdie, *Bye Bye Birdie,* Professional Children's School, New York City.

Stage Appearances; Plays:
Appeared as Kevin in *Dear Maudie,* John Houseman Theatre, New York City; appeared as Lysander in a production of *A Midsummer Night's Dream.*

Major Tours; Musicals:
Chip, *Disney's "Beauty and the Beast"* (also known as *Beauty and the Beast*), U.S. cities, c. 1994.
Prince Edward Tudor, *The Prince and the Pauper,* U.S. cities, c. 2000–2001.

Also toured U.S. cities as Friedrich and Kurt in the musical *The Sound of Music.*

Radio Appearances:
Young monk and member of the ensemble, *Becket or the Honor of God,* L.A. Theatre Works, KPCC, 2005.

RECORDINGS

Albums; with V Factory:
These Are the Days (EP), Reprise, 2008.
Love Struck: The Remixes (DMD maxi), Reprise, 2009.

With V Factory, released the singles and music videos "These Are the Days," c. 2008, and "Love Struck," 2009.

Albums; with Others:
Fame (film soundtrack), Lakeshore Records, 2009.

Audiobooks:
(As a young monk and a member of the ensemble) Jean Anouilh, *Becket or the Honor of God,* L.A. Theatre Works, 2005.

Electronic:
Asher Book: The Official Website, http://www. asherbook.com, August 4, 2010.

BOURNE, Douglas
See DOUG, Doug E.

BOUTTE, Denise 1982–

PERSONAL

Original name, Denise Joseph; born January 19, 1982, in Maurice, LA; married Kevin Boutte, 2003. *Education:* Louisiana State University, B.A., communication; studied acting with different instructors. *Avocational Interests:* Cooking, collecting recipes, entertaining, in-line skating.

Addresses: *Agent*—Innovative Artists Talent and Literary Agency, 1505 10th St., Santa Monica, CA 90401. *Manager*—Charles Newman, Newman/Thomas Management, 8306 Wilshire Blvd., Suite 996, Beverly Hills, CA 90211.

Career: Actress. Appeared in advertisements; worked as a motivational speaker; also a presenter at awards presentations. Worked as an advertising account manager in Dallas, TX. Involved in the Greater Than AIDS movement.

Member: Alpha Kappa Alpha.

Awards, Honors: Valedictorian of her high school graduating class; Artistic Director Achievement awards (with others), best ensemble cast, 2004 and 2005, for different projects.

CREDITS

Film Appearances:
Mandy, *Death Valley: The Revenge of Bloody Bill* (also known as *Bloody Bill* and *Death Valley*), The Asylum, 2004.
(Uncredited) Hitchhiker, *A Killer Within,* Showcase Entertainment, 2004, Fireside Releasing, 2005.
Arianna, *Way of the Vampire* (also known as *Bram Stoker's "Way of the Vampire," Van Helsing's "Way of the Vampire," Van Helsing vs. Dracula,* and *Way of the Vampire*), The Asylum, 2005.

Charlotte, *Black Leather Soles* (short film), 2005.
Andrea, *Only in Your Dreams* (short film), Axe Attractions/The Suber Group, 2006.
Brianna Douglas, *Pieces of Eight,* Secondhand Films/ Wildcard Productions, 2006.
Title role, *Nola* (also known as *NOLA*), Blue Bayou Entertainment/Ransack Films, 2006.
Aunt Dee, *Restraining Order,* Codeblack Entertainment, 2006, Polychrome Pictures/Warner Home Video, 2007.
Lady at the piano, *Behind the Smile,* 2006, THINKFilm, 2007.
Diane, *Sister's Keeper,* Offset Filmworks/SEE Entertainment, 2007.
News reporter, *Splitting Hairs* (short film), Shining Pictures, 2007.
Trina, *Why Did I Get Married?* (also known as *Tyler Perry's "Why Did I Get Married?"*), Lions Gate Films, 2007.
Candy, *15 Minutes of Fame,* 2008.
New Tabitha, *Extreme Movie* (also known as *Everything You Always Wanted to Know about Teen Sex ... but Were Afraid to Ask, Hotdogs & Doughnuts,* and *Parental Guidance Suggested*), Dimension Films, 2008.
Tina Simpson, *N–Secure* (also known as *Insecure* and *N Secure*), N–Secure Films, 2009.

Appeared in other films, including *Welcome to Hollywood.*

Television Appearances; Series:
Danielle Calder, *Days of Our Lives* (also known as *Cruise of Deception: Days of Our Lives, Days, DOOL, Tropical Temptation, Tropical Temptation: Days of Our Lives, Des jours et des vies, Horton–sagaen, I gode og onde dager, Los dias de nuestras vidas, Meres agapis, Paeivien viemaeae, Vaara baesta aar, Zeit der Sehnsucht,* and *Zile din viata noastra*), NBC, 2007.
Sasha Brown, *Tyler Perry's "Meet the Browns"* (also known as *Meet the Browns*), TBS, beginning 2009.

Appeared in a lottery program on Texas television.

Television Appearances; Episodic:
Guest, *Caliente,* Univision, 1995.
Hostess, *Days of Our Lives* (also known as *Cruise of Deception: Days of Our Lives, Days, DOOL, Tropical Temptation, Tropical Temptation: Days of Our Lives, Des jours et des vies, Horton–sagaen, I gode og onde dager, Los dias de nuestras vidas, Meres agapis, Paeivien viemaeae, Vaara baesta aar, Zeit der Sehnsucht,* and *Zile din viata noastra*), NBC, 2004.
Court clerk, "Got 'til It's Gone," *Noah's Arc,* Logo, 2005.

Wedding planner, *Days of Our Lives* (also known as *Cruise of Deception: Days of Our Lives, Days, DOOL, Tropical Temptation, Tropical Temptation: Days of Our Lives, Des jours et des vies, Horton-sagaen, I gode og onde dager, Los dias de nuestras vidas, Meres agapis, Paeivien viemaeae, Vaara baesta aar, Zeit der Sehnsucht,* and *Zile din viata noastra*), NBC, 2005.

Lisa, "Black Don't Crack," *Cuts,* UPN, 2006.

Mrs. Johnson, "Everybody Hates Valentine's Day," *Everybody Hates Chris* (also known as *Alle hassen Chris* and *Todo el mundo odia a Chris*), UPN, 2006.

Sixth reporter, "BL: Los Angeles," *Boston Legal* (also known as *Fleet Street, The Practice: Fleet Street,* and *The Untitled Practice*), ABC, 2006.

Waitress, "Just Joan," *Girlfriends,* The CW, 2006.

Happy Hour, Fox, 2006.

Herself, *The Mo'Nique Show,* Black Entertainment Television, 2010.

Television Appearances; Pilots:

Dante, NBC, c. 2005.

Sharice, *Notes from the Underbelly,* ABC, 2007.

Television Work; Pilots:

(With Jasper Cole) Producer, *CIT* (also known as *Crisis Intervention Team*), c. 2010.

Stage Appearances:

The Tangled Snarl and *Murder Me Once* (one-act plays), Fremont Centre Theatre, South Pasadena, CA 2004.

Rachel Robinson, *National Pastime,* Fremont Centre Theatre, 2005.

Appeared in *Fear Itself* and *Whatever Happened to Baby Jane?,* both Swine Palace, Baton Rouge, LA.

Internet Appearances:

Appeared in footage posted on the Internet.

RECORDINGS

Videos; Short Documentaries; as Herself:

Death Valley: The Revenge of Bloody Bill—Behind the Scenes, The Asylum Home Entertainment, 2004.

Way of the Vampire: Behind the Scenes, The Asylum Home Entertainment, 2005.

WRITINGS

Teleplays; Pilots:

(With Jasper Cole) *CIT* (also known as *Crisis Intervention Team*), c. 2010.

OTHER SOURCES

Periodicals:

Precious Times, fall, 2007, pp. 26–29.

Smashing Interviews, June 1, 2010.

Electronic:

Denise Boutte, http://www.denisejboutte.com, August 4, 2010.

BOYD, Dwayne 1972–

PERSONAL

Born March 6, 1972, in Kansas City, MO. *Education:* Studied acting with Gaylor Parsons, Robert Townsend, Jason Wood, Chez Bentley–Griffith, Joanne Bassa, Munirah Baptiste, and H. M. Coakley.

Career: Actor. Premier Actor's Network, founder; Mandara Pictures (a production company), cofounder. Appeared in industrial films for Macy's department stores, Popeye's restaurants, Grady Healthcare, Domino's pizza, Walmart, Coca–Cola, Home Depot home improvement stores, Cingular Wireless telecommunication, The Baby Network, Embassy Suites hotels, and Emory Healthcare. Also worked as a barber. *Military service:* Served in U.S. Army.

CREDITS

Film Appearances:

Mike Thompson, *Bill Collectors,* 2003.

Bar patron, *Fate,* Alpha Film Group, 2003.

Buddhist worshipper, *Delivery Boy Chronicles,* Breakthrough Distribution, 2004.

Oscar, *The Gospel,* Screen Gems, 2005.

Kalfani, *The Walk,* 2005.

Officer Rod Williams, *Motives 2* (also known as *Motives 2: Retribution*), Sony Pictures, 2007.

Mike Martin, *Standing Reign* (short film), 2007.

First guy, *Three Can Play That Game,* Sony Pictures, 2007.

Kyle Hanson, *Grapes on a Vine,* Urban Home Entertainment, 2008.

First juke joint man, *Hope & Redemption: The Lena Baker Story* (also known as *The Lena Bake Story*), B.D. Fox Independent, 2008.

Johnson, *Losing Ground,* 2008.

Omar, *4 Minutes,* 2009.

Carl, *The Way Home,* Lions Gate Films, 2010.

Delivery guy, *Stomp the Yard 2: Homecoming,* Screen Gems, 2010.

Also appeared as Jamal, *Exposure*; J. T., *Ruthless Company*; Alvin Harrison, *Video Girl*; Evan Stokley, *Peachtree Shadows;* Jason, *Cheatin';* bus patron, *Sweet Home Alabama.*

Film Work:
Producer, director, and original casting, *4 Minutes,* 2009.

Television Appearances; Series:
Jonathan Reed, *Playhouse 22,* 2006.

Television Appearances; Movies:
(Uncredited) Martin Luther King supporter, *Boycott,* HBO, 2001.

Television Appearances; Episodic:
James Pretlow, "Firestorm," *Critical Rescue,* 2003.
Second cutter technician, *Surface,* NBC, 2005.
(As G. Wayne Boyd) Emergency room doctor, *Surface,* NBC, 2006.
Captain Jolivette, "Only the Lonely," *Army Wives,* Lifetime, 2007.
Security guard, "The Chinese Wall," *Drop Dead Diva,* 2009.
Captain, "Shrapnel and Alibis," *Army Wives,* Lifetime, 2009.
Security officer, "Running on Empty," *Past Life,* Fox, 2010.

Stage Appearances:
Appeared as Reverend Sykes, *To Kill a Mockingbird,* Cobb Playhouse, Atlanta, GA; Otis Claymore, *Wrong Decision,* Van Horn Players; Superman Doll, *A Special Christmas,* Van Horn Players; Charles and David, *CAS Showcase,* CAS Productions; host, *Bill E. Kool,* Fulton County Productions; in *A Man's World,* Atlanta, GA.

WRITINGS

Screenplays:
4 Minutes, 2009.

BROWN, Brennan

PERSONAL

Married Jenna Stern (an actress), 1988. *Education:* Yale University, degree in drama, 2000.

Career: Actor.

CREDITS

Stage Appearances:
Shakespeare, Claudius, Polonius, Moon, Magnus, and Inspector, *The Real Inspector Hound* [and] *The Fifteen Minute Hamlet,* Roundabout Theatre Company, Criterion Center Stage Right Theatre, New York City, 1992.
Tom, *Have You Spoken to Any Jews Lately?,* American Jewish Theatre, New York City, 1995.
Bilton, Snobby Price, and Charles Lomax, *Major Barbara,* Roundabout Theatre Company, American Airlines Theatre, New York City, 2001.
Bob Lamb, *Museum,* Company at Connelly Theatre, New York City, 2002.
David, *Absolution,* American Repertory Theatre, Hasty Pudding Theatre, Cambridge, MA, 2002.
Lucidi, Scazzochio, and other roles, *Edgardo Mine,* Hartford Stage Company, Hartford, CT, 2002.
Herald, *The Persians,* Michael Schimmel Center for the Arts, New York City, 2003.
Signor Ponza, *Right You Are,* Michael Schimmel Center for the Arts, 2003.
Russell, *Celebration and the Room,* Linda Gross Theatre, New York City, 2005–2006.
Investigator/colleague number two, *Offices,* Linda Gross Theatre, 2009.

Appeared in *Asylum* and *Fair Night,* both Naked Angels; as Thomas Diafoirus, *The Imaginary Invalid,* and in the title role, *Richard III,* both Yale Repertory Theatre, New Haven, CT; and in *The Second Man,* Keen Theatre, New York City; also appeared in productions at Florida Studio Theatre and Fulton Opera House.

Television Appearances; Movies:
Bob Goodrich, *Monday Night Mayhem,* TNT, 2002.
Hailey Preston, *Marple: The Mirror Crack'd from Side to Side,* 2010.

Television Appearances; Episodic:
Attorney Brendan Walsh, "Asunder," *Law & Order: Special Victims Unit,* NBC, 2000.
Forensic technician, "Teenage Wasteland," *Law & Order,* NBC, 2001.
Engineer, "Somebody's Fool," *Deadline,* NBC, 2001.
Ron Zinn, "A Very Great Man," *The Education of Max Bickford,* CBS, 2001.
Attorney for Bates, "Paranoia," *Law & Order: Special Victims Unit,* NBC, 2001.
Donald Houseman, "The Ring," *Law & Order,* NBC, 2002.
Jerry Rivers, "The Gift," *Law & Order: Criminal Intent* (also known as *Law & Order: CI*), NBC, 2003.
"Sorry, Wrong Number," *Kidnapped* (also known as *Kidnap*), 2006.

Robert Treat Paine, "Independence," *John Adams,* 2008.
Robert Treat Paine, "Join or Die," *John Adams,* 2008.
Mr. Smith, "Bonfire of the Vanity," *Gossip Girl,* 2008.
Arthur Phillips, "I Agree, It Wasn't Funny," *Damages,* FX Network, 2009.
Miles Foster, "A Mother of a Problem," *Ugly Betty,* ABC, 2009.
Miles Foster, "Rabbit Test," *Ugly Betty,* ABC, 2009.
Attorney Hoyt, "Doped," *Law & Order,* NBC, 2009.

Film Appearances:

Randolph, *Turn the River* (also known as *T.T.R.*), Screen Media Films, 2007.
Larry Bukheim, *I Love You Phillip Morris,* Independent, 2009.
Andrew Pell, *State of Play,* United International, 2009.

BROWN, Max 1981–

PERSONAL

Full name, Max Barnaby Brown; born February 10, 1981, in Ilkley, Yorkshire, England; married Pollyanna Rose Williams (an actress), December 18, 2005 (divorced).

Addresses: *Agent*—Dallas Smith, United Agents, 12–26 Lexington St., London W1F 0LE, England. *Manager*—Lena Roklin, Luber Rocklin Entertainment, 8530 Wilshire Blvd., 5th Floor, Beverly Hills, CA 90211.

Career: Actor.

CREDITS

Television Appearances; Series:
Danny Hartston, *Grange Hill,* BBC, 2001–2002.
Mark Russell, a recurring role, *Crossroads,* ITV, 2001, 2002.
Kristian Hargreaves, *Hollyoaks,* E4, 2002–2004.
Sam Grey, a recurring role, *Mistresses,* BBC America, 2008.
Edward Seymour, *The Tudors,* Showtime, 2008–10.

Television Appearances; Episodic:
The Saturday Show, BBC, 2002.
Leon, "Tall Tales," *Down to Earth,* BBC, 2005.
Kenny Parks, "Is There a Doctor in the House?," *Doctors,* BBC, 2005.
Simon Broughton, "Brief Encounters," *Casualty,* BBC1, 2005.

Pete Grimshaw, "Give Peace a Chance," *Heartbeat,* ITV, 2006.
Dimitri Levendis, *MI–5* (also known as *Spooks*), Arts and Entertainment, 2010.
Adam Wainwright, "The Russian House," *Foyle's War,* PBS, 2010.
Adam Wainwright, "Killing Time," *Foyle's War,* PBS, 2010.
Adam Wainwright, "The Hide," *Foyle's War,* PBS, 2010.
Breakfast, BBC, 2010.

Film Appearances:

Brad, *Fallen Angels,* Avrio Filmworks, 2002.
Chad, *True True Lie* (also known as *Girls Club*), Verve Pictures, 2006.
Liam, *Turistas* (also known as *Blood Paradise* and *Turistas: Holiday of Horror*), Fox Atomic, 2006.
Doctor, *Daylight Robbery,* Liberation Entertainment, 2008.
Richard Short, *Act of God,* AOG Films/Giant Films/Spectrum Media Entertainment, 2009.
Wagner, *Flutter,* Silver Reel, 2010.

RECORDINGS

Videos:
It's Not a Movie, It's Real Life: The Making of "Turistas," Twentieth Century–Fox Home Entertainment, 2007.

BRUENING, Justin 1979(?)–

PERSONAL

Full name, Justin S. Bruening; born September 24, 1979 (some sources cite 1974), in Chadron (some sources cite St. Helena), NE; married Alexa Havins (an actress), June 5, 2005; children: Lexington Grace. *Education:* Attended Chadron State College; trained with Caymichael Patten.

Addresses: *Agent*—Marnie Sparer, Innovative Artists Talent and Literary Agency, 1505 10th St., Santa Monica, CA 90401. *Publicist*—WKT Public Relations, 9350 Wilshire Blvd., Suite 450, Beverly Hills, CA 90212.

Career: Actor. Worked as a model and appeared in advertisements.

Awards, Honors: *Soap Opera Digest* Award, outstanding male newcomer, 2005, for *All My Children.*

CREDITS

Television Appearances; Series:
James Edward "Jamie" Martin, *All My Children* (also known as *All My Children: The Summer of Seduction* and *La force du destin*), ABC, 2003–2007.
James Edward "Jamie" Martin, *One Life to Live* (also known as *Between Heaven and Hell, OLTL,* and *One Life to Live: The Summer of Seduction*), ABC, 2004–2005.
Mike Traceur, *Knight Rider,* NBC, 2008–2009.

Television Appearances; Movies:
Whitt Sheffield, *Class,* Hallmark Channel, 2010.

Television Appearances; Specials:
Himself, *Macy's Thanksgiving Day Parade* (also known as *2008 Macy's Thanksgiving Day Parade*), NBC, 2008.

Television Appearances; Awards Presentations:
Presenter, *The 32nd Annual Daytime Emmy Awards,* CBS, 2005.
Presenter, *The 33rd Annual Daytime Emmy Awards,* ABC, 2006.

Television Appearances; Episodic:
Jake, "Do I Look Frat in This?," *Hope & Faith,* ABC, 2004.
Himself, "Justin Bruening," *Soapography,* SOAPnet, 2004.
"Hold the Phone," *Hope & Faith,* ABC, 2004.
Guest, *The View,* ABC, 2004.
Guest, *Soap Talk,* SOAPnet, multiple episodes, 2004, 2006.
Guest, *The Tony Danza Show,* syndicated, 2005.
Himself, *Entertainment Tonight* (also known as *Entertainment This Week, E.T., ET Weekend,* and *This Week in Entertainment*), syndicated, 2005, multiple episodes, 2008.
Personal trainer, "The Cutting Edge," *3 lbs.* (also known as *3 Lbs, 3 Lbs.,* and *3 lbs*), CBS, 2006.
Craig Abbott, "CSI: My Nanny," *CSI: Miami* (also known as *CSI Miami* and *CSI: Weekends*), CBS, 2007.
Spencer Mason in 1989, "Thick as Thieves," *Cold Case* (also known as *Anexihniastes ypothesis, Caso abierto, Cold case—affaires classees, Cold Case—Kein Opfer ist je vergessen, Doegloett aktak, Kalla spaar, Todistettavasti syyllinen,* and *Victimes du passe*), CBS, 2007.
Guest, *The Bonnie Hunt Show,* syndicated, 2008.
Himself, *Today* (also known as *NBC News Today* and *The Today Show*), NBC, multiple episodes, 2008.

Television Appearances; Pilots:
Mike Traceur, *Knight Rider,* NBC, 2008.

Film Appearances:
Bobby, *Fat Girls,* 2006, Regent Releasing, 2007.

RECORDINGS

Videos:
Himself, *Knight Rider: The Icon Reborn* (short film), Universal Studios Home Entertainment, 2009.

Appeared in the music video "Boys (Co–Ed Remix)" by Britney Spears, 2002.

OTHER SOURCES

Periodicals:
Starlog, December, 2008, pp. 70–73.
TV Zone, February, 2008, pp. 36–40.

BUCHMAN, Michael
  See SILVER, Michael B.

BURNETT, Carol 1933–

PERSONAL

Full name, Carol Creighton Burnett; born April 26, 1933, in San Antonio, TX; daughter of Joseph "Jodie" Thomas (a movie theatre manager) and Ina Louise (a Hollywood publicity writer; maiden name, Creighton; some sources site maiden name as Melton) Burnett; married Don Saroyan (an actor), December 15, 1955 (divorced, 1962); married Joseph Hamilton (a television producer), May 4, 1963 (divorced, 1984); married Brian Miller (a musician and composer), November 24, 2001; children: (second marriage) Erin Kate (a singer), Jody Ann, Carrie Louise (an actress, singer, filmmaker, and writer; deceased), and eight stepchildren. *Education:* Attended University of California, Los Angeles, c. 1952–54.

Addresses: *Agent*—Brian Mann, International Creative Management, 10250 Constellation Way, 9th Floor, Los Angeles, CA 90067; (voice work and commercials) Tim Curtis, WME Entertainment, 9601 Wilshire Blvd., 3rd Floor, Beverly Hills, CA 90210. *Manager*—Bill Robinson, Bill Robinson Management, P.O. Box 6284, Malibu, CA 90264.

Career: Actress, singer, and comedian. Kalola Productions, Beverly Hills, CA, cofounder and president. Began career as a nightclub performer at the Blue

Angel, New York City, 1957; appeared in commercials, including voice work for Nyquil cold medicine. Pasadena Playhouse, member of board of directors. Emerson College, Franklin D. Murphy Associate and board member; University of California, Los Angeles, established the "Carol Burnett Musical Competition Award" at Theatre Arts School. Worked as a restaurant hat check girl in New York City and as an usher.

Awards, Honors: American Guild of Variety Artists Award, outstanding comedienne, and *Theatre World* Award, both 1960, and Outer Critics Circle Award, outstanding performance, 1965, all for *Once upon a Mattress; TV Guide* Awards, outstanding female performer, 1961, 1962, and 1963, and Emmy Award, outstanding performance in a variety or musical program or series, 1962, all for *The Garry Moore Show;* Emmy Award, outstanding performance in a variety or musical program or series, 1963, for *Julie and Carol at Carnegie Hall* and *An Evening with Carol Burnett;* Personal Peabody Award, 1963; Golden Laurel Award nomination, top female new face, 1964; Golden Globe Award, best television actress, 1968, Emmy Award nominations, 1969, 1970, 1971, 1973, 1976, 1977, 1978, and Emmy Awards, 1972, 1974, 1975, all outstanding variety or musical series (with others), Golden Globe Awards, 1970, 1972, 1977, 1978, and Golden Globe Award nominations, 1971, 1973, 1974, 1975, 1976, 1979, all best actress in a musical or comedy television series, and Legend Award (with others), TV Land Awards, 2005, all for *The Carol Burnett Show;* Special Antoinette Perry Award, 1969; named Hasty Pudding Woman of the Year, Hasty Pudding Theatricals, Harvard University, 1969; Golden Apple Award, star of the year, Hollywood Women's Press Club, 1970; Emmy Award nomination (with others), outstanding single variety or musical program, 1972, for *Julie and Carol at Lincoln Center;* Golden Globe Award nomination, best actress in a motion picture musical or comedy, 1973, for *Pete 'n' Tillie;* Emmy Award nomination, best actress in a drama, 1974, for *6 Rms Riv Vu;* People's Choice awards, favorite all–around female entertainer, 1975, 1976, 1977, 1978, 1979, 1980, and 1981; People's Choice awards, favorite female television performer, 1976, 1979, 1980, 1981; Emmy Award nomination (with others), outstanding comedy–variety or music special, Christopher Award, and Bronze Rose from Montreaux Television Contest, all 1977, for *Sills and Burnett at the Met;* National Critics' Circle Award, outstanding performance, 1977–78; first annual National Television Critics Circle Award, outstanding performance, 1977; Prize San Sebastian, best actress, San Sebastian International Film Festival, 1978, and Golden Globe Award nomination, best supporting actress in a motion picture, 1979, both for *A Wedding;* Emmy Award nomination, outstanding lead actress in a limited series or special, 1979, for *Friendly Fire;* Louella Parsons Award, Hollywood Women's Press Club, 1979; Crystal Award, Women in Film, 1980; honorary D.H.L., Emerson Col-

lege, 1980; American Guild of Variety Artists Award, favorite television performer, 1981; Jack Benny Humanitarian Award, March of Dimes, 1981; Golden Globe Award nomination, best actress in a motion picture comedy or musical, 1982, for *The Four Seasons;* Golden Globe Award nomination, best actress in a motion picture comedy or musical, 1983, for *Annie;* Golden Globe Award nomination, best actress in a miniseries or television movie, 1983, for *Life of the Party: The Story of Beatrice;* Emmy Award nomination, outstanding individual performance in a variety or music program, 1983, for *Texaco Star Theatre: Opening Night;* Humanitarian of the Year Award, Variety Clubs International, 1983; Gold Medal, International Radio and Television Society, 1984; Annual CableACE Award, best actress in a dramatic or theatrical program, National Cable Television Association, 1984, for *Between Friends;* inducted into Academy of Television Arts and Sciences Hall of Fame, 1985; Lifetime Achievement Award in Comedy, American Comedy Awards, 1987; Horatio Alger Distinguished Americans Award, Horatio Alger Association, 1988; People's Choice Award, favorite female performer in a new program, 1991; Emmy Award nomination, outstanding guest actress in a comedy series, 1993, for "The Spider Episode," *The Larry Sanders Show;* American Comedy Award, funniest female performer in a television special, 1990, for *Julie and Carol: Together Again!;* Golden Globe Award nomination, best actress in a television comedy or musical series, 1991, for *Carol and Company;* Emmy Award nomination, outstanding individual performance in a variety or music program, 1995, for *Men, Movies, and Carol;* Antoinette Perry Award nomination, 1995, for *Moon over Buffalo;* award for personal style and lifetime achievement in fashion, Dallas Market Center, 1995; Emmy Award, 1997, for "Jamie's Parents," and Emmy Award nomination, outstanding guest actress in a comedy series, 1998, for "Coming Home," both episodes of *Mad about You;* American Comedy Awards, 1997, 1998, and American Comedy Award nomination, 1999, all funniest female guest appearance in a television series, for *Mad about You;* American Comedy Award, funniest female performer in a television special, 1999, for *The Marriage Fool;* Garland Award, *Backstage West,* 1999; Emmy Award nomination (with others), outstanding variety, music, or comedy special, 2002, for *Carol Burnett: Show Stoppers;* Kennedy Center Honor, John F. Kennedy Center for the Performing Arts, Washington, DC, 2003; also honored by Museum of Radio and Television, 2003; Presidential Medal of Freedom, 2005; Career Achievement Award, Television Critics Association, 2006; inducted into California Hall of Fame, 2009; Emmy Award nomination, outstanding guest actress in a drama series, 2009, for "Ballerina," *Law & Order: Special Victims Unit;* Woman of the Year Awards, *Los Angeles Times* and Academy of Television Arts and Sciences; four Entertainer of the Year awards, best comedienne, American Guild of Variety Artists; Variety Club Award, top female star; named entertainer of the year, New York Friars Club; received star on

Hollywood Walk of Fame; also winner of various popularity and magazine reader polls.

CREDITS

Television Appearances; Series:
Member of regular cast, *The Garry Moore Show,* CBS, 1959–64.
Member of regular cast, *The Entertainers,* CBS, 1964–65.
Host, *The Carol Burnett Show* (repeat compilations broadcast as *Carol Burnett and Friends*), CBS, 1967–78, 1977.
Host, *Carol Burnett and Company,* ABC, 1979.
Eunice Harper Higgins, a recurring role, *Mama's Family,* NBC, 1983–84.
Host, *Carol & Company,* NBC, 1990–91.
Theresa Stemple, a recurring role, *Mad about You,* NBC, between 1996 and 1999.

Television Appearances; Specials:
The General Motors 50th Anniversary Show, NBC, 1957.
"The American Cowboy," *The United States Steel Hour* (also known as *The U.S. Steel Hour*), CBS, 1960.
The Carol Burnett Show, 1960.
No Place Like Home, 1960.
CBS Fall Preview Special: Seven Wonderful Nights, 1961.
Julie and Carol at Carnegie Hall, CBS, 1962.
Carol and Company, CBS, 1963.
Title role, *Calamity Jane,* CBS, 1963.
An Evening with Carol Burnett, 1963.
Princess Winnifred the Woebegone, *Once upon a Mattress,* CBS, 1964.
Host, *The Entertainers,* CBS, 1964.
Carol + 2, CBS, 1967.
The Perry Como Christmas Show, NBC, 1968.
Girl Friends and Nabors, CBS, 1968.
The Ann–Margret Show, 1968.
Talking Pictures, 1968.
Carol Channing Proudly Presents the Seven Deadly Sins, ABC, 1969.
Bing Crosby and Carol Burnett—Together Again for the First Time, NBC, 1969.
A Last Laugh at the 60's, ABC, 1970.
Rowan and Martin Bite the Hand that Feeds Them, NBC, 1970.
The Tim Conway Special, CBS, 1970.
Host, *The Carol Burnett Show in London,* 1970.
Li'l Abner, NBC, 1971.
Cohost, *Julie and Carol at Lincoln Center,* CBS, 1971.
Super Comedy Bowl 1, CBS, 1971.
Bing Crosby and His Friends, NBC, 1972.
Burt Bacharach: Close to You, ABC, 1972.
Princess Winnifred the Woebegone, *Once upon a Mattress,* CBS, 1972.
Keep U.S. Beautiful, NBC, 1973.

Burt and the Girls, NBC, 1973.
Shirley MacLaine: If They Could See Me Now, CBS, 1974.
Anne Miller, *6 Rms Riv Vu,* CBS, 1974.
Out to Lunch, 1974.
Emily, Celia, Dorothy, and Mother, *Twigs,* CBS, 1975.
Cohost, *Sills and Burnett at the Met,* CBS, 1976.
CBS Salutes Lucy: The First 25 Years, 1976.
Steve & Eydie Celebrate Irving Berlin, NBC, 1978.
A Special Evening with Carol Burnett, CBS, 1978.
Dolly and Carol in Nashville, CBS, 1978.
Musical Comedy Tonight, 1979.
The Sensational, Shocking, Wonderful, Wacky '70s, NBC, 1980.
Where Have All the Children Gone?, 1980.
The Bert Convy Special—There's a Meeting Here Tonight, syndicated, 1981.
Christmas in Hawaii (also known as *Jim Nabors' Christmas in Hawaii*), 1981.
"A Lincoln Center Special: Beverly! Her Farewell Performance," *Great Performances,* PBS, 1981.
The Barbara Walters Special (also known as *Barbara Walters: Interviews of a Lifetime* and *The Barbara Walters Summer Special*), ABC, 1982.
Cheryl Ladd: Scenes from a Special, ABC, 1982.
Miss Hannigan, *Lights, Camera, Annie!,* 1982.
Cohost, *Hollywood: The Gift of Laughter,* ABC, 1982.
Eunice Higgins, *Eunice,* CBS, 1982.
Texaco Star Theatre: Opening Night, NBC, 1982.
All–Star Party for Carol Burnett, 1982.
All–Star Party for Frank Sinatra, 1983.
The Kennedy Center Honors: A Celebration of the Performing Arts, CBS, 1983, 1985, 1991, 2001, 2003.
Host, *Burnett "Discovers" Domingo,* CBS, 1984.
Mike Douglas Presents, 1984.
The Night of 100 Stars II, ABC, 1985.
Here's Television Entertainment, syndicated, 1985.
Alberta Johnson, *The Laundromat,* HBO, 1985.
Narrator, "Happily Ever After" (animated), *Wonder-Works,* PBS, 1985.
The American Film Institute Salute to Billy Wilder, NBC, 1986.
Neil Diamond ... Hello Again, CBS, 1986.
Carlotta Campion, "Follies in Concert," *Great Performances,* PBS, 1986.
(In archive footage) *The Muppets: A Celebration of 30 Years,* 1986.
A Carol Burnett Special: Carol, Carl, Whoopi, and Robin (also known as *Carol, Carl, Whoopi, and Robin*), ABC, 1987.
James Stewart: A Wonderful Life, PBS, 1987.
Karen Nash, "Visitor from Mamaroneck," Muriel Tate, "Visitor from Hollywood," and Norma Hubley, "Visitor from Forest Hills," *Plaza Suite,* ABC, 1987.
Happy Birthday, Hollywood! (also known as *Happy 100th Birthday, Hollywood!*), ABC, 1987.
Host, *Great Moments in Disney Animation,* ABC, 1987.
Secrets Women Never Share, NBC, 1987.
A Star–Spangled Celebration, ABC, 1987.

This Is Your Life, NBC, 1987.

Host, *Superstars and Their Moms,* ABC, 1987, 1988.

A Conversation with Carol, The Disney Channel, 1988.

Walt Disney World 4th of July Spectacular, 1988.

America's All–Star Tribute to Elizabeth Taylor, ABC, 1989.

Julie and Carol: Together Again!, ABC, 1989.

Herself, *One for the Road,* 1989.

The Muppets Celebrate Jim Henson, CBS, 1990.

The Los Angeles Music Center's 25th Anniversary Celebration (also known as *The Music Center's 25th Anniversary*), PBS, 1990.

The Tube Test, ABC, 1990.

Segment host, *Funny Women of Television: A Museum of Television and Radio Tribute* (also known as *Funny Women of Television*), NBC, 1991.

Host, *The Very Best of the Ed Sullivan Show,* CBS, 1991.

Voices of narrator, Mrs. Rabbit, and Mr. McGregor's cat, "The Tale of Peter Rabbit," *HBO Storybook Musicals* (animated), HBO, 1991.

Children's Miracle Network Telethon, syndicated, 1991.

The Dream Is Alive: The 20th Anniversary Celebration of Walt Disney World (also known as *Walt Disney World's 20th Anniversary Celebration*), CBS, 1991.

In a New Light (also known as *In a New Light: A Call to Action in the War Against AIDS*), ABC, 1992.

Jack Benny: Comedy in Bloom (also known as *Comedy in Bloom*), HBO, 1992.

"Total Exposure—Privacy and the Press," *First Person with Maria Shriver,* NBC, 1992.

Host, *The American Film Institute Salute to Elizabeth Taylor,* ABC, 1993.

Bob Hope: The First Ninety Years, NBC, 1993.

The Carol Burnett Show: A Reunion, CBS, 1993.

The Harry Connick, Jr. Christmas Special, CBS, 1993.

In a New Light '93, ABC, 1993.

Legend to Legend Night, NBC, 1993.

Host, *Carol Burnett: The Special Years,* CBS, 1994.

Men, Movies & Carol, CBS, 1994.

Comic Relief VI, HBO, 1994.

Host, *The All My Children 25th Anniversary Special,* ABC, 1995.

CBS Soap Break, CBS, 1995.

Who Makes You Laugh?, 1995.

(In archive footage) *Ed Sullivan All–Star Comedy Special,* 1995.

"Boris Karloff: The Gentle Monster," *Biography,* Arts and Entertainment, 1995.

"Betty Grable: Behind the Pin–up," *Biography,* Arts and Entertainment, 1995.

"Julie Andrews: Back on Broadway," *Great Performances,* PBS, 1995.

(In archive footage) *50 Years of Funny Females,* 1995.

Host and narrator, *Jimmy Stewart,* The Disney Channel, 1996.

Happy Birthday Elizabeth—A Celebration of Life, ABC, 1997.

"Alan Alda: More than Mr. Nice Guy," *Biography,* Arts and Entertainment, 1997.

At Home with Carol Burnett, Home and Garden Television, 1997.

"Jimmy Stewart," *Biography,* Arts and Entertainment, 1997.

CBS: The First 50 Years, CBS, 1998.

(In archive footage) *Sonny & Me: Cher Remembers,* CBS, 1998.

Grand marshal, "The Tournament of Roses Parade," *Coming Up Roses,* CBS, 1998.

Intimate Portrait: Carol Burnett, Lifetime, 1998.

"Roddy McDowell: Hollywood's Best Friend," *Biography,* Arts and Entertainment, 1998.

Grand marshal, *The 109th Tournament of Roses Parade,* ABC, 1998.

Tony Bennett: An All–Star Tribute—Live by Request, Arts and Entertainment, 1998.

"William S. Paley: The Eye of CBS," *Biography,* Arts and Entertainment, 2000.

"Lucille Ball: Finding Lucy," *American Masters,* PBS, 2000.

The 70s: The Decade that Changed Television, ABC, 2000.

Wife, *Putting It Together,* Broadway Television Network, 2000.

Narrator, *Rosemary Clooney: Girl Singer,* PBS, c. 2000.

Host, *Carol Burnett: Show Stoppers* (also known as *The Carol Burnett Show: Show Stoppers*), CBS, 2001.

The Honeymooners 50th Anniversary, CBS, 2001.

Host, *CBS: 50 Years from Television City,* CBS, 2002.

Intimate Portrait: Lucille Ball, Lifetime, 2002.

"Carol Burnett: Just to Have a Laugh," *TVography,* Arts and Entertainment, 2002.

"Tim Conway: Just Clowning Around," *Biography,* Arts and Entertainment, 2002.

Intimate Portrait: Vicki Lawrence, Lifetime, 2003.

Intimate Portrait: Florence Henderson, Lifetime, 2003.

Intimate Portrait: Linda Lavin, Lifetime, 2003.

Intimate Portrait: Susan Lucci, Lifetime, 2003.

Great Women of Television Comedy: A Museum of Television & Radio Special, NBC, 2003.

Presenter, *CBS at 75: A Primetime Celebration,* CBS, 2003.

The Desilu Story: The Rags to Riches Success of the Desilu Empire, Bravo, 2003.

(In archive footage) *Cher: The Farewell Tour,* NBC, 2003.

(In archive footage) *TV Land Online Special,* TV Land, 2003.

Host, *The Carol Burnett Show: Let's Bump Up the Lights,* CBS, 2004.

Emmy's Greatest Moments (also known as *TV Land Presents: Emmy's Greatest Moments*), TV Land, 2004.

Queen Aggravain, *Once upon a Mattress,* ABC, 2005.

"Carol Burnett: A Woman of Character," *American Masters,* PBS, 2007.

TV's Funniest Moments, Fox, 2007.

Entertainment Weekly & TV Land Present: The 50 Greatest TV Icons, TV Land, 2007.
Mr. Prince, Ovation, 2009.
(In archive footage) *TV's 50 Funniest Phrases,* 2009.

Television Appearances; Movies:
Dorothy Benson, *The Grass Is Always Greener over the Septic Tank,* CBS, 1978.
Peg Mullen, *Friendly Fire,* ABC, 1979.
Dori Grey, *The Tenth Month,* CBS, 1979.
Beatrice O'Reilly, *Life of the Party: The Story of Beatrice,* CBS, 1982.
Mary Catherine Castelli, *Between Friends* (also known as *Nobody Makes Me Cry*), HBO, 1983.
Martha Madden, *Hostage* (also known as *Against Her Will*), CBS, 1988.
Vivian Levinson, *Seasons of the Heart* (also known as *The Winter Garden*), NBC, 1994.
Grace, 1998.
Florence, *The Marriage Fool* (also known as *Love after Death*), CBS, 1998.

Television Appearances; Miniseries:
Cohost, *CBS: On the Air,* CBS, 1978.
Charlotte Kensington, *Fresno,* CBS, 1986.
A Century of Women (also known as *A Family of Women*), TBS, 1994.
(Uncredited; in archive footage) *Cronkite Remembers,* CBS, 1997.
Broadway: The American Musical, PBS, 2004.
Make 'em Laugh: The Funny Business of America, PBS, 2009.

Television Appearances; Episodic:
Jerry Mahoney's girlfriend, *The Paul Winchell–Jerry Mahoney Show* (also known as *The Speidel Show*), NBC, 1955.
Celia, premiere episode, *Stanley,* NBC, 1956.
Celia, "The New Year's Party," *Stanley,* NBC, 1956.
"The American Musical Comedy," *Omnibus,* 1956.
The Ed Sullivan Show (also known as *Toast of the Town*), CBS, multiple appearances, between 1957 and 1970.
Pantomime Quiz (also known as *Mike Stokey's Pantomime Quiz* and *Stump the Stars*), ABC, 1958.
I've Got a Secret, multiple appearances, between 1960 and 1966.
Narrator, "The Wonderful World of Toys," *The DuPont Show of the Week,* NBC, 1961.
Person to Person, 1961.
Mystery guest, *What's My Line?,* 1961, 1964, 1966.
Agnes Grep, "Cavender Is Coming," *The Twilight Zone,* CBS, 1962.
Password (also known as *Password All–Stars*), multiple appearances, between 1962 and 1974.
"Jack Plays Tarzan," *The Jack Benny Show* (also known as *The Jack Benny Program* and *The Lucky Strike Program*), CBS, 1962.

Talent Scouts, 1963.
"Riverboat Sketch," *The Jack Benny Show* (also known as *The Jack Benny Program* and *The Lucky Strike Program*), CBS, 1963.
Hollywood Talent Scouts (also known as *Art Linkletter's Hollywood Talent Scouts*), 1966.
Carol Bradford, "Lucy and Carol in Palm Springs," *The Lucy Show* (also known as *The Lucille Ball Show*), CBS, 1966.
Carol Bradford, "Lucy Gets a Roommate," *The Lucy Show* (also known as *The Lucille Ball Show*), CBS, 1966.
Carol Bradford, "Lucy and Carol Burnett: Parts 1 & 2," *The Lucy Show* (also known as *The Lucille Ball Show*), CBS, 1967.
Corporal Carol Barnes, "Corporal Carol," *Gomer Pyle, U.S.M.C.,* CBS, 1967.
Ozark Annie, "One of Our Olives Is Missing," *Get Smart,* NBC, 1967.
Our Place, 1967.
Personality, 1967.
The Smothers Brothers Comedy Hour, 1967.
(Uncredited) Goodfellow's wife, *The Bob Hope Show,* 1968.
The Art Linkletter Show, 1968.
The Barbara McNair Show, 1969.
Sergeant Carol Barnes, "Showtime with Sgt. Carol," *Gomer Pyle, U.S.M.C.,* CBS, 1969.
Sesame Street (also known as *The New Sesame Street, Open Sesame,* and *Sesame Street Unpaved*), 1969, 1970, 1971.
Playboy after Dark, 1970.
Carol Krausmauer, "Lucy and Carol Burnett: Part 2," *Here's Lucy,* CBS, 1971.
The Ken Berry "Wow" Show, 1972.
Rowan & Martin's Laugh–In, 1972.
The Sonny and Cher Comedy Hour, 1972, 1973.
The Electric Company, 1973.
Sammy and Company, 1975.
The Sonny and Cher Show, 1976.
Eve, "This Side of Eden," *Insight,* 1977.
Premiere episode, *3 Girls 3,* 1977.
The Jim Nabors Show, 1978.
America 2–Night, 1978.
Password Plus, 1979, 1980.
Herself and cleaning lady, *The Muppet Show,* syndicated, 1980.
Omnibus, 1980.
Verla Grubb, *All My Children* (also known as *AMC*), ABC, 1983.
Woman in courtroom, "Midnight Cowboy II," *SCTV Network* (also known as *S.C.T.V., SCTV Comedy Network,* and *SCTV Network 90*), 1983.
Susan Johnson, "Rembrandt's Girl," *Magnum, P.I.,* CBS, 1984.
Saturday Night Live (also known as *SNL*), NBC, 1985.
Super Dave, Showtime, 1987.
Susan Johnson, "A Girl Named Sue," *Magnum, P.I.,* CBS, 1988.
Rose, "Reggie and Rose," *Fame,* c. 1988.

Alan King: Inside the Comedy Mind, Comedy Central, 1991.

Herself, "The Spider Episode," *The Larry Sanders Show,* HBO, 1992.

The Price Is Right (also known as *The New Price Is Right*), 1992.

Contestant, *Jeopardy!,* 1992.

Herself, "One Down, Three to Go," *Evening Shade,* CBS, 1993.

Mrs. Johnson and Verla Grubb, *All My Children* (also known as *AMC*), ABC, 1995.

Inside the Actors Studio (also known as *Actors Interview* and *Inside the Actors Studio: The Craft of Theatre and Film*), Bravo, 1995.

The Movie That Changed My Life, AMC, 1995.

"Women in Film," *Women of the House,* 1995.

"Carol Burnett," *Charles Grodin,* 1995.

Lillian Bennett, "The Comeback," *Touched by an Angel,* CBS, 1997.

Herself, "Flip," *The Larry Sanders Show,* HBO, 1998.

Hollywood Squares (also known as *H2* and *H2 Hollywood Squares*), syndicated, multiple appearances, 1999, 2000.

Host, "I Will Walk with You: Parts 1 & 2," *Touched by an Angel,* CBS, 2003.

The CBS Morning News, CBS, 2003.

CBS News Up to the Minute (also known as *Up to the Minute* and *UTTM*), CBS, 2003.

Eleanor Mason, "Don't Look at Me," *Desperate Housewives,* ABC, 2006.

Entertainment Tonight (also known as *E.T.* and *This Week in Entertainment*), syndicated, multiple appearances, beginning 2007.

Corazon de ..., 2007.

Bridget "Birdie" Sulloway, "Ballerina," *Law & Order: Special Victims Unit* (also known as *Law & Order: SVU* and *Special Victims Unit*), NBC, 2009.

Doris Sylvester, "Furt," *Glee,* Fox, 2010.

Television Talk Show Guest Appearances; Episodic:

The Jack Paar Show (also known as *The Jack Paar Tonight Show* and *Tonight Starring Jack Paar*), NBC, 1957, 1958.

The Arlene Francis Show, 1957, 1958.

The Dinah Shore Chevy Show (also known as *The Dinah Shore Show*), 1958.

Dinah's Place, 1970.

The David Frost Show, 1970, 1971.

The Tonight Show Starring Johnny Carson, CBS, 1972, 1973.

Good Morning America (also known as *G.M.A.*), ABC, 1979, 2005.

The Dick Cavett Show, ABC, 1986.

A Conversation with Dinah, The Nashville Network, 1990.

Sally Jessy Raphael (also known as *Sally*), 1990.

Late Night with David Letterman, NBC, 1991.

The Tonight Show with Jay Leno, NBC, 1993.

Charlie Rose (also known as *The Charlie Rose Show*), PBS, 1994, 2010.

Late Show with David Letterman (also known as *The Late Show* and *Letterman*), CBS, 1995.

The Rosie O'Donnell Show, syndicated, several appearances, between 1996 and 1999.

Larry King Live, Cable News Network, 2000, 2005.

The View, ABC, 2005.

The Tony Danza Show, syndicated, 2005.

The Megan Mullally Show, syndicated, 2006.

The Oprah Winfrey Show (also known as *Oprah*), syndicated, 2008.

Rachael Ray, syndicated, 2008, 2010.

Ellen: The Ellen DeGeneres Show, syndicated, 2009.

Tavis Smiley, PBS, 2010.

Live with Regis and Kelly, syndicated, 2010.

The Bonnie Hunt Show, NBC, 2010.

Television Appearances; Awards Presentations:

Presenter, *The ... Annual Primetime Emmy Awards,* 1963, 1976, Fox, 1990, ABC, 1993, ABC, 1994, ABC, 1996, CBS, 1997.

Presenter, *The ... Annual Tony Awards,* 1967, CBS, 1994, 1995, 1999, 2000.

Cohost, *The 45th Annual Academy Awards,* 1973.

The ... Annual Primetime Emmy Awards, 1978, 1979, ABC, 1985, Fox, 1991.

Presenter, *The ... Annual Academy Awards,* 1982, 1983.

Presenter, *The 1st Academy TV Hall of Fame,* 1984.

Soap Opera Digest Awards, NBC, 1988, 1996.

The 9th Annual ACE Awards, HBO, 1988.

The ... Annual American Comedy Awards, ABC, 1989, 1990.

The Walt Disney Company Presents the American Teacher Awards, The Disney Channel, 1990.

Presenter, *The ... Annual Golden Globe Awards,* TBS, 1991, TBS, 1994, NBC, 1997, NBC, 2003.

The 17th Annual People's Choice Awards, CBS, 1991.

Presenter, *The ... Annual CableACE Awards,* Lifetime, 1993, TNT, 1997.

Presenter, *The ... Annual People's Choice Awards,* CBS, 1993, 1994, 1999, 2002, 2004.

The First Annual Comedy Hall of Fame, NBC, 1993.

American Comedy Honors, Fox, 1997.

The 3rd Annual TV Land Awards, TV Land, 2005.

Presenter, *The 5th Annual TV Land Awards,* TV Land, 2007.

2009 Creative Arts Emmy Awards, 2009.

Presenter, *The 2009 Primetime Creative Arts Emmy Awards,* E! Entertainment Television, 2009.

Television Appearances; Pilots:

Host, *The Carol Burnett Show,* CBS, 1991.

Television Executive Producer; Specials:
Plaza Suite, ABC, 1987.
A Conversation with Carol, The Disney Channel, 1988.
The Carol Burnett Show: A Reunion, CBS, 1993.
Carol Burnett: The Special Years, CBS, 1994.
Men, Movies & Carol, CBS, 1994.
Carol Burnett: Show Stoppers (also known as *The Carol Burnett Show: Show Stoppers*), CBS, 2001.
The Carol Burnett Show: Let's Bump Up the Lights, CBS, 2004.
Once upon a Mattress, ABC, 2005.

Television Producer and Director; Specials:
Fred Astaire: Puttin' On His Top Hat, 1980.
Fred Astaire: Change Partners and Dance, 1980.
Starring Katharine Hepburn, 1981.
Judy Garland: The Concert Years, 1985.
James Stewart: A Wonderful Life, PBS, 1987.
Bacall on Bogart, 1988.
The Fred Astaire Songbook, 1991.
Katharine Hepburn: All about Me, 1992.
Southern Star: A Portrait of Atlanta, 1996.

Television Director; Specials:
The Universal Story, 1995.

Television Executive Producer; Pilots:
The Carol Burnett Show, CBS, 1991.

Film Appearances:
(Film debut) Stella Irving, *Who's Been Sleeping in My Bed?,* Paramount, 1963.
Miss Grebs, *Star Spangled Salesman,* 1966.
Herself, *Rowan and Martin at the Movies,* 1968.
Tillie Schlaine, *Pete 'n' Tillie,* Universal, 1972.
Mollie Malloy, *The Front Page,* Universal, 1974.
Katherine "Tulip" Brenner, *A Wedding,* Twentieth Century–Fox, 1978.
Gloria Burbank, *HealtH* (also known as *H.E.A.L.T.H.*), Twentieth Century–Fox, 1980.
Chu–Chu/Emily, *Chu Chu and the Philly Flash,* Twentieth Century–Fox, 1981.
Kate Burroughs, *The Four Seasons,* Universal, 1981.
Miss Hannigan, *Annie,* Columbia, 1982.
Dotty Otley and Mrs. Clackett, *Noises Off,* Buena Vista, 1992.
(In archive footage) Herself, *Wisecracks* (documentary), Alliance Releasing, 1992.
Herself, *Moon over Broadway,* Artistic License, 1997.
Herself, *Get Bruce!,* Miramax, 1999.
Voice of Mrs. Hammerbotham, *The Trumpet of the Swan* (animated), TriStar, 2001.
(Uncredited; in archive footage) Herself, *The Kid Stays in the Picture,* 2002.

Broadway: The Golden Age, by the Legends Who Where There (documentary; also known as *Broadway, Broadway: The Golden Age,* and *Broadway: The Movie*), Dada Films/Second Act Productions, 2003.
(Uncredited) *ShowBusiness: The Road to Broadway* (documentary), Regent Releasing, 2007.
Voice of Kangaroo, *Horton Hears a Who!* (animated; also known as *Dr. Seuss' "Horton Hears a Who"* and *Horton*), Twentieth Century–Fox, 2008.
Grandma Maureen, *Post Grad,* Fox Searchlight, 2009.
(In archive footage) *Muppets 201: Rarities from the Henson Vault,* Jim Henson Legacy, 2009.

Film Work:
Executive producer, *Made in America,* Warner Bros., 1993.

Stage Appearances:
(Off–Broadway debut) Princess Winnifred the Woebegone, *Once upon a Mattress* (musical), Phoenix Theatre, 1959, then (Broadway debut) Alvin Theatre, 1960.
Hope Springfield and Lila Tremaine, *Fade Out—Fade In* (musical), Mark Hellinger Theatre, New York City, 1964.
Karen Nash, "Visitor from Mamaroneck," Muriel Tate, "Visitor from Hollywood," and Norma Hubley, "Visitor from Forest Hills," *Plaza Suite,* Huntington Hartford Theatre, Los Angeles, 1970.
Agnes, *I Do! I Do!,* Huntington Hartford Theatre, 1973.
Doris, *Same Time, Next Year,* Huntington Hartford Theatre, 1977, then Burt Reynolds' Jupiter Dinner Theatre, Jupiter, FL, 1980.
The Night of 100 Stars II, Radio City Music Hall, New York City, 1985.
Melissa Gardner, *Love Letters,* Canon Theatre, Los Angeles, 1990.
Charlotte Hay, *Moon over Buffalo,* Martin Beck Theatre, New York City, 1995–96.
Amy, *Putting It Together* (musical revue), Center Theatre Group, Mark Taper Forum, Los Angeles, 1998, then Ethel Barrymore Theatre, New York City, 1999–2000.
Broadway on Broadway (outdoor concert), Times Square, New York City, 2002.

Appeared in *Follies,* Lincoln Center Theatre, New York City, 1980s.

RECORDINGS

Videos:
(In archive footage) *A Bing Crosby Christmas,* 1998.
(In archive footage) *Cher: Live in Concert,* 1999.

(In archive footage) Verla Grubbs, *Daytime's Greatest Weddings,* Buena Vista Home Video, 2004.

(In archive footage) *Cavett Remembers the Comic Legends,* Sony BMG Music Entertainment, 2006.

(In archive footage) Tulip Brenner, *A Wedding: Altman Style,* Twentieth Century–Fox Home Entertainment, 2006.

The Making of "The Larry Sanders Show," Sony Pictures Home Entertainment, 2007.

(In archive footage) *Mike Douglas: Moments & Memories,* American Public Television, 2008.

Albums:

Let Me Entertain You, Decca, 2000.

Audio Books:

This Time Together: Laughter and Reflection, by Carol Burnett, Books on Tape, 2010.

WRITINGS

Television Specials:

Katharine Hepburn: All about Me, 1992.

(With others) *Men, Movies & Carol,* CBS, 1994.

The Universal Story, 1995.

Southern Star: A Portrait of Atlanta, 1996.

Stage Plays:

(With daughter Carrie Hamilton) *Hollywood Arms* (two-act; based on Burnett's book *One More Time: A Memoir*), Goodman Theatre, Chicago, IL, 2002, then Cort Theatre, New York City, 2002–2003.

Books:

What I Want to Be When I Grow Up, created by George Mendoza and Sheldon Secunda, photographs by Secunda, Simon & Schuster, 1975.

One More Time: A Memoir, Random House, 1986.

This Time Together: Laughter and Reflection (memoir), Harmony, 2010.

OTHER SOURCES

Books:

Burnett, Carol, *One More Time: A Memoir,* Random House, 1986.

Burnett, Carol, *This Time Together: Laughter and Reflection,* Harmony, 2010.

Encyclopedia of World Biography Supplement, Volume 23, Gale, 2003.

Newsmakers 2000, Issue 3, Gale, 2000.

Taraborrelli, J. Randy, *Laughing Till It Hurts: The Complete Life and Career of Carol Burnett,* 1988.

Periodicals:

Entertainment Weekly, September 15, 2000, p. 84.

Good Housekeeping, October, 2002, pp. 98–100, 102, 104.

Interview, March, 1990, p. 122; October, 1994, p. 174.

New Yorker, August 21, 1995, p. 56.

New York Observer, May 17, 2004, p. 21.

Parade, December 18, 2005, p. 22.

People Weekly, December 17, 2001, p. 17; February 4, 2002, pp. 50–55.

TV Guide, August 30, 2003, p. 9; December 12, 2005, pp. 42–43; November 5, 2007, p. 48.

USA Today, December 14, 2005, p. 4D.

Washington Post, December 7, 2003, pp. N1, N8.

Television Specials:

Intimate Portrait: Carol Burnett, Lifetime, 1998.

"Carol Burnett: Just to Have a Laugh," *TVography,* Arts and Entertainment, 2002.

"Carol Burnett: A Woman of Character," *American Masters,* PBS, 2007.

BYRNE, Alexandra 1962–
(Alex Byrne)

PERSONAL

Born in 1962; married Simon Shepherd (an actor), 1980; children: four.

Addresses: *Agent*—International Creative Management, 10250 Constellation Blvd., 9th Floor, Los Angeles, CA 90067.

Career: Costume designer. Designed numerous productions in regional theatre in England; worked with the Royal Shakespeare Company.

Awards, Honors: Antoinette Perry Award nomination, best scenic designer, 1990, for *Some Americans Abroad;* Television Award nomination, best costume design, British Academy of Film and Television Arts, 1994, for *The Buddha of Suburbia;* Television Award, best costume designer, British Academy of Film and Television Arts, 1996, for *Persuasion;* Academy Award nomination, best costume design, Film Award nomination, best costume designer, British Academy of Film and Television Arts, 1997, both for *Hamlet;* Academy Award nomination, best costume design, Film Award nomination, best costume designer, British Academy of Film and Television Arts, Golden Satellite Award, best motion picture costume designer, International Press

Academy, 1999, both for *Elizabeth;* Academy Award nomination, best costume design, Film Award nomination, best costume designer, British Academy of Film and Television Arts, 2005, both for *Finding Neverland;* Costume Designer Guild Award nomination, excellence in costume design for film—period/fantasy, Golden Satellite Award nomination, best costume design, Saturn Award nomination, best costumes, Academy of Science Fiction, Fantasy, and Horror Films, 2005, all for *The Phantom of the Opera;* Satellite Award, best costume design, 2007, Academy Award, best costume design, Film Award nomination, best costume designer, British Academy of Film and Television Arts, Costume Designer Guild Award nomination, excellence in costume design for film—period, 2008, all for *Elizabeth: The Golden Age.*

CREDITS

Film Costume Designer:
Persuasion, Sony Pictures Classics, 1995.
Hamlet (also known as *William Shakespeare's "Hamlet"*), Columbia, 1996.
Elizabeth (also known as *Elizabeth: Virgin Queen*), Gramercy, 1998.
Captain Corelli's Mandolin, Universal, 2001.
Finding Neverland, Miramax, 2004.
The Phantom of the Opera (also known as *Andrew Lloyd Webber's "The Phantom of the Opera"*), Warner Bros., 2004.
Sleuth, Sony Pictures Classics, 2007.
Elizabeth: The Golden Age (also known as *Elizabeth: Golden Age*), Universal, 2007.

The Garden of Eden, 2008.
Thor (also known as *Mighty Thor*), Paramount, 2011.

Film Work; Other:
(As Alex Byrne) Art department assistant, *Grotesque,* Live Entertainment, 1997.

Film Appearances:
Princess Fleur–de–Lys, *Louis the Fourteenth Street,* 2004.
(Uncredited) Herself, *The Making of "The Phantom of the Opera"* (documentary), 2005.

Television Costume Designer; Miniseries:
The Buddha of Suburbia, BBC, 1993.

Television Appearances; Specials:
The 80th Annual Academy Awards, ABC, 2008.

Stage Work:
Costume designer and scenic designer, *Some Americans Abroad,* Mitzi E. Newhouse Theatre, then Vivian Beaumont Theatre, New York City, 1990.

Also worked on *Life of Napoleon.*

B–ZAR
    See GETTY, Balthazar

C

CALLOW, Simon 1949–

PERSONAL

Full name, Simon Phillip Hugh Callow; born June 15, 1949, in London (some sources cite Cumbria), England; son of Neil Francis (in business) and Yvonne Mary (a secretary; maiden name, Guise) Callow. *Education:* Attended Queen's University, Belfast (or according to some sources, Queen's College, Cambridge), 1967–68; trained for the stage at London Drama Centre.

Addresses: *Agent*—Clifford Stevens, Paradigm, 360 Park Ave. S., 16th Floor, New York, NY 10010.

Career: Actor, director, writer, and translator. Worked as a box office attendant at a London theatre (Old Vic Theatre, according to some sources). London Institute, member of board of governors, 2000; Theatres Trust, member of board of trustees, 2004.

Awards, Honors: Film Award nomination, best supporting actor, British Academy of Film and Television Arts, 1987, for *A Room with a View;* Drama Desk Award nomination, best director, 1989, for *Shirley Valentine;* Laurence Olivier Theatre Award, best director of a musical, Society of West End Theatre, 1991, for *Carmen Jones;* nomination for Golden Berlin Bear, Berlin International Film Festival, 1991, for *The Ballad of the Sad Cafe;* Film Award nomination, best supporting actor, British Academy of Film and Television Arts, 1995, for *Four Weddings and a Funeral;* Screen Actors Guild Award (with others), outstanding cast performance, 1999, for *Shakespeare in Love;* Patricia Rothermere Award, *Evening Standard* Theatre Awards, 1999; decorated commander, Order of the British Empire, 1999; honorary D.L.L., Queen's University, Belfast, 1999, and University of Birmingham, 2000; *Theatre World* Award, outstanding new performer, 2002, for *The Mystery of Charles Dickens.*

CREDITS

Stage Appearances:
(Stage debut) *The Thrie Estates,* Assembly Hall, Edinburgh, Scotland, 1973.
Crown Prince Maximilian, *Schippel,* Open Space Theatre, London, then Traverse Theatre, Edinburgh, 1974, produced as *Plumber's Progress* (previously known as *Schippel*), Prince of Wales Theatre, London, 1975.
Passing By, Gay Sweatshop (theatre company), 1975.
Redpenny, *The Doctor's Dilemma,* Mermaid Theatre, London, 1975.
Mrs. Grabowski's Academy, Theatre Upstairs, London, 1975.
Pieter de Groot, *Soul of the White Ant,* Bush Theatre, London, 1976.
Oliver, Jack, Putter, and Rider, *Blood Sports,* Bush Theatre, 1976.
Juvenalia (solo show), Bush Theatre, 1976.
Kutchevski, *Devil's Island,* Joint Stock Company, Royal Court Theatre, London, 1977.
Sayers, *A Mad World, My Masters,* Joint Stock Company, Young Vic Theatre, London, 1977.
Sandy, *Epsom Downs,* Joint Stock Company, Round House Theatre, London, 1977.
Title role, *Titus Andronicus,* Bristol Old Vic Theatre, Bristol, England, 1978.
Boyd, *Flying Blind,* Royal Court Theatre, 1978.
Title role, *The Resistible Rise of Arturo Ui,* Half Moon Theatre, London, 1978.
Ure, the old reaper, and a drunk, *The Machine Wreckers,* Half Moon Theatre, 1978.
Eddie, *Mary Barnes,* Birmingham Repertory Studio, Birmingham, England, then Royal Court Theatre, both 1978.
Orlando, *As You Like It,* Royal National Theatre, Olivier Theatre, London, 1979.
Mozart, *Amadeus,* Royal National Theatre, Olivier Theatre, 1979.
Stafford, *Sisterly Feelings,* Royal National Theatre, Olivier Theatre, 1979.

Beefy, *The Beastly Beatitudes of Balthazar B.,* Bristol Old Vic Theatre, 1981, then Duke of York's Theatre, London, 1982.

Verlaine, *Total Eclipse,* Lyric Hammersmith Theatre, London, 1982.

Lord Are, *Restoration,* Royal Court Theatre, 1982.

Lord Foppington, *The Relapse,* Lyric Hammersmith Theatre, 1983.

Perelli, *On the Spot,* Watford, then Albery Theatre, London, 1984.

Rousseau, *Melancholy Jacques,* Traverse Theatre, then Bush Theatre, 1984.

Kiss of the Spider Woman, Bush Theatre, 1985.

Title role, *Faust,* Lyric Hammersmith Theatre, 1988.

Guy Burgess, "An Englishman Abroad," *Single Spies,* National Theatre Company, Queen's Theatre, London, 1988–89.

Ned, *The Destiny of Me,* Leicester Haymarket Theatre, Leicester, England, 1993.

Face, *The Alchemist,* Birmingham production, then Royal National Theatre, 1996.

The Importance of Being Oscar (solo show), Savoy Theatre, London, 1997.

Falstaff, *Chimes at Midnight,* Chichester Festival Theatre, Chichester, England, 1998.

The Mystery of Charles Dickens (solo show), London, 2000–2001, then Belasco Theatre, New York City, 2002.

Through the Leaves, Southwark Playhouse, then London, 2003.

The Holy Terror, London, 2004.

Count Fosco, *The Woman in White,* Palace Theatre, London, c. 2005.

Sir John Falstaff, *The Merry Wives of Windsor,* Royal Shakespeare Company, Royal Shakespeare Theatre, Stratford–upon–Avon, England, 2006.

Aladdin, Richmond, 2006.

Present Laughter, 2006.

There Reigns Love, Stratford Festival, Stratford, Ontario, Canada, 2008.

A Festival Dickens, Edinburgh Fringe Festival, Edinburgh, Scotland, 2008.

Peter Pan, Richmond, 2008.

Doctor Marigold and Mr. Chops (solo show), Riverside Studio Theatre, London, 2010.

Also appeared in repertory in Lincoln, England, 1973–74.

Major Tours:

The Mystery of Charles Dickens, international cities, c. 2002.

The Holy Terror, 2004.

Equus, British cities, 2008.

Stage Director:

Loving Reno, Bush Theatre, London, 1983.

The Passport, Offstage Downstairs Theatre, London, 1985.

Nicholson Fights Croydon, Offstage Downstairs Theatre, 1986.

The Infernal Machine, Lyric Hammersmith Theatre, London, 1986.

Amadeus, Clwyd, Wales, 1986.

Cosi fan tutte, Lucerne Theatre, Lucerne, Switzerland, 1987.

Jacques and His Master, Los Angeles Theatre Center, Los Angeles, 1987.

Shirley Valentine, Vaudeville Theatre, London, 1988, then Really Useful Theatre Company, Booth Theatre, New York City, 1989.

Die Fledermaus, Scottish Opera Theatre, 1988.

Facades, Lyric Hammersmith Theatre, 1988.

(With Alan Bennett) "An Englishman Abroad," *Single Spies,* National Theatre Company, Queen's Theatre, 1988–89.

Die Fledermaus, Scottish Opera Theatre, 1989–90.

Stevie Wants to Play the Blues, Los Angeles Theatre Center, 1990.

Carmen Jones, Old Vic Theatre, London, 1991.

Shades, Albery Theatre, London, 1992.

The Destiny of Me, Leicester Haymarket Theatre, Leicester, England, 1993.

Il trittico, Broomhill Opera Theatre, 1995.

Les enfants du paradis, Royal Shakespeare Company, Barbican Theatre, London, 1996.

Il turco in italia, Broomhill Opera Theatre, 1997.

HRH, Playhouse Theatre, 1997.

The Pajama Game, Birmingham Repertory Company, Birmingham, England, 1999.

The Consul, Holland Park Opera, 1999.

Jus' like That, London, 2003.

Everyman, Norwich Festival Theatre, 2003.

Le Roy Malgre Lui, Grange Park Theatre, 2003.

The Magic Flute, Holland Park Theatre, 2008.

Stage Director; Major Tours:

My Fair Lady, British cities, 1992.

Carmen Jones, British and Japanese cities, 1994.

Film Appearances:

Gossip, Boyd's Company, 1983.

Emanuel Schikaneder, *Amadeus* (also known as *Amadeus: The Director's Cut* and *Peter Shaffer's Amadeus: Director's Cut*), Orion, 1984.

Mark Varda, *The Good Father,* Skouras, 1986.

Reverend Arthur Beebe, *A Room with a View,* Cinecom, 1986.

Mr. Ducie, *Maurice,* Cinecom, 1987.

Police Chief Hunt, *Manifesto* (also known as *For a Night of Love*), Cannon, 1988.

Dr. Alexis Sauer, *Mr. & Mrs. Bridge,* Miramax, 1990.

Simon Asquith, *Postcards from the Edge,* Columbia, 1990.

(Uncredited) "Music and Meaning" lecturer, *Howards End,* Sony Pictures Classics, 1992.

Eddie Cherdowski, *Soft Top, Hard Shoulder,* 1992.

Gareth, *Four Weddings and a Funeral,* Gramercy, 1994.

A.N. official, *Street Fighter* (also known as *Street Fighter: The Battle for Shadaloo, Street Fighter: The Movie,* and *Street Fighter: The Ultimate Battle*), Universal, 1994.

Charles II, *England, My England,* 1995.

Richard Cosway, *Jefferson in Paris,* Buena Vista, 1995.

Vincent Cadby, *Ace Ventura: When Nature Calls* (also known as *Ace Ventura Goes to Africa*), Warner Bros., 1995.

Voice of Grasshopper, *James and the Giant Peach* (animated), Buena Vista, 1996.

Captain John Fairfax, *The Scarlet Tunic,* Marie Hoy Film & Television, 1997.

Mr. Zangiacomo, *Victory,* Miramax, 1997.

Tilney, Master of the Revels, *Shakespeare in Love,* Miramax, 1998.

Keith, *Bedrooms and Hallways,* First Run Features, 1999.

Junk, 1999.

(Uncredited) Himself in film within film, *Notting Hill,* 1999.

Phileas Fogg, *Around the World in 80 Days,* 1999.

Colonel Soft, *No Man's Land,* United Artists, 2001.

Voices of Ebenezer Scrooge and Charles Dickens, *Christmas Carol: The Movie,* Planeta 2010, 2001.

Sir John Osgood, *Thunderpants,* United Artists, 2002.

King Edgar, *George and the Dragon* (also known as *Dragon Sword*), First Look International, 2003, American World Pictures, 2006.

Andre, *The Phantom of the Opera* (also known as *Andrew Lloyd Webber's "The Phantom of the Opera"*), Warner Bros., 2004.

Bob, *Merci Docteur Rey,* Here Films, 2004.

King of Anatolia, *Bright Young Things,* THINKFilm, 2004.

Fat Boy, *Rag Tale,* Becker Films, 2005.

Theatre director, *Ripley Under Ground,* Fox Searchlight, 2005.

Mr. Wroth, *The Civilization of Maxwell Bright,* 2005, Grass Roots Film Distribution, 2007.

Some Break (short film), Primafilm, 2006.

St. John, *Surveillance 24/7* (also known as *Surveillance*), Peccadillo Pictures/Visual Factory, 2007.

Father Henry, *Arn: The Knight Templar* (also known as *Arn—Tempelriddaren*), Svensk Filmindustri, 2007.

Haddo/Crowley, *Chemical Wedding,* Warner Bros., 2008.

Narrator, *The Pantomime* (short documentary), 2008.

Professor Gwynson, *Natural Selection* (short film), RSA Films, 2010.

Voice of the Swinesbury's boss, *Save Our Bacon* (animated short film), 2010.

Godfrey, *Acts of Godfrey,* 2010.

Guy Witherspoon, *No Ordinary Trifle,* Just Nuts Films/Trifle Films, 2010.

Prime minister, *Ice,* Power, 2010.

Film Director:
The Ballad of the Sad Cafe, Angelika, 1991.

Television Appearances; Miniseries:
Hugo Silver, *Dead Head,* BBC, 1984.

Mr. Wilkins Micawber, *David Copperfield,* BBC, 1986, broadcast by *Masterpiece Theatre,* PBS, 1988.

Edward Feathers, *Little Napoleons,* BBC, 1994.

Voice of Menephtah, *Testament: The Bible in Animation,* HBO, 1997.

Mr. Rupert Halliday, *Trial & Retribution,* YTV, 1998, ITV, 1999, 2002.

Charles Dickens, *Hans Christian Anderson: My Life as a Fairy Tale,* Hallmark Channel, 2001.

Prior Walter's second ancestor, *Angels in America,* HBO, 2003.

George Russell, *The Curse of King Tut's Tomb,* Hallmark Channel, 2006.

Himself, *The Play's the Thing,* Channel 4, 2006.

Pliny, *The Roman Mysteries,* BBC, 2007.

Elihu Epstein, *The Company,* TNT, 2007.

Interviewee, *British Film Forever,* BBC, 2007.

Himself, *Rude Britannia,* BBC, 2010.

Television Appearances; Specials:
"Instant Enlightenment, Including V.A.T.," *Play for Today,* BBC, 1979.

Napoleon, *The Man of Destiny,* BBC, 1981.

The poet, *La ronde,* BBC, 1982.

The Madness Museum, 1986.

Raimondi, "Cariani and the Courtesans," *Screenplay,* Granada Television, 1987.

Nathaniel Quass, "Old Flames," *Screen Two,* BBC, 1989.

Franciscus Palloy, "The Patriot," *Revolutionary Witness,* BBC, 1989.

Vicar Ronnie, "Femme Fatale," *Screen Two,* BBC, 1993.

Himself, *Camp Christmas,* 1993.

Title role, *An Audience with Charles Dickens,* 1996.

Count Fosco, *The Woman in White,* PBS, 1998.

Dear Boy: The Story of Michael Mac Liammoir, 1999.

Voice of Don Quixote de la Mancha, *Don Quixote* (also known as *Animated Epics: Don Quixote*), HBO, 2000.

Title role, *The Mystery of Charles Dickens,* 2000.

Judi Dench: A BAFTA Tribute, BBC, 2002.

(In archive footage) *Retrosexual: The 80's,* VH1, 2004.

Admiral, *Comic Relief: Red Nose Night Live 05,* BBC, 2005.

Foley & McColl: This Way Up, BBC, 2005.

It's Christmas with Jonathan Ross, BBC, 2005.

Narrator, *The Madness of Boy George,* Channel 4, 2006.

How Gay Sex Changed the World, Channel 4, 2007.

Presenter, *Orson Wells over Europe,* 2009.

Also appeared in *All the World's a Stage* and *The Dybbuk.*

Television Appearances; Movies:
George Frideric Handel, *Honor, Profit, and Pleasure,* Channel 4, 1985.
Jacob, *The Christmas Tree,* 1986.
John Mortimer, *The Trials of Oz,* BBC, 1991.
Inspector Lestrade, *The Crucifer of Blood,* TNT, 1991.
Friar Morcheno, *Bye Bye Columbus,* BBC, 1992.
Major Owens, *Le passager clandestin,* 1994.
Rick Spencer, *Deadly Appearances* (also known as *Criminal Instinct: Deadly Appearances*), Lifetime, 2000.
Florestan/Eusebius, *Robert's Rescue,* 2000.
Colonel Terence Melchett, *Marple: The Body in the Library,* ITV, 2004, broadcast as an episode of *Agatha Christie's Marple,* PBS, 2005.
Mr. Butler, *Bob the Butler,* The Disney Channel, 2005.
Big–time publisher, *The Best Man* (also known as *Best Man, Worst Friend* and *Unhitched*), ABC Family, 2006.

Television Appearances; Series:
Tom Chance, *Chance in a Million,* Thames Television, 1984–86.
Fox & Bear, *Don't Eat the Neighbours* (also known as *Big Teeth, Bad Breath*), YTV, 2001.
Voice of Wolfgang the Wolf, *Shoebox Zoo,* BBC, 2004.
Host, *Classical Destinations,* 2006–2007.

Television Appearances; Pilots:
Dr. George Griffen, *Anatomy of Hope,* HBO, 2009.

Television Appearances; Episodic:
Wally, "36–Hour Pass," *Get Some In!,* Thames Television, 1975.
Duval, "Skittles," *Victorian Scandals,* Granada Television, 1976.
Detective Sergeant, "Down to You, Brother," *The Sweeney,* ITV, 1976.
Wings of Song, Granada Television, 1977.
Raymond Craft, "Association," *Crown Court,* ITV, 1978.
Panelist, *The Theatre Quiz,* 1981.
Haddy Kemp, "The Times They Are a Changin'," *Scarecrow and Mrs. King,* CBS, 1984.
Voice of the Dragon, "The Reluctant Dragon," *Long Ago and Far Away,* PBS, 1987.
"Simon Callow: On Acting in Restoration Comedy," *Acting,* 1987.
Dr. Theodore Kemp, "The Wolvercote Tongue," *Inspector Morse,* Granada Television, 1987, broadcast on *Mystery!,* PBS, 1988.
Politically Incorrect, Comedy Central, 1996.
Himself, "Giacomo Puccini 1858–1924," *Great Composers,* PBS, 1997.
Voice of Hugo Trenchfoot, "The Trial," *Dennis the Menace,* 1998.
Galileo Galilei, "Galileo's Battle for the Heavens," *Nova,* PBS, 2002.

Charles Dickens, "The Unquiet Dead," *Doctor Who,* BBC1, 2005, Sci–Fi Channel, 2006.
Publius Servilius, "Egeria," *Rome,* HBO, 2005.
Presenter, "Actresses," *Britain's Finest,* Channel 5, 2005.
Dr. Wellow, "Dead Letters," *Midsomer Murders,* Arts and Entertainment, 2006.
"Four Weddings and a Funeral," *Movie Connections,* 2007.
"Shakespeare in Love," *Movie Connections,* 2007.
Actor, *What's on Theatre,* c. 2008.
Vernon Oxe, "Counter Culture Blues," *Inspector Lewis* (also known as *Lewis*), PBS, 2009.
Voice of Tree Blathereen, "The Gift: Parts 1 & 2," *The Sarah Jane Adventures,* 2009.

Television Talk Show Guest Appearances; Episodic:
Breakfast Time, 1985.
Brunch, 1997.
Loose Women, ITV, 1999.
Parkinson, BBC, 1999.
"Alex Guinness: A Secret Man," *Arena,* BBC, 2003.
Today with Des and Mel, ITV, 2004.
The Frank Skinner Show, ITV, 2004.
Breakfast, BBC, 2004, 2009.
News 24 Sunday, BBC, 2005.
Richard & Judy, Channel 4, 2005.
Ant & Dec's Saturday Night Takeaway, ITV, 2005.
The Wright Stuff, Channel 5, 2005, 2008.
This Week, BBC, 2006, 2009.
Derren Brown: Trick or Treat, 2007.
HARDtalk Extra, BBC, 2007.
Sunday AM, BBC, 2008.
"Paul Scofield," *Arena,* BBC, 2008.
The ONE Show, 2009, 2010.

Television Director; Specials:
Charles Laughton, BBC, 1987.
Stage director, *Richard Rodgers: Some Enchanted Evening,* 2002.

Radio Appearances:
Michael MacLiammoir, BBC, 1991.
Dr. Johnson, *Poonsh,* BBC, 1994.
Shakespeare's Sonnets, BBC, 1994.
Orson Welles, 1999.

Radio Director:
Tomorrow Week, 1999.
The Man Who Came to Dinner, 2000.
The Judas Kiss, 2000.
I'll Be George, 2001.
Third Soldier, 2004.
Put Money in Thy Purse, 2005.
Single Spies, 2006.

RECORDINGS

Videos:
In Ismail's Custody, 1994.

Making "Christmas Carol: The Movie," Metro–Goldwyn–Mayer Home Entertainment, 2003.

(Uncredited) *The Making of "The Phantom of the Opera,"* Really Useful Films, 2005.

Men of Mystery, Criterion Collection, 2006.

Reviving Harry Lime, Criterion Collection, 2006.

The Dark Secrets of the Hellfire Council, Echo Bridge Home Entertainment, 2006.

Shooting "Egypt" in India, Echo Bridge Home Entertainment, 2006.

Locked in the Tower: The Men behind "Jane Eyre," Twentieth Century–Fox Home Entertainment, 2007.

Audio Books; Reader:

Shooting the Actor by Simon Callow, 1992.

Fairy Tales by Oscar Wilde, 1995.

Handful of Dust, 1995.

Dance to the Music of Time, 1995.

Swann's Way, 1996.

Oscar Wilde: The Road to Xanadu by Simon Callow, 1996.

The Witches, 1997.

The Twits, 1998.

The Plato Papers, 1999.

London: A Biography, 2000.

What Ho Jeeves, 2000.

English Passengers, 2001.

Death in Venice, 2004.

Shakespeare, 2005.

The Aeneid, 2006.

Practical Cats, 2008.

Also reader for the audio book series "Jeeves," 2003.

WRITINGS

Plays:

(Translator) Denis Diderot, *Jacques and His Master,* Royal Shakespeare Company, Almeida Theatre, London, 1985, then Los Angeles Theatre Center, Los Angeles, 1987, published by Faber, 1986.

(Translator) Jean Cocteau, *The Infernal Machine,* 1986.

(Adaptor) *Les enfants du paradis* (based on screenplay by Jacques Prevert), Royal Shakespeare Company, Barbican Theatre, London, 1996.

Henry IV, Part 1, Faber, 2002.

Henry IV, Part 2, Faber, 2003.

Television Specials:

Orson Wells over Europe, 2009.

Books:

Being an Actor (autobiography), Methuen, 1984, St. Martin's Press, 1986, revised edition, Vintage, 2004.

(With Adam Godley and Mark McGlynn) *Zero Hour,* 1986.

Charles Laughton: A Difficult Actor, Methuen, 1987, corrected edition, 1988, Grove Press, 1988.

(With Dusan Makavejev) *Shooting the Actor; or, The Choreography of Confusion,* Hern, 1990, revised edition, Vintage, 2004.

Acting in Restoration Comedy, Applause Theatre Books, 1991.

Orson Welles: The Road to Xanadu, Jonathan Cape, 1995, Viking, 1996.

The National: The Theatre and Its Work 1963–97; and a Chronology of Productions 1963–1997, Nick Hern, 1997.

Love Is Where It Falls: An Account of a Passionate Friendship (memoir), Fromm International, 1999.

Oscar Wilde and His Circle, National Portrait Gallery, 2000.

The Night of the Hunter (criticism), BFI Publishing, 2000.

(Compiler) *Shakespeare on Love,* Frances Lincoln, 2000.

Dickens' Christmas: A Victorian Celebration, Frances Lincoln, 2002.

Orson Welles: Hello Americans, Jonathan Cape, 2006.

Contributor to books, including foreword, *The Great Stage Directors: 100 Distinguished Careers of the Theatre,* Facts on File, 1994; and introduction, *Snowdon on Stage: With a Personal View of the British Theatre 1954–1996,* Pavilion, 1996. Also contributor of book reviews to periodicals, including *Evening Standard, Observer, Sunday Times,* and *Times* (London).

OTHER SOURCES

Books:

Callow, Simon, *Being an Actor,* Methuen, 1984, St. Martin's Press, 1986.

Callow, Simon, *Love Is Where It Falls: An Account of a Passionate Friendship,* Fromm International, 1999.

Periodicals:

Independent: Education & Careers, April 6, 2004, p. 6.

Radio Times, February 25, 2006, p. 154.

CAMERON, Earl 1917–

PERSONAL

Born August 8, 1917, in Pembroke, Bermuda; married Audrey, 1954 (died February, 1994); married Barbara, September 20, 1994; children: (first marriage) five. *Education:* Studied acting with Amanda Aldridge; studied speech and singing. *Religion:* Baha'i Faith.

Addresses: *Agent*—Linda Kremer, Billy Marsh Drama, Ltd., 11 Henrietta St., Covent Garden, London WC2E 8PY, England.

Career: Actor. Participated in events in the entertainment industry. Worked as a dishwasher, as a kitchen porter, and on ships. *Military service:* British Merchant Navy, c. 1939–40.

Awards, Honors: British Film Institute held a retrospective of Cameron's career, National Film Theatre, London, 2002; Prospero Award, lifetime achievement, Bermuda International Film Festival, 2007; decorated Commander, Order of the British Empire, 2009.

CREDITS

Film Appearances:
Johnny Lambert, *Pool of London,* Universal, 1951.
Ginger Jones, *Wall of Death* (also known as *There Is Another Sun*), Realart Pictures, 1952.
George Robinson, *The Hundred Hour Hunt* (also known as *Emergency Call*), Abner J. Greshler Productions, 1953.
(Uncredited) Ali, *The Heart of the Matter,* British Lion, 1953, Associated Artists, 1954.
Karanja, *Simba,* Lippert Pictures, 1955.
Lemmie, *The Woman for Joe,* J. Arthur Rank, 1955.
Hassan, *Odongo,* Columbia, 1956.
Jeroge, *Safari,* Columbia, 1956.
(English–language dubbed version) Johnny Brown, *Torpedo Zone* (also known as *The Great Hope, Submarine Attack,* and *La grande speranza;* originally released in Italy in Italian), I.F.E. Releasing, 1956.
Victor Conway, *The Heart Within,* J. Arthur Rank, 1957.
Prosecutor, *The Mark of the Hawk,* Universal, 1958.
Dr. Robbins, *Sapphire* (also known as *Operation Scotland Yard*), Universal, 1959.
Witch doctor, *Killers of Kilimanjaro,* Columbia, 1959.
Tate, *Tarzan the Magnificent,* Paramount, 1960.
Father, *Beware of Children* (also known as *No Kidding*), American International Pictures, 1961.
Gabriel Gomez, *Flame in the Streets,* J. Arthur Rank, 1961.
(Uncredited) Chard, *Term of Trial,* Warner Bros., 1963.
Mang, *Tarzan's Three Challenges,* Metro–Goldwyn–Mayer, 1963.
Captain Abraham, *Guns at Batasi,* Twentieth Century–Fox, 1964.
Pinder Romania, *Thunderball* (also known as *Ian Fleming's "Thunderball," James Bond, Secret Agent,* and *Longitude 78 West*), United Artists, 1965.
Bernard, *The Sandwich Man,* J. Arthur Rank, 1966.
Verger, *Two a Penny,* 1967, World Wide Pictures, 1969.
Sergeant Seth Hawkins, *Battle beneath the Sea* (also known as *Battle beneath the Earth*), Metro–Goldwyn–Mayer, 1968.

Charles (Jane's father), *Two Gentlemen Sharing,* American International Pictures, 1969.
Speaker, *The Revolutionary,* United Artists, 1970.
Ambassador George Oswandu, *A Warm December,* National General, 1973.
Employee in toilet, *Scorpio* (also known as *The Scorpio File*), United Artists, 1973.
(English–language dubbed version) Annajashi, *The Message* (also known as *Mohammad: Messenger of God, Mohammed, Messenger of God,* and *Al–risalah;* originally released in other countries in Arabic), Filmco International Productions, 1976, Tarik Film Distributors, 1977.
Colonel Rosell y Leyva, *Cuba* (also known as *Explosion in Cuba*), United Artists, 1979.
Doctor, *Deja Vu,* Lions Gate Films, 1997, Rainbow Releasing, 1998.
(English–language dubbed version) Rui, *Sand Bride* (also known as *Heikkamorsian;* originally released in Finland in Finnish), Marianna Films/Oblomovies, c. 1998.
Cardinal Chisamba, *Revelation,* First Look International/Miracle Communications, 2001.
Edward Zuwanie, *The Interpreter,* Universal, 2005.
Portrait artist, *The Queen,* Miramax, 2006.
Himself, *Don't Knock Yourself Out* (documentary; other versions also released), 2007.
Elderly bald man, *Inception* (also known as *Oliver's Arrow;* IMAX version known as *Inception: The IMAX Experience*), Warner Bros., 2010.

Appeared in other films, including appearances as an extra.

Television Appearances; Series:
Yusel, *The Andromeda Breakthrough,* BBC, 1962.
Storyteller for Brer Rabbit stories, *Jackanory* (also known as *Jackanory: Brer Rabbit Stories*), BBC, 1971.

Television Appearances; Miniseries:
Vic, *Men Only,* Channel 4, 2001.

Television Appearances; Movies:
Hank Christians, *The End Begins,* BBC, 1956.
Joseph Brent, *A Man from the Sun,* BBC, 1956.
Bargie Meade, *A World Inside,* BBC, 1962.
Carlton, *The Great Kandinsky,* broadcast as part of *Screen One,* BBC, c. 1994, and broadcast as part of *Masterpiece Theatre* (also known as *ExxonMobil Masterpiece Theatre, Masterpiece,* and *Mobil Masterpiece Theatre*), PBS, 1995.

Television Appearances; Specials:
Joseph Blake, "Thunder on Sycamore Street," *ITV Television Playhouse,* ITV, 1957.
Adam Hezdral, "The Green Pastures," *Sunday–Night Theatre* (also known as *BBC Sunday–Night Theatre*), BBC, 1958.

Dr. Jennings, "The Concert," *Sunday–Night Theatre* (also known as *BBC Sunday–Night Theatre*), BBC, 1959.

Cab driver, *The Dark Man*, BBC, 1960.

Christopher Davis–Robinson, "The Gentle Assassin," *Play of the Week* (also known as *ITV Play of the Week*), ITV, 1962.

William Jones, "The Chocolate Tree," *Armchair Theatre*, Associated British Picture Corporation, 1963.

Mike, "I Can Walk Where I Like Can't I?," *Play of the Week* (also known as *ITV Play of the Week*), ITV, 1964.

Ramsay, "A Fear of Strangers," *Drama '64* (also known as "Drama '64: A Fear of Strangers" and "A Fear of Strangers," *Drama 61–67*), ITV, 1964.

Jack, "The Death of Bessie Smith," *Play of the Week* (also known as *ITV Play of the Week*), ITV, 1965.

M'Landa, "The Minister," *Theatre 625*, BBC, 1965.

Chief Ozuomba, "Wind versus Polygamy," *Theatre 625*, BBC, 1968.

Dr. Henry Mbala, "Number Ten," *ITV Playhouse*, ITV, 1968.

Matthew Ramsey, "Murder: An Even Chance," *ITV Playhouse*, ITV, 1968.

"Anything You Say," *Thirty–Minute Theatre*, BBC, 1969.

"Soldier Ants," *Thirty–Minute Theatre*, BBC, 1971.

First king, "The Coming of the Kings," *Jackanory Playhouse*, BBC, 1972.

Television Appearances; Episodic:

Josh Barsey, "Cable Street," *Big City*, ITV, 1956.

Sam, "The Slave Ship," *The Buccaneers*, ITV, 1956.

Domani, "Port Jeopardy," *Sailor of Fortune*, ITV, 1957.

Dr. Ant Eater, "The Carefulness of Kleiber," *The Killing Stones*, ITV, 1958.

Dr. Ant Eater, "The Holiness of Ant Eater," *The Killing Stones*, ITV, 1958.

Komo, "The Day of Reckoning," *White Hunter*, ITV and syndicated, 1958.

Komo, "The Fugitive," *White Hunter*, ITV and syndicated, 1958.

Mr. Alexander, *Probation Officer*, ITV, 1959.

Symeon, "To the Gentiles," *Paul of Tarsus*, BBC, 1960.

Professor Moma, "Deadline," *Danger Man* (also known as *Dangerman, John Drake, Secret Agent*, and *Secret Agent aka Danger Man*), Associated Television, Incorporated Television Company, and CBS, 1961.

Lucky Jones, *Emergency–Ward 10* (also known as *Calling Nurse Roberts*), ITV, 1962.

Jerome, "The Dawn," *First Night*, BBC, 1963.

M'Bata, "Once a Spy ...," *Espionage*, NBC, 1964.

The Negro, "The Respectful Prostitute," *Festival*, BBC, 1964.

Thomas Kassawari, "The Galloping Major," *Danger Man* (also known as *Dangerman, John Drake, Secret Agent*, and *Secret Agent aka Danger Man*), Associated Television, Incorporated Television Company, and CBS, 1964.

Darcy, "Parallel Lines Sometimes Meet," *Danger Man* (also known as *Dangerman, John Drake, Secret Agent*, and *Secret Agent aka Danger Man*), Associated Television, Incorporated Television Company, and CBS, 1965.

Prime minister, "Loyalty Always Pays," *Danger Man* (also known as *Dangerman, John Drake, Secret Agent*, and *Secret Agent aka Danger Man*), Associated Television, Incorporated Television Company, and CBS, 1965.

Sergeant Floyd Latham, "Operation Makeshift," *Court Martial*, ABC, 1965.

Chand, "Someone Is Liable to Get Hurt," *Danger Man* (also known as *Dangerman, John Drake, Secret Agent*, and *Secret Agent aka Danger Man*), Associated Television, Incorporated Television Company, and CBS, 1966.

Jordan Kobola, "The Chicken Run," *The Power Game*, Associated Television, 1966.

Jordan Kobola, "Safe Conduct," *The Power Game*, Associated Television, 1966.

Thomas, "Thea," *Mogul* (also known as *The Troubleshooters*), BBC, 1966.

Williams, "The Tenth Planet: Episodes 1 & 2," *Doctor Who* (also known as *Dr. Who*), BBC, 1966.

Supervisor, "The Schizoid Man," *The Prisoner* (also known as *Prisoner No. 6*), ITV and CBS, 1967.

John Tate, "English—Born and Bred," *Dixon of Dock Green*, BBC, 1968.

Freddy Hafiz, "The Hafiz Affair," *Spyder's Web*, ITV, 1972.

Maynard, "A Private Nuisance," *Six Days of Justice*, Thames Television, 1972.

Antoine Mbula, "Wise Child: Parts 1–3," *Crown Court*, ITV, 1973.

Daniel Rocco, "To Suffer a Witch: Parts 1–3," *Crown Court*, ITV, 1973.

Jombote, "African Misfire," *The Zoo Gang*, ITV, 1974.

Fogerty, "Holding the Baby," *Lovejoy*, BBC and Arts and Entertainment, 1994.

Mr. Tambo Senior, "Doctor Death," *Health and Efficiency*, BBC, 1995.

The abbot of Blackfriars, "As Above, So Below," *Neverwhere*, BBC2, 1996.

The abbot of Blackfriars, "Blackfriars," *Neverwhere*, BBC2, 1996.

Joseph Cook, "In God We Trust," *Kavanagh QC* (also known as *Kavanagh Q.C.*), Central, 1997.

Theo, "Food of Love," *Maisie Raine*, BBC, 1998.

Bookshop owner, "Part Two," *Babyfather*, BBC, 2001.

Bookshop owner, "Part Four," *Babyfather*, BBC, 2001.

Mr. Lambert, *EastEnders* (also known as *East 8, London Pride, Round the Houses, Round the Square, Square Dances*, and *Victoria Square*), BBC, 2001.

Boss, "Part One" (first episode of second season), *Babyfather* (also known as *Babyfather 2*), BBC, 2002.

Guiness, "Two Plus Two Makes Five," *Offenders*, Channel 4, 2002.

"15 Storeys High," *Pool Kids*, BBC Choice, 2002.

Carlton Jordan, "Final Cut: Parts 1 & 2," *Waking the Dead*, BBC, 2003.

Lenny Henry in Pieces, BBC, 2003.

Arthur Nolan, "Houdini's Ghost: Parts 1 & 2," *Dalziel and Pascoe* (also known as *Dalziel & Pascoe*), BBC, 2006.

Himself, "Hardship, Humour and Heroes: The Story of British Realism," *British Film Forever* (documentary), BBC2, 2007.

Himself, "'Cold Feet' to 'A Touch of Frost,'" *Drama Trails* (documentary), ITV, 2008.

Horace Mumford, "Where's the Art in Heartache?," *Casualty* (also known as *Casual+y* and *Front Line*), BBC, 2008.

Stage Appearances:

Chu Chin Chow (musical), London, 1941.

The Petrified Forest, London, 1943.

All God's Chillun Got Wings, Colchester Repertory Theatre, Colchester, England, 1944.

Understudy, *Deep Are the Roots,* London, 1946.

In White America (also known as *In White America: A Documentary Play*), Arts Theatre, London, 1964.

Janie Jackson, London, 1968.

Major Tours:

Understudy, *Deep Are the Roots,* British cities, c. 1946.

13 Death Street, Harlem, British cities, c. 1950.

Radio Appearances:

Deep Are the Roots, 1949.

The Green Pastures, 1956.

Christophe, 1958.

Under the Sun, 1958.

The University of Hunger, 1960.

Come Along to Freedom, 1961.

Brother Man, 1964.

Wind versus Polygamy, 1966.

OTHER SOURCES

Books:

Contemporary Black Biography, Volume 44, Gale, 2004.

CASSARO, Nancy 1959–
(Nancy Ellen Cassaro)

PERSONAL

Born May 28, 1959, in Massapequa, NY. *Education:* Attended Hofstra University; studied tap dancing with Jerry Ames.

Addresses: *Agent*—Dan Baron, Agency for the Performing Arts, 405 South Beverly Dr., Beverly Hills, CA 90212.

Career: Actress and writer. Artificial Intelligence (improvisational theatre company), New York City, member of company.

CREDITS

Television Appearances; Series:

Sheila DeMattis, *Family Album,* CBS, 1993.

Ann Marie, *Temporarily Yours* (also known as *Temp Yours, Temp Mine*), CBS, 1997.

Shelly Tucci, *Getting Personal,* Fox, 1998.

Connie O'Keefe, a recurring role, *Grounded for Life,* Fox, between 2002 and 2004.

Suzanne Epstein, a recurring role, *Nip/Tuck,* FX Network, 2003–2004.

Television Appearances; Movies:

Maria, *Casualties of Love: The Long Island Lolita Story,* CBS, 1993.

Maria, *A Mother's Prayer,* USA Network, 1995.

Tour guide, *Hefner: Unauthorized* (also known as *Hugh Hefner: The True Story*), USA Network, 1999.

Television Appearances; Pilots:

Sheila DeMattis, *Family Album,* CBS, 1993.

Linda, *Girl's Best Friend,* CBS, 1994.

"Oh, My God! Jerry!," *Partners,* Fox, 1996.

Ann Marie, *Temporarily Yours* (also known as *Temp Yours, Temp Mine*), CBS, 1997.

Television Appearances; Episodic:

Doris Blynn, "Alien Aided Affection," *Civil Wars,* ABC, 1993.

Alice, "George Looks down the Wrong End of a Thirty–Eight," *The George Carlin Show,* Fox, 1994.

Nancy Caruso, "The Homecoming Queen," *Dream On,* HBO, 1994.

Shelly, "The One Where Nana Dies Twice," *Friends,* NBC, 1994.

Dominique Garfolo, *Madman of the People,* ABC, c. 1994.

Alice, *The Home Court,* NBC, c. 1995.

Angela, "The Apartment Show," *Platypus Man,* UPN, 1995.

Angela Cusomano, "Little Italy," *Northern Exposure,* CBS, 1995.

Paula, "We Ought to Be in Pictures," *High Society,* CBS, 1995.

Michelle Sitkowitz, "Just Say Noah," *Lois & Clark: The New Adventures of Superman,* ABC, 1995.

Mona Feigenbaum, "Chapter Twelve," *Murder One,* ABC, 1996.

Simone, "Tainted Love," *Hope & Gloria,* NBC, 1996.

Mohawk secretary, "Defending Your Life," *Murphy Brown,* CBS, 1996.

Gloria, "It Takes a Village," *NYPD Blue* (also known as *N.Y.P.D.*), ABC, 1997.

Salesperson, "The Big, Flouncy Thing," *Cybill*, CBS, 1997.

Libby, "California, Here We Come," *The Nanny*, CBS, 1999.

Libby, "The Baby Shower," *The Nanny*, CBS, 1999.

Joanne Moltisanti, "From Where to Eternity," *The Sopranos*, HBO, 2000.

Sarah Rutigliano, "The Quick Hit," *Bull*, TNT, 2000.

Instructor, "Another Moving Script," *Two Guys and a Girl* (also known as *Two Guys, a Girl, and a Pizza Place*), ABC, 2000.

Mrs. Horowitz, "Hi Def–Jam," *The King of Queens*, CBS, 2001.

"Exposure," *Providence*, NBC, 2001.

Toni Crispes–Santo, "Russian Winter" (also known as "The Russian Wars"), *The District*, CBS, 2002.

Janet Price, "Night Five," *The West Wing* (also known as *The White House*), NBC, 2002.

Wedding planner, "There Goes the Bride," *Without a Trace* (also known as *W.A.T.*), CBS, 2003.

Kristi Haines, "Nude Awakening," *NYPD Blue* (also known as *N.Y.P.D.*), ABC, 2003.

Gwen, "Trade Talks," *Clubhouse*, CBS, 2004.

Gwen, "Spectator Interference," *Clubhouse*, CBS, 2004.

Gwen, "Stealing Home," *Clubhouse*, CBS, 2005.

Perry Tatum, "In Lieu of Flowers," *Dirt*, FX Network, 2008.

Television Appearances; Other:

Flora, *The 70s* (miniseries), NBC, 2000.

The Mayor of Oyster Bay (special), ABC, 2002.

Film Appearances:

(As Nancy Ellen Cassaro) Joe Buddha's wife, *Goodfellas*, Warner Bros., 1990.

Esther, *Deuces Wild*, Metro–Goldwyn–Mayer, 2002.

Newton's Law (short film), 2003.

Christy in 1978 poetry club, *Running with Scissors*, TriStar, 2006.

Stage Appearances:

Valentina Lynne Vitale Nunzio, *Tony n' Tina's Wedding*, St. Luke's Theatre, New York City, 1988.

Stage Work:

Cocreator, *Tony n' Tina's Wedding*, St. Luke's Theatre, New York City, 1988–2003.

WRITINGS

Screenplays:

Shortcut to Happiness (also known as *The Devil and Daniel Webster*), 2001, Yari Film Group, 2004.

CAVILL, Henry 1983–

PERSONAL

Full name, Henry William Dalgliesh Cavill; born May 5, 1983, in Jersey, Channel Islands. *Education:* Attended boarding school in Buckingham, England.

Addresses: *Agent*—Creative Artists Agency, 2000 Avenue of the Stars, Los Angeles, CA 90067; Dallas Smith, United Agents, 12–26 Lexington St., London W1F 0LE, England.

Career: Actor. Appeared in television commercials and print advertisements for Dunhill London fragrance for men.

CREDITS

Film Appearances:

Thomas Aprea, *Laguna*, Allumination Filmworks/Fries Film Group, 2001.

Albert Mondego, *The Count of Monte Cristo* (also known as *Alexandre Dumas' "The Count of Monte Cristo"*), Buena Vista, 2003.

Stephen Colley, *I Capture the Castle*, Samuel Goldwyn, 2003.

The hunter, *Red Riding Hood*, Twentieth Century–Fox, 2005.

Mike, *Hellraiser: Hellworld*, Dimension Home Video, 2005.

Melot, *Tristan + Isolde* (also known as *Tristan & Isolde*), Twentieth Century–Fox, 2006.

Humphrey, *Stardust*, Paramount, 2007.

Evan Marshall, *Blood Creek* (also known as *Town Creek*), Gold Circle Films, 2009.

Randy James, *Whatever Works*, Sony Pictures Classics, 2009.

Will, *The Cold Light of Day*, Summit Entertainment, 2011.

Television Appearances; Series:

Charles Brandon, Duke of Suffolk, *The Tudors*, Showtime, 2007–10.

Television Appearances; Movies:

Soldier Colley, *Goodbye, Mr. Chips*, ITV, 2002, PBS, 2003.

Television Appearances; Episodic:

Chas Quilter, "Well Schooled in Murder," *The Inspector Lynley Mysteries*, BBC1, 2002.

Simon Mayfield, "The Green Man," *Midsomer Murders,* Arts and Entertainment, 2003.
Xpose, TV3, 2009.

Television Appearances; Specials:
(In archive footage) *Reinventando Hollywood,* 2008.
Los Tudor: Rodaran cabezas, 2009.

CHOU, Robin
    See SHOU, Robin

CLABAUGH, Richard 1960–

PERSONAL

Born February 26, 1960, in St. Petersburg, FL; married Fran (a film editor and writer); children: Laurel, Ivory.

Career: Cinematographer, camera operator, gaffer, and director. Also worked as a special effects photographer, producer, film editor, writer, and composer; cinematographer for short documentary films, music videos, film trailers, and commercials. WTVT (television station), Tampa, FL, worked as a laboratory technician and film editor; WTOG (television station), St. Petersburg, FL, worked as a camera operator and editor for *Eyewitness News* for eight years; Crimson Wolf Productions, founding partner, 2005, and president, beginning 2005. Teacher of cinematography at the School of Filmmaking at the North Carolina School of the Arts, 1996–2007, the Oklahoma Summer Arts Institute, and Columbia College, CA; also an instructor at other institutions.

Awards, Honors: Won several awards for news photography, including a regional Emmy Award nomination, and awards from United Press International for best news photography and best news feature; also received awards and recognition from the Ann Arbor Film Festival, Central Florida Film Festival, Florida Independent Film Festival, Kinetic Image Film Festival, and WEDU Young Filmmakers Festival.

CREDITS

Film Cinematographer:
Dragonfly, c. 1980.
(And second unit cinematographer) *Mankillers* (also known as *Death Squad* and *12 Wild Women*), c. 1986.

Hollywood's New Blood, Raedon Home Entertainment, 1988.
Meanwhile in Santa Monica (also known as *Russian Nights*), 1988.
Necromancer (also known as *Necromancer: Satan's Servant*), Bonaire Film/Spectrum Entertainment, 1988.
The Ivory Tower (short film), Fine Grain Films, 1989.
L.A. Bounty, Leighton & Hilpert Production/Adventuress Productions International, 1989.
Pale Blood, Noble Entertainment, 1990.
Suburban Commando (also known as *Urban Commando*), New Line Cinema, 1991.
(And second unit cinematographer) *Ulterior Motives* (also known as *The Japan Connection*), Imperial Entertainment, 1991.
(And second unit cinematographer) *Lower Level,* NEO Motion Pictures/First Look International, c. 1992.
American Yakuza (also known as *Yakuza vs mafia*), Toei Company, 1993.
(And second unit cinematographer) *Infested* (also known as *Parasites, Ticks,* and *Ticks attack*), Republic Pictures/First Look International, c. 1993.
The Prophecy (also known as *God's Army, God's Secret Army,* and *Seraphim*), Miramax/Dimension Films, 1995.
Children of the Corn: The Gathering (also known as *Children of the Corn IV* and *Deadly Harvest*), Dimension Home Video, 1996.
Campfire Tales, New Line Cinema, 1997.
(And second unit cinematographer) *Drive* (also known as *Fugue*), Road to Ruin, 1997.
(And second unit cocinematographer) *The Killing Jar* (also known as *The Killing Game*), Curb Entertainment, c. 1997.
(And second unit cinematographer) *Palmetto* (also known as *Just Another Sucker*), Columbia, 1998.
Phantoms (also known as *Dean Koontz's "Phantoms"* and *Phantom*), Miramax/Dimension Films, 1998.
The Prophecy II (also known as *Ashtown: Prophecy II, God's Army II,* and *Prophecy II: Ashtown*), Dimension Films, 1998.
Children of the Corn 666: Isaac's Return (also known as *Children of the Corn 666*), Buena Vista Home Video/Highlight Video, 1999.
Deep Core (also known as *Deep Core 2000*), Paramount/New City Releasing, 2000.
The Prophecy 3: The Ascent (also known as *God's Army III*), Dimension Films/New Films International, 2000.
A Union in Wait (short documentary), Digital Social Productions, 2001.
Fall Down Dead, New Films International, 2007.
Off–Ramp to Eden (also known as *Dangerous Curves*), Blindside Illuminations, 2010.

Worked on other projects, including *Tarcon Mission* (also known as *Alien Plague*).

Film Additional Photography:
Hollywood's New Blood, Raedon Home Entertainment, 1988.
Lobster Men from Mars, c. 1989.
Pale Blood, Noble Entertainment, 1990.
(With others) *Suburban Commando* (also known as *Urban Commando*), New Line Cinema, 1991.
(With others) *Campfire Tales,* New Line Cinema, 1997.

Worked on photography for other films, including short documentary films.

Film Camera Operator:
Waxwork, Vestron Pictures, 1988.
Project Eliminator (also known as *The Eliminator* and *Stroker*), Victory Pictures Production, 1991.
Hellraiser III: Hell on Earth (also known as *Hellraiser III* and *Hellraiser 3*), Miramax/Dimension Films, 1992.
Waxwork II: Lost in Time (also known as *Lost in Time, Spaceshift, Space Shift: Waxwork II,* and *Waxwork II*), Electric Pictures/Contemporary Films, 1992.
Warlock: The Armageddon (also known as *Warlock II*), Trimark Pictures, 1993.

Film Gaffer:
Gaffer: additional photography, *The Dark Side of the Moon* (also known as *Parasite*), 1990.
Project Eliminator (also known as *The Eliminator* and *Stroker*), Victory Pictures Production, 1991.

Film Director:
(Uncredited) Second unit director, *Palmetto* (also known as *Just Another Sucker*), Columbia, 1998.
Smitty (short film), North Carolina School of the Arts, 2002.
Little Chicago, 2005, York Entertainment, 2007.
Eyeborgs, Image Entertainment, 2009.

Film Supervisor:
Faith, North Carolina School of the Arts, 2003.
Justice, North Carolina School of the Arts, 2003.

Film Assistant:
Sanctuary, 1985 (some sources cite 1979).
Stepfather II (also known as *Stepfather II, Stepfather II: Make Room for Daddy, Stepfather 2: Make Room for Daddy,* and *The Stepfather 2: Make Room for Daddy*), Millimeter Films, 1989.
Lobster Men from Mars, c. 1989.

Film Work; Other:
Special effects photographer, *Dr. Otto and the Riddle of the Gloom Beam* (also known as *Dr. Otto*), Web Productions, 1986.

Pick–ups photographer, *L.A. Bounty,* Leighton & Hilpert Production/Adventuress Productions International, 1989.
Film editor, *Yeah Vous!,* Second Chance Films, 1998.
Producer, *Eyeborgs,* Image Entertainment, 2009.

Film Appearances:
Himself, *Trekkies* (documentary), Paramount, 1997.

Television Work; News Programs:
Worked as a camera operator and editor for television documentaries, including *Growing Older, Impact: Tomorrow, Moving Day,* and *The Singer,* all broadcast as part of *Eyewitness News,* WTOG (St. Petersburg, FL).

Television Cinematographer; Movies:
No Way Back, HBO, 1996.
Plato's Run, HBO, 1996.
Escape under Pressure (also known as *The Cruel Deep* and *Under Pressure*), HBO, 2000.

Television Work; Other; Movies:
Director of photography: additional photography, *Maniac Cop 3: Badge of Silence* (also known as *Badge of Silence: Maniac Cop III, Maniac Cop 3, Maniac Cop III: Badge of Silence,* and *MC3: Maniac Cop 3*), HBO, 1993.
Camera operator, *Back to Back* (also known as *American Yakuza II, American Yakuza 2, Back to Back: American Yakuza II,* and *Back to Back: American Yakuza 2*), HBO, 1996.
Director, *Python,* 2000.

Television Work; Specials:
Second unit cinematographer, *Why Colors?,* Showtime, c. 1992.

RECORDINGS

Video Cinematographer:
Playboy: Fabulous Forties (also known as *Fabulous Forties* and *Playboy's "Fabulous Forties"*), Playboy Entertainment Group, 1994.

Cinematographer for music videos, including "Cruisin'" by Pat Garrett and the Straight Shooters, and "Tic–Toc" by Big Mack; and for street scenes in "Run for Your Life" by Eric Burdon, c. 1988.

WRITINGS

Screenplays:
(With Fran Clabaugh) *Eyeborgs,* Image Entertainment, 2009.

Film Music Themes:
Eyeborgs, Image Entertainment, 2009.

Nonfiction:
Author of a college textbook. Contributor to periodicals, including *American Cinematographer* and *Film Newsletter.*

OTHER SOURCES

Electronic:
Richard Clabaugh, http://www.rclabaugh.com, August 5, 2010.

CLARKE, Jason

PERSONAL

Education: Graduate of Victorian College of the Arts, Melbourne, Australia.

Addresses: *Agent*—United Talent Agency, 9560 Wilshire Blvd., Suite 500, Beverly Hills, CA 90212; RGM Artist Group, PO Box 128, Surry Hills, New South Wales 2010, Australia. *Manager*—Robert Stein, Robert Stein Management, 345 North Maple Dr., Suite 217, Beverly Hills, CA 90210.

Career: Actor.

CREDITS

Film Appearances:
Second guy, *Dilemma,* 1997, York Entertainment, 1999.
First young cop, *Twilight,* Paramount, 1998.
Frank, *Praise,* 1998, Strand Releasing, 2000.
Band, *Schmooze* (short film), 1999.
Nicholas Ratcliff, *Kick,* Beyond Films, 1999.
Mac, *Our Lips Are Sealed,* Dualstar Home Video, 2000.
Christ, *Risk,* Roadshow Entertainment, 2000.
Guy C, *Better than Sex,* Samuel Goldwyn, 2001.
Free (short film), 2002.
Constable Riggs, *Rabbit–Proof Fence* (also known as *Long Walk Home*), Miramax, 2002.
Slade, *You Can't Stop the Murders,* Buena Vista International, 2003.
Fenris, *Get Rich Quick,* Vivo Films, 2004.
Howard Ferp, *Hole in the Paper Sky* (short film), Iron Ocean Films, 2008.
Ulrich, *Death Race,* Universal, 2008.
Julian Wright, *The Human Contract,* Eagle Films, 2008, Sony Pictures Home Entertainment, 2009.

Andrew, *Still Waters* (also known as *Under Still Waters*), 2008, MPI Home Video, 2010.
John "Red" Hamilton, *Public Enemies,* Universal, 2009.
Jack Schwietzer, *Wall Street: Money Never Sleeps* (also known as *Wall Street*), Twentieth Century–Fox, 2010.
Doug Tate, *Trust,* Lions Gate Films, 2010.
Frank, *Swerve,* Duo Art Productions, 2010.
Gordon O'Hara, *Yelling to the Sky,* YTTS LLC, 2011.
Rule, *The Fields,* IPA Asia Pacific, 2011.

Film Producer:
Free (short film), 2002.

Television Appearances; Series:
Nathan Cohan, *Mercury,* Australian Broadcasting Corporation, 1996.
Christopher "Kick" Johnson, a recurring role, *Home and Away,* Seven Network, 2002.
Brett Linton, a recurring role, *Stingers,* between 2000 and 2003.
Tommy Caffee, *Brotherhood,* Showtime, 2006–2008.

Television Appearances; Movies:
Detective, *Halifax f.p: Hard Corps,* 1993.
Ray Childress, *The Outsider,* Showtime, 2002.
Tony Seaton, *BlackJack,* Ten Network, 2003.

Television Appearances; Miniseries:
Willy, *Knots Landing: Back to the Cul–de–Sac,* CBS, 1997.

Television Appearances; Pilots:
Michael Ryan, *U.S. Attorney,* CBS, 2009.
Jarek Wysocki, *Ridealong,* Fox, 2010.

Television Appearances; Specials:
Following the Rabbit–Proof Fence, 2002.

Television Appearances; Episodic:
Rick "Slick" Brooks, "A Model Murder," *Diagnosis Murder* (also known as *Dr. Mark Sloan*), CBS, 1996.
Hank, "Two Guys, a Girl, and a Recovery," *Two Guys, a Girl, and a Pizza Place* (also known as *Two Guys and a Girl*), ABC, 1998.
Adam Jarvis, "Sample," *The Net,* USA Network, 1998.
Warren, *Heartbreak High,* Australian Broadcasting Corporation, 1998.
Detective Constable Paul Moss, *Wildside,* Australian Broadcasting Corporation, 1998.
Zac Hartman, "A View to a Kill," *Murder Call,* Nine Network, 1998.
Troy Harris, "An Eye for an Eye," *Blue Heelers,* Seven Network, 1999.

Eddie Furlong, "Blood and Water," *All Saints,* Seven Network, 1999.

Eddie Furlong, "Valley of the Shadow: Part 1," *All Saints,* Seven Network, 2000.

"Dark & Stormy Night," *Flat Chat,* Nine Network, 2001.

Constable Rogers, "Out of the Blue," *Head Start,* 2001.

Agent Vinten, "Beech on the Run," *The Bill,* ITV1, 2001.

Jenek, "Prayer," *Farscape,* Sci–Fi Channel, 2003.

Jenek, "We're So Screwed, Part 1: Fetal Attraction," *Farscape,* Sci–Fi Channel, 2003.

Jenek, "We're So Screwed, Part 2: Hot to Katratzi," *Farscape,* Sci–Fi Channel, 2003.

Jenek, "We're So Screwed, Part 3: La Bomba," *Farscape,* Sci–Fi Channel, 2003.

Ray Jarvis, *White Collar Blue,* Ten Network, 2002, 2003.

Stage Appearances:

Appeared in Australian stage productions of *Hamlet* and *The Tempest.*

Stage Director:

Directed a musical stage production of *A Clockwork Orange.*

RECORDINGS

Videos:

Human Contract: Roll of Film, Sony Pictures Home Entertainment, 2009.

The Last of the Legendary Outlaws, Universal Studios Home Entertainment, 2009.

Michael Mann: Making "Public Enemies," Universal Studios Home Entertainment, 2009.

CLAYBURGH, Jill 1944–2010

PERSONAL

Full name, Jill Clayburgh; born April 30, 1944, in New York City, NY; died of leukemia, November 5, 2010, in Lakeville, CT. Actress. Known for her performances as strong, liberated women in difficult personal circumstances, stage, movie, and television actress Clayburgh particularly shone in the 1970s during the feminist movement. Her first movie role was opposite Robert DeNiro in *The Wedding Party,* which was filmed in 1963 but not released until 1969. She made her off-Broadway debut in the 1968 play *The Sudden and Accidental Re-Education of Horse Johnson.* Among her numerous Broadway performances were leading roles in the musicals *The Rothschilds* in 1970 and *Pippin* in 1972. From 1969 to 1970 she appeared in the popular television soap opera *Search for Tomorrow,* and her

1975 performance as a New York prostitute in the television movie *Hustling* earned an Emmy Award nomination. Clayburgh also won two Academy Award nominations during her career, one for her signature role in Paul Mazursky's 1978 film *An Unmarried Woman* (for which she won the Cannes Film Festival's best actress award) and the other for the 1979 romantic comedy *Starting Over.*

Other film credits include her breakthrough role in the 1972 comedy-drama *Portnoy's Complaint* and leading parts in the 1976 comedy *Silver Streak* (opposite Gene Wilder), the 1977 football movie *Semi-Tough* (opposite Burt Reynolds), the 1981 supreme court dramedy *First Monday in October* (opposite Walter Matthau), and the 1982 biopic *I'm Dancing as Fast as I Can.* In the late 1990s she had a recurring role on the television series *Ally McBeal* and was named one of Hollywood's twenty-five greatest actresses by *Entertainment Weekly.* After a long break from Hollywood, Clayburgh acted in the 2002 romantic comedy *Never Again.* Her final appearance on Broadway was in a 2006 revival of *Barefoot in the Park,* and her last film was 2010's *Love and Other Drugs.*

PERIODICALS

Entertainment Weekly, November 5, 2010.
Los Angeles Times, November 6, 2010.
New York Times, November 5, 2010.
Washington Post, November 6, 2010.

CLENNON, David 1943–
(Dave Clennon)

PERSONAL

Born May 10, 1943, in Waukegan, IL; son of Cecil (an accountant) and Virginia (a homemaker) Clennon; married Perry Adelman (a writer and camera assistant), 1996; children: Daisy Virginia and Harry Francis (twins). *Education:* University of Notre Dame, B.S., 1965; Yale University, M.F.A.

Addresses: *Agent*—Michael Greene, Greene and Associates Talent Agency, 190 North Canon Dr., Suite 202, Beverly Hills, CA 90210.

Career: Actor. Also appears as a political activist.

Awards, Honors: Emmy Award nomination, outstanding supporting actor in a drama series, 1991, for *thirtysomething;* Emmy Award, outstanding guest actor in a comedy series, 1993, for "For Peter's Sake," *Dream On;* Golden Satellite Award, best supporting actor in a television miniseries or movie, International Press Academy, 1999, for *From the Earth to the Moon.*

CREDITS

Film Appearances:

Toombs, *The Paper Chase,* Twentieth Century–Fox, 1973.

Carl (man in gas station), *Bound for Glory,* 1976.

Tim, *Coming Home,* United Artists, 1977.

Captain, *The Greatest,* Columbia, 1977.

Crew member on *U.S.S. Neptune, Gray Lady Down,* Universal, 1977.

Lieutenant Finley Wattsberg, *Go Tell the Spartans,* Avco Embassy, 1978.

Social worker, *Billy in the Lowlands,* FIF Inc., 1978.

Psychiatrist, *On the Yard,* Midwest Film, 1978.

(As Dave Clennon) Thomas Franklin, *Being There* (also known as *Chance*), United Artists, 1979.

Richard Fieldston, *Hide in Plain Sight,* Metro–Goldwyn–Mayer, 1980.

Dave Robell, *Ladies and Gentlemen, the Fabulous Stains* (also known as *All Washed Up*), Paramount, 1981.

Consul Phil Putnam, *Missing,* Universal, 1981.

Geb, *Star 80,* Warner Bros., 1982.

Palmer, *The Thing* (also known as *John Carpenter's "The Thing"*), Universal, 1982.

Newspaper editor, *The Escape Artist,* Orion/Warner Bros., 1982.

Liaison man, *The Right Stuff,* Warner Bros., 1983.

Amnon, *Hannah K.,* Universal, 1983.

Brian Gilmore, *Falling in Love,* Paramount, 1984.

Randy Hughes, *Sweet Dreams,* TriStar, 1985.

Lars, *The Trouble with Dick,* Frolix, 1986.

Blanchard, *Legal Eagles,* Universal, 1986.

Mason Mogan, *He's My Girl,* Scotti Brothers, 1987.

Lawrence Baird, *The Couch Trip,* Orion, 1988.

Jack Carpenter, *Betrayed,* Metro–Goldwyn–Mayer, 1988.

Jerome Sweet, *Downtown,* Twentieth Century–Fox, 1990.

Robert, *Light Sleeper,* Fine Line, 1992.

Lewie Duart, *Man Trouble,* Twentieth Century–Fox, 1992.

Jack, *Matinee,* Universal, 1993.

Jim, *Two Crimes* (also known as *Kissing Cousin* and *Dos crimenes*), 1994.

Dr. Jones/"Jonesy", *Grace of My Heart,* Gramercy, 1996.

Street Preacher, *Mad City,* Warner Bros., 1997.

(Uncredited) Martin, *Playing by Heart* (also known as *My Heart, My Love*), Miramax, 1998.

Bill Brenner, *The Visit,* Shoreline Entertainment, 2000.

(Uncredited) Barry Linder, *Antitrust* (also known as *Conspiracy.com* and *Surveillance*), 2001.

Mort Seymour, *Silver City,* Newmarket Films, 2004.

Jack, *Life of the Party,* Warner Bros., 2005.

Bear Korngold, *Constellation,* 2005, Twentieth Century–Fox, 2007.

Donald Farish III, *Syriana,* Warner Bros., 2005.

White House official, *Flags of Our Fathers,* Paramount, 2006.

Reynold Sherman, *Rocketboy* (short film), Graduate School of Cinema and Television, University of Southern California, 2006.

Instructor, *With God on Our Side* (short film), Military Religious Freedom Foundation, 2007.

Senator Chuck McGee, *Convention* (also known as *The Heart of the Possible*) 2008.

General, *1945A* (short film), 2010.

Dr. Renzler, *Extraordinary Measures,* CBS Films, 2010.

Hamilton, *Callers,* Taos Land & Film/Adobe Noir Productions/Existential Films/Pendragon Film, 2010.

Television Appearances; Series:

Miles Drentell, a recurring role, *thirtysomething,* ABC, 1989–91.

Neal Luder, *Almost Perfect* (also known as *You Can't Have It All*), CBS, 1995–97.

Miles Drentell, a recurring role, *Once and Again,* ABC, 2000–2001.

Joshua Nankin, *The Agency* (also known as *CIA: The Agency*), CBS, 2001–2003.

Dr. Martin Cole (some sources cite the character as Leon Cole), *Saved,* TNT, 2006.

Carl Sessick (Carl the Watcher), a recurring role, *Ghost Whisperer,* CBS, 2009–10.

Television Appearances; Movies:

Tom Trimpin, *The Migrants,* CBS, 1974.

Peter Karpf, *Crime Club,* CBS, 1975.

Panic in Echo Park, NBC, 1977.

Steve Rawlin, *Reward,* ABC, 1980.

James Fitzpatrick, "Gideon's Trumpet," *Hallmark Hall of Fame,* CBS, 1980.

The Day the Bubble Burst, NBC, 1982.

Dr. Bruce Lyman, *Special Bulletin,* NBC, 1983.

Reverend Werner, *Best Kept Secrets,* ABC, 1984.

U.S. Attorney Richard Schultz, *Conspiracy: The Trial of the Chicago 8,* HBO, 1987.

Dr. Sigmond Grampton, *The Image,* HBO, 1990.

Reverend Dwight Moore, *Black Widow Murders: The Blanche Taylor Moore Story,* NBC, 1993.

Mr. Johnstone, *And the Band Played On,* HBO, 1993.

Dr. Ruland Beesley (some sources spell the name as Rulon Beesley), *Nurses on the Line: The Crash of Flight 7* (also known as *Lost in the Wild* and *Race Against the Dark: The Crash of Flight 7*), CBS, 1993.

Jimbo, *Original Sins* (also known as *Acts of Contrition*), CBS, 1995.

William Henry Harrison, *Tecumseh: The Last Warrior,* TNT, 1995.

Mr. Filger, *The Staircase,* CBS, 1998.
Homeless man, *Saving Sarah Cain,* Lifetime, 2007.

Television Appearances; Miniseries:
Harry Jones, *Helter Skelter* (also known as *Massacre in Hollywood*), CBS, 1976.
Phillip Murray, *Blood & Orchids,* CBS, 1986.
Dr. Lee Silver, *From the Earth to the Moon,* HBO, 1998.

Television Appearances; Pilots:
David, *Marriage Is Alive and Well,* NBC, 1980.
Lester Brotman, *First Time, Second Time,* CBS, 1980.
(In archive footage) Leader of Martian High Council, *Toonces, the Cat Who Could Drive a Car* (also known as *Toonces and Friends*), NBC, 1992.
Mr. Reed, *Class of '96,* 1993.
Joshua Nankin, *The Agency,* CBS, 2001.
Ralph Gravis, *LAX,* NBC, 2004.

Television Appearances; Specials:
"Story Theatre," *NET Playhouse,* PBS, 1969.
Medvedenko, "The Seagull," *Theatre in America,* PBS, 1975.

Television Appearances; Episodic:
Bodhisattva, "Abduction," *Barney Miller,* ABC, 1977.
Stevens, "Asylum," *Barney Miller,* ABC, 1977.
George Martin, "The Summer of '69: Parts 1 & 2," *Kojak,* 1977.
Dr. Calvin, *Rafferty,* CBS, 1977.
Chester Monahan, "Identity," *Barney Miller,* ABC, 1979.
Howard Speer, "The Architect," *Barney Miller,* ABC, 1980.
Jeff O'Neil, "Revenge," *Park Place,* CBS, 1981.
Jeff O'Neil, "Benign Neglect," *Park Place,* CBS, 1981.
Jeff O'Neil, "Marooned," *Park Place,* CBS, 1981.
Jeff O'Neil, "Crazy Judge," *Park Place,* CBS, 1981.
Howard Weckler, "Homeless," *Barney Miller,* ABC, 1981.
Norris Breeze, "The Consultant," *WKRP in Cincinnati,* CBS, 1981.
Professor John Tate, "Revenge," *Alfred Hitchcock Presents,* NBC, 1985.
Harold Bell, "Sledge in Toyland," *Sledge Hammer!* (also known as *Sledge Hammer: The Early Years*), ABC, 1987.
Cullen, "Fever," *Beauty and the Beast,* CBS, 1988.
Wilton Tibbles, "Benedict Arnold Slipped Here," *Murder, She Wrote,* CBS, 1988.
Mitch Duprete, "Jersey Blues," *Almost Grown,* CBS, 1989.
Peter Brewer, "For Peter's Sake," *Dream On,* HBO, 1992.
Barry, "As the World Turns to Crap," *Cybill,* CBS, 1995.
Judge, "Rose Bowl," *NewsRadio,* NBC, 1996.
Nathan Cahill, "Good Dog Karl," *Maximum Bob,* ABC, 1998.

Dr. Crell Moset, "Nothing Human," *Star Trek: Voyager* (also known as *Voyager*), UPN, 1998.
Martin Spencer, "Maya's Nude Photos," *Just Shoot Me,* NBC, 1999.
Andrew Weller, "The Nanny," *Family Law,* CBS, 1999.
Voice of the boss, "Unemployment: Part 2" (also known as "Theory of the Leisure Ass"), *Mission Hill,* The WB, 2002.
Voice of the boss, "Stories of Hope and Forgiveness" (also known as "Day of the Jackass"), *Mission Hill,* The WB, 2002.
Ralph Gravis, "The Longest Morning," *LAX,* NBC, 2004.
Ralph Gravis, "Out of Control," *LAX,* NBC, 2004.
Attorney Braxton Mason, "An Eye for an Eye," *Boston Legal,* ABC, 2004.
Health spa owner, "Recreation," *Joan of Arcadia,* CBS, 2004.
Judge, "Gunshot Wedding," *Strong Medicine,* Lifetime, 2005.
Garner Swain, "Cost of Freedom," *In Justice,* ABC, 2006.
Charles Gibson, "Blame Game," *Crossing Jordan,* NBC, 2006.
Braden Marter, "Used, Abused, and Unenthused," *Huff,* Showtime, 2006.
Jim, "The Last Hurrah," *The West Wing* (also known as *The White House*), NBC, 2006.
Arthur Stanton, "Legacy," *Close to Home,* CBS, 2006.
Dr. Turner, "My Coffee," *Scrubs* (also known as *Scrubs: Med School*), NBC, 2006.
Mel Oliver, "Finders Keepers," *Numb3rs* (also known as *Num3ers*), CBS, 2007.
Jared Morgan, "The War Comes Home," *ER,* NBC, 2007.
Jack Shandley, "Haunt You Every Day," *Grey's Anatomy,* ABC, 2007.
Randall Farmer, "Deck the Howls," *October Road,* ABC, 2007.
Attorney Braxton Mason, "The Gods Must Be Crazy," *Boston Legal,* ABC, 2008.
Senator Conrad Dallow, "Deal or No Deal," *Prison Break,* Fox, 2008.
"Myanmar," *The Philanthropist,* NBC, 2009.

Also appeared as Stan Pooch, *Birdland;* in *Earth 2;* and as Prosser, *Michael Hayes,* CBS.

Stage Appearances:
Messenger to King John, *King John,* New York Shakespeare Festival, Delacorte Theatre, Public Theatre, New York City, 1967.
Martius, *Titus Andronicus,* New York Shakespeare Festival, Delacorte Theatre, Public Theatre, 1967.
"The Golden Goose," *Story Theatre,* Yale Repertory Theatre, New Haven, CT, 1968.
The Blood Knot, Long Wharf Theatre, New Haven, CT, 1970.

Kid, *The Unseen Hand,* and Emmett, *Forensic and the Navigators* (double–bill), Astor Place Theatre, New York City, 1970.

Loot, Hartford Stage Company, Hartford, CT, 1972.

Marat/Sade (also known as *The Persecution and Assassination of Jean–Paul Marat As Performed by the Inmates of the Asylum of Charenton under the Direction of the Marquis de Sade*), Actors' Theatre of Louisville, Louisville, KY, 1972.

Oliver, *As You Like It,* New York Shakespeare Festival, Delacorte Theatre, Public Theatre, 1973.

Boy, *Welcome to Andromedia,* and narrator, *Variety Obit* (double–bill), Cherry Lane Theatre, New York City, 1973.

Alfred Allmers, *Little Eyolf,* Manhattan Theatre Club, New York City, 1974.

The Seagull, Long Wharf Theatre, 1974.

Doctor, *Medal of Honor Rag,* Folger Theatre Group, Washington, DC, then Theatre De Lys (now Lucille Lortel Theatre), New York City, both 1976.

Pyotr Sergeyevich Trofimov, *The Cherry Orchard,* New York Shakespeare Festival, Vivian Beaumont Theatre, Lincoln Center, New York City, 1977.

Tales from the Vienna Woods, Yale Repertory Theatre, 1978.

Mistaken Identities, Yale Repertory Theatre, 1978.

S.S. Glencairn, Long Wharf Theatre, 1978.

Beyond Therapy, Los Angeles Public Theatre, Los Angeles, 1983.

Jeremy M., *Talking Things Over with Chekhov,* Victory Theatre, Hollywood, CA, 1987.

Also appeared in *Operation Sidewinder* and *Rosencrantz and Guildenstern Are Dead,* both Williamstown Theatre Festival, Williamstown, MA.

Radio Appearances:

Performed the role of Admiral Motti for a broadcast of *Star Wars,* National Public Radio.

RECORDINGS

Videos:

Realizing "The Right Stuff," Warner Bros., 2003.

OTHER SOURCES

Periodicals:

People Weekly, October 8, 1990, pp. 51–52.

COLCHART, Thomas
    See COPPOLA, Francis Ford

COLEY, Caia 1968–

PERSONAL

Born May 9, 1968, in Atlanta, GA; married Michael Feifer (a producer), April 14, 2001.

Career: Actress, producer, and director. Miss Atlanta, 1986. Creator of children's video *Baby Dance.*

Awards, Honors: Best Film Performance Award, Beverly Hills Festival, 2009, for *Drifter: Henry Lee Lucas.*

CREDITS

Film Appearances:

Gayle, *Looking for Bruce,* 1996.

Annie, *348,* 1999.

Claire Smith, *The Miracle Letter,* 2000.

Maggie, *Choosing Matthias,* 2001.

Cobalt, *Elements of Society,* 2001.

Cell phone woman, *Target,* First Look International, 2004.

Tenant, *Lethal Eviction* (also known as *Grayson Arms*), Asylum Home Entertainment, 2005.

Louise, *El Cortez,* Brazos Productions, 2006.

(Uncredited) Detective Wilkins, *Are You Scared?* (also known as *Jigsaw: Game of Death*), Lions Gate Films, 2006.

Mrs. Sullivan, *A Dead Calling,* Barnholtz Entertainment, 2006.

Karen, *Grim Reaper* (also known as *Re: Play*), MRG Entertainment, 2007.

Sue Layton, *Ed Gein: The Butcher of Plainfield,* Barnholtz Entertainment, 2007.

Nurse Boyd, *Chicago Massacre: Richard Speck* (also known as *The Nurse Killer*), Barnholtz Entertainment, 2007.

Nurse, *Drive Thru* (also known as *Death Burger*), Lions Gate Films, 2007.

Janice, *Dear Me,* 2008.

Mrs. Murray, *Dracula's Guest,* Lions Gate Entertainment, 2008.

Annie, *A Christmas Proposal,* Peace Arch Home Entertainment, 2008.

Prosecution attorney, *Bundy: An American Icon* (also known as *Bundy: A Legacy of Evil*), Lions Gate Films, 2008.

Mary Ann, *B.T.K.,* Barnholtz Entertainment, 2008.

Michelle Marsden, *Boston Strangler: The Untold Story,* Weinstein Company, 2008.

Viola, *Drifter: Henry Lee Lucas,* Barnholtz Entertainment, 2009.

Cindy Williams, *The Perfect Student,* 2010.

Jackie, *Groupie,* VVS Films, 2010.

Nurse Jennifer, *Abandoned,* Anchor Bay Entertainment, 2010.

Herodius/desert sequence, *Wilde Salome,* 2010.

Judy, *A Valentine's Date,* 2011.

Film Work:

Producer and director, *She Wasn't Mine* (short film), 2000.

Executive producer and director, *Choosing Matthias,* 2001.

Director, *Workout with a Knockout,* 2004.

Casting director, *Drifter: Henry Lee Lucas,* Barnholtz Entertainment, 2009.

Television Appearances; Movies:

Woman, *An Element of Truth,* CBS, 1995.

Donna Jameson, *The Dog Who Saved Christmas,* ABC Family, 2009.

WRITINGS

Screenplays:

She Wasn't Mine (short film), 2000.

COPPOLA, Francis Ford 1939–
(Thomas Colchart, Francis Coppola)

PERSONAL

Born April 7, 1939, in Detroit, MI; son of Carmine (a musician and composer) and Italia (an actress; maiden name, Pennino) Coppola; brother of Talia Shire (an actress); married Eleanor Neil (an artist), February, 1963; children: Sophia (an actress and filmmaker), Gian–Carlo (died, 1987), Roman (an actor). *Education:* Attended New York Military Academy; graduated from Great Neck High School, Great Neck, NY, 1955; Hofstra University, B.A., theatre, 1959; University of California, Los Angeles, M.F.A., cinema, 1967.

Addresses: *Agent*—International Creative Management, 8942 Wilshire Blvd., Beverly Hills, CA 90211. *Contact*—c/o Zoetrope Studios, 916 Kearny St., San Francisco, CA 94133–5107.

Career: Director, producer, editor, screenwriter, and composer. Worked for director, producer, and film executive Roger Corman during the late 1950s and early 1960s; American Zoetrope (now Zoetrope Studios), San Francisco, CA, founder (with George Lucas) and film producer, beginning in 1969; Directors Company, founder with Peter Bogdanovich and Wil-

liam Friedkin, 1972; City, publisher, 1975–76; Zoetrope: All–Story, founder, 1996. Niebaum–Coppola (winery), owner, 1978—.

Member: Directors Guild of America, Writers Guild of America.

Awards, Honors: Samuel Goldwyn Award, best screenplay written by a student, 1962, for *Pilma, Pilma;* WGA Screen Award nomination, best written American comedy, Writers Guild of America, Golden Palm Award nomination, Cannes International Film Festival, 1967, both for *You're a Big Boy Now;* Golden Seashell Award, San Sebastian International Cinema Festival, 1970, for *The Rain People;* Academy Award (with Edmund H. North), best screenplay, WGA Screen Award, best drama written directly for the screen, Writers Guild of America, 1971, both for *Patton;* Academy Award nomination, Golden Globe Award, both best director, Directors Guild Award (with others), outstanding directorial achievement in motion pictures, Academy Award and Golden Globe Award (both with Mario Puzo), both best screenplay, WGA Screen Award (with Puzo), best drama adapted from another medium, Writers Guild of America, Kansas City Film Critics Circle Award, best director, 1973, all for *The Godfather;* Academy Award nomination (with Gary Kurtz), best picture, 1974, for *American Graffiti;* Golden Palm Award and Prize of the Ecumenical Jury—special mention, Cannes International Film Festival, National Board of Review Award, best director, 1974, Academy Award nominations, best picture and best screenplay, WGA Screen Award nomination, best drama written directly for the screen, Writers Guild of America, Golden Globe Award nominations, best director—motion picture and best screenplay—motion picture, Edgar Award nomination, best motion picture, Edgar Allan Poe Awards, Directors Guild of America Award nomination, outstanding directorial achievement in motion pictures, Film Award nominations, best direction and best screenplay, British Academy of Film and Television Arts, 1975, Video Premiere Award nomination, best DVD audio commentary, 2001, all for *The Conversation;* Directors Guild of America Award (with others), outstanding directorial achievement in motion pictures, Academy Awards, best picture (with Gray Frederickson and Fred Roos), best director, and best screenplay (with Puzo), WGA Screen Award (with Puzo), best drama adapted from another medium, Writers Guild of America, National Society of Film Critics Award, best director, Golden Globe Award nominations, best director—motion picture and best screenplay—motion picture (with Puzo), Kansas City Film Critics Circle Award, best director, 1975, all for The Godfather, Part II; honorary degree from Hofstra University, 1977; Golden Palm Award and FIPRESCI Prize, Cannes International Film Festival, Grammy Award nomination (with Carmine Coppola), best original score, National Academy of Recording Arts and Sciences, 1979,

Academy Award nominations, best picture, best director, and best screenplay (with John Milius), Golden Globe Awards, best director and best original score (with Carmine Coppola), Film Award, best direction, British Academy of Film and Television Arts, Anthony Asquith Award for film music nomination (with Carmine Coppola), British Academy of Film and Television Arts, WGA Award nomination (with John Milius), best drama written directly for the screen, Writers Guild of America, Directors Guild of America Award nomination, outstanding directorial achievement in motion pictures, David Award, best director—foreign film, David di Donatello Awards, Cesar Award nomination, best foreign film, 1980, all for *Apocalypse Now;* David Award (with George Lucas), best producer—foreign film, 1981, for *Kagemusha;* Golden Prize Award nomination, Moscow International Film Festival, 1983, for The Outsiders; FIPRESCI Award and OCIC Award, San Sebastian International Film Festival, 1984, both *Rumble Fish;* Golden Globe Award nomination, best director—motion picture, 1985, for *The Cotton Club;* Golden Prize Award nomination, Moscow International Film Festival, 1987, for *Gardens of Stone;* Academy Award nominations, best director and best picture, Golden Globe Award nomination, best director—motion picture and best screenplay—motion picture (with Puzo), Directors Guild of America Award nomination, outstanding directorial achievement in motion pictures, 1991, Fotogrames de Plata, best foreign film, 1992, all for *The Godfather: Part III;* Berlinale Camera, Berlin International Film Festival, 1991; Career Golden Lion, Venice Film Festival, 1992; Saturn Award, best director, Academy of Science Fiction, Fantasy, and Horror Films, 1993, Fotogrames de Plata, best foreign film, 1994, for *Dracula;* CEC Career Award, Cinema Writers Circle Awards, 1994; Emmy Award nomination (with others), outstanding miniseries, 1997, for *The Odyssey;* Billy Wilder Award, National Board of Review, 1997; Emmy Award nomination (with others), outstanding miniseries, 1998, for *Moby Dick;* USC Scripter Award nomination (with John Grisholm), 1998, for *The Rainmaker;* Board of Governors Award, American Society of Cinematographers, 1998; Lifetime Achievement Award, Directors Guild of America, 1998; Video Premiere Award nomination, best audio commentary, 2001, for The Godfather; Mary Pickford Award, Golden Satellite Awards, International Press Academy, 2001; Special 50th Anniversary Award, San Sebastian International Film Festival, 2002; Gala Tribute, Film Society of Lincoln Center, 2002; Lifetime Achievement Award, Denver International Film Festival, 2003.

CREDITS

Film Director:

(As Thomas Colchart) *Nebo zovyot* (also known as *Battle Beyond the Sun, The Heavens Call, The Sky Calls,* and *The Sky Is Calling*), 1960.

(With Fritz Umgelter) *The Playgirls and the Bellboy* (also known as *The Bellboy and the Playgirls* and *Mit Eva fing die suende an*), United Producers, 1962.

Tonight for Sure (also known as *Tonite for Sure* and Wide Open Spaces), Premier, 1962.

The Terror (also known as *Lady of the Shadows,* The Castle of Terror, and The Haunting), American International Pictures, 1963.

(As Francis Coppola) *Dementia 13* (also known as *The Haunted and the Hunted*), American International Pictures, 1963.

You're a Big Boy Now, Seven Arts, 1966.

Finian's Rainbow, Warner Bros./Seven Arts, 1968.

The Rain People, Twentieth Century–Fox, 1969.

The Godfather (also known as *Mario Puzo's ''The Godfather''*), Paramount, 1972.

The Godfather, Part II (also known as *Mario Puzo's ''The Godfather: Part II''*), Paramount, 1974.

The Conversation, Paramount, 1974.

Apocalypse Now (also known as *Apocalypse Now Redux*), United Artists, 1979.

One from the Heart, Columbia, 1982.

Rumble Fish, Universal, 1983.

The Outsiders, Warner Bros., 1983.

(As Francis Coppola) *The Cotton Club,* Orion, 1984.

Peggy Sue Got Married, TriStar, 1986.

Captain Eo, 1986.

(As Francis Coppola) *Gardens of Stone,* TriStar, 1987.

Tucker: The Man and His Dream, Paramount, 1988.

(As Francis Coppola) ''Life without Zoe,'' *New York Stories,* Buena Vista, 1989.

The Godfather, Part III (also known as *Mario Puzo's ''The Godfather: Part III''*), Paramount, 1990.

The Godfather Trilogy: 1901–1980, 1992.

Bram Stoker's Dracula (also known as *Dracula*), Columbia, 1992.

Jack, Buena Vista, 1996.

John Grisham's ''The Rainmaker'' (also known as *The Rainmaker*), Paramount, 1997.

Supernova, 2000.

Megalopolis, DreamWorks, 2003.

Youth without Youth, Sony, 2007.

Tetro, Lions Gate Films, 2009.

Film Producer:

Nebo zovyot (also known as *Battle Beyond the Sun,* The Heavens Call, The Sky Calls, and The Sky Is Calling), 1960.

Tonight for Sure (also known as *Tonite for Sure* and Wide Open Spaces), Premier, 1962.

I Am Cuba, 1964.

The Making of ''The Rain People,'' 1969.

American Graffiti, Universal, 1973.

The Godfather, Part II (also known as *Mario Puzo's ''The Godfather: Part II''*), Paramount, 1974.

The Conversation, Paramount, 1974.

Apocalypse Now (also known as *Apocalypse Now Redux*), United Artists, 1979.

The Outsiders, Warner Bros., 1983.

(As Francis Coppola) *Gardens of Stone,* 1987.

The Godfather, Part III (also known as *Mario Puzo's ''The Godfather: Part III''*), Paramount, 1990.

Bram Stoker's Dracula (also known as *Dracula*), Columbia, 1992.

The Godfather Trilogy: 1901–1980, 1992.

The Junky's Christmas, 1993.

Mary Shelley's "Frankenstein" (also known as *Frankenstein*), TriStar, 1994.

Don Juan DeMarco, New Line Cinema, 1995.

One Night Stand, New Horizons, 1995.

Jack, Buena Vista, 1996.

Lanai–Loa (also known as *Lani Loa: The Passage*), 1998.

The Florentine, Bcb Productions, Inc., 1999.

The Virgin Suicides (also known as *Sofia Coppola's "The Virgin Suicide"*), 1999.

On the Road, United Artists, 2003.

(Restoration) *One from the Heart,* Sony, 2003.

Youth without Youth, Sony, 2007.

Tetro, Lions Gate Films, 2009.

Film Executive Producer:

THX–1138, Warner Bros., 1971.

The Black Stallion, United Artists, 1979.

(With George Lucas) *Kagemusha* (also known as *The Double, Kagemusha (The Shadow Warrior), Kagemusha the Shadow Warrior,* and *Shadow Warrior*), 1980.

Hammett, Warner Bros., 1982.

The Escape Artist, Warner Bros., 1982.

Rumble Fish, Universal, 1983.

The Black Stallion Returns, Metro–Goldwyn–Mayer/United Artists, 1983.

Koyaanisqatsi (also known as *Koyaanisqatsi: Life Out of Balance*), 1983.

(With Lucas) *Mishima: A Life in Four Chapters* (also known as *Mishima*), Warner Bros., 1985.

Tough Guys Don't Dance, Cannon, 1987.

Lionheart (also known as *Lionheart: The Children's Crusade*), Orion, 1987.

Barfly, Cannon, 1987.

Powaqqatsi (also known as *Powaqqatsi: Life in Transformation*), 1988.

(Uncredited), *Wait Until Spring, Bandini* (also known as *Aspetta primavera Bandini, Bandini, John Fante's Wait Until Spring, Bandini,* and *Le ragioni del cuore*), 1989.

Wind, TriStar, 1992.

The Secret Garden, Warner Bros., 1993.

Haunted, October Films, 1995.

My Family, Mi Familia (also known as *Cafe con leche* and *East L.A.*), New Line Cinema, 1995.

John Grisham's "The Rainmaker" (also known as *The Rainmaker*), Paramount, 1997.

Buddy, Columbia, 1997.

The Third Miracle, Sony Pictures Classics, 1999.

Goosed, 1999.

Sleepy Hollow, 1999.

Suriyothai, New Line Cinema, 2001.

CQ, United Artists, 2001.

No Such Thing, Metro–Goldwyn–Mayer/United Artists, 2001.

Jeepers Creepers (also known as *JEEpERs CrEEpers*), United Artists, 2001.

Pumpkin, Metro–Goldwyn–Mayer/United Artists, 2002.

Assassination Tango, Metro–Goldwyn–Mayer, 2002.

The Legend of Suryiothai, Sony Pictures Classics, 2003.

Lost in Translation, Universal, 2003.

Jeepers Creepers II, United Artists, 2003.

Kinsey, Twentieth Century–Fox, 2004.

Forever Is a Long, Long Time, The Verve Music Group, 2004.

Marie Antoinette, Columbia, 2006.

The Good Shepherd, Universal, 2006.

Somewhere, Focus Features, 2010.

Also executive producer for *Indigo; The Florentine;* and *Gunfighter.*

Film Work:

Assistant director, *The Premature Burial,* American International Pictures, 1962.

Sound recorder and second unit director, *The Young Racers,* American International Pictures, 1963.

Second unit director and associate producer, *The Terror* (also known as *Lady of the Shadows, The Castle of Terror,* and *The Haunting*), American International Pictures, 1963.

(As Francis Coppola) Second unit director, *The Wild Racers,* 1968.

(Uncredited) Assistant to director, *Return to Oz,* 1985.

(Uncredited) Editor, *Supernova,* 2000.

(Uncredited) Editor, *The Fantasticks,* 2000.

Film Appearances:

(Uncredited) Army truck driver, *War Hunt,* 1962.

(Uncredited) *The Young Racers,* 1963.

Filmmaker (also known as *Filmmaker: A Diary by George Lucas*), 1968.

The World Premiere of "Finian's Rainbow," 1968.

Bald: The Making of "THX 1138," 1971.

Th Godfather: Behind the Scenes, 1971.

(Uncredited) Himself, *The Lion Roars Again,* 1975.

The Godfather Comes to Sixth St., 1975.

Himself, *Cultural Celebrities,* 1979.

(Uncredited) Member of television camera crew, *Apocalypse Now* (also known as *Apocalypse Now Redux*), United Artists, 1979.

American Mythologies, 1981.

The Making of "One from the Heart," 1982.

Reverse Angle (also known as *Reverse Angle: NYC March '82*), 1982.

Hollywood Mavericks, 1990.

Hearts of Darkness: A Filmmaker's Apocalypse, 1991.

Writing with Light: Vittorio Storaro, 1992.

A Personal Journey with Martin Scorsese Through American Movies, 1996.

Himself, *The Unauthorized Star Wars Story,* Visual Entertainment, 1999.

(Uncredited) Himself, *R2–D2: Beneath the Dome,* Twentieth Century–Fox, 2001.

Himself, *Whether You Like It or Not: The Story of Hedwig,* New Line Home Video, 2001.

(Uncredited; in archive footage) Himself, *The Kid Stays in the Picture,* USA Films, 2002.

Himself, *A Decade under the Influence,* IFC Films, 2003.

Easy Riders, Raging Bulls: How the Sex, Drugs and Rock 'N' Roll Generation Saved Hollywood, Shout! Factory, 2003.

(As Francis Coppola) *Dennis Hopper: Create (or Die),* Easy Rider, 2003.

Dean Tavoularis, le magicien d'Hollywood, CineCinema, 2003.

The Dream Studio, American Zoetrope, 2004.

Tying the Knot, Roadside Attractions, 2004.

(As Francis Coppola) Vieux monsieur rue Pinocchio, *L'enquete Corse* (also known as *The Corsican File*), Eurocine Films, 2004.

There Is No Direction, Central Films, 2005.

Inside Deep Throat, Universal, 2005.

(As Francis Coppola) On Location in Tulsa: The Making of *"Rumble Fish,"* Universal Studios Home Video, 2005.

Boffo! Tinseltown's Bombs and Blockbusters, HBO, 2006.

(As Francis Coppola) Francis Ford Coppola Directs *"John Grisham's The Rainmaker,"* Paramount Home Video, 2007.

Fog City Mavericks, Leva Film Works, 2007.

I Knew It Was You: Rediscovering John Cazale, HBO, 2009.

Television Executive Producer; Series:
The Outsiders, Fox, 1989–90.
First Wave, Sci–Fi Channel, 1998.
Platinum, UPN, 2003.

Television Executive Producer; Movies:
The People, ABC, 1972.
White Dwarf, Fox, 1995.
Tecumseh: The Last Warrior, 1995.
Dark Angel, 1996.
Survival on the Mountain, NBC, 1997.
Outrage, ABC, 1998.
Dr. Jeykll & Mr. Hyde, syndicated, 1999.
Another Day, USA Network, 2001.

Television Executive Producer; Miniseries:
Kidnapped, 1995.
The Odyssey (also known as *Homer's "The Odyssey,"* Odissea, and Die Abenteuer des Odysseus), NBC, 1997.
Moby Dick, USA Network, 1998.

Television Producer; Episodic:
The Godfather: A Novel for Television (also known as Mario Puzo's *"The Godfather": A Novel for Television;* The Godfather 1902–1959: The Complete Epic; The Godfather Novella; The Godfather Saga; and *The Godfather: The Complete Novel for Television*), 1977.

Television Director; Specials:
Making Bram Stoker's "Dracula," 1992.

Television Work; Pilots:
Executive producer, *The Conversation,* NBC, 1995.

Television Director; Episodic:
The Godfather: A Novel for Television (also known as Mario Puzo's *"The Godfather": A Novel for Television;* The Godfather 1902–1959: The Complete Epic; The Godfather Novella; The Godfather Saga; and *The Godfather: The Complete Novel for Television*), 1977.

"Rip Van Winkle," *Faerie Tale Theatre* (also known as Shelley Duvall's *"Faerie Tale Theatre"*), Showtime, 1987.

Television Appearances; Series:
The Kennedy Center Honors: A Celebration of the Performing Arts (also known as *The 30th Annual Kennedy Center Honors*), 2007.

Television Appearances; Movies:
Fog City Mavericks, Starz!, 2007.

Television Appearances; Specials:
The 45th Annual Academy Awards, 1973.
The 47th Annual Academy Awards, 1975.
Copresenter, *The 51st Annual Academy Awards,* 1979.
Reverse Angle, 1982.
The Making of "Captain Eo," 1986.
The Godfather Family: A Look Inside, HBO, 1990.
Hearts of Darkness: A Filmmaker's Apocalypse, Showtime, 1991.
Crazy About the Movies: Dennis Hopper, 1991.
The 63rd Annual Academy Awards, 1991.
The Godfather Family: A Look Inside, 1991.
Memory and Imagination: New Pathways to the Library of Congress, PBS, 1992.
Blood Lines: Dracula–The Man. The Myth. The Movies, 1992.
The World of Jim Henson, PBS, 1994.
Marlon Brando, Wild One, Channel 4, 1994.
It's Alive: The True Story of Frankenstein, 1994.
A Personal Journey with Martin Scorsese through American Movies, 1995.
Anatomy of Horror, UPN, 1995.
In Search of Dracula with Jonathan Ross, 1996.

The Making of "American Graffiti," 1998.
Mickey Rourke: The E! True Hollywood Story, E! Entertainment Television, 1999.
Heart of Darkness, The Learning Channel, 1999.
I Lars von triers rige, 1999.
Kurosawa: The Last Emperor, Independent Film Channel, 2000.
Martha Stewart's Home for the Holidays, CBS, 2001.
R2–D2: Beneath the Dome, 2001.
Hollywood Salutes Nicolas Cage: An American Cinematheque Tribute, TNT, 2002.
George Lucas: Creating an Empire, Arts and Entertainment, 2002.
101 Biggest Celebrity Oops, E! Entertainment Television, 2004.
The 2004 IFP/West Independent Spirit Awards, Independent Film Channel and Bravo, 2004.
Presenter, *The 76th Annual Academy Awards,* ABC, 2004.
AFI Life Achievement Award: A Tribute to George Lucas, 2005.
Saturday Night Live in the '80s: Lost & Found, NBC, 2005.
The Godfather and the Mob, Channel 4, 2006.
Cannes 2006: Cronica de Carlos Boyero, 2006.
Brando, TCM, 2007.
Cannes, 60 ans d'histoires, France 3, 2007.
Camara negra. Teatro Victoria Eugenia, Television Espanola, 2007.
Presenter, *The 30th Annual Kennedy Center Honors,* CBS, 2007.
Presenter, *The 79th Annual Academy Awards,* ABC, 2007.
Lights! Action! Music!, WLIW–21, 2007.
Coda: Thirty Years After, Starz!, 2007.
Ciak Point Torino, 2009.
I Knew It Was You, HBO, 2009.

Television Appearances; Episodic:
The Mike Douglas Show, 1974.
"Francis Ford Coppola," *The South Bank Show,* 1979.
"A Pretty British Affair," *Arena,* 1981.
Late Night with David Letterman, NBC, 1982.
Saturday Night Live (also known as *SNL*), NBC, 1986.
"George Lucas: Heroes, Myths, and Magic," *American Masters,* PBS, 1993.
"John Barry's Moviola," *Great Performances,* PBS, 1993.
Late Night with Conan O'Brien, NBC, 1997.
Howard Stern, 1998.
Inside the Actors Studio (also known as *Inside the Actors Studio: The Craft of Theatre and Film* and *Actors Interview*), 2001.
"Troldspejlet special: Bag Klonernes angreb," *Troldspejlet,* 2002.
Tinseltown TV, International Channel, 2003.
"Francis Ford Coppola's Napa & Belize," *Travel Channel Secrets,* Travel Channel, 2004.
Dateline NBC (also known as *Dateline*), NBC, 2004.
"Brando," *Imagine,* BBC, 2004.

Cinema mil, Televisio de Catalunya, 2005.
Sunday Morning Shootout (also known as *Hollywood Shootout* and Shootout), AMC, 2005, 2006.
"Marlon Brando," *The Hollywood Greats,* BBC1, 2006.
Corazon de ..., 2006.
La tele de tu vida, 2007.
Up Close with Carrie Keagan, 2007.
Le grand journal de Canal+, 2009.
Dias de cine, 2009.
Cinema 3, 2009.
Tavis Smiley, PBS, 2009.
Jornal Nacional, 2009.
"Directing," *Made in Hollywood: Teen Edition,* 2009.
Che tempo che fa, 2009.

Stage Director:
Enrico IV, American Conservatory Theatre, San Francisco, CA, 1971.
Private Lives, American Conservatory Theatre, 1972.
The Visit of the Old Lady (opera), San Francisco Opera Company, San Francisco, 1972.

RECORDINGS

Videos:
Under the Hood: Making "Tucker," 2000.
Breaking the Silence: The Making of "Hannibal," 2001.
Francis Coppola's Notebook, 2001.
On the Set of "CQ," 2002.
Whether You Like It or Not: The Story of Hedwig, New Line Home Video, 2003.
Artifact from the Future: The Making of "THX 1138," Warner Home Video, 2004.
A Legacy of Filmmakers: The Early Years of American Zoetrope, Warner Home Video, 2004.
"Rumble Fish": The Percussion–Based Score, Universal Studios Home Video, 2005.
(As Francis Coppola) *Staying Gold: A Look Back at "The Outsiders,"* 2005.
The Birth of 5.1 Sound, American Zoetrope, 2006.
Celebrating Schlesinger, Sony, 2006.
(As Francis Coppola) *Heard Any Good Movies Lately?: The Sound Design of "Apocalypse Now,"* Paramount, 2006.
(As Francis Coppola) *A Million Feet of Film: The Editing of "Apocalypse Now,"* Paramount, 2006.
(As Francis Coppola) *The Music of "Apocalypse Now,"* Paramount, 2006.
The Making of "Marie Antoinette," Sony, 2007.
The Costumes Are the Sets: The Design of Eiko Ishioka, Sony, 2007.
Method and Madness: Visualizing "Dracula," Sony, 2007.
In Camera: The Naive Visual Effects of "Bram Stoker's Dracula," Sony, 2007.
The Blood Is the Life: The Making of "Bram Stoker's Dracula," Sony, 2007.
The Masterpiece That Almost Wasn't, Paramount, 2008.

Soundtracks:

The Godfather: Part III (also known as *Mario Puzo's ''The Godfather: Part III''* and *Godfather Part III*), 1990.

WRITINGS

Screenplays:

Tonight for Sure (also known as *Tonite for Sure* and *Wide Open Spaces*), 1961.

(With Dieter Hildebrandt and Margh Malina; extra scenes) *The Playgirls and the Bellboy* (also known as *The Bellboy and the Playgirls* and *Mit Eva fing die suende an*), United Producers, 1962.

The Magic Voyage of Sinbad (adaptation), Filmgroup, 1962.

Pilma, Pilma, 1962.

(Uncredited) Additional dialogue, *The Haunted Palace* (also known as *Edgar Allan Poe's ''The Haunted Palace''* and *The Haunted Village*), 1963.

Battle Beyond the Sun (adaptation), American International Pictures, 1963.

(As Francis Coppola) *Dementia 13* (also known as *The Haunted and the Hunted*), American International Pictures, 1963.

(With Gore Vidal, Jean Aurenche, Pierre Bost, and Claude Brule) *Is Paris Burning?* (also known as *Paris brule–t–il?*), Paramount, 1966.

(With Fred Coe and Edith Sommer) *This Property Is Condemned,* Paramount, 1966.

You're a Big Boy Now, Seven Arts, 1966.

Reflections in a Golden Eye (adaptation), 1967.

The Rain People, Twentieth Century–Fox, 1969.

(With Edmund H. North) *Patton* (also known as *Blood and Guts, Patton: A Salute to a Rebel,* and *Patton: Lust for Glory*), Twentieth Century–Fox, 1970.

(With Mario Puzo) *The Godfather* (also known as *Mario Puzo's ''The Godfather''*), Paramount, 1972.

The Conversation, Paramount, 1974.

(With Puzo) *The Godfather, Part II* (also known as *Mario Puzo's ''The Godfather: Part II''*), Paramount, 1974.

The Great Gatsby, Paramount, 1974.

(With John Milius) *Apocalypse Now* (also known as *Apocalypse Now Redux*), United Artists, 1979.

(With Armyan Bernstein) *One from the Heart,* Columbia, 1982.

(With S. E. Hinton) *Rumble Fish* (based on the book by Hinton), Universal, 1983.

(With William Kennedy; as Francis Coppola) *The Cotton Club,* Orion, 1984.

Captain Eo, 1986.

''Life without Zoe,'' *New York Stories,* Touchstone, 1989.

The Outsiders, Fox, 1989.

The Godfather, Part III (also known as *Mario Puzo's ''The Godfather: Part III''*), Paramount, 1990.

The Godfather Trilogy: 1901–1980, 1992.

John Grisham's ''The Rainmaker'' (also known as *The Rainmaker;* based on the novel by Grisham), Paramount, 1997.

Megalopolis, DreamWorks, 2003.

Youth without Youth, Sony, 2007.

Tetro, Lions Gate Films, 2009.

Film Scores:

(With father, Carmine Coppola) *Apocalypse Now* (also known as *Apocalypse Now Redux*), United Artists, 1979.

Hearts of Darkness: A Filmmaker's Apocalypse, 1991.

Television Episodic:

The Godfather: A Novel for Television (also known as *Mario Puzo's ''The Godfather'': A Novel for Television; The Godfather 1902–1959: The Complete Epic; The Godfather Novella; The Godfather Saga;* and *The Godfather: The Complete Novel for Television*), 1977.

Other Writings:

(With James V. Hart) *Bram Stoker's Dracula: The Film and the Legend,* Newmarket Press, 1992.

(With Eiko Ishioka) *Coppola and Eiko on "Bram Stoker's Dracula,"* Collins, 1992.

(Author of essay) Ishioka, Eiko, *Eiko on Stage,* Callaway, 2000.

(Author of introduction) Brodeur, Adrienne, and Samantha Schnee, eds., *Francis Ford Coppola's Zoetrope All Story,* Harcourt, 2000.

OTHER SOURCES

Books:

Authors and Artists for Young Adults, Volume 39, Gale Group, 2001.

Cowie, Peter, *Coppola,* Andre Deutsch, 1989, Scribner, 1990.

Browne, Nick, ed., *Francis Ford Coppola's ''The Godfather,''* Cambridge University Press, 2000.

Goodwin, Michael, and Naomi Wise, *On the Edge: The Life and Times of Francis Coppola,* Morrow, 1989.

Johnson, Robert K., *Francis Ford Coppola,* Twayne, 1977.

Lewis, Jon, *Whom God Wishes to Destroy ... Francis Coppola and the New Hollywood,* University Press, 1995.

Schumacher, Michael, *Francis Ford Coppola: A Filmmaker's Life,* 1999.

Zucker, Joel S., *Francis Ford Coppola: A Guide to References and Resources,* G. K. Hall, 1984.

Periodicals:

American Film, June, 1988, pp. 21–27.

Entertainment Weekly, November 21, 1997, p. 56; July 24, 1998, p. 10; November 1, 1999, p. 107.
Film Comment, January/February, 1993.
Gentlemen's Quarterly, December, 1992.
Interview, November, 1992.
New York Times Magazine, July 24, 1988.
People, April 4, 1994.
Rolling Stone, February 7, 1991.
Variety, January 12, 1998, p. 152; July 20, 1998, p. 7.

Electronic:

Zoetrope Studios, http://www.zoetrope.com, May 5, 2010.

COTILLARD, Marion 1975–

PERSONAL

Born September 30, 1975, in Paris, France; raised in Orleans, France; daughter of Jean–Claude Cotillard (an actor, mime, teacher, and theatre director) and Niseema Theillaud (an actress and acting teacher). *Education:* Attended Conservatoire National Superieur d'Art Dramatique, Orleans, France. *Avocational Interests:* Singing, visiting museums, environmental causes.

Addresses: *Agent*—Hylda Queally, Creative Artists Agency, 2000 Avenue of the Stars, Los Angeles, CA 90067; Laurent Gregoire, Adequat, 80 rue d'Amsterdam, Paris 75009, France. *Publicist*—Bryna Rifkin, I/D Public Relations, 8409 Santa Monica Blvd., West Hollywood, CA 90069.

Career: Actress. Appeared in advertisements, including the Dior spots *Lady Blue Shanghai,* directed by David Lynch. Participated in various events, including galas. Greenpeace France, celebrity spokesperson.

Member: Screen Actors Guild, Academy of Motion Picture Arts and Sciences.

Awards, Honors: Special jury mention, film festivals, c. 1998, for *Affaire classee;* Cesar Award nomination, most promising actress, Academie des Arts et Sciences du Cinema, 1999, for *Taxi;* Cabourg Romantic Film Festival Award, best new actress, 2000, for *Taxi 2;* Verona Love Screens Film Festival Award, best actress, 2001, for *Lisa;* Cesar Award nomination, most promising actress, 2002, for *Les jolies choses;* Chopard Trophy, female revelation, Cannes International Film Festival, 2004; Jury Award, feature film—best actress—drama, Newport Beach Film Festival, 2004, for *Jeux d'enfants* (also known as *Love Me If You Dare);* Cesar

Award, best supporting actress, 2005, for *Un long dimanche de fiancailles;* Hollywood Film Festival Award, actress of the year, 2007; Los Angeles Film Critics Association Award, Boston Society of Film Critics Award, Golden Space Needle Award, Seattle International Film Festival, Cabourg Romantic Film Festival Award, Chicago Film Critics Association Award nomination, and European Film Award nomination, all best actress, all 2007, Satellite Award, best actress in a motion picture, drama, International Press Academy, and NRJ Cine awards, French actress of the year and best look, all 2007, Academy Award, best performance by an actress in leading role, Film Award, best leading actress, British Academy of Film and Television Arts, Golden Globe Award, best performance by an actress in a motion picture—musical or comedy, and ALFS Award, London Critics Circle Film awards, actress of the year, all 2008, Cesar Award, Kansas City Film Critics Circle Award, Critics Choice Award nomination, Broadcast Film Critics Association, Vancouver Film Critics Circle Award, Lumiere Award, Czech Lion, Etoile d'Or, and Online Film Critics Society Award nomination, all best actress, Breakthrough Performance Award, Palm Springs International Film Festival, and Screen Actors Guild Award nomination, outstanding performance by a female actor in a leading role, all 2008, all for *La vie en rose* (also known as *La mome);* Virtuoso Award, Santa Barbara International Film Festival, 2008; Satellite Award nomination, best actress in a motion picture, comedy or musical, and Special Satellite Achievement Award (with others), best ensemble in a motion picture, both International Press Academy, and Washington, DC Area Film Critics Association Award nomination (with others), best ensemble, all 2009, Desert Palm Achievement Award, Palm Springs International Film Festival, Golden Globe Award nomination, best performance by an actress in a motion picture—musical or comedy, Critics Choice Award nomination, best supporting actress, Broadcast Film Critics Association, Audience Award nomination, best international actress, Irish Film and Television awards, and Screen Actors Guild Award nomination (with others), outstanding performance by a cast in a motion picture, all 2010, all for *Nine;* decorated Chevalier of the Order of Arts and Letters (l'Ordre des Arts et des Lettres), France, 2010.

CREDITS

Film Appearances:

Mathilde, *L'histoire du garcon qui voulait qu'on l'embrasse* (also known as *The Story of a Boy Who Wanted to Be Kissed),* MKL Distribution, 1994.
Snuff Movie (short film), Ministrie de la Communiate Francaise de Belgique, c. 1994.
Macha, *La belle verte,* TF1 Films/Cinemussy, 1996.
Insalata mista (short film), c. 1996.
Student, *Comment je me suis dispute ... (ma vie sexuelle)* (also known as *Ma vie sexuelle—Paul Ded-*

alus' Journey and *My Sex Life ... or How I Got into an Argument*), France 2 Cinema/La Sept Cinema, 1996, subtitled version, Zeitgeist Films, 1997.

Affaire classee, c. 1997.

Keo (short film), Ministrie de la Communiate Francaise de Belgique, c. 1997.

La sentence (short film; also known as *The Sentence*), c. 1997.

Lilly Bertineau, *Taxi* (also known as *Taxi Express*), Lions Gate Films, 1998.

La surface de reparation (short film), c. 1998.

Elia, *Furia,* Bac Films, 1999.

Julie Bonzon, *La guerre dans le Haut Pays* (also known as *War in the Highlands*), Rezo Films, 1999.

Rachel, *L'appel de la cave* (short film), Aurelien Bonzon–Alpha Key Productions, 1999.

Solange, *Du bleu jusqu'en Amerique* (also known as *Blue Away to America*), Noria Films, 1999.

Lilly Bertineau, *Taxi 2* (also known as *Taxi Taxi*), Lions Gate Films, 2000.

Le marquis (short film), 2000.

Quelques jours de trop (short film), 2000.

Title role (younger version), *Lisa,* Capitol Films, 2001.

Lucie and Marie, *Les jolies choses* (also known as *Pretty Things*), United International Pictures, 2001.

Mme. Boomer, *Boomer* (short film), Les Productions du Tresor, 2001.

Heureuse (short film), 2001.

Clarisse Entoven, *Une affaire privee* (also known as *A Private Affair*), Bac Films, 2002.

Josephine, *Big Fish,* Columbia, 2003.

Lilly Bertineau, *Taxi 3* (also known as *Taxi 2003*), EuropaCorp, 2003.

Sophie Kowalsky, *Jeux d'enfants* (also known as *Love Me If You Dare*), Mars Distribution, 2003, subtitled version, Paramount Classics, 2004.

Tina Lombardi, *Un long dimanche de fiancailles* (also known as *A Very Long Engagement*), Warner Bros., 2004.

Mademoiselle Eva, *Innocence,* 2004, subtitled version, Leisure Time Features, 2005.

Alice, *Ma vie en l'air* (also known as *Love Is in the Air*), TFM Distribution, 2005.

Alizee, *Cavalcade,* Mars Distribution, 2005.

Celine (la chanteuse du reve), *Edy,* Mars Distribution, 2005.

Isabelle Kruger and Alice, *La boite noire* (also known as *Black Box* and *The Black Box*), EuropaCorp, 2005.

Lisa, *Sauf le respect que je vous dois* (also known as *Burnt Out*), Haut et Court, 2005.

Gretchen, *Mary* (also known as *Maria* and *Mary: This Is My Blood*), Pan Europeenne Distribution/Mikado, 2005, IFC Films, c. 2007.

Fanny Chenal, *A Good Year,* Fox 2000, 2006.

Lena, *Toi et moi,* Pyramide Distribution, 2006.

Nadine, *Dikkenek,* EuropaCorp, 2006.

Nicole, *Fair Play,* TFM Distribution, 2006.

Edith Piaf, *La vie en rose* (also known as *Life in Pink, The Little Girl,* and *The Passionate Life of Edith Piaf;* originally known as *La mome*), Picturehouse Entertainment, 2007.

Billie Frechette, *Public Enemies,* Universal, 2009.

Luisa Contini, *Nine* (musical; also known as *Untitled Rob Marshall Project*), The Weinstein Company, 2009.

Marie Vallieres de Beaumont, *Le dernier vol* (also known as *The Last Flight* and *The Last Voyage of Lancaster*), Gaumont, 2009.

Voice of sea turtle and narrator of French version, *OceanWorld 3D* (documentary; also known as *Oceans 3D: Into the Deep* and *Oceans 3D: Voyage of a Turtle*), Walt Disney Studios Motion Pictures, 2009.

Mal, *Inception* (also known as *Oliver's Arrow;* IMAX version known as *Inception: The IMAX Experience*), Warner Bros., 2010.

Marie, *Les petits mouchoirs* (also known as *Little White Lies*), EuropaCorp, 2010.

Muse, *Midnight in Paris,* 2011.

Appeared in other films, including *La fee electrique* and *Le jeu.* Some sources cite appearances in other films.

Television Appearances; Movies:

Title role, *Chloe,* [Belgium and France], 1996.

Abigail Dougnac, *Interdit de vieillir,* [Belgium and France], 1998.

Florence Lacaze, *Une femme piegee,* [France], 2001.

Television Appearances; Specials:

Comedienne, *Homo cinematographicus* (documentary), 1998.

Herself, *Un jour dans la vie du cinema francais* (documentary), 2002.

Herself, *Un long dimanche de fiancailles; le making–of* (documentary), Canal+, 2004.

Herself, *Une americaine a Paris,* 2005.

Herself, "Hommage a Piaf," *Generation duo,* TF1, c. 2007.

Herself, *An Evening at the Academy Awards,* ABC, 2008.

(In archive footage) Herself, *Generation duo,* TF1, 2008.

Herself, *Golden Globes Announcement Special,* NBC, 2008.

Herself, *Golden Globe Winner Special,* NBC, 2008.

Herself, *La noche de los Oscar,* Canal+ Espana, 2008.

Herself, *Live from the Red Carpet: The 2008 Academy Awards,* E! Entertainment Television, 2008.

Herself, *Mon clown* (documentary), Canal+, 2008.

Herself, *Oscar's Red Carpet 2008 with Regis Philbin,* ABC, 2008.

Herself, *13th Annual Critics' Choice Awards Red Carpet Premiere,* VH1, 2008.

Herself, *The Red Carpet Issue,* Sundance Channel, 2010.

Television Appearances; Awards Presentations:
Presenter, *The 14th Annual Screen Actors Guild Awards* (also known as *Screen Actors Guild 14th Annual Awards*), TNT and TBS, 2008.
The 80th Annual Academy Awards, ABC, 2008.
The Orange British Academy Film Awards, BBC and BBC America, 2008.
La nuit des Cesars, 2008, 2009, 2010.
Presenter, *The 81st Annual Academy Awards,* ABC, 2009.
Presenter, *The Orange British Academy Film Awards,* BBC and BBC America, 2009.
15th Annual Critics' Choice Movie Awards, VH1, 2010.
16th Annual Screen Actors Guild Awards (also known as *Screen Actors Guild 16th Annual Awards*), TNT and TBS, 2010.
The 67th Annual Golden Globe Awards, NBC, 2010.

Television Appearances; Episodic:
Lori Bellian, "Nowhere to Run," *Highlander* (also known as *Highlander: The Series*), syndicated, 1993.
Sophie Colbert, "La pistonnee," *Extreme limite,* TF1, c. 1994.
Laurence, "La mouette" (also known as "The Seagull"), *L'@mour est a reinventer* (also known as *Love Reinvented*), Arte, 1996.
"La nouvelle de la semaine," *Theo la tendresse,* 1996.
Gabby, "Doggy dog" (also known as "Doggy Dog"), *Les redoutables,* 13eme Rue, 2001.
Herself, *Vivement dimanche,* France 2, 2005, 2007.
Herself, *Jour de fete,* 2007.
Herself, *Entertainment Tonight* (also known as *Entertainment This Week, E.T., ET Weekend,* and *This Week in Entertainment*), syndicated, multiple episode, 2008 and 2009.
Herself, "Making 'Public Enemies,'" *HBO First Look,* HBO, 2009.
Herself, *Le journal de 20 heures,* TF1, 2009.
Herself, *Xpose,* TV3 Television Network, multiple episodes, 2009.
Herself, "Inception," *HBO First Look,* HBO, 2010.
Herself, *Mark at the Movies,* 2010.

Television Talk Show Guest Appearances; Episodic:
Tout le monde en parle, France 2, 2000, 2003, 2007.
On ne peut pas plaire a tout le monde (also known as *ONPP, O.N.P.P., ONPP vu de la loge, ONPP vu de la plage, ONPP vu du bocal,* and *ONPP vu du desert*), 2004.
Le grand journal de Canal+, Canal+, several episodes, beginning 2005.
"And the Nominees Are ...," *The Oprah Winfrey Show* (also known as *Oprah* and *Oprah Winfrey Show*), syndicated, 2008.

"Oscar Nominees Special," *Sunday Morning Shootout* (also known as *Hollywood Shootout* and *Shootout*), AMC, 2008.
The Late Late Show with Craig Ferguson (also known as *The Late Late Show*), CBS, 2008, 2009, multiple episodes, 2010.
Larry King Live, Cable News Network, 2009.
Late Night with Jimmy Fallon, NBC, 2009.
The Oprah Winfrey Show (also known as *Oprah* and *Oprah Winfrey Show*), syndicated, 2009.
(In archive footage) *This Morning* (also known as *This Morning with Richard and Judy*), ITV, 2009.
Up Close with Carrie Keagan, 2010.

Some sources cite appearances in other programs.

Internet Appearances; Videos:
Appeared in the short video clip *Forehead Tittaes,* posted on *Funny or Die,* http://www.funnyordie.com. Appeared in other footage posted on the Internet.

Stage Appearances:
Y'a des nounours dans les placard, Theatre Contemporain de la Danse, Paris, c. 1997.

Began appearing in stage appearances as a child.

RECORDINGS

Videos; Documentaries; as Herself:
(Uncredited) *Making of: Taxi* (short film), TF1 Video, 2000.
(Uncredited) *Making of: Taxi 2* (short film), TF1 Video, 2000.
Une annee au front, les coulisses de "Un long dimanche de fiancailles" (also known as *A Year at the Front: Behind the Scenes of "A Very Long Engagement"*), Warner Bros., 2004.
Postcards from Provence, Twentieth Century–Fox Home Entertainment, 2007.
The Last of the Legendary Outlaws (short film), Universal Studios Home Entertainment, 2009.
Michael Mann: Making "Public Enemies" (short film), Universal Studios Home Entertainment, 2009.

Albums; Film Soundtracks:
(Including song "La fille de joie") *Les jolies choses,* BMG, 2001.
La vie en rose, EMI Classics, 2007.
Nine, Geffen Records, 2009.

With Hawksley Workman, recorded "The Strong Ones," c. 2008; with others, recorded "Beds Are Burning," 2009; and with Franz Ferdinand, recorded "The Eyes of Mars," c. 2010. Appeared in music videos, including

"No Reason to Cry out Your Eyes (On the Highway Tonight)," by Hawksley Workman, 2003; and "Givin' Up," by Tommy Hools featuring Richard Archer, c. 2003. Some sources cite appearances in other recordings.

WRITINGS

Film Music:
(With others) Song "La fille de joie," *Les jolies choses* (also known as *Pretty Things*), United International Pictures, 2001.

With Hawksley Workman, wrote "The Strong Ones," c. 2008.

OTHER SOURCES

Books:
Newsmakers, issue 1, Gale, 2009.

Periodicals:
USA Today, February 15, 2008, p. 7E.

CRAIG, Carl 1954–

PERSONAL

Born August 1, 1954, in Tallahassee, FL; son of Walter O. (a music professor) and Ruth (a secretary; maiden name, Roper) Craig; married Angela E. Fong (an airline worker). *Education:* University of Rochester, B.A., 1976; studied with Stella Adler in New York City. *Religion:* Roman Catholic.

Addresses: *Office*—FarCor Studios, 6725 Sunset Blvd., Suite 450, Los Angeles, CA 90028.

Career: Actor, singer, and producer. Also worked as production manager and music consultant. FarCor Studios, Los Angeles, producer.

Member: Actors' Equity Association, American Federation of Television and Radio Artists, Screen Actors Guild.

Awards, Honors: Independent Spirit Award nomination, best first feature, Independent Features Project/West, 1988, and Annual CableACE Award, best variety

special or series, National Cable Television Association, 1991, both (with others) for *Hollywood Shuffle;* Enzian Award, Florida Film Festival, 1994, for creative achievement.

CREDITS

Film Producer:
Executive producer, *Hollywood Shuffle* (also known as *Robert Townsend's "Hollywood Shuffle"*), Samuel Goldwyn, 1987.
I'm Gonna Git You Sucka, Metro–Goldwyn–Mayer, 1988.
Coproducer, *Mo' Money,* Columbia, 1992.
House Party 3, New Line Cinema, 1994.
The Players Club, New Line Cinema, 1998.
Book of Love, Artisan Entertainment, 2002, broadcast on television as *Book of Love: The Definitive Reason Why Men Are Dogs,* Black Entertainment Television, 2005.
Coproducer, *Playas Ball,* Summertime Films, 2003.
The Salon, Freestyle Releasing, 2006.
Young Cesar, Codeblack Entertainment, 2007.

Film Appearances:
Jacques Le Monde, *Bummer!* (also known as *The Sadist*), 1972.
Willie, *Tom* (also known as *The Bad Bunch, The Brothers,* and *Mothers, Fathers, and Lovers*), 1973.
Type, reporter, fool, Beaner Gang member, basketball player, and actor in audition, *Hollywood Shuffle* (also known as *Robert Townsend's "Hollywood Shuffle"*), Samuel Goldwyn, 1987.
Man in love, *I'm Gonna Git You Sucka,* Metro–Goldwyn–Mayer, 1988.

Television Producer; Series:
Who's Got Jokes?, 2006.
Baisden after Dark, TV One, 2007–2008.

Television Producer; Specials:
"The Best of Robert Townsend and His Partners in Crime," *HBO Comedy Hour,* HBO, 1987.
"Damon Wayans: The Last Stand?," *HBO Comedy Hour,* HBO, 1991.

Television Work; Pilots:
Associate producer, *Hammer, Slammer, and Slade,* ABC, 1990.

Television Appearances; Specials:
"The Best of Robert Townsend and His Partners in Crime," *HBO Comedy Hour,* HBO, 1987.

Stage Appearances:
My Fair Lady, Arizona Theatre Company, Phoenix, 1985–86.

Also appeared as Tony, *Black Sheep,* Billie Holiday Theatre, New York City; in *The Brownsville Raid,* Negro Ensemble Company, New York City; in *Ceremonies in Dark Old Men,* GeVa Theatre, Rochester, NY; as Shine, *The Great Mac Daddy,* Negro Ensemble Company; Universal Man, *Poets from the Inside,* Public Theatre, New York City; Catesby, *Richard III,* U.R.S.T., Rochester, NY; Bubba, *Second Thoughts,* Afro American Total Theatre, New York City; and Pierre, *Sister Racher and the Ton Ton Maconte,* La MaMa Experimental Theatre Club, New York City.

RECORDINGS

Video Producer:

The Big Black Comedy Show, Volume 2, 2005.
The Big Black Comedy Show, Volume 4: *Live from Los Angeles,* 2005.
Bobby Jones Comedy All Stars: Volume 1, Lions Gate Films, 2007.

CRIBBINS, Bernard 1928–

PERSONAL

Born December 29, 1928, in Oldham, England; son of John Edward and Ethel (maiden name, Clarkson) Cribbins; married Gillian Isabella McBarnet, 1955. *Education:* Attended elementary school in Oldham, England. *Avocational Interests:* Fly fishing, golf, shooting clay pigeons.

Addresses: *Agent*—Gavin Barker, Gavin Barker Associates, 2D Wimpole St., London W1G 0EB, England; (voice work) Voice Shop, 1A Devonshire Rd., 1st Floor, London W4 2EU, England.

Career: Actor. Oldham Repertory Company, Oldham, England, actor, 1942–43; also former member of Piccolo Players, Manchester, England, and Queen's Players, Hornchurch, England; appeared in commercials, including voice of Buzby in commercials for British Telecom, beginning 1976, and narrator of "Tufty" British public information films, 1970s. Sport Aiding Medical Research for Children (also known as SPARKS), president, 1999–2000; White Lodge Centre (for the disabled), patron. *Military service:* British Army, Parachute Regiment, 1947–49; served in Palestine and Germany.

Awards, Honors: Film Award nomination, best supporting actor, British Academy of Film and Television Arts, 1971, for *The Railway Children;* Saturn Award nomination, best guest–starring role on television, Academy of Science Fiction, Fantasy, and Horror Films, 2010, for *Doctor Who.*

CREDITS

Television Appearances; Series:

Thomas Traddles, a recurring role, *David Copperfield,* 1956.
Storyteller, *Jackanory,* BBC1, multiple appearances, 1966–91.
Cribbins, 1969–70.
The Val Doonican Show, 1971.
Narrator, *The Wombles,* 1973–75.
Narrator, *Simon in the Land of Chalk Drawings,* 1976.
Narrator, *Moschops,* 1983.
Seth Raven, *Langley Bottom,* 1986.
Voice, *Edward and Friends* (animated), 1987.
Narrator, *Bertie the Bat,* 1990.
Member of ensemble, *Noel's House Party,* BBC, 1991.
Narrator, *A Passion for Angling,* 1993.
Himself, *... And It's Goodnight from Him ...,* 1996.
Wilfred Mott, a recurring role, *Doctor Who,* BBC America, beginning 2007.

Television Appearances; Specials:

Member of Now Cranks revue, *Cranko at Work,* 1960.
Corporal Pearce, "The Night of the Big Heat," *ITV Play of the Week,* ITV, 1960.
"Charley's Aunt," *BBC Sunday–Night Play,* BBC, 1961.
Ghost of Sir Simon de Canterville, "The Canterville Ghost," *BBC Sunday–Night Play,* BBC, 1962.
Cakebreak, "Visiting Day," *Comedy Playhouse,* BBC, 1962.
Mr. Spooner, "Impasse," *Comedy Playhouse,* BBC, 1963.
Ambrose Twombly, "Here I Come Whoever I Am," *Comedy Playhouse,* BBC, 1965.
Arnold, "Judgement Day for Elijah Jones," *Comedy Playhouse,* BBC, 1966.
Larry, "The Loser," *Theatre 625,* BBC, 1967.
(In archive footage) Bradley Mahler, *Light Entertainment Killers,* 1969.
Jimmy Sampson, "Who's Your Friend?," *Comedy Playhouse,* BBC, 1970.
Patrick, Dear Patrick, an Evening with Patrick Cargill and His Guests, 1972.
(English–language version) Narrator, *Sagan om Karl–Bertil Jonssons julafton,* 1975.
Narrator, *The Elstree Story,* 1976.
Pinchwife, "The Country Wife," *BBC Play of the Month,* BBC, 1977.
House painter, *The Plank,* ITV, 1979.
Night of One Hundred Stars, 1980.
Herbert Soppitt, *When We Are Married,* BBC, 1987.
Comic Relief: The Invasion of the Comic Tomatoes, BBC, 1993.
(In archive footage) Tom Campbell, "Doctor Who": *Thirty Years in the Tardis,* BBC, 1993.
The Very Best of Sid James, Thames Television, 1996.
(Uncredited) Harold Crump and himself, *What's a Carry On?,* 1998.

I Love a 1970's Christmas, BBC, 2000.
The 100 Greatest Kids TV Shows, Channel 4, 2001.
(In archive footage) *Cilla in Black & White,* 2003.
The Wonderful World of Roald Dahl, Channel 5, 2005.
The 100 Greatest Family Films, Channel 4, 2005.
Fawlty Towers Revisited, 2005.
Station guard, *The Children's Party at the Palace,* BBC, 2006.
National Television Awards, ITV, 2010.

Television Appearances; Movies:
Moneytrap, *The Confederacy of Wives,* 1975.
Title role, *Dangerous Davies* (also known as *The Last Detective*), 1980.
Neighbor, *It's Your Move,* Thames Television, 1982.

Television Appearances; Miniseries:
Arrivano I mostri, 1977.
Ron Archer, *High and Dry,* 1987.
I Love 1970's, BBC, 2000.
British Film Forever, BBC, 2007.
Doctor Who Greatest Moments, BBC, 2009.

Television Appearances; Episodic:
Prince's guard, "Danger," *The Black Tulip,* 1956.
Driver, "The Missing Hours," *The Vise* (also known as *Detective's Diary* and *The Vise: Mark Saber*), 1957.
"Peanuts" Perry, "Don't Send My Boy to Prison," *The Army Game,* Granada Television, 1960.
Sid, "Slow Boat to Amsterdam," *Interpol Calling,* 1960.
Pasquale, "The Santino Case," *International Detective,* 1960.
Thank Your Lucky Stars, 1962.
"Studio '64: The Close Prisoner," *Drama 61–67,* 1964.
Chas Wilson, "Driver of the Year," *Mogul* (also known as *The Troubleshooters*), 1965.
Arkwright, "The Girl from Auntie," *The Avengers,* ITV, 1966.
"Reunion," *Mr. Aitch,* 1967.
Honeybone, "The Wind in a Tall Paper Chimney," *Armchair Theatre,* ABC England, 1968.
Bradley Mahler, "Look (Stop Me if You've Heard This One) but There Were These Two Fellers ...," *The Avengers,* ITV, 1968.
It's Tommy Cooper, 1970.
"Lionel Jeffries," *This Is Your Life,* ITV, 1971.
Petypon, "The Lady from Maxims," *Ooh La La!,* BBC, 1973.
The Good Old Days, BBC, multiple appearances, 1973–82.
Cilla, 1974.
Mr. Hutchinson, "The Hotel Inspectors," *Fawlty Towers,* BBC, 1975.
Record Breakers, 1975.
Pyramid, "Night Ferry," *Once Upon a Classic,* 1976.
King Ferdinand, "The Sleeping Princess," *Jackanory Playhouse,* 1976.

Captain Michael, "Brian the Brain," *Space: 1999,* syndicated, 1976.
(In archive footage) "Lionel Jeffries: Part 1," *Clapper Board,* 1979.
Blankety Blank, BBC, 1980.
Looks Familiar, ITV, 1981.
Cuffy, "The Shillingbury Tinker," *Shillingbury Tales,* 1981.
Cuffy, "The Shillingbury Daydream," *Shillingbury Tales,* 1981.
Jolly Jack, "The Golden Hind," *Worzel Gummidge,* Southern, 1981.
"Hands across the Sea," *Tonight at Eight–Thirty,* BBC, 1981.
"Bernard Cribbins," *This Is Your Life,* ITV, 1981.
Charlie Krebs/Mr. King, "The Memory Man," *Tales of the Unexpected,* syndicated, 1983.
Cuffy, "Cuffy and a Green Eye," *Cuffy,* 1983.
Voice of Mock Turtle, "The Mock Turtle's Story, The Lobster Quadrille, and Who Stole the Tarts?," *Alice in Wonderland,* CBS, 1985.
Officer P. Brain, "Supergran and the Birthday Dambusters," *Super Gran,* 1987.
Miscellaneous characters, "The Russ Abbot Christmas Show," *The Russ Abbot Show,* BBC, 1988.
Contestant, *Treasure Hunt,* 1988.
Mr. Wadhurst, "Hands across the Sea," *Tonight at 8:30,* 1991.
Voice of snowman, "The Snowman," *I, Lovett,* 1993.
Pebble Mill at One, 1994.
"Barry Cryer," *This Is Your Life,* BBC, 1995.
"1962," *Noel's Telly Years,* 1996.
Captain Hook, *Bruce Forsyth and the Generation Game,* 1997.
Give Us a Clue, 1997.
Voice of Katzenburger, "Oil Strike!," *Dennis the Menace,* 1998.
"Barbara Windsor," *The Best of British,* BBC, 1998.
"Celebrity Special," *Wipeout,* 1998.
Uncle Henry, "Time to Go," *Dalziel and Pascoe,* BBC, 1999.
Voice of carpenter, "The Journey Back," *The Canterbury Tales,* HBO, 2000.
(In archive footage) "Sidney James," *Heroes of Comedy,* Channel 4, 2002.
Gavin Hinchcliffe, "In Which Gavin Hinchcliffe Loses the Gulf Stream," *Last of the Summer Wine,* BBC, 2003.
Frank, "Guy Fawkes," *Barbara,* ITV, 2003.
Wally Bannister, *Coronation Street,* ITV, 2003.
This Morning, ITV, 2003.
Frank Cosgrove, "Hot Air," *Down to Earth,* BBC, 2005.
Frank Cosgrove, "Tall Tales," *Down to Earth,* BBC, 2005.
Frank Cosgrove, "Trouble 'n' Strife," *Down to Earth,* BBC, 2005.
"The Kids' Verdict," *Children's TV on Trial,* 2007.
"Kylie Meets the Doctor," *Doctor Who Confidential,* BBC, 2007.

"Send In the Clones," *Doctor Who Confidential*, BBC, 2008.

Breakfast, BBC, 2008.

The Alan Titchmarsh Show, ITV, 2008, 2009.

The ONE Show, BBC, 2008, 2009.

Loose Women, ITV, 2008, 2009, 2010.

"The Doctor Who Special," *Never Mind the Buzzcocks*, BBC, 2009.

"Lords and Masters," *Doctor Who Confidential*, BBC, 2009.

(In archive footage) "Where Are They Now?," *Never Mind the Buzzcocks*, BBC, 2009.

The Sunday Night Project, Channel 4, 2009.

"Allons–y!," *Doctor Who Confidential*, BBC, 2010.

Look North, 2010.

Also appeared in an episode of *Call My Bluff*.

Film Appearances:

(Uncredited) Sonar operator, *Battle Hell* (also known as *Yangtse Incident: Thte Story of H.M.S. Amethyst*), 1957.

(Uncredited) Thirsty sailor, *Dunkirk*, Metro–Goldwyn–Mayer, 1958.

(Uncredited) Stage hand at Collins Music Hall, *Davy*, Metro–Goldwyn–Mayer, 1958.

Jack, *Make Mine a Million* (also known as *Look before You Laugh*), British Lion, 1959, Schoenfeld, 1965.

Paco, *Tommy the Toreador*, Warner Bros., 1960.

Otis, *The World of Suzy Wong*, Paramount, 1960.

Lennie Price, *Two–Way Stretch*, International Show Corporation of America, 1961.

Newspaperman, *Nothing Barred*, British Lion, 1961.

Pereira, *Passport to China* (also known as *Visit to Canton*), Columbia, 1961.

Peters, *The Girl on the Boat*, Knightsbridge, 1962.

Colonel Brownlow, *The Best of Enemies*, Columbia, 1962.

Midshipman Albert Poop–Decker, *Carry On Jack*, Warner Bros., 1963.

Vincent Mountjoy, *The Mouse on the Moon*, United Artists, 1963.

Nervous O'Toole, *The Wrong Arm of the Law*, Continental Distributing, 1963.

(Uncredited) Man on stretcher, *The Fast Lady*, 1963.

Harold Crump, *Carry On Spying*, Warner Bros., 1964.

Squirts McGinty, *Crooks in Cloisters*, Associated British Film, 1964.

Mason, *A Home of Your Own*, 1964.

Bob (Agent 202), *The Counterfeit Constable* (also known as *Allez France!*), 1964, Seven Arts, 1966.

Policeman, *Cup Fever*, CFF, 1965.

Job, *She*, Metro–Goldwyn–Mayer, 1965.

Sergeant Clegg, *You Must Be Joking!*, Columbia, 1965.

The Bargain, 1965.

Tom Campbell, *Daleks' Invasion Earth: 2150 A.D.* (also known as *Daleks Invade Earth 2150 A.D.* and *Dr. Who: Daleks Invasion Earth 2150 A.D.*), British Lion, 1966.

Harold, *The Sandwich Man*, J. Arthur Rank, 1966.

Taxi driver, *Casino Royale*, Columbia, 1967.

Fred Davies, *Don't Raise the Bridge, Lower the River*, Columbia, 1968.

Ron, *A Ghost of a Chance*, 1968.

Neighbor, *It's Your Move*, 1969.

Albert Perks, *The Railway Children*, Universal, 1971.

Felix Forsythe, *Frenzy*, Universal, 1972.

(In archive footage) Multiple roles, *That's Carry On*, 1977.

Mr. Masterman and voice of Eel, *The Water Babies*, Penthurst International, 1979.

Narrator and Gertrude Stein, *The Adventures of Picasso* (also known as *Picassos aeventyr*), Svensk Film Industries, 1980.

Mordecai "Mort" Mendoza, *Carry On Columbus*, Laurenfilm, 1992.

(In archive footage) *Laugh with the Carry Ons*, 1993.

Mutley, *Blackball* (also known as *National Lampoon's "Blackball"*), Icon Film Distribution, 2003, Palisades Pictures, 2004.

Stage Appearances:

(Stage debut) *Lavender Ladies*, Oldham Repertory Company, Coliseum Theatre, Oldham, England, 1942.

(London debut) Both Gromios, *The Comedy of Errors* (musical), Arts Theatre, 1956.

Salad Days, Vaudeville Theatre, London, 1956.

Chicken, *The Chicken Play*, New Lindsey Theatre, London, 1957.

Tony Peters, *Harmony Close*, Lyric Hammersmith Theatre, London, 1957.

Boris (the dog), *Antarctica*, Players' Theatre, London, 1957.

Fernando Fernandez, *Lady at the Wheel*, Lyric Hammersmith Theatre, then Westminster Theatre, London, 1958.

Deadly Mortimer, *The Big Tickle*, Duke of York's Theatre, London, 1958.

Kiki Reger, *Hook, Line, and Sinker*, Piccadilly Theatre, London, 1958.

New Cranks, Lyric Hammersmith Theatre, 1960.

And Another Thing, Fortune Theatre, London, 1960.

Corporal Billy Jester, *Little Mary Sunshine*, Comedy Theatre, London, 1962.

Reader, *The Fire of London*, Mermaid Theatre, London, 1966.

Arnold Crouch, *Not Now, Darling*, Strand Theatre, London, 1968–69.

Timothy Westerby, *There Goes the Bride*, Criterion Theatre, London, 1974.

Murray, *Forty Love*, Arnaud Theatre, Guildford, England, 1978.

Herr Von Cuckoo, *The Gingerbread Man*, Royalty Theatre, London, 1979.

Mother Goose (pantomime), Guildford, 1981.

Run for Your Wife, Adelaide, Australia, and Shaftesbury Theatre, London, both 1983, then Criterion Theatre, London, 1984.

Nathan Detroit, *Guys and Dolls* (musical), National Theatre, London, 1984.

Dick Whittington (pantomime), Plymouth, England, 1988.

Moonface Martin, *Anything Goes,* Prince Edward Theatre, London, 1989.

Doolittle, *My Fair Lady* (musical), Houston Opera House, Houston, TX, 1991.

Professor Otto Marvuglia, *La Grande Magia,* Royal National Theatre, London, 1995.

Appeared as Ada, *Dick Whittington* (pantomime), Wimbledon Theatre and Leeds Grand Theatre, Leeds, England; Watty Watkins, *Lady Be Good,* Open Air Theatre at Regents Park and elsewhere; and as Hans Anderson, *The Snow Queen* (pantomime), Guildford; reader for children's concerts, including *Carnival of the Animals, Peter and the Wolf,* and *The Snowman;* actor in pantomime presentations at Richmond Theatre, Surrey, England, including role of Widow Twankey in *Aladdin.*

Major Tours:

The Love Game, Australian cities, 1973.
Old Time Music Hall, British and Danish cities, 1982.
Run for Your Wife, Australian cities, 1985.

Radio Appearances:

Arnold Korns, *Doctor Who: Horror of Glam Rock,* 2007.

Reader for *80 Not Out,* BBC4.

RECORDINGS

Videos:

Narrator, *Original Sylvanian Families,* 1988.

(Uncredited; in archive footage) Tom Campbell, "*Dr. Who.*" *Daleks—The Early Years,* BBC Video, 1993.

(In archive footage) Tom Campbell, *Dalekmania,* Lumiere Films, 1995.

(Uncredited; in archive footage) Midshipman Albert Poop–Decker, *Carry On Quizzing* (video game), 2006.

Albums:

Recorded the singles "Gossip Calypse," "Hold in the Ground," and "Right Said Fred," all 1962.

Audio Books:

Reader for children's books, including *Bedtime Stories,* CBeebies; *The House at Pooh Corner; The Mudds,* CBeebies; *Return to the Hundred Acre Wood* and *Winnie the Pooh;* and books in the "Sophie" series; also reader for the audio–book version of the autobiography of Roy Castle.

OTHER SOURCES

Periodicals:

Independent on Sunday, December 13, 2009, pp. 26–27.

Other:

"Bernard Cribbins" (television episode), *This Is Your Life,* ITV, 1981.

CRONENBERG, David 1943–

PERSONAL

Born March 15, 1943 (some sources say May 15), in Toronto, Ontario, Canada; son of Milton (a writer, editor, and book store owner) and Esther (a musician; maiden name, Sumberg) Cronenberg; brother of Denise Cronenberg (a costume designer); married Margaret Hindson, 1970 (divorced, 1977); married Carolyn Zeifman, 1979; children: (first marriage) Cassandra (an assistant director); (second marriage) Caitlin, Brandon. *Education:* University of Toronto, degree (with distinction, literature), 1967; also attended North Toronto College and Harbord College. *Avocational Interests:* Cars, auto racing, bugs and insects.

Addresses: *Office*—Toronto Antenna Ltd., 244 Dupont St., 2nd Floor, Toronto, Ontario M5R 1V7, Canada. *Agent*—WME Entertainment, One William Morris Pl., Beverly Hills, CA 90212. *Manager*—881 Alma Real Drive 317, Pacific Palisades, CA 90272.

Career: Director, screenwriter, editor, producer, cinematographer, and actor. Producer of short films at the University of Toronto; Toronto Antenna Film Ltd., principal. Cannes International Film Festival, Cannes, France, president of feature film jury, 1999.

Awards, Honors: Medella Sitgues en Oro de Ley, best director, 1975, for *Shivers;* Medella Sitgues en Oro de Ley, best screenplay, 1977, for *Rabid;* Prize of the International Critics' Jury—Special Mention, 1981, for *The Brood;* Genie Award nominations, best achievement in direction and best original screenplay, Academy of Canadian Cinema and Television, 1982, International Fantasy Film Award, best film, 1983, all for *Scanners;* Best Science Fiction Film Award, Brussels

International Festival of Fantasy Film, Genie Award, best achievement in direction, Genie Award nomination, best screenplay, 1983, Best Science–Fiction Film, Brussels International Festival of Fantasy Film, 1984, all for *Videodrome;* Audience Award and Best Film Award, both Fantafestival, Critics Award and Grand Prize nomination, Avoriaz Fantastic Film Festival, 1984, all for *The Dead Zone;* International Fantasy Film Award nomination, best film, 1987, for *The Fly;* Los Angeles Film Critics Association Award, best director, and Genie Awards, best achievement in direction, best adapted screenplay, and best motion picture (with Marc Boyman), 1988, International Fantasy Film Award nomination, best film, Grand Prize, Avoriaz Fantastic Film Festival, 1989, all for *Dead Ringers;* Saturn Awards, Academy of Science Fiction, Fantasy, and Horror Films, and George Pal Memorial Award, all 1989; National Society of Film Critics Awards, best director and best screenplay, New York Film Critics Circle Award, best screenplay, Genie Award, best achievement in direction, Boston Society of Film Critics Award, best screenplay 1991, International Fantasy Film Award nomination, best film, Golden Berlin Bear nomination, 1992, all for *Naked Lunch;* Genie Awards, best achievement in direction and best adapted screenplay, Special Jury Prize and Golden Palm nomination, both Cannes International Film Festival, Genie Award nomination, best motion picture, Golden Reel Award (with others), 1996, all for *Crash;* Catalonian International Film Festival Award nomination, best film, Silver Berlin Bear, outstanding artistic achievement, Golden Berlin Bear nomination, Silver Scream Award, Amsterdam Fantastic Film Festival, 1999, Genie Award nomination (with others), best motion picture, 2000, all for *eXistenZ;* Genie Award nomination (with Jody Shapiro), best live action short—drama, 2002, for *Camera;* Special Jury Prize, Flanders International Film Festival, 2002; Time–Machine Honorary Award, Catalonian International Film Festival, 2002; Catalonian International Film Festival Award, best director, Catalonian International Film Festival Award nomination, best film, Best Canadian Feature Film, Toronto International Film Festival, Screen International Award nomination, Golden Palm Award nomination, 2002, Directors Guild of Canada Team Award (with others), outstanding achievement in feature film, Directors Guild of Canada Craft Award, outstanding achievement in direction—feature film, Genie Award, best achievement in direction, 2003, all for *Spider;* Lifetime Achievement Award, Stockholm Film Festival, 2005; Billy Wilder Award, National Board of Review, 2005; Golden Palm nomination, Cannes Film Festival, Gotham Award nomination, best film, Toronto Film Critics Association Award, best director, 2005, ALFS Award nomination, director of the year, London Critics Circle Award, Bodil Award, best American film, Central Ohio Film Critics Association, best direction, Cesar Award nomination, best foreign film, Chicago Film Critics Association Award, best director, Critics Award, best foreign film, French Syndicate of Cinema Critics, David di Donatello Award nomination, best foreign film, Directors Guild of

Canada Craft Award, outstanding direction—feature film, National Society of Film Critics Award, best director, Online Film Critics Society Award, best director, Sant Jordi Award, best foreign film, 2006, for *A History of Violence;* Sonny Bono Visionary Award, Palm Springs International Film Festival, 2006; Golden Coach, Cannes Film Festival, 2006; British Independent Film Award nomination, best director, People's Choice Award, Toronto International Film Festival, Satellite Award nomination, best director, International Press Academy, 2007, Film Award nomination (with others), best British film, British Academy of Film and Television Arts, Bodil Award nomination, best non–American film, Cesar Award nomination, best foreign film, Directors Guild of Canada Team Award (with others), feature film, Directors Guild of Canada Craft Award, direction—feature film, Fotogramas de Plata, best foreign film, Genie Award nomination, best achievement in direction, Online Film Critics Society Award nomination, best director, Sant Jordi Award, best foreign film, Vancouver Film Critics Circle Award, best director in a Canadian film, 2008, all for *Eastern Promises;* Medal of Knight, French National Order of the Legion of Honor, 2009.

CREDITS

Film Work:

Director, producer, editor, and cinematographer, *Transfer* (short film), 1966.

Director, producer, editor, and cinematographer, *From the Drain* (short film), 1967.

Director, producer, editor, and cinematographer, *Stereo,* Emergent Films, 1969.

Director, producer, editor, and cinematographer, *Crimes of the Future,* Emergent Films, 1970.

Director, producer, editor, and cinematographer, *Jim Ritchie, Sculptor,* 1971.

Assistant production manager, *Across This Land with Stompin' Tom Connors,* 1973.

Director, *They Came from Within* (also known as *Frissons, Orgy of the Blood Parasites, The Parasite Murders,* and *Shivers*), American International Pictures, 1975.

Director, *Rabid* (also known as *Rage*), New World Pictures, 1977.

Director, *Fast Company,* Topar, 1978.

Director, *The Brood* (also known as *La clinique de la terreur* and *David Cronenberg's "The Brood"*), New World Pictures, 1979.

Director, *Scanners* (also known as *Telepathy 2000*), Avco Embassy, 1981.

Director, *Videodrome,* Universal, 1983.

Director, *The Dead Zone,* Paramount, 1983.

Director, *The Fly,* Twentieth Century–Fox, 1986.

Director and (with Marc Boyman) producer, *Dead Ringers* (also known as *Gemini* and *Twins*), Twentieth Century–Fox, 1988.

Director, *Naked Lunch,* Twentieth Century–Fox, 1991.
Director, *M. Butterfly,* Warner Bros., 1993.
Director and producer, *Crash,* Fine Line, 1996.
Executive producer, *I'm Losing You,* Lions Gate Films, 1998.
Director and producer, *eXistenZ,* Miramax, 1999.
Director, *Camera* (short film), 2000.
Producer and director, *Spider,* Sony Pictures Classics, 2002.
Director, *Painkillers,* 2003.
Director, *A History of Violence,* New Line Cinema, 2005.
Director, "At the suicide of the last Jew in the world in the last cinema in the world," *To Each His Own Cinema* (also known as *Chacun son cinema ou ce petit coup au coeur quand la lumiere s'eteint et que le film commence*), 2007.
Director, *Eastern Promises,* Focus Features, 2007.
Executive producer, *The Plan,* 2008.
Director, *A Dangerous Method,* 2011.

Film Appearances:
Group supervisor, *Into the Night,* Universal, 1985.
Gynecologist, *The Fly,* Twentieth Century–Fox, 1986.
(Uncredited) Obstetrician, *Dead Ringers* (also known as *Gemini* and *Twins*), Twentieth Century–Fox, 1988.
Dr. Philip K. Decker, *Nightbreed* (also known as *Clive Barker's "Nightbreed"*), Twentieth Century–Fox, 1990.
Himself, *Untitled "Naked Lunch" Featurette,* 1991.
Himself, *Naked Making Lunch,* 1992.
Blue, Miramax, 1993.
The director, *Trial by Jury,* Warner Bros., 1994.
Doc Fisher, *Henry and Verlin,* Original Motion Picture Company, 1994.
Stan Coleburn, *Boozecan,* 1994.
Man at lake, *To Die For,* Columbia, 1995.
Stephen, *Blood & Donuts,* Malofilm, 1995.
(Uncredited) Voice of auto salesperson, *Crash,* Fine Line, 1996.
Postal supervisor, *The Stupids,* New Line Cinema, 1996.
Hospital attorney, *Extreme Measures* (also known as *Body Bunk*), Columbia, 1996.
Psychiatrist, *The Grace of God,* 1997.
Duncan, *Last Night,* Lions Gate Films, 1998.
Himself, *Cronenberg Interview: Shivers,* 1998.
Himself, *Cronenberg Interview: Rabid,* 1998.
Father Rousell, *Resurrection,* 1999.
Himself, *David Cronenberg: I Have to Make the Word Be Flesh,* 1999.
Himself, *The American Nightmare,* 2000.
Dr. Wimmer, *Jason X,* New Line Cinema, 2001.
Himself/Dr. Wimmer, *By Any Means Necessary: The Making of "Jason X,"* New Line Home Video, 2002.
Himself, *Je t'aime ... moi non plus: Artistes et critiques* (documentary), Colifilms Distribution, 2004.

Himself, *The Best of Secter & the Rest of Secter* (documentary), 2005.
Himself, *Acts of Violence* (documentary), New Line Home Video, 2005.
Himself, *Too Commercial for Cannes* (short film), New Line Home Video, 2006.
Himself, *Violence's History: United States Version vs. International Version* (short documentary), New Line Home Video, 2006.
Himself, *The Politics of "The Dead Zone"* (short film), Paramount Home Entertainment, 2006.
Himself, *Memories from "The Dead Zone"* (short film), Paramount Home Entertainment, 2006.
Himself, *Visions and Horrors from "The Dead Zone"* (short film), Paramount Home Entertainment, 2006.
Himself, *The Look of "The Dead Zone"* (short film), Paramount Home Video, 2006.
The suicidal man, "At the suicide of the last Jew in the world in the last cinema in the world," *To Each His Own Cinema* (also known as *Chacun son cinema ou ce petit coup au coeur quand la lumiere s'eteint et que le film commence*), 2007.
Himself, *William S. Burroughs: A Man Within* (documentary), Oscilloscope Laboratories, 2009.

Television Work; Specials:
Director, editor, and cinematographer, *Tourettes,* 1971.
Director, editor, and cinematographer, *Letter from Michelangelo,* 1971.
Director, editor, and cinematographer, *Winter Garden,* 1972.
Director, editor, and cinematographer, *Scarborough Bluffs,* 1972.
Director, editor, and cinematographer, *Lakeshore,* 1972.
Director, editor, and cinematographer, *In the Dirt,* 1972.
Director, editor, and cinematographer, *Fort York,* 1972.
Director, editor, and cinematographer, *Don Valley,* 1972.

Television Director; Episodic:
"Secret Weapons," *Programme X,* 1972.
"The Lie Chair," *Peep Show,* 1976.
"The Victim," *Peep Show,* 1976.
"The Italian Machine," *Teleplay,* CBC, 1976.
"Faith Healer," *Friday the 13th: The Series* (also known as *Friday's Curse, Friday's Game,* and *Friday the 13th*), syndicated, 1988.
"Regina vs. Horvath," *Scales of Justice,* CBC, 1990.
"Regina vs. Logan," *Scales of Justice,* CBC, 1990.

Television Appearances; Miniseries:
Detective Stobel, *The Judge* (also known as *Steve Martini's "The Judge"*), NBC, 2001.

Television Appearances; Movies:
Clem Clayton, *Moonshine Highway,* Showtime, 1996.
Father Rousell, *Resurrection,* HBO, 1999.

Television Appearances; Specials:

Long Live the New Flesh: The Films of David Cronenberg (documentary), CBC, 1987.

David Cronenberg and the Cinema of the Extreme, 1997.

The Fly Papers: The Buzz on Hollywood's Scariest Insect, AMC, 2000.

The American Nightmare, Independent Film Channel, 2000.

Masters of Horror (also known as *Boogeyman II: Masters of Horror*), 2002.

Ceremonia de apertura—55 degree festival internacional de cine de San Sebastian, 2007.

Presenter, *The 28th Annual Genie Awards,* 2008.

Television Appearances; Episodic:

Cinema 3, 1989, 1996, 2007.

"Idella's Breakdown," *Maniac Mansion,* The Family Channel, 1992.

"Meltdown: Part 1," *The Newsroom,* CBC, 1997.

"New Years Eve 1999," *Royal Canadian Air Farce* (also known as *Air Farce Live* and *Air Farce: Final Flight*), CBC, 1999.

"The Films of David Cronenberg," *The Directors,* Encore, 1999.

"David Cronenberg: I Have to Make the Word Be Flesh," *Cinema, de notre temps,* 1999.

Festival Pass with Chris Gore, Starz!, 2002.

Open Mike with Mike Bullard (also known as *Open Mike* and *The Mike Bullard Show*), 2003.

Charlie Rose (also known as *The Charlie Rose Show*), PBS, 2003.

"Dark Desires: Sexuality in the Horror Film," *SexTV,* 2003.

"Romantic Love/Strip Club DJ's/A Moment with ... David Cronenberg," *SexTV,* 2003.

Dr. Brezzel, "Conscious," *Alias,* ABC, 2003.

Dr. Brezzel, "Remnants," *Alias,* ABC, 2003.

La caja negra, 2004.

Le grand journal de Canal+, 2005.

Comme au cinema, 2005.

"A History of Violence," *HBO First Look,* HBO, 2005.

Go'morgen Danmark, 2005.

Magacine, 2005.

Tout le monde en parle, 2005.

"Monstrous Desires: Sexuality and Horror/A Moment ... with David Cronenberg," *SexTV,* 2005.

L'hebdo cinema, 2006.

Torrent, 2006.

"David Lynch Special," *Tracks,* 2007.

Up Close with Carrie Keegan, 2007.

El blog de Cayetena, 2007.

The Culture Show, 2007.

"Armin Mueller–Stahl," *Deutschland, deine Kunstler,* 2008.

Jornal Nacional, 2009.

Dr. Leichman, "Polly Wants a Crack at Her," *Happy Town,* ABC, 2009.

RECORDINGS

Taped Readings:

"Sneakers," *Nightmares and Dreamscapes,* Volume 2, Penguin HighBridge Audio, 1994.

WRITINGS

Screenplays:

Transfer (short film), 1966.

From the Drain (short film), 1967.

Stereo, Emergent Films, 1969.

Crimes of the Future, Emergent Films, 1970.

Jim Ritchie, Sculptor, 1971.

They Came from Within (also known as *Frissons, Orgy of the Blood Parasites, The Parasite Murders,* and *Shivers*), American International Pictures, 1975.

Rabid (also known as *Rage*), New World Pictures, 1977.

Fast Company, Topar, 1978.

The Brood (also known as *La clinique de la terreur* and *David Cronenberg's "The Brood"*), New World Pictures, 1979.

Scanners (also known as *Telepathy 2000*), Avco Embassy, 1981.

Videodrome, Universal, 1983.

(With Charles Pogue) *The Fly* (based on a story by George Langelaan), Twentieth Century–Fox, 1986.

(With Norman Snider) *Dead Ringers* (also known as *Gemini* and *Twins;* based on the book *The Twins* by Bari Wood and Jack Geasland), Twentieth Century–Fox, 1988.

Naked Lunch (based on the novel by William S. Burroughs), Twentieth Century–Fox, 1991.

Crash (based on a novel by J. G. Ballard), Fine Line, 1996.

eXistenZ (also known as *Crimes of the Future*), Miramax, 1999.

Camera (short film), 2000.

Television Specials:

Tourettes, 1971.

Letter from Michelangelo, 1971.

Winter Garden, 1972.

Scarborough Bluffs, 1972.

Lakeshore, 1972.

In the Dirt, 1972.

Fort York, 1972.

Don Valley, 1972.

Television Episodes:

"The Italian Picture," *Teleplay,* CBC, 1976.

Nonfiction:

Cronenberg on Cronenberg, edited by Chris Rodley, Faber & Faber, 1992.

OTHER SOURCES

Books:

Dompierre, Louise, *Prent/Cronenberg: Crimes Against Nature,* Power Plant, 1987.

Gruenberg, Serge, *David Cronenberg,* Cahiers du Cinema, 1992.

Rodley, Chris, ed., *Cronenberg on Cronenberg,* Faber & Faber, 1992.

Handling, Piers, editor, *The Shape of Rage: The Films of David Cronenberg,* General Publishing, 1993.

International Dictionary of Films and Filmmakers, Volume 2: *Directors,* St. James Press, 1996.

Morris, Peter, *David Cronenberg: A Delicate Balance,* Eclipse Books, 1994.

Grant, Michael, ed., *The Modern Fantastic: The Films of David Cronenberg,* Praeger, 2000.

Periodicals:

Artforum, March, 1997, p. 76.

Film Comment, March/April, 1997, p. 14.

Interview, January, 1992, p. 80; August, 1996, p. 64.

Maclean's, June 3, 1996, p. 54; November 11, 1996, p. 72.

Rolling Stone, February 6, 1992, p. 66.

Saturday Night, September, 1993, p. 42; October, 1996, p. 119.

CRONENBERG, Denise
(Denise Woodley)

PERSONAL

Born in Toronto, Ontario, Canada; sister of David Cronenberg (a film director, producer, and writer); married Raymond Woodley (died, 2002); children: Aaron (a director). *Education:* Graduated from Ryerson Polytech; studied ballet at the American Ballet Theatre.

Addresses: *Agent*—International Creative Management, 10250 Constellation Blvd., 9th Floor, Los Angeles, CA 90067.

Career: Costume designer and producer. Appeared as a ballet dancer with the Royal Winnipeg Ballet; appeared as a dancer on CBS variety shows for fifteen years, through 1983.

Awards, Honors: Genie Award nomination, best achievement in costume design, 1989, Academy of Canadian Cinema and Television, Saturn Award nomination, best costumes, Academy of Science Fiction, Fantasy, and Horror Films, both for *Dead Ringers;*

Genie Award nomination, best achievement in costume design, 1992, for *Naked Lunch;* Genie Award nomination, best achievement in costume design, 2003, for *Spider;* Genie Award nomination, best achievement in costume design, 2008, for *Eastern Promises.*

CREDITS

Film Costume Designer:

The Fly, Twentieth Century–Fox, 1986.

Dead Ringers, Twentieth Century–Fox, 1986.

The Long Road Home, 1989.

The Guardian, 1990.

Naked Lunch, Twentieth Century–Fox, 1991.

M. Butterfly, Warner Bros., 1993.

Moonlight and Valentino, Gramercy, 1995.

Crash, Fine Line, 1996.

Murder at 1600, Warner Bros., 1997.

A Cool, Dry Place (also known as *Dance Real Slow*), Twentieth Century–Fox, 1998.

The Wager, 1998.

eXistenZ, Miramax, 1999.

The Third Miracle, Sony Pictures Classics, 1999.

Camera, 2000.

Bless the Child (also known as *Die Prophezeiung*), Paramount, 2000.

Dracula 2000 (also known as *Dracula 2001* and *Wes Craven Presents "Dracula 2000"*), Miramax, 2000.

The Caveman's Valentine (also known as *Caveman*), MCA/Universal, 2001.

Spider, Sony Pictures Classics, 2002.

Avenging Angelo, Warner Bros., 2002.

Rhinoceros Eyes, Madstone Films, 2003.

Dawn of the Dead (also known as *Zack Snyder's "Dawn of the Dead"*), Universal, 2004.

A History of Violence, New Line Cinema, 2005.

Dead Silence, Universal, 2007.

Shoot 'Em Up, New Line Cinema, 2007.

Eastern Promises, Focus Features, 2007.

The Incredible Hulk, Universal, 2008.

Toronto Stories, Christal Films, 2008.

Resident Evil: Afterlife (also known as *Resident Evil: Afterlife: An IMAX Experience* and *Biohazard IV: Afterlife*), Screen Gems, 2010.

A Dangerous Method, 2011.

Film Work; Other:

(As Denise Woodley) Wardrobe trainee, *Videodrome,* 1983.

(As Denise Woodley) Wardrobe mistress, *The Dead Zone,* 1983.

Costumes, *Shoot Me,* 1988.

Wardrobe for Alan Alda, *Mad City,* 1997.

Executive producer, *The Wager,* 1998.

Costumes for Milla Jovovich, *Resident Evil: Afterlife* (also known as *Resident Evil: Afterlife: An IMAX Experience* and *Biohazard IV: Afterlife*), Screen Gems, 2010.

Film Appearances:
Herself, *Acts of Violence* (documentary), New Line Home Video, 2006.

Television Costume Designer; Miniseries:
Master Spy: The Robert Hanssen Story, CBS, 2002.

Also worked as costume designer, *Murder Ordained,* CBS.

Television Costume Designer; Movies:
Child of Rage, CBS, 1992.
Sugartime, HBO, 1995.
Friends at Last, CBS, 1995.
Mistrial, HBO, 1996.
Rebound: The Legend of Earl "The Goat" Manigault (also known as *Rebound*), HBO, 1996.
Madness of Method, 1996.
Martha Behind Bars, CBS, 2005.

Also worked as costume designer, *Scales of Justice.*

Television Costume Designer; Pilots:
The Tower, CBS, 2008.

CUMMINGS, Brian 1948–

PERSONAL

Born March 4, 1948, in Youngstown, OH. *Education:* Attended Sherwood Oaks College; trained at Film Industry Workshops and Off the Wall workshop, and with Joan Gerber and Larry Moss.

Addresses: *Agent*—(voice work) Jeff Danis, Danis Panaro Nist, 9201 West Olympic Blvd., Beverly Hills, CA 90212.

Career: Actor, voice artist, and teacher. Worked for KISS–FM Radio and other national radio programs; worked as an announcer for many of the major television and cable networks; made commercials for dozens of products, including CocaCola, McDonald's restaurants, Home Depot home improvement stores, Disneyland, Hasbro toys, and Safeway stores. Teacher of quarterly voice–acting workshops; performer and recording artist with the band Media Monsters.

CREDITS

Television Appearances; Animated Series:
Voice, *Spider–Man* (also known as *Spiderman 2000* and *Spiderman*), NBC, 1981.
Voice of Dr. Mindbender, *G.I. Joe,* syndicated, 1983.

Voice, *The New Scooby and Scrappy–Doo Show,* ABC, 1983.
Voice of Dimmy Finster, *The Snorks,* NBC, 1984.
Voice, *Pole Position,* CBS, 1984.
Voices of Papa Q. Bear and other characters, *The Berenstain Bears,* CBS, 1985.
Voice, *The New Jetsons,* syndicated, 1985.
Voice, *Saber Rider and the Star Sheriffs* (also known as *Bismarck the Star Musketeers*), syndicated, 1986.
Voice, *Pound Puppies,* ABC, 1986.
Voices of Sir Tuxford and others, *Adventures of the Gummi Bears* (also known as *Disney's "Adventures of the Gummi Bears"* and *Disney's "Gummi Bears"*), NBC, 1987–89, then ABC, 1990–91.
Voices of Doofus Drake, Bubba the Caveduck, and others, *DuckTales* (also known as *Disney's "DuckTales"*), ABC and syndicated, 1988–89.
Voice, *The California Raisin Show,* 1989.
Voice of Bully, *Zazoo U,* Fox, 1990.
Voice, *The Adventures of Don Coyote and Sancho Panda,* syndicated, 1990.
Voice of Garlic Man, *Little Dracula,* 1991.
Voice, *ProStars,* NBC, 1991.
Voice, *Mr. Bogus,* syndicated, 1991.
Voices of Morton Fizzback and Professor Funt, *Denver, the Last Dinosaur,* 1992.
Voice of Hollywood, *2 Stupid Dogs,* syndicated, 1993–94.
Voices of vulture police and others, *Timon and Pumbaa,* 1995–96.
Voice of Master Phantom, *Space Strikers,* 1995.
Voice, *Zorro,* syndicated, 1997–2000.
Voices, *The Emperor's New School,* The Disney Channel, 2006–2008.
Voice of Omar, *Ben & Izzy,* 2007.

Television Appearances; Animated Specials:
Voice, *Stanley, the Ugly Duckling,* ABC, 1982.
Voice, "The Pig Plantagenet," *CBS Storybreak,* CBS, 1985.
Voice, "Harry, the Fat Bear Spy," *CBS Storybreak,* CBS, 1985.
Voice of Harry, "The Velveteen Rabbit," *ABC Weekend Specials,* ABC, 1985.
Voice, "The Shy Stegosaurus of Cricket Creek," *CBS Storybreak,* CBS, 1987.
Voice, "Mama Don't Allow," *CBS Storybreak,* CBS, 1987.
Voice, "Jeffrey's Ghost," *CBS Storybreak,* CBS, 1987.
Voice, *Raisins Sold Out: The California Raisins II,* 1989.
Voices of Lick Broccoli and Leonard Limabean, *The Raisins Sold Out!:,* CBS, 1990.
Voice, *Claymation Comedy of Horrors Show,* CBS, 1991.
Voice, *Christmas Every Day,* syndicated, 1991.
Voice of Christmas Present, *Flintstone Christmas Carol,* 1994.

Television Appearances; Live–Action Specials:
Voice, *Smithsonian's Great Battles of the Civil War,* The Learning Channel, 1994.
Voice, *Russia's Last Tsar,* NBC, 1996.

Television Appearances; Animated Episodes:
Voices of Bumblelion and Flizzard, "Bulls of a Feather," *The Wuzzles,* CBS, 1985.
Voice of Jack Case, "A Spy in the Ointment," *Tale Spin,* 1990.
Voices of Arnould Mousenegger and hapless mouse, "Mind Your Cheese and Q's," *Chip 'n Dale Rescue Rangers,* 1990.
Voices of Arnould Mousenegger, kid with boat, and toy store owner, "The SS Drainpipe," *Chip 'n Dale Rescue Rangers,* 1990.
Voice of Clyde, "Penthouse Mouse/Twelve Angry Sheep/The Ant Attack," *Tom & Jerry Kids Show,* 1990.
Voice, "The Pizza Patrol/The Son Also Rises/Rolling Romance," *Garfield and Friends,* 1991.
Voice, "The Automated, Animated Cartoon/It's a Wonderful Wade/Truckin' Odie," *Garfield and Friends,* 1991.
Voice of reporter, "Perchance to Dream," *Batman* (also known as *The Adventures of Batman & Robin* and *Batman: The Animated Series*), Fox, 1992.
Voice of Simon, "Message in a Bottle," *The Little Mermaid,* 1992.
Voice of Weasal Loman, "The Merchant of Menace," *Darkwing Duck,* ABC and syndicated, 1992.
Voice of announcer, "Oh, Oh, Ethel/Meet John Brain/Smell Ya Later/Spike," *Animaniacs* (also known as *Steven Spielberg Presents "Animaniacs"*), 1994.
Voice, "The Once and Future Duck," *Duckman* (also known as *Duckman: Private Dick/Family Man*), USA Network, 1996.
Voices of male Eskimo, guard, and gator, "Pizza Boy in No Tip," *The Cartoon Cartoon Show* (also known as *The What a Cartoon Show*), 1996.
Voices of whaling captain and fourth pirate, "Dishonest Abe/Blackbeard, Warm Heart," *Time Squad,* 2001.
Voice of Trode, "Wild Styles," *Totally Spies!* (animated; also known as *Totally Spies Undercover!*), 2002.
Voices of anchor, guy, and assistant, "Wishbones," *The Grim Adventures of Billy & Mandy* (also known as *Grim & Evil*), Cartoon Network, 2005.
Voices of cop, clown, and hillbilly dad, "Jeffy's Web/Irwin Gets a Clue," *The Grim Adventures of Billy & Mandy* (also known as *Grim & Evil*), Cartoon Network, 2005.
Voices of radio speaker and Uncle Frosty, "The Firebird Sweet/The Bubble with Billy," *The Grim Adventures of Billy & Mandy* (also known as *Grim & Evil*), Cartoon Network, 2005.
Voices of Orc and television host, "Dumb–Dumbs and Dragon/Fear and Loathing in Endsville," *The Grim Adventures of Billy & Mandy* (also known as *Grim & Evil*), Cartoon Network, 2006.

Also voice for episodes of *Beethoven.*

Television Appearances; Other:
Voice, *The Pink Panther in "Pink at First Sight,"* 1981.
Voice of Dr. Mindbender, *G.I. Joe: Arise, Serpentor, Arise!* (animated), 1986.
Voices of driver, guard, and sultan, *Scooby–Doo in Arabian Nights* (animated movie; also known as *Scooby Doo's Arabian Nights*), syndicated, 1994.

Television Work; Live–Action Series:
Announcer, *Let's Make a Deal,* 1984–85.
Narrator, *World's Wildest Vacation Videos,* truTV, 2008–2009.
Announcer, *Most Daring,* truTV, 2009–10.

Television Work; Additional Voices; Animated Series:
Widget, the World Watcher (also known as *Widget*), syndicated, 1990.
Midnight Patrol: Adventures in the Dream Zone (also known as *Potsworth & Co.*), 1990.
Darkwing Duck, ABC and syndicated, 1991.
Where's Waldo? (also known as *Where's Wally?*), CBS, 1991.
Capitol Critters, ABC, 1992.
Raw Toonage (also known as *Disney's "Raw Toonage"*), CBS, 1992.
Problem Child, USA Network, 1993.

Also worked for the series *The Jetsons.*

Television Work; Specials:
Announcer, *Wake Up Your Smile: The Best of the Ben Stiller Show,* Comedy Central, 2003.
Announcer, *Kathy Griffin: The D–List,* Bravo, 2004.
Announcer, *Knots Landing Reunion: Together Again,* CBS, 2005.

Television Work; Episodic:
Voices, *Saturday Night Live* (also known as *SNL*), NBC, 2001, 2002.
Announcer, "Busted in the Buff 3," *Most Shocking,* truTV, 2009.

Provided additional voices for *Kissyfur; A Pup Named Scooby Doo;* and *Teenage Mutant Ninja Turtles.*

Film Appearances:
Assistant director, *Hughes and Harlow: Angels in Hell,* PRO International Pictures, 1977.
Autograph seeker, *California Suite* (also known as *Neil Simon's "California Suite"*), Columbia, 1978.
Voice of Richard Nixon, *Where the Buffalo Roam,* Universal, 1980.
Voice of Dr. Mindbender, *G.I. Joe: The Movie* (animated; also known as *Action Force: The Movie*), 1987.

English–speaking arena announcer, *Ice Pawn,* 1989.

Voice of Stove, *Beauty and the Beast* (animated; also released as *Beauty and the Beast: Special Edition* and *Beauty and the Best 3–D*), Buena Vista, 1991.

Voice of Ock, *FernGully: The Last Rainforest* (animated; also known as *FernGully 1*), Twentieth Century–Fox, 1992.

Voice of Brewster, *Annabelle's Wish,* 1997.

Voice of Snarls/Dawg, *The Legend of Sasquatch* (animated), Gorilla Pictures, 2006.

Voice of robot, *Super Capers,* Roadside Attractions, 2009.

Film Work:

Singer, *Little Nemo: Adventures in Slumberland* (animated; also known as *Little Nemo*), 1990.

Additional voices, *Jetsons: The Movie* (animated), Universal, 1990.

Additional voice, *The Jungle Book 2,* Buena Vista, 2003.

RECORDINGS

Videos; Narrator:

Mary Poppins Practically Perfect in Every Way: The Magic behind the Masterpiece (also known as *Walt Disney's Mary Poppins Practically Perfect in Every Way: The Magic Behind the Masterpiece*), 1997.

Once Upon a Dream: The Making of Walt Disney's "Sleeping Beauty," 1997.

Under the Sea: The Making of Disney's Masterpiece "The Little Mermaid," 1998.

Animated Videos; Voice Performer:

Hoomania (also known as *Hoomania: A Journey into Proverbs*), 1985.

Mad Scientist, 1988.

The Story Keepers: Roar in the Night, 1996.

The Story Keepers: Sink or Swim, 1996.

The Story Keepers, Catacomb Rescue, 1996.

The Story Keepers: Captured!, 1996.

The Story Keepers: To the Ends of the Earth, 1997.

The Story Keepers: Tricked by a Traitor, 1997.

The Story Keepers: Trapped!, 1997.

The Story Keepers: Caught at the Crossroads, 1997.

The Story Keepers: Tried and True, 1997.

Voices of God, Aaron, and Raca, *Kids' Ten Commandments: A Life and Seth Situation,* Nest Learning, 2003.

Voices of God and Aaron, *Kids' Ten Commandments: The Not So Golden Calf,* Nest Learning, 2003.

The Emperor's New Groove 2: Kronk's New Groove, Buena Vista Home Video, 2005.

Video Games:

Voice of MCP, *TRON Solar Sailer,* 1983.

Voice, *M.A.X.: Mechanized Assault and Exploration,* 1996.

Voices of Enric and Dwarf, *Die by the Sword,* 1998.

Voice, *Die by the Sword: Limb from Limb,* 1998.

Voice of Sully, *Monsters, Inc.,* Disney Interactive, 2002.

Voice of Baumusu, *The Mark of Kri,* Sony Computer Entertainment America, 2002.

Voice, *Evil Dead: A Fistful of Boomstick* (also known as *Evil Dead V*), THQ, 2003.

More than a dozen voices, *EverQuest II,* Sony Online Entertainment, 2004.

Voice of Sokolov, *Metal Gear Solid 3: Snake Eater* (also known as *Metal Gear Solid 3* and *MGS3*), Konami Digital Entertainment America, 2004.

Voice of Victor5, *Area 51,* Midway, 2005.

Voice of Baumusu, *Rise of the Kasai,* Sony Computer Entertainment America, 2005.

Voices of Nikolai Stepanovich Sokolov and soldiers, *Metal Gear Solid 3: Subsistence,* Konami Digital Entertainment America, 2005.

Voices of Sokolov and ghost, *Metal Gear Solid: Portable Ops,* Konami Digital Entertainment America, 2006.

Voices, *Bee Movie Game,* Activision, 2007.

OTHER SOURCES

Electronic:

Brian Cummings Official Site, http://www.voiceatility. com, August 19, 2010.

CURRY, Shea

PERSONAL

Born in Hattiesburg, MS; married Justin Levy, August 5, 2006. *Education:* Marymount Manhattan College, B.F.A., acting. *Avocational Interests:* Rollerblading, waterskiing, snow skiing, horseback riding, canoeing, fishing, and swimming.

Career: Actress.

Awards, Honors: Garland Award nomination, best actress in a play, 2001, for *Beirut.*

CREDITS

Film Appearances:

Girl in park, *Nice Guys Sleep Alone,* The Asylum, 1999.

Whitney, *Little Indiscretions,* Singa Home Entertainment, 1999.

All bad female roles, *Jonni Nitro* (animated), Eruptor Entertainment, 2000.

Lisa, *Karma to Burn*, 2001.

(Uncredited) Dream girl, *Diary of a Sex Addict* (also known as *Sex Diary*), Nu Image Films, 2001.

Jen, *Ask Curtis*, 2003.

Lisa, *Every 43 Seconds*, 2003.

Starlet, *Straight–Jacket*, Regent Releasing, 2004.

Lady's maid Brigitte, *The Princess Diaries 2: Royal Engagement*, Buena Vista, 2004.

Mary Anne, *Bigger Than the Sky*, Metro–Goldwyn–Mayer, 2005.

Chloe, *I–See–You.com*, 2006.

Pig owner Melody, *Georgia Rule*, Universal, 2007.

Shaana Martell, *Screw Cupid*, 2008.

(Uncredited) Second reporter, *Hancock* (also known as *Hidden from Earth*), Columbia, 2008.

Kara Lysander, *Kink* (short film), 2008.

Dana, *Only for You*, Singa Home Entertainment, 2008.

Receptionist, *Tom Cool*, 2009.

Marge, *Maneater*, Lightning Media, 2009.

Indian restaurant friend Elise, *Valentine's Day*, New Line Cinema, 2010.

Film Coproducer:

Screw Cupid, 2008.

Kink (short film), 2008.

Television Appearances; Episodic:

Tina, "Marci's Job," *One World*, NBC, 1998.

Dina, "Lois vs. Evil," *Malcolm in the Middle*, Fox, 2000.

Croupier, "Something for Everyone," *Lucky*, FX Network, 2003.

Carla, *Days of Our Lives* (also known as *DOOL* and *Days*), NBC, 2003.

Tina, *Days of Our Lives* (also known as *DOOL* and *Days*), NBC, 2003.

Jill, "All the Young Nudes," *Grounded for Life*, The WB, 2003.

Janine, "Donny, We Hardly Knew Ye," *Las Vegas*, NBC, 2004.

Ann Wylie, "Two of a Kind," *Las Vegas*, NBC, 2004.

Anne Harding, "To Kill a Predator," *CSI: Miami*, CBS, 2008.

Rebecca, "Dan Daly," *Nip/Tuck*, FX Network, 2010.

Jenni, "Nerds Gone Wild," *The Hard Times of R J Berger*, MTV, 2010.

Also appeared as Emily, *The IT Crowd*, Channel 4.

Stage Appearances:

Appeared in *The Little Prince*, Promenade Theatre, New York City; *The 25th Anniversary of Lyrics and Lyricists—An Evening with Charles Strouse*, Broadway production; *Can't Stop Dancin'*; *West Side Story*; as Pamina, *The Magic Flute*, Falcon Theatre; Blue, *Beirut*.

Major Tours:

Toured in *Show Boat*, U.S. cities; *The Little Prince*, U.S. cities; as Maria, *West Side Story*, U.S. cities; Philia, *A Funny Thing Happened on the Way to the Forum*, U.S. cities; Annie, *Annie Get Your Gun*, U.S. cities; Lucy, *The Three Penny Opera*, U.S. cities; Tuptim, *The King & I*, U.S. cities; Shelby, *Steel Magnolias*, U.S. cities; Angelique, *La Malade Imaginaire*, U.S. cities; Caitlin, *Waiting for Ophelia*, U.S. cities.

D

DANIELS, Keli

PERSONAL

American. *Education:* Attended New York University; trained at Beverly Hills Playhouse, West End Theatre Company, Actor's Lab, and Margie Haber Studios, all Los Angeles, with Stella Adler and at HB Studios and National Improv Theatre, all New York City.

Addresses: *Agent*—Sally Kadison, TGMD, 6767 Forest Lawn Dr., Suite 101, Los Angeles, CA 90068.

Career: Actress. Appeared in commercials, industrial films, Internet broadcasts, and music videos; also voice actor.

Member: American Federation of Television and Radio Artists, Screen Actors Guild.

CREDITS

Film Appearances:
Civility (also known as *The Day October Died*), SoHo Entertainment/VCL Communications, 2000.
Fitness club lady, *Beautiful,* Destination Films, 2000.
Didi, *Crocodile Dundee in Los Angeles,* Paramount, 2001.
Fedora, *The Dry Spell,* Brothers Dowdle Films/Group W Films, 2005.
Out of the Woods (short film), Edit This Productions, 2006.
Kay's mother, *Maneater,* Arsenal Pictures, 2009.
Narrator, *Portrait: Audrey* (short film), 2010.

Television Appearances; Movies:
Hanna Richardson, *Malaika* (also known as *Tons of Trouble*), HBO, 1999.

Darcy, *A Table for One* (also known as *Wicked Ways*), Cinemax, 1999.
Rachael, *Better People,* 2010.

Television Appearances; Pilots:
The Weekend, NBC, 2005.
Patient, *Windfall,* NBC, 2006.
Brenda, *Notes from the Underbelly,* ABC, 2007.
Special Agent Oso, The Disney Channel, 2008.

Television Appearances; Episodic:
Laurel, "10,000 Steps," *Judging Amy,* CBS, 2005.
Nurse, "My Rite of Passage," *Scrubs* (also known as *Scrubs: Med School*), NBC, 2006.
Nurse, "My Intern's Eyes," *Scrubs* (also known as *Scrubs: Med School*), NBC, 2006.
Hotel employee, "Chuck versus the Tango," *Chuck,* NBC, 2007.
Vera–Joan's friend, "Beaverland," *Hung,* HBO, 2010.

Stage Appearances:
Appeared as Carla, *Between Daylight and Boonesville,* Thirteenth Street Theatre, New York City; Simi, *Broccoli Romance,* Cinegrill; Babe, *Crimes of the Heart,* Thirteenth Street Theatre; Madeline LaRue, *Guess Who's Coming Out for Dinner,* Melrose Theatre; Phoebe Bubka, *Life Is a Bad Cabaret,* Melrose Theatre; Helena, *A Midsummer Night's Dream,* Artists Repertory Theatre; Hazel, *My Controllable Zombie,* Skylight Theatre; Ms. Alabama, *Queen for a Year,* Theatre Geo; and Veronica, *Showcase,* Melrose Theatre.

DAVIS, Don 1957–

PERSONAL

Full name, Donald Romain Davis; born February 4, 1957, in Anaheim, CA; married Megan Jeanne Mac-

Donald, May 25, 1986; children: two. *Education:* University of California, Los Angeles, graduated; studied composition with Henri Lazarof and orchestration with Joe Harnell and Albert Harris.

Addresses: *Agent*—First Artists Management, 4764 Park Granada, Suite 210, Calabasas, CA 91302.

Career: Composer, orchestrator, music director, conductor, and musician (trumpet and piano). Participant in workshops and concerts. Member of American Music Center, Opera America, and Center for Contemporary Opera; also member of MoveOn.org, Act Now to Stop War and End Racism, and Progressive Democrats of America.

Member: American Federation of Musicians, National Academy of Recording Arts and Sciences, Academy of Motion Picture Arts and Sciences, Broadcast Music Inc., American Composers Forum, Hispanics for Los Angeles Opera, Amnesty International, American Civil Liberties Union, Sierra Club, Alumni Association of University of California, Los Angeles.

Awards, Honors: Grammy Award (with others), best rhythm and blues song, National Academy of Recording Arts and Sciences, 1976, for "Disco Lady"; Emmy Award (with others), outstanding achievement in creative technical crafts, 1981, for *Astronomical Artists, Cosmos, The Shores of the Cosmic Ocean;* Emmy Award nomination, 1988, and Emmy Award, 1990, both best composition of a dramatic underscore for a series, for *Beauty and the Beast;* two Emmy Award nominations, best composition of a dramatic underscore for a series, 1991, one for *My Life and Times,* the other for *Lies before Kisses;* BMI Television Music Award (with others), Broadcast Music Inc., 1991, for *Matlock;* Emmy Award nomination, best composition of a dramatic underscore for a series, 1992, for *A Little Piece of Heaven;* Emmy Award nomination, 1994, and Emmy Award, 1995, both best composition of a dramatic underscore for a series, for *SeaQuest DSV;* Emmy Award nomination, best composition of a dramatic underscore for a series, 1998, for *House of Frankenstein;* BMI Film Music Award, 1999, for *The Matrix;* World Soundtrack Award nomination, best original score of the year not released on an album, 2001, for *AntiTrust;* BMI Film Music Award, 2002, for *Jurassic Park III;* BMI Film Music Awards, 2004, for both *The Matrix Reloaded* and *The Matrix Revolutions;* other awards include first prize from Mark Taper Foundation commission competition and prize from Henri Dutilleux International Composition Competition.

CREDITS

Film Work; Music Orchestrator:
(Uncredited) Additional orchestrations, *Aliens* (also known as *Alien 2*), 1986.

Additional orchestrations, *Police Academy 3: Back in Training,* Warner Bros., 1986.
Additional orchestrations, *Police Academy 4: Citizens on Patrol,* Warner Bros., 1987.
The In Crowd, 1988.
Die Hard 2 (also known as *Die Hard 2: Die Harder*), Twentieth Century–Fox, 1990.
Robin Hood: Prince of Thieves, 1991.
If Looks Could Kill (also known as *Teen Agent*), 1991.
Hudson Hawk, TriStar, 1991.
Ricochet, Warner Bros., 1991.
Death Becomes Her, Universal, 1992.
We're Back! A Dinosaur's Story (animated), Universal, 1993.
Cop & ½ (also known as *Cop and a Half*), Universal, 1993.
Hocus Pocus, Buena Vista, 1993.
(Uncredited) *Last Action Hero,* Columbia, 1993.
The Pelican Brief, Warner Bros., 1993.
Legends of the Fall, TriStar, 1994.
(Uncredited) *Clean Slate,* United International Pictures, 1994.
I Love Trouble, Buena Vista, 1994.
Maverick, Warner Bros., 1994.
Clear and Present Danger, Paramount, 1994.
The Pagemaster (animated), Twentieth Century–Fox, 1994.
Additional orchestrations, *When a Man Loves a Woman* (also known as *To Have and To Hold*), Buena Vista, 1994.
Casper, Universal, 1995.
(Uncredited) *Apollo 13* (also known as *Apollo 13: The IMAX Experience*), Universal, 1995.
Toy Story (animated; also released as *Toy Story in 3–D*), Buena Vista, 1995.
Balto (animated), Universal, 1995.
(And song arranger) *James and the Giant Peach,* Buena Vista, 1996.
(Uncredited) *The Phantom,* Paramount, 1996.
(Uncredited) *Courage under Fire,* Twentieth Century–Fox, 1996.
Ransom, Buena Vista, 1996.
Michael, New Line Cinema, 1996.
Additional orchestrations, *Titanic,* Paramount, 1997.
Pleasantville (also known as *Color of Heart*), New Line Cinema, 1998.
A Bug's Life (animated), Buena Vista, 1998.
Lost in Space (also known as *LS*), New Line Cinema, 1998.
The Matrix, Warner Bros., 1999.
House on Haunted Hill, Warner Bros., 1999.
Meet the Parents, Universal, 2000.
The Unsaid (also known as *The Ties that Bind*), Universal Studios Home Video, 2001.
Toy Story 3 (animated; also known as *Toy Story 3: An IMAX Experience* and *3*), Walt Disney, 2010.

Film Work; Music Orchestrator and Conductor:
A Goofy Movie, Buena Vista, 1995.
Warriors of Virtue, 1997.

The Lesser Evil, Orion Home Entertainment, 1998.

The Matrix, Warner Bros., 1999.

The Unsaid (also known as *The Ties that Bind*), Universal Studios Home Video, 2001.

(And song producer) *The Matrix Reloaded* (also known as *The Matrix Reloaded: The IMAX Experience*), Warner Bros., 2003.

(And song performer) *The Matrix Revolutions* (also known as *The Matrix Revolutions: The IMAX Experience*), Warner Bros., 2003.

The Marine, Twentieth Century–Fox, 2006.

The Good Life, Epic Pictures Group, 2007.

Film Work; Music Conductor:

Flowers in the Attic, New World, 1987.

Jurassic Park III (also known as *JP3*), Universal, 2001.

Behind Enemy Lines, Twentieth Century–Fox, 2001.

Film Work; Other:

Song producer, *La Bamba,* Columbia, 1987.

Score performer, *Fear of Flying* (also known as *Turbulence 2: Fear of Flying* and *Turbulence II: Fear of Flying*), 2000.

Score producer and theme song performer, *Ballistic: Ecks vs. Sever,* Warner Bros., 2002.

Television Music Orchestrator and Conductor; Movies:

Eagles: Hell Freezes Over, 1995.

Personally Yours (also known as *Wilderness Love*), CBS, 2000.

Television Music Orchestrator; Other:

(Uncredited) *V* (miniseries; also known as *V: The Original Mini Series*), 1983.

Also orchestrator for the series *The Incredible Hulk.*

Television Appearances; Episodic:

So You Think You Can Dance (also known as *S.Y.T.Y.C.D.* and *American Dance Idol*), Fox, 2009.

WRITINGS

Film Music; Musical Underscores:

Hyperspace (also known as *Gremloids*), 1985.

Police Academy 3: Back in Training, Warner Bros., 1986.

Police Academy 4: Citizens on Patrol, Warner Bros., 1987.

Blackout (also known as *The Attic*), Ambient Light Entertainment, 1988.

Die Hard 2 (also known as *Die Hard 2: Die Harder*), Twentieth Century–Fox, 1990.

Hudson Hawk, TriStar, 1991.

Tiny Toon Adventures: How I Spent My Vacation (animated; also known as *How I Spent My Vacation*), 1992.

We're Back! A Dinosaur's Story (animated), Universal, 1993.

Hocus Pocus, Buena Vista, 1993.

The Pelican Brief, Warner Bros., 1993.

I Love Trouble, Buena Vista, 1994.

Additional music (and song "Mike & Alice's Restaurant"), *When a Man Loves a Woman* (also known as *To Have and To Hold*), Buena Vista, 1994.

Maverick, Warner Bros., 1994.

Clear and Present Danger, Paramount, 1994.

The Pagemaster (animated), Twentieth Century–Fox, 1994.

Casper, Universal, 1995.

Toy Story (animated), Buena Vista, 1995.

Additional music, *A Goofy Movie,* Buena Vista, 1995.

James and the Giant Peach, Buena Vista, 1996.

Ransom, Buena Vista, 1996.

Michael, New Line Cinema, 1996.

Bound, Gramercy, 1996.

(And song "Inside of You") *Warriors of Virtue,* 1997.

The Lesser Evil, Orion Home Entertainment, 1998.

A Bug's Life (animated), Buena Vista, 1998.

A League of Old Men, 1998.

Lost in Space (also known as *LS*), New Line Cinema, 1998.

The Matrix, Warner Bros., 1999.

House on Haunted Hill, Warner Bros., 1999.

Universal Soldier: The Return (also known as *Universal Soldier IV*), TriStar, 1999.

Fear of Flying (also known as *Turbulence 2: Fear of Flying* and *Turbulence II: Fear of Flying*), 2000.

Well Met in Osaka, 2000.

AntiTrust (also known as *Conspiracy.com* and *Surveillance*), Metro–Goldwyn–Mayer, 2001.

Valentine, Warner Bros., 2001.

New music, *Jurassic Park III* (also known as *JP3*), Universal, 2001.

The Unsaid (also known as *The Ties that Bind*), Universal Studios Home Video, 2001.

Behind Enemy Lines, Twentieth Century–Fox, 2001.

Long Time Dead, Universal, 2002.

(And theme song) *Ballistic: Ecks vs. Sever,* Warner Bros., 2002.

(And songwriter) *The Matrix Reloaded* (also known as *The Matrix Reloaded: The IMAX Experience*), Warner Bros., 2003.

(And songwriter) *The Matrix Revolutions* (also known as *The Matrix Revolutions: The IMAX Experience*), Warner Bros., 2003.

The Animatrix, Warner Home Video, 2003.

The Animatrix: The Second Renaissance Part 1 (also known as *The Second Renaissance Part I*), Warner Bros., 2003.

The Animatrix: The Second Renaissance Part 2 (also known as *The Second Renaissance Part II*), Warner Bros., 2003.

The Animatrix: Final Flight of the Osiris (also known as *Final Flight of the Osiris*), Warner Bros., 2003.
The Animatrix: Kid's Story (short animated film; also known as *Kids' Story*), Studio 4C, 2003.
The Marine, Twentieth Century–Fox, 2006.
The Good Life, Epic Pictures Group, 2007.
Ten Inch Hero, Indies Home Entertainment, 2007.
Main title theme music, *Return to House on Haunted Hill,* Warner Bros., 2007.

Songs Featured in Films:
"Somebody's Gettin' It," *She's So Lovely,* Miramax, 1997.
"Who's Making Love," *Gangster No. 1,* 2000.
"Rowdy Booty Time," *Where the Heart Is,* Twentieth Century–Fox, 2000.
"That's a Team," *Down to Earth,* 2001.
"Jody's Got Your Girl and Gone," *Baby Boy,* Columbia, 2001.

Television Music; Series:
Beauty and the Beast, CBS, 1987–90.
Tiny Toon Adventures (animated; also known as *Steven Spielberg Presents … Tiny Toon Adventures*), 1990–93.
My Life and Times, 1991.
Capitol Critters, between 1992 and 1995.
SeaQuest DSV (also known as *SeaQuest 2032*), NBC, 1994–95.

Television Music; Movies:
Additional music, *I Dream of Jeannie: 15 Years Later,* 1985.
A Stoning in Fulham County, NBC, 1988.
Quiet Victory: The Charlie Wedemeyer Story, CBS, 1988.
"Home Fires Burning," *Hallmark Hall of Fame,* CBS, 1989.
Running against Time, USA Network, 1990.
Lies before Kisses, CBS, 1991.
A Little Piece of Heaven, NBC, 1991.
Notorious, Lifetime, 1992.
Woman with a Past, NBC, 1992.
Murder of Innocence, CBS, 1993.
Leave of Absence, NBC, 1994.
A Little Tailor's Christmas Story, 1994.
Sleep, Baby, Sleep, ABC, 1995.
In the Lake of the Woods, Fox, 1996.
For Love Alone: The Ivana Trump Story (also known as *Ivana Trump's "For Love Alone"*), CBS, 1996.
The Perfect Daughter, USA Network, 1996.
Not in This Town, USA Network, 1997.
The Alibi, ABC, 1997.
A Match Made in Heaven, CBS, 1997.
Weapons of Mass Distraction, HBO, 1997.
Life of the Party: The Pamela Harriman Story (also known as *Life of the Party: Pamela Harriman*), Lifetime, 1998.

The Agency, 1998.
The Lake, NBC, 1998.
Route 9, HBO, 1998.
In the Company of Spies, Showtime, 1999.
Hell Swarm, UPN, 2000.
Personally Yours (also known as *Wilderness Love*), CBS, 2000.
Race Against Time, TNT, 2000.
Murder in Greenwich (also known as *Dominick Dunne Presents: Murder in Greenwich*), USA Network, 2002.
Augusta, Gone, Lifetime, 2006.

Television Music; Miniseries:
Bluegrass, CBS, 1988.
In the Best of Families: Marriage, Pride & Madness (also known as *Bitter Blood*), CBS, 1994.
The Beast (also known as *Peter Benchley's "The Beast"*), NBC, 1996.
Pandora's Clock (also known as *Doomsday Virus*), NBC, 1996.
Invasion (also known as *Robin Cook's "Invasion"*), NBC, 1997.
House of Frankenstein, NBC, 1997.
The Third Twin (also known as *Ken Follett's "The Third Twin"*), CBS, 1997.
Space Odyssey: Voyage to the Plants (also known as *Voyage to the Planets and Beyond*), The Science Channel, 2004.

Television Music; Specials:
Session Man, Showtime, 1992.
"Between Mother and Daughter," *CBS Schoolbreak Special,* CBS, 1995.
Mighty Times: The Children's March, HBO, 2004.

Television Music; Pilots:
Country Estates, ABC, 1993.

Television Music; Episodic:
"Long Lost Love," *Hart to Hart,* 1984.
"Slam Dunk," *Hart to Hart,* 1984.
"Always, Elizabeth," *Hart to Hart,* 1984.
"Meanwhile, Back at the Ranch," *Hart to Hart,* 1984.
"Comrade Hammer," *Sledge Hammer!* (also known as *Sledge Hammer: The Early Years*), 1987.
"Wild about Hammer," *Sledge Hammer!* (also known as *Sledge Hammer: The Early Years*), 1987.
"The Personal Trainer," *Matlock,* 1990.
"Face of the Enemy," *Star Trek: The Next Generation* (also known as *Star Trek: TNG*), 1993.
Additional music, "Watergate," *SeaQuest DSV* (also known as *SeaQuest 2032*), NBC, 1995.

Video Music Composer:
The Special Effects of "Jurassic Park III," 2001.
The Sound and Music of "Jurassic Park III," 2001.

The Art of "Jurassic Park III," 2001.
The Fanimatrix: Run Program, Plutonian Shore Productions, 2003.

Video Game Music Composer:
Theme music, *Enter the Matrix,* 2003.
The Matrix Online (also known as *MxO*), Warner Bros. Interactive Entertainment, 2005.
CR: Enter the Matrix, Daiichi Shokai, 2009.

Other:
Rio de Sangre (opera), Florentine Opera Company and Milwaukee Symphony Orchestra, 2010.

Composer of numerous concert works including "The Eye and the Pyramid," Los Angeles Pops Orchestra, 1990; "Going On," 1991; "Green Light," 1992; "What Is the Silence," 1993; "Afterimages," 1994; "Of the Illuminated," Joseph and Loretta Law Foundation, 1995; "Flurry," 1996; "No Exit," 1996; "Pain," 1998; "Illicit Felicity," 1999; "Critical Mass," 2000; "A Lunatic Air (On Fire)," 2002; and "Wandering," New Hollywood String Quartet, 2002.

RECORDINGS

Albums:
Albums featuring Davis's music include *Ballistic: Ecks vs. Sever,* Varese Sarabande; *The Beast,* Varese Sarabande; *Bound,* Screen Archives Entertainment; *House of Frankenstein,* Screen Archives Entertainment; *House on Haunted Hill,* Varese Sarabande; *Hyperspace/Beauty and the Beast,* Prometheus; *Invasion,* Screen Archives Entertainment; *Jurassic Park III,* Decca; *The Matrix,* Varese Sarabande; *The Matrix Reloaded* and *The Matrix Revolutions,* Warner Sunset/Maverick; *The Matrix: The Deluxe Edition,* Varese Sarabande; *Turbulence 2: Fear of Flying,* Pacific Time Entertainment; *Universal Soldier: The Return,* Varese Sarabande; *The Unsaid,* Prometheus; and *Warriors of Virtue,* Prometheus; music also represented in recordings by others and in collections.

Video Appearances:
Beyond Jurassic Park, 2001.
The Matrix Revisited, Warner Bros., 2001.
The Sound and Music of "Jurassic Park III," 2001.
Ben–Hur: The Epic that Changed Cinema, Warner Home Video, 2005.
The Art of Imagination: A Tribute to Oz, Warner Home Video, 2005.

ADAPTATIONS

Davis's music from the television series *Beauty and the Beast* was also included in the video *Beauty and the Beast Season 2: Introductions with Ron Perlman and Linda Hamilton,* Paramount Home Video, 2007.

OTHER SOURCES

Electronic:
Don Davis Official Site, http://www.dondavis.net, August 9, 2010.

De LAURENTIIS, Dino 1919–2010

PERSONAL

Full name, Agostino De Laurentiis; born August 8, 1919, in Torre Annunziata, Campania, Italy; died November 10, 2010, in Beverly Hills, CA. Producer. Prolific, world-renowned producer, De Laurentiis made hundreds of films in a wide variety of genres, from high art to lowbrow commercial entertainment, during his more than sixty-year career. He left his village in the late 1930s to work in Rome as a movie extra and stagehand. After World War II, he worked avidly to revive Italy's film industry, joining the early Italian New Wave to produce his first international success, *Bitter Rice* (1949). His critical breakthrough came in 1954 with Federico Fellini's *La Strada,* which starred Anthony Quinn and Giulietta Masina; it and Fellini's 1957 *Nights of Cabiria* both won Academy Awards for Best Foreign Film. Hoping to attract an international audience, he and coproducer Carlo Ponti initiated several epic-scale films in English, including *War and Peace* (starring Audrey Hepburn and Henry Fonda) in 1956, the 1962 biblical story *Barabbas* (starring Anthony Quinn), and *The Bible* in 1966. In 1968 De Laurentiis produced the infamous *Barbarella,* a comic-book-based science fiction film starring Jane Fonda.

One of the first producers to promote international film partnerships, he collaborated during his career with such renowned European and American directors as Fellini, Ingmar Bergman, Vittorio De Sica, David Lynch, John Huston, Sydney Pollack, and Robert Altman. After moving to New York City in the early 1970s, De Laurentiis made the successful American films *Serpico* in 1973, *Death Wish* in 1974, *Three Days of the Condor* in 1975, and *The Shootist,* which featured John Wayne's last movie appearance, in 1976. His triumphs were mixed with expensive failures, such as a 1976 remake of *King Kong,* the 1979 *Hurricane,* and *Dune* in 1984. The 1980s also afforded him more popular achievements, including Milos Forman's 1981 *Ragtime,* the 1982 *Conan the Barbarian,* and a series of movies based on Stephen King novels, including *The Dead Zone* in 1983 and *Firestarter* in 1985. In 1986 he produced the critically acclaimed art film *Blue Velvet,* which many regard as director David Lynch's best work. De Laurentiis continued to produce films until 2007. The Academy of Motion Picture Arts and Sciences awarded him the Irving G. Thalberg Memorial Award for lifetime achievement in 2001.

PERIODICALS

Los Angeles Times, November 12, 2010.
New York Times, November 12, 2010.
Washington Post, November 11, 2010.

DEL RIVERO, Conchita
See RIVERA, Chita

DEMING, Peter 1957–

PERSONAL

Born December 13, 1957, in Beirut, Lebanon; raised in Wisconsin. *Education:* American Film Institute, graduated, 1980; also attended University of Wisconsin.

Addresses: *Office*—Agogo Films, 927 Fourth St., Santa Monica, CA 90403. *Manager*—Marsh, Best, and Associates, 9150 Wilshire Blvd, Suite 220, Beverly Hills, CA 90212.

Career: Cinematographer. Also worked as camera assistant, camera operator, second unit photographer, and consultant; cinematographer for commercials, and as a director and cinematographer of music videos. Presenter of seminars.

Member: American Society of Cinematographers.

Awards, Honors: Sundance Film Festival Award, best dramatic cinematography, 1990, and Independent Spirit Award nomination, best cinematography, Independent Features Project/West, 1991, both for *House Party;* nomination for Golden Frog, Camerimage, Fennecus Award nomination, best composition in cinematography, Apex Award nomination, best cinematography for an action, mystery, or suspense film, 2001, Independent Spirit Award, Chicago Film Critics Association Award nomination, and Online Film Critics Association Award nomination, all best cinematography, 2002, all for *Mulholland Dr.*

CREDITS

Film Cinematographer:
The Silence (short film), 1982.
Evil Dead II (also known as *Evil Dead 2: Dead by Dawn* and *Evil Dead II, the Sequel to the Ultimate Experience in Grueling Terror*), Rosebud Communications, 1987.
Hollywood Shuffle (also known as *Robert Townsend's "Hollywood Shuffle"*), Samuel Goldwyn, 1987.
Scarecrows, Sandstar, 1988.
Purple People Eater, Concorde, 1988.
It Takes Two (also known as *My New Car*), United Artists, 1988.
The Carrier, Magnum Video, 1988.
From Hollywood to Deadwood, Island Pictures, 1989.
Why Me?, Triumph Releasing, 1990.
House Party, New Line Cinema, 1990.
Martians Go Home, Taurus Entertainment, 1990.
Book of Love, New Line Cinema, 1990.
Drop Dead Fred (also known as *My Special Friend*), New Line Cinema, 1991.
Scorchers (also known as *Jumper: Hot Lover*), Goldcrest, 1991.
My Cousin Vinny, Twentieth Century–Fox, 1992.
Loaded Weapon 1 (also known as *National Lampoon's "Loaded Weapon 1"*), New Line Cinema, 1993.
Son–in–Law, Buena Vista, 1993.
S.F.W. (also known as *So Fucking What?*), Gramercy, 1994.
Joe's Apartment, Warner Bros., 1996.
Lost Highway, October Films, 1997.
Austin Powers: International Man of Mystery, New Line Cinema, 1997.
Scream 2, Miramax, 1997.
Music of the Heart, Miramax, 1999.
Mystery, Alaska, Buena Vista, 1999.
Scream 3, Miramax, 2000.
Mulholland Dr. (also known as *Mulholland Drive*), Universal, 2001.
From Hell, Twentieth Century–Fox, 2001.
Austin Powers in Goldmember (also known as *Austin Powers: Goldmember*), New Line Cinema, 2002.
People I Know, Miramax, 2002.
Coney Island Baby, Frontlot Productions/double A Films, 2002.
I Heart Huckabees (also known as *I Love Huckabees*), Fox Searchlight, 2003.
Twisted, Paramount, 2004.
The Jacket, Warner Bros., 2005.
Rumor Has It ..., Warner Bros., 2005.
Lucky You, Warner Bros., 2007.
Married Life, Sony Pictures Classics, 2007.
The Love Guru, Paramount, 2008.
Drag Me to Hell (also known as *Spell*), Universal, 2009.
Last Night, Miramax, 2010.
The Cabin in the Woods, Metro–Goldwyn–Mayer, 2011.

Film Appearances:
Popcorn boy, *Scream 2,* 1997.
(Uncredited) Man eating popcorn on studio tour, *Scream 3,* 2000.
Cinema Style (documentary), T–Stop Production, 2006.

Television Cinematographer; Specials:
Cosmic Slop, HBO, 1994.

Television Cinematographer; Movies:
"2000" segment, *If These Walls Could Talk 2,* HBO, 2000.

Television Cinematographer; Pilots:
Key West, Fox, 1993.
The Last Days of Russell, ABC, 1995.
Cashmere Mafia, ABC, 2008.

Television Cinematographer; Episodic:
On the Air, ABC, 1992.
"Tricks," *Hotel Room* (also known as *David Lynch's "Hotel Room"*), 1993.
"Getting Rid of Robert," *Hotel Room* (also known as *David Lynch's "Hotel Room"*), 1993.
"Blackout," *Hotel Room* (also known as *David Lynch's "Hotel Room"*), 1993.
"Gimme Shelter," *Key West,* Fox, 1993.
"Crossroads," *Key West,* Fox, 1993.

RECORDINGS

Videos:
Behind the "Scream," 2000.
I Heart Huckabees: Production Surveillance, Twentieth Century–Fox Home Entertainment, 2005.

De NIRO, Drena 1971–

PERSONAL

Born in 1971, in New York, NY; daughter of Diahnne Abbott; adopted daughter of Robert De Niro (an actor); children: (with Carlos Rodriguez, an artist) one son.

Addresses: *Agent*—Mindel–Shaw Donegan, 9057 Nemo St., West Hollywood, CA.

Career: Actress and director. Previously worked as a deejay, model, and fashion consultant; worked for Giorgio Armani as a musical supervisor for stores and shows.

CREDITS

Film Appearances:
First receptionist, *Grace of My Heart,* Gramercy, 1996.

Gate stewardess, *Wag the Dog,* New Line Cinema, 1997.
Waitress, *Too Tired to Die* (also known as *New York Daydream*), Phaedra Cinema, 1998.
Marcy, *Great Expectations,* Twentieth Century–Fox, 1998.
Rita, *On the Run* (also known as *Em fuga* and *On the Run*), Phaedra Cinema, 1998.
Caroline, *At First Sight,* Metro–Goldwyn–Mayer, 1999.
Lori, *The 24 Hour Woman,* Artisan Entertainment, 1999.
Sherie, *Personals* (also known as *Hook'd Up*), Unapix Entertainment, 1999.
Waitress, *Entropy* (also known as *Without You*), 1999.
RBTV Lackey, *The Adventures of Rocky & Bullwinkle* (also known as *Die Abenteuer von Rocky und Bullwinkle*), Universal, 2000.
Keechie, *Giravolte* (also known as *Freewheeling in Roma*), 2001.
Annie, Chase's production assistant, *Showtime,* Warner Bros., 2002.
Semi, *Ghetto Dawg,* Jersey Bred Productions, 2002.
Vanessa Hansen, *City by the Sea* (also known as *The Suspect*), Warner Bros., 2002.
Kara, *Soliloquy,* 2002.
Several characters, *DV Workshop,* 2002.
Female staff writer, *Death of a Dynasty,* TLA Releasing, 2003.
Betsy Vandercleef, *Love & Orgasms,* 2003.
Nada the handler, *Freezerburn,* The Brookturn Co., 2005.
The Collection, Arco Films, 2005.
Stella Clark, *The Lovebirds,* 2007.
Megan, *Karma, Confessions and Holi,* 2009.
Dr. Press, *ExTerminators,* 2009.
P, *A Day in the Life,* Lions Gate Films, 2009.

Film Producer:
Karma, Confessions and Holi, 2009.

Television Appearances; Miniseries:
Girl in beauty shop, *Witness to the Mob,* NBC, 1998.

Television Appearances; Specials:
Spring Break Rave, ABC, 1993.
Voice of Glindy, *The Groovenians* (animated), Cartoon Network, 2002.
AFI Life Achievement Award: A Tribute to Robert De Niro, 2003.

Television Work; Specials:
Director, executive producer, and additional photography, *Girls and Dolls* (documentary), PBS, 2001.

WRITINGS

Television Specials:
Girls and Dolls (documentary short film), PBS, 2001.

DOMINGO, Placido 1941–

PERSONAL

Born January 21, 1941, in Madrid, Spain; immigrated to Mexico, 1950; son of Placido (a singer) and Pepita (a singer; maiden name, Embil) Domingo; married first wife, 1958 (divorced, 1959); married Marta Ornelas (a lyric soprano), 1962; children: (first marriage) Jose; (second marriage) Placido, Alvaro Maurizio. *Education:* Attended National Conservatory of Music, Mexico City.

Addresses: *Contact*—c/o Vincent and Farrell Associates, 157 West 57th St., Suite 502, New York, NY 10019–2210.

Career: Opera singer, actor, and producer. Performed as lead tenor with opera companies all over the world, including La Scala, Covent Garden, Hamburg State Opera, Vienna State Opera, New York City Opera, San Francisco Opera, and National Hebrew Opera, Tel Aviv, Israel; Mexican National Opera, member of company, 1959–61; Israel National Opera Company (now New Israeli Opera), Tel Aviv, member of company, 1962–65; New York City Opera, New York City, member of company, 1965—, opera conductor, 1973—; Washington Opera, Washington, DC, artistic director, c. 1994—; Los Angeles Opera, artistic director, 2000—; Los Angeles Music Center Opera, cofounder; Placido Domingo Operalia (competition), founder. Domingo (restaurant), New York City, owner; appeared in magazine ad for Quorum perfume, 1988.

Awards, Honors: Grammy Award nomination, best classical vocal soloist, National Academy of Recording Arts and Sciences, 1973, for *La voce d'oro;* Grammy Award nomination (with others), best classical vocal soloist, 1975, for *Verdi and Puccini Duets;* named Musician of the Year, *Musical America,* 1977; Grammy Award nomination (with others), best opera recording, 1981, for *Puccini: Le villi;* Grammy Award nomination, video of the year, 1982, for *The Tales of Hoffmann;* Grammy Award nomination (with others), best opera recording, 1982, for *Puccini: Tosca;* honorary degree, Royal College of Music, 1982; Grammy Award nomination, best Latin pop performance, 1983, for *Besame mucho;* Grammy Award nomination (with others), best opera recording, 1983, for *Verdi: La traviata;* Emmy Award, best classical program in the performing arts, 1984, for "Placido Domingo Celebrates Seville," *Great Performances;* Grammy Award, best Latin pop performance, 1984, for *Always in My Heart;* Grammy Award nomination (with others), best opera recording, 1985, for *Leoncavallo: Pagliacci;* Grammy Award nomination (with others), best classical vocal soloist, 1985, for *Zarzuela Arias and Duets;* Emmy Award, best performer in classical music or dance programming, 1986, for "Cavalleria Rusticana," *Great Performances;* Grammy Award nomination, best opera recording, 1986, for *Verdi: Otello;* Emmy Award, best performer in classical music or dance programming, 1988, for "Aida: From the Houston Grand Opera," *Great Performances;* Grammy Award (with others), best opera recording, 1988, for *Wagner: Lohengrin;* awarded honorary degree from Complutense de Madrid, 1989; Grammy Award (with others), best classical vocal soloist performance, 1990, for *Carreras, Domingo, Pavarotti in Concert;* Emmy Award, best classical music or dance programming, 1992, for "The Metropolitan Opera Silver Anniversary Gala," *Great Performances;* Kennedy Center Honors, 2000; decorated Knight Commander of the British Empire, 2002; Ella Award, Society of Singers, 2002; decorated chevalier of Arts and Letters of France and member of French Legion of Honor.

CREDITS

Stage Appearances; Operas:
Zarzuela gigantes y cabezudos, Mexico, 1957.
Rigoletto, Mexican National Opera, 1960.
Alfredo, *La traviata,* Mexican National Opera, Monterrey, 1961.
Edgardo, *Lucia di Lammermoor,* Fort Worth, TX, 1962.
Don Jose, *Carmen,* New York City Opera, New York City, 1965.
Pinkerton, *Madame Butterfly,* New York City Opera, 1965.
Title role, *Don Rodrigo,* New York City Opera, 1966.
Maurizio, *Adriana Lecouvreur,* Metropolitan Opera House, New York City, c. 1968.
Tosca, Covent Garden, London, 1969.
Manon Lescaut, Barcelona, Spain, 1969.
Vasco da Gama, *L'africaine,* San Francisco, CA, 1972.
Title role, *Otello,* Hamburg, Germany, then Paris, 1975.
My Fair Lady, Mexico, 1986.
Verdi: Il trovatore, Royal Opera, Covent Garden, 1989.
Puccini: Tosca, Los Angeles Music Center, Los Angeles, 1989.
Giordano: Andrea Chenier, with National Philharmonic, 1989.
Verdi: Otello, Metropolitan Opera House, 1990, then 1994.
Puccini: La boheme, Metropolitan Opera House, 1990.
Puccini: La fanciulla del west, Metropolitan Opera House, 1991.
Wagner: Parsifal, Metropolitan Opera House, 1991, then La Scala, Milan, Italy, 1992.
Bizet: Carmen, Los Angeles Music Center, 1992.
Offenbach: Les contes d'Hoffmann (also known as *Tales of Hoffmann*), Metropolitan Opera House, 1992–93.
Giordano: Fedora, La Scala, 1993.
Verdi: Rigoletto, Los Angeles Music Center, 1993.

Wagner: Die Walkure, Vienna State Opera, Vienna, Austria, 1993.

Verdi: La traviata, Metropolitan Opera House, 1993.

Verdi: Stiffelio, Metropolitan Opera House, 1993–94.

Verdi: Il trovatore, Metropolitan Opera House, 1994.

Wagner: Die Walkure, Metropolitan Opera House, 1994.

Offenbach: Les contes d'Hoffmann, Vienna State Opera, 1994.

Bizet: Carmen, Vienna State Opera, 1994.

Puccini: Il tabarro, Metropolitan Opera House, 1994.

Mozart: Idomeneo, Metropolitan Opera House, 1994.

Wagner: Lohengrin, Vienna State Opera, 1994.

Bellini: I puritani, Vienna State Opera, 1994.

Penella: El gato montes, Los Angeles, 1994.

Sly, Metropolitan Opera House, 2002.

Dick Johnson, *The Girl of the Golden West,* Dorothy Chandler Pavilion, Los Angeles Music Center, Los Angeles, 2002.

Also performed in *Don Giovanni,* Israel National Opera Company, Tel Aviv; as Arrigo, *Les vepres siciliennes,* Paris, then New York City.

Television Appearances; Episodic:

Duke, "Rigoletto," *Live from the Metropolitan Opera,* 1977.

Turiddu/Canio, "Cavalleria Rusticana/Pagliacci," *Live from the Metropolitan Opera,* 1978.

The Tonight Show Starring Johnny Carson, 1979.

The Big Show, 1980.

"Verdi: Requiem," *Live from Lincoln Center,* 1980.

"A Lincoln Center Special: Beverly! Her Farewell Performance," *Great Performances,* 1981.

Alfredo Germont, "La Traviata," *Live from the Metropolitan Opera,* 1981.

Parkinson, 1982.

"Placido Domingo Celebrates Seville," *Great Performances,* PBS, 1983.

Paolo, "Francesca da Rimini," *Live from the Met,* PBS, 1985.

Mario Cavaradossi, "Tosca," *Live from the Met,* PBS, 1985.

"Gian Carlo Menotti: The Musical Musician," *Great Performances,* PBS, 1986.

Turiddu, "Cavalleria rusticana," *Great Performances,* PBS, 1986.

Don Francisco Goya y Lucientes, "Goya" (also known as "Goya with Placido Domingo"), *Great Performances,* PBS, 1986.

"An Evening with Placido Domingo," *Live from Lincoln Center* (also known as *Great Performances*), PBS, 1987.

Radames, "Aida: From the Houston Grand Opera," *Great Performances,* PBS, 1987.

Duke of Mantua, "Rigoletto," *Live from the Met,* PBS, 1987.

Wogan, 1987.

Alberto, *The Cosby Show,* NBC, 1988.

Calaf, "Turandot," *The Metropolitan Opera Presents,* PBS, 1988.

Vasco DaGama, "L'africaine," *Great Performances,* PBS, 1989.

Radames, "Aida," *The Metropolitan Opera Presents,* PBS, 1989.

Alberto Santiago, "Birthday Blues," *The Cosby Show,* 1989.

La luna, 1989.

Verstehen Sie Spass, 1989.

"Jose Carreras, Diana Ross, Placido Domingo: Christmas in Vienna," *Great Performances,* PBS, 1992.

"Placido Domingo: The Concert for Planet Earth," *Great Performances,* PBS, 1992.

Otello, "The Metropolitan Opera Silver Anniversary," *Great Performances,* PBS, 1992.

"My World of Opera," *A&E Stage,* Arts and Entertainment, 1992.

Dick Johnson/Ramirrez, "The Girl of the Golden West from the Metropolitan Opera," *Great Performances,* PBS, 1992.

De tu a tu, 1992.

"Passing the Baton," *Great Performances,* PBS, 1993.

"Christmas in Vienna," *A&E Stage,* Arts and Entertainment, 1993.

Title role, "Stiffelio," *The Metropolitan Opera Presents,* PBS, 1993.

Mario Cavaradossi, "Tosca from Rome," *Great Performances,* PBS, 1993.

Dick Johnson, Hoffmann, and Ernani, "Opera Favorites with Domingo and Te Kanawa," *A&E Stage,* Arts and Entertainment, 1994.

Luigi, "Il tabarro," "Il tabarro and Pagliacci," *The Metropolitan Opera Presents,* PBS, 1994.

"Placido Domingo: A Musical Life," *American Masters,* PBS, 1995.

Cita con la vida, 1995.

Cartelera, 1995.

Pasa la vida, 1996.

Mundo VIP, 1996 and 1998.

The Royal Opera House, PBS, 1997.

(In archive footage) "Los carnavales," *Mitomania,* 1998.

Nit d'arts, 2000.

"Wetten, dass ...? aus Basel," *Wetten, dass ...?,* 2000.

Un dia con Vicente Galvez, 2003.

"Pavarotti: The Last Tenor," *Arena,* BBC, 2004.

"Die schonsten weihnachtslieder des Nordens," *Hitlisten des Nordens,* 2004.

Las Cerezas, 2005.

Corazon de ..., 2005.

"Wetten, dass ...? aus Hannover," *Wetten, dass ...?,* 2005.

De cerca, 2006.

"Vienna State Opera 50th Anniversary Reopening Gala," *Great Performances,* PBS, 2006.

(In archive footage) "30 Years of 'Live from Lincoln Center'," *Live from Lincoln Center,* PBS, 2006.

Emperor Qin, "Tan Dun's The First Emperor," *Metropolitan Opera: Live in HD* (also known as *Great Performances at the Met*), 2007.

Late Night with Conan O'Brien, NBC, 2007.
"Homer of Seveille," *The Simpsons,* Fox, 2007.
(In archive footage) *Les grands du rire,* 2007.
(In archive footage) *La tele de tu vida,* 2007.
(In archive footage) "Karajan or Beauty as I See It," *Great Performances,* PBS, 2007.
(In archive footage) *Memories de la tele,* 2007, 2008, and 2010.
La 2 noticias, 2008.
Miradas 2, 2008.
(In archive footage) *De par en par,* 2008.
Wilkommen bei Carmen Nebel, 2009.
"Wetten, dass ...? aus Palma de Mallorca," *Wetten, dass ...?,* 2009.
Beckmann, 2009.
En noches como esta, 2009.
"Vaya tela!," *El club de Pizzicato,* 2009.
"Placido Domingo," *Masterclass,* 2010.

Also appeared as himself, *Sesame Street,* PBS.

Television Appearances; Miniseries:
Presenter, *Tales from the Opera,* 1994.
2006 FIFA World Cup (also known as *Fifa World Cup: Germany 2006*), 2006.

Television Appearances; Specials:
Bernstein on Beethoven: A Celebration in Vienna (also known as *Beethoven's Birthday: A Celebration in Vienna with Leonard Bernstein*), 1970.
Bernstein in Vienna: Beethoven—The Ninth Symphony in D Minor, 1970.
Gustavus, *Un ballo in maschera,* 1975.
Benjamin Franklin Pinkerton, *Madame Butterfly,* 1976.
Title role, *Otello,* 1976, 1979, 1992, PBS, 1996.
Mario Cavaradossi, *Tosca,* 1976.
Canio, *Pagliacci,* 1978.
Manrico, *Il trovatore,* 1978.
Turiddu, *Cavalleria Rusticana,* 1978.
The Kennedy Center Honors, 1979.
Don Jose, *Carmen,* 1979.
Rodolfo, *Luisa Miller,* 1979.
Host, *Placido Domingo ... Stepping Out with the Ladies,* 1980.
Des Grieux, *Manon Lescaut,* 1980.
Rodolfo, *La boheme,* 1980.
Hoffmann, *The Tales of Hoffmann* (also known as *Les contes d'Hoffmann*), 1981.
Himself, *Hommage a Seville,* 1981.
Title role, *Andrea Chenier,* 1981.
Samson, *Samson and Delilah,* 1981.
Alfredo Germont, *La traviata,* 1981 and 1983.
The Nativity, syndicated, 1982.
Texaco Star Theatre: Opening Night, NBC, 1982.
Live from Studio 8H: Caruso Remembered, 1982.
In Concert at the Met, 1982.
Placido Domingo! The Tenor, the Teacher, 1982.
Title role, *Ernani,* 1982.

Dick Johnson, *La fanciulla del west,* 1982.
Night of 100 Stars, 1982.
Narrator, *Mario Lanza: The American Caruso,* 1983.
Metropolitan Centennial Gala Telecast, 1983.
Aeneas, *Les troyens,* 1983.
Des Grieux, *Manon Lescaut,* 1983.
Gala of Stars 1984, 1984.
Placido Domingo Celebrates Seville, PBS, 1984.
Bob Hope Special: Bob Hope's Super Birthday Special, NBC, 1984.
Cohost, *Burnett "Discovers" Domingo,* CBS, 1984.
Mario Cavaradossi, *Tosca,* PBS, 1984.
Host, Canio, *Pagliacci,* PBS, 1984.
Paolo, *Francesca Da Rimini,* PBS, 1984.
Title role, *Don Carlo,* 1984.
In Concert at the Met (also known as *In Concert at the Met: A Century of the Performing Arts*), 1984.
Night of 100 Stars II, 1985.
Host, *Placido Domingo: Stepping Out with the Ladies,* 1985.
Himself, *Requiem Mass* (also known as *Lloyd Weber's Requiem Mass*), 1985.
Title role, *Andrea Chenier,* 1985.
Turiddu, *Cavalleria Rusticana,* PBS, 1985.
Don Francisco Goya y Lucientes, *Goya,* PBS, 1986.
Gian Carlo Menotti: The Musical Magician (documentary), PBS, 1986.
Placido Domingo Sings Zarzuela!, PBS, 1986.
Liberty Weekend, ABC, 1986.
Enzo Grimaldi, *La gioconda,* 1986.
16 Days of Glory, The Disney Channel, 1987.
Julie Andrews: The Sound of Christmas, ABC, 1987.
Solti at 75: A Celebration!, PBS, 1987.
An Evening with Placido Domingo, 1987.
Radames, *Aida,* PBS, 1987.
The New York Philharmonic New Year's Eve Gala (also known as *Live from Lincoln Center*), PBS, 1988.
Sesame Street ... 20 and Still Counting, NBC, 1989.
Paris '89, PBS, 1989.
Title role, *Andrea Chenier,* Arts and Entertainment, 1989.
Sanson, *Sanson y Dalila,* 1989.
Riccardo, *Un ballo in maschera,* 1989.
The Music Center 25th Anniversary (also known as *The Los Angeles Music Center's 25th Anniversary Celebration*), PBS, 1990.
Title role, *Lohengrin,* 1990.
Great Moments from the Met, PBS, 1990.
American Tribute to Vaclav Havel and a Celebration of Democracy in Czechoslovakia, PBS, 1990.
Carreras, Domingo, Pavarotti, Mehta (also known as *Three Tenors in Concert* and *The Original Three Tenors in Concert*), PBS, 1991.
Carnegie Hall: Live at 100! The Gala Celebration, PBS, 1991.
Otello, *Panasonic Presents: 25th Anniversary Gala at the Met,* syndicated, 1991.
Dick Johnson, *La fanciulla del west,* 1991.
Otello, *The Metropolitan Opera Silver Anniversary Gala,* 1991.

Hoffman, *Dame Kiri Te Kanawa: My World of Opera,* 1991.

Mario Cavaradossi, *Tosca: In the Settings and at the Times of Tosca* (also known as *Tosca, nei luoghi e nelle ore di Tosca*), 1992.

My World of Opera, Arts and Entertainment, 1992.

From Vienna: The New Year's Celebration 1992, PBS, 1992.

Cerimonia d'inauguracio jocs olimpics Barcelona '92, 1992.

Placido Domingo: The Concert for Planet Earth, PBS, 1992.

Jose Carreras, Diana Ross, Placido Domingo: Christmas in Vienna, PBS, 1992.

Placido Domingo in der Staatsoper Berlin, 1993.

Three Tenors: The Impossible Dream, PBS, 1993.

The Best of Disney Music II: A Legend in Song, CBS, 1993.

Rodolfo Muller, *Stiffelio,* 1993.

The Best of Disney Music: A Legacy in Song–Part II, 1993.

Gala Tribute to Tchaikovsky, 1993.

Passing the Baton (documentary), 1993.

(In archive footage) *Carol Burnett: The Special Years,* 1994.

Tibor Rudas Presents Carreras, Domingo, Pavarotti with Mehta: The Three Tenors in Concert 1994 (also known as *The 3 Tenors in Concert* and *Tibor Rudas Presents: The Three Tenors in Concert 1994*), PBS, 1994.

Cristina Presents: Latin Lovers of the 90s, syndicated, 1994.

The Three Tenors—Backstage Live!, PBS, 1994.

Carreras, Domingo and Pavarotti with Mehta, 1994.

The Vision: The Making of the Three Tenors in Concert, 1994.

Hoffman, Dick Johnson, and Ernani, *Opera Favorites with Domingo and Te Kanawa,* Arts and Entertainment, 1994.

Host, *Operalia,* 1994.

Luigi, *Il Tabarro and Pagliacci,* PBS, 1994.

Rafael/El Gato Montes, *El gato montes from the Los Angeles Music Center Opera* (also known as *The Wild Cat* and *El gato montes*), 1995.

Gabriele Adorno, *Simon Boccanegra,* 1995.

Christmas in Vienna '94, 1995.

Placido Domingo: A Musical Life, 1995.

Telemaraton, 1995.

Placido Domingo at the Roman Amphitheater of Verona, Arts and Entertainment, 1995.

Carreras, Domingo, Pavarotti with Levine: The Three Tenors in Concert 1996 (also known as *Three Tenors in Concert*), PBS, 1996.

James Levine 25th Anniversary Gala, PBS, 1996.

Don Alvaro, *La forza del destino,* PBS, 1996.

Siegmund, *Die Walkure,* 1996.

Merry Christmas from Vienna, 1996.

The Three Tenors at Giants Stadium, 1996.

Die Verwandlung der welt in musik: Bayreuth vor der premiere, 1996.

The Royal Opera House, PBS, 1996.

San Francisco Opera Gala Celebration, PBS, 1997.

Placido Domingo—The Covent Garden Gold and Silver Gala, PBS, 1997.

Loris Ipanov, *Fedora,* PBS, 1997.

Don Jose, *Carmen,* PBS, 1997.

Tenor, *A Gala Christmas in Vienna,* 1997.

Tibor Rudas Presents Carreras, Domingo, Pavarotti with Levine—The Three Tenors Live in Concert—Paris 1998 (also known as *Carreras, Domingo, Pavarotti with Levine*), PBS, 1998.

Samson, *Samson et Dalila,* PBS, 1998.

Enrico Caruso: Voice of the Century, Arts and Entertainment, 1998.

Host, *Opera Stamps—Dedications at the Met,* PBS, 1998.

Canio, *Pagliacci* (also known as *The Washington Opera Production of "Pagliacci"*), PBS, 1998.

Star Crossed Lovers, PBS, 1999.

Title role, *Parsifal: The Search for the Holy Grail,* PBS, 1999.

Ghermann, *The Queen of Spades,* 1999.

Master of ceremonies, *The Richard Tucker Opera Gala Hosted by Placido Domingo,* PBS, 1999.

Requiem, PBS, 2000.

The Three Tenors Christmas, PBS, 2000.

Our Favorite Things: Christmas in Vienna, 2000.

Honoree, *The Kennedy Center Honors* (also known as *The Kennedy Center Honors: A Celebration of the Performing Arts*), CBS, 2000.

Don Juan de Alarcon, *Margarita la tonera,* 2000.

Rodrigue Diaz de Vivar, *Le cid* (also known as *The Washington Opera Presents "El cid"*), 2001.

The Three Tenors in the Forbidden City, Arts and Entertainment, 2001.

Otello, *Otello,* 2001.

A Prayer for America: Yankee Stadium Memorial, 2001.

Samson, *Samson et Delila,* 2002.

Zwischen Wustensand und Traumpalasten—Placido Domingo in Dubai, ARD, 2003.

Kurt Rydl—Der Gladiator, Osterreichischer Rundfunk, 2003.

Maria Callas: Living and Dying for Art and Love, Iambic Productions, 2004.

(Uncredited) *Boda real,* 2004.

(In archive footage) *Celebremos Mexico: Hecho en Mexico,* Televisa S.A. de C.V., 2005.

(In archive footage) Rodolfo, *Tatort Oper,* Osterreichischer Rundfunk, 2006.

Hollywoods Oper—Eine Oper fur Los Angeles, Raphaela Film GmbH, 2006.

Antoinia Gades, la etica de la danza, 2007.

Placido Domingo: Celebrating 40 Years in Los Angeles, 2008.

Bambi Verleihung, 2008.

Placido y la copla, 2008.

(In archive footage) *Catalunya.cat,* TV3, 2008.

La noche de los Oscar, 2009.

The Simpsons: Celebrity Friends, 2010.

Television Appearances; Awards Presentations:

Presenter, *The ... Annual Academy Awards,* 1983, 1985.

The Classical Music Awards, Arts and Entertainment, 1988.

The ... Annual Grammy Awards, CBS, 1991, 2010.

The 65th Annual Academy Awards Presentation, ABC, 1993.

Presenter, *The ... Annual Grammy Awards,* CBS, 1994, 1995.

Presenter, *The 1994 World Music Awards,* ABC, 1994.

The 13th Annual Hispanic Heritage Awards, NBC, 1999.

The 1st Annual Latin Grammy Awards, CBS, 2000.

NRJ 12 Grammys Awards 2010, 2010.

Television Work; Specials:

Conductor, *Die Fledermaus,* 1984.

Executive producer, *Goya,* 1986.

Conductor, *Solti at 75: A Celebration!,* PBS, 1987.

Conductor, *From Vienna: The New Year's Celebration 1992,* PBS, 1992.

Conductor, *Gala Tribute to Tchaikovsky,* 1993.

Conductor, "La Traviata," *Only You,* 1994.

Artistic consultant (Los Angeles Music Center Opera), *El gato montes from the Los Angeles Music Center Opera,* 1995.

Music director, *La rondine,* 1998.

Artistic director (Washington Opera Chorus), *The Washington Opera Production of "La rondine,"* PBS, 1999.

Executive producer, *The Other Conquest,* Hombre de Oro, 2000.

Artistic director (Washington Opera), *The Washington Opera Presents "El cid,"* PBS, 2001.

Conductor, *La traviata,* 2002.

Conductor, "Gounod's Romeo et Juliette," *Metropolitan Opera: Live in HD* (also known as *Great Performances at the Met*), 2007.

Film Appearances:

Mario Cavaradossi, *Tosca,* 1976.

Alfredo Germont, *La traviata,* Universal, 1982.

Canio, *Pagliacci* (also known as *Der Bajazzo*), 1982.

Turiddu, *Cavalleria rusticana,* 1982.

Don Jose, *Bizet's Carmen* (also known as *Carmen*), Triumph, 1984.

Title role, *Otello,* Cannon, 1986.

Himself, *Why Havel?,* 1991.

Hoffmann/Ernani, *Dame Kiri Te Kanawa: My World of Opera,* 1991.

Tenor, *Symphony for the Spire* (also known as *HRH The Prince of Wales Symphony for the Spire* and *A Spectacle of Music and Theatre in Aid of the Salisbury Cathedral Spire Appeal*), 1992.

Dick Johnson, *La fanciulla del west,* 1992.

Himself, *Gold and Silver Gala with Placido Domingo,* 1998.

Voice of man in the moon, *Moulin Rouge!,* Twentieth Century–Fox, 2001.

Caballe, mas alla de la musica (also known as *Caballe Beyond Music*), Morena Films, 2003.

Sacred Stage, First Run Features, 2005.

Democracy: The Making of an American Opera (short film), 2008.

Cyrano, *Cyrano de Bergerac,* Salzgeber & Company, 2008.

Voice of Monte, *Beverly Hills Chihuahua,* Walt Disney Studios, 2008.

Also appeared as voice in *Sian Ka'an,* Universal.

Film Work:

Conductor, *Only You* (also known as *Just in Time* and *Him*), TriStar, 1994.

Executive producer, *The Other Conquest* (also known as *La otra conquista*), Twentieth Century–Fox, 1998.

Conductor, *Gounod: Romeo et Juliette,* Metropolitan Opera, 2007.

RECORDINGS

Albums:

Romantic Arias, RCA, 1969.

Domingo Conducts Milnes! Milnes Conducts Domingo!, RCA, 1972.

Siempre En Mi Corazon: Y Las Canciones De Ernesto Lecuona, Sony, 1972.

La voce d'oro, RCA, 1973.

Caballe: Romances de Zarzuelas, Decca, 1974.

Aida, Angel, 1974.

Verdi and Puccini Duets, RCA, 1975.

Carmen, London, 1975.

Otello, RCA, 1978.

Placido Domingo and the Vienna Choir Boys, RCA Red Seal, 1980.

Music of My Country (zarzuela arias), 1980.

Beethoven IX: Symphonie d–Moll, op. 25, Deutsche Grammophon, 1981.

Puccini: Le villi, CBS, 1981.

Berlioz: Requiem, Deutsche Grammophon, 1981.

Opera Arias, Angel, 1981.

Opern–Gala, Deutsche Grammophon, 1981.

Perhaps Love, CBS Masterworks, 1981.

Un ballo in maschera, Deutsche Grammophon, 1981.

Viva Domingo, Deutsche Grammophon, 1981.

Puccini: Tosca, Angel, 1981.

Tangos, Pansera/DG, 1981.

Adoro, CBS Masterworks, 1982.

Placido Domingo, Zacosa, 1982.

Aida, Deutsche Grammophon, 1982.

Opera Duets, Angel, 1982.

Berlioz: Beatrice et Benedict, Deutsche Grammophon, 1982.

Bravissimo, Domingo!, RCA Red Seal, 1982.

Canciones mexicanas, Discos CBS International, 1982.

Domingo: Con Amore, RCA Victor, 1982.

My Life for a Song, CBS Records, 1983.

Ernani: Verdi, Angel, 1983.

The Best of Domingo, Popular and Classical, Deutsche Grammophon, 1983.

Besame mucho, CBS Masterworks, 1983.

La rondine: Giacomo Puccini, CBS Records, 1983.

Turandot, Deutsche Grammophon, 1983.

Nabucco, Deutsche Grammophon, 1983.

Verdi: La traviata, Elektra, 1983.

Verdi Arias, Deutsche Grammophon, 1983.

Il trovatore, Deutsche Grammophon, 1984.

Bizet: Carmen, Musical Heritage Society, 1984.

Placido Domingo Sings Great Love Scenes with Renata Scotto, CBS Masterworks, 1984.

Carmen, RCA, 1984.

Romanzas de Zarzuelas, MMG, 1984.

Golden Voices of Zarzuela, MMG, 1984.

Always in My Heart (also known as *Great Tenors of Our Time*), Angel, 1984, released as *Siempre en mi corazon*, Discos CBS International, 1984.

Pagliacci: Ruggiero Leoncavallo, Philips, 1984.

Christmas with Placido Domingo, CBS Masterworks, 1984.

Be My Love: An Album of Love, EMI Angel, 1984.

Zarzuelas, Discos CBS International, 1985.

Romanzas de Zarzuelas, Forlane, 1985.

Leoncavallo: Pagliacci, Polygram Classics/Philips, 1985.

Fiesta de la Zarzuela, Forlane, 1985.

Zarzuela Arias and Duets, CBS Masterworks, 1985.

Save Your Nights for Me, CBS, 1985.

Placido Domingo Sings Grand Opera, Angel, 1985.

Requiem: Andrew Lloyd Webber, Angel, 1985.

Don Carlo, Deutsche Grammophon, 1985, released by Angel, 1986.

Christmas with Placido Domingo: Trumpets Sound and Angels Sing, Cherry Lane Music Co., 1986.

Un ballo in maschera, Angel, 1986.

La forza del destino, Angel, 1986.

Verdi: Otello, Angel, 1986.

Die Fledermaus, Angel, 1986.

Listen to the Joy, Hallmark Cards, 1986.

Vienna, City of My Dreams, Angel, 1986.

Nights at the Opera, BCS, 1986.

A Love Until the End of Time, CBS Records, 1988.

Wagner: Lohengrin, 1988.

Greatest Love Songs, SCL, 1988.

Live in Tokyo 1988, 1989.

Verdi: Messa da Requiem, 1989.

Domingo at the Philharmonic, 1989.

Covent Garden Gala Concert, EMI, 1989.

Goya: A Life in Song, Columbia, 1989.

Sonadores de Espana, Discos CBS International, 1989.

Donizetti: L'Elisire d'Amore/Pritchard, Cotrubas, Domingo, CBS Masterworks, 1989.

The Unknown Puccini, 1990.

Wagner: Tannhauser, 1990.

Puccini: Songs, 1990.

Donizetti: Anna Bolena, 1990.

Songs, 1990.

Mascagni: Iris, 1990.

Cilea: Adriana Lecouvreur, 1990.

Schifrin: Song of the Aztecs, 1990.

(With Jose Carreras and Luciano Pavarotti) *Carreras, Domingo, Pavarotti in Concert*, 1990.

Donizetti: L'elisir d'amore, 1990.

Sonadores De Espana, Sony, 1990.

Canciones Mexicanas, Sony, 1990.

Zarzuelas, Sony, 1990.

Zarzuela Arias & Duets, 1990.

Opera Arias, Columbia, 1990.

Belcanto Domingo, 1991.

Mascagni, 1991.

Boito: Mefistofele, 1991.

(With the London Symphony Orchestra) *The Broadway I Love*, Atlantic, 1991.

Be My Love ... An Album of Love, Angel, 1991.

(With Paloma San Basilio) *Por fin juntos*, Capitol/EMI Latin, 1991.

Noche de Zarzuela, Radio Nacional, 1991.

Por Fin Juntos, EMI Latin, 1991.

Canta Para Todos, Polygram Latino, 1991.

Louise, 1991.

Favorite Arias by the World's Favorite Tenors, Sony, 1991.

My Latin Soul, CCT, 1991.

Canta para todos, Capitol/EMI Latin, 1991, reissued PolyGram Latino, 1993.

Together, 1992.

Mascagni: Cavalleria rusticana, 1992.

Arias, Songs, and Tangos, 1992.

Toselli: Serenata; Ponce: Estrellita; Massenet: Elegie; Kalman: Wisst du es noch? From Die Scardas-furstin; Kreisler: The Old Refrain; and Others, 1992.

Verdi: Aida, 1992.

The Domingo Songbook, 1992.

Puccini: Il tabarro, 1992.

Leoncavallo: I pagliacci, 1992.

Placido Domingo: Mozart Arias, Duets, 1992.

Strauss: Die Frau Ohne Schatten, 1992.

Sleighride! Classic Christmas Favorites, 1992.

Entre Dos Mundos, Sony, 1992.

Giacomo Puccini: La Fanciulla Del West, Sony, 1992.

Greatest Love Songs, Sony, 1992.

Verdi: Luisa Miller, 1993.

Puccini: La fanciulla del west (also known as *Placido: The Girl of the Golden West*), 1993.

Domingo Sings Caruso, 1993.

Puccini: Tosca, 1993.

Penella: El gato montes, 1993.

Gala lirica, 1993.

From the Official Barcelona Games Ceremony, 1993.

Espana, 1993.

Entre dos mundos, 1993.

Donizetti: Lucia di Lammermoor, 1993.

Verdi: Otello, 1993.

Verdi: Aida, 1993.

Verdi: I lombardi alla prima crociata, 1993.
Beethoven: Missa solemnis, 1993.
Rossini: El barbiere di Seviglia (also known as *Rossini: The Barber of Seville*), 1993.
Saint–Saens: Samson et Dalila, 1993.
Puccini: Madama Butterfly, 1993.
(With Pavarotti and Carreras) *Domingo, Pavarotti, Carreras in Concert with Mehta,* Mobile Fidelity, 1993.
Canta Para Mexico, Polygram, 1993.
(With Pavarotti and Carreras) *The Three Tenors in Concert,* Atlantic, 1994.
Verdi: Il trovatore, 1994.
Zandonai: Francesca da Rimini, 1994.
Verdi: Don Carlo, 1994.
Tchaikovsky: Romeo and Juliet, 1994.
Capriccio Italian, 1994.
1812 Overture, 1994.
None But the Lonely Heart, 1994.
Lensky's Aria, 1994.
Placido Domingo, 1994.
Opera Duets, 1994.
Verdi: Requiem, 1994.
Bizet: Carmen, 1994.
Verdi: I vespri siciliano, 1994.
(With Pavarotti and Carreras) *The Three Tenors in Paris 1994,* PolyGram, 1994.
De mi alma latina, Angel, 1994.
Granada: The Greatest Hits of Placido Domingo, Deutsche Grammophon, 1994.
All–Star Tenors Salute the World, Sony, 1994.
Premier Concours International de Voix d'Opera Placido Domingo: Paris 1993, Sony, 1994.
Verdi: Aida, Sony, 1994.
De Mi Alma Latina, EMI Angel, 1994.
Nativo, Musical, 1995.
Vienna Noel, Sony, 1995.
Songs of Love, 1995.
Amadeo Vives: Dona Francisquita, Sony, 1995.
De Coleccion, Universal, 1995.
Herodiade Opera en Quatre Actes et Sept Tableaux Opera in Four Acts, Sony, 1995.
Bajo el cielo espanol, Sony, 1996.
Popular Favorites, Cema Special, 1996.
Man of la mancha, Sony, 1996.
Il Guarany—Opera in Quattro Atti, Sony, 1996.
Pure Domingo, CCT, 1996.
Opera Heroes, Capitol, 1997.
The Domingo Collection, Sony, 1997.
De Mi Alma Latina, Vol. 2, EMI Latin, 1997.
Coleccion Mi Historia, Universal Music Latino, 1997.
Por amor, Warner Music International, 1998.
(With Pavarotti and Carreras) *The Three Tenors: Live 1998,* Atlantic, 1998.
Desires, Bci, 1998.
A Gala Christmas in Vienna, Sony, 1998.
Sempre Belcanto: The Legendary First Recital Recording, Teldec, 1998.
798, Sony, 1999.
The Greatest Arias, BMG Special, 1999.
100 Anos de Mariachi, 1999.

Placido Domingo Greatest Arias, BMG, 1999.
Live in America, Hallmark Recordings, 1999.
The Young Domingo, RCA, 1999.
Christmastime in Vienna, SCL, 1999.
Placido Domingo in Concert, Koch Records, 1999.
Super Hits: Placido Domingo, Sony, 2000.
Aida: Highlights, Sony Classical, 2000.
Songs of Love, EMI, 2000.
Canciones de Amor: Songs of Love, EMI Latin, 2001.
The Three Tenors at Christmas, K–Tel Distribution, 2002.
(With Pavarotti and Carreras) *Romantic Tenors,* Atlantic, 2002.
Quiereme Mucho, EMI Latin, 2002.
Wagner: Scenes from "The Ring," 2002.
Placido Domingo Sings ..., Great Opera Tenors, 2002.
Live from Miami, Immortal, 2003.
Placido Domingo, Vol 1, BCI Music, 2003.
Placido Domingo, Vol 2, BCI Music, 2003.
Placido Domingo, Vol 3, BCI Music, 2003.
Bravo Domingo: The Best of Placido Domingo, EMI Music, 2003.
Domingo Sings Caruso, RCA/BMG, 2004.
The Essential Placido Domingo, Sony, 2004.
Vienna, City of My Dreams, EMI Music, 2004.
The Best of Placido Domingo: 20th Century Masters/ The Millennium Collection, 2004.
From My Latin Soul, Vol. 2, Angel, 2005.
Italia, Ti Amo, Polygram, 2006.
Alborada, EMI–Televisa/Mixed Repertoire, 2006.
Moments of Passion, Sony, 2006.
Verdi Otello Giuseppe Verdi, EMI Music, 2006.
Moreno Torroba: Luisa Fernanda, Universal, 2007.
The Great Placido Domingo, Goldies, 2007.
Placido Domingo Sings Tangos, EMI Music, 2007.
Nostalgias ... Lo Mejor de Mi, Universal Music Latino, 2007.
Amore Infinito, Siente Music, Deutsche Grammophon, 2008.
Pasion Espanola, Deutsche Grammophon, 2008.
Domingo!, Third Side, 2009.
Cuore de Tenore, Sony, 2009.
My Greatest Roles: The Documentary, 2009.

Videos:
Caruso Remembered, NBC Enterprises, 1982.
The Tales of Hoffmann, Pioneer Artists, 1982.
Requiem, Kultur, 1986.
Puccini: Turandot, 1990.
Great Arias with Placido Domingo and Friends, 1991.
Hommage a Sevilla, 1992.
Verdi: Aida, 1992.
Three Tenors: Encore, 1992.
Placido Domingo: Grandissimi, 1993.
Symphony for the Spire, 1993.
Verdi: Otello, 1994.
Puccini: Tosca, 1994.
Wagner: Lohengrin, 1994.

Placido Domingo with Mstislav Rostropovich, St. Clair Vision, 2004.

Manuel Barrueco: A Gift and a Life, Michael Lawrence, 2006.

(In archive footage) *Diva,* EMI–Espana, 2006.

Placido Domingo: My Greatest Roles, Kultur Video, 2009.

WRITINGS

Autobiography:
My First Forty Years, Knopf, 1983.

Television Music; Specials:
Julie Andrews: The Sound of Christmas, ABC, 1987.

Jose Carreras, Diana Ross, Placido Domingo: Christmas in Vienna, PBS, 1992.

Tibor Rudas Presents Carreras, Domingo, Pavarotti with Levine—The Three Tenors Live in Concert—Paris 1998, PBS, 1997.

Merry Christmas from Vienna, 1996.

Film Songs:
"Un ballo in maschera," *La luna* (also known as *Luna*), 1979.

OTHER SOURCES

Books:
Contemporary Hispanic Biography, Volume 1, Gale Group, 2002.

Contemporary Musicians, Volume 20, Gale, 1997.

Dictionary of Hispanic Biography, Gale Research, 1996.

Encyclopedia of World Biography, Gale Research, 1998.

Snowman, Daniel, *The World of Placido Domingo,* McGraw, 1985.

Stefoff, Rebecca, *Placido Domingo,* Chelsea House, 1992.

Periodicals:
Americas, English edition, September/October, 1997, p. 22.

Billboard, August 22, 1998, p. 37.

Opera News, September, 1998, p. 24; December, 1998, p. 86.

DOUG, Doug E. 1970–
(Douglas Bourne)

PERSONAL

Original name, Douglas Bourne; born January 7, 1970, in Brooklyn, NY. *Education:* Attended St. Johns University, Jamaica, NY.

Addresses: *Agent*—Brian Stern, Brillstein Entertainment Partners, 375 Greenwich St., 7th Floor, New York, NY 10013.

Career: Actor, producer, director, and writer. Began career as standup comedian at age seventeen, appearing at the Apollo Theatre, the Comic Strip, and other venues across the United States. Horace E. Greene Day Care Center, Brooklyn, NY, volunteer counselor; once worked as a security guard at offices of National Broadcasting Co.

Member: Screen Actors Guild.

Awards, Honors: Independent Spirit Award nomination, best male lead, Independent Features Project/West, 1992, for *Hangin' with the Homeboys;* Young Artist Award nomination, best youth comedian, 1994, for *Where I Live;* Image Award nominations, outstanding supporting actor in a comedy series, National Association for the Advancement of Colored People, 1998, 1999, 2000, all for *Cosby.*

CREDITS

Film Appearances:
(As Douglas Bourne) Jimmy the busboy, *Mo' Better Blues,* 1989.

Friend of Livin' Large, *Jungle Fever,* Universal, 1991.

Willie Stevens, *Hangin' with the Homeboys,* New Line Cinema, 1991.

Trotter, *Dr. Giggles,* Universal, 1992.

Popsicle, *Class Act,* Warner Bros., 1992.

Sanka Coffie, *Cool Runnings,* Buena Vista, 1993.

Harvey "H. A." Ashford, *Operation Dumbo Drop* (also known as *Dumbo Drop*), Buena Vista, 1995.

Zeke Kelso, *That Darn Cat,* Buena Vista, 1997.

Voice of Turbo the Turtle, *Rusty: A Dog's Tale* (also known as *Rusty: The Great Rescue*), 1997.

Taxi driver, *Everything's Jake,* 1999.

Title role, *Citizen James,* 2000.

Harlan Griffith, *Eight Legged Freaks* (also known as *Arac Attack* and *Spider Panic!*), Warner Bros., 2002.

Voice of Bernie, *Shark Tale* (animated), DreamWorks, 2004.

Leonard Garvey, *Snowmen,* NeMetro Distribution, 2010.

Barry Humfries, *A Novel Romance,* MEGA Films/StudioB, 2010.

Film Producer:
(And director) *Citizen James,* 2000.

Slap the Donkey (documentary), Harlem Edit, 2009.

Television Appearances; Series:
Douglas St. Martin, *Where I Live,* ABC, 1993.

Griffen Vesey, *Cosby,* CBS, 1996–2000.

Also appeared as host, *The New Music Report,* WNBC, and *Rock of Ages,* VH1.

Television Appearances; Specials:
Host, *The Making of "Operation Dumbo Drop,"* The Disney Channel, 1995.
Night of About 14 CBS Stars, Comedy Central, 1996.
Host, *Caribbean Music Awards,* syndicated, 1997.
Host from Milwaukee, *Safe Night USA,* PBS and Black Entertainment Television, 1999.
Reporter from New York City, *The All–American Thanksgiving Parade,* CBS, 1999.
Voice, *The Snow Queen: An Animated Special from the "Happily Ever After: Fairy Tales for Every Child'* Series, HBO, 2000.
Shark Tale: Gettin' Fishy with It, HBO, 2004.
Nicky Lolo, *Wyclef Jean in America,* 2006.
(In archive footage) *I Was a Network Star,* 2006.
Even Scarier Movie Moments, Bravo, 2006.

Television Appearances; Pilots:
Toby James, *Conviction,* NBC, 2006.

Television Appearances; Episodic:
The Chevy Chase Show, 1993.
The Tonight Show with Jay Leno, NBC, 1995.
Oddville, MTV, 1997.
Himself, "Must Kill TV," *Diagnosis Murder* (also known as *Dr. Mark Sloan*), CBS, 1997.
Late Show with David Letterman (also known as *The Late Show* and *Letterman*), CBS, 1997.
The Martin Short Show, syndicated, 1999.
General Dread, "My Spy," *Cosby,* CBS, 1999.
Voice of Percy Mulch, "The Zoo/My Pet Elephant," *Little Bill* (animated), Nickelodeon, 2000.
Ronnie, "Monica's Bad Day," *Touched by an Angel,* CBS, 2000.
Voice of Percy Mulch, "Elephant on the Loose/If a Bird Rings, Answer It," *Little Bill* (animated), Nickelodeon, 2000.
Sesame Street (also known as *The New Sesame Street, Open Sesame,* and *Sesame Street Unpaved*), 2000.
Hollywood Squares (also known as *H2* and *H2: Hollywood Squares*), several appearances, 2000.
Rudy Lemcke, "Criminal," *Law & Order: Special Victims Unit* (also known as *Law & Order: SVU* and *Special Victims Unit*), NBC, 2004.
"'Shark Tale': Gettin' Fishy with It," *HBO First Look,* HBO, 2004.
Life & Style, BBC, 2004.
(Uncredited) Voices of four–year–old kid and dog, "Mindless," *Harvey Birdman, Attorney at Law* (animated), Cartoon Network, 2005.
Contestant, *Celebrity Poker Showdown,* Bravo, 2006.
Voice of bear, "Mongoosed/Mellow Fellows," *My Gym Partner's a Monkey* (animated), Cartoon Network, 2007.
Michael Reed, "Immortal," *Law & Order,* NBC, 2010.

Israel Fandi, "Fire in the Hole," *Justified,* FX Network, 2010.
Israel Fandi, "The Hammer," *Justified,* FX Network, 2010.

According to some sources, appeared as Antoine Jamison in an episode of *The Jury,* Fox, c. 2004.

Television Appearances; Awards Presentations:
Host, *NAACP ACT–SO Awards,* 1998.
Presenter, *The 30th NAACP Image Awards,* Fox, 1999.

Television Work; Series:
Coproducer, *Where I Live,* ABC, 1993.

RECORDINGS

Videos:
A Fishified World, DreamWorks Home Entertainment, 2005.

WRITINGS

Television Series:
Writer for *The New Music Report,* WNBC.

Screenplays:
Citizen James, 2000.

Other:
Contributor to *Spin.*

WRITINGS

Screenplays:
Slap the Donkey (documentary), Harlem Edit, 2009.

OTHER SOURCES

Periodicals:
NEA Today, November, 1998, p. 46.

DOUGHTY, Kenny 1975–

PERSONAL

Born 1975, in Barnsley, England; married Caroline Carver (an actress). *Education:* Graduated from Guildhall School of Music and Drama, 1997.

Addresses: *Agent*—United Agents, 12–26 Lexington St., London W1F 0LE, England. *Manager*—Alan Siegel Entertainment, 345 North Maple Dr., Suite 375, Beverly Hills, CA 90210.

Career: Actor.

Awards, Honors: Palm Beach International Film Festival Award, best actor, for *The Aryan Couple.*

CREDITS

Film Appearances:
Smokey's friend, *I Want You,* Gramercy, 1998.
Sir Thomas Elyot, *Elizabeth* (also known as *Elizabeth: The Virgin Queen*), Gramercy, 1998.
Quintas, *Titus,* Fox Searchlight, 1999.
Denis, *Lover's Prayer* (also known as *All Forgiven*), Seven Hills Productions, 2000.
Jed Willis, *Crush,* Sony Pictures Classics, 2001.
Putting Down the King (short film), 2002.
Nick, *My First Wedding,* Cinema Libre Studio, 2004.
Hans Vassman, *The Aryan Couple* (also known as *The Couple*), Hemdale Film, 2004.
Pitt, *The Great Raid,* Miramax, 2005.
Ratter, *The Crew,* Image Entertainment, 2008.
Olly, *City Rats,* 2009.
Himself, *The Making of "City Rats"* (short documentary), Revolver Entertainment, 2009.
David, *Irreversi,* Bigfoot Entertainment, 2010.
Drake, *I Against I,* Stray Dog Films, 2010.

Also appeared as Ringo, *Don't Stop Dreaming.*

Film Director:
You Me and Captain Longbridge (short film), 2008.

Television Appearances; Series:
William Forrest, *Servants,* BBC, 2003.
Liam Woolf, *Funland,* 2005.
Coll, *Goldplated,* 2006.
Jake Harman, *Coronation Street,* ITV and CBC, 2009.

Television Appearances; Miniseries:
Police constable Simon Lincoln, *The Second Coming,* BBC America, 2003.
Danny Absolon, "The Miller's Tale," *Canterbury Tales,* BBC and BBC America, 2003.

Television Appearances; Movies:
Gus Gascoigne, *Anorak of Fire,* BBC2, 1998.
Young Scrooge, *A Christmas Carol,* TNT, 1999.
Para 027, *Sunday,* 2002.

Jamie Gilliam, *Gifted,* 2003.
Joe Orton, *Kenneth Williams: Fantabulosa!,* BBC4, 2006.

Television Appearances; Episodic:
Barry Hadfield, "Pat–a–Cake," *Heartbeat,* ITV, 1998.
Clint, "Scandal," *Dinnerladies,* BBC, 1998.
Billy, "Reproduction," *Love in the 21st Century,* Channel 4, 1999.
Grant Allen, "Half Man Half Cop," *City Central,* 2000.
Jason, "Shadows Rising: Parts 1 & 2," *Wire in the Blood,* ITV and BBC America, 2002.
Joe Breeley, "Make Believe," *Blue Murder,* 2006.
Mark, *Shameless,* 2008.
Jake, "The Empress's New Clothes," *Fairy Tales,* BBC, 2008.
Neil Mayhew, *Spooks: Code 9,* BBC3, 2008.
Billy Radford, "Shadow Snow," *New Tricks,* BBC, 2009.
Steve, "Regrets," *Casualty,* BBC1, 2009.
Gerry Mortimer, *Paradox,* BBC1, 2009.

Stage Appearances:
Appeared as Paul, *Accomplices,* Crucible Theatre, Sheffield, England; Patroclus, *Troillus and Cressida,* Old Vic Theatre, London; Fred, *Present Laughter,* Royal Exchange Theatre, Manchester, England; Gerard, *Small Change,* Sherman, Cardiff, Wales.

Radio Appearances:
Appeared as Keith, *London Pride,* BBC Radio 4; Freddie, *Mugsborough,* BBC Radio 4.

DOUGLAS, Peter 1955–
      (Peter Vincent Douglas)

PERSONAL

Full name, Peter Vincent Douglas; born November 23, 1955; son of Kirk Douglas (an actor and writer) and Anne Buydens; brother of Eric Douglas (an actor); half brother of Michael Douglas (an actor, director, and producer) and Joel Douglas (a producer, production manager, and director); married Lisa Marie Schoeder (a physiologist), June 15, 1991; children: Kelsey, Tyler, Ryan, Jason. *Education:* Graduate of the Directors Guild of America Training Program; also a licensed civilian pilot.

Addresses: *Office*—Vincent Pictures and Mission Entertainment, PO Box 5066, Santa Barbara, CA 93150. *Agent*—Creative Artists Agency, 2000 Avenue of the Stars, Los Angeles, CA 90067.

Career: Producer, director, writer, and actor. Mission Entertainment, Santa Barbara, CA, founder and president; Vincent Pictures and Mission Entertainment, Santa Barbara, CA, president. Worked as an assistant director and production manager for Columbia Pictures and Rastar Productions.

Member: Alliance of Motion Picture and Television Producers, Directors Guild of America, Writers Guild of America, West, Academy of Motion Picture Arts and Sciences, Academy of Television Arts and Sciences.

Awards, Honors: Emmy Award nomination (with others), outstanding drama or comedy special, 1986, for *Amos;* Emmy Award (with Robert Papazian), outstanding drama or comedy special, 1988, for *Inherit the Wind.*

CREDITS

Film Producer:
(As Peter Vincent Douglas) *The Final Countdown* (also known as *USS Nimitz* and *U.S.S. Nimitz: Lost in the Pacific*), United Artists, 1980.
(As Peter Vincent Douglas) *Something Wicked This Way Comes,* Buena Vista, 1983.
Fletch, Universal, 1985.
A Tiger's Tale, Atlantic Releasing, 1987.
Fletch Lives (also known as *Fletch Saved*), Universal, 1989.
Executive producer, *Whip It* (also known as *Bliss, Derby Girl, Roller Girl, Roller Girls Diary,* and *Whip It!*), Fox Searchlight, 2009.

Worked on other projects.

Film Work; Other:
Postproduction supervisor, *Posse,* Paramount, 1975.
Director, *A Tiger's Tale,* Atlantic Releasing, 1987.

Film Appearances:
(Uncredited) Young boy, *The Vikings* (also known as *Vikings* and *:The Vikings:*), United Artists, 1958.
Quartermaster, *The Final Countdown* (also known as *USS Nimitz* and *U.S.S. Nimitz: Lost in the Pacific*), United Artists, 1980.

Television Producer; Movies:
Amos, CBS, 1985.
Executive producer, *Inherit the Wind,* NBC, 1988.
Executive producer, *The Enemy Within,* HBO, 1994.

Television Appearances; Specials:
Himself, *... A Father ... a Son ... Once upon a Time in Hollywood,* HBO, 2005.

Television Appearances; Awards Presentations:
The Kennedy Center Honors: A Celebration of the Performing Arts (also known as *The Kennedy Center Honors*), CBS, 1994.

Television Appearances; Episodic:
Himself, "Kirk Douglas," *This Is Your Life,* NBC, 1958.
Himself, "Kirk Douglas," *Hollywood Greats* (also known as *The Hollywood Greats*), BBC, 2003.

RECORDINGS

Videos:
Himself, *The Life and Times of Kirk Douglas* (short documentary), Buena Vista Home Entertainment, 2000.

WRITINGS

Screenplays:
A Tiger's Tale (based on the novel *Love and Other Natural Disasters,* by Allen Hannay III), Atlantic Releasing, 1987.

DOW, Ellen Albertini 1918–
(Ellen R. Albertini, Ellen Dow)

PERSONAL

Original name, Ellen R. Albertini; born November 16, 1918, in Mount Carmel, PA; father, a car dealership owner; mother's name, Ellen Albertini; married Eugene Dow (a college theatre teacher, director, writer, and composer), June, 1951 (died October 11, 2004). *Education:* Cornell University, B.F.A., 1935, and M.F.A.; studied dance with Hanya Holm and Martha Graham; studied mime with Marcel Marceau and Macques LeCoq in Paris; studied acting with Michael Shurtleff and Uta Hagen. *Religion:* Roman Catholic. *Avocational Interests:* Collecting hats.

Addresses: *Agent*—Michael Greene, Greene and Associates Talent Agency, 190 North Canon Dr., Suite 202, Beverly Hills, CA 90210.

Career: Actress. Teacher of drama and dance, and director and choreographer of college musicals at Los Angeles City College and Pierce College for more than thirty years, retiring in 1985; Albertini Mime Players, creator and producer for about twenty years; performed as a comedian at Second Avenue Theatre, New York City, and at venues in the Catskill Mountains of New York; performed in summer stock productions in Massachusetts, New York, Pennsylvania, and South Carolina. Appeared in a television commercial for Double Delight Oreo cookies, 2002.

Member: Kappa Delta (sorority).

Awards, Honors: Rockefeller Foundation grant for work as a mime.

CREDITS

Film Appearances:
Allison, *American Drive–in,* 1985.
Old lady, *Tough Guys,* Buena Vista, 1986.
Organist, *Walk Like a Man,* Metro–Goldwyn–Mayer, 1987.
Little old lady, *Munchies,* Metro–Goldwyn–Mayer, 1987.
Organist, *Body Slam,* New Line Home Video, 1987.
Nun, *My Blue Heaven,* Warner Bros., 1990.
Receptionist, *Genuine Risk,* IRS Entertainment, 1990.
Old lady, *Blood and Concrete* (also known as *Blood and Concrete, a Love Story*), IRS Releasing, 1991.
Mrs. Coulson, *Memoirs of an Invisible Man,* Warner Bros., 1992.
Betsy, *Space Case* (also known as *Alien Invasion*), 1992.
Choir nun, *Sister Act,* Buena Vista, 1992.
Choir nun, *Sister Act 2: Back in the Habit,* Buena Vista, 1993.
Mrs. Norton, *Twogether,* 1994.
Radio organist, *Radioland Murders,* Universal, 1994.
Rosie, *The Wedding Singer,* New Line Cinema, 1998.
Disco Dottie, *54* (also known as *Studio 54*), Miramax, 1998.
Aggie Kennedy, *Patch Adams,* Universal, 1998.
Mrs. Meltzer, *Carnival of Souls* (also known as *Wes Craven Presents "Carnival of Souls"*), Trimark Pictures, 1998.
Mrs. MacKenzie, *Ready to Rumble* (also known as *Head Lock Go! Go! Professional Wrestling*), Warner Bros., 2000.
Grandma Manilow, *Road Trip,* DreamWorks, 2000.
Hildegard, *Conundrum,* 2000.
Mrs. Fleisher, *Longshot* (also known as *Jack of All Trades* and *Longshot: The Movie*), 2001.
Voice of See's Candies box, *Eight Crazy Nights* (also known as *Adam Sandler's "Eight Crazy Nights"*), Sony Pictures Entertainment, 2002.
Mrs. Kahn, *Halfway Decent,* 2005.
Grandma Mary Cleary, *Wedding Crashers,* New Line Cinema, 2005.

Mildred, *Fat Girls,* Regent Releasing, 2007.
Anabella, *The Blue Hour,* Orange Bird Productions/ Silver Blue Pictures/Fresco Films, 2007.
Lydia the librarian, *Lonely Street,* Echo Bridge Home Entertainment, 2009.
Mrs. Bessler, *Without a Paddle: Nature's Calling,* 2009.
Natalie Shaw, *The Invited,* Dark Portal/Relativity Media, 2010.
Rose, *Not Another Not Another Movie,* True Fiction Filmz, 2010.

Other film appearances include *Femme Fatale; Mighty Joe Young; The Minus Man;* and *Two Gether.*

Television Appearances; Movies:
Grandma Haldane, *Going to the Chapel* (also known as *Wedding Day* and *Wedding Day Blues*), NBC, 1988.
Lydia, "Things That Go Bump in the Night" (sometimes cited as an episode of *Christine Cromwell*), ABC, 1989.
Lila Duvane, *Problem Child 3* (also known as *Problem Child 3: Junior in Love*), NBC, 1995.
Louise Tette, *Annie's Point,* Hallmark Channel, 2005.

Television Appearances; Episodic:
Mrs. Hotchkiss, "Need to Know," *The Twilight Zone,* CBS, 1986.
Old lady, "Grandma," *Mr. Belvedere,* 1986.
Old woman, "The Storyteller," *The Twilight Zone,* CBS, 1986.
Lady, "A Mother and a Daughter," *Highway to Heaven,* 1987.
(As Ellen Dow) Anna Lausch, "Nor Iron Bars a Cage," *Beauty and the Beast,* 1987.
Mrs. Baer, "Los dos dipestos," *Moonlighting,* 1988.
"The Trip: Part 1," *Mr. Belvedere,* 1988.
Mrs. Leonard, "The Days and Nights of Sophia Petrillo," *The Golden Girls,* CBS, 1988.
Mrs. Crane, "Papa's Big Romance," *Webster,* 1988.
Old woman, "Black Tickets," *Freddy's Nightmares,* 1989.
"In the Still of My Pants," *Hooperman,* 1989.
Lillian, "Sophia's Choice," *The Golden Girls,* CBS, 1989.
Dorothy Benson, "Utley Exposed," *Newhart,* CBS, 1989.
Dorothy Benson, "Good Lord Louden," *Newhart,* 1989.
Miss Gilbert, "The Big Reunion," *Family Matters,* ABC, 1990.
Aunt Belle, "The Bitch's Back," *Murphy Brown,* CBS, 1990.
Tight Lips, "Miss Trial," *Designing Women,* CBS, 1990.
Mrs. Ferguson, "Have Yourself a Very Winslow Christmas," *Family Matters,* ABC, 1990.

Sarah, "Older and Wiser," *The Golden Girls,* NBC, 1991.

"Prisoners of Love," *True Colors,* 1991.

Sadie, "Splendor in the Basement," *True Colors,* 1991.

Jennifer Simpson–Riley, *Jack's Place,* ABC, c. 1991.

Grandma, "Dr. Ruth—April 25, 1985," *Quantum Leap,* NBC, 1992.

Debbie, "The Customer's Usually Right," *Wings,* NBC, 1992.

Mrs. Tambora, "Kevin Delivers," *The Wonder Years,* 1992.

Second woman, *Frannie's Turn,* CBS, 1992.

The old woman, "Atlantic City," *Down the Shore,* Fox, 1992.

The salesclerk, "Damned if You Do," *The Building,* CBS, 1993.

Elderly lady, "Scenes from a Mall," *Family Matters,* ABC, 1993.

Old woman, "Dirty Deeds," *The John Larroquette Show* (also known as *Larroquette*), NBC, 1993.

Emily, *Second Chances,* CBS, c. 1993.

Mrs. Ostendorf, "That's What Friends Are For," *Family Matters,* ABC, 1994.

Mildred, "The Woman Who Came to Dither," *Empty Nest,* NBC, 1994.

Miss Abbington, "It's My Party and I'll Cry if I Want To," *Hearts Afire,* CBS, 1994.

First little old lady, "Baby Blues," *On Our Own,* ABC, 1994.

Felisa M. Howard, "Sub Rosa," *Star Trek: The Next Generation* (also known as *Star Trek: TNG*), syndicated, 1994.

Elderly woman, "Death and Execs," *Cybill,* CBS, 1995.

Mrs. Riblet, "Hell and High Water," *ER,* NBC, 1995.

Momma, "The Secret Code," *Seinfeld,* NBC, 1995.

Betty, "Single White Teenager," *Sister, Sister,* ABC, 1995.

Edna Gunther, "Searching for Sarah Hansen," *The Boys Are Back,* CBS, 1995.

Miss Mae, "One Sorry Mother," *Hope & Gloria,* NBC, 1996.

Mrs. Porter, "Friends and Lovers," *Ned and Stacey,* Fox, 1996.

Mrs. Porter, "New Year's Eve," *Ned and Stacey,* Fox, 1996.

Aunt Ida Watherwax, "A Little Snag," *Sisters,* NBC, 1996.

Mrs. Porter, "The End?," *Ned and Stacey,* Fox, 1996.

Woman, "Something about Cheating," *Something So Right,* 1996.

"Something about a Christmas Miracle," *Something So Right,* 1996.

Craft granny, "Dave Barry, Call Your Agent," *Dave's World,* CBS, 1997.

Old lady, "A River of Candy Corn Runs through It," *Sabrina, the Teenage Witch* (also known as *Sabrina* and *Sabrina Goes to College*), ABC, 1997.

Esther Kettering, "Chapter Seventeen, Year Two," *Murder One,* 1997.

Esther Kettering, "Chapter Eighteen, Year Two," *Murder One,* 1997.

Aunt Connie, "Mystery Lock," *Beyond Belief: Fact or Fiction* (also known as *Beyond Belief*), 1997.

(Uncredited) Mr. Kent's mother, "Fran Gets Shushed," *The Nanny,* 1998.

Lily, "Seems like Old Times," *Suddenly Susan,* NBC, 1998.

Nurse, "Life Is a Beach," *Clueless,* UPN, 1998.

Amelia, "Cause and Effect," *Arli$$,* HBO, 1999.

Flo, "What Ever Happened to Baby Payne?," *Payne,* CBS, 1999.

Flo, "Gossip Checks In and a Cat Checks Out," *Payne,* CBS, 1999.

Flo, "Pacific Ocean Duck," *Payne,* CBS, 1999.

Mrs. Gallo, "Jack Vents," *Just Shoot Me!,* NBC, 1999.

Spooky Eleanor, "Underworld," *Good vs. Evil* (also known as *G vs. E*), USA Network, 2000.

Miss Marie, "The Next Step," *Nikki,* The WB, 2000.

Sylvia Walker, "The Young and the Tactless," *Will & Grace,* NBC, 2001.

Mrs. Powell, "Hold On Tight," *Judging Amy,* CBS, 2001.

Grandma Nan, "March Madness," *Yes, Dear,* CBS, 2003.

Clara Meeks, "Bye, Bye, Miss American Pie," *A Minute with Stan Hooper,* Fox, 2003.

Betty, "My Faith in Humanity," *Scrubs* (also known as *Scrubs: Med School*), NBC, 2005.

Roberta, "Time Flies," *Six Feet Under,* HBO, 2005.

Dottie Arkin, "Whatever Happened to Seymour Magoon?," *Las Vegas,* NBC, 2005.

Gertrude Balboa, "Broke Joy's Fancy Figurine," *My Name Is Earl,* NBC, 2005.

Voice, "Francine's Flashback," *American Dad!* (animated), Fox, 2005.

Voice of elderly woman, "Stewie Loves Lois," *Family Guy* (animated; also known as *Padre de familia*), Fox, 2006.

Mrs. Knapp, "Social Studies & Embarrassment," *Ned's Declassified School Survival Guide,* Nickelodeon, 2006.

Kathrine McCord, "Debt It Be," *Hannah Montana* (also known as *Hannah Montana Forever* and *Secret Idol Hannah Montana*), The Disney Channel, 2006.

Rose, "Let Go, Let Golf," *In Case of Emergency,* ABC, 2007.

Audrey Abruzzi in 2007, "Torn," *Cold Case,* CBS, 2007.

Voice of first old woman, "1600 Candles," *American Dad!* (animated), Fox, 2008.

Emily Rose, "Diamonds Are a Ghoul's Best Friend," *According to Jim,* ABC, 2009.

Also appeared as Mrs. DiNovio in an episode of *Cosby,* CBS; voice for *Out of Jimmy's Head* (animated), Cartoon Network.

Television Appearances; Other:
Mrs. Pitman, *K–9* (pilot), ABC, 1991.
Esther Kettering, *Murder One: Diary of a Serial Killer* (miniseries), ABC, 1997.
Grandma Harriet Krupp, *Maybe It's Me* (series), The WB, 2001–2002.

Stage Appearances; As Ellen R. Albertini:
Dancer, "The Eccentricities of Davey Crockett," and Little Juniper Tree, "Susanna and the Elders," in *Ballet Ballads* (triple–bill; also included "Willie the Weeper"), Maxine Elliott's Theatre, then Music Box Theatre, both New York City, 1948.

Director and choreographer of plays and operas, including productions of *The Beggars Opera,* Carnegie Recital Hall, New York City; *Julius Caesar;* and *The Magic Flute;* also appeared with Interplayers and at Provincetown Playhouse, Provincetown, MA, and Paper Mill Playhouse, Millburn, NJ.

RECORDINGS

Albums:
Sing a Happy Song, 2006.

OTHER SOURCES

Periodicals:
Entertainment Weekly, March 6, 1998, p. 79.

Electronic:
Ellen Albertini Dow Official Site, http://www. ellenalbertinidow.com, September 22, 2010.

DRISCOLL, Eddie

PERSONAL

Career: Actor.

CREDITS

Film Appearances:
Jenny's assistant, *Physical Evidence,* Columbia, 1989.
Paul the Apostle, *Breaking In,* Samuel Goldwyn, 1989.
Courier, *Subterfuge,* Avalanche Home Entertainment, 1996.

Detective, *Ladykiller* (also known as *Scene of the Crime*), Concorde, 1996.
The Pest, TriStar, 1997.
FBI Agent Driscoll, *Pros & Cons,* New Line Home Video, 1999.
Benjamin, *Ground Zero* (also known as *California Quake*), Euro Video, 2000.
Detective North, *NewsBreak,* MTI Home Video, 2000.
Freddie, *Sparkle and Charm,* Independent, 2000.
Security guard, *Dynamite* (also known as *Family under Siege*), 2002.
Bank guard, *Redemption of the Ghost,* Daniel Sladek Entertainment, 2002.
Detective Frank Hagen, *Borderline,* Motion Picture Corporation of America, 2002.
Lewis, *Pavement,* Film Afrika Worldwide, 2002.
Steward, *Boat Trip,* Artisan Entertainment, 2003.
Chuck, *Prey for Rock & Roll,* Mac Releasing, 2003.
Mike, *After School Special* (also known as *National Lampoon's "Barely Legal"*), Barely Legal Productions, 2003.
Crewcut officer, *Cellular,* New Line Cinema, 2004.
Jackson, *Blast,* DEJ Productions, 2005.
Delivery guy, *The Pleasure Drivers,* 2005, Anchor Bay Entertainment, 2007.
Larry Johnson, *The Final Season,* Yari Film Group, 2007.
Big Orange Head, *Life's a Joke* (short film), 2009.

Television Appearances; Movies:
Terry, *Plates,* ABC, 1990.
John, *Not of This Earth,* Showtime, 1995.
Supper Club maitre d', *Lansky,* HBO, 1999.
Detective Davis, *Ghost Dog: A Detective Tail,* PAX, 2003.
Second investigator, *The Meant to Be's,* CBS, 2008.

Television Appearances; Episodic:
Leon, "Forgive Me Father," *Night Heat,* CBS, 1987.
Gavin, "The Bride Wore Red," *Freddy's Nightmares,* syndicated, 1988.
Doug Jackson, "Hooray for Wood," *Evening Shade,* CBS, 1990.
Car salesman, "Royalty," *Tracey Takes On ...,* HBO, 1996.
Fendi man, "Sex and Another City," *Sex and the City* (also known as *S.A.T.C.* and *Sex and the Big City*), HBO, 2000.
John, "Chapter Forty–five," *Boston Public,* Fox, 2002.
Dog catcher, "Multiple Plots," *The King of Queens,* CBS, 2004.
Rick "The Hat" Carver, "Dog Day Afternoons," *Cold Case,* CBS, 2006.
Eddie Diamond, *Days of Our Lives* (also known as *Days* and *DOOL*), NBC, 2005, 2006.

Sergeant Doty, "I Love Sushi," *Drake & Josh,* Nickelodeon, 2006.
Mike, "What about Marjorie …," *What about Brian,* ABC, 2007.
Security station agent, "Day 6: 4:00 p.m.–5:00 p.m.," *24,* Fox, 2007.
First guard, "The Art of Reckoning," *Numb3rs* (also known as *Num3ers*), CBS, 2007.
Hal Weston, "The Thing about Heroes …," *CSI: NY,* CBS, 2007.
Cop, "The Plan," *Dirty Sexy Money,* ABC, 2008.
Adam Dietz, "A Necessary Evil," *Medium,* NBC, 2009.
Airport policeman, "Tailspin," *Eli Stone,* ABC, 2009.
Uniformed officer, "Chapter Eleven 'I Am Sylar,'" *Heroes,* NBC, 2009.
MDPD officer, "In Plane Sight," *CSI: Miami,* CBS, 2009.

Appeared as Officer Petzoldt and as a patrolman in various episodes of *Evening Shade,* CBS.

Television Appearances; Other:
Voice of Smithy, *Rapsittie Street Kids: Believe in Santa,* 2002.

Appeared as Bob in the series *Port Charles,* ABC.

Stage Appearances:
Uncle Ernie, *The Who's Tommy* (musical), Orpheum Theatre, Phoenix, AZ, 2000.
Knute Rockne, *Rockne the Musical,* La Mirada Theatre for the Performing Arts, La Mirada, CA, 2001.

Appeared as Windy, Jim, and backwoodsman, *Show Boat* (musical), Welk Resort Theatre, San Diego, CA; also appeared in regional productions of *Dorian Gray* and *Mephisto.*

E

EISENBERG, Ned 1957–

PERSONAL

Born January 13, 1957, in New York, NY.

Addresses: *Agent*—Richard Schmenner, Paradigm, 360 North Crescent Dr. N., Beverly Hills, CA 90210. *Manager*—Craig Dorfman, Frontline Management, 8265 Sunset Blvd., Suite 310, Los Angeles, CA 90046.

Career: Actor, director, and playwright. Appeared in a television commercial for Budweiser beer. Naked Angels (theatre company), founding member of company; Ensemble Studio Theatre, member of company.

Awards, Honors: DramaLogue Award, 1994, for *Fruits & Nuts;* Drama Desk Award, best ensemble, 2006, for *Awake and Sing!;* Lucille Lortel Award nomination, outstanding lead actor, 2009, for *Othello;* also recipient of a Fox fellowship.

CREDITS

Film Appearances:
Marty, *The Exterminator,* Avco Embassy, 1980.
Eddy, *The Burning* (also known as *Cropsy*), Filmways, 1981.
Israeli prisoner, *The Soldier* (also known as *Codename: The Soldier*), Embassy, 1982.
Lonzini, *Slayground,* Universal, 1983.
Rat game owner, *Deadly Force,* Embassy, 1983.
(Uncredited) Learner driver, *Firstborn* (also known as *Moving In*), Paramount, 1984.
Wink Barnes, *Moving Violations,* Twentieth Century–Fox, 1985.
Piero, *Key Exchange,* Twentieth Century–Fox, 1985.
Rodriguez, *Hiding Out* (also known as *Adult Education*), De Laurentiis Entertainment Group, 1987.
Nick Pirelli, *Air America,* TriStar, 1990.
Fredo Strozzi, *Last Man Standing,* New Line Cinema, 1996.
Brad Lieberman, *Primary Colors* (also known as *Perfect Couple*), Universal, 1998.
Elaine's book party guest, *Celebrity,* Miramax, 1998.
Uncle Pete, *A Civil Action,* Buena Vista, 1998.
Jimmy, *A Whole New Day* (short film), 1999.
Carl, *Snow Days* (also known as *Let It Snow*), Artistic License, 1999.
Mike Blake, *Head of State,* DreamWorks, 2003.
Sally Mendoza, *Million Dollar Baby,* Warner Bros., 2004.
Officer Polnicki, *World Trade Center,* Paramount, 2006.
Joe Rosenthal, *Flags of Our Fathers,* Paramount, 2006.
Morris, *The Dark Fields,* Rogue Pictures/Relativity Media, 2011.

Television Appearances; Series:
Anthony Fanelli, *The Fanelli Boys,* The Nashville Network, 1990.
James Granick, a recurring role, *Law & Order,* NBC, between 1997 and 2009.
Roger Kressler, a recurring role, *Law & Order: Special Victims Unit* (also known as *Law & Order: SVU* and *Special Victims Unit*), NBC, between 1999 and 2010.

Television Appearances; Movies:
Ace, *We're Fighting Back,* CBS, 1981.
Detective Richard Freedman, *A Murderous Affair: The Carolyn Warmus Story* (also known as *The Lovers of Deceit: The Carolyn Warmus Story*), ABC, 1992.
Mickey, *Star Struck,* CBS, 1994.
Emad Salem, *Path to Paradise: The Untold Story of the World Trade Center Bombing* (also known as *Path to Paradise*), HBO, 1997.
Jerry Kleinert, *Exiled* (also known as *Exiled: A Law & Order Movie*), NBC, 1998.

Lepke Buchlater, *Winchell,* HBO, 1998.
Bob Constantine, *Dash and Lilly,* Arts and Entertainment, 1999.
Robert Clifford, *Cheaters,* HBO, 2000.

Television Appearances; Pilots:
For Lovers Only, ABC, 1982.
Al Hattman, *Charlie,* ABC, 1989.
Anthony Fanelli, *The Fanelli Boys,* The Nashville Network, 1990.
Elliot Riis, *The Jury,* Fox, 2004.
Detective Frankie Stein, *The Black Donnellys,* NBC, 2007.

Television Appearances; Specials:
Sobel, *The First Seven Years,* PBS, 1998.
Jimmy, "A Whole New Day" (originally released as a short film), *Stories of Lost Souls,* Cinemax, 2000.

Television Appearances; Episodic:
Frederico Librizzi, "Lombard," *Miami Vice,* NBC, 1985.
Charlie Glide, "Yankee Dollar," *Miami Vice,* NBC, 1986.
Dr. Eisnberg, "Abrams for the Defense," *Crime Story,* NBC, 1986.
Frank Stevens, "Breakpoint," *The Equalizer,* 1986.
"The Rehearsal," *The Equalizer,* 1987.
Sal Castelli, "The Lost Madonna," *Miami Vice,* NBC, 1989.
Frederico Librizzi, "World of Trouble," *Miami Vice,* NBC, 1989.
"Brother's Keeper," *Reasonable Doubts,* NBC, 1992.
Howard Bannister, "Leap of Faith," *L.A. Law,* NBC, 1993.
"Missing," *Time Trax,* syndicated, 1994.
Butler, "Spare Parts," *New York Undercover,* Fox, 1998.
Ariel, "Denial, Anger, Acceptance," *The Sopranos,* HBO, 1999.
Jerry Kleinert, "Payback," *Law & Order: Special Victims Unit* (also known as *Law & Order: SVU* and *Special Victims Unit*), NBC, 1999.
Damien Roth, "20/20 Hindsight," *Wonderland,* ABC, 2000.
Rothberg, "Closure: Part 2," *Law & Order: Special Victims Unit* (also known as *Law & Order: SVU* and *Special Victims Unit*), NBC, 2000.
Danny Sussman, "Shandeh," *Law & Order: Criminal Intent* (also known as *Law & Order: CI*), NBC, 2002.
Vic Davis, "One in the Nuts," *NYPD Blue* (also known as *N.Y.P.D.*), ABC, 2002.
Lawyer, "The House Next Door," *Queens Supreme,* CBS, 2003.
Judge, "Shout," *Whoopi,* NBC, 2003.
Peter Radic/Vukov Regad, "Retribution," *L.A. Dragnet* (also known as *Dragnet*), ABC, 2004.
Burt, "Orphans," *Rescue Me,* FX Network, 2004.
Brad Ellis, "Heart Stopping," *3 lbs.,* 2006.

Artie Ableson, "30," *Law & Order: Criminal Intent* (also known as *Law & Order: CI*), NBC, 2007.
Detective Frankie Stein, "A Stone of the Heart," *The Black Donnellys,* NBC, 2007.
Detective Frankie Stein, "The Black Drop," *The Black Donnellys,* NBC, 2007.
Detective Frankie Stein, "Easy Is the Way," *The Black Donnellys,* NBC, 2007.
Fiske, "Love Hurts," *New Amsterdam,* Fox, 2008.

Also appeared as C. J. in an episode of *Dear John;* and as Frankie, *That's Life.*

Stage Appearances:
Saturninus, *Titus Andronicus,* Theatre for a New Audience, St. Clement's Church Theatre, New York City, 1994.
Ludlow Lowell, "Pal Joey" (concert), *City Center Encores!,* City Center Theatre, New York City, 1995.
Flea, *Antigone in New York,* Vineyard Theatre, New York City, 1996.
Truffaldino, *The Green Bird* (musical), Theatre for a New Audience, New Victory Theatre, New York City, 1996.
Dick, *The Red Address,* Second Stage Theatre, McGinn–Cazale Theatre, New York City, 1997.
Truffaldino, *The Green Bird,* Cort Theatre, New York City, 2000.
King John, *King John,* Theatre for a New Audience, American Place Theatre, New York City, 2000.
Aaron Greidinger, *Meshugah,* Kirk Theatre, New York City, 2003.
Voice of Mr. Dugan, "Crazy Eights," and Max, "Sleep Deprived," *The 24 Hour Plays* (benefit), American Airlines Theatre, New York City, 2003.
Uncle Morty, *Awake and Sing!,* Belasco Theatre, New York City, 2006.
Iago, *Othello,* Theatre for a New Audience, Duke Theatre on Forty–Second Street, New York City, 2009.

Also appeared in "Bloomer Girl," *City Center Encores!,* City Center Theatre, New York City; *The Cherry Orchard; Claus; Dream of a Blacklisted Actor; Fruits and Nuts,* Los Angeles; *Guys and Dolls* (musical), Long Wharf Theatre, New Haven, CT; *Hesh,* Naked Angels; *Midnight & Morning Rain; Middle of Nowhere* (musical),Prince Music Theatre; *Moving Targets,* Vineyard Theatre; *Oliver Twist,* New York City; *Saxophone Music; Street Scene* (musical), Williamstown Theatre Festival, Williamstown, MA; *Three Generations* (musical), John F. Kennedy Center for the Performing Arts, Washinton, DC; *True to You;* and *You Gotta Sing for Your Supper,* Los Angeles.

Major Tours:
Appeared as Uncle Louie, *Lost in Yonkers,* U.S. cities.

Stage Director:
Directed *Acapulco* and *Funky Crazy Boogaloo Boy,* both for Naked Angels; and *Suburban Tango,* Actor's Gang.

RECORDINGS

Videos:
Himself, *Scream Greats, Vol. 1: Tom Savini, Master of Horror Effects,* 1986.

WRITINGS

Stage Plays:
Author of *Fruits and Nuts* and *You Gotta Sing for Your Supper,* both produced in Los Angeles.

EISNER, Michael 1942–
(Michael D. Eisner)

PERSONAL

Full name, Michael Dammann Eisner; born March 7, 1942, in Mount Kisco, NY; son of Lester, Jr. (a lawyer, government administrator, and entrepreneur) and Margaret (a business executive; maiden name, Dammann) Eisner; married Jane Breckenridge (a computer programmer and business advisor), 1967; children: Michael "Breck" (a director), Eric (a producer), Anders. *Education:* Denison University, B.A., 1964. *Religion:* Jewish.

Addresses: *Office*—Tornante Co., 233 South Beverly Dr., Beverly Hills, CA 90212; Eisner Foundation, 9401 Wilshire Blvd., Suite 760, Beverly Hills, CA 90212.

Career: Producer and studio executive. National Broadcasting Co., began as page, 1963, became clerk, 1964; Federal Communications Commission logging clerk, 1964; Columbia Broadcasting System, worked in programming department, mid–1960s; American Broadcasting Companies, assistant to the national vice president in charge of programming, 1966–68, director of program development for the East Coast and manager of television specials and talent, 1968–71, vice president for daytime television programming, 1971–75, director of feature films and program development, 1969, vice president for children's programs, 1972–75, vice president for program planning and development, 1975–76, senior vice president for prime-time production and development for ABC Entertainment, 1976; Paramount Pictures, president and chief

operating officer, 1976–84; Walt Disney Co., Burbank, CA, board chair, 1984–c. 2003, chief executive officer, 1984–c. 2005, board member, 2005; Tornante Co. (animation venture capital group), Beverly Hills, CA, founder and chief executive officer, 2005—. Eisner Foundation, founder, 1996; Veoh Networks (Internet broadcasting company), member of board of directors, 2006; Vuguru, chair; Global Business Dialogue on Electronic Commerce, member of business steering committee. Member of board of trustees, Denison University and California Institute of the Arts; University of California, Los Angeles, member of executive board for medical science; Mighty Ducks of Anaheim (professional hockey team; also known as Anaheim Ducks), member of board of governors, 1993; also board member, American Film Institute, Conservatives International, American Hospital of Paris Foundation, Performing Arts Council of the Los Angeles Music Center, and Sega Enterprises (amusement game manufacturer).

Awards, Honors: Named advertising executive of the year, *Advertising Age,* 1988; IRTS Gold Medal Award, 1992; James A. Doolittle Award, for leadership in theatre, L.A. Ovation Awards, 2000, for work at Walt Disney Co.; named pioneer of the year, Will Rogers Motion Picture Pioneers Foundation, 2003; received star on Hollywood Walk of Fame, 2008.

CREDITS

Television Appearances; Series:
Host, *Conversations with Michael Eisner,* CNBC, 2006, 2007, 2008.

Host of various incarnations of the series originally known as *Disneyland;* under Eisner's tenure known as *Disney Sunday Movie, The Magical World of Disney,* and *The Wonderful World of Disney,* among other variations, between 1986 and 1997.

Television Appearances; Specials:
The Making of "Captain Eo," 1986.
Mickey's 60th Birthday (also known as *Mickey's 60th Birthday Anniversary Shorts Programme*), 1988.
Jungle Book Reunion, 1990.
Disneyland's 35th Anniversary Celebration, 1990.
The Best of Disney: 50 Years of Magic, ABC, 1991.
Host, *The Dream Is Alive: The 20th Anniversary Celebration of Walt Disney World* (also known as *Walt Disney World's 20th Anniversary Celebration*), CBS, 1991.
The Grand Opening of Euro Disney, 1992.
The Wonderful World of Disney: 40 Years of Television Magic, ABC, 1994.
Beauty and the Beast: The Broadway Musical Comes to L.A. (also known as *Disney's "Beauty and the Beast: The Broadway Musical Comes to L.A."*), 1995.

Leaders with David Faber, CNBC, 2001.
Disney's California Adventure TV Special, The Disney Channel, 2001.
Intimate Portrait: Cindy Williams, Lifetime, 2001.
(In archive footage) "Times Square," *Modern Marvels,* 2001.
Presenter, *ABC 50th Anniversary Celebration,* ABC, 2003.
The Pixar Story, Starz!, 2008.

Television Appearances; Episodic:
Larry King Live, Cable News Network, 1996.
The Rosie O'Donnell Show, syndicated, 1998.
Himself, "Home Alone," *Home Improvement,* ABC, 1999.
ABC News Nightline, ABC, 2004.
Live with Regis and Kelly, syndicated, 2005.
The View, ABC, 2005.
The Tony Danza Show, syndicated, 2005.
Charlie Rose (also known as *The Charlie Rose Show*), PBS, 2005, 2006.
(In archive footage) *The O'Reilly Factor,* Fox News Channel, 2008.

Also appeared in *American Cinema,* PBS.

Television Appearances; Awards Presentations:
The Television Academy Hall of Fame, Fox, 1987.
Fourth Annual Environmental Media Awards, TBS, 1994.
Presenter, *The 10th Annual Television Academy Hall of Fame,* The Disney Channel, 1994.
The 2nd Annual Family Television Awards, CBS, 2000.

Television Appearances; Other:
Host, "Polly" (movie), *The Magical World of Disney,* NBC, 1989.
Broadway: The American Musical, PBS, 2004.

Television Work; Series:
Producer, *Conversations with Michael Eisner,* CNBC, 2006, 2007, 2008.
Executive producer, *Prom Queen,* 2007.
Executive producer, *Foreign Body,* 2008.
Creator and executive producer, *Glenn Martin DDS,* Nickelodeon, 2009.
Executive producer, *The Booth at the End,* 2010.

Also creative producer of the series *Schoolhouse Rock* (also known as *ABC Schoolhouse Rock, America Rock, Grammar Rock, Multiplication Rock,* and *Science Rock*), ABC.

Film Appearances; Documentaries:
Michael & Mickey, 1991.
Junket Whore, 1998.

Sketches of Frank Gehry, Sony Pictures Classics, 2005.
Waking Sleeping Beauty, Walt Disney, 2009.

RECORDINGS

Videos:
(As Michael D. Eisner) *Tale as Old as Time: The Making of "Beauty and the Beast,"* 2002.
Treasures Untold: The Making of Disney's "The Little Mermaid," Buena Vista Home Entertainment, 2006.
Disneyland: Secrets, Stories & Magic, Walt Disney Studios Home Entertainment, 2007.

WRITINGS

Books:
(With Tony Schwartz) *Work in Progress: Risking Failure* (autobiography), Random House, 1988.
Camp (nonfiction), 2005.

OTHER SOURCES

Books:
Business Leader Profiles for Students, Volume 2, Gale, 2002.
Eisner, Michael, and Tony Schwartz, *Work in Progress: Risking Failure,* Random House, 1988.
Encyclopedia of World Biography Supplement, Volume 19, Gale, 1999.
Gale Encyclopedia of U.S. Economic History, Gale, 1999.
Masters, Kim, *The Keys to the Kingdom: How Michael Eisner Lost His Grip,* William Morrow, 2000.

Periodicals:
Broadcasting & Cable, August 10, 2009, p. 3.
Economist, July 26, 2003, p. 59.
Esquire, April, 2009, p. 122.
Forbes Global, October 17, 2005, p. 18.
Harvard Business Review, January, 2000, p. 115.
Newsweek, June 2, 2003, p. 40.
New York Times, March 3, 2008, pp. C1, C8; October 26, 2009, p. B3.
Parade, November 15, 1987.
USA Today, February 5, 2007, p. 3B; March 12, 2007, p. 3B; November 5, 2007, p. 5b.
Variety, September 28, 1998, p. 1.

ENGVALL, Bill 1957–

PERSONAL

Full name, William Ray Engvall, Jr.; born July 27, 1957, in Galveston, TX; son of William Ray Engvall (a public health service doctor); married Mary Gail Watson, December 18, 1982; children: Emily, Travis.

Addresses: *Agent*—Paradigm, 360 North Crescent Dr. N., Beverly Hills, CA 90210. *Manager*—J. P. Williams, Parallel Entertainment, 9420 Wilshire Blvd., Suite 250, Beverly Hills, CA 90210.

Career: Comedian, actor, producer, and writer. Blue Collar Comedy, member of company and performer on tour, 2000–09. Worked as a radio disc jockey in Dallas, TX; also performed as a standup comic at Dallas Comedy Corner.

Awards, Honors: American Comedy Award, funniest male standup comic, 1992; gold record certification (with Travis Tritt), Recording Industry Association of America, 1997, for the single "Here's Your Sign (Get the Picture)"; platinum record certification, Recording Industry Association of America, and award from National Association of Recording Merchandisers, bestselling album, 1997, both for *Here's Your Sign;* Grammy Award nomination, National Academy of Recording Arts and Sciences, c. 2006, for soundtrack recording of *Blue Collar Comedy Tour: One for the Road.*

CREDITS

Television Appearances; Series:
Buck Overton, *Delta,* ABC, 1992–93.
Bill Pelton, *The Jeff Foxworthy Show,* NBC, 1996–97.
Host, *TNN Sofa Cinema,* The Nashville Network, 1999–2000.
Blue Collar TV, The WB, 2004–2006.
Host, *Country Fried Home Videos,* Country Music Television, 2006.
Bill Pearson, *The Bill Engvall Show,* TBS, 2007–2009.
Country Fried Planet, Country Music Television, 2008.

Television Appearances; Specials:
A Pair of Jokers with Rosie O'Donnell & Bill Engvall, Showtime, 1989.
The Comedy Concert Hour, The Nashville Network, 1990.
Showtime Comedy Club All–Stars VI, Showtime, 1992.
Komedy All Stars, syndicated, 1993.
Host, *Wildhorse Concert Series Starring Radney Foster,* The Nashville Network, 1994.
Host, *American Originals,* 1997.
Host, *CMT Labor Day Top 100,* Country Music Television, 1997.
Host, *CMA Awards Backstage Pass,* pay–per–view, 1999.
Host, *Country Weekly Magazine Presents the TNN Music Awards Preview,* The Nashville Network, 2000.
CMT: 40 Greatest Fashion Statements, Country Music Television, 2003.

Bill Engvall: Here's Your Sign Live, Comedy Central, 2004.
Blue Comedy Tour Rides Again, 2004.
Boyz in the Woodz, The WB, 2004.
Last Laugh '04 (also known as *Comedy Central's Last Laugh '04*), Comedy Central, 2004.
VH1 Big in '04, VH1, 2004.
Mobile Home Disaster, The WB, 2005.
50 Hottest Vegas Moments, E! Entertainment Television, 2005.
Comedy Central Roast of Jeff Foxworthy, Comedy Central, 2005.
The Ron White Show, The WB, 2005.
Host, *CMT: 20 Sexiest Videos of 2005,* Country Music Television, 2005.
Blue Collar Comedy Summer Special, Comedy Central, 2006.
Blue Collar Comedy Tour: One for the Road, Comedy Central, 2006.
Redneck Comedy Roundup 2, Fox, 2006.
Henry Cho: What's That Clickin' Noise?, Comedy Central, 2006.
CMT: The Greatest—20 Greatest Country Comedy Shows, Country Music Television, 2006.
Bill Engvall: 15 Degrees Off Cool, Comedy Central, 2007.
Host, *Blue Collar Comedy: The Next Generation,* TBS, 2007.
Bill Engvall: Here's Your Sign Awards, Country Music Television, 2008.
Larry the Cable Guy's Star–Studded Christmas Extravaganza, Country Music Television, 2008.
Grand marshal of race, *2008 NASCAR Lifelock 400,* TBS, 2008.
Comedy Central Roast of Larry the Cable Guy, Comedy Central, 2009.
2009 CMT Music Awards Live Red Carpet Special, Country Music Television, 2009.
Bill Engvall: Aged & Confused, Comedy Central, 2009.
Blue Collar Comedy: Ten Years of Funny, Country Music Television, 2010.

Television Appearances; Movies:
Bill Dugan, *Bait Shop,* USA Network, 2008.

Television Appearances; Episodic:
Comedian challenger, *Star Search,* syndicated, 1984.
Bill, "Tough Enough," *Designing Women,* CBS, 1990.
Matthew Devereaux, "Say Goodbye, Rose," *The Golden Palace,* CBS, 1993.
Guest host, *Prime Time Country,* The Nashville Network, 1997.
Just for Laughs (also known as *Ed Byrne's "Just for Laughs,"* Just for Laughs Comedy Festival, and *Just for Laughs Montreal Comedy Festival*), CBC, 2003.
Balderdash, I Network, 2004.
Weekends at the DL, Comedy Central, 2005.

Voice of Duke Dillon, "Boys Do Cry," *Family Guy* (animated; also known as *Padre de familia*), Fox, 2007.

Celebrity judge, *Wanna Bet?*, ABC, c. 2007.

Contestant, "Bill Engvall vs. Larry the Cable Guy, Vivica A. Fox vs. Mo'Nique," *Celebrity Family Feud*, NBC, 2008.

Celebrity volunteer, *Extreme Makeover: Home Edition*, ABC, c. 2009.

CMT Insider, Country Music Television, 2009, 2010.

"The Boost Job," *Leverage*, TNT, 2010.

Hosted an episode of *Evening at the Improv*, Arts and Entertainment; also appeared in episodes of *London Underground*, Comedy Central, and *The Test*, FX Network.

Television Talk Show Guest Appearances; Episodic:

The Tonight Show with Jay Leno, NBC, multiple appearances, between 1992 and 2008.

The Rosie O'Donnell Show, syndicated, 1997.

Dennis Miller, CNBC, 2005.

Tavis Smiley, PBS, 2007.

The View, ABC, 2008.

The Late Late Show with Craig Ferguson, CBS, 2008.

The Tonight Show with Conan O'Brien, NBC, 2009.

Late Night with Jimmy Fallon, NBC, 2009.

Lopez Tonight, TBS, 2009.

The Bonnie Hunt Show, NBC, 2010.

Television Appearances; Awards Presentations:

The 32nd Annual Academy of Country Music Awards, NBC, 1997.

Presenter, *The ... Annual Academy of Country Music Awards*, CBS, 1998, 1999, 2000, 2003, 2004.

Presenter, *TNN Music City News Country Awards*, The Nashville Network, 1998, 1999.

Presenter, *Country Weekly Magazine Presents the TNN Music Awards*, The Nashville Network, 2000.

Presenter, *The CMT Music Awards*, Country Music Television, 2005.

Host, *2009 CMT Music Awards*, Country Music Television, 2009.

(In archive footage) *Best of CMT Music Awards*, Country Music Television, 2009.

Television Appearances; Other:

Panelist, *You Lie like a Dog* (miniseries), Animal Planet, 2000.

I Love the '90s: Part Deux (miniseries), VH1, 2005.

Host, *Trust Me, I'm a Game Show Host* (pilot), ABC, 2010.

Television Work; Series:

Producer, *Country Fried Home Videos*, Country Music Television, 2006.

Creator and executive producer, *The Bill Engvall Show*, TBS, 2007–2009.

Television Executive Producer; Specials:

Mobile Home Disaster, The WB, 2005.

Bill Engvall: 15 Degrees Off Cool, Comedy Central, 2007.

Blue Collar Comedy: The Next Generation, TBS, 2007.

Bill Engvall: Aged & Confused, Comedy Central, 2009.

Television Producer; Specials:

Bill Engvall: Here's Your Sign Awards, Country Music Television, 2008.

Film Appearances:

Student, *Split Image* (also known as *Captured*), Orion, 1982.

Second photographer, *Not for Publication*, Samuel Goldwyn, 1984.

Bill Little, *Delta Farce*, Lions Gate Films, 2007.

Bill, *Cowboy Dreams* (short film), Locked Horns Productions/Ronalds Brothers Films/University of Advancing Technology, 2009.

Mr. Mendelson, *All's Faire in Love*, On Pictures, 2009, Metro–Goldwyn–Mayer Home Entertainment, 2011.

Pete Sullivan, *Bed & Breakfast*, BB Film Productions, 2010.

RECORDINGS

Comedy Albums:

Here's Your Sign, Warner Bros., 1996.

Dorkfish, Warner Bros., 1998.

Here's Your Christmas Album, Warner Bros., 1999.

Now That's Awesome!, BMG, 2000.

(With others) *The Blue Collar Comedy Tour: Live*, Copyright.net, 2000.

(Contributor) *Favorite Country Duets: Volume 2*, Warner Bros., 2000.

Cheap Drunk: An Autobiography, Warner Bros., 2002.

Here's Your Sign: Reloaded, Warner Bros., 2003.

A Decade of Laughs, Warner Bros., 2003.

(With others) *The Blue Collar Comedy Tour, the Movie*, Warner Bros./Gaylord, 2003.

(With others) *Blue Collar Comedy Tour Rides Again*, Warner Bros., 2004.

(With others) *Blue Collar Comedy Tour: One for the Road*, two volumes, Warner Bros., 2006.

15 Degrees Off Cool, Warner Bros., 2007.

Aged and Confused, Warner Bros., 2009.

Singles include "Here's Your Sign (Get the Picture)," c. 1996, and "Redneck 12 Days of Christmas," 2003.

Videos:
Blue Collar Comedy Tour: The Movie, Warner Bros., 2003.
(Contributor) *A Decade of Laughs,* 2004.
Redneck Comedy Roundup, 2005.
Bill Little, *The Men of Delta Farce Salute the Troops,* Lions Gate Films Home Entertainment, 2007.
All the Way to ... LA?, Lions Gate Films Home Entertainment, 2007.
Hacienda Confidential, THINKFilm, 2007.
15 Degrees Off Cool, 2007.
Aged and Confused, Warner Bros., 2009.

Recorded the music videos "Here's Your Sign (Get the Picture)."

Audio Books:
Reader, *Just a Guy: Notes from a Blue Collar Life,* by Bill Engvall and Alan Eisenstock, Audio Renaissance, 2007.

WRITINGS

Books:
(With David Brown) *You Don't Have to Be Dumb to Be Stupid,* Longstreet Press, 1997.
Here's Your Sign!, illustrated by Bill Ross, Rutledge Hill Press, 2005.
(With Alan Eisenstock) *Just a Guy: Notes from a Blue Collar Life,* St. Martin's Griffin, 2007.

Television Series:
Blue Collar TV, The WB, 2004–2006.

Television Specials:
Bill Engvall: Here's Your Sign Live, Comedy Central, 2004.
Blue Comedy Tour Rides Again, 2004.
Blue Collar Comedy Tour: One for the Road, Comedy Central, 2006.
Bill Engvall: 15 Degrees Off Cool, Comedy Central, 2007.
Bill Engvall: Aged & Confused, Comedy Central, 2009.

Television Episodes:
"Feel Free to Say No," *The Bill Engvall Show,* TBS, 2007.

Videos:
Blue Collar Comedy Tour: The Movie, Warner Bros., 2003.

OTHER SOURCES

Books:
Engvall, Bill, and Alan Eisenstock, *Just a Guy: Notes from a Blue Collar Life,* St. Martin's Griffin, 2007.
Newsmakers, Issue 1, Gale, 2010.

Periodicals:
TV Guide, August 27, 2007, p. 58.

Electronic:
Bill Engvall Official Site, http://www.billengvall.com, September 6, 2010.

ESPOSITO, Jennifer 1973–

PERSONAL

Born April 11, 1973, in New York, NY; daughter of Bob (a music producer and computer consultant) and Phyllis (an interior decorator) Esposito; married Bradley Cooper (an actor), December 30, 2006 (divorced, 2007). *Education:* Studied acting at Lee Strasberg Institute (some sources cite Actors Studio), New York City.

Addresses: *Agent*—Paradigm, 360 North Crescent Dr. N., Beverly Hills, CA 90210; (voice work and commercials), Alix Gucovsky, Special Artists Agency, 9465 Wilshire Blvd., Suite 470, Beverly Hills, CA 90212. *Manager*—Kathy Atkinson, Washington Square Arts and Films, 310 Bowery, 2nd Floor, New York, NY 10012.

Career: Actress. Appeared in advertisements for Bongo jeans and Chevy Malibu autos, 2007, and in commercials for Swiffer cleaning products, 2004. Formerly worked as a waitress.

Awards, Honors: Gotham Award nomination, 2005, Screen Actors Guild Award, Black Reel Award, and (according to some sources) Broadcast Film Critics Association Award, all best ensemble cast (with others), 2006, all for *Crash.*

CREDITS

Film Appearances:
Donna Delgrosso, *A Brooklyn State of Mind,* Miramax, 1997.
Lucy, *A Brother's Kiss,* First Look Pictures Releasing, 1997.
Debbie, *Kiss Me, Guido,* Paramount, 1997.
Teresa, *No Looking Back* (also known as *Long Time, Nothing New*), Gramercy, 1997.
Nancy, *I Still Know What You Did Last Summer* (also known as *Last Summer*), Sony Pictures Entertainment, 1998.
Ms. Janus, *He Got Game* (also known as *Last Game*), Buena Vista, 1998.
Jessica, *Side Streets,* Cargo Films, 1998.

Michelle, *Just One Time* (short film), First Look Pictures Releasing, 1998, later included in *Boys Life 3*, Strand Releasing, 2000.

Michelle, *Just One Time* (feature film; expanded version of short film of the same title), 1999.

Ruby, *Summer of Sam*, Buena Vista, 1999.

Daphne, *The Bachelor* (also known as *Propose*), New Line Cinema, 1999.

Solina, *Dracula 2000* (also known as *Dracula 2001* and *Wes Craven Presents "Dracula 2000"*), Dimension Films, 2000.

Susan Reese, *The Proposal*, Curb Entertainment, 2001.

(Uncredited) Club girl, *Made*, Artisan Entertainment, 2001.

Detective Sandra Cassidy, *Don't Say a Word* (also known as *Sound of Silence*), Twentieth Century–Fox, 2001.

Olive Dee "Harley" Klintucker, *Backflash*, Paragon Film Group, 2001.

Carmela, *Welcome to Collinwood*, Warner Bros., 2002.

Jennifer Baker, *The Master of Disguise*, Sony Pictures Entertainment, 2002.

Helena Toretti, *Beyond the City Limits* (also known as *Rip It Off*), Spartan Home Entertainment, 2002.

Frankie Vitello, *Jesus, Mary and Joey* (also known as *Welcome Back Miss Mary*), 2003, Panorama Entertainment, 2006.

Rita Monroe, *Breakin' All the Rules*, Screen Gems, 2004.

Lieutenant Marta Robbins, *Taxi*, Twentieth Century–Fox, 2004.

Ria, *Crash*, Lions Gate Films, 2005.

Joanna, *Conspiracy*, Stage 6 Films, 2008.

Carlos, *American Crude*, Sony Pictures Home Entertainment, 2008.

Suzanne, *Four Single Fathers*, Indiana Production, 2009.

Television Appearances; Series:

Connie Soleito, *The City* (sequel to *Loving*), ABC, 1995–97.

Stacey Paterno, *Spin City* (also known as *Spin*), ABC, 1997–99.

Tanzy, *All My Children*, ABC, 1998.

Louann "Crystal" Turner, a recurring role, *Judging Amy*, CBS, 2004–2005.

Ginnie Sorelli, *Related*, The WB, 2005–2006.

Nona, *Rescue Me*, FX Network, 2007.

Andrea Belladonna, *Samantha Who?*, ABC, 2007–2009.

The Broadroom, 2009.

Jackie Curatola, *Blue Bloods*, CBS, 2010—.

Appeared as a dancer on *Club MTV*, MTV.

Television Appearances; Movies:

Jeannie, *The Sunshine Boys* (also known as *Neil Simon's "The Sunshine Boys"*), CBS, 1997.

Partners and Crime, 2003.

Pilar, *Snow Wonder*, CBS, 2005.

Sarah Fischer, *The Wish List*, Hallmark Channel, 2010.

Television Appearances; Pilots:

Sheila Leary, *Violent Crime*, CBS, 2003.

Ginnie Sorelli, *Related*, The WB, 2005.

Patience More, *More, Patience*, Fox, 2006.

Andrea Belladonna, *Samantha Who?*, ABC, 2007.

Television Appearances; Specials:

Presenter, *The 11th Annual Critics' Choice Awards*, The WB, 2006.

Big Night of Stars (also known as *Jimmy Kimmel's Big Night of Stars*), ABC, 2008.

Presenter, *The 35th Annual People's Choice Awards*, CBS, 2009.

Television Appearances; Episodic:

Gina Tucci, "Good Girl," *Law & Order*, NBC, 1996.

Flo, "Crash and Burn," *Feds*, 1997.

Gina Stone, "Spare Parts," *New York Undercover*, Fox, 1998.

Gina Stone, "Mob Streets," *New York Undercover*, Fox, 1998.

Gina Stone, "Signs o' the Times," *New York Undercover*, Fox, 1998.

Sara Logan, "Remorse," *Law & Order: Special Victims Unit* (also known as *Law & Order: SVU* and *Special Victims Unit*), NBC, 2000.

Abby Banks, "Obsession," *Hack*, CBS, 2002.

Justine Bailey, "In Vino Veritas," *Law & Order*, NBC, 2006.

Dancing with the Stars (also known as *D.W.T.S.*), ABC, 2007.

Access Hollywood, syndicated, 2008.

Jules Fattore, "Too Much Attitude and Not Enough Underwear," *Mercy*, NBC, 2010.

Jules Fattore, "That Crazy Bitch Was Right," *Mercy*, NBC, 2010.

According to some sources, appeared as Michelle Paxon in an episode of *Burn Notice*, USA Network.

Television Talk Show Guest Appearances; Episodic:

Late Night with Conan O'Brien, NBC, multiple appearances, between 1999 and 2007.

The Tonight Show with Jay Leno, NBC, 2001.

Movie House, 2002.

Late Show with David Letterman (also known as *The Late Show* and *Letterman*), NBC, 2002.

The Late Late Show with Craig Kilborn (also known as *The Late Late Show*), CBS, 2002.

Last Call with Carson Daly, NBC, 2003, 2004.

Dinner for Five, Independent Film Channel, 2004.

The Tony Danza Show, syndicated, 2004, 2005.

Jimmy Kimmel Live!, ABC, 2007.

Live with Regis and Kelly, syndicated, 2007.

The Late Late Show with Craig Ferguson, CBS, 2007, 2008.

The Bonnie Hunt Show, NBC, 2008.

The View, ABC, 2008.

Also appeared in the series *Anytime with Bob Kushell.*

Stage Appearances:

XXX Love Act, Ohio Theatre, New York City, 1995.

Painting X's on the Moon, Crane Theatre, New York City, 1995.

Renee and waitress, *Dark Rapture,* Second Stage Theatre, New York City, 1996.

Bob, "Notes on Camping," *The 24 Hour Plays 2008* (benefit performance), American Airlines Theatre, New York City, 2008.

RECORDINGS

Videos:

The Magic of Disguise, Columbia TriStar Home Entertainment, 2003.

Identity Crisis: The Making of a Master, Columbia TriStar Home Entertainment, 2003.

Welcome to Collinwood: Uncensored, Warner Home Video, 2003.

OTHER SOURCES

Periodicals:

Brandweek, January 18, 1999, p. 5.

InStyle, December, 2000, pp. 353–56.

Us, February, 1999.

F

FELLNER, Eric 1960–

PERSONAL

Born 1960 in the United Kingdom; married Gaby Dellal (an actress; divorced); children: (from marriage) three; (with Laura Bailey) Luc, additional child. *Education:* Attended Guildhall School of Music and Drama.

Addresses: *Office*—Working Title Films/Working Title Television, 26 Aybrook St., London W1U 4AN, England; British Film Institute, 21 Stephen St., London W1T 1LN, England.

Career: Producer. Working Title Films, founder and cochairman (with Tim Bevan), 1992—; Working Title Television, London, cochairman; Working Title 2 (with Bevan), founder, 2000. British Film Institute, London, England, member of board of directors, and governor, 2003—.

Awards, Honors: Alexander Korda Award nomination (with others), best British film, British Academy of Film and Television Arts, 1998, for *The Borrowers;* Bronze Wrangler (with others), theatrical motion picture, Western Heritage Awards, 1999, for *The Hi–Lo Country;* Academy Award nomination (with others), best picture, ALFS Award (with others), British producer of the year, London Critics Circle Film Awards, Australia Film Institute Award nomination, best foreign film, Film Award nomination (with others), best film, and Alexander Korda Award (with others), best British film, British Academy of Film and Television Arts, Golden Satellite nomination (with others), best motion picture— drama, International Press Academy, 1999, all for *Elizabeth;* European Film Award nomination (with others), best film, 2001, Alexander Korda Award nomination (with others), best British film, British Academy of

Film and Television Arts, 2002, both for *Bridget Jones's Diary;* Alexander Korda Award nomination (with others), best British film, British Academy of Film and Television Arts, 2004, for *Love Actually;* decorated Commander of the Order of the British Empire, 2005; Special Award (with Tim Bevan), *Evening Standard* British Film Awards, 2005; Special Award (with Bevan), Empire Awards, 2005; Alexander Korda Award nomination (with others), best British film, British Academy of Film and Television Arts, 2006, for *Pride & Prejudice;* ALFS Award (with others), British producer of the year, London Critics Circle Film Awards, 2007, for *United 93;* Academy Award nomination, best motion picture of the year, Film Award (with others), best film, and Film Award nomination (with others), best British film, British Academy of Film and Television Arts, 2008, both for *Atonement;* Academy Award nomination, best motion picture of the year, Film Award nomination (with others), best film, British Academy of Film and Television Arts, Motion Picture Producer of the Year Award nomination (with other), theatrical motion pictures, Producers Guild of America, 2009, both for *Frost/ Nixon;* Tribute Award (with Bevan), Gotham Awards, 2009.

CREDITS

Film Producer:
Sid and Nancy, New Line Cinema, 1986.
Straight to Hell, Island Pictures, 1987.
Pascali's Island, Avenue Entertainment, 1988.
Hidden Agenda, Hemdale Film, 1990.
Liebestraum, Metro–Goldwyn–Mayer, 1991.
Wild West, Samuel Goldwyn Company, 1992.
No Worries, 1994.
French Kiss, Twentieth Century–Fox, 1995.
Moonlight and Valentino, Gramercy, 1995.
Loch Ness, Gramercy, 1996.
Bean (also known as *Bean: The Movie* and *Bean: The Ultimate Disaster Movie*), Gramercy, 1997.
The MatchMaker, Gramercy, 1997.

The Borrowers, PolyGram Filmed Entertainment, 1997.

What Rats Won't Do, PolyGram Filmed Entertainment, 1998.

Elizabeth (also known as *Elizabeth: The Virgin Queen*), Gramercy, 1998.

The Hi–Lo Country, Gramercy, 1998.

Plunkett & Macleane, USA Films, 1999.

Bridget Jones's Diary, Miramax, 2001.

Captain Corelli's Mandolin, Universal, 2001.

40 Days and 40 Nights, Miramax, 2002.

Ali G Indahouse, Universal Focus, 2002.

About a Boy, Universal, 2002.

The Guru, Universal, 2002.

Johnny English, Universal, 2003.

Love Actually, Universal, 2003.

The Calcium Kid, Universal, 2004.

Thunderbirds, Universal, 2004.

Wimbledon, Universal, 2004.

Bridget Jones: The Edge of Reason, Universal, 2004.

The Interpreter, Universal, 2005.

Pride & Prejudice, Focus Features, 2005.

Nanny McPhee, Universal, 2005.

United 93, Universal, 2006.

Catch a Fire, Focus Features, 2006.

Sixty Six, First Independent Pictures, 2006.

Smokin' Aces, Universal, 2006.

Hot Fuzz, Rogue Pictures, 2007.

Mr. Bean's Vacation (also known as *Mr. Bean's Holiday*), Universal, 2007.

Atonement, Focus Features, 2007.

Elizabeth: The Golden Age (also known as *Elizabeth: Golden Age*), Universal, 2007.

Definitely, Maybe (also known as *Love Diaries*), Universal, 2008.

Wild Child, Universal, 2008.

Burn After Reading, Focus Features, 2008.

Frost/Nixon, Universal, 2008.

The Boat That Rocked (also known as *Pirate Radio* and *Pirates Rock*), Focus Features, 2009.

State of Play, Universal, 2009.

Senna (documentary), 2010.

Green Zone, Universal, 2010.

Nanny McPhee Returns (also known as *Nanny McPhee and the Big Bang*), Universal, 2010.

Hippie Hippie Shake, Universal, 2010.

Paul, Universal, 2010.

Film Executive Producer:

The Rachel Papers, United Artists, 1989.

A Kiss Before Dying, Universal, 1991.

Year of the Gun, Triumph, 1991.

Posse, 1993.

Romeo Is Bleeding, Gramercy, 1993.

The Hawk, Castle Hill, 1993.

Four Weddings and a Funeral, Gramercy, 1994.

The Hudsucker Proxy, Warner Bros., 1994.

Panther, Gramercy, 1995.

Dead Man Walking, Gramercy, 1995.

Fargo, Gramercy, 1996.

The Big Lebowski, Gramercy, 1998.

Notting Hill, Universal, 1999.

O Brother, Where Art Thou? (also known as *Oh, Brother!*), Buena Vista, 2000.

The Man Who Cried, Universal Focus, 2000.

The Man Who Wasn't There, USA Films, 2001.

Long Time Dead, Focus Features, 2002.

My Little Eye, Focus Features, 2002.

The Shape of Things, USA Films, 2002.

Thirteen, Twentieth Century–Fox, 2003.

Ned Kelly (also known as *Ned Kelly: Public Enemy No. 1*), Focus Features, 2003.

The Italian Job, Paramount, 2003.

Getting' Square, Universal, 2003.

Shaun of the Dead, Focus Features, 2004.

Mickybo and Me (also known as *Mickybo & Me*), Universal, 2004.

Rory O'Shea Was Here (also known as *Inside I'm Dancing*), Focus Features, 2004.

Naming No. 2, Cyan Pictures, 2006.

Gone, 2007.

The Soloist, Paramount, 2009.

A Serious Man, Focus Features, 2009.

Film Work; Other:

Assistance, *Walker,* 1987.

Film Appearances:

Himself, *Back to Hell* (documentary), 2002.

Television Executive Producer; Series:

The Tudors, Showtime, 2007–2008.

Television Executive Producer; Miniseries:

Underbelly, BBC, 1992.

Television Work; Movies:

Producer (United Kingdom), *Frankie's House,* Arts and Entertainment, 1992.

Executive producer, *Babycakes,* Showtime, 2005.

Television Executive Producer; Pilots:

Flat Stanley, 2009.

Love Bites, NBC, 2010.

Television Executive Producer; Episodic:

"Storm over Everest," *Frontline,* PBS, 2008.

Television Appearances; Episodic:

"Toronto Film Festival: Part 2," *Shootout* (also known as *Sunday Morning Shootout* and *Hollywood Shootout*), AMC, 2007.

RECORDINGS

Music Videos:
Producer, "Hungry Like the Wolf" and "Save a Prayer," *Duran Duran: Greatest–The Videos,* EMI Distribution, 1999.

OTHER SOURCES

Periodicals:
Variety, December 14, 1998, pp. 108, 114; June 25, 2001, p. 34.

FIELDS, Michael
(Michael David Fields)

PERSONAL

Addresses: *Agent*—International Creative Management, 10250 Constellation Blvd., 9th Floor, Los Angeles, CA 90067.

Career: Director, producer, and writer.

CREDITS

Television Director; Episodic:
"The Old and the Dead," *Homicide: Life on the Street* (also known as *H:LOTS* and *Homicide*), NBC, 1995.
Courthouse, 1995.
"M.E., Myself, and I," *Homicide: Life on the Street* (also known as *H:LOTS* and *Homicide*), NBC, 1996.
"A Ceremony of Innocence," *EZ Streets,* CBS, 1997.
"'Tis Pity She's a Whore," *Cracker* (also known as *Fitz*), ABC, 1997.
"Valentine's Day," *Relativity,* 1997.
"Boyfriend" (also known as "Escape from New York"), *Dawson's Creek,* The WB, 1998.
"Secret Sex," *Sex and the City,* HBO, 1998.
"The Turtle and the Hare," *Sex and the City,* HBO, 1998.
"Meat Market," *Cupid,* ABC, 1998.
"Finally," *Felicity,* The WB, 1998.
"Uncivilized," *Law & Order: Special Victims Unit* (also known as *Special Victims Unit*), NBC, 1999.
"Bad Blood," *Law & Order: Special Victims Unit* (also known as *Special Victims Unit*), NBC, 2000.
"Taken," *Law & Order: Special Victims Unit* (also known as *Special Victims Unit*), NBC, 2000.
"Ohio," *Third Watch,* NBC, 2000.
"A Thousand Points of Light," *Third Watch,* NBC, 2000.

"Toy House," *Roswell* (also known as *Roswell High*), The WB, 2000.
"Justice," *D.C.,* The WB, 2000.
"Father and Sons," *Prince Street,* 2000.
"Smothered," *Law & Order: Criminal Intent* (also known as *Law & Order: CI*), NBC, 2000.
"Somebody's Fool," *Deadline,* NBC, 2001.
"Seizure," *Law & Order: Criminal Intent* (also known as *Law & Order: CI*), NBC, 2001.
"The Egg and I," *The Education of Max Bickford,* CBS, 2002.
"Lust," *Law & Order: Special Victims Unit* (also known as *Special Victims Unit*), NBC, 2002.
"My Alibi," *Hack,* 2002.
"Molting," *Sex, Love & Secrets,* 2005.
"On the Jones," *The Shield,* FX Network, 2007.
"Train in Vain," *Women's Murder Club* (also known as *wmc*), 2007.
"Arrested Development," *Moonlight,* 2007.
"Roman Holiday," *Gossip Girl,* The CW, 2007.
"Homecoming," *Runaway,* 2008.
(As Michael David Fields) "Chapter Twelve: Scary, Scary Night!," *Lipstick Jungle,* 2008.
"Desperately Seeking Serena," *Gossip Girl,* The CW, 2008.
"Never Been Marcused," *Gossip Girl,* The CW, 2008.
"There Might be Blood," *Gossip Girl,* The CW, 2008.
"Cahuenga," *Melrose Place,* Fox, 2009.
"The Beautiful Triangle," *The Beautiful Live: TBL,* 2009.

Television Director; Series:
Queens Supreme, CBS, 2003.
Veronica Mars, 2004–2007.

Television Director; Pilots:
County 187, NBC, 2000.
D.C., The WB, 2000.

Television Executive Producer; Series:
Jane Nugent's Garden Party, Home and Garden Television, 1994.
Lucille's Car Care Clinic, Home and Garden Television, 1994.

Television Producer; Series:
Cupid, 2009.

Television Work; Specials:
Director, *Noon Wine* (also known as *Short Story Collection II: Noon Wine*), PBS, 1985.
Executive producer, *Marvin Hamlisch & the Pittsburgh Pops,* PBS, 1996.
Executive producer, *John Updike: In His Own Words,* 1997.

Film Director:
Bright Angel, Hemdale, 1991.

Film Work:
Second assistant editor, *3 by Cheever: The 5:48* (also known as *The Five Forty–Eight*), 1979.
Assistant editor, *Jane Austen in Manhattan,* 1980.
Assistant director, *Courtesans of Bombay,* New Yorker Films, 1986.

Stage Production Manager:
Hamlet, Roundabout Theatre, New York City, 1970.
Tug of War, Roundabout Theatre, 1970–71.
Uncle Vanya, Roundabout Theatre, 1971.
Chas, Abbott & Son, Roundabout Theatre, 1971.
She Stoops to Conquer, Roundabout Theatre, 1971.

Stage Work:
Set designer, *Tug of War,* Roundabout Theatre, New York City, 1970–71.

WRITINGS

Television Specials:
Noon Wine (also known as *Short Story Collection II: Noon Wine*), PBS, 1985.

FIMMEL, Travis 1979–

PERSONAL

Born July 15, 1979, near Echuca, Victoria, Australia; son of Chris (a dairy and beef farmer) and Jennie (a recreation officer for the disabled) Fimmel. *Education:* Briefly attended Royal Melbourne Institute of Technology (also known as RMIT University); trained with Ivana Chubbock in Los Angeles.

Addresses: *Agent*—Paradigm, 360 North Crescent Dr. N., Beverly Hills, CA 90210. *Manager*—David L. Seltzer, Management 360, 9111 Wilshire Blvd., Beverly Hills, CA 90210.

Career: Actor. Chadwick Modeling Agency, worked as a model in Australia and England, beginning c. 1990; worked as a model for Calvin Klein menswear, c. 2001.

CREDITS

Film Appearances:
Ron, *Restraint,* Accent Film Entertainment, 2008.
Johnny Doran, *Surfer, Dude,* Anchor Bay Entertainment, 2008.
Dale, *Pure Country 2: The Gift,* Warner Bros., 2010.

Jake, *Ivory,* Ivory Tower Productions, 2010.
Helweg, *The Experiment,* Sony Pictures Home Entertainment, 2010.
Marcus Rutherford, *Needle,* Polyphony Entertainment, 2010.

Television Appearances; Series:
John Clayton, *Tarzan,* The WB, 2003.
Ellis Dove, *The Beast,* Arts and Entertainment, 2009.

Television Appearances; Pilots:
John Clayton, *Tarzan,* The WB, 2003.
Taj Walters, *Rocky Point,* The WB, 2005.
Bobby Granger, *Southern Comfort,* Fox, 2006.
Ellis Dove, *The Beast,* Arts and Entertainment, 2009.
Mason Boyle, *Chase,* NBC, 2010.

Television Appearances; Episodic:
Extra (also known as *Extra: The Entertainment Magazine*), syndicated, 2003.
Total Request Live (also known as *Total Request with Carson Daly, TRL,* and *TRL Weekend*), MTV, 2003.
Jimmy Kimmel Live!, ABC, 2003.
The Sharon Osbourne Show (also known as *Sharon*), syndicated, 2003.

RECORDINGS

Videos:
Appeared in the music videos "Country Kid in the City" by Stephen Rowe, and "I'm Real" by Jennifer Lopez, and a music video by Janet Jackson.

OTHER SOURCES

Periodicals:
Chicago Tribune, November 19, 2008; December 6, 2008.
Movieline's Hollywood Life, September 1, 2003, p. 29.
TV Guide, July 12, 2003, pp. 32–34.

FINNIGAN, Judy 1948–

PERSONAL

Full name, Judith Finnigan; born May 16, 1948, in Manchester, England; daughter of David Henshaw (a journalist; divorced); married Richard Madeley (a television presenter and producer), November 21, 1986; children: (first marriage) Dan and Tom (twins); (second marriage) Jack Christopher, Chloe Susannah.

Education: University of Bristol, B.A. (with honors), 1971.

Addresses: *Agent*—Ali Clapperton, James Grant Media, 94 Strand on the Green, Chiswick, London W4 3NN, England.

Career: Television presenter and producer. Granada Television, Manchester, England, researcher, beginning 1971; Anglia Television, Norwich, England, news reporter, beginning 1974; Granada Television, presenter, beginning 1980.

Awards, Honors: Royal Television Society Award nomination, best female presenter, 1994, for *This Morning;* National Television Awards, most popular daytime program, 1998, 1999, 2000, 2001.

CREDITS

Television Appearances; Series:
Presenter, *Granada Reports,* Granada Television, beginning 1980.
Presenter, *This Morning,* ITV, 1988–2007.
The Richard and Judy Show, 1993.
Presenter, *Tonight with Richard Madeley and Judy Finnigan,* 1996.
We Can Work It Out, 1998–99.
Presenter of "Duets," *Top Ten,* Channel 4, 2001.
Presenter, *Richard & Judy,* Channel 4, 2001–2008.
Presenter, *Richard & Judy's New Position,* UKTV, 2008–2009.

Also presented *Get a Life.*

Television Appearances; Specials:
Presenter, *Classic Coronation Street,* 1991, 1993.
The Judy Finnigan Debate, 1993, 1994.
Audience member, *An Audience with the Spice Girls,* ITV, 1997.
Forty Years on Coronation Street, 2000.
(In archive footage) *100 Greatest TV Moments from Hell,* 2000.
(Uncredited; in archive footage) *Goodbye 2000,* 2000.
The Ultimate Pop Star, Channel 4, 2004.
The Big Fat Quiz of the Year, Channel 4, 2004, 2005.
TV's 50 Greatest Stars, Granada, 2006.
Presenter, *Richard & Judy's Christmas Books,* Channel 4, 2006, 2007.
(In archive footage) *Sex on Trial: The Soapstar Story,* Channel 4, 2007.
Happy Birthday Brucie!, BBC1, 2008.
Ant & Dec's Christmas Show, ITV, 2009.
Newsnight at 30, BBC2, 2010.

Television Appearances; Miniseries:
I Love 1980's, BBC, 2001.
The Second Coming, BBC America, 2003.

Television Appearances; Episodic:
"The Bolivian Connection," *Cluedo,* ITV, 1991.
Surprise Surprise!, ITV, 1996.
"Richard Madeley and Judy Finnigan," *This Is Your Life,* BBC, 1997.
"Dad's Army," *Selection Box,* 1997.
TV Nightmares, ITV, 1999.
"When the Fat Lady Sings," *Fat Friends,* BBC America, 2000.
So Graham Norton, Channel 4, 2001.
"Parallox," *Absolutely Fabulous,* BBC1, then Comedy Central, 2001.
Friday Night with Jonathan Ross, BBC America, 2002.
The Kumars at No. 42, BBC America, 2002.
The Late Late Show, 2002.
"Celebrity Christmas Puddings," *French and Saunders,* BBC, 2002.
Liquid News, BBC3, 2004.
The Keith Barret Show, 2004.
(In archive footage) *Room 101,* BBC, 2004.
Ant & Dec's Saturday Night Takeaway, ITV, 2005.
"The Trial," *Absolute Power,* BBC, 2005.
Little Britain, BBC America, 2005.
(Uncredited; in archive footage) "Boy George's Queerest TV Moments," *Favouritism,* Channel 4, 2005.
Footballers' Wives, BBC America, 2006.
"Daniel Radcliffe," *Extras,* HBO, 2006.
The Paul O'Grady Show, ITV, 2007.
(Uncredited) "A Heroes Welcome," *Heroes Unmasked,* BBC, 2007.
TV Burp, ITV, 2007, then uncredited appearances, 2008, and (in archive footage) in "The Best of TV Burp," 2009.
Happy Hour, 2008.
(Uncredited) *Chris Moyles Quiz Night,* Channel 4, 2009.
"Richard Madeley," *Piers Morgan's Life Stories,* ITV, 2009.

Also appeared in an episode of *Women of Substance.*

Television Appearances; Awards Presentations:
Cohost, *BAFTA British Academy Awards,* 1989.
The British Comedy Awards, ITV, 1993.
The National Television Awards, ITV, 1998, 2000, 2001.
Host, *The British Soap Awards,* 1999, 2000, 2001.
Pride of Britain Awards, ITV, 2003.

Television Work; Series:
Executive producer, *Richard & Judy,* Channel 4, 2001–2007.

Film Appearances:
Herself, *Ali G Indahouse,* Universal, 2002.

WRITINGS

Books:
(With husband, Richard Madeley) *Richard and Judy: The Autobiography,* Hodder & Stoughton, 2002.

OTHER SOURCES

Books:
Finnigan, Judy, and Richard Madeley, *Richard and Judy: The Autobiography,* Hodder & Stoughton, 2002.

Periodicals:
Daily Telegraph (London), April 7, 2004, p. 19.

Electronic:
Richard & Judy Official Site, http://www.officialrichardandjudy.com, July 30, 2010.

Other:
"Richard Madeley and Judy Finnigan" (television episode), *This Is Your Life,* BBC, 1997.

FLEISS, Noah 1984–

PERSONAL

Born April 16, 1984, in White Plains, NY.

Career: Actor.

Awards, Honors: YoungStar Award, outstanding young actor in a television movie or miniseries, *Hollywood Reporter,* and Young Artist Award nomination, best performance by a young actor—television special, Young Artist Foundation, both 1996, for *A Mother's Prayer;* Young Artist Award nomination, best performance in a television movie or miniseries—young actor, 1997, for *Chasing the Dragon;* Young Artist Award nomination, best performance in a feature film—leading young actor, 2000, for *Joe the King;* named a star of tomorrow, *Jane* magazine, 2002; other honors and recognition.

CREDITS

Film Appearances:
Samuel "Sam"/"Killer Sam" Whitney, *Josh and S.A.M.,* Columbia, 1993.

Michael at the age of five, *Roommates,* Buena Vista, 1995.
Jay, "Someone for Rose" segment, *Things You Can Tell Just by Looking at Her,* Metro–Goldwyn–Mayer/United Artists, 1999.
Joe Henry (title role), *Joe the King* (also known as *Pleasant View Avenue*), Trimark Pictures, 1999.
Bret, *Double Parked,* Castle Hill, 2000.
Steve, *The Favor* (short film; also known as *Mission*), Heartcore Productions, 2001.
Brady Livingston, "Non–Fiction" segment, *Storytelling* (also known as *Story Telling* and *Untitled Todd Solondz Project*), Fine Line, 2002.
Marcus Swords, *Bringing Rain,* Belladonna Productions, 2003.
Chat Turly, *Evergreen,* Evergreen Films, 2004.
Tugger, *Brick,* 2005, Focus Features, 2006.
Sol Rosenbaum, *Hard Luck* (also known as *Middleman*), Sony Pictures Home Entertainment, 2006.
Todd Hunter, *Off the Black,* THINKFilm, 2006.
Day on Fire (also known as *The Day on Fire*), Bleiberg Entertainment, 2006.
Vincent, *The Speed of Life* (also known as *Superheroes*), 2007, also 2009.
Bobby, *Mother's Day Massacre* (also known as *Hot Baby!*), Angel Baby Entertainment/Trucker Films, 2007, Maxim Media International and iTunes, 2009.
Eric, *Capers* (also known as *The Brooklyn Heist*), Capers Productions/Numeric Pictures, 2008, 2009.
Harley, *Red Canyon,* Red Canyon Pictures, 2008, Fireside Releasing, 2009.
Ben, *Further Lane* (short film), 2009.
Derek, *11:11* (also known as *Rocky Costanzo's "11:11"*), Hourglass Pictures, 2010.
Ryan, *Beware the Gonzo* (also known as *The Gonzo Files*), Corner Store Entertainment, 2010.
Ryan, *Consent,* Lili Pad Films, 2010.
Stoner, *The Last Film Festival,* Rebellion Rd Productions, 2010.

Television Appearances; Series:
Ivan, *Huge,* beginning 2008.

Television Appearances; Movies:
Charlie, *Past the Bleachers,* ABC, 1995.
T. J. Holmstrom, *A Mother's Prayer,* USA Network, 1995.
Matt Whitney, *An Unexpected Family,* USA Network, 1996.
Sean Kessler, *Chasing the Dragon,* Lifetime, 1996.
Zach Braverton, *Bad Day on the Block* (also known as *Dark Instinct, The Fireman,* and *Under Pressure*), HBO, 1997.
Matt Whitney, *An Unexpected Life,* USA Network, 1998.
Ned, *The Truth about Jane,* Lifetime, 2000.

Shannon Shingleton, *The Laramie Project,* HBO, 2002.
Army sergeant, *Taking Chance,* HBO, 2009.

Television Appearances; Episodic:
Andrew, "Mary Anne and the Brunettes," *The Baby-Sitters Club,* HBO, 1990.
Aaron, "How do You Spell Faith?," *Touched by an Angel,* CBS, 1998.
Denny Cannon, "Girl Most Likely," *Law & Order* (also known as *Law & Order Prime*), NBC, 2002.
Joe Risby, "The Offer," *Ed* (also known as *Stuckeyville*), NBC, 2003.
Nathan Angeli, "Brotherhood," *Law & Order: Special Victims Unit* (also known as *Law & Order's Sex Crimes, Law & Order: SVU,* and *Special Victims Unit*), NBC, 2004.

Luke Dempsey, "The No-Brainer," *Fringe,* Fox, 2009.
Sam Heden, "Win-Loss," *Three Rivers* (also known as *Untitled Barbee/Hanson Project*), CBS, 2010.

Stage Appearances:
Understudy, *Four Baboons Adoring the Sun,* Lincoln Center, Vivian Beaumont Theater, New York City, 1992.

RECORDINGS

Videos:
Himself, *Building "Brick"* (documentary), Senator Film, 2006.

G

GETTY, Balthazar 1975–
(B–Zar)

PERSONAL

Full name, Paul Balthazar Getty; born January 22, 1975, in Los Angeles, CA; son of J. Paul III (a writer and actor) and Gisela Martine (a photojournalist; maiden name, Zacher) Getty; great–grandson of business tycoon J. Paul Getty; married Rosetta Millington (a designer of children's clothing), May 3, 2000 (separated, 2008); children: Cassius Paul, Grace, Violet, June Catherine. *Education:* Attended Bel–Air Preparatory School, Los Angeles. *Avocational Interests:* Riding motorcycles.

Addresses: *Agent*—Gersh Agency, 9465 Wilshire Blvd., 6th Floor, Beverly Hills, CA 90212; (voice work and commercials) Alix Gucovsky, Special Artists Agency, 9465 Wilshire Blvd., Suite 470, Beverly Hills, CA 90212. *Manager*—The Collective, 8383 Wilshire Blvd., Suite 1050, Beverly Hills, CA 90211.

Career: Actor and producer. 5150 (film production company), founder. Performs as a rap music artist and music producer under the name B–Zar; founding member and performer with music groups, including Ringside, Tape, and Thirteenth Floor. Appeared in a commercial for iVote2.com, 2000. Formerly worked as a fashion model for designers Calvin Klein, Tommy Hilfiger, and Versace.

Awards, Honors: Young Artist Award nominations, outstanding young actor starring in a motion picture and outstanding young ensemble cast in a motion picture (with others), both 1991, for *Lord of the Flies;* Young Artist Award nomination, outstanding young supporting actor in a motion picture, 1991, for *Young Guns II;* Young Artist Award nomination, outstanding young actor starring in a motion picture, 1992, for *My Heroes Have Always Been Cowboys;* Golden Satellite Award nomination, best supporting actor in a series, miniseries, or movie made for television, International Press Academy, 2005, for *Traffic;* Fennecus Award nomination, outstanding juvenile performance.

CREDITS

Film Appearances:
Ralph, *Lord of the Flies,* Columbia, 1990.
Tom O'Folliard, *Young Guns II* (also known as *Young Guns II: Blaze of Glory*), Twentieth Century–Fox, 1990.
Jud Meadows, *My Heroes Have Always Been Cowboys,* Samuel Goldwyn, 1991.
Joe Don Dante, *The Pope Must Diet* (also known as *The Pope Must Die*), Miramax, 1991.
Allister Gibbs, *December,* IRS Releasing, 1991.
Little J, *Where the Day Takes You,* New Line Cinema, 1992.
Halfway House, Centre Films, 1992.
Alexi, *Red Hot,* SC Entertainment International, 1993.
Jimmy Lupont, *Natural Born Killers,* Warner Bros., 1994.
Jake, *Don't Do It,* Triboro Entertainment Group, 1994.
Leader, *Cityscrapes: Los Angeles,* Filmtribe Moving Pictures/High Octane Productions, 1994.
Rudy Dobbs, *Dead Beat* (also known as *The Phony Perfector*), Northern Arts Entertainment, 1995.
Cadet Nathan Olmeyer, *Judge Dredd,* Buena Vista, 1995.
Chad's friend, *Terrified* (also known as *Evil Never Sleeps* and *Tough Guy*), A–Pix Entertainment, 1995.
(Uncredited) Mr. Stadler as a student, *Mr. Holland's Opus,* Buena Vista, 1995.
Tod Johnstone, *White Squall,* Buena Vista, 1997.
Pete Dayton, *Lost Highway,* October Films, 1997.
A. J. Merchant, *Fait Accompli* (also known as *VooDoo Dawn*), Cutting Edge Entertainment, 1998.

Lefty, *Out in Fifty*, Avalanche Home Entertainment, 1999.

Walter, *Big City Blues*, Avalanche Home Entertainment, 1999.

Michael Holloway, *Shadow Hours*, Newmark Films, 2000.

Julian, *Four Dogs Playing Poker*, Warner Home Video, 2000.

Steve, *MacArthur Park*, Northshire Entertainment Group/Wirthwhile, 2001.

Brian Pivano, *The Center of the World*, Artisan Entertainment, 2001.

Jimmy Pockets, *Deuces Wild*, Metro–Goldwyn–Mayer, 2002.

Ray Gauquin, *Ladder 49*, Buena Vista, 2003.

Taylor, *Slingshot*, Weinstein Company, 2005.

Bozo, *Feast*, Weinstein Company, 2006.

Jimmy, *The Tripper*, NaVinci Films/Coquette Productions, 2006.

Himself, *My American Cousin* (documentary), Hochschule fuer Fernsehen und Film Muenchen, 2008.

Man at door, *West of Brooklyn*, Osiris Entertainment, 2009.

Film Work:

Coproducer, *Shadow Hours*, Newmark Films, 2000.

Co–executive producer, *Sluts & Losers*, 2001.

Television Appearances; Series:

Nate Greeley, *Pasadena*, Fox, 2001.

Corsairs (also known as *Rosebud*), 2002.

Richard Montana, a recurring role, *Charmed*, The WB, 2003–2004.

Thomas Grace, *Alias*, ABC, 2005–2006.

Thomas "Tommy" Walker, *Brothers & Sisters*, ABC, 2006—.

Television Appearances; Miniseries:

Ben Edmonds, *Traffic* (also known as *Traffic: The Miniseries*), USA Network, 2003.

David Wheeler, *Into the West*, TNT, 2005.

Project Greenlight 3, Bravo, 2005.

Television Appearances; Movies:

Andreas Symes, *Habitat*, Sci–Fi Channel, 1997.

Title role, *Sol Goode*, The WB, 2002.

Eddie, *Run for the Money* (also known as *Hard Cash*), USA Network, 2002.

Television Appearances; Specials:

Master Miles, "The Turn of the Screw," *Nightmare Classics*, Showtime, 1990.

Pretty as a Picture: The Art of David Lynch, 1997.

The Hunger: An MTV Sneak Preview, MTV, 1997.

Tommy Walker, *Brothers & Sisters: Family Album*, ABC, 2007.

The 2007 Alma Awards, ABC, 2007.

(In archive footage) Tommy Walker, *Brothers & Sisters: A Family Matter*, 2007.

(In archive footage) *Reinventando Hollywood*, Canal+ Espana, 2008.

Television Appearances; Pilots:

Nate Greeley, *Pasadena*, Fox, 2001.

Michael Adams, *Ghost Whisperer*, CBS, 2005.

Scotty, *Dirtbags*, Fox, 2006.

Television Appearances; Episodic:

James Chandler, "The Swords," *The Hunger*, Showtime, 1997.

Jimmy Kimmel Live!, ABC, 2005, 2007, 2009.

The View, ABC, 2007.

Entertainment Tonight (also known as *E.T.* and *This Week in Entertainment*), syndicated, 2008, 2009.

Christopher Dennis Snipes, "The First Bite Is the Deepest," *Medium*, NBC, 2009.

The Bonnie Hunt Show, NBC, 2009, 2010.

Tom Garvin, "Born to Run," *Rizzoli & Isles*, TNT, 2010.

Walton Dawkins, "Lanakila," *Hawaii Five–O*, CBS, 2010.

RECORDINGS

As B–Zar, producer of the album *Sedative* by Mannish.

OTHER SOURCES

Periodicals:

Interview, May, 2001, p. 99.

Movieline, August, 2000, p. 18.

Premiere, August, 1992; September, 2000, pp. 78–83, 88.

TV Guide, January 12, 2009, p. 13; November 16, 2009, p. 12.

USA Today, March 30, 2007, p. 3E.

GHAI, Jilon 1978–
(Jilon Van Over, Jilon Ghai VanOver)

PERSONAL

Born August 24, 1978, in CA. *Education:* Murray State University, B.S., theatre; attended junior college; studied with various instructors.

Addresses: *Agent*—Peter Young, Sovereign Talent Group, 10474 Santa Monica Blvd., Suite 301, Los Angeles, CA 90025.

Career: Actor. Appeared in industrial films and commercials; appeared in and worked on music videos; also worked as voice performer.

Member: Screen Actors Guild.

CREDITS

Film Appearances:

Randy, *Malibu Spring Break,* Crown International, 2003.

Willard Bell, *Eternal Bliss,* Counterflux Films/Fly Fast Films, 2004.

Kevin, *Boo!* (also known as *Boo*), Ventura Distribution, 2005.

Nathan (The Dreamer), *White Nights,* Pendragon Film/Plaster City Productions, 2005.

Thomas James, *Alien Abduction,* The Asylum, 2005.

Byron Oniskon, *Death by Engagement,* 2005, Maverick Entertainment Group, 2007.

Barbecue (BBQ) waiter, *Take Out,* 2005, Landau Motion Pictures, 2009.

Astor "Click" Upjohn III, *Bad Blood,* Conmar Productions, 2006.

Mason, *Death Tunnel,* Sony Pictures Home Entertainment, 2006.

Randy, *TV Face,* 99 Options/Paradox Opera, 2007.

Ronald, *L.A. Proper,* Minnie and Doug's Boy Productions/Produce a Crime Productions, 2007.

(Uncredited) Voice of creature, *I Am Legend* (IMAX version known as *I Am Legend: The IMAX Experience*), Warner Bros., 2007.

Young German driver, *Miriam,* Seventh Art Releasing, 2007.

Brett Kern, *Salvation, Texas* (short film), University of Southern California, 2008.

Brody, *Bryan Loves You,* Anchor Bay Entertainment, 2008.

Simon, *Marco Polo,* West Wing Films, 2008.

Astor "Click" Upjohn III, *Bad Blood ... the Hunger,* Miracon Pictures, 2009.

Alex, *Dream in American,* Saddle Ranch Productions, 2010.

(As Jilon Van Over) Geoffrey, *Being Killed,* Avalon Entertainment, 2010.

Junkyard man, *Bloodworth* (also known as *Provinces of Night*), Dax Productions/Buffalo Bulldog Films/Provinces of Night, 2010.

Rauch Orlaff, *Monster Heroes,* Tarnol Group Pictures, 2010.

Steve, *The Reflex* (short film), 2010.

Stan, *The Legends of Nethiah* (also known as *Legends of Nethiah: The Nameless* and *Untitled Jeremiah Sayys Sci–Fi/Fantasy Project*), WorldsLastHero Productions/Starruner, 2011.

Television Appearances; Episodic:

Hassenfeffer, "Black and Tan: A Crime of Fashion," *Psych,* USA Network, 2008.

Truitt "Spider" Leland, "Spiders," *Cold Case* (also known as *Anexihniastes ypothesis, Caso abierto, Cold case—affaires classees, Cold Case—Kein Opfer ist je vergessen, Doegloett aktak, Kalla spaar, Todistettavasti syyllinen,* and *Victimes du passe*), CBS, 2008.

Appeared in other programs, including *1000 Ways to Die,* Spike TV.

Television Appearances; Pilots:

Appeared in *Harry Nash* and *Thor's Hammer.*

Stage Appearances:

(As Jilon Ghai VanOver) Bluntschli, *Arms and the Man,* Long Beach Playhouse, Mainstage, Long Beach, CA, 2002.

Multiple roles, *A New War,* Theatre 68, Hollywood, CA, 2005.

Gene West, *Lost in Radioland,* Theatre Palisades, Pacific Palisades, CA, 2010.

Appeared as Billy D., *Bill W. and Dr. Bob,* Theatre 68; as Jilon Van Over, appeared as Jean–Paul Marat, *Marat/Sade,* Tamarind Theatre; also appeared in other stage productions.

Internet Appearances:

Appeared in footage posted on the Internet.

RECORDINGS

Music Videos:

Appeared in music videos. Directed and edited the music video "Blue Wolf," by Revolutionary Wordplay; as Jilon Ghai VanOver, directed, shot, and edited the music video "Heaven Is a Promise," by Dean Walker.

WRITINGS

Screenplays:

Worked on screenplays.

GILFORD, Zach 1982–

PERSONAL

Full name, Zachary Gilford; born January 14, 1982, in Evanston, IL. *Education:* Graduate of Northwestern University.

Addresses: *Agent*—Megan Silverman, WME Entertainment, 9601 Wilshire Blvd., 3rd Floor, Beverly Hills, CA 90210. *Manager*—Charles Mastropietro, D/F Management, 270 Lafayette St., Suite 402, New York, NY 10012. *Publicist*—Gina Hoffman, Baker, Winokur, Ryder, 5700 Wilshire Blvd., Suite 550, Los Angeles, CA 90036.

Career: Actor.

Awards, Honors: Gotham Award nomination (with others), best ensemble cast, 2007, for *The Last Winter.*

CREDITS

Film Appearances:
Jimmy, *Handbook to Casual Stalking* (short film), Studio 22 Productions/When Pigs Fly Productions, 2003.
Maxwell McKinder, *The Last Winter,* Antidode Films, 2006.
Sailor, *Rise* (also known as *Rise: Blood Hunter*), Samuel Goldwyn, 2007.
Johnny Drake, *Dare,* Image Entertainment, 2009.
Adam Davies, *Post Grad,* Fox Searchlight, 2009.
Evan, *Answers to Nothing,* Ambush Entertainment, 2010.
Gus, *The River Why,* Pelston Productions/Ambush Entertainment, 2010.
Jerry, *Super,* MG Film, 2010.
Himself, *Greenlit* (documentary), Ambush Entertainment, 2010.

Television Appearances; Series:
Matt Saracen, *Friday Night Lights* (also known as *F.N.L.*), NBC, 2006–2008, DirecTV, 2009, NBC, 2009–10.

Television Appearances; Pilots:
Matt Saracen, *Friday Night Lights,* NBC, 2006.
Off the Map, ABC, 2010.
Alex Galloway, *Matadors,* ABC, 2010.

Television Appearances; Episodic:
Kevin Wilcox, "Contagious," *Law & Order: Special Victims Unit* (also known as *Law & Order: SVU* and *Special Victims Unit*), NBC, 2005.
Entertainment Tonight (also known as *E.T.* and *This Week in Entertainment*), syndicated, 2007.
Charlie Lowell, "Here's to Future Days," *Grey's Anatomy,* ABC, 2009.
Up Close with Carrie Keagan, ABC, 2009.
Chelsea Lately, E! Entertainment Television, 2009, 2010.

Television Appearances; Specials:
The Teen Choice Awards 2009 (also known as *Teen Choice 2009*), Fox, 2009.

OTHER SOURCES

Periodicals:
Backstage, October 5, 2006, p. 8.
Moving Pictures, February, 2009, p. 65.

GINTY, James 1980–
   (James Francis Ginty)

PERSONAL

Full name, James Francis Lawrence Ginty; born December 4, 1980, in Los Angeles, CA; son of Robert Ginty (an actor, director, and writer) and Francine Tacker (an actress). *Education:* Attended Juilliard School and University of California, Los Angeles; studied ballet at American Ballet Theatre, Royal Ballet, and National Ballet of Canada; trained for the stage at British American Drama Academy, Royal Academy of Dramatic Art, and Interlochen Arts Academy. *Avocational Interests:* Attending plays, ballets, and operas, spectator sports, travel, cooking, fishing.

Addresses: *Manager*—Michael Einfeld, ME Management, 10630 Moorpark, Suite 101, Toluca Lake, CA 91602. *Publicist*—R. Couri Hay, 141 West 81st St., New York, NY 10024.

Career: Actor.

Member: American Federation of Television and Radio Artists, Actors' Equity Association, Screen Actors Guild.

CREDITS

Film Appearances:
(Uncredited) Altar boy, *Vietnam, Texas,* RCA/Columbia Pictures Home Video, 1990.
Anatoly, *K–19: The Widowmaker* (also known as *K–19* and *The Widowmaker*), New Films International/Paramount, 2002.
(As James Francis Ginty) Canter surrogate, *Surrogates* (also known as *Vicarious*), Walt Disney, 2009.

Television Appearances; Episodic:
Frick, "Lost in America," *ER,* NBC, 2006.
Dr. Deardon, *Days of Our Lives* (also known as *Days* and *DOOL*), NBC, 2007.
Emergency room intern, "In Which Cooper Finds a Port in His Storm," *Private Practice,* ABC, 2007.

(Uncredited) Trent, *Real Time with Bill Maher* (also known as *Real Time with Bill Maher: Electile Dysfunction '08*), HBO, 2008.

Dr. Russell, "The Time Warp," *Grey's Anatomy*, ABC, 2010.

Television Appearances; Pilots:

Philip, *The Wester Report*, CBS, 2004.

Stage Appearances:

Romeo, *Romeo and Juliet*, Seattle Repertory Theatre, Seattle, WA, 2003.

Bertram, *All's Well that Ends Well*, Folger Shakespeare Theatre, Washington, DC, 2003.

Jacob Milne, *Night and Day*, Wilma Theatre, Philadelphia, PA, 2005.

Title role, *Macbeth*, Interlochen Shakespeare Festival, Interlochen, MI, 2010.

Internet Appearances; Episodic:

Guest, *Live! from the Future*, LiveFromTheFuture.com, 2006.

OTHER SOURCES

Periodicals:

New York Post, June 15, 2009, p. 20.
Variety, June 12, 2008.

GOGGINS, Walton 1971–
(Walt Goggins, Walter Goggins)

PERSONAL

Full name, Walton Sanders Goggins, Jr.; born November 10, 1971, in Birmingham, AL; son of Walton Sanders, Sr. and Janet Goggins; married Leanne, 2001 (died, 2004). *Education:* Attended high school in Lithia Springs, GA; studied acting with Harry Mastrogeorge and David Le Grand. *Avocational Interests:* Photography, travel, scuba diving.

Addresses: *Agent*—Dan Baron, Agency for the Performing Arts, 405 South Beverly Dr., Beverly Hills, CA 90212. *Manager*—Darris Hatch, Darris Hatch Management, 9538 Brighton Way, Suite 308, Beverly Hills, CA 90210. *Publicist*—Nancy Iannios, Nancy Iannios Public Relations, Signal Mountain, TN 37377.

Career: Actor and producer. Ginny Mule Pictures, cofounder and partner, 2001—. Performed as a clog dancer as a child. Previously managed his own valet parking service. Supported of environmental and humanitarian causes.

Member: Global Green USA.

Awards, Honors: Spirit of Slamdance Award (with others), Slamdance Film Festival, 2001 (and, according to some sources, Academy Award for best live–action short film, also 2001), for *The Accountant*; Spirit of Slamdance Award (with others), 2001, for *Randy and the Mob*; Television Critics Association Award nomination, individual achievement in drama, 2009, for *The Shield*; Special Jury Award (with others), best ensemble cast, SXSW Film Festival, 2009, for *That Evening Sun*.

CREDITS

Film Appearances:

Shaky kid (uncredited), *Mr. Saturday Night*, Columbia, 1992.

(As Walt Goggins) Military police officer at gate, *Forever Young*, Warner Bros., 1992.

(As Walt Goggins) Charlie, *The Next Karate Kid*, Columbia, 1994.

Roddy, *Painted Hero* (also known as *Shadow of the Past*), Astra Cinema, 1996.

Sam, *The Apostle*, October Films, 1997.

(As Walt Goggins) Bud, *Switchback* (also known as *Zig Zag*), Paramount, 1997.

Billy "Downtown" Anderson, *Major League: Back to the Minors* (also known as *Major League III*), Warner Bros.,1998.

(As Walt Goggins) *Wayward Son*, 1999.

(As Walter Goggins) Stan Robbers, *The Crow: Salvation*, Dimension Films, 2000.

Lee Todd, *Red Dirt*, 2000.

Wallace, *Shanghai Noon*, Buena Vista, 2000.

(As Walt Goggins) Tommy O'Dell, *The Accountant*, Ginny Mule Pictures, 2001.

Tommy Christian, *Daddy and Them*, Miramax, 2001.

(Uncredited) Police officer in footage added to DVD release, *Joy Ride* (also known as *Never Play with Strangers, Road Kill,* and *Road Killer*), Twentieth Century–Fox, 2001.

Research technician, *The Bourne Identity*, Universal, 2002.

Moe Danyou, *Apple Jack* (short film; also known as *The Legend of Apple Jack*), Tranquility Pictures/Ocean of Storms Pictures, 2003.

Steve Naish, *House of 1000 Corpses*, Lions Gate Films, 2003.

(As Walt Goggins) Larry, *Chrystal*, Palisades Pictures, 2004.

Marty Dickerson, *The World's Fastest Indian*, Magnolia Pictures, 2005.

Joe, *The Architect*, Magnolia Pictures, 2006.

Tino Armani, *Randy and the Mob*, Lightyear Entertainment/Vivendi Entertainment, 2007.

Zack, *Fragments* (also known as *Winged Creatures*), Columbia, 2008.

Captain Nokes, *Miracle at St. Anna,* Touchstone/Walt Disney, 2008.

Paul Meecham, *That Evening Sun,* Freestyle Releasing, 2009.

Reno Paulsaint, *Damage,* Nasser Group, 2009.

Stans, *Predators,* Twentieth Century–Fox, 2010.

Film Producer:

The Accountant, Ginny Mule Pictures, 2001.

(As Walt Goggins) *Chrystal,* Palisades Pictures, 2004.

Randy and the Mob, Lightyear Entertainment/Vivendi Entertainment, 2007.

That Evening Sun, Freestyle Releasing, 2009.

Television Appearances; Series:

Detective Shane Vendrell, *The Shield,* FX Network, 2002–2008.

Boyd Crowder, *Justified,* FX Network, 2010—.

Television Appearances; Movies:

(As Walt Goggins) Lyle, *Murder in Mississippi,* NBC, 1990.

(As Walt Goggins) Buck, *For Love and Glory,* CBS, 1993.

Jim Bob, *The Cherokee Kid,* HBO, 1996.

Rod, *Humanoids from the Deep* (also known as *Roger Corman Presents "Humanoids from the Deep"*), Showtime, 1996.

(As Walt Goggins) Almanzo Wilder, *Beyond the Prairie: The True Story of Laura Ingalls Wilder,* CBS, 2000.

Billy Weber, *Murder, She Wrote: The Last Free Man,* CBS, 2001.

Almanzo Wilder, *Beyond the Prairie, Part 2: The True Story of Laura Ingalls Wilder,* CBS, 2002.

Television Appearances; Pilots:

Huff, *The Watcher,* UPN, 1995.

(As Walt Goggins) Harv, *Pacific Blue,* USA, 1996.

Detective Shane Vendrell, *The Shield,* FX Network, 2002.

Rectify, AMC, 2009.

Television Appearances; Miniseries:

(As Walt Goggins) Wayne Seagrove, *Stay the Night,* ABC, 1992.

First young man, *Queen,* CBS, 1993.

Television Appearances; Specials:

Bob, "A Voice from Home," *Miracles and Other Mysteries,* ABC, 1991.

Himself, *Speechless,* 2008.

Television Appearances; Episodic:

"Missing," *In the Heat of the Night,* NBC, 1989.

(As Walt Goggins) Darrell, "Crackdown," *In the Heat of the Night,* NBC, 1989.

(As Walt Goggins) Robbie Jeffries, "Shine On Sparta Moon," *In the Heat of the Night,* NBC, 1991.

"Rules of the Game," *I'll Fly Away,* NBC, 1991.

(As Walt Goggins) Mike Muchin, "The Pit and the Pendulum," *Beverly Hills, 90210* (also known as *Class of Beverly Hills*), Fox, 1992.

(As Walt Goggins) Garth Watkins, "A Frenzied Affair," *In the Heat of the Night,* NBC, 1992.

(Uncredited; in archive footage) Garth Watkins, "Discovery," *In the Heat of the Night,* NBC, 1992.

(As Walt Goggins) Langley, "What's in a Name?," *I'll Fly Away,* NBC, 1993.

(As Walt Goggins) Lance McBride, "Wheel Man," *Renegade,* USA Network, 1993.

Commanding officer, "Desert Son," *JAG,* NBC, 1995.

(As Walt Goggins) Harv, "Captive Audience," *Pacific Blue,* USA Network, 1996.

Mick, "True Crime," *The Sentinel,* UPN, 1996.

Terry, "Honeymoon at Viagra Falls," *NYPD Blue* (also known as *N.Y.P.D.*), ABC, 1998.

Bill Green, *Family Law,* CBS, 1999.

Agent Davis, "Lost and Found," *Hawaii,* NBC, 2005.

Marlon Frost, "Empty Eyes," *CSI: Crime Scene Investigation* (also known as *C.S.I.* and *CSI: Las Vegas*), CBS, 2007.

John Cooley, "Demonology," *Criminal Minds,* CBS, 2009.

Sean Echols, "Dissolved," *CSI: Miami,* CBS, 2009.

Television Work; Pilots:

Co–executive producer, *Rectify,* AMC, 2009.

RECORDINGS

Videos:

Voice of third border world pilot, *Wing Commander IV: The Price of Freedom* (video game), Electronic Arts, 1996.

(As Walt Goggins) Narl, *4 Selections from Plimpton County's Tuff Truck Jamboree,* Blue Milk Entertainment/Mentalland, 2003.

Detective Shane Vendrell, *Under the Skin,* Twentieth Century–Fox Home Entertainment, 2005.

Voice of Detective Shane Vendrell, *The Shield* (video game), Aspyr Media, 2007.

OTHER SOURCES

Periodicals:

Entertainment Weekly, February 20, 2004, p. 17.

GOLDENBERG, William
(Billy Goldenberg, William C. Goldenberg)

PERSONAL

Addresses: *Agent*—The Skouras Agency, 1149 Third St., 3rd Floor, Santa Monica, CA 90403.

Career: Film editor. Worked as an apprentice editor, assistant editor, and associate editor.

Member: American Cinema Editors.

Awards, Honors: Emmy Award nomination, outstanding individual achievement in editing for a miniseries or a special—single–camera, 1995, for *Citizen X;* Golden Satellite Award nomination, best motion picture film editing, International Press Academy, and Online Film Critics Society Award nomination, best film editing, both 1999, for *Pleasantville;* Academy Award nomination, best editing, Golden Satellite Award nomination, best film editing, and Eddie Award nomination, best–edited feature film—dramatic, American Cinema Editors, all with others, 2000, for *The Insider;* Phoenix Film Critics Society Award nomination (with others), best film editing, 2002, for *Ali;* Emmy Award nomination (with others), outstanding multicamera picture editing for a miniseries, movie, or a special, 2002, for *The 74th Annual Academy Awards;* Academy Award nomination, best editing, Golden Satellite Award nomination, best film editing, and Eddie Award nomination, best–edited feature film—dramatic, all 2004, for *Seabiscuit;* Satellite Award nomination, best film editing, International Press Academy, 2006, for *Miami Vice.*

CREDITS

Film Editor:
Apprentice editor, *The Breakfast Club* (also known as *Breakfast Club*), Universal, 1985.
Apprentice editor, *Jagged Edge,* Columbia, 1985.
Assistant editor, *Punchline,* Columbia, 1988.
Assistant editor, *Three Fugitives,* Buena Vista, 1989.
Assistant editor, *Arachnophobia,* Buena Vista, 1990.
Associate editor, *Welcome Home, Roxy Carmichael* (also known as *Roxy* and *Welcome Home Roxy Carmichael*), Paramount, 1990.
Touch of a Stranger, Raven Star, 1990.
Additional editor, *Hook* (also known as *Captain Hook*), TriStar, 1991.
Assistant editor, *Toy Soldiers* (also known as *Boy Soldiers*), TriStar, 1991.

Alive (also known as *Alive: The Miracle of the Andes*), Buena Vista, 1993.
Kangaroo Court (short film), Lava Entertainment, 1994.
The Puppet Masters (also known as *Alien Master, Puppet Masters,* and *Robert A. Heinlein's "The Puppet Masters"*), Buena Vista, 1994.
Heat (also known as *Tension*), Warner Bros., 1995.
(As William C. Goldenberg) *The Long Kiss Goodnight* (also known as *Spy*), New Line Cinema, 1996.
Pleasantville (also known as *Color of Heart*), New Line Cinema, 1998.
The Insider (also known as *Insider, Man of the People, The Man Who Knew Too Much, Revelations, 60 Minutes, Untitled Michael Mann Film,* and *The Untitled Tobacco Project*), Buena Vista, 1999.
Coyote Ugly (also known as *Coyote Bar, Coyote Girls,* and *Show Bar*), Buena Vista, 2000.
(With others) *Ali* (also known as *Muhammad Ali*), Columbia, 2001.
Kangaroo Jack (also known as *Down and Under*), Warner Bros., 2003.
Seabiscuit, Universal, 2003.
National Treasure (also known as *Sonomo*), Buena Vista, 2004.
Domino (also known as *Domino—Live Fast, Die Young*), New Line Cinema, 2005.
Miami Vice, Universal, 2006.
Gone Baby Gone, Miramax, 2007.
National Treasure: Book of Secrets (also known as *National Treasure 2* and *National Treasure 2: Book of Secrets*), Walt Disney Studios Motion Pictures, 2007.
Confessions of a Shopaholic (also known as *I Love Shopping*), Walt Disney Studios Motion Pictures, 2009.
The Sorcerer's Apprentice, Walt Disney Studios Motion Pictures, 2010.
Transformers 3, Paramount/DreamWorks, 2011.

Television Editor; Series:
Johnny Bago, CBS, 1993.

Television Editor; Movies:
The Witness (short; also known as *Witness*), Showtime, 1992, released on video as part of *Perverse Destiny, Volume 3,* MRA, c. 2002.
Body Language, HBO, 1995.
Citizen X, HBO, 1995.

Television Editor; Specials:
Assistant editor, "Promise," *Hallmark Hall of Fame* (also known as *Hallmark Television Playhouse*), CBS, 1986.

Television Editor; Awards Presentations:
(With others) *The 74th Annual Academy Awards,* ABC, 2002.

Television Editor; Pilots:
(As Billy Goldenberg) Assistant editor, *High School USA* (also known as *High School U.S.A.*), NBC, 1983.
Over There, FX Network, 2005.

Television Appearances; Episodic:
Himself, "Ali" (also known as "The Making of 'Ali'"), *HBO First Look,* HBO, 2001.

RECORDINGS

Video Appearances; Documentaries; as Himself:
The Making of "Seabiscuit" (short; also known as *Bringing the Legend to Life: The Making of "Seabiscuit"*), Universal Studios Home Video, 2003.
Invisible Art/Visible Artists, American Cinema Editors, 2004.

Video Work:
Editor for the short film *The Witness* (also known as *Witness*), released as part of *Perverse Destiny, Volume 3,* MRA, c. 2002, originally broadcast as a movie on Showtime, 1992.

GORDON, Kiowa 1990–

PERSONAL

Full name, Kiowa Joseph Gordon; born March 25, 1990, in Berlin, Germany; raised in the United States, beginning c. 1991, primarily in Peach Springs, AZ; father, an employee of U.S. government; mother's name Camille Nighthorse Gordon (an actress).

Addresses: *Agent*—Agency for the Performing Arts, 405 South Beverly Dr., Beverly Hills, CA 90212. *Manager*—Daniel Spilo, Industry Entertainment, 955 South Carrillo Dr., 3rd Floor, Los Angeles, CA 90048.

Career: Actor.

CREDITS

Film Appearances:
Embry Call, *New Moon* (also known as *New Moon: Twilight Saga, Twilight: New Moon, The Twilight Saga: New Moon,* and *Twilight 2*), Summit Entertainment, 2009.
Embry Call, *Eclipse* (also known as *Eclipse: Twilight Saga, Twilight: Eclipse, The Twilight Saga: Eclipse—The IMAX Experience,* and *Twilight 3*), Summit Entertainment, 2010.

Television Appearances; Specials:
2010 MTV Movie Awards, MTV, 2010.
Teen Choice Awards 2010, Fox, 2010.

Television Appearances; Episodic:
Made in Hollywood, 2009.
Up Close with Carrie Keagan, ABC, 2009.

GRANT, Saginaw 1936–

PERSONAL

Full name, Saginaw Morgan Grant; born 1936, in Pawnee, OK; son of Austin, Sr. and Sarah Grant; married; children: one son, one daughter. *Education:* Graduate of Bacon Indian College. *Avocational Interests:* Outdoor activities, spectator sports, Native pow-wow gatherings.

Career: Actor. Also works as counselor, lecturer, and mentor; appeared in commercials for Best Buy and Radio Shack electronics stores, Planter's peanuts snacks, Snicker's chocolate bars, MasterCard credit cards, and Jack in the Box restaurants; also appeared in public service announcements and print ads. Enrolled member of Sauk and Fox tribe, Iowa and Otoe Missouria Nation; traditional Native American dancer; worked for Bureau of Indian Affairs. *Military service:* Served in U.S. Marine Corps.

Awards, Honors: First Americans in the Arts Award and San Francisco Native American Award, both best supporting actor, 2002.

CREDITS

Film Appearances:
Freddie Man Wolf, *War Party* (also known as *War Game*), Hemdale, 1989.
The holy man, *Small Time,* Manga Films, 1996.
Pow wow chief, *Grey Owl,* New City Releasing, 1999.
Medicine man, *Dreamer,* 2000, Film Movement, 2007.
Medicine man, *Legend of the Phantom Rider,* A–Mark Entertainment, 2002.
Grandpa, *Black Cloud,* Old Post Films, 2004.
Jake, *The World's Fastest Indian,* Magnolia Pictures, 2005.
Hanbleceya (short film), Tribal Alliance Productions, 2005.
(Uncredited) Chief Standing Bear, *It Waits,* New Arc Entertainment, 2005.
Red Hightower, *Social Guidance* (also known as *Formosa*), KOAN, 2006.

Apparition, *Beyond the Quest,* Skywalk Films, 2007.

Eddie, *Slipstream* (also known as *Slipstream Dream*), Strand Releasing, 2007.

Catches the Bear, *Walking on Turtle Island,* 2009.

Stanley, *Maneater,* Arsenal Pictures, 2009.

Other film appearances include role of spirit, *Devil's Cove,* Golden Hour Productions; companion, *Follow Me Home;* elder, *Oyana,* American Film Institute; grandfather, *Passage;* and good spirit, *Trigon: The Legend of Pelgidium.*

Television Appearances; Movies:

Chief Luta, *Stolen Women, Captured Hearts,* CBS, 1997.

Gatekeeper, *Purgatory,* TNT, 1999.

Wilson Sam, *Skinwalkers,* PBS, 2002.

Joseph, *The Fallen Ones,* Sci–Fi Channel, 2005.

Price Tenderfoot, *Eagleheart,* Cartoon Network, 2010.

Television Appearances; Series:

Auggie Velasquez, *Harts of the West,* CBS, 1993–94.

Television Appearances; Episodic:

Grey Cloud, "Young Indiana Jones and the Mystery of the Blues," *The Young Indiana Jones Chronicles,* ABC, 1993.

"The Catamount," *The Lazarus Man,* TNT and syndicated, 1996.

Alaskan, "The One with the Friends' Theme," *The Last Frontier,* Fox, 1996.

Ol'Larry, "Inside Out," *Nash Bridges,* CBS, 1997.

Eyes that See at Night, "Homecoming," *Baywatch,* syndicated, 1997.

Medicine man, "A Bridge Too Far," *Auf Wiedersehen, Pet,* BBC, 2002.

Medicine man, "Another Country," *Auf Wiedersehen, Pet,* BBC, 2002.

Medicine man, "An Inspector Calls," *Auf Wiedersehen, Pet,* BBC, 2002.

Most respected elder, "The Bone Scatterer," *Miracles,* ABC, 2003.

Dakota, "White Lie Christmas," *My Name Is Earl,* NBC, 2005.

Mudwa, "Yeehaw, Geepaw," *Saving Grace,* TNT, 2007.

Also appeared as second chief, *Dr. Quinn, Medicine Woman;* in *The Dudesons,* MTV; in *Picket Fences,* CBS; guest, *Sally Jesse Raphael.*

Television Appearances; Other:

Auggie Velasquez, *Harts of the West* (pilot), CBS, 1993.

Pawnee shaman, *Ancient Prophecies II* (special), NBC, 1994.

Old medicine man, *DreamKeeper* (miniseries), ABC, 2003.

Appeared in *By Word of Mouth.*

RECORDINGS

Videos:

Appeared in music videos recorded by Louise Miguel and Bruce Springsteen.

OTHER SOURCES

Electronic:

Saginaw Grant Official Site, http://www.saginawgrant.com, September 7, 2010.

GUNN, Suzette
(Suzette Azariah Gunn)

PERSONAL

Education: Graduate of Howard University and Oxford University.

Addresses: *Contact*—Laurie Smith, Smith Talent Group, 14 Minetta St., 1st Floor, New York, NY 10012; Kerin–Goldberg Associates, 155 East 55th St., New York, NY 10022.

Career: Actress, producer, director, and writer. Also works as acting coach and performance artist. YOUr-Reels, creator and marketer of demonstrations reels for professional performers; Its Personal Films, creator and producer; Art of the Craft (workshop), developing partner.

Awards, Honors: Audelco Award nomination, best lead actress, Audience Development Committee, 2006.

CREDITS

Film Appearances:

Adrienne, *The Wannabe* (short film), 2006.

Sarita, *Premature* (short film), Mi Alma Films/Relative Noise, 2008.

(As Suzette Azariah Gunn) Minnie Ripperton, *Cadillac Records,* TriStar, 2008.

Isis Steele, *Spare Change,* 2010.

Lizette Santiago, *Roadie,* Hero Content, 2010.
Kiki, *You're Nobody 'til Somebody Kills You,* 2010.

Film Producer:
Spare Change, 2010.

Television Appearances; Episodic:
Detective Luisa Valenzuela, "Gunplay," *Law & Order,* NBC, 2004.
Elena Hernandez, "41 Shots," *Law & Order: Trial by Jury,* NBC, 2005.
(As Suzette Azariah Gunn) Norma "Nightshade" Robbins, "Flipped," *Law & Order: Criminal Intent* (also known as *Law & Order: CI*), NBC, 2007.
Alicia Spivey, "There Is No Superwoman," *Mercy,* NBC, 2010.

Stage Appearances; As Suzette Azariah Gunn:
The Phoenix Does Rise, Nuyorican Poets Cafe, New York City, 2004.
Sarah, *Funnyhouse of a Negro,* Classical Theatre of Harlem, HSA Theatre, New York City, 2006.
Birthright, Billie Holliday Theatre, Brooklyn, NY, 2007.

Appeared as Smiles, *Paradox of the Urban Cliche,* LAByrinth Theatre Company, New York City.

Stage Work:
(As Suzette Azariah Gunn) Coproducer, *The Phoenix Does Rise,* Nuyorican Poets Cafe, New York City, 2004.

WRITINGS

Screenplays:
Spare Change, 2010.

Stage Shows:
(As Suzette Azariah Gunn) *The Phoenix Does Rise,* Nuyorican Poets Cafe, New York City, 2004.

OTHER SOURCES

Periodicals:
Black Hands Review, January 10, 2007, p. 2.

Electronic:
Suzette Gunn Official Site, http://www.suzettegunn.com, August 2, 2010.

H

HALL, Arsenio 1955–
   (Arsenio)

PERSONAL

Born February 12, 1955, in Cleveland, OH; son of Fred (a Baptist minister) and Anne Hall. *Education:* Attended Ohio University; Kent State University, B.A., communications.

Addresses: *Agent*—Writers and Artists Agency, 8383 Wilshire Blvd., Suite 550, Beverly Hills, CA 90211; Creative Artists Agency, 9830 Wilshire Blvd., Beverly Hills, CA 90212–1825. *Manager*—c/o ML Management, 152 West 57th St., 47th Floor, New York, NY 10019. *Contact*—9701 Wilshire Blvd., 10th Floor, Beverly Hills, CA 90212.

Career: Talk show host, actor, comedian, producer, and composer. Performed stand–up comedy act throughout the United States, 1979; also appeared as a magician and a drummer with a pop music band; appeared in commercials for Tab, c. mid–1980s, and 1–800–COLLECT, 1999.

Awards, Honors: NAACP Image Award, best supporting actor in a motion picture, National Association for the Advancement of Colored People, 1988, and American Comedy Award, funniest supporting male in a motion picture, 1989, Image Award, outstanding supporting actor in a motion picture, 1990, for *Coming to America;* Soul Train Music Award, Entertainer of the Year, 1990; People's Choice Award, favorite late night talk show host, 1990; NAACP Image Award, Key of Life Award, 1991; Emmy Award nominations, outstanding variety, music or comedy series, 1989 and 1990, American Comedy Award nomination, funniest male performer in a television series—leading role network, cable or syndication, 1990, NAACP Image Award, outstanding variety series, 1991, for *The Arsenio Hall Show;* honorary degree, Central State University, 1992; star on Hollywood Walk of Fame.

CREDITS

Film Appearances:
More Laughing Room Only, 1986.
(Film debut; as Arsenio) Apartment victim, "Mondo Condo," *Amazon Women on the Moon* (also known as *Cheeseburger Film Sandwich*), Universal, 1987.
Semmi, Morris, extremely ugly girl, and Reverend Brown, *Coming to America* (also known as *Prince in New York*), Paramount, 1988.
Crying man, *Harlem Nights,* Paramount, 1989.
Host, *Time Out: The Truth about HIV, AIDS, and You,* 1992.
Himself, *Blankman,* Sony, 1994.
Playboy: The Best of Pamela Anderson, 1995.
Playboy: The Complete Anna Nicole Smith, 2000.
Tupac: Resurrection, 2003.
200 Greatest Pop Culture Icons, VH1, 2003.
TV in Black: The First Fifty Years, 2004.
The Naked Brothers Band: The Movie, 2005.
Voice of Captain Crothers, *Scooby–Doo! Pirates Ahoy,* 2006.
Heckler, 2007.
Be Funny, 2008.
Voice of Carl Cristall, *Igor,* 2008.
Tasty Freeze, *Black Dynamite,* 2009.

Film Executive Producer:
Time Out: The Truth about HIV, AIDS, and You, 1992.
Bopha!, Paramount, 1993.

Television Appearances; Series:
Cohost, *The Half Hour Comedy Hour,* ABC, 1983.

Guest panelist, *The Match Game/Hollywood Squares Hour,* 1983–84.

Cohost, *Thicke of the Night,* syndicated, 1984.

The New Love, American Style, ABC, 1985.

Motown Revue (also known as *The Motown Revue Starring Smokey Robinson*), NBC, 1985.

Voice of Winston Zeddmore, *The Real Ghostbusters* (animated; also known as *Slimer and the Real Ghostbusters*), ABC, 1986–87.

Cohost, *Solid Gold* (also known as *Solid Gold in Concert*), syndicated, 1986–88.

Guest host, *The Late Show* (also known as *The Late Show Starring Joan Rivers* and *The Late Show Starring Arsenio Hall*), Fox, 1987.

Comedy Club, 1987.

Host, *The Arsenio Hall Show,* syndicated, 1989–94.

Michael Atwood, *Arsenio,* ABC, 1996–97.

Terrell Parker, *Martial Law,* CBS, 1998–2000.

(In archive footage) Himself, *Arsenio Jams,* VH1, 2001.

Guest appearance, *Hollywood Squares* (also known as *H2: Hollywood Squares*), syndicated, 2002–2003.

The Jazzspel with Eric J, 2003.

The Blacklist: 100 Greatest Power Moves, 2008.

The World's Funniest Moments, 2008–2009.

Correspondent, *The Jay Leno Show,* 2009–10.

Television Appearances; Specials:

Uptown Comedy Express, HBO, 1987.

Going for Laughs, 1983.

The R.A.C.E., NBC, 1989.

Mike Tyson—A Portrait of the People's Champion, syndicated, 1989.

Comic Relief III, HBO, 1989.

The Comedy Store 15th Year Class Reunion, NBC, 1989.

A Laugh, A Tear, syndicated, 1990.

Face to Face with Connie Chung, CBS, 1990.

Racism: Points of View, MTV, 1991.

A Party for Richard Pryor, CBS, 1991.

First Person with Maria Shriver, NBC, 1991.

In a New Light: A Call to Action in the War against AIDS, ABC, 1992.

The Comedy Store's 20th Birthday, NBC, 1992.

Kathie Lee Gifford's Celebration of Motherhood, ABC, 1993.

Apollo Theatre Hall of Fame, NBC, 1993.

Host, *In a New Light '93,* ABC, 1993.

24 Hours in Rock and Roll, 1994.

Host, *The Soul Train 25th Anniversary Hall of Fame Special* (also known as *Soul Train's 25th Anniversary*), 1995.

50 Years of Funny Females, 1995.

Classic Stand–Up Comedy of Television, 1996.

Celebrate the Dream: 50 Years of Ebony, ABC, 1996.

Comic Relief American Comedy Festival, ABC, 1996.

Happy Birthday Elizabeth—A Celebration of Life, ABC, 1997.

Intimate Portrait: Patti LaBelle, Lifetime, 1998.

Narrator, *Intimate Portrait: Josephine Baker,* Lifetime, 1999.

The Politically Incorrect After Party, ABC, 2000.

The Comedy Store: The E! True Hollywood Story, E! Entertainment Television, 2001.

Inside TV Land: African Americans in Television, TV Land, 2002.

(Uncredited) Himself, *Inside the Playboy Mansion,* Arts and Entertainment, 2002.

Diet Coke with Lemon Celebrates 40 Years of Laughter: At the Improv, 2002.

Cohost, *World's Greatest Commercials,* CBS, 2002.

Laugh Out Loud: TV's 15 Greatest Comedians, Arts and Entertainment, 2002.

Host, *The 5th Annual Sears Soul Train Christmas Starfest,* The WB, 2002.

Cohost, *World's Greatest Commercials,* 2002.

The 6th Annual Sears Soul Train Christmas Starfest, UPN, 2003.

Boomer Nation, Arts & Entertainment Television, 2003.

TV's Illest Minority Moments Presented by Ego Trip, VH1, 2004.

When Stand–Up Comics Ruled the World, 2004.

Unforgettable Moments in Television Entertainment: A Museum of Television & Radio Special, NBC, 2004.

25 Strong: The BET Silver Anniversary Special, Black Entertainment Television, 2005.

Eddie Murphy: The Making of Delirious, MyNetworkTV, 2006.

Host, *The Harlem Globetrotters: A New Generation,* MyNetworkTV, 2007.

Magic & Bird, HBO, 2009.

Also host, *The Magic of Christmas,* broadcast on a local station in Cleveland, OH.

Television Appearances; Awards Presentations:

Host, *MTV's … Video Music Awards Show,* MTV, 1988, 1989, 1990, 1991.

The … Annual NAACP Image Awards, NBC, 1989, 1992, 1993, 1996, Fox, 2001.

The … Annual Emmy Awards, Fox, 1989, ABC, 2000.

The 3rd Annual American Comedy Awards, ABC, 1989.

The 15th Annual People's Choice Awards, CBS, 1989.

The 4th Annual Soul Train Music Awards, syndicated, 1990.

Soul Train Comedy Awards, syndicated, 1993.

The American Television Awards, ABC, 1993.

The 51st Annual Golden Globe Awards, TBS, 1994.

Tribute segment host, *The 23rd Annual American Music Awards,* 1996.

Host, *The 28th Annual NAACP Image Awards,* 1997.

Presenter, *The American Comedy Awards,* 1997.

Host, *The … Annual Soul Train Music Awards,* syndicated, 2002, The WB, 2003.

Presenter, *TV Land Awards: A Celebration of Classic TV,* TV Land, Nickelodeon, 2003.

Cohost, *9th Annual Soul Train Lady of Soul Awards,* The WB, 2003.

The 2nd Annual TV Land Awards, TV Land, 2004.

Television Appearances; Episodic:

Himself, "The Spinners/Skyy," *Soul Train,* 1981.

Himself, "The Four Tops/Stacy Lattisaw," *Soul Train,* 1981.

Madame's Place, 1982.

Dr. Mustapha Abdul Raheem Jamaal X Muhammad/ Tyrone, "Dr. Black, Mr. Hyde," *Movie Macabre* (also known as *Elvira's Movie Macabre*), 1982.

Cleavon, "Happy Birthday," *Alfred Hitchcock Presents,* NBC, 1986.

"Uptown Comedy Express," *On Location,* HBO, 1987.

Himself, "Where Nobody Knows Your Name," *Cheers,* NBC, 1990.

"Ask Dr. Doogie," *Doogie Howser, M.D.,* 1990.

Himself, "The Joke," *The Jackie Thomas Show,* ABC, 1992.

Himself, "The Last Laugh," *Blossom,* 1993.

Himself, "Friends Like These," *Living Single,* 1994.

Himself "The Cameo Show," *Muppets Tonight!,* 1997.

"M.C. Hammer," *Behind the Music* (also known as *VH1's Behind the Music*), 1997.

"Redd Foxx: Say It Like It Is," *Biography,* Arts and Entertainment, 2000.

Joe, "Norm vs. the Kids," *The Norm Show,* ABC, 2000.

"The Comedy Store," *E! True Hollywood Story,* 2001.

"Patti LaBelle: Surviving with Soul," *Biography,* Arts and Entertainment, 2001.

Tinseltown TV, International Channel, 2003.

Host, *Star Search,* 2003, 2004.

Chappelle's Show (also known as *Chappelle's Show: The Lost Episodes*), 2004.

"Paula Abdul," *Biography,* Arts and Entertainment, 2005.

"Eddie Murphy," *Biography,* Arts and Entertainment, 2008.

Memories de la tele, 2008.

WWF Raw Is War, 2009.

"Snoop/Fat Kid," *Brothers,* Fox, 2009.

Made in Hollywood, 2009.

Television Talk Show Guest Appearances; Episodic:

The Tonight Show Starring Johnny Carson, NBC, 1986.

Face to Face with Connie Chung, CBS, 1990.

The Howard Stern Show (also known as *The Howard Stern Summer Show*), 1991.

First Person with Maria Shriver, NBC, 1991.

The Late Show with David Letterman, 1995.

The Chris Rock Show, HBO, 1996–2002.

The Rosie O'Donnell Show, syndicated, 1997.

The Magic Hour, syndicated, 1998.

The Tonight Show with Jay Leno, NBC, 1998–2009.

The Wayne Brady Show, syndicated, 2004.

Tavis Smiley, PBS, 2004.

The Sharon Osbourne Show (also known as *Sharon*), syndicated, 2004.

Up Close with Carrie Keagan, 2009.

Television Appearances; Movies:

Voice of Dr. Carver/Bobby Proud, *The Proud Family Movie,* 2005.

The Naked Brothers Band, Nickelodeon, 2006.

Television Appearances; Miniseries:

Pioneers of Television, PBS, 2007.

Television Executive Producer; Series:

The Arsenio Hall Show (series), syndicated, 1989–94.

The Party Machine with Nia Peeples (series), syndicated, 1991.

Arsenio (series), ABC, 1996–97.

Television Executive Producer; Specials:

One on One with Magic Johnson (special), Fox, 1994.

RECORDINGS

Videos:

Paula Abdul: Straight Up, 1989.

Playboy Exposed: Playboy Mansion Parties Uncensored, 2001.

Comic interview, *Living in the Spirit Revue,* 2001.

Before They Were Kings: Vol 1, 2004.

Music Videos:

Appeared in "Straight Up" by Paula Abdul.

Albums:

Recorded (as Chunky A), *Large and In Charge.*

WRITINGS

Television Theme Songs; Series:

"Hall or Nothing," *The Arsenio Hall Show,* syndicated, 1989–94.

Television Episodes:

Motown Revue, NBC, 1985.

The Arsenio Hall Show, syndicated, 1989–94.

Television Specials:

Uptown Comedy Express, 1987.

Opening monologue, *The Soul Train 25th Anniversary Hall of Fame Special,* CBS, 1995.

Screenplays:
Before They Were Kings: Vol. 1, 2004.

Film Songs:
"Hall or Nothing," *Hot Shots! Part Deux,* 1993.

OTHER SOURCES

Periodicals:
Newsweek, March 10, 1997, p. 78.
New York Times Magazine, October 1, 1989, pp. 29–31, 65–66, 92–93.
Time, March 10, 1997, pp. 82–83.
TV Guide, September 30, 1989, pp. 16–19.
US, September 18, 1989, pp. 24–28, 30, 32–33.
Village Voice, May 23, 1989, pp. 27–31.

HAMMOND, Darrell 1955(?)–

PERSONAL

Born October 8, 1955 (some sources cite 1960), in Melbourne, FL; married Elizabeth (divorced, c. 1980s); remarried Elizabeth, May 9, 1990; children: Mia. *Education:* Graduate of University of Florida.

Addresses: *Agent*—WME Entertainment, 9601 Wilshire Blvd., 3rd Floor, Beverly Hills, CA 90210. *Manager*—Tim Sarkes, Brillstein Entertainment Partners, 9150 Wilshire Blvd., Suite 350, Beverly Hills, CA 90212.

Career: Actor and comedian. Appeared in commercial for MyTouch cellular phones, 2009. Radio 105.1 FM, Orlando, FL, worked as a disc jockey in the late 1980s; also worked as a waiter.

Awards, Honors: *TV Guide* Award nomination (with Will Ferrell), breakout star of the year, 2001, for *Saturday Night Live.*

CREDITS

Television Appearances; Series:
Member of ensemble, *Saturday Night Live Saturday Night Live* (also known as *SNL*), NBC, 1995–2010.
Member of ensemble, *Saturday Night Live: Weekend Update Thursday,* NBC, 2008–2009.
The Deacon, a recurring role, *Damages,* FX Network, 2009.

Television Appearances; Specials:
71st Annual Macy's Thanksgiving Day Parade, NBC, 1997.
(Uncredited; in archive footage) Jesse Jackson, *The Bad Boys of Saturday Night Live,* NBC, 1998.
(In archive footage) Jesse Jackson, *Saturday Night Live: The Best of Chris Rock,* NBC, 1999.
(Uncredited; in archive footage) *SNL: 25 Years of Music,* NBC, 1999.
(Uncredited) Audience member, *Saturday Night Live: 25th Anniversary* (also known as *Saturday Night Live: 25th Anniversary Primetime Special, Saturday Night Live 25,* and *SNL 25: 25 Years of Laughs*), NBC, 1999.
"Darrell Hammond," *Comedy Central Presents,* Comedy Central, 2000.
(In archive footage) *Saturday Night Live: Best of the Clinton Scandal,* NBC, 2000.
Member of ensemble, *Saturday Night Live: Presidential Bash,* NBC, 2000, 2004 (also known as *Saturday Night Live's Presidential Bash 2004: The Great Debates*), 2008.
(In archive footage) *Saturday Night Live: Best of Game Show Parodies,* NBC, 2000.
Member of ensemble, *Saturday Night Live: Mother's Day Special,* NBC, 2001.
Sports Illustrated's Night of Champions, NBC, 2001.
Member of ensemble, *Saturday Night Live Primetime Extra: Parts 1 & 2,* NBC, 2001.
Member of ensemble, *Saturday Night Live: TV Tales,* NBC, 2002.
(Uncredited; in archive footage) *Saturday Night Live: The Best of Will Ferrell,* NBC, 2003.
Night of Too Many Stars, NBC, 2003.
The Mark Twain Prize: Lily Tomlin, PBS, 2003.
Voice, *A Freezerburnt Christmas,* NBC, 2003.
Chris Matthews, *Saturday Night Live Weekend Update Halftime Special,* NBC, 2003.
(Uncredited; in archive footage) *Saturday Night Live: The Best of Chris Kattan,* NBC, 2003.
The Celebrity Hot 100 of Forbes, Arts and Entertainment, 2004.
(Uncredited; in archive footage) *Saturday Night Live: The Best of Cheri Oteri,* NBC, 2004.
(Uncredited; in archive footage) *Saturday Night Live: The Best of Christopher Walken,* NBC, 2004.
(In archive footage) *101 Most Unforgettable SNL Moments,* E! Entertainment Television, 2004.
Presenter, *On Stage at the Kennedy Center: The Mark Twain Prize Celebrating Lorne Michaels,* PBS, 2005.
(Uncredited; in archive footage) *Saturday Night Live: The Best of Jon Lovitz,* NBC, 2005.
(Uncredited; in archive footage) *Saturday Night Live: The Best of Commercial Parodies,* NBC, 2005.
(In archive footage) *Saturday Night Live: The Best of Alec Baldwin,* NBC, 2005.
(Uncredited; in archive footage) Skeeter, *Saturday Night Live: The Best of David Spade,* NBC, 2005.

Member of ensemble, *Saturday Night Live in the '90s: Pop Culture Nation,* NBC, 2007.

(Uncredited; in archive footage) *Saturday Night Live Sports Extra '09,* NBC, 2009.

(In archive footage) *Saturday Night Live: The Best of Amy Poehler,* NBC, 2009.

(Uncredited; in archive footage) *Saturday Night Live: Just Shorts,* NBC, 2009.

(Uncredited; in archive footage) *SNL Presents: A Very Gilly Christmas,* NBC, 2009.

Saturday Night Live in the 2000s: Time and Again, NBC, 2010.

(Uncredited; in archive footage) *Saturday Night Live Presents: Sports All–Stars,* NBC, 2010.

Television Appearances; Episodic:

Himself, "Sometimes When We Touch," *Apt. 2F,* 1997.

Oddville, MTV, MTV, 1997.

Premium Blend, Comedy Central, 1998.

The Martin Short Show, syndicated, 1999.

Hollywood Squares (also known as *H2* and *H2: Hollywood Squares*), multiple appearances, between 1999 and 2001.

Himself, "Dick'll Take Manhattan: Parts 1 & 2," *3rd Rock from the Sun* (also known as *Encounters of the Personal Kind* and *3rd Rock*), NBC, 2000.

Ted Bolger, "Runaway," *Law & Order: Special Victims Unit* (also known as *Law & Order: SVU* and *Special Victims Unit*), NBC, 2001.

Vice President Dick Cheney, *Primetime Glick,* Comedy Central, 2001.

Who Counts?, 2002.

Comic Remix, 2002.

(Uncredited) *60 Minutes* (also known as *TV Land Legends: The 60 Minutes Interviews*), CBS, 2004.

Leonard Timmons, "No Exit," *Law & Order: Criminal Intent* (also known as *Law & Order: CI*), NBC, 2005.

Josh, "3D," *Starved,* FX Network, 2005.

Ben Carlson, Carlos, and Ted Waters, "Double Down, Triple Threat," *Las Vegas,* NBC, 2005.

(In archive footage) *Howard Stern on Demand,* 2006.

(In archive footage) *Anderson Cooper 360 Degrees,* Cable News Network, 2008.

Entertainment Tonight (also known as *E.T.* and *This Week in Entertainment*), syndicated, 2008, 2010.

Television Appearances; Awards Presentations:

Cohost, *The 55th Annual Primetime Emmy Awards,* Fox, 2003.

Host, *25th Annual News and Documentary Emmy Awards,* The Discovery Channel, 2004.

Television Appearances; Pilots:

William & Ree Comedy Central, The Nashville Network, 1991.

Television Talk Show Guest Appearances; Episodic:

Late Show with David Letterman (also known as *The Late Show* and *Letterman*), CBS, 1995.

Late Night with Conan O'Brien, NBC, multiple appearances, between 1996 and 2008.

The Daily Show with Jon Stewart (also known as *The Daily Show* and *The Daily Show with Jon Stewart Global Edition*), Comedy Central, 1997.

The Rosie O'Donnell Show, syndicated, 2000, 2001.

The Wayne Brady Show, ABC, 2001.

The Tonight Show with Jay Leno, NBC, multiple appearances, between 2001 and 2005.

The Late Late Show with Craig Kilborn (also known as *The Late Late Show*), CBS, 2003.

Live with Regis and Kelly, syndicated, 2004.

Howard Stern on Demand (also known as *Howard TV on Demand*), 2006.

Charlie Rose (also known as *The Charlie Rose Show*), PBS, 2008.

Film Appearances:

Greenkeeper, *Greenkeeping,* Central Park Films, 1992.

Chris McCarthy, *Celtic Pride* (also known as *Dunk Brothers*), Buena Vista, 1996.

Mr. Robertson, *Blues Brothers 2000,* Universal, 1998.

Voice of Master Little, *The King and I* (animated), Warner Bros., 1999.

The Devil and Daniel Webster, Family Room Entertainment, 2001, released as *Shortcut to Happiness,* 2004.

Earl, *Agent Cody Banks,* Metro–Goldwyn–Mayer, 2003.

Father Muldoon, *Scary Movie 3* (also known as *Scary Movie 3.5*), Miramax/Dimension Films, 2003.

Hudson McGill, *New York Minute,* Warner Bros., 2004.

Michael, *Kiss Me Again,* Monarch Home Video, 2006.

Jonathan, *Puff, Puff, Pass,* Sony Pictures Home Entertainment, 2006.

Dr. Lawrence Rosenblum, *Ira & Abby,* Magnolia Pictures, 2007.

Captain Jack Swallows, *Epic Movie,* Twentieth Century–Fox, 2007.

Turner Claymore, *Netherbeast Incorporated,* Shoreline Entertainment, 2007.

Dr. Dwayne, *Wieners,* Screen Gems, 2008.

Karaoke Killer, *BuzzKill,* Buzz Kill production company, 2010.

Stage Appearances:

Douglas Panch, *The 25th Annual Putnam County Spelling Bee,* Circle in the Square, New York City, 2007.

Internet Appearances; Videos:

Bill Clinton, *Presidential Reunion,* FunnyOrDie.com, 2010.

RECORDINGS

Videos:

(Uncredited; in archive footage) *Saturday Night Live: The Best of Mike Myers,* 1998.

(Uncredited; in archive footage) Marge Schott, *Saturday Night Live: The Best of Molly Shannon*, 2001.

(Uncredited; in archive footage) Red Ships of Spain announcer, *Saturday Night Live: The Best of Will Ferrell—Volume 2*, Lions Gate Films Home Entertainment, 2004.

(Uncredited; in archive footage) *Saturday Night Live: The Best of Tracy Morgan*, 2004.

(Uncredited; in archive footage) *Saturday Night Live: The Best of Jimmy Fallon*, 2005.

(Uncredited; in archive footage) *Saturday Night Live: The Best of Saturday TV Funhouse*, 2006.

WRITINGS

Television Specials:
"Darrell Hammond," *Comedy Central Presents*, Comedy Central, 2000.

HAPKA, Mark 1982–

PERSONAL

Full name, Mark David Hapka; born May 29, 1982, in Buffalo, NY. *Education:* Onondaga Community College, music degree; studied at Playhouse West; attended workshops.

Addresses: *Agent*—The Gage Group, 14724 Ventura Blvd., Suite 505, Sherman Oaks, CA 91403.

Career: Actor. Participated in various events. Worked as a bartender.

CREDITS

Television Appearances; Series:
Nathan Horton, *Days of Our Lives* (also known as *Cruise of Deception: Days of Our Lives, Days, DOOL, Tropical Temptation, Tropical Temptation: Days of Our Lives, Des jours et des vies, Horton-sagaen, I gode og onde dager, Los dias de nuestras vidas, Meres agapis, Paeivien viemaeae, Vaara baesta aar, Zeit der Sehnsucht,* and *Zile din viata noastra*), NBC, 2007—.

Television Appearances; Episodic:
Zach, "The Gathering," *Ghost Whisperer*, CBS, 2007.
Johnny DiMera, *Days of Our Lives* (also known as *Cruise of Deception: Days of Our Lives, Days, DOOL, Tropical Temptation, Tropical Temptation: Days of Our Lives, Des jours et des vies, Horton-*

sagaen, *I gode og onde dager, Los dias de nuestras vidas, Meres agapis, Paeivien viemaeae, Vaara baesta aar, Zeit der Sehnsucht,* and *Zile din viata noastra*), NBC, 2007, 2008.

(And in archive footage) *Current TV*, 2007, 2010.
Jeff, "A Tale of Two Parties," *Greek*, ABC Family, 2008.
Zach, "Deadbeat Dads," *Ghost Whisperer*, CBS, 2008.
Austin Rain, "Cheat It," *Hannah Montana* (also known as *Hannah Montana Forever* and *Secret Idol Hannah Montana*), The Disney Channel, 2009.
Mark Callahan in 1976, "Jackals," *Cold Case* (also known as *Anexihniastes ypothesis, Caso abierto, Cold case—affaires classees, Cold Case—Kein Opfer ist je vergessen, Doegloett aktak, Kalla spaar, Todistettavasti syyllinen,* and *Victimes du passe*), CBS, 2009.

Film Appearances:
Mark, *Good Time Max*, IFC Films, 2008.
Photographer, *Real Fiction* (short film), Cittadino/Dugan Entertainment, 2008.
Matt, *Second Sight* (short film), 2009.
Store attorney, *The Cellar*, Invisible Forces/On Time and Sober Productions, 2009.
Bo Sanders, *Beyond the Mat* (also known as *Near Fall*), Catch 22 Entertainment, 2010.
Danny McKay, *The Danny McKay Project*, 2010.
Mark (Little Richard), *Midgets vs Mascots* (also known as *A Tribute to Big Red*), First Look International, 2010.

Film Work:
Producer, *Beyond the Mat* (also known as *Near Fall*), Catch 22 Entertainment, 2010.

Internet Appearances; Series:
Zach, *Ghost Whisperer: The Other Side*, http://www.cbs.com/primetime/ghost_whisperer/the_other_side and http://www.cbs.com/innertube, c. 2007–2008.
Chad Slutsky, *Private High Musical*, broadcast on YouTube, http://www.youtube.com, beginning 2008.

Stage Appearances:
Cohost and performer, *ACME Saturday Night*, ACME Comedy Theatre, Hollywood, CA, 2010.

WRITINGS

Writings for the Stage:
(With others) *ACME Saturday Night*, ACME Comedy Theatre, Hollywood, CA, 2010.

OTHER SOURCES

Electronic:
BuffaloNews.com, http://www.buffalonews.com, November 17, 2009.

HARRAS, Patricia
    (Patti Harras)

PERSONAL

Full name, Patricia Ann Harras; born in Winnipeg, Manitoba, Canada.

Addresses: *Agent*—Jamie Levitt, Lauren Levitt and Associates, 1525 West Eighth Ave., Vancouver, British Columbia V6J 1T5, Canada.

Career: Actress, director, and writer.

Awards, Honors: Gemini Award, outstanding lead actress, Academy of Canadian Cinema and Television, 1998, for *Jake and the Kid*; Gemini Award nomination, best gust actress in a dramatic series, 1998, for *Cold Squad*; Leo Award, best actress in a short drama, Motion Picture Arts and Sciences Foundation of British Columbia, 2001, for *Legs Apart*; Leo Award nomination, best guest actress in a dramatic series, 2003, for "Live Fast Die Young," *Cold Squad*.

CREDITS

Television Appearances; Movies:
Julie, *Have You Seen My Son?*, ABC, 1996.
(As Patti Harras) Well–dressed woman, *Nightmare Street*, ABC, 1998.
Dr. Vanderbosch, *Christmas Rush* (also known as *Breakaway*), TBS, 2002.
Mary, *Dawn Anna*, Lifetime, 2005.
Sandy Bradshaw, *Flight '93* (also known as *Airport United 93*), Arts and Entertainment, 2006.
Francoise Cloutier, *The Hunters*, Lifetime, 2006.
Mrs. Campbell, *Deep Cove* (also known as *Fear Island*), 2009.

Television Appearances; Series:
Sally Caulfield–MacBride, *The Marshal*, ABC, 1995.
Lydia Archer, *Tower Prep*, Cartoon Network, 2010.

Television Appearances; Episodic:
Yvonne Leed, "Battered," *Sirens*, ABC, 1993.
Millie, "Blast from the Past," *Cobra*, syndicated, 1994.
Debbie, "Sandkings," *The Outer Limits* (also known as *The New Outer Limits*), Showtime, 1995.
Barbara, "Off Broadway: Part 2," *The Commish*, ABC, 1995.
Julia Osborne, "We All Live in Crocus," *Jake and the Kid*, 1995.
Julia Osborne, "Grand Plans," *Jake and the Kid*, 1995.
Julia Osborne, "Long Live the Queen," *Jake and the Kid*, 1996.
Sandy Kilkenney, "Rita Brice," *Cold Squad* (also known as *Files from the Past*), CTV, 1998.
Deborah Wagner, "Seven Deadly Sins," *Dead Man's Gun*, Showtime, 1998.
Denise Kaylen, "Seminar from Hell," *Viper*, syndicated, 1999.
Karen Vincennes, "Dead to Rights," *The Crow: Stairway to Heaven*, syndicated, 1999.
Amy, "Breaking Point," *The Outer Limits* (also known as *The New Outer Limits*), Showtime, 2000.
Maggie Martin, "Code of Silence," *Just Cause*, PAX, 2002.
Meg Duffy, "Live Fast Die Young," *Cold Squad* (also known as *Files from the Past*), CTV, 2002.
Carol Sumlin, "Wake–up Call," *The 4400*, USA Network, 2005.
Carol, "Unlocking the Secrets," *The 4400*, USA Network, 2006.
Fake Carter, "Memento Mori," *Stargate SG–1*, Sci–Fi Channel, 2006.
Laura Wallace, "What about Bob?," *Eureka* (also known as *A Town Called Eureka*), Sci–Fi Channel, 2008.
Donna, "Swap Meat," *Supernatural*, The CW, 2010.

Appeared in "Janine Elston," an episode of *Cold Squad*, CTV.

Television Appearances; Pilots:
Sally Caulfield–MacBride, *The Marshal*, ABC, 1995.
Rebecca Stone, *Conspiracy*, 2007.

Film Appearances:
Tunes a Plenty, 1987.
Zombie, *Linnea Quigley's Horror Workout*, Cinema Home Video, 1990.
Van driver's wife, *Intersection*, Paramount, 1994.
Johnna, *Bliss*, Triumph Releasing, 1997.
NASA wife, *Mission to Mars* (also known as *M2M*), Buena Vista, 2000.
Di, *Legs Apart*, Toronto International Film Festival, 2000.
Dr. Simon, *Numb*, Scanbox Entertainment, 2007.
Fan Four receptionist, *Rise of the Silver Surfer* (also known as *Fantastic Four: Galaxy Crisis* and *Fantastic Four: Rise of the Silver Surfer*), Twentieth Century–Fox, 2007.
Howard's wife, *Things We Lost in the Fire*, Paramount, 2007.
Lorraine, *Love Happens*, Universal, 2009.

Stage Appearances:
Meg, *Crimes of the Heart*, 1986.
Lou Lou Belle Lee, *Frontier Psychiatrist*, 1986.
Marcia, *Ya Divvy*, 1986.
Hortensia, *The Rehearsal*, 1987.

Carol, *The Reunion,* 1987.
Louise, *After the Fall,* 1988.
Amanda, *Private Lives,* 1988.
Lady Anne, *Richard III,* 1988.
Susan Harder, *Heat,* 1990.
Amy Lee, *Laundry and Bourbon,* 1990.
Honey, *Who's Afraid of Virginia Woolf?,* 1996.
Curley's wife, *Of Mice and Men,* 1997.
Claire Harrison, *Whose Life Is It Anyway?,* First Impressions Theatre, Deep Cove Shaw Theatre, Deep Cove, British Columbia, Canada, 2001.
Julie, *Pizza Man,* 2005.
Doris, *Same Time Next Year,* 2009.

Appeared as Miss Lynch and Alice in a production of the musical *Grease.*

Stage Director:
The Scottish Play, 1998.

WRITINGS

Stage Plays:
The Scottish Play, 1998.

HAVEY, Allan 1954–

PERSONAL

Born September 19, 1954, in St. Louis, MO; married Susan Holcomb, 1995. *Education:* Florida State University, B.F.A., 1978.

Addresses: *Manager*—Naomi Odenkirk, Odenkirk Provissiero Entertainment, 650 North Bronson Ave., Building B145, Los Angeles, CA 90004.

Career: Actor and producer. Member of the comedy duo Two for Nothing, c. 1978–80; standup comedian, beginning in New York City, 1981, including appearances at the Improv; also appeared a colleges, comedy clubs, and comedy festivals; toured Europe and Australia. Appeared in commercials, including an ad for Wendy's restaurants, 2004. Worked as a waiter and bartender.

CREDITS

Film Appearances:
Pat Hagen, *Checking Out,* Warner Bros., 1989.

Love or Money (also known as *For Love or Money*), Hemdale, 1990.
Judson, *Internal Affairs,* Paramount, 1990.
Guberman, *Rounders,* Miramax, 1998.
Dean the greens keeper, *Knockaround Guys,* New Line Cinema, 2002.
Comedian, Miramax, 2002.
Husband, *Melvin Goes to Dinner,* Arrival Pictures, 2003.
Vet, *Wild Things 2,* Columbia TriStar Home Entertainment, 2004.
The Good Part (short film), Out West Studios/ Tullyvision, 2005.
Adam's dad, *Adam and Eve* (also known as *National Lampoon "Adam & Eve"*), New Line Cinema, 2005.
The Aristocrats (documentary; also known as *The @r!$t*(r@t$*), THINKFilm, 2005.
Convict, *Hancock* (also known as *Hidden from Earth*), Columbia, 2008.
Boxman, *Fragments* (also known as *Winged Creatures*), Columbia, 2008.
Chun Li's father, *Me, You, a Bag & Bamboo* (short film), Sweet Potato Productions, 2009.
FBI Special Agent Dean Paisley, *The Informant!,* Warner Bros., 2009.

Television Appearances; Series:
Member of ensemble, *The New Show,* 1984.
Host, *Night after Night with Allan Havey,* Comedy Central, 1989–92.
Bob Stahlings, *Free Ride,* Fox, 2006.

Television Appearances; Specials:
The 11th Annual Young Comedians, HBO, 1987.
Comic Relief IV, HBO, 1991.
Comic Relief V, HBO, 1992.
The Real Deal, Comedy Central, 1995.
Larry David: Curb Your Enthusiasm, HBO, 1999.

Television Appearances; Episodic:
Late Night with David Letterman, NBC, 1986.
One Night Stand, HBO, 1991, 1992.
Policeman, "The Wait Out," *Seinfeld,* NBC, 1996.
Jay Lowery, "Talk Is Cheap," *Viper,* 1996.
Homeowner, "Chet's Shirt," *Curb Your Enthusiasm,* HBO, 2002.
Comic Remix, Comedy Central, 2003.
Ask Rita, syndicated, 2003.
Field agent, *Punk'd,* MTV, 2003.
Late Show with David Letterman, CBS, multiple appearances, until 2003.
Judge, "The Mongolian Beef," *The Sarah Silverman Program,* Comedy Central, 2008.

Also appeared in episodes of *London Underground,* Comedy Central, *The Louie Show,* and *Tough Crowd with Colin Quinn,* Comedy Central.

Television Work; Series:
Creator and executive producer, *Night after Night with Allan Havey,* Comedy Central, 1989–92.

Internet Appearances; Episodic:
Frank, "S. Erland Hussen #76," *Easy to Assemble,* 2009.
Frank, "The Team Building Event," *Easy to Assemble,* 2009.

RECORDINGS

Videos:
Himself, *Totally Bill Hicks,* Manuel Salvador, 1994.

OTHER SOURCES

Electronic:
Allan Havey Official Site, http://www.allanhavey.com, August 3, 2010.

HAYDEN, Dennis 1952–

PERSONAL

Born April 7, 1952, in Girard, KS; son of hog and soybean farmers.

Career: Actor and producer. Appeared in stage productions and in commercials, including True Value hardware stores, 1996–97.

CREDITS

Film Appearances:
Bartender, *Tomboy,* Crown International Pictures, 1985.
Sonny, *Murphy's Law,* Cannon Films, 1986.
First police officer, *Jo Jo Dancer, Your Life Is Calling,* Columbia, 1986.
Mean drunk, *Slam Dance,* Island Pictures, 1987.
Shaker, *Action Jackson,* Twentieth Century–Fox, 1988.
Eddie, *Die Hard,* Twentieth Century–Fox, 1988.
Barroom tough guy, *Another 48 Hrs.* (also known as *Another 48 Hours*), Paramount, 1990.
Eddie Taylor, *One Man Army* (also known as *Kick & Fury*), Concorde–New Horizons, 1994.
Phil Coe, *Wild Bill,* Metro–Goldwyn–Mayer, 1995.
Senator James Lockholt, *The Random Factor,* Showbuzz Productions, 1995.
Detective Jim Kale, *Fatal Choice,* 1995.
Lieutenant Davis, *Beyond Desire,* Beyond Pictures, 1995.

Tom, *George B.,* Tango West, 1997.
Security guard, *Wishmaster* (also known as *Wes Craven Presents "Wishmaster"* and *Wes Craven's "Wishmaster"*), Live Film & Mediaworks, 1997.
D'Artagnan, *The Mask of Dumas* (also known as *The Man in the Iron Mask* and *The Three Musketeers Meet the Man in the Iron Mask*), Invisible Studio/Fastest Cheapest Best Film, 1999.
Merrill, *Stageghost* (also known as *Stage Ghost*), All Channel Films, 2000.
First cowboy, *Knight Club,* American World Pictures, 2001.
Frank Savage, *Echoes of Enlightenment,* Myogaku Productions, 2001.
Klete, *Sniper 2,* Columbia/TriStar, 2002.
T, *The Negative Pick–up,* 2003.
Bouncer, *The Librarians* (also known as *Strike Force*), Lions Gate Films Home Entertainment, 2004.
Red, *Carts,* Frazzled Man Productions, 2007.
First Satanist, *Revamped,* Millennium Concepts, 2007.
Earl, *Purple Heart,* 2005, Indican Pictures, 2008.
First launch guard, *Light Years Away,* 2008.
Title role, *Trucker,* Monterey Media, 2009.
Slim Sheppard, *Dead in Love,* Wild Range Productions, 2009.
"T"/"Tall Man", *A Way with Murder,* PFG Entertainment, 2009.
Ray, *Race to Witch Mountain* (also known as *Witch Mountain*), Walt Disney, 2009.

Film Work:
Associate producer, *The Random Factor,* Showbuzz Productions, 1995.
Executive producer, *The Mask of Dumas* (also known as *The Man in the Iron Mask* and *The Three Musketeers Meet the Man in the Iron Mask*), Invisible Studio/Fastest Cheapest Best Film, 1999.

Television Appearances; Movies:
The Animal, *Perry Mason: The Case of the Scandalous Scoundrel,* NBC, 1987.
Bounty hunter, *Grand Slam,* 1990.
Electrician, *Grave Secrets: The Legacy of Hilltop Drive* (also known as *Grave Secrets*), CBS, 1992.
Revenge on the Highway (also known as *Silent Thunder*), NBC, 1992.

Television Appearances; Episodic:
First bodyguard, "Our Fair City," *Simon & Simon,* 1984.
Renco, "The Man Who Cried Fox," *Crazy Like a Fox,* 1985.
Trucker, "Key to Angela," *Falcon Crest,* 1988.
(Uncredited) Gunfighter, "Stray Bullet," *Guns of Paradise* (also known as *Paradise*), CBS, 1988.
Nick, "Hard Choices," *Guns of Paradise* (also known as *Paradise*), CBS, 1989.
Larry, "Boozin' Buddies," *Who's the Boss?,* ABC, 1989.

Police officer, "The Things We Do for Love," *Sisters,* NBC, 1993.

Bud Poplin, "These Foolish Things," *The Marshal,* ABC, 1995.

First desperado, "The Magnificent T. K. R.," *Team Knight Rider,* 1997.

Television Appearances; Pilots:

Biker, *Them,* Fox, 2007.

RECORDINGS

Video Games:

Voices, *Jack Orlando,* 1997.

HAYES, Chip 1956–

PERSONAL

Born December 15, 1956; son of Bill Hayes (an airline captain) and Nancy Gates (an actress); married Deborah Adair (an actress), 1987; children: Lucy Taylor, Jeremy.

Addresses: *Agent*—The Sarnoff Company, 10 Universal City Plaza, 20th Floor, Universal City, CA 91608.

Career: Writer, producer, and director.

Member: Writers Guild of America, West, Directors of Guild of America.

Awards, Honors: Writers Guild of America Award nominations, best writing for a daytime serial, 2007 and 2010, and Daytime Emmy Award nomination, outstanding drama series writing team, 2009, all with others, for *All My Children.*

CREDITS

Television Producer; Series:

Executive producer in charge of production, *Hard Knocks,* Showtime, 1987.

Marblehead Manor, syndicated, 1987.

Hearts Are Wild, CBS, 1992.

Melrose Place (also known as *Place Melrose*), Fox, 1992–97.

Television Executive Producer; Movies:

Alien Cargo (also known as *UPN Special Presentation: Alien Cargo*), UPN, 1999.

Max Knight: Ultra Spy, UPN, 2000.

Virtual Nightmare, UPN, 2000.

Code Red (also known as *Code Red: The Rubicon Conspiracy*), UPN, 2001.

Curse of the Talisman (also known as *Malediction*), UPN, 2001.

Television Work; Other; Movies:

Researcher, *Who Is the Black Dahlia?,* NBC, 1975.

Associate producer, *Sizzle* (also known as *Golden Club*), ABC, 1981.

Television Director; Episodic:

"Devil in a Wet Dress," *Melrose Place* (also known as *Place Melrose*), Fox, 1996.

"Sole Sister," *Melrose Place* (also known as *Place Melrose*), Fox, 1996.

"Men Are from Melrose," *Melrose Place* (also known as *Place Melrose*), Fox, 1997.

"Ball n' Jane," *Melrose Place* (also known as *Place Melrose*), Fox, 1998.

"Coop de Grace," *Melrose Place* (also known as *Place Melrose*), Fox, 1998.

Television Producer; Pilots:

Melrose Place (also known as *Place Melrose*), Fox, 1992.

Television Appearances; Episodic:

Lab assistant, "The Inventor/On the Other Side," *Fantasy Island,* ABC, 1979.

Irving Marshall, Jr., "Pas de Trois," *Melrose Place* (also known as *Place Melrose*), Fox, 1993.

WRITINGS

Teleplays; Episodic:

(With others) *The Young and the Restless* (also known as *Y&R, The Innocent Years, Atithasa niata, Les feux de l'amour, Schatten der Leidenschaft,* and *Tunteita ja tuoksuja*), CBS, multiple episodes, c. 1983–85.

(With others) *General Hospital* (also known as *Hopital central* and *Hospital general*), ABC, multiple episodes, 1985–90.

"Now, for a Re–Butle," *Marblehead Manor,* syndicated, 1987.

"The Detour," *Brothers,* Showtime, 1988.

"Countdown," *Mission: Impossible,* ABC, 1989.

(With others) *Melrose Place* (also known as *Place Melrose*), Fox, multiple episodes, 1992–98.

(With others) *All My Children* (also known as *All My Children: The Summer of Seduction* and *La force du destin*), ABC, multiple episodes, 2004—.

HAYWARD, Rachel

PERSONAL

Born in Toronto, Ontario, Canada. *Education:* Graduate of Ontario College of Art.

Career: Actress. Worked as a model; appeared in commercials. Also worked as a freelance graphic designer.

CREDITS

Television Appearances; Series:
Florence, *Harsh Realm,* Fox, 1999–2000.
Executive Director Valerie Warner, a recurring role, *Jake 2.0,* UPN, 2003–2004.

Television Appearances; Movies:
Sonia Glatt, *Anything for Love* (also known as *Just One of the Girls*), Fox, 1992.
Ann Treadwell, *The Sea Wolf,* TNT, 1993.
Harriett, *A Stranger in the Mirror* (also known as *Sidney Sheldon's "A Stranger in the Mirror"*), ABC, 1993.
Barmaid Gabby, *The Final Cut,* HBO, 1995.
Jill Weitz, *She Woke Up Pregnant* (also known as *Crimes of Silence*), ABC, 1996.
Bookstore fan, *Bloodhounds II,* USA Network, 1996.
Alexa Stant, *Dead Fire,* Sci-Fi Channel, 1997.
Maggie Reid, *Voyage of Terror* (also known as *The Fourth Horseman*), Fox Family, 1998.
Rachel Castlemore, *Deadlocked* (also known as *Negotiator*), TNT, 2000.
Reece Robins, *Cabin Pressure,* 2001, PAX, 2003.
Amy, *The Snow Queen,* Hallmark Channel, 2002.
Jamie, *Sightings: Heartland Ghost,* Showtime, 2002.
Karen Sowells, *Devil Winds,* PAX, 2003.
Captain O'Brien, *Deep Evil,* 2004.
Judy, *Augusta, Gone,* Lifetime, 2006.
Katie Stratton, *Last Chance Cafe,* Lifetime, 2006.
Andi, *Cleaverville,* Lifetime, 2007.
Susan Shaw, *Unthinkable,* Lifetime, 2007.
Dr. Ferrel, *The Perfect Child,* Lifetime, 2007.
Marcia, *The Christmas Clause* (also known as *The Mrs. Clause*), Ion Television, 2008.
Judy Saunders, *Christmas in Wonderland,* ABC Family, 2008.

Television Appearances; Specials:
Mrs. Fulton, *Holiday Wishes* (also known as *All I Want for Christmas*), Lifetime, 2006.

Television Appearances; Episodic:
Beth, "John Doe," *Neon Rider,* syndicated, 1990.

Marie Pulaski, "A Matter of Life or Death: Part 1," *The Commish,* ABC, 1991.
Helen Rpinehart, "Kidnapped Boyfriend," *Robin's Hoods,* syndicated, 1994.
Karen the Summoner, "Eggheads," *Sliders,* Fox, 1995.
Valerie Meech, "Leader of the Pack," *Highlander* (also known as *Highlander: The Series*), syndicated, 1995.
Delila, "The End of Innocence," *Highlander* (also known as *Highlander: The Series*), syndicated, 1996.
Julianna "Jolie" Morrow, "Wheelman," *Viper,* syndicated, 1997.
Sergeant Carol Weterings, "Children of the Gods," *Stargate SG–1,* Showtime, 1997.
Lisa Landon, "All at Sea," *Police Academy: The Series,* syndicated, 1997.
Angela, "The Mikado," *Millennium,* Fox, 1998.
Emma Roe, "Go Like You Know," *The Net,* USA Network, 1998.
Megan Galloway, "Blue Champagne Resort," *Welcome to Paradox,* Sci-Fi Channel, 1998.
Susan Tannen, "Blue Agave," *First Wave,* Sci-Fi Channel, 1998.
Maureen Masters, "The Really Real Reenactment," *Viper,* syndicated, 1998.
Amazon, "Them Bones, Them Bones," *Xena: Warrior Princess,* syndicated, 1999.
Diane Armstrong, "Death, Lies, and Videotape," *Cold Squad* (also known as *Files from the Past*), CTV, 1999.
Elizabeth, "The Seductress," *The Hunger,* Showtime, 2000.
Adoley Thornton, "Molly Brown," *Call of the Wild* (also known as *Jack London's "Call of the Wild"*), Animal Planet, 2000.
Adoley Thornton, "Fool's Gold," *Call of the Wild* (also known as *Jack London's "Call of the Wild"*), Animal Planet, 2000.
Adoley Thornton, "Fox Fire," *Call of the Wild* (also known as *Jack London's "Call of the Wild"*), Animal Planet, 2000.
Adulasia Stalin, "Fear and Loathing in the Milky Way," *Andromeda* (also known as *Gene Roddenberry's "Andromeda"*), syndicated, 2001.
Cory, "Last Call at the Broken Hammer," *Andromeda* (also known as *Gene Roddenberry's "Andromeda"*), syndicated, 2001.
Amanda, "Office Management," *Bliss* (also known as *Bliss II*), Oxygen, 2003.
Christina, "Within These Walls," *Mutant X,* syndicated, 2003.
Alma/Rosemary, "The Man Who Never Was," *The Dead Zone* (also known as *The Dark Hall* and *Stephen King's "The Dead Zone"*), USA Network, 2003.
Ellie, "Losing It," *The L Word,* Showtime, 2004.
Adrian Barnes, "Drop Dead Gorgeous," *Tru Calling,* Fox, 2004.
Corporal Linda Macey, "Rather Be Wrong," *The Eleventh Hour,* CTV, 2004.

Mama, "Righteous," *Cold Squad* (also known as *Files from the Past*), CTV, 2004.
Suki, "The Bigger Man," *Godiva's*, Bravo, 2006.
Blonde woman, "Torn," *Battlestar Galactica* (also known as *BSG*), Sci–Fi Channel, 2006.
Jennifer Meyers, "Something Nasty in the Neighborhood," *Painkiller Jane*, Sci–Fi Channel, 2007.

Appeared as Mindy in an episode of *The Hat Squad*, CBS.

Television Appearances; Pilots:
Third guard, *Stargate SG–1: Children of the Gods*, Showtime and syndicated, 1997.
Florence, *Harsh Realm*, Fox, 1999.

Film Appearances:
Fun Park, New World, 1985.
Angie, *Breaking All the Rules*, New World, 1985.
Dr. Myers, *Xtro II: The Second Encounter* (also known as *Xtro II*), New Line Home Video, 1990.
(Uncredited) Woman in morgue, *Whispers*, 1990.
Last victim, *Knight Moves* (also known as *Face to Face*), Interstar, 1993.
Caroline Raynor, *Time Runner* (also known as *In Exile*), Alliance Atlantis Communications/North American Releasing, 1993.
Roxanne, *Suspicious Agenda* (also known as *Under the Gun*), WarnerVision, 1995.
T. K. Wallace, *Convergence* (also known as *Premonition*), New City Releasing, 1999.
Trish, *The Fear: Resurrection* (also known as *The Fear: Halloween Night*), A–Pix Entertainment, 1999.
Panama, *Y2K* (also known as *Terminal Countdown*), PM Entertainment Group, 1999.
Dr. Fishbourne, *Limp*, Goal Line Productions/Swell Entertainment, 1999.
Sonya Orlova, *The Operative*, Studio Home Entertainment, 2000.
Lola, *Apartment Hunting* (also known as *Lola*), Alliance Atlantis Communications, 2000.
Kate O'Conner, *Watchtower* (also known as *Cruel and Unusual*), Alliance Atlantis Communications, 2001.
Woman at phone booth, *Lola*, 2001.
Dr. Allison, *Hellraiser: Hellseeker*, Buena Vista Home Video, 2002.
Carrie, *Cellmates*, RBG Entertainment, 2003.
Verity Phillips, *Art History*, Gold Star Productions, 2003.
Spinning instructor, *Numb*, Scanbox Entertainment, 2007.
Lynn, *While She Was Out* (also known as *Alive*), Anchor Bay Films, 2008.
Carlson, *The Art of War II: Betrayal* (also known as *Art of War 2*), Stage 6 Films, 2008.
Sergeant Carol Weterings, *Stargate SG–1: Children of the Gods—Final Cut*, Twentieth Century–Fox Home Entertainment, 2009.

RECORDINGS

Videos:
Voice of third cowgirl, *Wirehead* (video game), 1995.
Inside "Harsh Realm," Twentieth Century–Fox Home Entertainment, 2004.

HICKEY, John Benjamin 1963–
(John B. Hickey)

PERSONAL

Born June 25, 1963, in Plano, TX. *Education:* Trained at Juilliard School.

Addresses: *Agent*—Paradigm, 360 North Crescent Dr. N., Beverly Hills, CA 90210.

Career: Actor and director. Narrator of television documentary specials.

Awards, Honors: Obie Award (with others), distinguished ensemble performance, *Village Voice*, 1995, for *Love! Valour! Compassion!*.

CREDITS

Film Appearances:
(As John B. Hickey) Henry, *The Bet*, 1992.
Old Baybrook police officer, *The Ref* (also known as *Hostile Hostages*), Buena Vista, 1994.
Dwayne, *Only You* (also known as *Him* and *Just in Time*), TriStar, 1994.
Priest, *Comfortably Numb*, Meistrich Corporation, 1995.
Bruce, *Sin #8*, 1996.
Joe Nader, *Eddie*, Buena Vista, 1996.
Arthur Pape, *Love! Valour! Compassion!*, Fine Line, 1997.
Mark Boland, *The Ice Storm*, Twentieth Century–Fox, 1997.
Travis Furlong, *Finding North*, Cowboy Booking International, 1999.
Captain Goodson, *The General's Daughter* (also known as *The General's Daughter: Elizabeth Campbell*), Paramount, 1999.
Dr. Barry Lehman, *The Bone Collector*, Universal, 1999.
Jerry Adams, *The Anniversary Party*, Fine Line, 2001.
Carlyle, *Changing Lanes*, Paramount, 2002.
David, *Flightplan*, Buena Vista, 2005.

Jack Dunphy, *Infamous,* Warner Independent Pictures, 2006.

Keyes Beech, *Flags of Our Fathers,* Paramount, 2006.

Wesley's dad, *The Ex* (also known as *Fast Track*), Metro–Goldwyn–Mayer, 2006.

Brian Gelford, *Freedom Writers,* Paramount, 2007.

John Stanton, *The Seeker: The Dark Is Rising,* Fox–Walden, 2007.

Alan, *Then She Found Me,* THINKFilm, 2008.

Deputy Mayor LaSalle, *The Taking of Pelham 1 2 3,* Columbia, 2009.

Galloway, *Transformers: Revenge of the Fallen* (also known as *Transformer: Revenge* and *Transformers: Revenge of the Fallen—The IMAX Experience*), DreamWorks/Paramount, 2009.

Television Appearances; Series:
Philip Stoddard, *It's All Relative,* ABC, 2003–2004.
Sean, *The Big C,* Showtime, 2010.

Television Appearances; Miniseries:
Detective Patterson, *Perfect Murder, Perfect Town,* CBS, 2000.
Horatio, *Hamlet,* Odyssey, 2000.
Roger Edens, *Life with Judy Garland: Me and My Shadows,* ABC, 2001.

Television Appearances; Movies:
Paul Kessler, *The Lady in Question,* Arts and Entertainment, 1999.
Commander Shelby, *A Glimpse of Hell,* FX Network, 2001.
Lawrence, *Silver Bells,* CBS, 2005.
Blake Rogers, *Living Proof,* Lifetime, 2008.

Television Appearances; Pilots:
Philip, *It's All Relative,* ABC, 2003.
President Russell, *A House Divided,* ABC, 2006.
Bill Bryce, *Heartland,* TNT, 2007.
Sean, *The Big C,* Showtime, 2010.

Television Appearances; Specials:
Voice of Verus, *Colosseum: A Gladiator's Story,* BBC, 2003, The Discovery Channel, 2004.
Narrator, *Inside the U.S. Secret Service,* PBS, 2004.
Narrator, *Secrets of the Moon Landings,* 2007.
Narrator, "Ocean Animal Emergency," *Nova,* PBS, 2008.
Narrator, *National Geographic's Most Incredible Photos: Afghan Warrior,* The Discovery Channel, 2009.
Narrator, *Lincoln: American Mastermind,* 2009.

Television Appearances; Episodic:
Paul Gaines, "Good Time Charlie," *NYPD Blue* (also known as *N.Y.P.D.*), ABC, 1994.

"You Thought the Pope Was Something," *New York News,* CBS, 1995.

Dr. Elliott, "Speaking in Tongues," *Nothing Sacred,* ABC, 1997.

Rick, "The Great Dickdater," *3rd Rock from the Sun* (also known as *Encounters of the Personal Kind* and *3rd Rock*), NBC, 1998.

Charles Thatcher, "Castoff," *Law & Order,* NBC, 1998.

Thomas John "Tom" Anderson, "Oh Come All Ye Faithful," *Sex and the City* (also known as *S.A.T.C.* and *Sex and the Big City*), HBO, 1998.

Dennis Kohler, "Zen and the Art of Murder," *Homicide: Life on the Street* (also known as *Homicide*), NBC, 1999.

Assistant district attorney, "Misleader," *Law & Order: Special Victims Unit* (also known as *Law & Order: SVU* and *Special Victims Unit*), NBC, 2000.

Rob, "Truth," *D.C.,* The WB, 2000.

Rob, "Justice," *D.C.,* The WB, 2000.

Congressman Owens, "Blame," *D.C.,* The WB, 2000.

Neil, "Party," *D.C.,* The WB, 2000.

Assistant district attorney, "Nocturne," *Law & Order: Special Victims Unit* (also known as *Law & Order: SVU* and *Special Victims Unit*), 2000.

John Smith, "The Stalker," *Welcome to New York,* 2001.

Dr. Sidney Cornfeld, "Slaves of Las Vegas," *CSI: Crime Scene Investigation* (also known as *C.S.I.* and *CSI: Las Vegas*), CBS, 2001.

Phillip Connor, "Mom's Away," *NYPD Blue* (also known as *N.Y.P.D.*), ABC, 2001.

Hank Rogers, "Loyalties," *The Guardian* (also known as *Ochita bengoshi Nick Fallin*), CBS, 2001.

Aaron Solomon, "DR 1–102," *Law & Order,* NBC, 2002.

Dr. Martin Shane, "Obsession," *Hack,* CBS, 2002.

Randall Fuller, "Con–Text," *Law & Order: Criminal Intent* (also known as *Law & Order: CI*), NBC, 2003.

Aaron Solomon, "C.O.D.," *Law & Order,* NBC, 2004.

Father Kampinski, "In Dreams …," *Alias,* ABC, 2005.

Aaron Solomon, "Mammon," *Law & Order,* NBC, 2005.

Lloyd Barrett, "Wrongful Death," *Justice,* Fox, 2006.

Aaron Solomon, "Profiteer," *Law & Order,* NBC, 2006.

Major Guinness, "Light the Lights," *Brothers & Sisters,* ABC, 2006.

Headmaster Keenan, "The Headmaster," *Stacked,* Fox, 2006.

Narrator, "Amelia Earhart," *Undercover History,* National Geographic Channel, 2006.

"A Moment in Time … Flags of Our Fathers," *HBO First Look,* HBO, 2006.

Narrator, "The Hunt for Hitler," *Undercover History,* National Geographic Channel, 2007.

Narrator, "The Hunt for the Boston Strangler," *Undercover History,* National Geographic Channel, 2007.

Narrator, "Nightmare on Mt. Hood," *Situation Critical,* 2007.

Donald Fraser/Donald Ferguson, "Don of the Dead," *In Plain Sight,* USA Network, 2008.

Narrator, "Undercover Titanic with Bob Ballard," *Undercover History,* National Geographic Channel, 2008.

Narrator, "Unabomber: The Secret History," *Inside,* 2008.

Narrator, "The Real Bonnie and Clyde," *Timewatch,* 2009.

Sid, *Past Life,* Fox, 2010.

Stage Appearances:

Jonathon Toffler and young Graydon, *The End of the Day,* Playwrights Horizons Theatre, New York City, 1992.

Oskar, *On the Bum,* Playwrights Horizons Theatre, 1992.

Arthur Pape, *Love! Valour! Compassion!,* Manhattan Theatre Club Stage I, New York City, 1994–95, then Walter Kerr Theatre, New York City, 1995.

Griever, *Blue Window,* Manhattan Theatre Club Stage I, 1996.

David, *God's Heart,* Mitzi E. Newhouse Theatre, New York City, 1997.

Jonathan Balton, *The Film Society,* Adams Memorial Theatre, Williamstown Theatre Festival, Williamstown, MA, 1997.

Clifford Bradshaw, *Cabaret* (musical), Roundabout Theatre Company, Kit Kat Klub, New York City, 1998.

Reverend John Hale, *The Crucible,* Virginia Theatre, New York City, 2002.

Reflections ... Post 9/11 through the Children's Eyes, Estelle R. Newman Theatre, Public Theatre, New York City, 2002.

Earl of Leicester, *Mary Stuart,* Broadhurst Theatre, New York City, 2009.

Also appeared in *Dreading Thekla,* Williamstown Theatre Festival, Williamstown, MA; *New Music,* Cleveland Playhouse, Cleveland, OH; *Snakebit,* New York Stage and Film Theatre, New York City; *The Substance of Fire,* Lincoln Center Theatre, New York City; and *Valued Friends,* Long Wharf Theatre, New Haven, CT.

Stage Director:

Bad Dates, Playwrights Horizons Theatre, New York City, 2003.

RECORDINGS

Videos:

The Human Factor: Exacting Revenge of the Fallen, Paramount Home Entertainment, 2009.

OTHER SOURCES

Periodicals:

Advocate, July 6, 1999, pp. 55–56.

HOBERMAN, David

PERSONAL

Addresses: *Office*—Mandeville Films, 500 South Buena Vista St., Old Animation Building, Suite 2G, Burbank, CA 91521.

Career: Executive, producer, and agent. American Broadcasting Companies, worked in mail room, 1970s; TAT Communications, production executive, 1978–82; worked as a motion picture agent for International Creative Management, Writers and Artists Agency, and Ziegler Associates, between 1982 and 1985; Walt Disney Pictures, Burbank, CA, vice president for production, 1985–87, senior vice president for production, 1987–88, president for production, 2988–89, president of Touchstone Pictures division, 1989–94, and president for motion pictures at Walt Disney Studios, 1994–95; Mandeville Films (also known as Mandeville Films and Television), Burbank, president and chief executive officer, 1995—. University of California, Los Angeles, professor. Board member, Anxiety Disorders Association of America and Starlight Starbright Foundation; Los Angeles Museum of Contemporary Art, member of collections and acquisitions committee; Los Angeles Free Clinic, former board member.

CREDITS

Film Producer:

The Sixth Man, Buena Vista, 1997.

George of the Jungle (also known as *Jungle George*), Buena Vista, 1997.

Senseless, Dimension Films, 1998.

The Negotiator, Warner Bros., 1998.

I'll Be Home for Christmas, Buena Vista, 1998.

Bandits, Metro–Goldwyn–Mayer, 2001.

Bringing Down the House, Buena Vista, 2003.

Walking Tall, Metro–Goldwyn–Mayer, 2004.

Raising Helen, Buena Vista, 2004.

The Last Shot, Buena Vista, 2004.

Beauty Shop, Metro–Goldwyn–Mayer, 2005.

Eight Below, Buena Vista, 2006.

The Shaggy Dog, Buena Vista, 2006.

Traitor, Overture Films, 2008.

Beverly Hills Chihuahua, Walt Disney, 2008.

The Lazarus Project, Sony Pictures Entertainment, 2008.

The Proposal, Walt Disney, 2009.

Surrogates (also known as *Vicarious*), Walt Disney, 2009.

Beverly Hills Chihuahua 2, Walt Disney, 2010.

The Fighter, Paramount, 2010.

Film Executive Producer:
Mr. Wrong, Buena Vista, 1996.
The Other Sister, Buena Vista, 1999.
Antitrust (also known as *Conspiracy.com* and *Surveillance*), Metro–Goldwyn–Mayer, 2001.
What's the Worst that Could Happen?, Metro–Goldwyn–Mayer, 2001.
Original Sin, Metro–Goldwyn–Mayer, 2001.
Moonlight Mile, Buena Vista, 2002.
Five Fingers, Lions Gate Films, 2006.

Film Associate Producer:
American Raspberry (also known as *Funny America* and *Prime Time*), Danton Films, 1977.

Film Appearances:
Airline passenger, *George of the Jungle 2* (also known as *Jungle George 2*), Walt Disney, 2003.
Himself, *Los Angeles* (short documentary), Parallax, 2005.

Television Executive Producer; Series:
Ryan Caulfield: Year One, Fox, 1999.
Monk, USA Network, 2002–2009.
Detroit 1-8-7, ABC, 2010.

Television Executive Producer; Movies:
Toothless, ABC, 1997.
Brink!, The Disney Channel, 1998.
Geek Charming, The Disney Channel, 2010.

Television Executive Producer; Pilots:
(And creator) *A.K.A.,* CBS, 2006.
The Kill Point, Spike TV, 2007.
Detroit 1-8-7, ABC, 2010.
Kegs, ABC, 2010.
Dorchester Heights, ABC, 2010.
Tarrytown, ABC, 2010.

Television Executive Producer; Episodic:
"No Meringue," *The Kill Point,* Spike TV, 2007.

Television Director; Episodic:
"Mr. Monk's Other Brother," *Monk,* USA Network, 2009.

HOBLIT, Gregory 1944–

PERSONAL

Full name, Gregory King Hoblit; born November 27, 1944, in Abilene, TX; son of Harold Foster (an FBI agent) and Elizabeth Hubbard (maiden name, King) Hoblit; married Debrah Farentino (an actress), September 10, 1994; children: Molly, Sophie. *Education:* Attended University of California, Berkeley; University of California, Los Angeles, B.A., history, B.A., political science, and graduate study.

Addresses: *Agent*—David Wirtschafter, WME Entertainment, 9601 Wilshire Blvd., 3rd Floor, Beverly Hills, CA 90210. *Manager*—Benderspink, 5870 West Jefferson Blvd., Studio E, Los Angeles, CA 90016.

Career: Producer and director. WLS–TV, Chicago, IL, worked as production assistant, associate producer, then producer of talk shows; MTM Enterprises, producer, beginning 1979; Creative Film Management, New York City, director of television commercials, beginning 1994; Abilene Pictures, Beverly Hills, CA, founder and producer, beginning 1996.

Member: Directors Guild of America.

Awards, Honors: Emmy Awards, 1981, 1982, 1983, 1984, and Emmy Award nomination, 1985, all best drama series (with others), and George Foster Peabody Broadcasting Award, Henry W. Grady School of Journalism and Mass Communications, University of Georgia, all for *Hill Street Blues;* Emmy Award and Directors Guild of America Award nomination, both outstanding directing in a drama series, 1987, for pilot episode, *L.A. Law;* Emmy Award, 1987, and Emmy Award nomination, 1988, both outstanding drama series (with others), and George Foster Peabody Broadcasting Award, all for *L.A. Law;* Emmy Award nomination, outstanding directing in a drama series, 1998, for "The Wizard of Odds," L.A. Law; Emmy Award, outstanding directing in a comedy series, 1988, for pilot episode, *Hooperman;* Emmy Award (with others), outstanding drama or comedy special, and Emmy Award nomination, outstanding directing in a mini-series or special, both 1989, for Roe vs. Wade; Emmy Award nomination, outstanding directing in a drama series, 1991, for pilot episode, *Cop Rock;* Directors Guild of America Award and Emmy Award nomination, both outstanding directing in a drama series, 1994, for pilot episode, *NYPD Blue;* Golden Laurel Award (with others), television producer of the year, Producers Guild of America, 1994, Emmy Award nomination, 1994, and Emmy Award, 1995, both outstanding drama series (with others), all for NYPD Blue; Directors Guild of America Award nomination, outstanding directing in a drama series, 1995, for "Simon Says," *NYPD Blue;* Humanitas Prize, Human Family Educational and Cultural Institute, and People's Choice Award.

CREDITS

Television Producer; Series:
Supervising producer, *Paris,* CBS, 1979.
Producer, *Hill Street Blues,* NBC, 1981.

Supervising producer, *Hill Street Blues,* NBC, 1981–82.
Co–executive producer, *Hill Street Blues,* NBC, 1982–85.
Executive producer, *Bay City Blues,* NBC, 1983.
Producer, *L.A. Law,* NBC, 1986.
Co–executive producer, *L.A. Law,* NBC, 1986–88.
Producer, *Hooperman,* ABC, 1987–89.
Co–executive producer, *Cop Rock,* ABC, 1990.
Producer, *Civil Wars,* ABC, 1991–93.
Producer, *NYPD Blue* (also known as *N.Y.P.D.*), ABC, 1993.
Co–executive producer, *NYPD Blue* (also known as *N.Y.P.D.*), ABC, 1993–94.

Television Director; Series:
Hill Street Blues, NBC, between 1981 and 1985.
NYPD Blue (also known as *N.Y.P.D.*), ABC, 1993–94.

Television Producer; Pilots:
Associate producer (and director), *Dr. Strange,* CBS, 1978.
Supervising producer, *Every Stray Dog and Kid,* NBC, 1981.
(And director) *L.A. Law,* NBC, 1986.
The Hall, CBS, 1999.
Executive producer (and director), *The E Team,* ABC, 2003.
Executive producer (and director), *NYPD Blue 2069,* Fox, 2003.

Television Director; Pilots:
Hill Street Blues, NBC, 1981.
Bay City Blues, NBC, 1983.
Civil Wars, ABC, 1991.
NYPD Blue (also known as *N.Y.P.D.*), ABC, 1993.
Solving Charlie, ABC, 2009.

Television Work; Movies:
Producer, *Vampire,* ABC, 1979.
Producer and director, *Roe vs. Wade,* NBC, 1989.
Director, *Class of '61,* ABC, 1993.

Television Work; Miniseries:
Associate producer, *Loose Change* (also known as *Those Restless Years*), NBC, 1978.

Television Director; Episodic:
"Those Lips, That Eye," *L.A. Law,* NBC, 1986.
"The Wizard of Odds," *L.A. Law,* NBC, 1987.
Premiere episode, *Hooperman,* ABC, 1987.
"The Answer My Friend, Is Passing in the Wind," *Hooperman,* ABC, 1987.
"Goodbye, Judge Green," *Equal Justice,* 1990.
Premiere episode, *Cop Rock,* ABC, 1990.
"Ill–Gotten Gains," *Cop Rock,* ABC, 1990.

Television Appearances; Episodic:
"Look Closely: The Making of 'Fracture,'" HBO First Look, HBO, 2007.
Up Close with Carrie Keagan, ABC, 2007.

Film Director:
Dawn Horse (documentary), 1972.
Primal Fear, Paramount, 1996.
Fallen, Warner Bros., 1998.
(And producer) *Frequency,* New Line Cinema, 1999.
(And producer) *Hart's War,* Metro–Goldwyn–Mayer, 2002.
Fracture, New Line Cinema, 2007.
Untraceable, Screen Gems, 2008.

RECORDINGS

Videos:
The Science & Technology Behind "Frequency," 2000.

WRITINGS

Television Episodes:
"The Most Likely to Succeed," *What Really Happened to the Class of '65",* 1978.
"Life, Death, Eternity," *Hill Street Blues,* NBC, 1981.

OTHER SOURCES

Periodicals:
Shoot, April 1, 1994, p. 7; March 29, 1996, p. S104.

HOCH, Danny 1970–

PERSONAL

Born November 23, 1970, in New York, NY (some sources specify boroughs of Brooklyn or Queens). *Education:* Attended High School of Performing Arts, New York City; attended North Carolina School of the Arts, 1988–89, British–American Drama Academy, London, 1990, and New York University, 1991–93. *Religion:* Jewish.

Addresses: *Agent*—Lindsay Porter, Gersh Agency, 41 Madison Ave., 33rd Floor, New York, NY 10010; (voice work and commercials) Robyn Starr, Don Buchwald and Associates, 10 East 44th St., 5th Floor, New York, NY 10017.

Career: Actor, writer, and director. New School, senior fellow at Vera List Center for Art and Politics, 2000–01; Sundance Theatre Lab, playwright in residence, 2007. New York University, performed with Creative Arts Team for adolescents in alternative high schools and correctional institutions; Active Element Foundation, founding board member; Hip–Hop Theatre Festival, founder, 2000.

Member: American Federation of Television and Radio Artists, Screen Actors Guild, Writers Guild of America.

Awards, Honors: Obie Award, outstanding performance, *Village Voice*, and Fringe First Award, Edinburgh Festival, both 1994, and Drama Desk Award nomination, outstanding solo show, 1995, all for *Some People*; Annual CableACE Award nomination, National Cable Television Association, 1996, for *Danny Hoch: Some People*; Sundance writers fellow, 1996; Bay Area Drama Critics Circle Award, Drama Desk Award nomination, outstanding solo show, and Best of Manhattan Award, *New York Press*, all 1998, both for *Evolution of a Homeboy: Jails, Hospitals & Hip–Hop*; CalArts/Alpert Award in theatre, 1998; Tennessee Williams fellow, 1999; honorable mention (with Mark Benjamin), best feature, Urbanworld Film Festival, 2000, for *Jails, Hospitals & Hip–Hop*; Wesleyan Millett writing fellowship, 2000; Guggenheim fellowship, 2008; solo theatre fellowship, National Endowment for the Arts; Drama League Award nomination, distinguished performance, 2009, for *Taking Over.*

CREDITS

Stage Appearances:
Pot Melting (solo show), Under One Roof Theatre Company, One Dream Theatre, New York City, 1992.
Multiple characters, *Some People* (solo show), Theatre at Performance Space 122, New York City, 1993, then New York Shakespeare Festival, Susan Stein Shiva Theatre, Public Theatre, New York City, 1994, later Stage II, Long Wharf Theatre, New Haven, CT, 1994–95.
Evolution of a Homeboy: Jails, Hospitals, and Hip–Hop (solo show), Julia Morgan Theatre, Berkeley, CA, 1997, then Public Theatre, New York City, 1998.
Sonny, *The Flattered Fifth*, New Group, Intar Hispanic American Theatre, New York City, 1997.
Taking Over (solo show), Martinson Hall, Public Theatre, beginning 2008.

Major Tours:
Toured in the solo show *Some People*, U.S. and international cities.

Stage Director:
Flow, New York Theatre Workshop, New York City, 2003.

Till the Break of Dawn, Culture Project, Harry De Jur Playhouse, Abrons Arts Center, New York City, 2007.

Also directed a production of *Representa*, Mission Cultural Center.

Film Appearances:
Shooter, *Sureshot*, 1996.
Lenny, *His and Hers*, Alliance Independent Films, 1997.
Private Carni, *The Thin Red Line*, Twentieth Century–Fox, 1998.
Flip, *Whiteboyz* (also known as *Whiteboys*), Fox Searchlight, 1999.
Timmi Hillnigger, *Bamboozled*, 2000.
Multiple characters, *Jails, Hospitals & Hip–Hop*, 2000.
Harris, *Prison Song*, New Line Cinema, 2001.
Dominick Pilla, *Black Hawk Down*, Columbia, 2001.
Mickey, *Washington Heights*, Mac Releasing, 2002.
Marty, *American Splendor*, Fine Line, 2003.
Cocinero, *The Other Shoe*, Family Productions, 2003.
Intersection guy cop, *War of the Worlds*, Paramount, 2005.
Clem, *Bam Bam and Celeste*, Salty Features/Nuit Blanche Productions/Cho Taussig Productions, 2005.
Pinchback, *Blackbird*, Blackbird Project, 2007.
Bobby Basketball, *Lucky You*, Warner Bros., 2007.
Jumbo Falsetti, *We Own the Night* (also known as *Undercover*), Columbia, 2007.
Something Out of Nothing (documentary), Robert Small Entertainment, 2008.
Joe, *Henry's Crime*, Ascot Elite Entertainment Group, 2010.

Film Director:
Jails, Hospitals & Hip–Hop, 2000.

Television Appearances; Movies:
Father, *3 A.M.*, Showtime, 2001.
Transportation Security Administration agent, *Taking Chance*, HBO, 2009.

Television Appearances; Specials:
Multiple characters, *Danny Hoch: Some People* (broadcast of his solo stage show), HBO, 1995.

Television Appearances; Episodic:
Edward, "Honey–Getter," *Subway Stories: Tales from the Underground*, HBO, 1997.
Russell Simmons Presents Def Poetry (also known as *Def Poetry* and *Def Poetry Jam*), HBO, 2002, 2003.
Kracker, "Soulless," *Law & Order: Special Victims Unit* (also known as *Law & Order: SVU* and *Special Victims Unit*), NBC, 2003.
"Race Is the Place," *Independent Lens*, PBS, 2005.

RECORDINGS

Videos:

Tension: Creating "We Own the Night," Sony Pictures Home Entertainment, 2008.

A Moment in Crime: Creating Late Eighties Brooklyn, Sony Pictures Home Entertainment, 2008.

The Making of "We Own the Night," Universal, 2008.

WRITINGS

Solo Shows for the Stage:

Pot Melting, Under One Roof Theatre Company, One Dream Theatre, New York City, 1992.

Some People (first performed at Theatre at Performance Space 122, New York City, 1993 produced by New York Shakespeare Festival, Susan Stein Shiva Theatre, Public Theatre, New York City, 1994, published in *Jails, Hospitals & Hip–Hop and Some People,* Villard Books, 1998.

Evolution of a Homeboy: Jails, Hospitals, and Hip–Hop (first performed at Julia Morgan Theatre, Berkeley, CA, 1997 produced at Public Theatre, 1998, published in *Jails, Hospitals & Hip–Hop and Some People,* Villard Books, 1998.

Till the Break of Dawn, Culture Project, Harry De Jur Playhouse, Abrons Arts Center, New York City, 2007.

Taking Over, Martinson Hall, Public Theatre, beginning 2008.

Stage Plays:

Clinic Con Class for the Pieces of the Quilt AIDS Theatre Project, Magic Theatre, San Francisco, CA, 1996.

Against the Wall, Mumia 911, Public Theatre, New York City, 1999.

Also author of the play *Children of War.*

Film Scripts:

Whiteboyz (also known as *Whiteboys;* also based on a story by Hoch), 1999.

Jails, Hospitals & Hip–Hop (based on his stage show), 2000.

Television Specials:

Wyclef Jean in America, 2006.

Television Episodes:

"Honey–Getter," *Subway Stories: Tales from the Underground,* HBO, 1997.

Other:

Work represented in anthologies, including *Creating Your Own Monologue; Extreme Exposure; Out of Character;* and *Total Chaos.* Contributor of articles to periodicals, including *American Theatre, Harper's, Nation, New Theatre Review, New York Times,* and *Village Voice.* Also writes poetry.

OTHER SOURCES

Periodicals:

American Theatre, July/August, 1998, p. 30.

Back Stage, November 11, 1994, p. 31.

New York Times, November 16, 2008.

Variety, November 3, 1997, p. 110.

Electronic:

Danny Hoch Official Site, http://www.dannyhoch.com, September 23, 2010.

HOLDEN, Alexandra 1977–

PERSONAL

Born April 30, 1977, in Northfield, MN; daughter of Barry and Kristi Holden; married Johnny Strong (an actor; divorced).

Addresses: *Agent*—Agency for the Performing Arts, 405 South Beverly Dr., Beverly Hills, CA 90212. *Manager*— Mary Putnam Greene, MPG Management, 1136 Roxbury Dr., Los Angeles, CA 90035.

Career: Actress. Formerly worked as a retail sales clerk.

CREDITS

Film Appearances:

Vicky, *The Last Time I Committed Suicide,* New City Releasing, 1997.

Meredith, *In & Out,* Paramount, 1997.

Vivian, *Dance, Texas Pop. 81,* TriStar, 1998.

Angelic girl, *Guinevere,* Miramax, 1999.

College girl, *Edtv* (also known as *Ed TV*), Universal, 1999.

Mary Johanson, *Drop Dead Gorgeous,* New Line Cinema, 1999.

Fern Rogers, *Sugar & Spice,* New Line Cinema, 2001.

Samantha Warren, *Wishcraft,* Wishcraft, 2002.

Mia, *American Gun,* Lightning Entertainment, 2002.

Nurse, *Four Reasons,* 2002.

Lulu, *The Hot Chick,* Buena Vista, 2002.

Sunny Burkhardt, *Purgatory Flats,* American Cinema International, 2002.

Dee Dee, *Moving Alan,* Destiny Entertainment/Roadkill Productions, 2002.

Marion Harrington, *Dead End,* Fox–Pathe, 2003, Lions Gate Films, 2004.

Scarlett Smith, *How to Deal,* New Line Cinema, 2003.

Kate, *Window Theory,* American World Pictures, 2004.

Casting About (documentary), 2004, Kino International, 2007.

Rosemary, *Everything's Gone Green* (short film), Sundance Film Festival, 2005.

Rachel Beckwith, *A Dead Calling,* Lions Gate Films Home Entertainment, 2006.

Maggie, *Special,* Revolver Entertainment, 2006, Magnet Releasing, 2008.

Amber, *Wasted,* Weinstein Company, 2007.

Alison, *All the Days before Tomorrow,* ViewCave, 2007.

Claire, *The Frequency of Claire,* Aquarius Films, 2008.

Scarlett May, *Dark Reel,* Barnholtz Entertainment, 2008.

Cute funky girl, *Post Grad,* Fox Searchlight, 2009.

Television Appearances; Series:

Elizabeth Stevens, a recurring role, *Friends,* NBC, 2000.

The Afterlife, 2003.

Suzy, a recurring role, *Friday Night Lights* (also known as *F.N.L.*), NBC, 2007.

Debbie Wilcox, *Franklin & Bash,* 2010.

Television Appearances; Movies:

Jessica Lindstrom, *Everything You Want,* ABC Family, 2005.

Jamie, *A Trick of the Mind* (also known as *Mind Games*), Lifetime, 2006.

Natasha, *Healing Hands,* Hallmark Channel, 2010.

Television Appearances; Miniseries:

Frania Beatus, *Uprising,* NBC, 2001.

Television Appearances; Pilots:

Bree Franklin, *The Afterlife,* Fox, 2003.

Sophie, *Peep Show,* Fox, 2005.

Candy, *The Eastmans,* CBS, 2009.

Devan, *Friends with Benefits,* NBC, 2010.

Television Appearances; Episodic:

Dani Swanson, "The Christmas Show," *Mr. Rhodes,* NBC, 1996.

Dani Swanson, "The Sexism Show," *Mr. Rhodes,* NBC, 1997.

Dani Swanson, "The Italian Show," *Mr. Rhodes,* NBC, 1997.

Debbie, "Hell Hath No Fury," *Cracker Mind over Murder* (also known as *Cracker* and *Cracker: The Complete Series*), ABC, 1997.

Debbie, "An American Dream," *Cracker Mind over Murder* (also known as *Cracker* and *Cracker: The Complete Series*), ABC, 1997.

Cassidy, "Sneaky Feelings," *Once and Again,* ABC, 2000.

Cassidy, "A Door, About to Open," *Once and Again,* ABC, 2000.

Jane Wilco, "The Getaway," *Ally McBeal* (also known as *Ally My Love*), Fox, 2001.

Jane Wilco, "Home Again," *Ally McBeal* (also known as *Ally My Love*), Fox, 2001.

Jane Wilco, "The Wedding," *Ally McBeal* (also known as *Ally My Love*), Fox, 2001.

Rebecca Leah "Becky Maxwell" Milford, "In the Game," *Six Feet Under,* HBO, 2002.

Jackie Connors, "Drop Dead Gorgeous," *Tru Calling,* Fox, 2004.

Jamie Carr, "Where the Boys Are," *Grey's Anatomy,* ABC, 2006.

Carla Hoyle, "Gone Baby Gone," *CSI: Miami,* CBS, 2008.

Laura, "Serving Two Masters," *Private Practice,* ABC, 2008.

Caroline Kemp/Bellowes in 1958, "Libertyville," *Cold Case,* CBS, 2009.

Zoey Hill, "Wonderland," *Royal Pains,* USA Network, 2009.

Crystal Hargrove, "Blood In, Blood Out," *The Mentalist,* CBS, 2010.

RECORDINGS

Music Videos:

Appeared in Aerosmith's "Hole in My Soul."

HOLDEN, Michael

PERSONAL

Education: Trained with Uta Hagen.

Addresses: *Agent*—Geddes Agency, 8430 Santa Monica Blvd., Suite 200, West Hollywood, CA 90069.

Career: Actor, singer, and writer.

Member: Screen Actors Guild, American Federation of Television and Radio Artists, Actors' Equity Association.

CREDITS

Television Appearances; Series:

District Attorney George Handeman, a recurring role, *L.A. Law,* NBC, between 1986 and 1992.

Joe, a recurring role, *Cheers,* NBC, between 1989 and 1992.

Judge Melvin Orrick, a recurring role, *Reasonable Doubts,* NBC, 1991–92.

Television Appearances; Movies:

Rivas (some sources cite the character as Ricos), *Sketch Artist II: Hands that See* (also known as *A Feel for Murder* and *Sketch Artist II*), Showtime, 1995.

Harry Dern, *Divas,* Fox, 1995.

Television Appearances; Pilots:

The attorney, *Eyes,* ABC, 2005.

Lawyer, *The Mentalist,* CBS, 2008.

Television Appearances; Episodic:

Artie Fonzarelli, "Arthur, Arthur," *Happy Days,* ABC, 1983.

Second air controller, "The Biggest Game in Town," *Automan,* ABC, 1984.

Customer, "Everyone Imitates Art," *Cheers,* NBC, 1986.

Scott Metoyer, premiere episode, *Hooperman,* ABC, 1987.

Bill, "The Game's Not Over 'til the Fat Lady Sings," *Spies,* CBS, 1987.

First man, "Whose Coup Is It Anyway?," *Throb,* 1987.

Neil, "The End of the World," *Freddy's Nightmares,* 1989.

Customer, "The Cranemakers," *Cheers,* NBC, 1989.

Officer Henry Ohlberg, "Trial," *Beauty and the Beast,* CBS, 1989.

Producer, "The Star," *Matlock,* NBC, 1989.

"Al Tells the Truth," *The Famous Teddy Z,* CBS, c. 1990.

Herb Stein, "Last Dance before an Execution—May 12, 1971," *Quantum Leap,* NBC, 1991.

Judge, "Church of Metropolis," *Lois & Clark: The New Adventures of Superman,* ABC, 1994.

Dr. Payson, "Postmortem Madness," *Melrose Place,* Fox, 1995.

Judge Cornell, "Bring Me the Head of Darnell Sims," *Charlie Grace,* ABC, 1995.

Caterer, "The Art of the Deal," *Hope & Gloria,* NBC, 1996.

Ron Zisk, "V–Fibbing," *Chicago Hope,* CBS, 1996.

Dr. Martin, "Insult to Injury," *Home Improvement,* ABC, 1997.

Joe Walsh, "Reasonable Doubts," *The Practice,* ABC, 1997.

The detective, "Faster than a Speeding Vixen," *Lois & Clark: The New Adventures of Superman,* ABC, 1997.

Henry Fields, "The Murder of Mark Sloan," *Diagnosis Murder* (also known as *Dr. Mark Sloan*), CBS, 1997.

Technician, "A Rip in Time," *Timecop,* ABC, 1997.

Technician, "Rocket Science," *Timecop,* ABC, 1997.

Technician, "Lost Voyage," *Timecop,* ABC, 1998.

Doctor, "Call Him Johnny," *Any Day Now,* Lifetime, 1998.

Dr. Wagner, "Call of the Wild," *Martial Law,* CBS, 1999.

Lyle McFarlan, "Letting Go," *Chicago Hope,* CBS, 2000.

Administrator, "Orphans," *Gideon's Crossing,* ABC, 2001.

District Attorney Duncan, "Recovery," *Family Law,* CBS, 2001.

Donald "Don" Herzig, "Obligations," *Family Law,* CBS, 2001.

Donald "Don" Herzig, "All in the Family," *Family Law,* CBS, 2001.

Dr. Buchbinder, "Death by Cycle," *NYPD Blue* (also known as *N.Y.P.D.*), ABC, 2002.

Fourth network news president, "The Black Vera Wang," *The West Wing* (also known as *The White House*), NBC, 2002.

Ron Wieland, "Day 2: 9:00 a.m.–10:00 a.m.," *24,* Fox, 2002.

Ron Wieland, "Day 2: 3:00 p.m.–4:00 p.m.," *24,* Fox, 2002.

Ron Wieland, "Day 2: 4:00 p.m.–5:00 p.m.," *24,* Fox, 2003.

Ron Wieland, "Day 2: 4:00 a.m.–5:00 a.m.," *24,* Fox, 2003.

First fabricator, "Go Ask Alice," *7th Heaven* (also known as *7th Heaven: Beginnings*), The WB, 2003.

Mr. Levine, "Wannabe," *Without a Trace* (also known as *W.A.T.*), CBS, 2004.

Cort Halliday, "The Dead Donald," *NYPD Blue* (also known as *N.Y.P.D.*), ABC, 2004.

(Uncredited) Tucker's attorney, "Iced," *CSI: Crime Scene Investigation* (also known as *C.S.I.* and *CSI: Las Vegas*), CBS, 2005.

Dr. Wayne Dobson, "Family Secret," *Navy NCIS: Naval Criminal Investigative Service* (also known as *NCIS* and *NCIS: Naval Criminal Investigative Service*), CBS, 2006.

Rabbi Saul Levine, "Last Call," *Boston Legal,* ABC, 2008.

Dr. Baron, "Mirror, Mirror," *Desperate Housewives,* ABC, 2008.

Dr. Baron, "If ...," *Desperate Housewives,* ABC, 2010.

Psychiatrist, *All My Children* (also known as *AMC*), ABC, 2010.

Also appeared in episodes of *Eddie Dodd, MD's,* and *General Hospital,* all ABC.

Film Appearances:

Daryl Perkins, *Uninvited,* New Star, 1988.

Accountant, *The Little Death,* PolyGram Filmed Entertainment, 1995.

Kormorov, *Fallout,* Hallmark Entertainment, 1998.

Mr. Geiger/concierge, *Punks,* Urbanworld Films, 2001.

Bo's lawyer, *Paparazzi,* Twentieth Century–Fox, 2004.

Funeral businessman, *The Green Hornet,* Columbia, 2011.

Film Work:

Post–production voice, *Frankie and Johnny Are Married,* Screen Media Films, 2005.

Stage Appearances:

Appeared as Zappy, *Angels Fall,* South Coast Repertory, Costa Mesa, CA; Shorty, *Bay City Blues,* Lex Theatre; Jimmy, *A History of the American Film,* CAST Theatre; Dr. Marty, *Isn't It Romantic,* Los Angeles Stage Company West; Walter, *Nobody,* Lex Theatre; George, *Suggs,* CAST Theatre; and Vicarro, *27 Wagons Full of Cotton,* Lex Theatre.

WRITINGS

Screenplays:

The Little Death, PolyGram Filmed Entertainment, 1995.
No Strings Attached, Redwood Communications, 1997.

HOPPER, Dennis 1936–2010

PERSONAL

Full name, Dennis Lee Hopper; born May 17, 1936, in Dodge City, KS; died of complications due to prostate cancer, May 29, 2010, in Venice Beach, CA; married Brooke Hayward, 1961 (divorced, 1969); married Michelle Phillips (an actress and singer), 1970 (divorced, 1970); married Daria Halprin (an actress), 1972 (divorced, 1976); married Katherine LaNasa (a dancer), June, 1989 (divorced, 1992); married Victoria Cane Duffy, April 13, 1996; children: (first marriage) Marin; (third marriage) Ruthana; (fourth marriage) Henry Lee. *Education:* Trained for the stage at Old Globe Theatre School, San Diego, CA; studied acting with Lee Strasberg at the Actors Studio.

Addresses: *Agent*—International Creative Management, 8942 Wilshire Blvd., Beverly Hills, CA 90211. *Manager*—Firm, 9465 Wilshire Blvd., Suite 212, Beverly Hills, CA 90212. *Contact*—c/o 330 Indiana Ave., Venice, CA 90291.

Career: Actor, writer, director, producer, editor, and photographer. Appeared in commercials for products such as Ford Focus autos, Nike sporting goods, Toyota Celica autos, Tsumura Bathing Essence, and The Gap clothing stores. Photographs have been exhibited at the Fort Worth Art Museum, Denver Art Museum, Wichita Art Museum, Cochran Art Museum, Spoleto Museum, Parco Gallery, and in Tokyo, Osaka, and Kumamoto, Japan.

Awards, Honors: Cannes Film Festival Award, best first work, Golden Palm Award nomination, Cannes Film Festival, National Society of Film Critics Special Award,

director, cowriter, and costar, Academy Award nomination (with Peter Fonda and Terry Southern), best writing, 1969, Writers Guild of America Screen Award nomination (with Fonda and Southern), best drama written directly for the screen, Golden Laurel Award nomination, male new face, Directors Guild of America Award nomination, outstanding directorial achievement in motion pictures, 1970, Kinema Junpo Award, best foreign language film, Kinema Junpo Awards, 1971, all for *Easy Rider;* Venice Film Festival Award, best film, 1971, for *The Last Movie;* Golden Palm Award nomination, best film, Cannes Film Festival, 1980, for *Out of the Blue;* Montreal World Film Festival Award, best actor, National Society of Film Critics Award, best supporting actor, 1986, and Los Angeles Film Critics and National Society of Film Critics Award, best supporting actor, Independent Spirit Award, best male lead, Golden Globe Award nomination, best supporting actor, and Boston Society of Film Critics Award, best supporting actor, 1987, all for *Blue Velvet;* Academy Award nomination, best supporting actor, and Golden Globe Award nomination, best supporting actor, 1987, both for *Hoosiers;* Lifetime Achievement Award, Stockholm Film Festival, 1991; Emmy Award nomination, outstanding lead actor in a miniseries or special, 1991, for *Paris Trout;* MTV Movie Award, best villain, 1995, for *Speed;* John M. Tiedtke Award, Florida Film Festival, 1994, for artistic vision; Empire Award, 1998, for lifetime achievement; Crystal Iris, Brussels International Film Festival, 1998; Feature Film Award, best antagonist actor, New York International Independent Film and Video Festival, 1998, for *The Blackout;* Maverick Award, Taos Talking Picture Festival, 1999; Role Model Award, Young Hollywood Awards, 2001; Video Premiere Award nomination, best supporting actor, DVDX Exclusive Awards, 2001, for *LAPD: To Protect and to Serve;* Donostia Lifetime Achievement Award, San Sebastian International Film Festival, 2002; Lifetime Achievement Award, Santa Monica Film Festival, 2003; Marquee Award, CineVegas International Film Festival, 2003; Lifetime Achievement Award, Method Fest, 2004.

CREDITS

Film Appearances:

(Uncredited) *Johnny Guitar,* 1954.
Goon, *Rebel Without a Cause,* Warner Bros., 1955.
Joe, *I Died a Thousand Times,* Warner Bros., 1955.
"Giant" Stars Are Off to Texas, 1955.
The Steel Jungle, Warner Bros., 1956.
Jordan Benedict III, *Giant,* Warner Bros., 1956.
Billy Clanton, *Gunfight at the O.K. Corral,* Paramount, 1957.
Napoleon Bonaparte, *The Story of Mankind,* Cambridge/Warner Bros., 1957.
(Uncredited) Himself (*Giant* premier footage), *The James Dean Story,* 1957.

(Uncredited) Voice of airman interviewing Major Gruver, *Sayonara,* 1957.

Tom Boyd, *From Hell to Texas* (also known as *The Hell–Bent Kid* and *Manhunt*), Twentieth Century–Fox, 1958.

Hatfield Carnes, *The Young Land,* Columbia, 1959.

William "Cowboy" Tomkins, *Key Witness,* Metro–Goldwyn–Mayer, 1960.

Johnny Drake, *Night Tide,* American International Pictures, 1963.

Tarzan and Jane Regained ... Sort Of, 1964.

The Thirteen Most Beautiful Boys, 1964.

Dave Hastings, *The Sons of Katie Elder,* Paramount, 1965.

Screen Test #1, 1965.

Screen Test #2, 1965.

Screen Test #3 (also known as *Suicide*), 1966.

Screen Test #4, 1966.

Paul, *Queen of Blood* (also known as *The Green Woman, Planet of Blood, Planet of Terror,* and *Planet of Vampires*), American International Pictures, 1966.

Chino, *The Glory Stompers,* American International Pictures, 1967.

Max, *The Trip,* American International Pictures, 1967.

Babalugats, *Cool Hand Luke,* Warner Bros., 1967.

Himself, *Luke,* 1967.

Goff, *Panic in the City,* Commonwealth, 1968.

The Prophet, *Hang 'em High,* United Artists, 1968.

(Uncredited) Himself, *Head,* 1968.

Backtrack!, 1969.

Billy, *Easy Rider,* Columbia, 1969.

Moon Garrett, *True Grit,* Paramount, 1969.

The Festival Game, 1970.

Kansas, *The Last Movie* (also known as *Chinchero*), Universal, 1971.

Himself, *The American Dreamer,* 1971.

The Other Side of the Wind, 1972.

Crush Proof, 1972.

Bickford Warner, *Kid Blue,* Twentieth Century–Fox, 1973.

Sergeant Jack Falen, *Tracks,* Trio, 1975.

Himself, *James Dean, the First American Teenager,* 1975.

Daniel Morgan, *Mad Dog Morgan* (also known as *Mad Dog*), Motion Picture Company, 1976.

Tom Ripley, *The American Friend* (also known as *Der Amerikanische Freund* and *L'ami americain*), New Yorker Films, 1977.

A spy, *Les apprentis sorciers* (also known as *The Sorceror's Apprentice*), 1977.

Medford, *L'ordre et la securite du monde* (also known as *Concorde Affair* and *Last In, First Out*), 1978.

Photojournalist, *Apocalypse Now,* United Artists, 1979.

Chicken, *Las flores del vicio* (also known as *Bloodbath, El cielo se cae, flores del vicio,* and *The Sky Is Falling*), 1979.

Mel, *Couleaur chair,* 1979.

Don Barnes, *Out of the Blue* (also known as *No Looking Back* and *Plus rien a perdre*), Discover, 1980.

Cal, *King of the Mountain,* Universal, 1981.

Reverend Tom Hartley, *Renacer* (also known as *Reborn*), 1981.

Cracker, *Neil Young: Human Highway,* Shakey, 1982.

Don Barnes, *Out of the Blue,* Discovery, 1982.

Scenes from the Life of Andy Warhol: Friendships and Intersections, 1982.

Richard Tremayne, *The Osterman Weekend,* Twentieth Century–Fox, 1983.

Father, *Rumble Fish,* Universal, 1983.

Kenneth Barlow, *White Star* (also known as *Let It Rock*), 1983.

Miller, *Slagskaempen* (also known as *The Inside Man*), 1984.

Euer Weg fuhrt durch die holle (also known as *Jungle Warriors*),1984.

Bob Roberts, *My Science Project,* Buena Vista, 1985.

A Hero of Our Time, 1985.

Running Out of Luck, 1985.

Frank Booth, *Blue Velvet,* De Laurentiis Entertainment Group, 1986.

Wilbur "Shooter" Flatch, *Hoosiers* (also known as *Best Shot*), Orion, 1986.

Lieutenant "Lefty" Enright—Texas Ranger, *The Texas Chainsaw Massacre Part 2* (also known as *TCM2* and *Texas Chainsaw Massacre Part 2*), Cannon, 1986.

Video director, *Running out of Luck,* CBS Records Group, 1986.

Captain (in the air), *The American Way,* 1986.

Ben Dumers, *Black Widow,* Twentieth Century–Fox, 1987.

Sponson, *O. C. and Stiggs,* Metro–Goldwyn–Mayer/United Artists, 1987.

Flash Jensen, *The Pick–up Artist,* Twentieth Century–Fox, 1987.

Feck, *River's Edge,* Island, 1987.

I. G. Farben, *Straight to Hell,* Island, 1987.

Photojournalist, *Apocalypse Pooh,* 1987.

Himself/host, *Rolling Stone Presents Twenty Years of Rock & Roll* (also known as *Rolling Stone: The First Twenty Years*), 1987.

Captain, *Riders of the Storm,* Miramax, 1988.

Monsters & Maniacs, 1988.

Himself, *Act, Acting, and the Suicide Chair: Dennis Hopper,* 1988.

Goon, *Forever James Dean,* 1988.

William Bradford Berrigan, *Blood Red,* 1989.

Milo, *Catchfire* (also known as *Backtrack* and *Do It the Hard Way*), 1989.

Huey Walker, *Flashback,* Paramount, 1990.

Walker Benson, *Chattahoochee,* Hemdale, 1990.

Himself, *Motion and Emotion,* 1990.

Himself, *Hollywood Mavericks,* Roxie, 1990.

Himself, *Superstar: The Life and Times of Andy Warhol,* 1990.

Himself, *Flashing on the Sixties: A Tribal Document,* 1990.

Caesar, *The Indian Runner,* Metro–Goldwyn–Mayer/Pathe, 1991.

A Hero of Our Time, 1991.

Himself, *Schneeweissrosenrot* (also known as *Snow-whiteRosered*), 1991.

Carl Madson, *Sunset Heat* (also known as *Midnight Heat*), 1991.

Hearts of Darkness: A Filmmaker's Apocalypse, 1991.

Picture This: The Times of Peter Bogdanovich in Archer City, Texas, 1991.

Paris Trout, *Paris Trout,* 1991.

Caesar, *The Indian Runner* (also known as *Indian Runner*), 1991.

Marvin Gladstone, *Eye of the Storm,* New Line Cinema, 1992.

Lyle from Dallas, *Red Rock West,* 1992.

Red Diamond, *Boiling Point* (also known as *L'extreme limite*), Warner Bros., 1993.

King Koopa, *Super Mario Bros.,* Buena Vista, 1993.

Clifford Worley, *True Romance,* Warner Bros., 1993.

Himself, *The Revenge of the Dead Indians,* 1993.

Doggie, *Chasers,* Warner Bros., 1994.

Howard Payne, *Speed,* Twentieth Century–Fox, 1994.

Dennis Hopper: L.A. Blues (also known as *L.A. Blues*), 1995.

Himself, *Who Is Henry Jaglom?* (documentary), Calliope Films, 1995.

Dr. Luther Waxling, *Search and Destroy* (also known as *The Four Rules*), October Films, 1995.

Deacon, *Waterworld,* Universal, 1995.

James Dean and Me, 1995.

Joseph Svendon, *Carried Away* (also known as *Acts of Love*), Fine Line, 1996.

John Canyon, *Space Truckers* (also known as *Star Truckers*), Pachyderm Productions, 1996.

Bruno Bischofberger, *Basquiat* (also known as *Build a Fort, Set It on Fire*), Miramax, 1996.

Cannes Man, Rocket Pictures Home Video, 1996.

Frankie, *The Last Days of Frankie the Fly,* 1996.

Mr. Golf, *The Good Life,* 1997.

Micky Wayne, *The Blackout,* Trimark Pictures, 1997.

Sheriff Gilchrist, *Road Ends,* New City Releasing/PM Entertainment Group, 1997.

Charles Atlas, *Top of the World* (also known as *Cold Cash* and *Showdown*), 1997.

Welcome to Hollywood, 1998.

Frank Slater, *Meet the Deedles* (also known as *The Deedles*), Buena Vista, 1998.

Peter Crawford, *Tycus,* 1998.

The Source, Winstar, 1999.

Henry "Hank" Pekurny, *EdTV* (also known as *Ed TV*), Universal, 1999.

Frank Hector, *Straight Shooter,* 1999.

Cleveland Carter, *Bad City Blues,* Showcase Entertainment, 1999.

Bill, *Jesus' Son,* Lions Gate Films, 1999.

Rick Chambers, *Lured Innocence,* Filmwave, 1999.

Roland/Salvatore, *The Venice Project,* 1999.

Vincent Swan, *The Prophet's Game,* Moonstone Entertainment, 1999.

Easy Rider clip, *Me and Will,* 1999.

Detective Ed Delongpre, *The Spreading Ground,* Smooth Pictures, 2000.

Gianti Ponti, *Luck of the Draw,* 2000.

Peter Crawford, *Tycus,* New City Releasing, 2000.

Himself, *Welcome to Hollywood,* PM Entertainment Group, 2000.

JD, *Held for Ransom,* Cutting Edge Entertainment, 2000.

Henry Clark, *Choke,* Artist View Entertainment, 2000.

Lewis Garou, *Michael Angel* (also known as *The Apostate*), 2000.

Swann, *Ticker,* Artisan Entertainment, 2001.

Benny Chains, *Knockaround Guys,* New Line Cinema, 2001.

Warden, *Unspeakable,* 2001.

LAPD: To Protect and Serve, Trinity Home Entertainment, 2001.

Jazz Seen: The Life and Times of William Claxton, 2001.

Himself, *1 Giant Leap,* Palm Pictures, 2002.

Himself, *I Don't Know Jack,* 2002.

Horace, *Leo,* 2002.

Robert Nile, *The Piano Player,* Splendid Pictures, 2002.

Himself, *Mysteries of Love,* Metro–Goldwyn–Mayer/United Artists Home Entertainment, 2002.

My Little Hollywood, 2002.

Himself, *The Art of Dennis Hopper,* 2002.

Venice: Lost and Found, 2002.

Red Light Runners, 2003.

Frank Sinatra, *The Night We Called It a Day,* 2003.

Frank, *Firecracker,* 2003.

Sam, *Dodge City,* 2003.

Easy Riders, Raging Bulls: How the Sex, Drugs and Rock 'N' Roll Generation Saved Hollywood, Shout! Factory, 2003.

A Decade Under the Influence, IFC Films, 2003.

Dennis Hopper: Create (or Die), Easy Rider, 2003.

New Scenes from America, Skandinavia, 2003.

Tell Them Who You Are, Arkles Entertainment, 2004.

And You Don't Stop: 30 Years of Hip–Hop, VH1, 2004.

CHP officer, *Legacy,* MagicQuest, 2004.

Krebs, *The Keeper,* Alliance Atlantis, 2004.

Harry Barlow, *Out of Season* (also known as *Final Shoot*), HBO, 2004.

Father Duffy, *House of 9,* Columbia TriStar Home Video, 2005.

Riccardo, *Americano,* Spirit Lake Pictures, 2005.

El Nino, *The Crow: Wicked Prayer,* Dimension Films, 2005.

Kaufman, *Land of the Dead* (also known as *George Romero's Land of the Dead*), Universal, 2005.

Sheriff Greer, *Hoboken Hollow,* Elephant Films, 2005.

On Location in Tulsa: The Making of "Rumble Fish," Universal Studios Home Video, 2005.

Narrator, *Inside Deep Throat,* Universal, 2005.

Going Through Splat: The Life and Work of Stewart Stern, Rosen/Ward, 2005.

Los Angeles, Parallax Corp., 2005.

Champion, The Film Emporium, 2005.

Sketches of Frank Gehry, Sony Pictures Classics, 2005.

The Holy Modal Rounders: Bound to Lose, Badbird, 2006.

Narrator, *Rising Son: The Legend of Skateboarder Christian Hosoi,* Quiksilver, 2006.

Ban the Sadist Videos!: Part 2, Anchor Bay Entertainment, 2006.

Andy Warhol: A Documentary Film (documentary), High Line, 2006.

3055 Jean Leon, Sagrera TV, 2006.

Matty Matello, *10th & Wolf,* THINKFilm, 2006.

Max Lichtenstein, *Memory,* Echo Bridge, 2006.

By the Ways: A Journey with William Eggleston, Noblesse Oblige, 2007.

Bananaz, Head Film Ltd., 2008.

The Cool School, Arthouse Films, 2008.

Generations 68 (also known as *Generation 68*), Arte, 2008.

Narrator, *Dennis Leary: The Art of Dying,* Long Tale, 2008.

No Subtitles Necessary: Laszlo & Vilmos, PBS, 2008.

Chelsea on the Rocks, Aliquot Films, 2008.

Dead On: The Life and Cinema of George A. Romero, New Eye Films, 2008.

Not Quite Hollywood: The Wild, Untold Story of Ozploitation!, Magnolia Pic., 2008.

The Brothers Warner, Warner Sisters Prod., 2008.

Shooting Palermo, *Rundfunk Berlin–Brandenbrug,* 2008.

Ferlinghetti: A City Light, Physical Features, 2008.

Eddie Zero, *Hell Ride,* Dimension Films, 2008.

Mr. Reedy, *Sleepwalking,* Anchor Bay Entertainment, 2008.

George O'Hearn, *Elegy,* Samuel Goldwyn, 2008.

Donald Greenleaf, *Swing Vote,* Walt Disney Studios, 2008.

Frank, *Palermo Shooting,* Odeon, 2008.

The judge, *An American Carol* (also known as *Big Fat Important Movie*), Vivendi Entertainment, 2008.

Sebring, 1010 Films, 2009.

Nick Twain the producer, *The Last Film Festival,* 2010.

Tony, *Alpha and Omega,* Lions Gate Films, 2010.

Also appeared in *Destiny.*

Film Director:

Easy Rider, Columbia, 1969.

The Last Movie (also known as *Chinchero*), Universal, 1971.

Out of the Blue (also known as *No Looking Back* and *Plus rien a perdre*), Discovery, 1983.

Colors, Orion, 1988.

The Hot Spot, Orion, 1990.

(As Alan Smithee) *Backtrack* (also known as *Catchfire* and *Do It the Hard Way*), Vestron, 1992.

Chasers, Warner Bros., 1994.

Homeless, 2004.

Film Work; Other:

(Uncredited) Second unit director, *The Trip,* 1967.

Producer, *Backtrack!,* 1969.

Editor supervisor, *The Last Movie* (also known as *Chinchero*), Universal, 1971.

Also produced *The Shooter.*

Television Appearances; Series:

Peter Vollmer, *The Twilight Zone,*1959.

Fishing with John, 1991.

Smith, *Flatland,* 2002.

Victor Drazen, a recurring role, *24,* Fox, 2002.

Autobiography, AMC, 2005.

Colonel Eli McNulty, *E–Ring,* 2005–2006.

Ben Cendars, *Crash,* 2008–2009.

Television Appearances; Miniseries:

Doc Holliday, *Wild Times,* syndicated, 1980.

General Tariq, *Samson and Delilah* (also known as *Sansone e Dalila*), TNT, 1996.

Pelias, *Jason and the Argonauts,* NBC, 2000.

James Richardson, *Firestarter 2: Rekindled* (also known as *Firestarter: Rekindled*), Sci–Fi Channel, 2002.

Television Appearances; Movies:

Fritz, *Swiss Family Robinson,* 1958.

Lieutenant Ron Bliss, *Stark,* CBS, 1985.

Lieutenant Ron Bliss, *Stark: Mirror Image* (also known as *Mirror Image* and *Stark II*), CBS, 1986.

Santabear's High Flying Adventure, 1987.

Narrator, *Black Leather Jacket,* 1988.

Title role, *Paris Trout* (also known as *Rage*), Showtime, 1991.

Barry Seal, *Doublecrossed* (also known as *The True Story of Barry Seal*), HBO, 1991.

Sunset Heat, HBO, 1991.

Harry "Nails" Niles, *Nails,* Showtime, 1992.

Austin Blair, "The Heart of Justice," *TNT Screenworks,* TNT, 1993.

H. Phillip Lovecraft, *Witch Hunt,* HBO, 1994.

Frankie, *The Last Days of Frankie the Fly* (also known as *Frankie and Fly*), HBO, 1996.

Atlas, *Top of the World,* HBO, 1997.

Gilchrist, *Road Ends,* Cinemax, 1998.

William S. Burroughs, *The Source,* 1999.

Justice, Cinemax, 1999.

Vincent Swan, *The Prophets Game,* 2000.

Lewis Garou, *The Apostate,* Cinemax, 2000.

Giant Ponti, *Luck of the Draw,* Cinemax, 2000.

Dad/King Normans, *The Groovenians,* 2002.

Ronnie Purnell, *The Last Ride,* 2004.

Television Appearances; Specials:

Fritz, *Swiss Family Robinson,* NBC, 1958.

Disneyland '59 (also known as *Kodak Presents Disneyland '59*), 1959.

James Dean: The First American Teenager, 1975.

Rolling Stone Magazine's 20 Years of Rock 'n' Roll (also known as *Rolling Stone Magazine's 20th Anniversary Special* and *Rolling Stone Presents 20 Years of Rock 'n' Roll*), ABC, 1987.

Out of the Blue and into the Black, 1987.

Farm Aid '87, 1987.

(Uncredited; in archive footage) Voice of Piglet, *Apocalypse Pooh,* 1987.

Himself, *No Frank in Lumberton,* 1988.

Narrator, *Black Leather Jacket,* 1988.

Art, Acting, and the Suicide Chair: Dennis Hopper, 1988.

"Montgomery Clift: His Place in the Sun," *Crazy about the Movies,* Cinemax, 1989.

Keith Haring: Drawing the Line, PBS, 1989.

Montgomery Clift: His Place in the Sun, Cinemax, 1989.

Jonathan Ross Presents for One Week Only: David Lynch, 1990.

Hearts of Darkness: A Filmmaker's Apocalypse, Showtime, 1991.

"Dennis Hopper," *Crazy about the Movies,* Cinemax, 1991.

Jonathan Ross Presents for One Week Only: Alejandro Jodorowsky, 1991.

Triers element (also known as *Trier's Element*), 1991.

Dennis Hopper as Collector and Artist, 1992.

"Superstar: The Life and Times of Andy Warhol," *American Masters,* PBS, 1992.

Kris Kristofferson: His Life and Work, 1993.

Bob Dylan: 30th Anniversary Concert Celebration, 1993.

Special segment host, *Willie Nelson The Big Six–O: An All–Star Birthday Celebration,* CBS, 1993.

The American Film Institute Salute to Elizabeth Taylor, ABC, 1993.

Great American Music: A Salute to Fast Cars, The Family Channel, 1994.

"Addicted to Fame," *First Person with Maria Shriver,* NBC, 1994.

Howard Payne the host, *The Making of "Speed,"* 1994.

The American Film Institute Salute to Jack Nicholson, 1994.

Biking USA, 1994.

James Dean and Me, 1995.

The NFL at 75: An All–Star Celebration (also known as *The NFL 75th Anniversary Special*), ABC, 1995.

Host, *Dennis Hopper: L.A. Blues,* 1995.

Caesars Palace 30th Anniversary Celebration, ABC, 1996.

Marlon Brando: The Wild One, Channel 4, 1996.

James Dean: A Portrait, The Disney Channel, 1996.

Goon, *Rediscovering a Rebel,* 1996.

American Dreamers, 1996.

MTV Europe Music Awards 1997 Pre–Show, 1997.

Willie Nelson: Down Home, 1997.

James Dean: Race with Destiny, 1997.

Pretty as a Picture: The Art of David Lynch, 1997.

MTV Europe Music Awards 1997: Nomination Special, 1997.

Happy Birthday Elizabeth—A Celebration of Life, ABC, 1997.

King Koopa, *The Making of "Super Mario Brothers,"* 1997.

Narrator, *U2: A Year in Pop,* ABC, 1997.

Vincent Price: The Versatile Villain, Arts and Entertainment, 1997.

Andy Warhol: A Life at the Edge, Arts and Entertainment, 1997.

Host, *The Fine Art of Separating People From Their Money,* Arts and Entertainment, 1998.

The Warner Bros. Story: No Guts, No Glory: 75 Years of Stars, TNT, 1998.

Warner Bros Story: No Guts, No Glory: 75 Years of Blockbusters, TNT, 1998.

Wie man die leute von ihrem geld trennt, 1998.

AFI's 100 Years ... 100 Movies: In Search of, 1998.

Roger Miller Remembered, 1998.

Where It's At: The Rolling Stone State of the Union, 1998.

Saturday Night Live: 25th Anniversary Primetime Special, NBC, 1999.

Narrator, *Robert Rauschenberg: Inventive Genius,* PBS, 1999.

Forever Hollywood, 1999.

An All–Star Tribute to Johnny Cash, 1999.

William S. Burroughs, *The Source,* 1999.

Dennis Hopper: Rebel Without a Pause, 2000.

A Hard Look (also known as *Emmanuelle: A Hard Look*), 2000.

Jazz Seen: The Life and Times of Photographer William Claxton, Bravo, 2001.

Presenter, *An All–Star Tribute to Brian Wilson,* TNT, 2001.

Die zehn gebote der kreativitat (also known as *The 10 Commandments of Creativity*), 2001.

Dennis Hopper: The Decisive Moments, 2002.

(Uncredited) Himself, *Reel Radicals: The Sixties Revolution in Film,* 2002.

Andy Warhol, the Complete Picture (also known as *The Whole Warhol*), 2002.

Intimate Portrait: Diane Lane, Lifetime, 2002.

Hollywood Salutes Nicolas Cage: An American Cinematheque Tribute, TNT, 2002.

24 Heaven, 2002.

24: The Postmortem, 2002.

Elvis Lives, NBC, 2002.

Peter Fonda: Fortunate Son, 2002.

The 100 Greatest Movie Stars, Channel 4, 2003.

Willie Nelson & Friends: Live and Kickin', USA Network, 2003.

AFI's 100 Years ... 100 Heroes & Villians (also known as *AFI's 100 Years, 100 Heroes & Villians: America's Greatest Screen Characters*), CBS, 2003.

The 100 Greatest Scary Moments, Channel 4, 2003.

The 100 Greatest War Films, Channel 4, 2005.

Premio Donostia a Willem Dafoe, 2005.

Premio Donostia a Max Von Sydow, 2006.

Premio Donostia a Matt Dillon, 2006.
Gorillaz: Live in Manchester (also known as *Gorillaz: Demon Days Live*), 2006.
The Art of Football from A to Z (also known as *The Art of Soccer with John Cleese*), BFS Video, 2006.
Wanderlust, Independent Film Channel, 2006.
50 Films to See Before You Die, Channel 4, 2006.
Cannes, 60 ans d'histoires, France 3, 2007.
Brando, TCM, 2007.
AFI's 100 Years ... 100 Movies: 10th Anniversary Edition, 2007.
Presenter, *Concert for Diana,* 2007.
Muss ich schreiben? (also known as *Must I Write?* and *Must I Write? Letters to a Young Poet*), 2007.
AFI's 10 Top 10: America's 10 Greatest Films in 10 Classic Genres, CBS, 2008.
Charity Poker Festival, 2008.

Television Appearances; Awards Presentations:
(Uncredited) *The ... Annual Academy Awards,* 1970, 1987.
Presenter, *The 1987 IFP/West Independent Spirit Awards,* 1987.
Presenter, *The 44th Annual Golden Globe Awards,* 1987.
The 16th Annual People's Choice Awards, CBS, 1990.
MTV's 1991 Video Music Awards, MTV, 1991.
(Uncredited) *The 43rd Annual Primetime Emmy Awards,* 1991.
Presenter, *The 13th Annual CableACE Awards,* 1992.
The ... Billboard Music Awards, Fox, 1993, 1999.
The 14th Annual CableACE Awards, Lifetime, 1993.
Jim Thorpe Pro Sports Awards, ABC, 1994.
Presenter, *The 1995 MTV Movie Awards,* MTV, 1995.
The ... ESPY Awards, ESPN, 1996, 1997.
Presenter, *The VH1 Fashion Awards,* VH1, 1996.
Presenter, *The Blockbuster Entertainment Awards,* 1996, UPN, 1997.
(Uncredited) *1997 VH1 Fashion Awards,* 1997.
Presenter, *The Screen Actors Guild Awards,* NBC, 1997.
Presenter, *The 1997 MTV Europe Music Awards,* MTV, 1997.
2000 Blockbuster Entertainment Awards, Fox, 2000.
Presenter, *ESPY Awards,* 2000.
Young Hollywood Awards, 2001.
ABC World Stunt Awards, ABC, 2001, 2002.
The 2001 IFP/West Independent Spirit Awards, 2001.
The 74th Annual Academy Awards, ABC, 2002.
Host, *2003 ABC World Stunt Awards,* 2003.
Presenter, *The 2004 IFP/West Independent Spirit Awards,* Independent Film Channel and Bravo, 2004.
Host, *2004 Taurus World Stunt Awards,* 2004.
Presenter, *The CMT Music Awards,* Country Music Television, 2005.
2005 Taurus World Stunt Awards, 2005.
Film Independent's 2007 Spirit Awards, 2007.
Presenter, *2007 Taurus World Stunt Awards,* AMC, 2007.

The 14th Annual Critics' Choice Awards, VH1, 2009.

Television Appearances; Pilots:
Vern, "The Sharpshooter" (re–edited version of *Zane Grey Theater* episode), *The Rifleman,* ABC, 1958.
Host, *Suspense,* NBC, 2003.
Narrator, *Nanette Burstein Celebrity Autobiography Project,* AMC, 2005.

Television Appearances; Episodic:
Loretta Young Show, NBC, 1954.
"A Medal for Miss Walker," *Cavalcade of America* (also known as *DuPont Presents the Cavalcade Theatre* and *DuPont Theater*), 1954.
"Boy in the Storm," *Medic,* NBC, 1955.
Frankie, "Mama's Boy," *Public Defender,* CBS, 1955.
"Inga," *Loretta Young Show,* NBC, 1955.
"The Wedding Gift," *King's Row,* ABC, 1955.
"The Traveler," *Cheyenne,* ABC, 1956.
Utah Kid, "Quicksand," *Cheyenne,* ABC, 1956.
Steve Redman, "High Air," *Screen Directors Playhouse,* NBC, 1956.
The Kaiser Aluminum Hour, NBC, 1956–57.
Abe Larson, "The Iron Trail," *Cheyenne,* ABC, 1957.
"A Question of Loyalty," *Conflict,* ABC, 1957.
"No Man's Road," *Conflict,* ABC, 1957.
Billy the Kid, "Brannigan's Boots," *Sugarfoot,* ABC, 1957.
"Trial by Slander," *Studio One,* CBS, 1958.
Vernon Tippert, "The Sharpshooter," *Zane Grey Theater,* CBS, 1958.
"The Last Summer," *Studio One,* CBS, 1958.
"Last Night in August," *Pursuit,* CBS, 1958.
Danny Sunrise, "The Sunrise Gun," *Zane Grey Theater,* CBS, 1959.
Johnny Clover, "Three Legged Terror," *The Rifleman,* ABC, 1959.
"Wake up to Terror," *Line–Up,* CBS, 1959.
"Goldie Meets Mike," *Betty Hutton Show,* CBS, 1960.
"Millionaire Julie Sherman," *Millionaire,* CBS, 1960.
"No One," *Barbara Stanwyck Theater,* NBC, 1960.
"Shoes for Vinnie Winford," *Naked City,* ABC, 1961.
"My Friend, My Enemy," *87th Precinct,* NBC, 1961.
"The Mind's Own Fire," *The Investigators,* CBS, 1961.
Fred Judson, "The Hold–Out," *General Electric Theater,* CBS, 1962.
"The Indelible Silence," *The Defenders,* CBS, 1962.
Trask, "Vendetta Arms," *Surfside 6,* 1962.
Peter Vollmer, "He's Alive," *Twilight Zone,* CBS, 1963.
"Requiem at Dancer's Hill," *The Dakotas,* ABC, 1963.
Emmett Lawton, "The Emmett Lawton Story," *Wagon Train,* ABC, 1963.
"The Weeping Baboon," *Defenders,* CBS, 1963.
"The Weakling," *Espionage,* NBC, 1963.
"The Wrecker," *Greatest Show on Earth,* ABC, 1963.
Peter Devlin, "To Set It Right," *The Lieutenant,* 1963.
Alan Landman, "Bobbie Jo and the Beatnik," *Petticoat Junction,* CBS, 1964.

"People in Glass Houses," *Arrest and Trial,* ABC, 1964.

Peter Devlin, "To Set It Right," *The Lieutenant,* NBC, 1964.

Dev Farnum, "The Dark Past," *Bonanza,* NBC, 1964.

Billy Kimbro, "One Killer on Ice," *Gunsmoke,* CBS, 1965.

"The Many Colors of Courage," *Convoy,* NBC, 1965.

"South Wind," *Legend of Jesse James,* ABC, 1966.

"Without Spear or Sword," *Court–Martial,* ABC, 1966.

Passenger, "Rendezvous with Yesterday," *The Time Tunnel,* ABC, 1966.

Zack Fender, "A Little Jazz," *Combat,* ABC, 1967.

Leon Grell, "Plunder at Hawk's Grove," *Big Valley,* ABC, 1967.

Pruitt Reed, "Find a Sonnett, Kill a Sonnett," *Guns of Will Sonnett,* ABC, 1967.

Jimmy Sweetwater, "Night of the Executioners," *Big Valley,* ABC, 1967.

The Johnny Cash Show, 1970.

The Dean Martin Show (also known as *The Dean Martin Comedy Hour*), 1972.

Host, "Dennis Hopper/Roy Orbison," *Saturday Night Live* (also known as *SNL*), NBC, 1987.

Cinema 3, 1992.

Tal cual, 1993.

Host, "The Making of 'Speed,'" *HBO First Look,* HBO, 1994.

Howard Payne, "om filmen 'Speed,'" *Nyhetsmorgon,* 1994.

Inside the Actors Studio, Bravo, 1995.

Narrator, "Cecil B. DeMille," *Sex and the Silver Screen,* Showtime, 1996.

Voice of himself, "Hank's Got the Willies," *King of the Hill* (animated), Fox, 1997.

Caiga quien caiga, 1997.

Lo + plus, 1998.

Fishing with John, Independent Film Channel, 1998.

"Andy Warhol: A Life at the Edge," *Biography,* Arts and Entertainment, 1998.

"Dennis Hopper," *E! True Hollywood Story,* E! Entertainment Television, 1999.

Egg: The Art Show, PBS, 1999.

Presenter, "The Fine Art of Separating People from Their Money," *Arena,* 2000.

MADtv, Fox, 2000.

"Jennifer Jones: Portrait of a Lady," *Biography,* Arts and Entertainment, 2001.

Seitenblicke, 2002.

NFL Monday Night Football, ABC, 2002.

"Diane Lane," *Intimate Portrait,* 2002.

"The Films of Tony Scott," *The Directors,* Encore, 2003.

"The Films of David Lynch," *The Directors,* Encore, 2003.

"Kentucky Derby," *10 Things Every Guy Should Experience,* Spike TV, 2004.

Jon Castille, "New Orleans," *Las Vegas,* 2004.

"Lauren Bacall," *The Hollywood Greats* (also known as *Hollywood Greats*), BBC1, 2005.

"Jane Fonda," *The Hollywood Greats* (also known as *Hollywood Greats*), BBC1, 2005.

"Andy Warhol," *Biography,* Arts and Entertainment, 2006.

"John at ESPY Awards," *Howard Stern on Demand,* 2006.

Sunday Morning Shootout (also known as *Hollywood Shootout* and *Shootout*), AMC, 2006.

"Just Say No!," *The Drug Years,* VH1, 2006.

Howard Payne, "Magnificent Movies," *20 to 1,* Nine Network, 2006.

Babalugats, "Sexiest Movie Moments," *20 to 1,* Nine Network, 2007.

"Virginia Madsen, Dennis Hopper, Gil Cates," *Sunday Morning Shootout* (also known as *Hollywood Shootout* and *Shootout*), AMC, 2007.

"Malibooty," *Entourage,* HBO, 2007.

"David Lynch Special," *Tracks,* 2007.

Entertainment Tonight (also known as *E.T.* and *This Week in Entertainment*), syndicated, 2007 and 2008.

"Charlize Theron," *E! True Hollywood Story,* E! Entertainment Television, 2008.

Ce soir (ou jamais!), 2008.

"Dennis Hopper," *Tracks,* 2008.

The Movie Loft, 2009.

Also appeared as Ross Martin, *Letter to Loretta;* himself, *Willemsens Woche.*

Television Talk Show Guest Appearances; Episodic:

The David Frost Show, 1970 and 1971.

Late Night with David Letterman, NBC, 1987, 1990, 1991.

The Tonight Show Starring Johnny Carson, NBC, 1990, 1991.

The Tonight Show with Jay Leno, NBC, 1993.

Late Show with David Letterman, CBS, 1994, 1996.

Dennis Miller Live, 1997.

The Rosie O'Donnell Show, syndicated, 1998.

The Howard Stern Radio Show, 2000.

V Graham Norton, Channel 4, 2002.

On the Record with Bob Costas, HBO, 2004.

Last Call with Carson Daly, NBC, 2004.

Larry King Live, Cable News Network, two episodes, 2005.

The Late Late Show with Craig Ferguson, CBS, 2005, 2007, and 2008.

Jimmy Kimmel Live!, ABC, 2005 and 2008.

Tavis Smiley, PBS, 2007.

The Graham Norton Show, BBC, 2007.

The Daily Show (also known as *A Daily Show with Jon Stewart, The Daily Show with Jon Stewart,* and *The Daily Show with Jon Stewart Global Edition*), Comedy Central, 2008.

Live with Regis & Kelly, syndicated, 2008.

The Charlie Rose Show (also known as *Charlie Rose*), PBS, 2008.

Le grand journal de Canal+, 2008.

The View, ABC, 2008.

Late Night with Conan O'Brien, NBC, 2008.

Stage Appearances:
Hammond Maxwell, *Mandingo,* Lyceum Theatre, New York City, 1961.

RECORDINGS

Video Games:
Voice of Mr. Beautiful, *Hell: A Cyberpunk Thriller,* 1995.
Walter Pensky, *Black Dahlia,* Take 2 Interactive, 1998.
Voice of Steve Scott, *Grand Theft Auto: Vice City,* 2002.
Deadly Creatures, Nintendo, 2009.

Videos:
Storyteller, *Rabbit Ears: The Ugly Duckling,* 1985.
Storyteller, *Rabbit Ears: The Steadfast Tin Soldier,* 1985.
Storyteller, *Rabbit Ears: The Tale of Mr. Jeremy Fisher,* 1986.
Storyteller, *Rabbit Ears: The Tale of Peter Rabbit,* 1987.
Monsters & Maniacs, 1988.
Storyteller, *Rabbit Ears: The Fisherman and His Wife,* 1989.
Storyteller, *Rabbit Ears: Thumbelina,* 1989.
Storyteller, *Rabbit Ears: How the Leopard Got His Spots,* 1989.
Storyteller, *Rabbit Ears: Paul Bunyan,* 1990.
Flashing on the Sixties: A Tribal Document, 1990.
Storyteller, *Rabbit Ears: King Midas and the Golden Touch,* 1991.
Storyteller, *Rabbit Ears: The Fool and the Flying Ship,* 1991.
Storyteller, *Rabbit Ears: Annie Oakley,* 1992.
Storyteller, *Rabbit Ears: Rip Van Winkle,* 1992.
Rabbit Ears: Jonah and the Whale, 1992.
The Making of "Space Truckers," 1996.
Peter Crawford, *Tycus,* 1998.
Easy Rider: Shaking the Cage (also known as *Shaking the Cage*), 1999.
Mysteries of Love, 2002.
Inside "Speed," 2002.
To Shoot a Mad Dog: The Making of "Mad Dog Morgan," 2003.
Return to "Giant," Warner Home Video, 2003.
Tune in to Trip Out, Metro–Goldwyn–Mayer/United Artist, 2003.
Victor Castiglione, *Bad Boy's 10th Anniversary ... The Hits,* Bad Boy Records, 2004.
Hoosier History: The Truth Behind the Legend, Metro–Goldwyn–Mayer, 2005.
Undead Again: The Making of "Land of the Dead," Universal Studios Home Video, 2005.
Land of the Dead: A Day with the Living Dead, Universal Studios Home Video, 2005.
Essential Gorillaz, MTV, 2006.
Real James Dean, EagleVision, 2006.

The Rise of Two Legends, Warner Home Video, 2006.
Brando: An Icon Is Born, Sony, 2008.
Stanley Kramer: A Man's Search for Truth, Sony, 2008.
That's Our Mad Dog: Dennis Hopper Interviewed by Phillipe Mora, 2009.

Music Videos:
Appeared in Puff Daddy's "Victory."

WRITINGS

Screenplays:
(With Peter Fonda and Terry Southern) *Easy Rider,* Columbia, 1969.
(With Stewart Stern) *The Last Movie* (also known as *Chinchero*), Universal, 1971.
The American Dreamer, 1971.
(Uncredited) *Out of the Blue* (also known as *No Looking Back* and *Plus rien a perdre*), 1980.

Nonfiction:
Out of the Sixties (photographs), text by Michael McClure, Twelvetrees, 1987.

OTHER SOURCES

Books:
St. James Encyclopedia of Popular Culture, St. James Press, 2000.

Periodicals:
Computer Gaming World, September, 1997, p. 26.
Interview, May, 2000, p. 92; April, 2001, p. 85.
New York Times, April 3, 1983; September 8, 1994, pp. C1, C10.
Premiere, June, 1988, pp. 21–23.

HOWARD, Sherman 1949–
  (Howard Sherman)

PERSONAL

Full name, Howard Lee Sherman; born June 11, 1949, in Chicago, IL; married Donna Bullock (an actress); children: Hannah.

Addresses: *Contact*—c/o Abrams Artists Agency, 9200 Sunset Blvd., Los Angeles, CA 90069.

Career: Actor. American Conservatory Theatre, San Francisco, CA, member of company; Actors Theatre of Louisville, member of company.

CREDITS

Television Appearances; Series:
(As Howard Sherman) Gordon Bradford Gray, *General Hospital*, ABC, 1973–74.
Vinnie Vincent, *Ryan's Hope*, ABC, 1986–87.
Japhet Harper, a recurring role, *Dallas*, 1988.
Lex Luthor, *Superboy* (also known as *The Adventures of Superboy*), syndicated, 1989–92.
Roger, *Good & Evil*, ABC, 1991.
Voice of Van Pelt, *Jumanji* (animated), UPN, 1996.
Voice of Blight/Derek Powers, *Batman Beyond* (animated; also known as *Batman of the Future*), The WB, 1999.

Television Appearances; Miniseries:
Director, *Celebrity* (also known as *Tommy Thompson's "Celebrity"*), NBC, 1984.
Dr. Dietz, *The Stand* (also known as *Stephen King's "The Stand"*), ABC, 1994.
OP Center (also known as *Tome Clancy's "OP Center"*), ABC, 1995.

Television Appearances; Movies:
(As Howard Sherman) *The Eagle and the Bear*, 1985.
Jack Martinelli, *Necessity*, CBS, 1988.
Bishop, *The Hit List*, Showtime, 1993.
Scoutmaster Phlim, *Problem Child 3: Junior in Love* (also known as *Problem Child 3*), NBC, 1995.
Trooper, *Retroactive*, HBO, 1997.
Voice of Derek Powers/Blight, *Batman Beyond: The Movie* (animated), 1999.

Television Appearances; Pilots:
On the Edge, NBC, 1987.
Nightingales, NBC, 1988.
General Craw, *Further Adventures*, 1988.
Steve Hobart, *The Ed Begley, Jr., Show*, CBS, 1989.
Mr. Lewis, *Parker Lewis Can't Lose*, Fox, 1990.
Hal Barber, *Melrose Place*, Fox, 1992.

Television Appearances; Episodic:
(As Howard Sherman) Arnold Baker, "Fear of Floating," *Tales from the Darkside*, syndicated, 1986.
Simon Peller, "Rakers," *Max Headroom*, 1987.
Simon Peller, "The Blanks," *Max Headroom*, 1987.
Colonel Andrew Baker, "Freefall," *Miami Vice*, NBC, 1989.
Ed Haley, "One Rat, One Ranger," *L.A. Law*, NBC, 1989.
Dick Sant, "Shelter Me," *Baywatch*, NBC, 1989.

Dr. Radford, "And They Swam Right Over the Dam," *Unsub*, 1989.
Dr. Lynch, "Monkey Dreams," *Freddy's Nightmares*, 1989.
Officer, "Consider Me Gone," *ALF*, NBC, 1990.
Captain Endar, "Suddenly Human," *Star Trek: The Next Generation*, syndicated, 1990.
Marshal Cole Lambert, "Blood Money," *The Young Riders*, ABC, 1990.
Hank Rickett, "Runaway–July 4, 1964," *Quantum Leap*, NBC, 1991.
Hal Barber, "Friends & Lovers," *Melrose Place*, Fox, 1992.
Grant Hoffler, *Likely Suspects*, Fox, 1992.
Weinblatt, *Good Advice*, CBS, 1992.
Kip, "Old Acquaintance," *Major Dad*, 1992.
Dr. Beldsoe, "To Plea or Not to Plea," *Rachel Gunn, R.N.*, 1992.
Prince Gor'Dah, "Death before Dishonor," *Space Rangers*, CBS, 1993.
Stephen Kane, "Heat," *Raven*, CBS, 1993.
Roy, "The Junior Mint," *Seinfeld*, NBC, 1993.
"Banshies," *Space Rangers*, CBS, 1993.
Joseph Talbot, "Lily," *Diagnosis Murder*, CBS, 1994.
Packard, "When We Dead Awaken," *SeaQuest DSV*, 1994.
Sonny Lyle, "Blue Movies," *Walker, Texas Ranger*, CBS, 1995.
Hendrick, "Prince of Wails," *Sliders*, Fox, 1995.
Syvar, "Shakaar," *Star Trek: Deep Space Nine*, syndicated, 1995.
Louis Zedek, "Hot Ice" (also known as "The Winter Star Intercept"), *Fortune Hunter*, Fox, 1995.
"Winning," *The Client*, CBS, 1996.
Bishop, "The Pipeline," *Renegade*, 1996.
Harvey, "The Practical Joke," *The Jeff Foxworthy Show*, 1996.
Explorer Channel executive, "The Weed," *Mad about You*, NBC, 1996.
Explorer Channel executive, "The Award," *Mad about You*, NBC, 1996.
Howard, "Workshop 'Til You Drop," *Home Improvement*, ABC, 1996.
Dr. Elton Greenleaf, "Lethal Injection," *The Burning Zone*, UPN, 1996.
Voices of Preserver and the collector, "The Main Man: Parts 1 & 2," *Superman* (animated), The WB, 1996.
Voice, *All Dogs Go to Heaven: The Series* (animated), syndicated, 1996–2000.
Mr. Burrows, "Mayday," *Walker, Texas Ranger*, CBS, 1997.
Franklin Quill, "Soft Targets," *Pacific Blue*, USA Network, 1997.
Jack Conrad, "The Counterfeiters," *Nash Bridges*, CBS, 1997.
Chamberlain, "Toy Story," *Life with Roger*, The WB, 1997.
Tow Tom, "Jingle Fever," *Malcolm & Eddie*, UPN, 1997.
"Ambush," *ER*, NBC, 1997.
"Retribution," *Michael Hayes*, CBS, 1997.

"The Buzzard Syndrome," *Men in Black,* 1997.

"The Symbiote Syndrome," *Men in Black,* 1997.

Voice, *Zorro* (animated), syndicated, 1997–2000.

Voice, "The Luck of the Irish," *Extreme Ghostbusters* (animated), syndicated, 1997.

Voice, *Disney's Hercules* (animated), ABC, 1998–2000.

Dr. Terdlington, "The Band Episode," *Sabrina, the Teenage Witch,* ABC, 1998.

Voice of Steppenwolf, "Apokolips ... Now!: Part 2," *Superman,* 1998.

Voice, "The Curse of the Blue Karbunkle," *Mad Jack the Pirate* (animated), 1998.

"Refuge: Part 2," *Law & Order,* NBC, 1999.

(As Howard Sherman) Clavon, "Scribbling Rivalry," *Once and Again,* ABC, 2001.

T'Greth, "Prophecy," *Star Trek: Voyager,* UPN, 2001.

Voice of Oog–Ah, "Planet Jackers," *Invader Zim* (animated), 2001.

Clyde, "A Paige from the Past," *Charmed,* The WB, 2002.

Voice of Captain Horoth, *The Mummy: The Animated Series* (animated; also known as *The Mummy: Secrets of the Medjai*), Kids' WB, 2003.

Tim Dorn, "Look Again," *Cold Case,* CBS, 2003.

Vanko, "Decks and Violence," *Las Vegas,* 2003.

Ivan, "Malcolm Dates a Family," *Malcolm in the Middle,* 2004.

Judge Josiah Bell, "Misbegotten," *Law & Order,* NBC, 2008.

Television Appearances; Specials:

Voice, *The Wild West* (documentary), syndicated, 1993.

Supervisor, *Seed: A Love Story,* Lifetime, 1998.

Film Appearances:

(As Howard Sherman) Alan, *Grace Quigley* (also known as *The Ultimate Solution of Grace Quigley*), Cannon, 1984.

(As Howard Sherman) Bub the Zombie, *Day of the Dead,* Image, 1985.

(As Howard Sherman) Boris, *The House on Carroll Street,* Orion, 1988.

(Uncredited) Canadian police officer, *Three Fugitives,* Buena Vista, 1989.

Dillon, *K–9,* Universal, 1989.

Hitman, *Lethal Weapon 2,* Warner Bros., 1989.

Court martial president, *Casualties of War,* Columbia, 1989.

Victor Manning, *I Come in Peace* (also known as *Dark Angel*), Image, 1990.

Kiley, *Ricochet,* Warner Bros., 1991.

Trooper, *Retroactive* (also known as *Reverse*), 1997.

Voice of Shere Khan, *The Jungle Book: Mowgli's Story* (animated), 1998.

Jesus, *Dante's View,* Showcase, 1998.

Voice of Haggis, *An American Tail: The Mystery of the Night Monster,* 1999.

Voice of McBrusque, *An American Tail: The Treasure of Manhattan Island* (animated; also known as *An American Tail 3: The Treasure of Manhattan Island*), Universal Studios Home Video, 2000.

Paul Pearson, *The Man from Elysian Fields,* Samuel Goldwyn, 2001.

Mr. Lloyd, *Dexter,* 2002.

Mr. Moffat, *Debating Robert Lee,* Radio London Films, 2004.

Funeral director, *Eulogy,* Lions Gate Films, 2004.

Stuart, *You Belong to Me,* Peccadillo, 2007.

Stage Appearances:

Enrico IV, New Jersey Shakespeare Festival, F. M. Kirby Shakespeare Theatre, Madison, NJ, 2002.

Henry Drummond, *Inherit the Wind,* Lyceum Theatre, New York City, 2007.

Dr. Jim Bayliss, *All My Sons,* Gerald Schoenfeld Theatre, New York City, 2008–2009.

Also appeared as title role, *Sheridan,* La Jolla Playhouse, San Diego, CA; title role, *Hamlet;* title role, *Macbeth;* Archie, *Jumpers;* and Charlie Castle, *The Big Knife.*

RECORDINGS

Video Games:

Voice of Belial/first filmmaker/Ssar priest, *Lands of Lore: Guardians of Destiny* (also known as *Lands of Lore 2*), 1997.

Voice of Red Sage, *Jak and Daxter: The Precursor Legacy,* Sony Computer Entertainment America, 2001.

Command & Conquer: Yuri's Revenge (also known as *Red Alert 2 Expansion Pack: Yuri's Revenge*), 2001.

Star Trek: Armada II, 2001.

Voice of Sopot, *Red Faction II,* THQ Inc., 2002.

Voice of ice demon/Blackbeard, *Pirates: The Legend of Black Kat,* 2002.

Command & Conquer: Renegade, 2002.

Voice of Azraman, *Summoner 2* (also known as *Summoner: A Goddess Reborn*), 2002.

Miner number one, *Run Like Hell* (also known as *RLH*), 2002.

Voice of Argosax, *Devil May Cry 2,* Capcom, 2003.

Voice of Kor, *Jak II* (also known as *Jak II: Renegade*), Sony, 2003.

Voice of Death's Hand, *Jade Empire,* Microsoft, 2005.

Voice of Kor, *Daxter,* Sony, 2006.

Videos:

The Many Days of "Day of the Dead," Anchor Bay Entertainment, 2003.

WRITINGS

Television Episodes:

"Mine Games," *Superboy* (also known as *The Adventures of Superboy*), 1991.

"Darla Goes Ballistic," *Superboy* (also known as *The Adventures of Superboy*), 1991.

HYATT, Michael

PERSONAL

Born in England; immigrated to the United States at the age of ten; daughter of Charles (an actor, broadcaster, and comedian) and Vera (an art historian and museologist) Hyatt. *Education:* Howard University, B.F.A.; New York University, M.F.A.

Addresses: *Agent*—Domain, 9229 Sunset Blvd., Suite 710, Los Angeles, CA 90069.

Career: Actress.

CREDITS

Film Appearances:
Trudy, *Pushing Tin,* Twentieth Century–Fox, 1999.
Digna, *Acts of Worship,* 2001, Manifesto Films, 2003.
Floberta, *The Good Girl,* Fox Searchlight, 2002.
Michelle, *Washington Heights,* 2002, Mac Releasing, 2003.
Nurse Gates, *Crazylove* (also known as *Committed* and *crazylove*), PorchLight Entertainment, 2005.
Carol, *Two Weeks,* Metro–Goldwyn–Mayer, 2006.
Delores, *Mississippi Damned,* Morgan's Mark, 2009.
Malik's mother, *Fame,* Metro–Goldwyn–Mayer, 2009.
Eve, *See You in September,* Steadfast Productions, 2010.

Television Appearances; Series:
Brianna Barksdale, *The Wire* (also known as *A escuta, Drot, Langalla, Oi dioktes tou eglimatos,* and *Sur ecoute*), HBO, between 2002 and 2006.
Angela Blake, a recurring role, *The West Wing* (also known as *West Wing, The White House,* and *El ala oeste de la Casablanca*), NBC, 2003–2004.
Connie Ruebens, *The Kill Point* (also known as *The Kill Pit*), Spike TV, 2007.
(Sometimes uncredited) Susan Chamblee, *Drive,* Fox, 2007.

Television Appearances; Episodic:
Doctor, "Unarmed and Dangerous," *Dharma & Greg,* ABC, 1998.
Rachel Willis, "Bad Girl," *Law & Order* (also known as *Law & Order Prime*), NBC, 1998.

Sadiya Khan, "Out o' Time," *Oz* (also known as *Kylmae rinki, Oz—A vida e uma prisao,* and *Oz—livet bak murene*), HBO, 1999.
Elan Holt, "Black, White and Blue," *Law & Order* (also known as *Law & Order Prime*), NBC, 2000.
The Beat (also known as *Flesh & Blood*), UPN, 2000.
Court clerk, "Myth of Fingerprints," *Law & Order* (also known as *Law & Order Prime*), NBC, 2001.
"What I'll Never Do for Love Again," *Ally McBeal* (also known as *Ally* and *Ally My Love*), Fox, 2002.
Josette Marshall, "Coming and Going," *Six Feet Under,* HBO, 2004.
Mary Wallace, "Out of Sight," *Joan of Arcadia,* CBS, 2004.
Agent Kathryn Thompson, "Cemetery Wind: Parts 1 & 2," *E–Ring* (also known as *Pentagon, D.O.S.—Division des operations speciales,* and *E–Ring—Aporrites apostoles*), NBC, 2005.
Defense attorney Julia Shinnear, "License to Kill," *Law & Order* (also known as *Law & Order Prime*), NBC, 2005.
Dr. Long, "Crazy Nuts & All Fucked Up," *Huff* (also known as *!Huff*), Showtime, 2005.
Marcy, "Day 4: 2:00 p.m.–3:00 p.m.," *24* (also known as *Twenty Four* and *24 Hours*), Fox, 2005.
Marian Davidson, "Grandma Got Run Over by a Reindeer," *Grey's Anatomy* (also known as *Complications, Procedure, Surgeons, Under the Knife,* and *Grey's Anatomy—Die jungen Aerzte*), ABC, 2005.
Women's studies professor, "One Angry Veronica," *Veronica Mars,* UPN, 2005.
Maisey, "The Focus Group," *Studio 60 on the Sunset Strip* (also known as *Studio 7 on the Sunset Strip* and *Studio 60*), NBC, 2006.
Maisey, "The West Coast Delay," *Studio 60 on the Sunset Strip* (also known as *Studio 7 on the Sunset Strip* and *Studio 60*), NBC, 2006.
Ruth Hartford, "Love Triangle," *Shark,* CBS, 2006.
Yvonne Devilliere, "Breach of Trust," *ER* (also known as *Emergency Room* and *E.R.*), NBC, 2007.
Charlotte, "The Bath Item Gift Hypothesis," *The Big Bang Theory,* CBS, 2008.
Dr. Barbara Morris, "Earthlings Welcome Here," *Terminator: The Sarah Connor Chronicles* (also known as *The Sarah Connor Chronicles* and *Terminator: S.C.C.*), Fox, 2008.
Dr. Ticona Roberts, "Conflicted," *Criminal Minds* (also known as *Quantico, Criminal Minds—FBI tutjijat, Esprits criminels, Gyilkos elmek, Kurjuse kannul,* and *Mentes criminales*), CBS, 2009.
Judy Williams, "Caged," *Navy NCIS: Naval Criminal Investigative Service* (also known as *Naval CIS, Navy CIS, Navy NCIS, NCIS,* and *NCIS: Naval Criminal Investigative Service*), CBS, 2009.
Sheriff Tina Mullins, "The Beaver in the Otter," *Bones* (also known as *Brennan, Bones—Die Knochenjaegerin, Dr. Csont,* and *Kondid*), Fox, 2009.
Cameron's attorney, "Bring Your Daughter to Work Day," *Medium* (also known as *Ghost and Crime* and *A medium*), CBS, 2010.

Dr. Katherine Cortez, "Run Baby Run," *Brothers & Sisters* (also known as *Brothers and Sisters*), ABC, 2010.

Dr. Katherine Cortez, "The Science Fair," *Brothers & Sisters* (also known as *Brothers and Sisters*), ABC, 2010.

Appeared as Officer Lauper in "Four," an episode of *Smith* (also known as *Dossier Smith*), CBS.

Television Appearances; Pilots:
Nurse in comprehensive psychiatric emergency unit, *Wonderland* (also known as *Bellevue*), ABC, 2000.

Officer Lauper, *Smith* (also known as *Dossier Smith*), CBS, 2006.

Connie Ruebens, *The Kill Point* (also known as *The Kill Pit*), Spike TV, 2007.

Emergency medical technician Frank, *Operating Instructions*, USA Network, 2009.

Some sources cite an appearance as Mrs. Prose, *Untitled Wyoming Project*, The CW, c. 2010.

Stage Appearances:
Sarah's friend, *Ragtime* (musical), Ford Center for the Performing Arts, New York City, between 1998 and 2000.

Rita, *Eclipsed*, Center Theatre Group, Kirk Douglas Theatre, Los Angeles, 2009.

Appeared in other productions, including *As You Like It, Hydrotaphia, or The Death of Dr. Browne* (also known as *Hydrotaphia, Hydriotaphia,* and *Hydriotaphia, or The Death of Dr. Browne*), *Rats, Twelfth Night* (also known as *Twelfth Night, or What You Will*), and *The Two Gentlemen of Verona.*

OTHER SOURCES

Electronic:
Michael Hyatt: Actor, http://www.michaelhyatttheactor.com, August 7, 2010.

I

IACONO, Paul 1988–

PERSONAL

Full name, Paul Stanley Iacono; born September 7, 1988, in Secaucus, NJ; son of Anthony (a town administrator) and Michele Iacono. *Education:* Graduate of the Professional Performing Arts School, New York City; attended Marymount Manhattan College. *Avocational Interests:* Writing.

Addresses: *Agent*—Abrams Artists Agency, 275 Seventh Ave., 26th Floor, New York, NY 10001.

Career: Actor. Performed as a cabaret singer; appeared in advertisements. Worked as an intern for a theatrical public relations firm; worked as a waiter and held other jobs. National spokesperson and former national patient youth ambassador (as a survivor) for the Leukemia & Lymphoma Society; also a spokesperson for the Tomorrows Children's Fund. Participated in various events.

Member: Actors' Equity Association.

Awards, Honors: Life of the Theatre Award, Paper Mill Playhouse, 2000.

CREDITS

Stage Appearances:
King Island Christmas (musical), c. 1990.
Tiny Tim, *A Christmas Carol,* Park Theatre, c. 1993.
(As Paul S. Iacono) Child storyteller, *Children of Eden* (musical), Paper Mill Playhouse, Millburn, NJ, 1997.

The Will Rodgers Follies (musical), Paper Mill Playhouse, 1998.
Alvin Lush, *Sail Away* (concert staging of musical), Carnegie Hall, Weill Recital Hall, New York City, 1999.
(As Paul S. Iacono) Patrick Dennis, *Mame* (musical), Paper Mill Playhouse, 1999.
Dear Maudie, The Triad, New York City, 2004.
Donny, *Landscape of the Body,* Signature Theatre Company, Peter Norton Space, New York City, 2006.
Paul, *And Somewhere Men Are Laughing,* New York International Fringe Festival (also known as Fringe-NYC), Connelly Theatre, New York City, 2007.
Punky Givens, *The Dark at the Top of the Stairs,* Transport Theatre Company, Connelly Theatre, 2007.

Appeared in other productions, including an appearance as Mark Brayne, *Welcome to Tourettaville* (musical); and an appearance in *Oliver!* (musical). Cabaret singer at Don't Tell Mama, New York City, c. 1992.

Major Tours:
The Wizard of Oz (musical), U.S. cities, c. 1998.

Film Appearances:
(Uncredited) Junior, *Winter Solstice,* Paramount, 2004.
Younger version of Shakes Mohamedi (title role), *Shakes* (short film), 2005.
Party boy, *The Naked Brothers Band: The Movie,* 2005, broadcast on television by Nickelodeon, 2007.
Ricky Lopefrawitz, *Glow Ropes: The Rise and Fall of a Bar Mitzvah Emcee,* 2005, Echo Bridge Home Entertainment, 2006.
Pee Pee, *Return to Sleepaway Camp* (also known as *Nightmare Vacation V* and *Sleepaway Camp V: The Return*), Magnet Releasing/Magnolia Pictures, 2008.
Neil Baczynsky, *Fame,* Metro–Goldwyn–Mayer, 2009.

Mickey, *Consent,* Lili Pad Films, 2010.

Tony Cafiero, *No God, No Master,* Strata Productions, 2010.

Television Appearances; Series:

RJ Berger, *The Hard Times of RJ Berger* (also known as *Hard Times* and *The Hard Times of R. J. Berger*), MTV, beginning 2010.

Television Appearances; Movies:

Party boy, *The Naked Brothers Band: The Movie,* Nickelodeon, 2007, released as a film, 2005.

Television Appearances; Awards Presentations:

2010 MTV Video Music Awards (also known as *MTV Video Music Awards 2010*), MTV, 2010.

Television Appearances; Episodic:

Jake, Jr., *Another World* (also known as *Another World: Bay City* and *AW: Bay City*), NBC, 1995, 1996.

Birthday party guest, *Guiding Light* (also known as *The Guiding Light*), CBS, 1997.

Hospital patient, *As the World Turns,* CBS, 1997.

Guest, *The Rosie O'Donnell Show,* syndicated, multiple appearances, 1997–2002.

Guest, *Late Night with Conan O'Brien,* NBC, 1998.

James (the lost boy), *Guiding Light* (also known as *The Guiding Light*), CBS, 1999.

Trick–or–treater, *As the World Turns,* CBS, 1999.

Voice of Benny the Bull, "Maestra," *Dora the Explorer* (animated; also known as *Dora*), Nickelodeon, 2000.

Billy Boy, "Let's Go," *Human Giant,* MTV, 2007.

Billy Boy, "Mosh Pit!," *Human Giant,* MTV, 2007.

Himself, *Entertainment Tonight* (also known as *Entertainment This Week, E.T., ET Weekend,* and *This Week in Entertainment*), syndicated, 2009.

Television Appearances; Pilots:

RJ Berger, *The Hard Times of RJ Berger* (also known as *Hard Times* and *The Hard Times of R. J. Berger*), MTV, 2010.

RECORDINGS

Videos:

Himself, *Return to Sleepaway Camp: Behind the Scenes* (short documentary), Magnolia Pictures, 2008.

Albums; Cast Recordings; with Others:

(As Paul S. Iacono) *Children of Eden,* RCA Victor Broadway, 1998.

King Island Christmas, KIC Music, 1999.

WRITINGS

Writings for the Stage:

Prince/Elizabeth (staged reading; also known as *Prince Elizabeth*), Columbia University, New York City, 2008.

IGHODARO, Osas
(Martha Ighodaro)

PERSONAL

Born in The Bronx, New York, NY. *Education:* Pennsylvania State University, B.A.; graduate study at Pace University; trained at Screen Actors Guild Conservatory, HB Studios, Actors Connection, and Alvin Ailey Dance Theatre.

Addresses: *Manager*—Ingrid French, Ingrid French Management, 928 Broadway, Suite 302, New York, NY 10010.

Career: Actress. Performer at New York Fringe Festival. Selected Miss Black Connecticut, 2010. Supporter of charities, including City Harvest, New York Cares, and SAG Book Pals.

Member: Screen Actors Guild.

CREDITS

Film Appearances:

(As Martha Ighodaro) *My African Uncle* (short film), 2006.

(As Martha Ighodaro) Shinae, *Killa Season,* The Asylum/The Diplomats/Killa Entertainment, 2006.

Singing voice of Sade's sister, *Luggage* (short film), Ndolo Films, 2007.

Delilah, *Hookers in Revolt,* 2008.

Nafisa, *Across a Bloodied Ocean* (short film), K'Alpha Innovations, 2008.

Vicky the maid, *Cadillac Records,* TriStar, 2008.

Neglected girlfriend, *Park Sharks,* Tuxedofight Films, 2009.

(Uncredited) Party girl, *Notorious,* Fox Searchlight, 2009.

Chastity, *Computer Love,* Computer Lov Group, 2010.

Adinike, *Restless City,* Clam Productions, 2010.

Sheena, *The Tested,* Shoebox Pictures, 2010.

Appeared as Rochelle, *Jewslim,* Midnite Oil Productions, and as Chioma, *The Wedding,* Real Livin' Films.

Television Appearances; Episodic:
(Uncredited) Desmond's date, "Breakup," *Conviction*, NBC, 2006.
(Uncredited) Model, "Bling," *Law & Order*, NBC, 2007.

Television Appearances; Other:
Appeared as host of *Diaspora TV*; appeared as Arlene McClain in the pilot *Bodies of Work*, and as Yvonne Dawkin in the pilot *City Hall East*.

Stage Appearances:
Afi, *Revenge of a King*, National Black Theatre Festival, 2006.
Afi and Osas, *Revenge of a King*, National Black Theatre Festival, 2007.
Mother Warrior, *Voices of Africa*, Estrogenius Festival, 2009.

Appeared as spirit of the ancestors, *Auction Block*, Between the Lines Productions; Lawanda and super model, *The Colored Museum*, Citizen Bank Theatre; Michelle, *Extreme Truth*, WinceyCompany; Martha Pentecost, *Joe Turner's Come and Gone*, August Wilson Play Festival; Josephine Baker, *Ladies @ the Cotton Club*, Loaves and Fish Traveling Repertory; and Malady in *Platanos and Collard Greens*, Between the Lines Productions, New York City.

OTHER SOURCES

Electronic:
Osas Ighodaro Official Site, http://www.osas-online. com, August 3, 2010.

IRONSIDE, Michael 1950–
(Mike Ironside)

PERSONAL

Born February 12, 1950, in Toronto, Ontario, Canada; son of Robert Walter and Patricia June (maiden name, Passmore) Ironside; married second wife Karen Virginia (an actress), c. 1983 (marriage ended); married Karen Dimwiddie, 1994; children: (first marriage) Adrienne Katrina; (with Dimwiddie), Findlay. *Education:* Graduated from Ontario College of Art; also trained there as a teaching aide.

Addresses: *Agent*—Abrams Artists Agency, 9200 Sunset Blvd., Suite 1130, Los Angeles, CA 90069; Gold Liedtke Associates, 3500 West Olive Ave., Suite 1400, Burbank,

CA 91505. *Manager*—Insight, 1134 Cloverdale Ave., Los Angeles, CA 90019.

Career: Actor, producer, director, and writer. Wilmont Productions (a production company), cofounder, 1991; appeared in commercials for Big Brother and provided voice work for World Wildlife Foundation.

Member: Association of Canadian Television and Radio Artists, Screen Actors Guild.

Awards, Honors: Genie Award nomination, best supporting actor, Academy of Canadian Cinema and Television, 1982, for *Scanners*; Gemini Award nomination, best performance by a lead actor in a dramatic program or miniseries, Academy of Canadian Cinema and Television, 1988, American Cable Entertainment Award nominations, best actor in a series, both for "The Fruit at the Bottom of the Bowl," *The Ray Bradbury Theatre*; Gemini Award nomination, best performance by a supporting actor, 1989, for *One Boy, One Wolf, One Summer*; Genie Award nomination, best supporting actor, for *I, Maureen*; Gemini Award nomination, best performance by a supporting actor, 2002, for *Le dernier chapitre: La Suite*; Gemini Award nomination, best performance by an actor in a continuing leading dramatic role, 2003, for *The Last Chapter II: The War Continues*.

CREDITS

Film Appearances:
Drunk, *Outrageous!*, Almi Cinema V, 1977.
Butch, *High–Ballin'*, American International, 1978.
Dr. Paul Johnson, *I, Maureen* (also known as *The Last Campaign*), New Cinema, 1978.
Torturer, *Power Play*, 1978.
Stone Cold Dead, Dimension, 1979.
Pimp, *Summer's Children*, 1979.
Jimmy, *Suzanne*, Ambassador, 1980.
Darryl Revok, *Scanners* (also known as *Telepathy 2000*), Avco Embassy, 1980.
Gateway, *Coming Out Alive*, 1980.
Edgar, *Double Negative* (also known as *Deadly Companion*), Quadrant Films, 1980.
Wayne, *Surfacing*, Pan–Canadian Film Distributors, 1981.
Colt Hawker, *Visiting Hours* (also known as *The Fright, Get Well Soon*, and *Terreur a l'hopital central*), Twentieth Century–Fox, 1981.
Detective Skylar, *American Nightmare*, Mano, 1982.
Detective Sergeant Ed Roersch, *Cross–Country*, Metro–Goldwyn–Mayer/United Artists, 1983.
Overdog/Dr. McNabb, mutant ruler of planet Terra 11, *Spacehunter: Adventures in the Forbidden Zone* (also known as *Road Gangs* and *Adventures in the Creep Zone*), Columbia, 1983.

Dealer, *Best Revenge* (also known as *Misdeal*), RKR Releasing, 1984.

George Kyber, *The Surrogate* (also known as *Blind Rage*), Cinepix, 1984.

Coming Out Alive, TransWorld Entertainment, 1984.

(In archive footage) Darryl Revok (segment *Scanners*), *Terror in the Aisles* (also known as *Time for Terror*), 1984.

FBI agent, *The Falcon and the Snowman,* Orion, 1985.

Detective Lawrence, *Jo Jo Dancer, Your Life Is Calling,* Columbia, 1986.

Lieutenant Commander Dick "Jester" Heatherly, *Top Gun,* Paramount, 1986.

Major Paul Hackett, *Extreme Prejudice,* TriStar, 1987.

Principal Bill Nordham, *Hello Mary Lou: Prom Night II* (also known as *The Haunting of Hamilton High* and *Prom Night II*), Norstar, 1987.

Ben, *Nowhere to Hide* (also known as *Fatal Chase*), New Century–Vista, 1987.

Lem Johnston, *Watchers,* Carolco, 1988.

Larry Gaylord, *Hostile Takeover* (also known as *Office Party* and *The Devastator*), SC Films, 1988.

Thunderground, 1989.

Kellen O'Reilly, *Mindfield,* Allegro, 1989.

Kenrick, *Destiny to Order,* Atlantis/Cineplex Odeon, 1989.

Richter, *Total Recall,* TriStar, 1990.

Sheriff Pete, *Payback,* Republic Pictures Home Video, 1991.

Frank Bruce, *McBain,* Shapiro/Glickenhaus Entertainment, 1991.

General Katana, *Highlander II: The Quickening* (also known as *Highlander II: The Renegade Version* and *Highlander–Le retour*), Interstar Releasing, 1991.

Lieutenant Ralf Barfuss, *The Vagrant,* Metro–Goldwyn–Mayer/United Artists Home Video, 1992.

Harry M. Stark, *Neon City,* Vidmark Entertainment, 1992.

Luther Kane, *Killer Image* (also known as *Meurtre dans l'objectif*), Groundstar Entertainment, 1992.

J. T. Blake, *Common Bonds* (also known as *Chaindance*), Academy Entertainment, 1992.

Natino, *Cafe Romeo,* Republic Pictures Home Video, 1992.

Quinn, *Black Ice* (also known as *A Passion for Murder*), Prism, 1992.

Mr. Kincaid, *Guncrazy,* 1992.

Detective Garcia, *Sweet Killing,* Paramount Home Video, 1993.

Bishop, *Mardi Gras for the Devil* (also known as *Night Trap*), Prism, 1993.

Dial, *Free Willy,* Warner Bros., 1993.

Jerry, *Father Hood* (also known as *Desperado, Honor Among Thieves,* and *Mike Hardy*), Buena Vista, 1993.

Roberto Largo, *Point of Impact* (also known as *Spanish Rose* and *In Too Deep*), Trimark Home Video, 1993.

Tokyo Cowboy, Cinexus/Famous Players Distribution, 1994.

Oliver, *Save Me,* Columbia/TriStar Home Video, 1994.

Sheriff Wilson, *Forced to Kill,* PM Home Video, 1994.

Mr. Green, *The Killing Man* (also known as *The Killing Machine*), A–Pix Entertainment, 1994.

Colonel Dugan, *The Next Karate Kid,* Columbia, 1994.

Carl Pimmler, *Fortunes of War,* Columbia/TriStar Home Video, 1994.

Billy Niles, *Bolt* (also known as *Rebel Run*), Avalanche Home Entertainment, 1994.

Captain Meisler, *Red Sun Rising,* 1994.

Detective Gene Baker, *The Glass Shield* (also known as *The Johnny Johnson Trial*), Miramax, 1995.

Colonel West, *Red Scorpion 2,* Universal Studios Home Video, 1995.

Lieutenant Colonel Stone, *Major Payne,* Universal, 1995.

Sergeant Ernie Hansen, *Portraits of a Killer* (also known as *Portraits of Innocence*), Live Entertainment, 1996.

Captain Floyd Anderson, *Too Fast Too Young,* Monarch Home Video, 1996.

Walt, *One Way Out,* Arrow Video, 1996.

Moravian Massacre (documentary), 1996.

Mr. Capelli, *The Destiny of Marty Fine,* 1996.

Slammers, 1997.

Frank Parr, *Cold Night into Dawn* (also known as *The Bomb Squad*), Showcase Entertainment, 1997.

Jean Rasczak, *Starship Troopers,* TriStar, 1997.

Butch Scarsdale, *Kids of the Round Table,* 1997.

Mr. Capelli, *The Destiny of Marty Fine,* Plaza Entertainment, 1998.

Al, *Chicago Cab* (also known as *Hellcab*), Castle Hill, 1998.

Detective Briscoe, *Captive,* Blackwatch Releasing, 1998.

Inspector Frank Schumann, *Black Light,* Peachtree Entertainment, 1998.

Detective Jack Connor, *The Arrangement* (also known as *Blood Money* and *Deadly Arrangement*), Avalanche Home Entertainment, 1998.

Mike Malone, *Going to Kansas City,* Mandart Entertainment, 1998.

Detective Jack Cooper, *One of Our Own,* 1998.

The Godson, Sterling Home Entertainment, 1998.

Judge, *Death Row the Tournament,* 1998.

Marshall Wallace, *Ivory Tower,* 1998.

Agent Bellows, *Desert Blue,* Samuel Goldwyn, 1999.

Dominic, *The Omega Code,* Providence Entertainment, 1999.

Southern Cross, Fries Film Group, 1999.

Alex Hunt, *A Twist of Faith* (also known as *Beyond Redemption*), Avalanche Home Entertainment, 1999.

Lieutenant Robert Ingram, *Question of Privilege,* 1999.

Fred Skolnik, *Crime and Punishment in Suburbia,* United Artists, 2000.

Voice of Tyler, *Heavy Metal 2000* (animated; also known as *Heavy Metal F.A.K.K.2*), Columbia TriStar Home Video, 2000.

Bob Brown, *The Perfect Storm,* Warner Bros., 2000.

Coach Rehmer, *Borderline Normal,* 2000.
Jonas Phifer, *Cause of Death,* 2000.
Senator Bill Armitage, *Mindstorm,* 2001.
Voice of Mr. M, *Soulkeeper,* 2001.
Skay, *Dead Awake,* 2001.
Steinberg (Gunter), *Down* (also known as *The Elevator*), 2001.
Priest, *Children of the Corn: Revelation,* Dimension Films, 2001.
Baker, *Extreme Honor* (also known as *Last Line of Defence 2*), Hollywood Feature Entertainment LLC, 2001.
Russo, *Ignition,* Saturn Home Entertainment, 2001.
Sheriff Ed Rooney, *Fallen Angels,* Avrio Filmworks, 2002.
Justice Coulton, *Fairytales and Pornography,* 2002.
Himself, *Death from Above: The Making of "Starship Troopers,"* Columbia TriStar Home Video, 2002.
General Amberson, *Maximum Velocity,* 2003.
Depressor, *The Failures,* 2003.
Miller, *The Machinist,* Paramount Home Video, 2004.
Henry, *Reeker* (also known as *Dead People 2*), Bac Films, 2005.
Walnut, *Deepwater,* Lightning Entertainment, 2005.
Guy X, *Guy X,* First Look, 2005.
Daniel's father, *On That Day,* Summer Pictures, 2005.
Theo, *1st Bite,* Singa, 2006.
Captain Nathan Norcross, *The Alphabet Killer,* Anchor Bay Entertainment, 2008.
Captain Billings, *Surveillance,* Warner Home Video, 2008.
Colonal Gauge, *Mutants* (also known as *Outbreak X*), Spotlight Pictures, 2008.
Captain Jones, *Abduction of Jesse Bookman,* Films In Motion, 2008.
General Ashdown, *Terminator Salvation* (also known as *T4: Salvation* and *Terminator 4*), Warner Bros., 2009.
Teddy Carmichael, *The Butcher,* Twentieth Century–Fox, 2009.
Tom Riggins, *Level 26: Dark Origins,* Dare to Pass, 2009.
Bernie, *The Jazzman,* Summer Pictures, 2009.
Officer Ned Hutton, *The Beacon,* Eagle Films, 2009.
Hal, *Hardwired,* Sony, 2009.
Eva, Hallmark, 2009.
Chief Bannen, *The Bannen Way,* Sony, 2010.
Blaine, *Beneath the Blue* (also known as *Way of the Dolphin*), Blue Sky Film, 2010.
Colonel Dodd, *Conduct Unbecoming,* 2010.
Fischer, *Liberty,* Silver Screen, 2010.

Also appeared in *Down Where the Lights Are;* and *Manhunt.*

Film Work:
Co–executive producer, *Common Bonds* (also known as *Chaindance*), Academy Entertainment, 1992.

Director, *The Arrangement* (also known as *Blood Money* and *Deadly Arrangement*), 1999.

Also directed, produced, and edited *Down Where the Lights Are.*

Television Appearances; Series:
Ham Tyler, *V: The Series,* NBC, 1984–85.
Dr. William "Wild Willy" Swift, a recurring role, *ER,* NBC, 1995.
Captain Oliver Hudson, *SeaQuest DSV* (also known as *SeaQuest 2032*), NBC, 1995–96.
Cardinal Mazarin, *Young Blades,* Ion Television, 2005.
Voice of Colonel Moss, *Wolverine and the X–Men* (animated), Nicktoons Network, 2008–2009.

Television Appearances; Miniseries:
Ham Tyler, *V: The Final Battle,* NBC, 1984.
Werner Heisenberg, *Race for the Bomb,* CBC, 1986.
Harry Bennett, *Ford: The Man and the Machine,* syndicated, 1987.
Colonel Burton C. Andrus, *Nuremberg,* TNT, 2000.
Bob Durelle, *Le dernier chapitre: La suite* (also known as *The Last Chapter*), CBS, 2002.
Bob Durelle, *The Last Chapter: The War Continues,* 2003.

Television Appearances; Movies:
Bartender, *The Family Man,* CBS, 1979.
Max, *Clown White,* 1980.
The July Group, 1981.
(As Mike Ironside) Victor, *Off Your Rocker,* 1982.
Alan Campbell, *The Sins of Dorian Gray,* ABC, 1983.
The Cap, 1984.
Captain Neal Braddock, *Murder in Space,* Showtime, 1985.
One Boy, One Wolf, One Summer, 1988.
Detective Lieutenant Carl Madsen, *Murder by Night* (also known as *Memory Lane*), USA Network, 1989.
Dr. Allard, *Drop Dead Gorgeous* (also known as *Victim of Beauty*), USA Network, 1991.
Rick Fender, *Deadly Surveillance,* Showtime, 1991.
Mr. Kincaid, *Guncrazy,* Showtime, 1992.
Bats O'Bannion, *Marked for Murder* (also known as *The Sandman and Hard Time* and *The Sandman*), NBC, 1993.
Captain Meisler, *Red Sun Rising,* HBO, 1994.
Luck Hatcher, *Dead Man's Revenge* (also known as *You Only Die Once*), USA Network, 1994.
West, *Red Scorpion 2,* HBO, 1994.
Gary Yanuck, *Probable Cause* (also known as *Sleepless*), Showtime, 1994.
Steiger, *Singapore Sling: Road to Mandalay* (also known as *Asian Connection: Road to Mandalay*), 1995.
Butch Scarsdale, *Kids of the Round Table,* 1995.

Sterling Rombauer, *Robin Cook's "Terminal"* (also known as *Terminal*), NBC, 1996.

Frank Donahue, *Johnny 2.0,* Sci–Fi Channel, 1997.

CIA Director, *The Arrow* (also known as *Projet arrow*), 1997.

McBride, *Voyage of Terror* (also known as *The Fourth Horseman* and *Die Schreckensfahrt der Orion Star*), Fox Family, 1998.

Inspector Frank Schumann, *Black Light,* Showtime, 1998.

Steiger, *Asian Connection: Road to Mandalay,* ABC, 1999.

Lieutenant Ingram, *Question of Privilege,* Lifetime, 1999.

Marshall Wallace, *The Ivory Tower,* Showtime, 2000.

Shopkeeper, *Soulkeeper,* Sci–Fi Channel, 2001.

(Uncredited) Voice of Mr. M, *Soulkeeper,* Sci–Fi Channel, 2001.

Senator Bill Armitage, *Mindstorm,* Sci–Fi Channel, 2001.

Skay, *Dead Awake,* Cinemax, 2001.

Jonas Phifer, *Cause of Death,* Cinemax, 2001.

Dr. Kragg, *Jett Jackson: The Movie,* The Disney Channel, 2001.

Bremer, *The Red Phone,* 2001.

Borderline Normal, USA Network, 2002.

Alaska, ABC, 2003.

Harry, *Hemingway vs. Callaghan* (also known as *Hemingway: That Summer in Paris*), 2003.

Muco, *Bloodsuckers* (also known as *Vampire Wars: Battle for the Universe*), Sci–Fi Channel, 2005.

Levering, *Disaster Zone: Volcano in New York,* Sci–Fi Channel, 2006.

Mark "Doc" Jordan, *The Veteran,* 2006.

Wade, *The Terrorist Next Door,* 2008.

James, *Storm Cell,* Lifetime, 2008.

Television Appearances; Specials:

Agent's boss, *The Sacrifice,* HBO, 1989.

The Making of "Total Recall," 1990.

Sharon Stone—Una mujer de 100 caras, 1998.

Narrator, *Supercarrier Is Burning: The U.S.S. Enterprise,* The Discovery Channel, 2000.

Narrator, *Inside the Kill Box: Fighting the Gulf War,* The Discovery Channel, 2001.

Television Appearances; Pilots:

Roger Prescott, *The Circle,* ABC, 2003.

Television Appearances; Episodic:

Policeman, "A Matter of Choice," *For the Record,* 1978.

Bill, "Silent Witness," *The Little Hobo,* 1979.

Crane, "The Taxicab Wars," *The A–Team,* NBC, 1983.

Schrader, "Midway to What?," *Hill Street Blues,* NBC, 1983.

Wade Bennett, "Warpath," *Mickey Spillane's Mike Hammer,* 1984.

Lee, "Dead Man's Curve," *The Hitchhiker,* HBO, 1985.

Lieutenant Rick Muldoon, "Man on the Edge," *Alfred Hitchcock Presents,* USA Network, 1987.

Charles Fuller, "Pilot Error," *Danger Bay,* 1987.

Acton, "The Fruit at the Bottom of the Bowl," *The Ray Bradbury Theatre,* USA Network, 1988.

Jerry, the agent's boss, "The Sacrifice," *Tales from the Crypt,* HBO, 1990.

Luther Kane, *Joe Bob's Drive–In Theater,* 1994.

Sergeant Burrows, "Comes the Dawn," *Tales from the Crypt,* HBO, 1995.

Montree, "Get Fast," *F/X: The Series,* 1997.

Voice of Darkseid, "Tools of the Trade," *Superman* (also known as *The New Batman/Superman Adventures*), The WB, 1997.

Voice of Darkseid, "Father's Day," *Superman* (also known as *The New Batman/Superman Adventures*), The WB, 1997.

Voice of '80s Batman, "Legends of the Dark Knight," *Batman: Gotham Knights* (animated), 1998.

Dr. William "Wild Willy" Swift, "Think Warm Thoughts," *ER,* NBC, 1998.

Voice of Darkseid, "Apokolips: Parts 1 & 2," *Superman* (also known as *The New Batman/Superman Adventures*), The WB, 1998.

Voice of Darkseid, "Little Girl Lost: Part 2," *Superman* (also known as *The New Batman/Superman Adventures*), The WB, 1998.

Vladimir Lenin, "Vladimir Lenin," *Witness to Yesterday,* 1998.

Prosser, "Summit," *The Outer Limits,* Showtime and syndicated, 1999.

The inspector, "Deadly Games: Parts 1 & 2," *Cold Squad,* CTV, 1999.

The inspector, "Dead of Night: Part 1," *Cold Squad,* CTV, 1999.

"The Films of David Cronenberg," *The Directors,* 1999.

Voice of Darkseid, "Legacy: Parts 1 & 2," *Superman* (also known as *The New Batman/Superman Adventures*), The WB, 2000.

Roland "The Chairman" Pierce, "Winds of Change," *Walker, Texas Ranger,* CBS, 2000.

Roland "The Chairman" Pierce, "Lazarus," *Walker, Texas Ranger,* CBS, 2000.

Roland "The Chairman" Pierce, "Turning Point," *Walker, Texas Ranger,* CBS, 2000.

Roland "The Chairman" Pierce, "Retribution," *Walker, Texas Ranger,* CBS, 2000.

General Quince, "Rule of Law," *The Outer Limits,* Showtime and syndicated, 2001.

Dimitri Putin, "Russian Winter" (also known as "The Russian Wars"), *The District,* CBS, 2002.

Dimitri Putin, "Daughter for Daughter," *The District,* CBS, 2002.

"Top Gun," *VH–1 Behind the Movie,* VH1, 2002.

The Patriarch, "Twilight of the Idols," *Andromeda* (also known as *Gene Roddenberry's Andromeda*), Sci–Fi Channel, 2003.

The Patriarch, "Abridging the Devil's Divide," *Andromeda* (also known as *Gene Roddenberry's Andromeda*), Sci–Fi Channel, 2003.

Voice of Darkseid, "Twilight: Parts 1 & 2," *Justice League* (animated; also known as *JL* and *Justice League Unlimited*), Cartoon Network, 2003.

General Sam Lane, "Gone," *Smallville* (also known as *Smallville Beginnings*), The WB, 2004.

General Sam Lane, "Facade," *Smallville* (also known as *Smallville Beginnings*), The WB, 2004.

Dragon Scout leader, "Dragon Scouts," *Jackie Chan Adventures,* 2004.

Ben Graybridge, "Price of Pleasure," *Medical Investigation,* NBC, 2004.

Curtis Monroe, "Coming Home," *Desperate Housewives,* ABC, 2005.

Curtis Monroe, "One More Kiss," *Desperate Housewives,* ABC, 2006.

Seevis, "Crusade," *Stargate SG–1,* Showtime, 2006.

Mr. Chaney, "The V Word," *Masters of Horror,* Showtime, 2006.

John, "Elephant's Memory," *Criminal Minds,* CBS, 2008.

Commandant Murillo, "The Long Blue Line," *Cold Case,* CBS, 2009.

Commandant Murillo, "Into the Blue," *Cold Case,* CBS, 2009.

Commandant Murillo, "The Crossing," *Cold Case,* CBS, 2009.

Victor Racine, "Den of Thieves," *Castle,* ABC, 2010.

Television Executive Producer; Movies:

Probable Cause (also known as *Sleepless*), Showtime, 1994.

Stage Appearances:

Appeared in *Look Back in Anger.*

RECORDINGS

Video Games:

Voice of Commander Mason, *Run Like Hell* (also known as *RLH*), 2002.

Voice of Sam Fisher, *Splinter Cell* (also known as *Tom Clancy's "Splinter Cell"*), Ubi–Soft, 2002.

Voice of Sam Fisher, *Splinter Cell: Pandora Tomorrow* (also known as *Tom Clancy's "Splinter Cell": Pandora Tomorrow*), Ubi–Soft, 2004.

Voice of Sam Fisher, *Splinter Cell: Chaos Theory,* 2005.

Voice of Sam Fisher, *Splinter Cell: Essentials,* Sony, 2006.

Voice of Sam Fisher, *Splinter Cell: Double Agent,* Ubisoft, 2006.

Voice of Jack Granger—GDI General, *Command & Conquer 3: Tiberium Wars,* Electronic Arts, 2007.

Voice of Doctor Krone, *TimeShift,* Vivendi, 2007.

Voice of Sam Fisher, *Splinter Cell: Conviction,* Ubisoft, 2010.

Videos:

Highlander 2: To Be or Not to Be a Sequel, 1997.

Heavy Metal 2000: Voice Talent Featurette, 2000.

Danger Zone: The Making of "Top Gun," Paramount, 2004.

Sreveillance: The Watched Are Watching, Magnolia, 2009.

WRITINGS

Screenplays:

(With Alan Aylward) *Common Bonds* (also known as *Chaindance*), Academy Entertainment, 1992.

The Arrangement (also known as *Blood Money* and *Deadly Arrangement*), Illusion Entertainment, 1998.

Also wrote *Down Where the Lights Are.*

Plays:

The Shelter, Canadian production, 1965.

OTHER SOURCES

Periodicals:

People Weekly, July 16, 1990, p. 47; April 3, 1995, p. 18.

Starlog, June, 1990, pp. 29–32, 64; September, 1997.

Variety, November 3, 1997, p. 98.

J

JEAN, Cassandra 1985–
(Cassandra Whitehead)

PERSONAL

Born October 5, 1985, in Houston, TX. *Education:* Studied marketing and public relations at Texas A&M University at Corpus Christi.

Career: Actress. Worked as a commercial print model in Houston, TX. Miss Houston Teen USA, 2003; Miss Corpus Christi, 2005. Miss Newport Beach pageant, judge, 2009.

Member: American Federation of Television and Radio Artists, Screen Actors Guild, Delta Delta Delta.

CREDITS

Film Appearances:
Second hot girl, *2 Dudes and a Dream,* Gravitas Ventures, 2009.
Ellen, *Kill Katie Malone,* 2010.
Johnette Rickards, *Level 26: Dark Prophecy* (short film), 2010.

Television Appearances; Series:
(As Cassandra Whitehead) Herself, *America's Next Top Model* (also known as *ANTM, America's Next Top Model with Tyra Banks,* and *Top Model*), UPN, 2005.

Television Appearances; Specials:
Muse, *Spike TV VGA Video Game Awards,* Spike TV, 2006.

Television Appearances; Episodic:
(As Cassandra Whitehead) Herself, "Top Model: Cycle 5 Fan Choice Awards," *The Tyra Banks Show,* UPN, 2006.
(Uncredited) Murder victim number one, "Born to Kill," *CSI: Miami,* CBS, 2007.
(Uncredited) Pretty girl, "Sleepwalk This Way," *Hannah Montana* (also known as *Hannah Montana Forever* and *Secret Idol Hannah Montana*), The Disney Channel, 2007.
(Uncredited) Bikini contestant, "Head Games," *Las Vegas,* NBC, 2007.
Pola Chesterwood, "The Chick Chop Flick Shop," *CSI: Crime Scene Investigation* (also known as *C.S.I.* and *CSI: Las Vegas*), CBS, 2007.
Dana Barrett, "The Ectoplasmic Panhellenic Investigation," *The Middleman,* ABC Family, 2008.
Herself, "Exposed: Parts I & II," *America's Next Top Model* (also known as *ANTM, America's Next Top Model with Tyra Banks,* and *Top Model*), The CW, 2008.
Missy, "Screenwriter's Blues," *One Tree Hill,* The CW, 2009.
Missy, "Forever and Almost Always," *One Tree Hill,* The CW, 2009.

JEFFERIES, Marc John 1990–
(Marc John Jeffries)

PERSONAL

Born May 16, 1990, in New York, NY; father a photography director; mother a teacher; brother of LaShawn Jefferies (an actress). *Avocational Interests:* Family travels, collecting cars.

Addresses: *Agent*—Mitchell Gossett, United Talent Agency, 9560 Wilshire Blvd., Suite 500, Beverly Hills, CA 90212; CESD Talent Agency, 257 Park Avenue S., New York, NY 10010–7304.

Career: Actor. Worked as a child model; became standup comedian and impersonator, including appearances at the Laugh Factory, Los Angeles. Appeared in commercials for Wendy's restaurants, 1999, and Band–Aid bandages, 2002; spokesperson for People PC computer and Internet service, 2002—. Affiliated with a series of young adult novels featuring "Agent Mjj," c. 2005–06.

Member: American Federation of Television and Radio Artists, Screen Actors Guild.

Awards, Honors: Young Artist Award nomination, best guest–starring young actor in a television drama series, 2002, for "Honor Code," *The Practice;* Young Artist Award nomination, best young supporting actor in a feature film, 2004, for *The Haunted Mansion;* Black Reel Award nomination (with others), best ensemble, 2010, for *Notorious.*

CREDITS

Film Appearances:
Title role, *Losing Isaiah,* Paramount, 1995.
Will, *Stuart Little 2,* Columbia, 2002.
Young Dre, *Brown Sugar,* Twentieth Century–Fox, 2002.
(Uncredited) Kid, *Friday after Next,* New Line Cinema, 2002.
Kid at bus stop, *Charlie's Angels: Full Throttle,* Columbia, 2003.
Michael, *The Haunted Mansion* (also known as *Disney's "The Haunted Mansion"*), Buena Vista, 2004.
Amazed kid, *Spider–Man 2* (also known as *Spider–Man 2.1* and *Spider–Man 2: The IMAX Experience*), Columbia, 2004.
Young Marcus, *Get Rich or Die Tryin',* Paramount, 2005.
Mikey, *Whitepaddy,* Big Six Film, 2006.
(As Marc John Jeffries) Tim, *Keeping Up with the Steins,* Miramax, 2006.
Ali, *Jackson Ward* (short film), TBY Productions, 2008.
Elliot Duncan, *Assassination of a High School President* (also known as *The High School Conspiracy*), Freestyle Releasing, 2008.
Maishee, *Running from the Devil,* KHOP Entertainment, 2008.
Lil Cease, *Notorious,* Fox Searchlight, 2009.
Little Hercules in 3–D, Gravitas Ventures, 2010.
Stone, *Beware the Gonzo,* Corner Store Entertainment, 2010.
Leon, *Slow Moe,* Feature Films for Families/PorchLight Entertainment, 2010.
Troy Shawn Welcome, *The Troy Shawn Welcome Story* (short film), Black Noise Media/Reel Works Teen Filmmaking, 2010.
Lil' man, *Yelling to the Sky,* YTTS LLC, 2010.

Rembrandt, *Big Mommas: Like Father, like Son,* Twentieth Century–Fox, 2011.

Other films include *Beanstalk of Brooklyn,* Urban Entertainment; *Doctor Dolittle,* Twentieth Century–Fox; *Love Changes,* Desert Films; and *Something Kind'a Wonderful,* Jamal & Hanalore Williams.

Film Work; Additional Voices:
Monsters, Inc. (animated), Buena Vista, 2001.
Finding Nemo (animated), Buena Vista, 2003.

Television Appearances; Series:
Derrick Mitchell, *The Tracy Morgan Show,* NBC, 2003–2004.
Voice of Roy Bindlebeep, *Fatherhood* (animated), Nickelodeon, 2004–2005.
Darius, *Treme,* HBO, 2010—.

Television Appearances; Episodic:
The Jon Stewart Show, MTV, 1995.
(As Marc John Jeffries) Kevin Wolfred, "Bad Girls," *New York Undercover,* Fox, 1995.
Showtime at the Apollo (also known as *It's Showtime at the Apollo*), syndicated, 1996.
Davy, "Anniversary Waltz," *Cosby,* CBS, 1997.
Davy, "I'm OK, You're Hilton," *Cosby,* CBS, 1997.
Jack Collins, "Blood Ties: Part 3," *Homicide: Life on the Street* and *Homicide*), NBC, 1997.
Second kid, "No Secrets," *Trinity,* NBC, 1998.
Jonathan, "Nocturne," *Law & Order: Special Victims Unit* (also known as *Law & Order: SVU* and *Special Victims Unit*), NBC, 2000.
Jason Lees, "Honor Code," *The Practice,* ABC, 2001.
Marcus Jackson, "To Protect and Serve," *Family Law,* CBS, 2002.
Miguel White, "To Protect ...," *Third Watch,* NBC, 2002.
Miguel White, "Crime and Punishment: Parts 1 & 2," *Third Watch,* NBC, 2002.
The Sharon Osbourne Show (also known as *Sharon*), syndicated, 2003.
Voice of the young Green Lantern, "Kid Stuff," *Justice League* (animated; also known as *JL* and *Justice League Unlimited*), Cartoon Network, 2004.
Victor Hopkins, "Back in the World," *ER,* NBC, 2005.
Jimmy Kimmel Live!, ABC, 2005.
Adam, "Plugged In," *3 lbs.,* CBS, 2006.
Wendell Owens, "Our Father," *Dexter,* Showtime, 2008.
Wendell Owens, "Turning Biminese," *Dexter,* Showtime, 2008.
Wendell Owens, "Si se puede," *Dexter,* Showtime, 2008.
The Mo'Nique Show, Black Entertainment Television, 2009.

Appeared as Herman in an episode of *Hangin' with Mr. Cooper,* ABC; also appeared in *The Guiding Light,* CBS.

Television Appearances; Awards Presentations:

Presenter, *The Ninth Annual Trumpet Awards,* TBS, 2001.

The WIN Awards, PAX, 2005.

Television Appearances; Other:

Hall, *Cry Baby Lane* (movie), Nickelodeon, 2000.

Derrick Mitchell, *The Tracy Morgan Show* (pilot), NBC, 2003.

The 6th Annual Sears Soul Train Christmas Starfest (special), UPN, 2003.

Appeared in the pilot *Wyclef Jean in America,* HBO; also appeared in *Hair Story,* HBO, and *Kindred,* USA Network.

Stage Appearances:

Milton, *Taller than a Dwarf,* Longacre Theatre, New York City, 2000.

Appeared in *The Lamb,* Edgemar Theatre.

WRITINGS

Songs Featured in Films:

"It's Happening," *Get Rich or Die Tryin',* Paramount, 2005.

JENNINGS, Alex 1957–

PERSONAL

Born May 10, 1957, in Essex, England (some sources say Upminster, England); son of Michael Thomas and Peggy Patricia (maiden name, Mahoney) Jennings; companion of Lesley Moors (a landscaper), beginning c. 1990; children: Ralph, Georgia. *Education:* University of Warwick, B.A.; trained at Bristol Old Vic Theatre School, Bristol, England.

Addresses: *Agent*—Paul Lyon–Maris, Independent Talent Group, Oxford House, 76 Oxford St., London W1D 1BS, England.

Career: Actor. Associate artist, Royal Shakespeare Company and Royal National Theatre.

Awards, Honors: Laurence Olivier Award, comedy performance of the year, Society of West End Theatre, and London Critic's Circle Theatre Award, best actor, 1988, both for *Too Clever by Half;* Actor of the Year Award, *Plays and Players,* 1988; Laurence Olivier Award nomination, best comedy performance, c. 1990, for *The Liar;* Laurence Olivier Award, best actor, 1996, for *Peer Gynt;* Helen Hayes Award, best lead actor in a non–resident production, Washington Theatre Awards Society, 1999, for *Hamlet;* honorary D.Litt., University of Warwick, 1999; *Evening Standard* Award, best actor, 2001, for *The Winter's Tale* and *The Relapse;* Laurence Olivier Award, best actor in a musical, 2003, for *My Fair Lady.*

CREDITS

Stage Appearances:

Mr. Darbey, *Dandy Dick,* Arts Theatre, Cambridge, England, 1981.

Chief rat, *Toad of Toad Hall,* Leeds Playhouse, Leeds, England, 1983.

Aguecheek, *Twelfth Night,* Chichester Festival Theatre, Chichester, England, 1985.

Tim, *Cavalcade,* Chichester Festival Theatre, 1985.

The groom, *A Respectable Wedding,* Chichester Festival Theatre, then London production, 1985.

The Scarlet Pimpernel, Her Majesty's Theatre, London, 1985.

Hargreves, *For King and Country,* Greenwich Theatre, London, 1986.

Mr. Sparkish, *The Country Wife,* Royal Exchange Theatre, Manchester, England, 1986–87.

Lucio, *Measure for Measure,* Royal Shakespeare Company, Royal Shakespeare Theatre, Stratford–upon–Avon, England, 1987, then Theatre Royal, Newcastle–upon–Tyne, England, and Barbican Theatre, London, both 1988.

Lucentio, *The Taming of the Shrew,* Royal Shakespeare Company, Royal Shakespeare Theatre, 1987, then Theatre Royal, and Barbican Theatre, both 1988.

Fairfield, *Hyde Park,* Royal Shakespeare Company, Swan Theatre, Stratford–upon–Avon, 1987, then Pit Theatre, London, 1988.

Gloumov, *Too Clever by Half,* Old Vic Theatre, London, 1988.

Oedipus, Royal Shakespeare Company, Other Place Theatre, Stratford–upon–Avon, then Live Theatre, Newcastle–upon–Tyne, both 1988.

Kittel, *Ghetto,* Royal National Theatre, London, 1989.

Hjalmar Ekdal, *The Wild Duck,* Peter Hall Company, Phoenix Theatre, London, 1990.

Dorante, *The Liar,* Old Vic Theatre, 1990.

Title role, *Richard II,* Royal Shakespeare Company, Royal Shakespeare Theatre, 1990, then Theatre Royal, and Barbican Theatre, both 1991.

Captain Plume, *The Recruiting Officer,* Royal National Theatre, 1992.

Jack Worthing, *The Importance of Being Earnest,* Aldwych Theatre, London, 1993.

Title role, *Peer Gynt,* Royal Shakespeare Company, Swan Theatre, Stratford–upon–Avon, 1994, then Newcastle Playhouse, Newcastle–upon–Tyne, and Young Vic Theatre, London, both 1995.

Angelo, *Measure for Measure,* Royal Shakespeare Company, Royal Shakespeare Theatre, 1994, then Theatre Royal, and Barbican Theatre, both 1995.

Theseus and Oberon, *A Midsummer Night's Dream,* Royal Shakespeare Company, Royal Shakespeare Theatre, 1994, then Theatre Royal, and Barbican Theatre, 1995, later (Broadway debut) Lunt–Fontanne Theatre, 1996.

Dr. Sobriety Mede, *Redskin,* Royal Shakespeare Company, Other Place Theatre, 1995.

Robespierre, *The Scarlet Pimpernel,* Chichester Festival Theatre, then London production, 1995.

Benedick, *Much Ado about Nothing,* Royal Shakespeare Company, Royal Shakespeare Theatre, 1996, then Barbican Theatre, 1998.

Easter Bonnet Competition, Palace Theatre, New York City, 1996.

Title role, *Hamlet,* Royal Shakespeare Company, Royal Shakespeare Theatre, Theatre Royal, and Barbican Theatre, all 1997, then Opera House, Brooklyn Academy of Music, New York City, 1998.

Title role, *Albert Speer,* Royal National Theatre, Lyttelton Theatre, London, 2000.

Leontes, *The Winter's Tale,* Royal National Theatre, New York City, 2001.

Foppington, *The Relapse,* Royal National Theatre, 2001.

Theseus and Oberon, *A Midsummer Night's Dream,* Royal Shakespeare Company, Barbican Hall, Barbican Centre, London, 2001.

Henry Higgins, *My Fair Lady* (musical), Theatre Royal Drury Lane, London, 2002.

Brand, Theatre Royal Haymarket, London, 2003.

George W. Bush, *Stuff Happens,* Royal National Theatre, 2004.

Subtle, *The Alchemist,* Royal National Theatre, 2006.

Major Tours:

Theseus and Oberon, *A Midsummer Night's Dream,* U.S. cities, c. 1996.

Television Appearances; Miniseries:

Police Constable Hall, *Smiley's People,* BBC, 1982.

Title role, *Alfonso Bonzo,* 1990.

John Ashenden, *Ashenden,* Arts and Entertainment, 1992.

Sebastian Parish, "Death at the Bar," *The Inspector Alleyn Mysteries* (also known as *Alleyn Mysteries;* broadcast in the United States on *Mystery!*), PBS, 1995.

Bitzer, *Hard Times,* PBS, 1995.

King George III, *Liberty! The American Revolution,* PBS, 1997–1998.

Julian Edgbaston–Bowles, *Too Much Sun,* BBC, 2000.

James Sinclair, *The State Within,* BBC, 2000.

Voice, *Fire, Plague, War, and Treason,* Channel 4, 2001.

Reverend Hutton, *Return to Cranford,* BBC1, 2007, PBS, 2008.

Roger Bateman, "Rapunzel," *Fairy Tales,* 2008.

Vincent, *10 Days to War,* BBC, 2008.

Commander Anderson, *Whitechapel,* ITV1, 2009.

Television Appearances; Movies:

Nevil Bennet, *The Franchise Affair,* BBC, 1988.

King Ferdinand, *Bye Bye Columbus,* BBC, 1991.

Byron, *Dread Poets' Society,* 1992.

Lieutenant Alexander, *The Hunley,* TNT, 1999.

Joe Harker, *Bad Blood,* Carlton, 1999.

Stephen Spender, *London,* 2004.

Alastair Campbell, *A Very Social Secretary,* Channel 4, 2005.

Sergei Diaghilev, *Riot at the Rite,* BBC, 2005.

John Le Mesurier, *Hancock & Joan,* 2008.

Captain Kell, *The 39 Steps,* PBS, 2008.

Inspector Curry, *Marple: They Do It with Mirrors,* Arts and Entertainment, 2009.

Timothy "Tim" Geithner, *The Last Days of Lehman Brothers,* BBC2, 2009.

Andrew Walker, *On Expenses,* 2010.

Television Appearances; Specials:

Victor Preece, "The Sins of the Fathers," *Inspector Morse,* PBS, 1992.

Reader, *The Noel Coward Story,* PBS, 1999.

Butler, "Joseph and the Amazing Technicolor Dreamcoat," *Great Performances,* PBS, 2000.

Voice, *Adolf Eichmann—Begegningen mit einem Moerder,* NDR, 2003.

The Laurence Olivier Awards, 2003.

Television Appearances; Series:

Narrator, *The Restaurant,* NBC, 2007.

Television Appearances; Episodic:

Police Constable Woods, "A Sick Society," *Kit Curran,* Channel 4, 1986.

Jeremy, "The Gospel According to Shelley," *The Return of Shelley,* 1989.

Dr. Roberts, "Cards on the Table," *Agatha Christie: Poirot,* Arts and Entertainment, 2005.

James Allan, *MI–5* (also known as *Spooks*), Arts and Entertainment, 2006.

Film Appearances:

Blind soldier, *War Requiem,* Anglo International, 1988.

Theseus and Oberon, *A Midsummer Night's Dream,* Miramax, 1996.

Lord Mark, *The Wings of the Dove,* Miramax, 1997.

Solo Shuttle, 1998.

Colonel Hamilton, *The Four Feathers,* Paramount, 2002.

Father, *Five Children and It,* Capitol Films, 2004.

Horatio, *Bridget Jones: The Edge of Reason,* Universal, 2004.

Ken Clifford, *Babel,* Paramount Vantage, 2006.

Prince Charles, *The Queen,* Miramax, 2006.

Adrian Ballan, *The Disappeared,* 2009, IFC Films, 2010.

Henry/Benjamin Britten, *The Habit of Art,* NT Live, 2010.

RECORDINGS

Audio Books; Reader:

Not a Penny More, Not a Penny Less, 1997.

Undercurrents by Frances Fyfield, Chivers Audiobooks, 2001.

The Horse and His Boy by C. S. Lewis, 2003.

The Secret Adversary by Agatha Christie, 2004.

The Theft of the Master by Edwin Alexander, Garev Publishing International, 2007.

Also narrator of *By the Pricking of My Thumbs by Agatha Christie.*

Videos:

Butler, *Joseph and the Amazing Technicolor Dreamcoat* (video recording of television special; also known as *Great Performances: Joseph and the Amazing Technicolor Dreamcoat*), 1999.

OTHER SOURCES

Periodicals:

Interview, May, 1990, p. 44.

JOHNSON, Lamont 1922–2010

PERSONAL

Full name, Ernest Lamont Johnson, Jr.; born September 30, 1922, in Stockton, CA; died of congestive heart failure, October 24, 2010, in Monterey, CA. Director. Known primarily as a director of made-for-television movies, Johnson took on controversial subjects and epic narratives of the lives of historical figures. During his forty-five-year career, he directed more than 150 movies-of-the-week, miniseries, and television shows and was nominated eleven times for Emmy Awards. An actor in radio, stage, and television for ten years after college, Johnson entertained troops during World War

II. He directed stage plays after the war, moving to television in 1955 with a one-hour adaptation of *Wuthering Heights* for NBC's *Matinee Theater.* During the next two years he directed 78 live productions for the series. He worked on episodes of *Have Gun? Will Travel, Peter Gunn* and *The Twilight Zone* before settling into his niche in television movies and miniseries.

In the 1970 movie *My Sweet Charlie,* he delved into interracial relationships, and in 1972 he directed one of the first treatments of homosexuality in television or film, *That Certain Summer.* Both won awards from the Directors Guild of America. *The Last American Hero,* in 1973 was one of Johnson's few feature film directorial credits. His interest in World War II let him to dramatize William Bradford Huie's nonfiction book *The Execution of Private Slovik* in 1974. In 1975 he addressed blacklisting in his television movie *Fear on Trial,* and in 1981 *Crisis at Central High* portrayed an episode in the Civil Rights Movement. His 1985 miniseries *Wallenberg: A Hero's Story* told the story of the Swedish diplomat who saved a hundred thousand Hungarian Jews during the Holocaust. It won an Emmy, and his 1988 TV movie *Gore Vidal's Lincoln* earned both an Emmy and a Directors Guild award. Among his final works in the 1990s was a four-hour television miniseries on multiple personality disorder, *Voices Within: The Lives of Truddi Chase*

PERIODICALS

Los Angeles Times, October 26, 2010.

New York Times, October 27, 2010.

Washington Post, October 27, 2010.

JORDAN, Michael B. 1987–
(Michael Jordan)

PERSONAL

Full name, Michael Bakari Jordan; born February 9, 1987, in Santa Ana, CA.

Addresses: *Publicist*—Mona Loring, MLC Public Relations, 5030 Chesebro Rd., Suite 202, Agoura Hills, CA 91301.

Career: Actor. Began career as a model.

Awards, Honors: Prime Award for Excellence and Support in Movies and Television, NJ Moviemakers, 2003; *Soap Opera Digest* Award nomination, favorite teen,

2005, and Image Award nominations, outstanding actor in a daytime drama series, National Association for the Advancement of Colored People, 2005, 2006, 2007, all for *All My Children*.

CREDITS

Television Appearances; Series:
Wallace, *The Wire*, HBO, 2002.
Reginald "Reggie" Porter Montgomery, *All My Children* (also known as *AMC*), ABC, 2003–2006.
Nate Warren, *The Assistants*, The N, 2009.
Vince Howard, *Friday Night Lights* (also known as *F.N.L.*), DirecTV, 2009, NBC, 2009–10.

Television Appearances; Movies:
C. J., *Blackout*, Black Entertainment Television, 2007.

Television Appearances; Specials:
"All My Children," *Biography*, Arts and Entertainment, 2003.
The 18th Annual Soap Opera Digest Awards, SoapNet, 2003.
The ... Annual Daytime Emmy Awards, ABC, 2003, NBC, 2004, CBS, 2005.

Television Appearances; Episodic:
(As Michael Jordan) Rideland kid, "Down Neck," *The Sopranos*, HBO, 1999.
Michael, "The Vesey Method," *Cosby*, CBS, 1999.
The View, ABC, 2003.
Morris, "Poppin' Tags," *CSI: Crime Scene Investigation* (also known as *C.S.I.* and *CSI: Las Vegas*), CBS, 2006.
Jesse Lewis, "The Calm Before," *Without a Trace* (also known as *W.A.T.*), CBS, 2006.
Michael Carter, "Wunderkind," *Cold Case*, CBS, 2007.
Corey Jensen, "Hot Spot," *Burn Notice*, USA Network, 2009.
Perry Wilson, "The Plain in the Prodigy," *Bones*, Fox, 2009.
Danny Ford, "Inhumane Society," *Law & Order: Criminal Intent* (also known as *Law & Order: CI*), USA Network, 2010.

Television Work; Series:
Assistant producer, *Souled Out*, 2004.

Film Appearances:
Second teen, *Black and White*, Screen Gems, 2000.
(As Michael Jordan) Jamal, *Hard Ball*, Paramount, 2001.
Tariq Brown, *Pastor Brown*, Rock Capital Films, 2010.
Maurice "Bumps" Wilson, *Red Tails*, Lucasfilm/Partnership Pictures, 2010.

RECORDINGS

Videos:
(In archive footage) Reginald "Reggie" Porter Montgomery, *Daytime's Greatest Weddings*, Buena Vista Home Video, 2004.

Appeared in the music video "Did You Wrong" by Pleasure P, 2008.

OTHER SOURCES

Periodicals:
Los Angeles Times, February 10, 2010.
TV Guide, May 3, 2010.

JUSTICE, Victoria 1993–

PERSONAL

Full name, Victoria Dawn Justice; born February 19, 1993, in Hollywood, FL.

Addresses: *Agent*—Mitchell Gossett, United Talent Agency, 9560 Wilshire Blvd., Suite 500, Beverly Hills, CA 90212. *Manager*—Larry Rudolph, ReignDeer Entertainment, Burbank, CA. *Publicist*—Shannon Barr, Shannon Barr Public Relations, 3619–1/2 Crest Dr., Manhattan Beach, CA 90266.

Career: Actress. Worked as a model for Jet Set Models, Union Bay, and others; appeared in commercials for Cinnamon Toast Crunch cereal, 2004, J. C. Penney department stores, 2007, and other products.

Awards, Honors: Young Artist Awards, 2006, 2007, and Young Artist Award nomination, 2008, all best young ensemble in a television comedy or drama series (with others), and Young Artist Award nomination, best young supporting actress in a television comedy or drama series, 2007, all for *Zoey 101*.

CREDITS

Television Appearances; Series:
Lola Martinez, *Zoey 101*, Nickelodeon, 2005–2008.
Tori Vega, *Victorious*, Nickelodeon, 2010.

Television Appearances; Movies:
Rose, *Silver Bells*, CBS, 2005.

Lola Martinez, *Zoey 101: Spring Break–up*, Nickelodeon, 2006.
Star gust, *Shredderman Rules*, Nickelodeon, 2007.
Lola Martinez, *Zoey 101: The Curse of P.C.A.*, Nickelodeon, 2007.
Lola Martinez, *Goodbye Zoey*, Nickelodeon, 2008.
Tammi, *Spectacular!*, Nickelodeon, 2009.
Jordan Sands, *The Boy Who Cried Werewolf*, Nickelodeon, 2010.

Television Appearances; Episodic:
The second Jill, "The Hobbit, the Sofa, and Digger Stiles," *Gilmore Girls* (also known as *Gilmore Girls: Beginnings*), The WB, 2003.
Rebecca, "The Fairest of Them All," *The Suite Life of Zack and Cody* (also known as *Suite Life* and *TSL*), The Disney Channel, 2005.
Thalia Thompson, "Enjoy the Ride," *Everwood*, The WB, 2006.
Vivian, "True Crush," *True Jackson, VP*, Nickelodeon, 2009.
Shelby Marx, "iFight Shelby Marx," *iCarly*, Nickelodeon, 2009.
Eric Fairy, "Speed," *The Troop*, Nickelodeon, 2010.
Shelby Marx, "iBloop," *iCarly*, Nickelodeon, 2010.
Voice of Badger, "Badger Pride," *The Penguins of Madagascar*, Nickelodeon, 2010.

Television Appearances; Specials:
Nickelodeon Kids' Choice Awards, Nickelodeon, 2006, 2007, 2008, 2009, 2010.
Presenter, *Teen Choice Awards*, Fox, 2010.

Film Appearances:
Stella, *Mary*, Sundance Film Festival, 2005.
Young Nikki, *When Do We Eat?*, THINKFilm, 2006.
Holly, *The Garden*, Anchor Bay Entertainment, 2006.
Daughter, *Unknown*, IFC First Take/Weinstein Company, 2006.
Betsy, *The Kings of Appletown*, Moresco Productions/Oak Films, 2009.

Stage Appearances:
Appeared in a production of the musical *Annie*.

RECORDINGS

Videos:
Lola Martinez, *Zoey 101: Behind the Scenes*, 2008.

OTHER SOURCES

Periodicals:
American Girl, April, 2006.
Daily Variety, October 3, 2008, p. 1.
Hollywood Reporter, November 16, 2005; September 3, 2008.
New York Post, August 13, 2008; October 26, 2009, p. 1.
Sweet 16, September, 2007.
Teen, March, 2006, p. 2; December, 2009, p. 2.
Teen Vogue, April, 2009, p. 1; September, 2010, pp. 194, 196, 199.
Variety, August 26, 2009, p. 2.

K–L

KANDA, Rome
(Kai Kato)

PERSONAL

Born in Osaka, Japan; immigrated to the United States, 1999. *Education:* Sapientia University, B.A., 1987; trained at Neighborhood Playhouse, New York City, and Actors Studio; also trained in Japan.

Career: Actor. Appeared as a standup comedian at Boston Comedy Club, New York Comedy Club, Theatre Sports Japan, and elsewhere; original member of the sketch comedy group New York Commedia Dell Arte; also appeared as a sword dancer in a Samurai sword fighting show in Europe and guest clown with a show in Thailand; teacher of sword fighting classes; appeared as a sushi chef in a commercial for the New York Mets baseball team.

Member: American Federation of Television and Radio Artists, Screen Actors Guild.

Awards, Honors: Finalist in World Asia Comedy Contest, 2004.

CREDITS

Film Appearances:
Minoru, *Tokyo Pop,* Warner Home Video, 1988.
Gangster, *Sonatine,* Miramax, 1993.
Kids Return (also known as *Kizzu ritan*), Mongrel Media, 1996.
Tour guide, *Memory & Desire,* Steward, 1997.
Mitani, *Spin Cycle Tokyo* (short film), 1999.
Zuki, *Just My Luck* (also known as *Lucky Girl*), Twentieth Century–Fox, 2006.

Akira, *Hooligan,* Halcyon International Pictures, 2006.
Dealer, *Brooklyn Rules,* City Lights Pictures, 2007.
Zhang Yang, *The Drucker Files* (short film), NBC Universal, 2007.
Club manager, *Lock and Roll Forever,* Scanbox Entertainment, 2009.
Hirokazu Ikeda, *The Informant!,* Warner Bros., 2009.

Appeared as Musashi Miyamoto, *Musashi;* as a Chinese gangster in *The Pink Panther;* and as an announcer, *Rollerball.*

Television Appearances; Episodic:
Samurai, "Field Trips, Permission Slips, Signs, and Weasels: Part 1," *Ned's Declassified School Survival Guide,* Nickelodeon, 2007.
Host, premiere episode, *I Survived a Japanese Game Show,* ABC, 2008.
Yuki, "Sin City Blue," *CSI: Crime Scene Investigation* (also known as *C.S.I.* and *CSI: Las Vegas*), CBS, 2010.
The 7PM Project, Ten Network, 2010.
Tetsuko's Room (also known as *Tetsuko no heya*), 2010.

Appeared as a Japanese businessman in an episode of *The Conan O'Brien Show,* NBC; also appeared on *Saturday Night Live* (also known as *SNL*), NBC.

Television Appearances; Other:
Yatsuhaka–mura: Kindaichi Kosuke no kessaku suiri, 1991.

Credited as Kei Kato, appeared in the Japanese program *Kinniku Banzuke.*

Stage Appearances:
Appeared as the moor, *Petrushka,* New Jersey Symphony Orchestra; and in Japanese stage productions.

WRITINGS

Books:

Author of a Japanese–language memoir whose title could be translated as *Samurai Spirit*.

OTHER SOURCES

Electronic:

Rome Kanda Official Site, http://www.romekanda.com, August 4, 2010.

KATO, Kai
    See KANDA, Rome

KATZ, Claudia 1971–

PERSONAL

Born July 12, 1971, in Peterborough, Cambridgeshire, England; naturalized U.S. citizen, 2007. *Education:* Attended secondary school in Peterborough, England; trained at The Actors Edge and the Praxis Acting Studio, Los Angeles; studied with Larry Moss. *Avocational Interests:* Traveling.

Addresses: *Agent*—Valentina Graham, ValMaur Talent Agency, 6671 Sunset Blvd., Building 1585, Suite 108, Los Angeles, CA 90028; Judy Rich, Brady, Brannon & Rich (BBR), 5670 Wilshire Blvd., Suite 820, Los Angeles, CA 90036.

Career: Actress. Appeared in advertisements. Worked for publishers in Great Britain.

Member: Screen Actors Guild, American Federation of Television and Radio Artists.

CREDITS

Film Appearances:

Frankie, *V–Town,* Vital Sign Films, 2001.

(Uncredited) Mecha robot, *Artificial Intelligence: AI* (also known as *A.I., A.I. Artificial Intelligence,* and *A.I.: Artificial Intelligence*), Warner Bros., 2001.

(Uncredited) Robbie's assistant, *Spider–Man* (also known as *Spiderman, Spider–Man: The Motion Picture, El hombre arana, Homem–Aranha, Omul paianjen, Pokember, Spider–Man—Haemaehaek-kimies,* and *Spindelmannen*), Columbia, 2002.

Housekeeper Freda, *The Princess Diaries 2: Royal Engagement* (also known as *The Princess Diaries 2*), Buena Vista, 2004.

(Uncredited) Robbie's assistant, *Spider–Man 2* (also known as *The Amazing Spider–Man, Spiderman 2, Spider–Man: No More,* and *Spider–Man 2 Lives;* IMAX version released as *Spider–Man 2: The IMAX Experience;* recut version known as *Spider–Man 2.1*), Columbia, 2004.

Leona, *Way of the Vampire* (also known as *Bram Stoker's "Way of the Vampire," Van Helsing's "Way of the Vampire," Van Helsing vs. Dracula,* and *Way of the Vampire*), The Asylum, 2005.

Major Shakti, *Alien Abduction,* The Asylum, 2005.

Secretary, *My Big Fat Independent Movie* (also known as *My Big Fat Indie Movie* and *My Big Fat Indy Movie*), Anchor Bay Entertainment, 2005.

Frolic bartender, *The Black Dahlia* (also known as *Black Dahlia*), Universal, 2006.

Nun, *Flight of the Living Dead: Outbreak on a Plane* (also known as *Plane Dead, Plane Dead: Zombies on a Plane,* and *Plane of the Dead*), New Line Home Video, 2007.

(Uncredited) Robbie's assistant, *Spider–Man 3* (also known as *3;* IMAX version released as *Spider–Man 3: The IMAX Experience*), Columbia, 2007.

Selina Smith, *Rainy Day,* c. 2011.

Some sources cite an appearance as Madelaine Gardner, *Be Not Afraid.*

Film Work:

Executive producer and producer, *Rainy Day,* c. 2011.

Television Appearances; Episodic:

Athletic girl, "Tug of War," *The District* (also known as *Washington Police, The District—Einsatz in Washington, Mannions distrikt,* and *Poliisipaeaellikkkoe Mannion*), CBS, 2001.

Enya, *Dog Eat Dog,* NBC, 2002.

Fourth cult member, "Shooting Stars," *CSI: Crime Scene Investigation* (also known as *C.S.I., CSI, CSI: Las Vegas, CSI: Weekends,* and *Les experts*), CBS, 2005.

Made an uncredited appearance as a nanny in "Habeas Corpse," an episode of *First Years,* NBC.

Stage Appearances:

Appeared in stage productions and recitals.

Internet Appearances:

Appeared in Internet programs.

RECORDINGS

Videos:
Herself, *Way of the Vampire: Behind the Scenes* (short documentary), The Asylum Home Entertainment, 2005.

WRITINGS

Screenplays:
Rainy Day, c. 2011.

KING, Rob Wilson
    See WILSON KING, Robb

KOSUGI, Kane 1974–
    (Kosugi Kane Takeshi)

PERSONAL

Born October 11, 1974, in Los Angeles, CA; son of Sho Kosugi (a martial arts actor and choreographer); brother of Shane Kosugi (an actor). *Avocational Interests:* Martial arts.

Addresses: *Agent*—The Geddes Agency, 8430 Santa Monica Blvd., Suite 200, West Hollywood, CA 90069. *Manager*—The Pitt Group, 9465 Wilshire Blvd., Suite 420, Beverly Hills, CA 90212.

Career: Actor. Also hosted a Japanese sports show; competed in *Ninja Warrior,* a Japanese show, several times with brother Shane.

CREDITS

Film Appearances:
Kane Osaki, *Revenge of the Ninja* (also known as *Way of the Ninja*), Cannon, 1983.
Kane, *Nine Deaths of the Ninja,* Crown International Pictures, 1985.
Takeshi Saito, *Pray for Death,* Trans World Entertainment, 1985.
Brian Tani, *Black Eagle,* Taurus Entertainment Company, 1988.
Yourimune, *Journey of Honor* (also known as *Kabuto* and *Shogun Warrior*), Rocket Pictures, 1991.
Ken Oshiro, *The Fighting King* (also known as *Za kakuto oh*), Toei Company, 1993.

Zero Woman (also known as *Zero Woman 2*), Media Blasters, 1995.
Jiraiya/Ninja Black, *Choriki sentai Ohranger vs Kakuranger,* 1995.
Cat's Eye, 1997.
(As Kosugi Kane Takeshi) Commando, *Wo shi shei,* Columbia TriStar Home Video, 1998.
Voice of Ryu, *Street Fighter Alpha* (animated; also known as *Street Fighter Zero*), 1999.
Joe Jinno, *Muscle Heat* (also known as *Masuuruhiito* and *Blood Heat*), Toho Company, 2002.
M–Facility soldier, *Godzilla: Final Wars* (also known as *Gojira: Fainaru uozu*), Sony Pictures Home Entertainment, 2004.
Ryu Hayabusa, *DOA: Dead or Alive* (also known as *DOA*), Dimension Films, 2006.
Temple Garden warrior, *War* (also known as *Rogue Assassin*), Lions Gate Films, 2007.
Voice of Satan, *Baton* (animated), 2009.
Coweb (also known as *Zhang wu shuang*), 2009.

Film Stunts:
Muscle Heat (also known as *Masuuruhiito* and *Blood Heat*), Toho Company, 2002.

Television Appearances; Series:
Kenichi Kai, *Ultraman: The Ultimate Hero* (also known as *Ultraman Powered*), 1993.

Television Appearances; Specials:
Himself, *Kyukyoku no sabaibaru atakku Sasuke,* 1997.

Television Appearances; Episodic:
"A Place to Call Home," *The Master* (also known as *Master Ninja*), NBC, 1984.
Jiraiya and Ninja Black, "Ninja de gozaru," *Ninja sentai Kakurenja,* 1994.
Competitor, *Sasuke,* 1997, 1998, 1999, 2000, 2001.
"Nebumi Camera," *Fujiko F. Fujio's Parallel Space* (also known as *Fujiko F. Fujio no parareru supesu*), 2008.

RECORDINGS

Video Games; as Work:
Motion capture performer for Onikage, *Tenchu: Stealth Assassins,* 1998.

KULZER, Robert

PERSONAL

Addresses: *Office*—Constantin Film, 9200 Sunset Blvd., Suite 800, Los Angeles, CA 90069.

Career: Producer. Constantin Film, Los Angeles, CA, copresident and executive producer, 2005.

CREDITS

Film Coproducer:
Manta, Manta (also known as *Racin' in the Streets*), Neue Constantin Films, 1991.

Film Co–Executive Producer:
Prince Valiant, Paramount, 1997.
Wrongfully Accused, Warner Bros., 1998.

Film Executive Producer:
The Calling, 2000.
Resident Evil (also known as *Biohazard*), Screen Gems, 2002.
Resident Evil: Apocalypse (also known as *Biohazard 2: Apocalypse*), Screen Gems, 2004.
The Dark, 2005.
Skinwalkers, After Dark Films, 2006.
Wrong Turn 2: Dead End (also known as *Wrong Turn 2*), Twentieth Century–Fox, 2007.
Wrong Turn 3: Left for Dead (also known as *Wrong Turn III: Left for Dead*), Twentieth Century–Fox Home Entertainment, 2009.

Film Producer:
Wrong Turn, Twentieth Century–Fox, 2003.
Autobahnraser (also known as *A2 Racer*), 2004.
DOA: Dead or Alive (also known as *DOA*), Weinstein Company, 2006.
Resident Evil: Extinction (also known as *Biohazard III*), Screen Gems, 2007.
Pandorum, Overture Films, 2009.
Resident Evil: Afterlife (also known as *Resident Evil: Afterlife: An IMAX Experience* and *Biohazard IV: Afterlife*), Screen Gems, 2010.

Film Work; Other:
Gaffer, *Kies,* Kora–Film, 1987.
(Uncredited) Production executive, *Wrong Turn,* Twentieth Century–Fox, 2003.

Film Appearances:
Himself, *Game Over: "Resident Evil" Reanimated* (documentary), Columbia TriStar Home Video, 2004.
Himself, *The Players: The Cast of "Extinction"* (short documentary), Sony Pictures Home Entertainment, 2008.
Himself, *"Resident" Road Map: Reflections on the Future of the Series* (short documentary), Sony Pictures Home Entertainment, 2008.

Himself, *Band of the Sand: Actors Unite* (short documentary), Sony Pictures Home Entertainment, 2008.
Himself, *Beyond Raccoon City: Unearthing "Resident Evil: Extinction"* (short documentary), Screen Gems, 2008.

Television Executive Producer; Movies:
A Girl Called Rosemary (also known as *Das Madchen Rosemarie*), 1996.
Charleys Tante, 1996.
Es geschah am hellichten tag, 1997.

Television Coproducer; Movies:
Die Halbstarken, 1996.

Television Appearances; Episodic:
Himself, "Skinwalkers," *Making of ...,* 2007.

WRITINGS

Screenplays:
Autobahnraser (also known as *A2 Racer*), 2004.

Film Stories:
Voll normaal, Neue Constantin Film, 1994.

Television Movies:
Charleys Tante, 1996.

LAKIN, Christine 1979–

PERSONAL

Full name, Christine Helen Lakin; born January 25, 1979, in Dallas, TX; daughter of James Daley and Karen (maiden name, Niedwick) Lakin. *Education:* University of California, Los Angeles, B.A. (cum laude), 2003.

Addresses: *Agent*—Fortitude, 8619 Washington Blvd., Culver City, CA 90232. *Manager*—Gordon Gilbertson, Gilbertson Management, 1334 Third St., Suite 201, Santa Monica, CA 90401.

Career: Actress and choreographer. Performer at area schools with Atlanta Workshop Players, beginning c. 1985; Troubadour Theatre Company, member of company; appeared in numerous commercials, including ads for T.G.I. Friday's restaurants, 2006, and Bud Lite beer, 2007.

Awards, Honors: Young Artist Award nominations, best young actress starring in a television series, 1993, and outstanding youth ensemble in a television series (with others), 1994, both for *Step by Step;* Ovation Award nomination, best featured actress in a musical, Los Angeles Stage Alliance, 2006, for *The Breakup Notebook: A Lesbian Rock Musical;* Ovation Award nomination and Los Angeles Drama Critics Circle nomination, both for *Zanna Don't!;* L.A. Weekly Award, best female comedic performance, and award nominations from Los Angeles Drama Critics Circle and Gay and Lesbian Alliance against Defamation, both 2009, for *Dog Sees God;* Ovation Award nominations and Los Angeles Drama Critics Circle award nominations, both 2009, for *Alice 2: Through the Looking Glass* and for *As U2 Like It.*

CREDITS

Television Appearances; Series:
Alicia "Al" Lambert, *Step by Step,* CBS, 1991–98.
Kate Providence, *Valentine,* The CW, 2008–2009.
Barbie Pedderson, *The Iceman Chronicles,* 2010.
Cohost, *The Kilborn File,* syndicated, 2010.

Also appeared as Alicia Lambert in *ABC TGIF,* ABC.

Television Appearances; Movies:
Little Rose, *The Rose and the Jackal,* TNT, 1990.
Kelly Harrington, *Finding Kelly* (also known as *Mystery Kids*), Showtime, 2000.
Macy, *Big Monster on Campus* (also known as *Boltneck*), Cinemax, 2000.
Carmen, *Combustion* (also known as *Silent Killer*), Lifetime, 2004.
Joan of Arc and female dancer, *Reefer Madness: The Movie Musical,* Showtime, 2005.
Christine, *In Memory of My Father,* 2005, Sundance Channel, 2009.
Francy, *Mystery Woman: At First Sight,* Hallmark Channel, 2006.
Luanne King, *The Cutting Edge: Going for the Gold* (also known as *The Cutting Edge 2: Going for the Gold*), ABC Family, 2006.

Television Appearances; Pilots:
Alicia "Al" Lambert, *Step by Step,* CBS, 1991.
Lisa, *Opposite Sex,* Fox, 2000.
Jade, *Lost in Oz* (also known as *Tim Burton's "Lost in Oz"*), syndicated, 2000.
Sara Olszewski, *Ruling Class,* Fox, 2001.
Tanya Bremer, *Dirty Famous,* VH1, 2005.
Kate Providence, *Valentine,* The CW, 2008.

Television Appearances; Episodic:
Cassandra, "Let's Talk about Sex," *7th Heaven* (also known as *7th Heaven: Beginnings*), The WB, 1998.

Michelle Solomon, "Dick Solomon of the Indiana Solomons," *3rd Rock from the Sun* (also known as *Encounters of the Paranormal Kind* and *3rd Rock*), NBC, 1999.
Dawn Sterling, "In the Money," *Promised Land,* CBS, 1999.
Gwen, "My Life as a Dog," *Odd Man Out,* ABC, 2000.
Karen, "Witch Way to the Prom," *Seven Days,* UPN, 2000.
Lisa, "The Field Trip Episode," *Opposite Sex,* Fox, 2000.
Cindy, "Chapter Forty–Two," *Boston Public,* Fox, 2002.
Ashlee, "Two Sides to Every Angel," *Touched by an Angel,* CBS, 2002.
Ms. Preston, "Teacher," *Rodney,* ABC, 2004.
Susan Knight, "Mars vs. Mars," *Veronica Mars,* UPN, 2005.
Sydney, "Karaoke," *Sons & Daughters,* ABC, 2006.
Sydney, "House Party," *Sons & Daughters,* ABC, 2006.
Erin, "I Love L.A.: Part 1," *One on One,* UPN, 2006.
(Uncredited) Ethan Parker's girl, "Death Pool 100," *CSI: Miami,* CBS, 2006.
Nick Cannon Presents: Wild 'n Out, MTV, 2006.
Leeza, "Stride," *The Loop,* Fox, 2007.
Margo Delphi, "The Theory of Everything," 2008.
Last Call with Carson Daly, NBC, 2008.
Up Close with Carrie Keagan, ABC, 2008.
Vanessa Newcomb, "The Bones that Foam," *Bones,* Fox, 2009.
Voice, "Quagmire's Baby," *Family Guy* (animated; also known as *Padre de familia*), Fox, 2009.
Stephanie, "The Jealous Kind," *Rita Rocks,* Lifetime, 2009.
Rachel Wells, "Double Identity," *NCIS: Naval Criminal Investigative Service* (also known as *Navy NCIS: Naval Criminal Investigative Service* and *NCIS*), CBS, 2010.

Also appeared in *Boy Meets World,* ABC; *Doggstyle,* Fox; and *The Owners,* ABC.

Television Appearances; Other:
Alicia "Al" Lambert, *ABC Sneak Peek with Step by Step* (special), ABC, 1994.
Undateable (miniseries), VH1, 2010.

Television Choreographer; Episodic:
"The Berger Cometh," *The Hard Times of R. J. Berger,* MTV, 2010.

Film Appearances:
Sloane, *Whatever It Takes,* Columbia, 2000.
Becca, *Buck Naked Arson* (also known as *Eyes of Fire; Feel the Heat*), Velocity Home Entertainment, 2001.
Natasha, *Getting Out* (short film), Fishman Productions, 2002.
Jamie, *Going Down,* Ardustry Home Entertainment, 2003.

Kate Reeves, *Who's Your Daddy?,* 2003, Screen Media Films, 2005.

Katie, *Blue Demon,* Regent Worldwide, 2004.

Danielle, *Suits on the Loose,* Halestone Distribution, 2005.

Grace Cunningham, *Georgia Rule,* Universal, 2007.

Tammy, *Dark Mirror,* 2007, IFC Films, 2009.

Nichole, *The Game Plan,* Buena Vista, 2007.

June Phigg, *The Hottie & and Nottie,* Regent Releasing, 2008.

Kelly, *Chronic Town,* Grey Jumper Productions, 2008.

Title role, *Patsy,* 11: Eleven Pictures, 2008.

High school girlfriend, *Naked: A Guy's Musical* (short film), Shorts International, 2008.

Regina, *Red Canyon,* Fireside Releasing, 2009.

Sunday, *Race to Witch Mountain* (also known as *Witch Mountain*), Walt Disney, 2009.

Red, *Super Capers,* Roadside Attractions, 2009.

Skyler, *Buttf**cker* (short film), Drama 3/4, 2009.

Kiki Hamilton, *Screwball: The Ted Whitfield Story,* Camelot Entertainment Group, 2010.

Heather, *Valentine's Day,* New Line Cinema, 2010.

Venus Azucar, *Elektra Luxx,* Myriad Pictures, 2010.

Tracy, *Caught in the Crossfire,* Fabrication Films, 2010.

News reporter, *Beverly Hills Chihuahua 2,* Walt Disney, 2010.

Rebecca, *Life's a Beach,* Bronx Born Films/Miracle Entertainment, 2010.

Voice of Reba, *Alpha and Omega* (animated; also known as *Alpha and Omega in 3D*), Lions Gate Films, 2010.

Taylor, *You Again,* Touchstone, 2010.

Wilimina Stansbury, *Darnell Dawkins: Mouth Guitar Legend,* A Common Thread, 2010.

Film Work:

Associate producer, *The Making of "The Nutcracker,"* Predator Productions, 2009.

Stage Appearances:

Darla and Sissy, *Sneaux* (musical), Matrix Theatre, Los Angeles, 2003–2004.

Cindy, *Cindy and the Discoball,* Falcon Theatre, Los Angeles, 2005.

Anita and nurse, *Wrong Turn at Lungfish,* Falcon Theatre, 2005.

Joanie Cunningham, *Happy Days: A Family Musical,* Falcon Theatre, 2006.

Casey and Sheila, *The Breakup Notebook: A Lesbian Rock Musical,* Hudson Theatre, Los Angeles, 2006.

Tricia, *Dog Sees God,* Hudson Theatre, 2009.

Appeared as Alice, *Alice in One–Hit Wonderland,* Troubadour Theatre Company, Los Angeles; Olivia Whorebucks, *Anne E. Wrecksick,* Cavern Club Theatre, Los Angeles; Heather Duke, *Heathers* (workshop production), Los Angeles; and Antigone, *Oedipus the King, Mama!,* Getty Villa Theatre, Los Angeles.

Stage Choreographer:

Zanna Don't! (musical), Lyric Theatre, Los Angeles, 2007.

Alice 2: Through the Looking Glass, Troubadour Theatre Company, Los Angeles, 2009.

Also choreographer of the musical *Big: The Musical* and *As U2 Like It,* Troubadour Theatre Company, Los Angeles, 2009.

Internet Appearances; Episodic:

Nan, "Nan and Lucy," *Wainy Days,* WainyDays.com, 2008.

RECORDINGS

Videos:

Behind the Scenes of "Going Down," PAIA Pictures, 2004.

OTHER SOURCES

Periodicals:

Hollywood Life, May, 2007; July, 2007, pp. 83, 85, 87.

Six Degrees, March, 2007, p. 91.

Electronic:

Christine Lakin Official Site, http://www.christine-lakin.com, August 19, 2010.

LAWTON, J. F. 1960–

(J. D. Athens)

PERSONAL

Full name, Jonathan Frederick Lawton; born August 11, 1960, in Riverside, CA; son of Harry (a writer) and Georgeann (a pianist) Lawton; married wife (a money manager), c. 1987. *Education:* Studied filmmaking at California State University Long Beach, graduated.

Addresses: *Manager*—Industry Entertainment, 955 South Carrillo Dr., 3rd Floor, Los Angeles, CA 90048.

Career: Screenwriter, producer, and director. Also producer of website Inner Object. An advocate for dyslexia and ADHD (attention deficit hyperactivity disorder).

Member: British Academy of Film and Television Arts, Academy of Motion Picture Arts and Sciences.

Awards, Honors: Film Award nomination, best screenplay—original, British Academy of Film and Television Arts, WGA Screen Award nomination, best screenplay written directly for the screen, Writers Guild of America, 1991, both for *Pretty Woman.*

CREDITS

Film Work:
Creative consultant and editor, *Talking Walls,* 1987.
(As J. D. Athens) Director, *Cannibal Women in the Avocado Jungle of Death* (also known as *Jungle Heat* and *Piranha Women in the Avocado Jungle of Death*), Paramount Home Video, 1989.
(As J. D. Athens) Director, *Pizza Man,* Megalomania, 1991.
Executive producer, *Under Siege,* Warner Bros., 1992.
Director, *The Hunted,* Universal, 1995.
Director and executive producer, *Jackson,* 2008.

Also worked as director, *Renascence.*

Television Work; Series:
Creator and executive producer, *V.I.P.,* syndicated, 1998–2002.

Television Director; Episodic:
"Beats Working at a Hot Dog Stand," *V.I.P.,* syndicated, 1998.
"One Wedding and Val's Funeral," *V.I.P.,* syndicated, 1998.
"The Quiet Brawler," *V.I.P.,* syndicated, 1999.
"Chasing Anna," *V.I.P.,* syndicated, 2001.

WRITINGS

Screenplays:
(As J. D. Athens) *Cannibal Women in the Avocado Jungle of Death* (also known as *Jungle Heat* and *Piranha Women in the Avocado Jungle of Death*), Paramount Home Video, 1989.
Pretty Woman, Buena Vista, 1990.
(As J. D. Athens) *Pizza Man,* Megalomania, 1991.
Mistress (also known as *Hollywood Mistress*), Rainbow Releasing, 1992.
Under Siege, Warner Bros., 1992.
Blankman, Columbia, 1994.
The Hunted, Universal, 1995.
Chain Reaction, Twentieth Century–Fox, 1996.
DOA: Dead or Alive (also known as *DOA*), Dimension Films, 2006.
Jackson, 2008.

Film Stories:
DOA: Dead or Alive (also known as *DOA*), 2006.

Television Episodes:
"Beats Working at a Hot Dog Stand," *V.I.P.,* syndicated, 1998.

Television Episode Stories:
"Bloody Vale–entine," *V.I.P.,* syndicated, 1998.

LAYNE, Chyna

PERSONAL

Born in the Philippines; raised in New York City; daughter of Sharon Bush (a community activist). *Education:* Trained with CityKids Repertory Company, Black Spectrum Theatre, African American Theatre of Harlem, Negro Ensemble Company, and Atlantic Acting School. *Avocational Interests:* Filipino stick fighting, Chinese martial arts.

Addresses: *Agent*—Suzanne Wohl, TalentWorks, 3500 West Olive Ave., Suite 1400, Burbank, CA 91505. *Manager*—Glenn Rigberg, Inphenate, 9701 Wilshire Blvd., 10th Floor, Beverly Hills, CA 90212.

Career: Actress and producer. Lawrence Layne Productions, cofounder; appeared in commercials for Dunkin Donuts, 2007, and Dr. Miracle's hair care products, 2007–08. Community volunteer in New York City, including operating the girls' dance team No Self Control.

Awards, Honors: Best Actress Award, short film category, New York International Independent Film and Video Festival, 2007, for *Silent Cries of a Child;* Boston Society of Film Critics Award nomination and Washington DC Area Film Critics Association Award nomination, both best ensemble (with others), 2009, for *Precious: Based on the Novel "Push" by Sapphire.*

CREDITS

Film Appearances:
(Uncredited) Bar patron, *The Last Laugh,* Last Laugh Films, 2005.
Tori, *Maya's Soul,* Maverick Entertainment Group, 2006.
Gina, *A Deeper Love,* Terry D. Films, 2007.
Debbie, *Back Stab,* A Small Production Company, 2007.

Trina, *STD: Sexually Transmitted Demons* (short film), 2007.
DOA (Daughters of America) (short film), 2007.
Doreen, *Hardrock,* Lions Gate Films Home Entertainment, 2007.
Silent Cries of a Child (short film), c. 2007.
Teenisha, *All Screwed Up,* Red Line Studios, 2008.
Pot's girlfriend Juanita, *Cadillac Records,* TriStar, 2008.
Rio, *10,000 A.D.: The Legend of a Black Pearl,* Indican Pictures, 2008.
Everything Goes, Everything Green Films, 2008.
Nicole, *Ordinance H5n1* (short film), Aramak Productions, 2009.
Kelly, *The Eddie Black Story,* Polychrome Pictures, 2009.
Rhonda, *Precious: Based on the Novel "Push" by Sapphire* (also known as *Precious*), Lions Gate Films, 2009.
Asia, *Left Unsaid,* Urban Romances, 2010.
Shee–Lee, *We Are Family,* Tri Destined Independent, 2010.

Film Producer:
A Deeper Love, Terry D. Films, 2007.

Television Appearances; Movies:
Deyeh, *Life Support,* HBO, 2007.

Television Appearances; Specials:
Nicole, *NY Actor's Showcase,* 2004.

Television Appearances; Episodic:
Nervous woman, "No More Good Days," *FlashForward,* ABC, 2009.
Good Day New York, WNYW, 2009.

Internet Appearances; Videos:
Honey, *Psionics,* YouTube, 2008.

OTHER SOURCES

Electronic:
Beautiful Minds Bodies and Souls, http://www.bmbsfamily.com, August 4, 2010.
Chyna Layne Official Site, http://www.chynalayne.com, August 20, 2010.

LE, Cung 1972–

PERSONAL

Born May 25, 1972, in Saigon, Vietnam; immigrated to the Philippines, 1975, then to the United States; son of Anne Le; married second wife, Suzanne, August, 2009; children: (first marriage) two sons; (second marriage) Robert Eric. *Education:* Attended West Valley College, Saratoga, CA. *Avocational Interests:* Movies, sports, fitness activities.

Addresses: *Office*—The Gym, Universal Strength Headquarters, 720 Montague Expressway, Milpitas, CA 95035. *Agent*—Brett Norensberg, Gersh Agency, 9465 Wilshire Blvd., 6th Floor, Beverly Hills, CA 90212. *Manager*—Scott Karp, 10203 Santa Monica Blvd., Los Angeles, CA 90067.

Career: Actor, fight choreographer, and martial artist (san shou/san da kung fy). The Gym: Universal Strength Headquarters, Milpitas, CA, principal; professional, competitive martial artist; martial arts teacher and coach; appeared in commercials.

Member: Screen Actors Guild.

Awards, Honors: More than thirty–five martial arts awards, including winner of U.S. Open international martial arts championships, 1994, 1995, 1996, and U.S. national championships, 1994, 1995, 1997; world champion kick–boxer, 1998–2007; StrikeForce mixed martial arts middleweight champion, 2008–09.

CREDITS

Film Appearances:
Victor, *Sleight of Hand,* 1997.
Mort Ission, *Kwoon,* Hollywood Wizard, 2004.
The assassin, *Dark Assassin,* Hart Sharp Video, 2006.
Erik, *Blizhniy Boy: The Ultimate Fighter,* Universal Vision Pictures, 2007.
Dragon Le, *Fighting,* Rogue Pictures, 2009.
Manh, *Pandorum,* Overture Films, 2009.
Sa Zhen–shan, *Bodyguards and Assassins* (also known as *Shi yue wei cheng*), E1 Entertainment, 2009.
Marshall Law, *Tekken,* TVA Films, 2010.
Militia leader, *True Legend* (also known as *The Legend of Beggar Su, Beggar Su,* and *Su Qi–Er*), Golden Village Pictures/Scorpio East/EDKO Film, 2010.

Television Appearances; Specials:
Audience member, *CBS StrikeForce—1 Global Saturday Night Fights,* CBS, 2009.

Also appeared in *Human Weapon,* History Channel; *Kung Fu Fighter,* History Channel; and *On the Inside of Chinese Martial Arts,* The Discovery Channel.

Television Appearances; Episodic:
Himself, "Legends," *Walker, Texas Ranger,* CBS, 2001.
Inside MMA, 2008.
The Hot List, 2008.

"Season Finale," *The Jace Hall Show,* 2008.

"Zach Levi! Cliffy B! and Cung Le!," *The Jace Hall Show,* 2008.

"MMA vs. Street Fighter 4," *The Jace Hall Show,* 2008.

"Nor Cal MMA Scene," *MMA Worldwide,* 2009.

Guest, "Burning Plain & Paradorum," *Sidewalks Entertainment,* 2009.

MMA H.E.A.T., 2009.

"Hand–to–Hand," *NCIS: Los Angeles,* CBS, 2010.

Also appeared in episodes of *Journey of a Champion; Toe to Toe with Goldberg,* Showtime; and *Warrior Nation,* MSNBC.

OTHER SOURCES

Periodicals:
Black Belt, December, 2004.

Electronic:
Cung Le Official Site, http://www.cungle.com, August 4, 2010.

LEET, Scott Anthony 1962–
   (Scott Leet, Brogan Rafter)

PERSONAL

Born December 26, 1962, in San Francisco, CA. *Education:* San Francisco State University, B.S.; trained at One on One and at Actors Studio, Los Angeles.

Addresses: *Agent*—Theo Caesar, 90210 Talent, 9595 Wilshire Blvd., Suite 900, Beverly Hills, CA 90212; (commercials) Brick Entertainment, 18663 Ventura Blvd., Suite 201, Tarzana, CA 91356.

Career: Actor, celebrity impersonator, voice performer, producer, director, and writer. Performed at comedy clubs in Los Angeles and San Francisco, CA; Ten Richter (music group), founder, lead singer (as Brogan Rafter), musician, and songwriter; appeared in commercials for Turbo–Tax computer software, Full Throttle energy drinks, Starburst candy bars, and other products and services. National Football League, former professional football player with the St. Louis Rams and Dallas Cowboys.

Member: Screen Actors Guild.

Awards, Honors: *Los Angeles Weekly* Award nomination (with others), best ensemble cast, 2006, for *Our*

Lady of 121st Street; selected as best new young comedian, San Francisco State University Comedy Festival.

CREDITS

Film Appearances:
T. J. McKay, *Solitaire,* Mystique Films, 1996.

Raymond Frye, *Out in Fifty,* Xscapade Pictures, 1999.

Jack Farrell, *L.A. Twister,* Indican Pictures, 2004.

Duwayne Fux, *Life on Mars* (also known as *Doctor Cloud*), 2006.

Officer Willoughby, *Dark Reel,* Barnholtz Entertainment, 2008.

Doyle Reid, *The Perfect Student,* Hybrid, 2010.

David Doyle, *The Prometheus Project,* Ominous Productions, 2010.

William Bonin, *Freeway Killer,* Image Entertainment, 2010.

Davis Holmes, *Groupie* (also known as *Backstage Pass*), Ovation Entertainment/VVS Films, 2010.

John Holloway, *Abandoned,* Anchor Bay Entertainment, 2010.

Other film appearances include role of Johnny Mirage, *A Vicious Cycle.*

Film Producer and Director:
Out in Fifty, Xscapade Pictures, 1999.

Television Appearances; Episodic:
Ray Packer, "Bad Blood," *Silk Stalkings,* USA Network and CBS, 1992.

Tommy Bannon, "The Two Renos," *Renegade,* USA Network and syndicated, 1993.

(As Scott Leet) Davis Lee, "Cadillac Jack," *Silk Stalkings,* USA Network, 1995.

Farrell Riggs, "Black and Blue," *Silk Stalkings,* USA Network, 1995.

Agent Woods, "Gee Your Hair Smells Evil," *Good vs Evil* (also known as *G vs E*), USA Network, 1999.

(As Scott Leet) Mad Dog Murphy, "Aww, Here It Goes to Hollywood: Part 1," *Kenan & Kel,* Nickelodeon, 1999.

Karl Petersen, "Four Corners," *ER,* NBC, 2001.

Joel Youngblood, "Lolita?," *The Guardian* (also known as *Ochita bengoshi Nick Fallin*), CBS, 2001.

Nick Reed, *The Young and the Restless* (also known as *Y&R*), CBS, four episodes, 2004.

Harold Flynn, "Carpe Demon," *Charmed,* The WB, 2005.

Jason Edom, "Ravenous," *NCIS: Naval Criminal Investigative Service* (also known as *Navy NCIS: Naval Criminal Investigative Service* and *NCIS*), CBS, 2006.

Jesse Wayne, "No Opportunity Necessary," *Women's Murder Club* (also known as *wmc*), ABC, 2007.

Tough–looking guy, *Days of Our Lives* (also known as *Days* and *DOOL*), NBC, 2009.
Tim Malone in 2010, "One Fall," *Cold Case,* CBS, 2010.

Appeared as Gary Ryan in an episode of *Baywatch,* NBC; and as a delivery boy, *The Bold and the Beautiful,* CBS.

Stage Appearances:

Appeared as Balthazar, *Our Lady of 121st Street,* Matrix Theatre, Los Angeles; Danny, *Sexual Perversity in Chicago,* Barbary Coast, San Francisco, CA; and Rodolpho, *A View from the Bridge,* Barbary Coast.

RECORDINGS

Videos:

Performed with Ten Richter for the album *Off the Charts,* Checkmate HQ.

WRITINGS

Screenplays:

Out in Fifty, Xscapade Pictures, 1999.

OTHER SOURCES

Electronic:

Scott Anthony Leet Official Site, http://www.scottleet.com, September 7, 2010.

LELAND, Brad 1954–
(Brad LeLand, Bradley Williams, Bradley Leland Williams)

PERSONAL

Full name, Bradley Leland Williams; born September 15, 1954, in Lubbock, TX; son of Bill and Shirley Williams; married Freda Ramsey (an actress), March 18, 1978; children: three, including Thea and Leah. *Education:* Texas Tech University, B.A. *Avocational Interests:* Golf, sports.

Addresses: *Agent*—Nancy Campbell, Campbell Agency, 3838 Oak Lawn Ave., Suite 900, Dallas, TX 75219.

Career: Actor. Turnkey Productions II, owner and manager. Disneyland, performed as a child at Crazy Horse Saloon, 1959.

Member: Screen Actors Guild, American Federation of Television and Radio Artists.

CREDITS

Film Appearances:

First rowdy, *The Texas Chainsaw Massacre Part 2,* Cannon Releasing, 1986.
Drunk cowboy, *Square Dance* (also known as *Home Is Where the Heart Is*), Island Pictures, 1987.
Second "scrutineer", *Winners Take All,* Apollo Pictures, 1987.
Larry, *Shy People,* Cannon, 1987.
Drive–in boy, *Blood Rage,* Film Concept Group, 1987.
Drug dealer, *Under Cover,* Cannon, 1987.
Dufee, *Blaze,* Buena Vista, 1989.
Patrolman, *Ruby,* Triumph Releasing, 1992.
Armored truck driver, *Love and a .45,* Trimark Pictures, 1994.
Man delivering money, *Underneath,* Gramercy, 1995.
Booking deputy, *Cadillac Ranch,* Legacy Releasing, 1996.
Deputy, *Painted Hero,* Cabin Fever Entertainment, 1997.
Louis Quillet, *The Only Thrill,* Legacy Releasing, 1998.
Barnard, *Abilene,* Clear Stream Pictures/Farmland Pictures, 1999.
Jim, *The Operator,* First Look International, 2000.
Earl, *World without Waves,* Abamedia/Texas 377 Partners, 2001.
Sheriff, *American Outlaws,* Warner Bros., 2001.
Truck driver, *The Anarchist Cookbook,* Innovation Film Group, 2002.
Big Rig Bob, *The Texas Chainsaw Massacre* (also known as *Texas Chainsaw*), New Line Cinema, 2003.
John Aubrey, *Friday Night Lights,* Universal, 2004.
Mr. Henderson, *The Ringer,* Fox Searchlight, 2005.
(As Bradley Williams) Ronnie, *Inside Man,* Universal, 2006.
Mr. Jonathan Marlin, *The Return,* Rogue Pictures, 2006.
Mitch, *Walking Tall: The Payback* (also known as *Wild Town 2*), Sony Pictures Home Entertainment, 2007.
Executive, *Hancock* (also known as *Hidden from Earth*), Columbia, 2008.
(As Bradley Williams) Trueheart Frazier, *Miracle at St. Anna,* Touchstone, 2008.

According to some sources, appeared as Corporal Sandy, *Silverado,* 1985; Agent Farley, *Born on the Fourth of July,* 1989; and Tex, *Dr. T and the Women,* 2000.

Television Appearances; Series:

Buddy Garrity, *Friday Night Lights* (also known as *F.N.L.*), NBC, 2006–2008, DirecTV, 2009, NBC, 2009–10.

Television Appearances; Miniseries:

Officer Manley, *Trial: The Price of Passion*, NBC, 1992.

Beaufort, *Heaven & Hell: North & South, Book III* (also known as *North and South Book III: Heaven and Hell*), ABC, 1994.

Stan Farr, *Texas Justice* (also known as *Blood Will Tell*), ABC, 1995.

Militia commander, *Comanche Moon*, CBS, 2008.

Television Appearances; Movies:

(As Bradley Leland Williams) Deputy Hackett, *Dalton: Code of Vengeance II*, NBC, 1986.

Sergeant Quinn, *Houston: The Legend of Texas*, CBS, 1986.

Fire captain, *Perry Mason: The Case of the Ruthless Reporter*, NBC, 1991.

Officer Grissom, *A Seduction in Travis County*, CBS, 1991.

Alan Fletcher, *Stranger at My Door*, CBS, 1991.

Otis, *The Last Prostitute*, Lifetime, 1991.

Andy Buckley, *An American Story*, CBS, 1992.

Jimmy Fortune, *Revenge on the Highway* (also known as *Overdrive*), NBC, 1992.

First cop, *Fatal Deception: Mrs. Lee Harvey Oswald*, NBC, 1993.

Police officer, *Witness to the Execution*, NBC, 1994.

Vince Clark, *The Curse of Inferno*, The Movie Channel, 1995.

Big Bob, *The Patriot*, HBO, 1998.

Deputy sheriff, *Dallas: War of the Ewings*, CBS, 1998.

Tubby, *Still Holding On: The Legend of Cadillac Jack* (also known as *Cadillac Jack*), CBS, 1998.

Dot Thomas the waitress, *Rolling Kansas*, Comedy Central, 2003.

Appeared as Chance, *Long Arm*.

Television Appearances; Pilots:

Officer, *Code of Vengeance*, NBC, 1985.

Travis, "Travelin' Man," *CBS Summer Playhouse*, CBS, 1987.

Buddy Garrity, *Friday Night Lights*, NBC, 2006.

Tom, *Trauma*, NBC, 2009.

Television Appearances; Episodic:

First man in bar, "Trompe L'Oeil," *Dallas*, CBS, 1986.

Mace Trapnell, "Fate," *In the Heat of the Night*, NBC, 1988.

Dill, "Ten–Cent Hero," *The Young Riders*, ABC, 1989.

Frank Banner, "The French Defection," *Dangerous Curves*, CBS, 1993.

Ridgeway, "Deadly Reunion," *Walker, Texas Ranger*, CBS, 1994.

Bobby, "Right Man, Wrong Time," *Walker, Texas Ranger*, CBS, 1994.

Deputy Roy, "Badge of Honor," *Walker, Texas Ranger*, CBS, 1994.

Horton, "Flashback," *Walker, Texas Ranger*, CBS, 1995.

Luke, "Last Hope," *Walker, Texas Ranger*, CBS, 1997.

Carl Wade, "Circle of Life," *Walker, Texas Ranger*, CBS, 1998.

Joey Dunbar, "Trackdown," *Walker, Texas Ranger*, CBS, 1998.

Detective John "Sully" Sullivan, "Out of Time," *CSI: Miami*, CBS, 2009.

Detective John "Sully" Sullivan, "Die by the Sword," *CSI: Miami*, CBS, 2010.

(As Brad LeLand) John "Sully" Sullivan, "Mommie Deadest," *CSI: Miami*, CBS, 2010.

John "Sully" Sullivan, "Time Bomb," *CSI: Miami*, CBS, 2010.

Voice of Slim Biggins, "Cleveland's Angels," *The Cleveland Show* (animated), Fox, 2010.

According to some sources, appeared as a valet in "I Don't Do Cuddles," an episode of *Unnatural Pursuits*, Arts and Entertainment, 1992.

Stage Appearances:

Appeared as Michael, *I Do! I Do!*, Hayloft Dinner Theatre; Randle McMurphy, *One Flew Over the Cuckoo's Nest*, Calm Eddy's Theatre, Dallas, TX; and Mac Sam, *Miss Firecracker Contest*, Stage One, Dallas.

LEVY, Eugene 1946–

PERSONAL

Born December 17, 1946, in Hamilton, Ontario, Canada; married Deborah Divine, 1977; children: Dan, one more. *Education:* Attended McMaster University.

Addresses: *Agent*—WME Entertainment, 9601 Wilshire Blvd., 3rd Floor, Beverly Hills, CA 90210. *Manager*—Anonymous Content, 3532 Hayden Ave., Culver City, CA 90067.

Career: Actor, comedian, producer, director, and writer. Second City (improvisational comedy troupe), Toronto, Ontario, member of company. Voice for radio commercials, including voice of the devil for the Seattle Seahawks football team commercials, 2001. McMaster University, officer of McMaster Film Board, 1967–68.

Member: Screen Actors Guild, American Federation of Television and Radio Artists.

Awards, Honors: Medalla Sitges en Plata de Ley, best actor, Catalonian International Film Festival, 1973, for *Cannibal Girls*; Academy of Canadian Cinema and

Television awards, best variety writer, 1978 and 1984; Emmy awards (with others), best writing for a comedy program, 1982 and 1983, both for *SCTV Network 90;* ACE Award nomination, performance in a comedy special, 1985, for *The Last Polka;* Earle Grey Award (with others), Academy of Canadian Cinema and Television, 1988, for *Second City TV;* Gemini Award nominations, best comedy series, Academy of Canadian Cinema and Television, 1992, 1993, and 1994, and best writing in a comedy or variety program or series, 1992, all for *Maniac Mansion;* Sir Peter Ustinov Award, Banff Television Festival, 1994; Earle Grey Award (with others), Gemini Awards, 1995; Independent Spirit Award nomination (with Christopher Guest), best screenplay, 1998, for *Waiting for Guffman;* American Comedy Award nomination, funniest supporting actor in a motion picture, and Blockbuster Entertainment Award, favorite supporting actor in a comedy, both 2000, for *American Pie;* Canadian Comedy awards, pretty funny male performance in a film and pretty funny writing in a film, and WGA Screen Award nomination (with Guest), best original screenplay, Writers Guild of America, all 2001, for *Best in Show;* Canadian Comedy Award, pretty funny male performance in a film, 2002, for *American Pie 2;* also awards from Alliance of Canadian Cinema, Television, and Radio Artists; Teen Choice Award nomination (with Queen Latifah), choice movie chemistry, 2003, for *Bringing Down the House;* New York Film Critics Circle Award, best supporting actor, Seattle Film Critics Award (with others), best music, 2003, Critics Choice Award (with others), best song, Broadcast Film Critics Association Awards, Canadian Comedy Awards, film—pretty funny performance male and film—pretty funny writing, Florida Film Critics Circle Award (with others), best ensemble cast, Grammy Award, best song written for a motion picture, Independent Spirit Award nomination, best screenplay, Independent Features Project/West, Phoenix Film Critics Society Award nomination (with others), best ensemble acting, Golden Satellite Award, best performance by an actor in a supporting role, comedy or musical, International Press Academy, Phoenix Film Critics Society Award nomination (with others), best ensemble acting, 2004, for *A Mighty Wind;* Teen Choice Award nomination, choice movie liar, 2004, for *New York Minute;* Gotham Award nomination (with others), best ensemble cast, 2006, for *For Your Consideration.*

CREDITS

Film Appearances:

Foxy Lady, 1971.

Clifford Sturges, *Cannibal Girls* (also known as *Des filles cannibales*), American International Pictures, 1973.

Richard "Ritchie" Rosenberg, *Running,* Universal, 1979.

Marty, *Nothing Personal,* American International Pictures/Filmways, 1980.

Matt, *Double Negative* (also known as *Deadly Companion*), 1980.

Voices of Edsel, Sternn, and male reporter, *Heavy Metal* (animated), Columbia, 1981.

Sal DiPasquale, *Going Berserk,* Universal, 1983.

Car salesman, *National Lampoon's Vacation* (also known as *American Vacation, National Lampoon's Summer Vacation,* and *Vacation*), Warner Bros., 1983.

Walter Kornbluth, *Splash,* Buena Vista, 1984.

Himself, *Tears Are Not Enough,* 1985.

Norman Kane, *Armed and Dangerous,* Columbia, 1986.

The Canadian Conspiracy, HBO Films, 1986.

Barry Steinberg, *Club Paradise,* Warner Bros., 1986.

Eugene Levy Discovers Home Safety, 1987.

Sherman Tully, *Ghostbusters II* (also known as *Ghostbusters 2*), 1989.

Leo Ross, *Speed Zone!* (also known as *Cannonball Fever*), Orion, 1989.

Singer at audition, *Father of the Bride,* Buena Vista, 1991.

Crowley, *Stay Tuned,* Warner Bros., 1992.

Casino cashier, *Once Upon a Crime ...,* Metro–Goldwyn–Mayer, 1992.

Good Samaritan, *For Goodness Sake,* 1993.

Justice of the peace, *I Love Trouble,* Buena Vista, 1994.

Mr. Habib, *Father of the Bride Part II,* 1995.

Dr. Allan Pearl, *Waiting for Guffman,* Sony Pictures Classics, 1996.

Vic, *Multiplicity,* 1996.

Professor Keanbean, *Richie Rich's Christmas Wish* (also known as *Richie Rich: A Christmas Story*), Warner Bros. Home Video, 1998.

Stanford Wharton, *Akbar's Adventure Tours* (also known as *Akbar's Adventure Ride*), Praxi's Film Works, 1998.

Guy Fontenot, *Almost Heroes,* Warner Bros., 1998.

Guy on background television, *Holy Man,* Buena Vista, 1998.

Hugh Sanford, *Unglued* (also known as *The Secret Life of Girls*), Her Way/Ocean Park Pictures, 1999.

Larry, *Dogmatic,* 1999.

Jim's dad, *American Pie,* Universal, 1999.

Gerald "Gerry" Fleck, *Best in Show* (also known as *Dog Show!*), Warner Bros., 2000.

Bucky Kent, *The Ladies Man,* Paramount, 2000.

Leon, *Silver Man,* Annex Entertainment, 2000.

Mr. Keyes, *Down to Earth* (also known as *Einmal Himmel und zurueck*), Paramount, 2001.

Himself, *Josie and the Pussycats,* MCA/Universal, 2001.

Jim's dad, *American Pie 2,* Universal, 2001.

Bloomingdale's salesman, *Serendipity,* Miramax, 2001.

Jonas, *Repli-Kate,* Fusion International, 2002.

Frank Bernard, *Like Mike,* Twentieth Century–Fox, 2002.

Howie Rosenthal (some sources cite Howie Rottman), *Bringing Down the House,* Buena Vista/Touchstone, 2003.

Mitch, *A Mighty Wind,* Warner Bros., 2003.

Principal Collins, *When Harry Met Lloyd: Dumb and Dumberer*, New Line Cinema, 2003.

Mr. Levinstien, *American Wedding*, Universal, 2003.

Car salesman, *The Family Truckster*, Warner Home Video, 2003.

Max Lomax, *New York Minute*, Warner Bros., 2004.

Andy Fiddler, *The Man*, New Line Cinema, 2005.

Jimmy Murtaugh, *Cheaper by the Dozen 2*, Twentieth Century–Fox, 2005.

Mr. Noah Levenstein, *American Pie Presents Band Camp*, Universal, 2005.

Noah Levenstein, *American Pie Presents The Naked Mile*, Universal, 2006.

Noah Levenstein, *American Pie Presents Beta House*, Universal, 2006.

Noah Levenstein, *American Pie Presents: The Book of Love*, Universal, 2006.

Voice of Clovis, *Curious George*, Universal, 2006.

Voice of Lou, *Over the Hedge* (animated), Dream-Works, 2006.

Morley Orfkin, *For Your Consideration*, Warner Bros., 2006.

Mr. Nerdlinger, *Gooby*, Monterey Media, 2009.

Voice of Einstein, *Night at the Museum: Battle of the Smithsonian* (also known as *Night at the Museum 2*, *Night at the Museum: Battle of the Smithsonian–The IMAX Experience*), Twentieth Century–Fox, 2009.

Max Yasgur, *Taking Woodstock*, Focus Features, 2009.

Voice of Orrin, *Astro Boy*, Summit, 2009.

Peace, Love and Cinema, Focus Features, 2009.

Film Work:

Cinematographer, *The Columbus of Sex*, 1969.

Director, *Once Upon a Crime ...*, Metro–Goldwyn–Mayer, 1992.

Television Appearances; Series:

Stay Tuned, 1976.

The Sunshine Hour, 1976.

Earl Camembert, Sid Dithers, and other roles, *Second City TV* (also known as *SCTV*), syndicated, 1977–81.

SCTV Network 90 (also known as *SCTV Comedy Network* and *SCTV Network*), NBC, 1981–83.

SCTV Channel, NBC, 1983.

Camp Candy, 1989.

(And creator) *Maniac Mansion*, syndicated, 1990–93.

Alex Trebel, *The Martin Short Show*, NBC, 1994.

Gordon Schermerhorn, *Hiller and Diller*, ABC, 1997–98.

Committed, 2001.

Gil Bender, *Greg the Bunny*, Fox, 2002.

Television Appearances; Specials:

The Magic of David Copperfield (also known as *The Magic of David Copperfield V: The Statue of Liberty Disappears*), CBS, 1983.

Stan Schmenge and Ma Schmenge, *The Last Polka*, HBO, 1985.

Stupid Eddie, *The Martin Short Concert for the North Americas*, Showtime, 1985.

First soldier, *Dave Thomas: The Incredible Time Travels of Henry Osgood*, Showtime, 1986.

Josh Smenge, *Comic Relief*, HBO, 1986.

Morty Arnold, *Billy Crystal—Don't Get Me Started*, HBO, 1986.

Morty Arnold, *Billy Crystal: Don't Get Me Started—The Lost Minutes* (also known as *The Lost Minutes of Billy Crystal*), 1987.

Second City's 15th Anniversary Reunion (also known as *The Second City Reunion*), Showtime, 1988.

The Best of SCTV, ABC, 1988.

Bertrand, *The Second City Toronto 15th Anniversary*, 1988.

Saturday Night Live: 15th Anniversary, NBC, 1989.

The Family Channel's Fall Sneak Preview, The Family Channel, 1990.

Friends of Gilda, 1993.

John Candy: A Tribute, Arts and Entertainment, 1995.

Various characters, *The Best of John Candy on SCTV*, 1996.

Gilda Radner: The E! True Hollywood Story, E! Entertainment Television, 1997.

Sea World/Busch Gardens Adventures: The Hidden Key, Nickelodeon, 1998.

Bobby Bittman, *Just for Laughs: Montreal Comedy Festival*, 1999.

Comedy Central Presents the Second Annual Kennedy Center Mark Twain Prize Celebrating the Humor of Jonathan Winters, Comedy Central, 2000.

Inside TV Land: The Andy Griffith Show, 2000.

Making the Movie: American Pie II, MTV, 2001.

The 2nd Annual Canadian Comedy Awards, 2001.

Presenter, *AFI Awards 2001*, CBS, 2002.

AFI Life Achievement Award: A Tribute to Tom Hanks, USA Network, 2002.

Gilda Radner's Greatest Moments, 2002.

Comedy Central Presents: The Commies, Comedy Central, 2003.

Weird Sex and Snowshoes: A Trek Through the Canadian Cinematic Psyche, Moving Images Dist., 2004.

Live from the Red Carpet: The 2004 Grammy Awards, E! Entertainment Television, 2004.

The 76th Annual Academy Awards, ABC, 2004.

E! Entertainer of the Year 2003, E! Entertainment Television, 2004.

Steve Martin: An American Cinematheque Tribute, 2005.

Dr. Vaughn, *Super Bowl XXXIX*, 2005.

Host, *Canada's Walk of Fame*, 2007.

Canada for Haiti, 2010.

Television Appearances; Episodic:

Freddie Cohen, "Half–Way Home," *King of Kensington*, syndicated, 1975.

Bernie, "Home Is Where the Heartburn Is," *King of Kensington,* syndicated, 1979.
Second City TV (also known as *SCTV* and *Second City Revue*), 1979.
"Alpha Channel," *Second City TV* (also known as *SCTV* and *Second City Revue*), 1981.
"The Cisco Kid," *Second City TV* (also known as *SCTV* and *Second City Revue*), 1981.
Various, *SCTV Network 90,* 1981.
"Home for Dinner," *George Burns Comedy Week,* CBS, 1985.
"Home for Christmas," *George Burns Comedy Week,* CBS, 1985.
"SNL Film Festival," *Saturday Night Live* (also known as *SNL*), 1985.
Bert Harris, "Skeleton," *The Ray Bradbury Theatre* (also known as *Ray Bradbury Theatre III*), syndicated, 1988.
Himself, "The Cliffhanger," *Maniac Mansion,* syndicated, 1991.
Doc Ellis, "Freddie Had a Little Lamb," *Maniac Mansion,* syndicated, 1993.
Rudy Blaine, "King of the Great White Way," *Road to Avonlea,* 1996.
Voice of Dr. Craig Ehrlich, "They Craved Duckman's Brain!," *Duckman* (animated), 1996.
Voice of Dr. Craig Ehrlich, "Bev Takes a Holiday," *Duckman* (animated), 1997.
Voice of bus driver, *Nightmare Ned,* ABC, 1997.
"Gilda Radner," *E! True Hollywood Story,* E! Entertainment Television, 1997.
Dr. Rider, "The Engagement," *The Drew Carey Show,* ABC, 1998.
Doctor, "Nat and Arley," *Mad about You,* NBC, 1998.
Voice of King Midas, "Hercules and the Golden Touch," *Disney's Hercules* (animated), ABC and syndicated, 1998.
"Filmen 'American Pie'/Nyheter och vader," *Nyhetsmorgon,* 1999.
Showbiz Today, 2000.
Voice of Comp–u–Comp guard, "The Return," *Dilbert,* UPN, 2000.
Dr. Barry Wasserman, "The Unkindest Cut," *Off Centre,* The WB, 2002.
Dr. Barry Wasserman, "P.P. Doc II: The Examination Continues," *Off Centre,* The WB, 2002.
"The Making of Ivan Reitman," *Life and Times,* 2002.
"American Pie," *VH-1 Behind the Movie,* VH1, 2002.
"Bringing Down the House," *Reel Comedy,* Comedy Central, 2003.
CBS News Sunday Morning, CBS, 2003.
Bobby Bittman, *Just for Laughs* (also known as *Ed Byrne's "Just for Laughs," Just for Laughs Comedy Festival,* and *Just for Laughs Montreal Comedy Festival*), CBC, 2003.
Fox News, Fox News, 2004.
Channel 4 News, Channel 4, 2004.
"Eugene Levy," *Distinguished Artists,* 2004.
Dr. Vaughn, a professor of physics, "Super Bowl XXXIX Pregame Show," *Fox NFL Sunday,* Fox, 2005.

Getaway, Nine Network, 2005 and 2006.
MTV News, MTV, 2006.
Film '72, BBC, 2007.
Made in Hollywood, 2009.

Also appeared as Kirk, *The David Steinberg Show.*

Television Talk Show Guest Appearances; Episodic:
Late Night with David Letterman, NBC, 1985, 1986.
The Martin Short Show, 1999.
The Daily Show (also known as *A Daily Show with Jon Stewart, The Daily Show with Jon Stewart,* and *The Daily Show with Jon Stewart Global Edition*), 2000.
Late Night with Conan O'Brien, NBC, 2000, 2003, and 2005.
Primetime Glick, 2001.
Late Show with David Letterman, CBS, 2001, 2003, 2009.
The Rosie O'Donnell Show, 2002.
The Tonight Show with Jay Leno, NBC, 2002.
Jimmy Kimmel Live!, ABC, 2003.
The View, ABC, 2003.
Richard & Judy, Channel 4, 2004.
The Terry and Gaby Show, Channel 5, 2004.
Live with Regis and Kelly, syndicated, 2005, 2009.

Television Appearances; Movies:
The Canadian Conspiracy, 1985.
Tom Lynch, "Bride of Boogedy," *The Disney Sunday Movie,* ABC, 1987.
Bobby Bittman, *Biographies: The Enigma of Bobby Bittman,* 1988.
Voice of studio head, *I, Martin Short, Goes Hollywood,* 1989.
David Grodin, *Partners 'n Love,* syndicated, 1992.
President McCloskey, *Kurt Vonnegut's "Harrison Bergeron"* (also known as *Harrison Bergeron*), 1995.
Larry Palmer, *Dogmatic,* ABC, 1996.
Bellerman Arthur, *The Journey of Allen Strange: Alien Vacation,* Nickelodeon, 1999.
Mr. White, "The Heidi Bowl," *The Sports Pages,* HBO, 2001.
Philly Green, *Club Land,* Showtime, 2001.
Voice of the father, *The Kid* (also known as *Gahan Wilson's "The Kid"*), Showtime, 2001.

Television Appearances; Pilots:
Bobby Bittman, Fred Wexelblatt, and other roles, *The Lovebirds,* CBS, 1979.
From Cleveland, CBS, 1980.
Bobby Bittman, "Autobiographies: The Enigma of Bobby Bittman" (also known as "Biographies: The Enigma of Bobby Bittman"), *Cinemax Comedy Experiment,* Cinemax, 1988.
Orfkin, *D.O.A.,* HBO, 1999.

Television Work; Series:
Creator, executive producer, and director, *Maniac Mansion*, syndicated, beginning 1990.

Television Work; Specials:
Executive producer, *The Last Polka*, HBO, 1985.
Producer and director, *Second City's 15th Anniversary Special* (also known as *The Second City Reunion*), Showtime, 1986.
Director, "I, Martin Short, Goes Hollywood," *HBO Comedy Hour*, HBO, 1989.
Director, *The Show Formerly Known As The Martin Short Show*, 1995.

Television Work; Movies:
Director, *Partners 'n Love*, 1992.
Executive producer and director, *Sodbusters*, Showtime, 1994.

Television Work; Pilots:
Executive producer and director, "Autobiographies: The Enigma of Bobby Bittman" (also known as "Biographies: The Enigma of Bobby Bittman"), *Cinemax Comedy Experiment*, Cinemax, 1988.

Television Director; Episodic:
"The Joker Is Me," *The Martin Short Show*, NBC, 1994.
"A Hippo Never Forgets," *The Martin Short Show*, NBC, 1994.
"Who's Afraid of Snowball Fortensky?," *The Martin Short Show*, NBC, 1994.
"The Steve Martin Show," *The Martin Short Show*, NBC, 1994.

Stage Appearances:
Godspell, Toronto, Ontario, 1971.
Mr. Dobitch, *Promises, Promises*, City Center Theatre, New York City, 1997.

Also appeared in Canadian productions of *Love Times Four* and *The Owl and the Pussycat*.

RECORDINGS

Video Games:
Voice, *Creature Crunch*, 1996.
Voice of Albert Einstein Bobbleheads, *Night at the Museum: Battle of the Smithsonian*, Majesco Entertainment, 2009.

Videos:
Good Times with Cast and Crew of "American Pie 2," 2002.
Making a "Splash," Buena Vista, 2004.

Meet the Cast of "Over the Hedge," Blue Collar Prod., 2006.

Albums:
Performed (with Northern Lights) "Tears Are Not Enough" on the album *We Are the World*.

WRITINGS

Screenplays:
(With Christopher Guest) *Waiting for Guffman*, Sony Pictures Classics, 1996.
(With Guest; and composer of the songs "God Loves a Terrier" and "Terrier Style") *Best in Show* (also known as *Dog Show!*), Warner Bros., 2000.
A Mighty Wind, Warner Bros., 2003.
For Your Consideration, 2006.

Soundtracks:
For Your Consideration, 2006.

Film Songs:
"God Loves a Terrier," "Terrier Style," *Best in Show* (also known as *Dog Show!*), 2000.
"When You're Next to Me," "One More Time," "A Mighty Wind," *A Mighty Wind*, 2003.
"The Purim Song," "You Were Never There for Me," *For Your Consideration*, 2006.

Television Series:
Second City TV (also known as *SCTV*), syndicated, 1977–81.
SCTV Network 90 (also known as *SCTV Comedy Network* and *SCTV Network*), NBC, 1981–83.
SCTV Channel, NBC, 1983.

Television Pilots:
(With others) *From Cleveland*, CBS, 1980.
"Autobiographies: The Enigma of Bobby Bittman" (also known as "Biographies: The Enigma of Bobby Bittman"), *Cinemax Comedy Experiment*, Cinemax, 1988.
D.O.A., HBO, 1999.

Television Specials:
The Last Polka, HBO, 1985.
The Best of SCTV, 1988.

Television Movies:
Biographies: The Enigma of Bobby Bittman, 1988.
(Including the song "The Sodbusters Song") *Sodbusters*, 1994.
D.O.A., 1999.

OTHER SOURCES

Periodicals:
Current Biography, January, 2002, pp. 77–80.
Entertainment Weekly, July 19, 1996, p. 58.
Maclean's, March 19, 2001, p. 47.
Newsweek, February 10, 1997, p. 66.
People Weekly, July 22, 1996, p. 19; September 22, 1997, p. 21.

LIOTTA, Ray 1955(?)–

PERSONAL

Surname is pronounced "Lee–oh–ta"; born December 18, 1955 (some sources cite 1954), in Newark, NJ; adopted son of Alfred (an auto parts store owner, politician, and personnel director) and Mary Liotta; married Michelle Grace (a model and producer), February 15, 1997 (divorced, 2004); children: Karsen (daughter). *Education:* University of Miami, Coral Gables, FL, B.F.A., 1978; studied acting with Harry Mastrogeorge.

Addresses: *Office*—Tiara Blu Films, 215 East 68th St., New York, NY 10021. *Agent*—Endeavor Talent Agency, 9701 Wilshire Blvd., 10th Floor, Beverly Hills, CA 90212. *Manager*—Management 360, 9111 Wilshire Blvd., Beverly Hills, CA 90210.

Career: Actor and producer. Tiara Blu Films, New York City, partner. Appeared in commercials. Also worked as a bartender at theatres and as a groundskeeper at a cemetery.

Member: Screen Actors Guild, American Federation of Television and Radio Artists.

Awards, Honors: Boston Society of Film Critics Award and Golden Globe Award nomination, best supporting actor, both 1987, for *Something Wild;* named male star of tomorrow, Motion Picture Bookers Club, 1989; MTV Movie Award nomination, best villain, 1993, for *Unlawful Entry;* Screen Actors Guild Award nomination, outstanding performance by a male actor in a television movie or miniseries, 1999, for *The Rat Pack;* Independent Spirit Award nomination, best supporting actor, Independent Features Project/West, Phoenix Film Critics Society Award nomination, best actor in a supporting role, 2003, for *Narc;* Glow Award, best voice performance—male, G–Phoria Awards, 2003, for *Grand Theft Auto: Vice City;* Emmy Award, outstanding guest actor in a drama series, Prism Award, performance in a drama series episode, 2005, for *ER.*

CREDITS

Film Appearances:
(Film debut) Joe Heron, *The Lonely Lady,* Universal, 1983.
Ray Sinclair, *Something Wild,* Orion, 1986.
The Artist, *Arena Brains,* 1987.
Eugene "Gino" Luciano, *Dominick and Eugene* (also known as *Nicky and Gino*), Orion, 1988.
Shoeless Joe Jackson, *Field of Dreams,* Universal, 1989.
Henry Hill, *Goodfellas,* Warner Bros., 1990.
Officer Pete Davis, *Unlawful Entry,* Twentieth Century–Fox, 1992.
Dr. Richard Sturgess, *Article 99,* Orion, 1992.
Robbins, *No Escape* (also known as *Escape from Absolom*), Savoy, 1994.
Manny Singer, *Corrina, Corrina,* New Line Cinema, 1994.
Captain T. C. Doyle, *Operation Dumbo Drop* (also known as *Dumbo Drop*), Buena Vista, 1995.
Dr. David Krane, *Unforgettable,* Metro–Goldwyn–Mayer, 1996.
Ryan Weaver, *Turbulence,* Metro–Goldwyn–Mayer, 1997.
Gary "Figgsy" Figgis, *Cop Land,* Buena Vista, 1997.
Harry Collins, *Phoenix,* 1998.
Mark Brice, *Forever Mine,* 1999.
First guardian of the gate, *Muppets from Space,* 1999.
Nathan Neubauer, *A Rumor of Angels,* Metro–Goldwyn–Mayer/United Artists, 2000, Cinetel Films, 2002.
Jack, *Pilgrim* (also known as *Inferno*), 2000.
Paul Krendler, *Hannibal,* Metro–Goldwyn–Mayer, 2001.
Dean Cumanno and Vinny Staggliano, *Heartbreakers,* Metro–Goldwyn–Mayer, 2001.
Fred Jung, *Blow,* New Line Cinema, 2001.
Detective Lieutenant Henry R. Oak, *Narc,* Paramount, 2002.
Chief Monroe, *John Q,* New Line Cinema, 2002.
FBI agent, *The Hire: Ticker,* BMW Films, 2002.
Detective Rhodes, *Identity,* Columbia, 2003.
Ray Liotta, *Boyz Up Unauthorized,* 2003.
Jack Devine, *The Last Shot,* Buena Vista, 2004.
Lee Ray Oliver, *Control,* Lions Gate Films, 2004.
Dorothy Macha, *Revolver,* Lions Gate Films, 2005.
Ford Cole, *Slow Burn,* Lions Gate Films, 2005.
Tom Carver, *Even Money,* New City, 2006.
John Talia Sr., *Local Color,* Monterey Media, 2006.
Walter Pearce, *Comeback Season,* First Look, 2006.
Donald Carruthers, *Smokin' Aces,* Universal, 2006.
Gallian, *In the Name of the King: A Dungeon Siege Tale,* Twentieth Century–Fox, 2007.
Jack, *Wild Hogs* (also known as *Blackberry*), Buena Vista, 2007.
Voice of Ray Liotta, *Bee Movie* (animated), Paramount, 2007.
Mayor Jim Tobin, *Battle in Seattle,* RCV, 2007.
Detective Terry Subcott, *Hero Wanted,* Sony, 2008.

Adult Mickey, *Chasing 3000,* Maya Entertainment, 2008.
The Grand, Anchor Bay Entertainment, 2008.
Jack Doheny, *Powder Blue,* Image, 2009.
Mark Shields, *La linea* (also known as *The Line, La Linea (The Line),* and *La Linea—The Line),* Eagle Films, 2009.
Cole Frankel, *Crossing Over,* Manga, 2009.
Detective Harrison, *Observe and Report,* Warner Bros., 2009.
Lance Wescott, *Youth in Revolt,* Dimension Films, 2009.
Gray, *Crazy on the Outside,* Freestyle Releasing, 2010.
Reggie Kirkfield, *Snowmen,* Italia Film, 2010.
Peter, *The Details,* Liddell Entertainment, 2010.
Jim, *Ticket Out,* Minds Eye Entertainment, 2010.
Donald Carruthers, *Behind the Scenes with Joe Carnahan,* Universal Studios, 2010.

Also appeared as Tommy, *Only in New York.*

Film Work:
Coproducer, *Phoenix,* 1998.
Producer, *Narc,* Paramount, 2002.
Co–executive producer, *Slow Burner,* 2005.
Executive producer, *Take the Lead,* New Line Cinema, 2006.
Executive producer, *La linea* (also known as *The Line, La Linea (The Line),* and *La Linea–The Line),* Eagle Films, 2009.

Television Appearances; Series:
Joey Perrini, *Another World* (also known as *Another World: Bay City),* NBC, 1978–81.
Sacha, *Casablanca,* NBC, 1983.
Officer Ed Santini, *Our Family Honor,* NBC, 1985–86.
Late Night with Conan O'Brien, NBC, 1998–2008.
Inside the Mafia, National Geographic Channel, 2005.
Bobby Stevens, *Smith,* CBS, 2006–2007.

Television Appearances; Movies:
Family member, *Hardhat and Legs,* CBS, 1980.
Johnny "Wizard" Lazarra, *Crazy Times,* ABC, 1981.
Women and Women: Stories of Seduction, 1990.
Martin Meadows, "A Domestic Dilemma," *Women and Men II* (also known as *Women and Men: In Love There Are No Rules),* HBO, 1991.
Frank Sinatra, *The Rat Pack,* HBO, 1998.
Harry Collins, *Phoenix,* HBO, 1998.
Mark Brice, *Forever Mine,* Starz!, 1999.
Jack, *Pilgrim* (also known as *Inferno),* Cinemax, 1999.
John Orr, *Point of Origin,* HBO, 2002.
Walter Pearce, *Comeback Season,* Lifetime, 2007.

Television Appearances; Episodic:
Murray, "Rain," *St. Elsewhere,* 1983.

Tony Cable, "Kill Devil," *Mickey Spillane's Mike Hammer,* CBS, 1985.
"Wetten, dass ...? aus Hannover," *Wetten, dass..?,* 1994.
Late Show with David Letterman (also known as *Letterman* and *The Late Show),* CBS, 1995, 1997 and 2006.
Voice of Bob, "Frasier Grinch," *Frasier,* NBC, 1995.
American Cinema, PBS, 1995.
The Rosie O'Donnell Show, syndicated, 1997, 2001, and 2002.
"The Films of Martin Scorsese," *The Directors,* 2000.
The Howard Stern Radio Show, 2001.
"Narc," *Anatomy of a Scene,* 2001.
Voice, "Brian Does Hollywood," *Family Guy,* Fox, 2001.
"Christmas? Christmas!," *Just Shoot Me,* NBC, 2001.
"Liotta? Liotta!," *Just Shoot Me,* NBC, 2002.
This Week in Baseball, 2002.
Listen Up! Charles Barkley with Ernie Johnson (also known as *Listen Up!),* 2002.
The Daily Show (also known as *A Daily Show with Jon Stewart, The Daily Show with Jon Stewart,* and *The Daily Show with Jon Stewart Global Edition),* Comedy Central, 2003.
Richard & Judy, Channel 4, 2003.
Jimmy Kimmel Live, ABC, 2003 and 2007.
Punk'd, MTV, 2003.
V Graham Norton, Channel 4, 2003.
The View, 2003.
Guest host, *Saturday Night Live* (also known as *SNL),* NBC, 2003.
Corazon de ..., 2005.
Charlie Metcalf, "300 Patients," *ER,* NBC, 2007.
"Wetten, dass ...? aus Freiburg," *Wetten, dass ...?,* 2007.
Deadline, 2007.
Entertainment Tonight (also known as *E.T.* and *This Week in Entertainment),* syndicated, 2007.
Xpose, TV3, 2007.
"Wild Hogs & Shooter," *Planet Voice,* 2007.
"WhoBob WhatPants?," *SpongeBob SquarePants* (animated; also known as *SpongeBob),* Nickelodeon, 2008.
Charlie Metcalf, "Previously on ER," *ER,* NBC, 2009.
Late Night with Jimmy Fallon, NBC, 2009.
The Morning Show with Mike & Juliet, Fox, syndicated, 2009.
"Observe and Report," *HBO First Look,* HBO, 2009.
Up Close with Carrie Keagan, 2009.

Television Appearances; Specials:
Masters of Illusion: The Wizards of Special Effects, 1994.
Gary "Figgsy" Figgis, *Venice Report,* 1997.
A Home for the Holidays, CBS, 1999.
Narrator, *High Stakes: Bet Your Life on Las Vegas,* The Learning Channel, 2001.
Back in the U.S., ABC, 2002.
G–Phoria, G4, 2003.
Precinct Hollywood, 2005.

Revolver: Movie Premiere Special, ITV, 2005.
AFI's 10 Top 10: America's 10 Greatest Films in 10 Classic Genres, 2008.
Oscar, que empiece el espectacula, 2008.

Television Appearances; Pilots:
Johnny "Wizard" Lazarra, *Crazy Times,* ABC, 1981.

Television Appearances; Miniseries:
Bravo Profiles: The Entertainment Business, 1998.

Television Appearances; Awards Presentations:
Henry Hill, *The 63rd Annual Academy Awards,* 1991.
Presenter, *GQ's 2000 Men of the Year Awards,* Fox, 2000.
Presenter, *The 60th Annual Golden Globe Awards,* NBC, 2003.
Spike TV VGA Video Game Awards, Spike TV, 2003.
9th Annual Prism Awards, 2005.
The 58th Annual Primetime Emmy Awards, 2006.
13th Annual Critics' Choice Awards, VH1, 2008.

Television Producer; Movies:
(With others) *Phoenix,* HBO, 1998.

Stage Appearances:
Mike, *Match,* Plymouth Theatre, New York City, 2004.

RECORDINGS

Videos:
The Directors: Martin Scorsese (also known as *AFI's the Directors: Martin Scorsese*), Media Home Entertainment, 2000.
Breaking the Silence: The Making of "Hannibal," 2001.
Behind the Scenes of "John Q," New Line Home Video, 2002.
Narc: Shooting Up, Paramount Home Video, 2003.
Narc: Making the Deal, Paramount Home Video, 2003.
Field of Dreams: Passing Along the Pastime, Universal, 2004.
Getting Made: The Making of "GoodFellas" (also known as *Getting Made*), Warner Home Video, 2004.

Video Games:
Voice of Tommy Vercetti, *Grand Theft Auto: Vice City,* Rockstar Games/Take 2 Interactive, 2002.

OTHER SOURCES

Periodicals:
Cable TV, August, 1998, pp. 22–23.
Empire, August, 1997, pp. 66–67.
Entertainment Weekly, November 22, 1996, p. 16.

Movieline, August, 1998, pp. 70–71; December, 2002, pp. 76–79.
Parade, March 31, 1996.
People Weekly, January 27, 1997, p. 122; March 10, 1997, p. 39.
Premiere, October, 1990, p. 58.
Starlog, June, 1994.
Video Business, March 23, 1998, p. 21.
Washington Post, January 12, 2003, p. G1.

LOOK, Lydia

PERSONAL

Married Jen Sung Outerbridge (an actor), August, 2005.

Career: Actress and stunt performer.

Member: Writers Guild of America, Screen Actors Guild, Actors Equity Association, American Federation of Television and Radio Artists.

CREDITS

Film Appearances:
Mei, *Deadly Target,* 1994.
Foo Chow waitress, *Rush Hour,* New Line Cinema, 1998.
Psych ward receptionist, *Bark!,* First Look International, 2002.
Girl raver, *Avatar* (also known as *Cyber Wars* and *Matrix Hunter*), 2004.
Lu Wan Chang, *Tremors 4: The Legend Begins,* 2004.
Herself, *You're on the Set of "Tremors 4: The Legend Begins,"* 2004.
Voice actor, *4: Rise of the Silver Surfer* (also known as *Fantastic Four: Rise of the Silver Surfer* and *Fantastic Four: Galaxy Crisis*), 2007.
Ms. Okata, *Bed & Breakfast,* 2010.
Ms. Okata, *Terror Trap,* 2010.

Film Stunts:
The Fast and the Furious: Tokyo Drift (also known as *Fast and Furious 3: Tokyo Drift* and *Wild Speed X3: Tokyo Drift*), 2006.

Television Appearances; Series:
Voice of the Chang triplets, *The Proud Family* (animated), The Disney Channel, 2001–2004.

Television Appearances; Episodic:
Leigh Woo, "Fools Night Out," *Ally McBeal* (also known as *Ally My Love*), Fox, 1998.

Jili Lee, "November Heat," *Ryan Caufield: Year One,* Fox, 1999.

Emily Fong, "Sticks and Stones," *ER,* NBC, 1999.

Laurie Chang, "Black Dragons," *Walker, Texas Ranger,* CBS, 2000.

Madam, "Empty the Dragon," *Son of the Beach,* FX Network, 2002.

Tracy Pok, "Riceburner," *The Shield,* FX Network, 2004.

Mercedes, "Check Please," *Jake in Progress,* ABC, 2005.

Heather Hundin, "Bitches," *Pushing Daisies,* ABC, 2007.

Yurika, "Why not to Cheat on Your Best Friend," *Emily's Reasons Why Not,* ABC, 2008.

Theresa Ming, "The Passenger in the Oven," *Bones,* Fox, 2008.

Stage Appearances:

Amelia, *The House of Bernarda Alba,* Mark Taper Forum, Los Angeles, 2002.

RECORDINGS

Video Games:

Voice of female Chinese solider, *The Mummy: Tomb of the Dragon Emperor,* 2008.

Commander Naomi Shirada, *Command & Conquer: Red Alert 3,* 2008.

WRITINGS

Television Movies:

Wendy Wu: Homecoming Warrior (also known as *Kang-fu Princess: Wendy Wu*), The Disney Channel, 2006.

Television Episodes:

"Love Kills," *The Sentinel,* UPN, 1998.

The Proud Family (animated), The Disney Channel, 2001.

LOVITZ, Jon 1957–

PERSONAL

Full name, Jonathan M. Lovitz; born July 21, 1957, in Tarzana, CA; father, a doctor. *Education:* University of California, Irvine, B.A., 1979; studied acting with Tony Barr at Film Actors Workshop, and at Groundlings (comedy improvisation studio), Los Angeles, 1982.

Addresses: Agent—Adam Venit, Endeavor Talent Agency, 9701 Wilshire Blvd., 10th Floor, Beverly Hills, CA 90212; (personal appearances) Jackie Miller, Agency for the Performing Arts, 9200 Sunset Blvd., Suite 900, Los Angeles, CA 90069. *Manager*—Marc Gurvitz, Brillstein–Grey Entertainment, 9150 Wilshire Blvd., Suite 350, Beverly Hills, CA 90212. *Publicist*—Jonas Public Relations, 240 26th St., Suite 3, Santa Monica, CA 90402.

Career: Actor, comedian, producer, and writer. Groundlings, Los Angeles, performed with Sunday company, 1983, then with main company. Appeared in television commercials for the Yellow Pages; voice of the red candy for M&Ms chocolates commercials; voice of penguin for Bud Ice beer commercials. Previously worked as an orderly in a hospital, a waiter, a sales clerk, and a messenger.

Awards, Honors: Emmy Award nominations, individual performance in a variety or music program, 1986 and 1987, for *Saturday Night Live;* National Board of Review Award (with others), best acting by an ensemble, 1998, for Happiness.

CREDITS

Film Appearances:

(Film debut) Bartender, *The Last Resort* (also known as *She Knew No Other Way*), Concorde/Cinema Group/Trinity, 1986.

Security guard, *Hamburger ... the Motion Picture* (also known as *Hamburger U.*), 1986.

Doug, *Jumpin' Jack Flash,* Twentieth Century–Fox, 1986.

Morty, *Three Amigos!,* Orion, 1986.

Party guest, *Ratboy,* Warner Bros., 1986.

Voice of the radio, *The Brave Little Toaster* (animated), Hyperion/Kushner–Locke, 1987.

Scotty Brennen, *Big,* Twentieth Century–Fox, 1988.

Ron Mills, *My Stepmother Is an Alien,* Weintraub Entertainment Group, 1988.

Right brain, *Cranium Command,* 1989.

Clip Metzler, *Mr. Destiny,* Buena Vista, 1990.

Voice of T. R. Chula, *An American Tail: Fievel Goes West* (animated), Universal, 1991.

Various characters, *Saturday Night Live: The Best of Robin Williams,* 1991.

Various characters, *Best of Saturday Night Live: Special Edition,* 1992.

Emperor Tod Spengo, *Mom and Dad Save the World,* Warner Bros., 1992.

Ernie Capadino, *A League of Their Own,* Columbia, 1992.

The Buzz, 1992.

Becker, *National Lampoon's Loaded Weapon I* (also known as *Loaded Weapon I*), New Line Cinema, 1993.

Dr. Rudolph, *Coneheads,* Paramount, 1993.

Glen Robbins, *City Slickers II: The Legend of Curly's Gold* (also known as *City Slickers: The Legend of Curly's Gold* and *City Slickers II*), Columbia, 1994.

Dave Firpo, *Trapped in Paradise,* Twentieth Century–Fox, 1994.

Arthur Belt, *North,* New Line Cinema, 1994.

Sol, *The Great White Hype,* Twentieth Century–Fox, 1996.

Million Dollar Sticky Host, *Matilda* (also known as *Roald Dahl's "Matilda"*), 1996.

Richard Clark, *High School High,* Columbia/TriStar, 1996.

For Goodness Sake II, 1996.

Andy Kornbluth, *Happiness,* Good Machine, 1998.

Jimmie Moore, *The Wedding Singer,* New Line Cinema, 1998.

Uncle Harry Epstein, *Lost & Found,* Warner Bros., 1999.

Hanukkah Harry/Mr. Potter/master thespian, *Saturday Night Live Christmas,* 1999.

Benny Borkowshi, *Small Time Crooks,* DreamWorks, 2000.

Peeper, *Little Nicky,* New Line Cinema, 2000.

Kirby, *Sand* (also known as *Sandstorm*), Showcase Entertainment, 2000.

Jay Peterson, *3000 Miles to Graceland,* Warner Bros., 2001.

Voice of Calico, *Cats & Dogs,* Warner Bros., 2001.

Randall "Randy" Pear, *Rat Race,* Paramount, 2001.

Barry Sherman, *Good Advice,* 2001.

Voice of Tom Baltezor, *Eight Crazy Nights* (also known as *Adam Sandler's "8 Crazy Nights"*), Columbia TriStar, 2002.

Sidney, *Dickie Roberts: Former Child Star,* Paramount, 2003.

Dave Markowitz, *The Stepford Wives,* Paramount, 2004.

Voice of Bailey, *Bailey's Billion$,* Echo Bridge, 2005.

Pancho's Pizza, Out of theWoods, 2005.

Mr. Marks, *The Producers,* Columbia, 2005.

Mel, *The Benchwarmers,* 2006.

Bart Bookman, *Southland Tales,* United International, 2006.

Voice of My Eyes Up Here Penguin, *Farce of the Penguins,* Lions Gate Films, 2006.

Heckler, Stardust, 2007.

Nathn, *I Could Never Be Your Woman,* Eagle Films, 2007.

Hilary! Uncensored: Banned by the Media, Equal Justice Foundation of America, 2008.

Secrets of Life, Karim Movies, 2009.

Adam Kidan, *Casino Jack,* Eagle Films, 2010.

Also appeared as Paul DeCrosta, *Hitting the Wall.*

Television Appearances; Series:

Mole, a recurring role, *Foley Square,* CBS, 1985–86.

Cast member, *Saturday Night Live* (also known as *SNL*), NBC, 1985–90.

Voice of Jay Prescott Sherman, *The Critic* (animated), ABC, 1993–94, Fox, 1994–95.

Max Louis, *NewsRadio* (also known as *The Station*), NBC, 1998–99.

Voice of Jay Prescott Sherman, *The Critic* (animated), 2000.

Television Appearances; Episodic:

(Television debut) Law student, *The Paper Chase,* CBS, 1984.

Dolly's date, *Dolly,* ABC, 1987.

Barry Blye, "Top Billing," *Tales from the Crypt,* HBO, 1991.

Voices of Artie Ziff and Mr. Seckofsky, "The Way We Was," *The Simpsons* (animated), Fox, 1991.

Voice of Professor Dean Lombardo, "Brush with Greatness," *The Simpsons* (animated), Fox, 1991.

Voice of Aristotle Amadopoulis, "Homer Defined," *The Simpsons* (animated), Fox, 1991.

Jeff Littlehead, "Kelly Does Hollywood, Part 2," *Married ... with Children,* Fox, 1991.

Saturday Night Live (also known as *SNL*), NBC, multiple appearances, beginning 1991.

Himself, "The Spider Episode," *The Larry Sanders Show,* HBO, 1992.

Voice of Llewellyn Sinclair, "A Streetcar Named Marge," *The Simpsons* (animated), Fox, 1992.

Showbiz Today, 1992, 1995.

Ernie "Cappy" Capadino, "Dottie's Back," *A League of Their Own,* CBS, 1993.

Himself, "Larry Loses a Friend," *The Larry Sanders Show,* HBO, 1994.

Voice of Artie Ziff, "Another Simpsons Clip Show," *The Simpsons,* Fox, 1994.

Gary Fogel, "The Scofflaw," *Seinfeld,* NBC, 1995.

Voice of Jay Sherman, "Hurricane Neddy," *The Simpsons* (animated), Fox, 1995.

Steve, "The One with the Stoned Guy," *Friends,* NBC, 1995.

Voice of Jay Sherman, "A Star Is Burns," *The Simpsons* (animated), Fox, 1996.

The Rodman World Tour (also known as *Dennis Rodman's World Tour*), 1996.

Acer Predburn, "The Scoop," *The Naked Truth,* ABC, 1997.

Fred, "Our Fiftieth Episode," *NewsRadio,* NBC, 1997.

Mike Johnson, "Jumper," *NewsRadio,* NBC, 1997.

"Liars, Windbags, and Blowhards," *Turn Ben Stein On,* Comedy Central, 1999.

Who Wants to Be a Millionaire, ABC, 2000, 2002.

"Polterguest," *Bette!,* CBS, 2001.

Voice of Artie Ziff, "Half–Decent Proposal," *The Simpsons* (animated), Fox, 2002.

Father of B. J.'s baby, "Bad News, Mr. Johnson," *Son of the Beach,* USA Network, 2002.

Primetime Glick, 2002.

Steve, "The One with the Blind Dates," *Friends*, NBC, 2003.

"Penny Marshall," *Intimate Portrait*, Lifetime, 2003.

Roland Devereaux, "A Simple Kiss of Fate," *Just Shoot Me!*, 2003.

Voice of Cheapo, "Crime Doesn't Pay ... Seriously, It Doesn't," *Stripperella* (also known as Stan Lee's "Stripperella"), Spike TV, 2003.

Voice of Cheapo, "Cheapo by the Dozen," *Stripperella* (also known as Stan Lee's "Stripperella"), Spike TV, 2004.

Fred Puterbaugh, "Things That Go Jump in the Night," *Las Vegas*, 2004.

Fred Puterbaugh, "The Count of Montecito," *Las Vegas*, 2004.

Dave Markowitz, "Bette Midler," *Biography*, Arts and Entertainment, 2004.

The Best Damn Sports Show Period, Fox Sports, 2004.

Voice of Artie Ziff/Jay Sherman, "The Ziff Who Came to Dinner," *The Simpsons* (animated), Fox, 2004.

Unscripted, 2005.

Fred Puterbaugh, "Magic Carpet Fred," *Las Vegas*, 2005.

"Southern California," *Open Access*, The Tennis Channel, 2005.

"Charity Season," *Open Access*, The Tennis Channel, 2006.

"Jon Lovitz," *Sit Down Comedy with David Steinberg*, 2006.

"Heavy Petting," *The Girls Next Door*, E! Entertainment Television, 2006.

Comics Unleashed, 2006.

Archie Baldwin, "The Unfortunate Little Schnauzer," *Two and A Half Men*, 2006.

Voice of Enrico Irritazio, "Homerazzi," *The Simpsons* (animated), Fox, 2007.

Last Comic Standing (also known as *Last Comic Standing: The Search for the Funniest Person in America*), 2008.

Entertainment Tonight (also known as *E.T.* and *This Week in Entertainment*), syndicated, 2009.

The Bachelor (also known as *The Bachelor: London Calling* and *The Bachelor: On The Wings of Love*), ABC, 2010.

WWF Raw is War (also known as *Raw Is War*, WWE Monday Night RAW, *WWE Raw*, and *WWF Raw*), 2010.

Appeared as guest host, *Talk Soup*, E! Entertainment Television; as voice of Jay Sherman for *Cartoon All Stars to the Rescue: Stop Digimon!*; voice for "King of the Hill," and an episode of *Toon Survivor: Hawaii*.

Television Talk Show Guest Appearances; Episodic:

Late Night with David Letterman, NBC, multiple episodes, 1988–93.

Late Show with David Letterman, CBS, multiple episodes, beginning 1993.

The Rosie O'Donnell Show, syndicated, 1996, 2001.

Dennis Miller Live, multiple episodes, beginning 1997.

Late Night with Conan O'Brien, NBC, 1997, 1998, 1999, 2003, and 2006.

Howard Stern, 1998.

The Roseanne Show, 1998.

The Martin Short Show, 1999.

Last Call with Carson Daly, NBC, 2006.

The Tonight Show with Jay Leno, NBC, 2006.

The Tonight Show with Conan O'Brien, NBC, 2009.

Television Appearances; Specials:

Injun Larry, "I'll Do It Guy's Way," *Cinemax Comedy Experiment*, Cinemax, 1987.

Comic Relief, HBO, 1987.

Comic Relief II, HBO, 1987.

Host, *Coca-Cola Presents Live: The Hard Rock* (also known as *Live: The Hard Rock*), NBC, 1988.

Saturday Night Live 15th Anniversary, NBC, 1989.

Voices That Care, Fox, 1991.

Saturday Night Live Goes Commercial, NBC, 1991.

The Please Watch the Jon Lovitz Special (also known as *The Jon Lovitz Show* and *Please Watch the Jon Lovitz Show*), Fox, 1992.

Governor Michael Dukakis, *Saturday Night Live: Presidential Bash*, NBC, 1992.

Comic Relief: Baseball Relief '93, 1993.

The Second Annual Comedy Hall of Fame, NBC, 1994.

1995 Young Comedians Special, 1995.

Canned Ham: High School High, Comedy Central, 1996.

Catch a Rising Star 50th Anniversary—Give or Take 26 Years, CBS, 1996.

Comic Relief's 10th Anniversary, HBO, 1996.

I Am Your Child, ABC, 1997.

Ira Gershwin at 100: A Celebration at Carnegie Hall, PBS, 1997.

To Life! America Celebrates Israel's 50th, CBS, 1998.

Saturday Night Live: The Best of Phil Hartman, NBC, 1998.

Saturday Night Live: The Best of Steve Martin, 1998.

Host, *Billboard 40 Top Forty Singles (1959–1998)*, VH1, 1999.

The 27th American Film Institute Life Achievement Award: A Salute to Dustin Hoffman (also known as *The American Film Institute Salute to Dustin Hoffman*), ABC, 1999.

Michael Dukakis and other characters, *Saturday Night Live: The Best of Dana Carvey*, NBC, 1999.

Opera man's brother, *Saturday Night Live: The Best of Adam Sandler*, NBC, 1999.

Saturday Night Live: 25th Anniversary (also known as *Saturday Night Live: 25th Anniversary Primetime Special*), NBC, 1999.

The Rock to Erase MS Concert, VH1, 1999.

NFL All-Star Comedy Blitz, CBS, 1999.

(In archive footage) Michael Dukakis and Caspar Weinberger, *Saturday Night Live: Presidential Bash 2000*, NBC, 2000.

One Night with Robbie Williams, BBC, 2001.

AFI Life Achievement Award: A Tribute to Tom Hanks, USA Network, 2002.

Presenter, *Hollywood Salutes Nicolas Cage: An American Cinematheque Tribute,* TNT, 2002.

Playboy: Inside the Playboy Mansion, 2002.

Brilliant But Cancelled: Pilot Season, Trio Network, 2003.

When Stand–Up Comics Ruled the World, VH1, 2004.

Michael Dukakis, *Saturday Night Live: Presidential Bash 2004,* NBC, 2004.

101 Most Unforgettable SNL Moments, NBC, 2004.

Saturday Night Live: The Best of Tom Hanks, NBC, 2004.

Music Cares Person of the Year: Brian Wilson, 2005.

Steve Martin: An American Cinemateque Tribute, 2005.

Saturday Night Live in the '80s: Lost & Found, NBC, 2005.

Reel Comedy: The Benchwarmers, Comedy Central, 2005.

Presenter, *Billy Crystal: The Mark Twain Prize,* PBS, 2007.

Comedy Central Roast of Bob Saget, Comedy Central, 2008.

Godfrey Live, 2008.

Michael Dukakis, *Saturday Night Live Presidential Bash '08,* NBC, 2008.

SNL Presents: A Very Gilly Christmas, NBC, 2009.

Comedy Central Roast of Joan Rivers, Comedy Central, 2009.

Television Appearances; Awards Presentations:

The ... Annual American Comedy Awards, ABC, 1988, 1991, 1992.

Jason Voorhees, *1992 MTV Movie Awards,* MTV, 1992.

Presenter, *1993 MTV Movie Awards,* MTV, 1993.

Presenter, *The 65th Annual Academy Awards,* ABC, 1993.

Presenter, *VH1 Honors,* VH1, 1994.

Presenter, *1994 MTV Video Music Awards,* MTV, 1994.

Presenter, *1994 Billboard Music Awards,* Fox, 1994.

Host, *The 1995 MTV Movie Awards,* MTV, 1995.

The Blockbuster Entertainment Awards, UPN, 1996.

Presenter, *The 50th Emmy Awards,* NBC, 1998.

The 51st Annual Primetime Emmy Awards, 1999.

The 10th Annual Critics' Choice Awards, The WB, 2004.

24th Annual Genesis Awards, 2010.

Television Appearances; Movies:

Barry Sherman, *Good Advice,* HBO, 2001.

Television Appearances; Miniseries:

Heroes of Jewish Comedy, Comedy Central, 2003.

Television Appearances; Pilots:

Leave Me Alone, NBC, 2002.

Television Work; Specials:

Creator and executive producer, *The Please Watch the Jon Lovitz Special* (also known as *The Jon Lovitz Show* and *Please Watch the Jon Lovitz Show*), Fox, 1992.

Television Work; Series:

Additional voices, *The Critic* (animated), ABC, 1993–94, Fox, 1994–95.

Stage Appearances:

Chick Hazzard: Olympic Trials, Groundlings Sunday Company, Los Angeles Olympic Art Festival, Los Angeles, 1983.

Very Warm for May, Weill Recital Hall, New York City, 1994.

The Dinner Party, Music Box Theatre, New York City, 2001.

RECORDINGS

Videos:

Back in the Saddle: The Making of ''City Slickers II,'' 1994.

Master thespian, *Saturday Night Live Christmas,* Trimark Video, 1999.

Wild Desk Ride (also known as *Conan O'Brien's ''Wild Desk Ride'*), 2001.

Making "Rat Race," Fireworks Pictures/Paramount, 2001.

Playboy Exposed: Playboy Mansion Parties Uncensored, 2001.

The Stepford Husbands, Paramount Home Video, 2004.

A Perfect World: The Making of ''The Stepford Wives,'' Paramount Home Video, 2004.

Stepford: A Definition, Paramount Home Video, 2004.

The Wallflowers: Rearrange, Interscope Records, 2005.

USIDent TV: Surveilling the Southland, Sony, 2008.

The Best Comics of Unleashed with Byron Allen, Entertainment Studios, 2008.

Appeared in "Voices That Care."

Albums:

(Contributor) Robbie Williams, *Swing When You're Winning,* 2001.

Performed for the single "Voices That Care."

WRITINGS

Television Series:

(With others) *Saturday Night Live* (also known as *SNL*), NBC, 1985–90.

Television Specials:

The Please Watch the Jon Lovitz Special (also known as *The Jon Lovitz Show* and *Please Watch the Jon Lovitz Show*), Fox, 1992.

Saturday Night Live: The Best of Jon Lovitz, NBC, 2005.

OTHER SOURCES

Periodicals:

Entertainment Weekly, February 11, 1994, pp. 26–27; August 17, 2001, pp. 40–42.

Mediaweek, February 17, 1997, p.3; July 13, 1998, p. 25.

People Weekly, November 4, 1996, p. 30.

Playboy, July, 1997, pp. 138–42.

Starlog, March, 1992.

LUKE, Derek 1974–

PERSONAL

Born April 24, 1974, in Jersey City, NJ; son of Maurice (an actor) and Marjorie (a pianist; maiden name, Dixon) Luke; brother of Maurice Luke, Jr. (a musician) and Daniel Luke (an actor); married Sophia Adella Hernandez (a singer and actress), 1998. *Education:* Briefly attended New Jersey City University.

Addresses: *Agent*—Brad Slater, WME Entertainment, 9601 Wilshire Blvd., 3rd Floor, Beverly Hills, CA 90210. *Publicist*—WKT Public Relations, 9350 Wilshire Blvd., Suite 450, Beverly Hills, CA 90212.

Career: Actor. Appeared in commercials for Gap clothing, 2002, and Roc a Wear clothing line, 2006. Worked for the U.S. Postal Service in New Jersey, c. 1992–95, and at a film studio gift shop in southern California; also worked as a banquet waiter and usher.

Awards, Honors: BET Award, favorite actor, Black Entertainment Television, 2003; National Board of Review Award, best breakthrough performance by an actor, 2002, Independent Spirit Award, best male lead, Independent Features Project/West, Special Achievement Award for outstanding new talent, Satellite Awards, International Press Academy, Chicago Film Critics Association Award nomination, most promising performer, Phoenix Film Critics Society Award nomination, best newcomer, Black Reel Awards, best theatrical actor and viewer's choice for best breakthrough performance, Online Film Critics Society Award nomination, best breakthrough performance, MTV Movie Award nomination, best breakthrough male

performance, and Teen Choice Award nomination, choice male movie breakout star, all 2003, all for *Antwone Fisher;* Hollywood Film Festival Award, breakthrough actor, 2006; Satellite Award nomination, best actor in a motion picture drama, 2005, and Black Reel Award nomination, best actor, 2007, both for *Catch a Fire;* Black Reel Award nominations, best actor and best ensemble (with others), 2008, and Image Award nomination, outstanding actor in a motion picture, National Association for the Advancement of Colored People, 2009, both for *Miracle at St. Anna;* Black Reel Award nomination, best supporting actor, 2010, for *Madea Goes to Jail;* Black Reel Award nomination (with others), best ensemble, 2010, for *Notorious.*

CREDITS

Film Appearances:

Antwone Quenton "Fish" Fisher (title role), *Antwone Fisher,* Fox Searchlight, 2002.

Bobby, *Pieces of April,* Metro–Goldwyn–Mayer, 2003.

Kid, *Biker Boyz,* DreamWorks, 2003.

Curtis, *Spartan,* Warner Bros., 2004.

Bobbie Miles, *Friday Night Lights,* Universal, 2004.

Bobby Joe Hill, *Glory Road,* Buena Vista, 2006.

Patrick Chamusso, *Catch a Fire,* Focus Features, 2006.

Arian Finch, *Lions for Lambs,* Metro–Goldwyn–Mayer, 2007.

Russell T. McCormack, *Definitely, Maybe* (also known as *Love Diaries*), Universal, 2008.

Second Staff Sergeant Aubrey Stamps, *Miracle at St. Anna,* Touchstone, 2008.

Sean "Puffy" Combs, *Notorious,* Fox Searchlight, 2009.

Joshua Hardaway, *Madea Goes to Jail* (also known as *Tyler Perry's "Madea Goes to Jail"*), Lions Gate Films, 2009.

Television Appearances; Series:

Cameron Boone, *Trauma,* NBC, 2009–10.

Television Appearances; Episodic:

Orderly, "White Collar," *The King of Queens,* CBS, 1999.

Delivery man, "Dark Meet," *The King of Queens,* CBS, 2000.

Ruckus, "Mayhem at the Jam," *Moesha,* UPN, 2001.

Total Request Live (also known as *Total Request with Carson Daly, TRL,* and *TRL Weekend*), MTV, 2002.

"Antwone Fisher," *HBO First Look,* HBO, 2003.

The Late Late Show with Craig Ferguson, CBS, 2006.

Tavis Smiley, PBS, 2006.

Entertainment Tonight (also known as *E.T.* and *This Week in Entertainment*), syndicated, 2006, 2008, 2009.

Up Close with Carrie Keagan, ABC, 2008.

The Bonnie Hunt Show, NBC, 2009.

Last Call with Carson Daly, NBC, 2009.

Television Appearances; Pilots:
Cameron Boone, *Trauma*, NBC, 2009.

Television Appearances; Specials:
The Making of "Antwone Fisher," 2001.
(In archive footage) Arian Finch, *Irak–Afganistan, la guerra llega al cine,* Canal+ Espana, 2008.
Host, *Rip the Runway,* Black Entertainment Television, 2009.

Television Appearances; Awards Presentations:
The 34th NAACP Image Awards, Fox, 2003.
The 17th Annual Soul Train Music Awards, The WB, 2003.
The 2003 IFP Independent Spirit Awards, Independent Film Channel, 2003.
BET Awards '08, Black Entertainment Television, 2008.

RECORDINGS

Videos:
"Friday Night Lights:" The Story of the 1988 Permian Panthers, Universal Studios Home Video, 2005.
I Believe in Miracles, RAI Cinema, 2009.

Also appeared in music videos, including "Take Care of U" by Shanice, 2006; "I Want You" by Common, 2007; "Teenage Love Affair" by Alicia Keys, 2008; "Knock Knock/Get It Off" by Monica; and "So Gone" by Monica and Missy Elliot.

OTHER SOURCES

Books:
Contemporary Black Biography, Volume 61, Gale, 2007.

Periodicals:
Best Life, February, 2007, pp. 112–13.
Complex, February, 2004, pp. 76–80.
Elle, November, 2006, p. 174.
Esquire, February, 2007, p. 109.
Essence, February, 2006, p. 78; December, 2007, p. 198.
Flaunt, October, 2006, pp. 108–13; January, 2007, p. 103.
GQ, November, 2004, p. 142.
Interview, November, 2006, pp. 64–68.
Men's Health, March, 2005, p. 28.
Playboy, January, 2006, p. 20.
Rolling Out, October 7, 2004, pp. 28–29.
Venice, November, 2006, pp. 56–62.
Vibe, November, 2006, p. 72.
Vixen, March, 2006, p. 98.
Washington Post, January 13, 2006, pp. 31, 36.

Electronic:
Pop Entertainment Online, http://www.pop entertainment.com, October 18, 2009.

M

MACARTHUR, James 1937–2010

PERSONAL

Full name, James Gordon MacArthur; born December 8, 1937, in Los Angeles, CA; died October 28, 2010, in Jacksonville, FL. Actor. Best known as Detective Danny "Danno" Williams from the original *Hawaii Five-O* television series, MacArthur was the son of actress Helen Hayes and playwright Charles MacArthur and the godson of silent-film star Lillian Gish. For more than four decades, he worked on stage, in television, and in Hollywood films. His first notable role was in a 1955 television production, *Deal a Blow,* which was adapted into a 1957 film titled *The Young Stranger;* MacArthur starred in both. His Broadway debut in the 1960 play *Invitation to a March* won him a best new actor Theatre World Award. Other stage credits included a lead part in a 1981 production of *The Front Page,* which his father cowrote in the late 1920s.

MacArthur turned seriously to movies in the early 1960s, appearing in Walt Disney's *Kidnapped* and *Swiss Family Robinson* and in the dramas *The Interns* and *Spencer's Mountain.* In the mid-1960s he played a small but noteworthy role in the cold war thriller *The Bedford Incident* and performed in the war action film *Battle of the Bulge* and the exuberant flower child movie *The Love-Ins.* As a guest performer, he appeared in such television series as *Gunsmoke, Bonanza, The Love Boat,* and *The Untouchables.* His role in the 1968 spaghetti western film *Hang 'Em High,* starring Clint Eastwood, caught the attention of *Hawaii Five-O* creator Leonard Freeman. Filmed in Hawaii, the crime show's 278 episodes made it one of the longest-running in television history, and it was broadcast in more than eighty countries. MacArthur acted in the show from 1968 to 1980, leaving the year before the run ended.

PERIODICALS

Los Angeles Times, October 29, 2010.

New York Times, October 29, 2010.
Washington Post, October 28, 2010.

MADELEY, Richard 1956–

PERSONAL

Born May 13, 1956, in Romford, England; son of Christopher and Mary Claire (maiden name, McEwan) Madeley; married, wife's name, Lynda, 1977 (divorced, 1983); married Judy Finnigan (a television presenter and producer), November 21, 1986; children: (second marriage) Dan and Tom (twin stepsons), Jack Christopher, Chloe Susannah. *Education:* Attended school in London.

Addresses: *Agent*—Ali Clapperton, James Grant Media, 94 Strand on the Green, Chiswick, London W4 3NN, England.

Career: Television presenter and producer. *Brentwood Argus,* reporter, 1972–74; *East London Advertiser,* news editor and assistant editor, 1975–76; BBC Cumbria, Carlisle, England, news producer and presenter, c. 1975–78; BBC Radio Carlisle, reporter, news producer, and presenter, 1976–78; Border Television, reporter and presenter, 1978–80; Yorkshire Television, reporter and presenter, 1980–82; Granada Television, presenter, 1982–2001; Cactus Television, presenter, 2001–09.

Awards, Honors: Royal Television Society Award nomination, best male presenter, 1994, for *This Morning;* National Television Awards, most popular daytime program, 1998, 1999, 2000, 2001.

CREDITS

Television Appearances; Series:
Presenter, *Calendar Goes Pop,* 1980.
Presenter, *This Morning,* ITV, 1988–2007.
Cluedo, ITV, 1991–93.
The Richard and Judy Show, 1993.
Presenter, *Tonight with Richard Madeley and Judy Finnigan,* 1996.
Presenter of "Duets," *Top Ten,* Channel 4, 2001.
Presenter, *Richard & Judy,* Channel 4, 2001–2008.
Presenter, *Richard & Judy's New Position,* UKTV, 2008–2009.

Television Appearances; Specials:
An Audience with the Spice Girls, ITV, 1997.
Presenter, *Eye of the Storm,* Granada Television, 1999.
Forty Years on Coronation Street, 2000.
(In archive footage) *100 Greatest TV Moments from Hell,* 2000.
(Uncredited; in archive footage) *Goodbye 2000,* 2000.
The Ultimate Pop Star, Channel 4, 2004.
The Big Fat Quiz of the Year, Channel 4, 2004, 2005.
TV's 50 Greatest Stars, Granada, 2006.
Presenter, *Richard & Judy's Christmas Books,* Channel 4, 2006, 2007.
(In archive footage) *Sex on Trial: The Soapstar Story,* Channel 4, 2007.
Happy Birthday Brucie!, BBC1, 2008.
(In archive footage; with the Spice Boys) *TV's Funniest Music Moments,* 2008.
Ant & Dec's Christmas Show, ITV, 2009.
Newsnight at 30, BBC2, 2010.

Television Appearances; Miniseries:
I Love 1980's, BBC, 2001.
The Second Coming, BBC America, 2003.
Presenter, *Fortune: Million Pound Giveaway,* 2007.

Television Appearances; Movies:
(Uncredited) Himself on television, *A Very Social Secretary,* Channel 4, 2005.

Television Appearances; Episodic:
Host, *Connections,* 1988.
Presenter, *Runway,* 1991.
Surprise Surprise!, ITV, 1996.
"Richard Madeley and Judy Finnigan," *This Is Your Life,* BBC, 1997.
"Dad's Army," *Selection Box,* 1997.
Late Lunch, Channel 4, 1998.
TV Nightmares, ITV, 1999, 2000.
"When the Fat Lady Sings," *Fat Friends,* BBC America, 2000.
So Graham Norton, Channel 4, 2001.
"Parallox," *Absolutely Fabulous,* BBC1, then Comedy Central, 2001.

Friday Night with Jonathan Ross, BBC America, 2002.
The Kumars at No. 42, BBC America, 2002.
The Late Late Show, 2002.
"Celebrity Christmas Puddings," *French and Saunders,* BBC, 2002.
"Is This the World We Created?," *Grumpy Old Men,* BBC, 2003.
"Stuff," *Grumpy Old Men,* BBC, 2003.
"So Who's to Blame?," *Grumpy Old Men,* BBC, 2003.
Liquid News, BBC3, 2004.
The Keith Barret Show, 2004.
(In archive footage) *Room 101,* BBC, 2004.
Derren Brown: Trick of the Mind, 2005.
Ant & Dec's Saturday Night Takeaway, ITV, 2005.
"The Trial," *Absolute Power,* BBC, 2005.
Little Britain, BBC America, 2005.
(Uncredited; in archive footage) "Boy George's Queerest TV Moments," *Favouritism,* Channel 4, 2005.
8 Out of 10 Cats, Channel 4, 2005, 2006.
Footballers' Wives, BBC America, 2006.
"Daniel Radcliffe," *Extras,* HBO, 2006.
Celebrity guest, *Gazza's Trip,* Channel 5, 2006.
The Bigger Picture (also known as *The Bigger Picture with Graham Norton*), BBC, 2006.
Question Time, 2006, 2010.
The Paul O'Grady Show, ITV, 2007.
(Uncredited) "A Heroes Welcome," *Heroes Unmasked,* BBC, 2007.
Deadline, 2007.
Guest presenter, *Have I Got News for You,* BBC, 2007.
TV Burp, ITV, 2007, then uncredited appearances, 2008, and (in archive footage) in "The Best of TV Burp," 2009.
Happy Hour, 2008.
Loose Women, ITV, 2008.
Xpose, TV3, 2008.
(Uncredited) *Chris Moyles Quiz Night,* Channel 4, 2009.
"Richard Madeley," *Piers Morgan's Life Stories,* ITV, 2009.
This Week, BBC, 2010.
The David Dickinson Show, 2010.

Television Appearances; Awards Presentations:
Cohost, *BAFTA British Academy Awards,* 1989.
The British Comedy Awards, ITV, 1993.
The National Television Awards, ITV, 1998, 2000, 2001.
Host, *The British Soap Awards,* 1999, 2000, 2001.
Pride of Britain Awards, ITV, 2003.
The Variety Club Showbusiness Awards, 2004.

Television Work; Series:
Executive producer, *Richard & Judy,* Channel 4, 2001–2007.

Film Appearances:
Ali G Indahouse, Universal, 2002.

Internet Appearances; Episodic:
Guest presenter, *Have I Got News for You: The Inevitable Internet Spin–off,* BBC.co.uk, 2007.

RECORDINGS

Videos:
Men in Black Training Video: UK, Columbia TriStar Home Video, 2002.

WRITINGS

Books:
(With wife, Judy Finnigan) *Richard and Judy: The Autobiography,* Hodder & Stoughton, 2002.

OTHER SOURCES

Books:
Madeley, Richard, and Judy Finnigan, *Richard and Judy: The Autobiography,* Hodder & Stoughton, 2002.

Periodicals:
Daily Telegraph (London), April 7, 2004, p. 19.
Guardian Weekend, October 4, 2008, pp. 32–33, 35, 37–38.
Times Magazine, January 27, 2007, pp. 20–25.

Electronic:
Richard & Judy Official Site, http://www.officialrichardandjudy.com, July 30, 2010.

Other:
"Richard Madeley and Judy Finnigan" (television episode), *This Is Your Life,* BBC, 1997.

McKEAN, Michael 1947–

PERSONAL

Born October 17, 1947, in New York, NY; son of Gilbert and Ruth McKean; married Susan Russell, 1970 (divorced, 1993); married Annette O'Toole (an actress), March 20, 1999; children: (first marriage) Colin Russell, Fletcher. *Education:* Studied theatre at Carnegie Institute of Technology (now Carnegie–Mellon University) and New York University.

Addresses: *Agent*—Jenny Delaney, William Morris Agency, 151 El Camino Dr., Beverly Hills, CA 90212–2704.

Career: Actor, musician, producer, director, and writer. Appeared with bands, including the Left Banke, the Folksmen, and Little Tip Lohengren and the Tip–Top Boys. Credibility Gap (radio comedy group), member in the late 1960s and early 1970s. Appeared as David St. Hubbins in commercials.

Awards, Honors: *Theatre World* Award, 1990, for *Accomplice;* CableACE Award nomination, actor in a comedy series, 1993, for *Sessions;* CableACE Award nominations, actor in a comedy series, 1994 and 1996, for *Dream On;* Video Premiere Award (with others), best DVD audio commentary, 2001, for *This Is Spinal Tap;* DVD Premiere Award (with Ritsuko Notani), best animated character performance, 2003, for *The Hunchback of Notre Dame II;* Seattle Film Critics Award (with others), best music, 2003, Academy Award nomination, best music—original song, Critics Choice Award (with others), best song, Broadcast Film Critics Association Awards, Florida Film Critics Circle Award (with others), best ensemble cast, Grammy Award, best song written for a motion picture, Phoenix Film Critics Society Award nomination (with others), best ensemble acting, Golden Satellite Award nomination (with Annette O'Toole), best original song, International Press Academy, 2004, for *A Mighty Wind;* Lifetime Achievement Award, Newport International Film Festival, 2005; Gotham Award nomination (with others), best ensemble cast, 2006, for *For Your Consideration;* TV Land Award nomination, the "who knew they could sing?" award, 2007.

CREDITS

Television Appearances; Series:
Leonard "Lenny" Kosnowski, *Laverne & Shirley* (also known as *Laverne & Shirley & Company* and *Laverne & Shirley & Friends*), ABC, 1976–83.
The $10,000 Pyramid (also known as *New $25,000 Pyramid, The $100, 000 Pyramid, The $20,000 Pyramid, The $25,000 Pyramid, The $50,000 Pyramid,* and *The New $100,000 Pyramid*), 1977–1985.
Tom Smithson, *Grand* (also known as *Grosse Pointe*), NBC, 1990.
Dan Carver, *Sessions,* HBO, 1991.
Gibby Fiske, a recurring role, *Dream On,* 1991–96.
Fox News, Fox News, 1992–2007.
Saturday Night Live (also known as *SNL*), NBC, 1994–95.
Voice of Shere Khan, *Disney's Jungle Cubs* (animated; also known as *Jungle Cubs*), ABC, 1996.
Frank McClellan, *Secret Service Guy,* Fox, 1996.

Barrington "Barry" LeTissier, *Tracey Takes On ...*, HBO, 1996–99.

Politically Incorrect (also known as *P.I.*), 1997–2002.

Jasper Badun, *101 Dalmatians: The Series*, 1997–98.

Host, *Totally Ridiculous*, 1998.

Jeopardy, syndicated, 1999–2010.

Voices of Professor Ram and village shaman, *Clerks* (animated; also known as *Clerks: The Animated Series, Clerks TAS, Clerks: The Cartoon,* and *Clerks: Uncensored*), ABC, 2000.

Marek Kohler, *Life's Too Short*, 2000.

Adrien Van Voorhees, *Primetime Glick*, Comedy Central, 2001–2002.

Festival Pass with Chris Gore, 2002.

David St. Hubbins, *I Love the '80s*, 2002.

David St. Hubbins, *Channel 4 News*, Channel 4, 2004–2009.

Mel Wax, *Hopeless Pictures*, Independent Film Channel, 2005.

Broadway Beat, 2006–2009.

Television Appearances; Movies:

Terry Christopher, *More Than Friends* (also known as *Love Me and I'll Be Your Best Friend*), 1978.

Various characters, *The T.V. Show*, 1979.

Likely Stories, Vol. 1, 1981.

Pete Newly, *Classified Love*, CBS, 1986.

Reverend Prufrock, *The History of White People in America: Volume II*, 1986.

Wexler Hatch, *Daniel and the Towers*, 1987.

Dr. Warren Starbinder/Jason Star, "Double Agent," *The Disney Sunday Movie*, ABC, 1987.

Martin Mull in "Portrait of a White Marriage" (also known as *Portrait of a White Marriage* and *Scenes from a White Marriage*), Cinemax, 1988.

Michael, *A Father's Homecoming* (also known as *Oakmont, The Oakmont Stories,* and *Town and Gown*), NBC, 1988.

Phil Dreyer, *Hider in the House*, 1989.

Pettibone, *Murder in High Places* (also known as *Out of Season*), NBC, 1991.

Ozzie Evans, "MacShayne: The Final Roll of the Dice" (also known as "MacShayne's Big Score"), *NBC Friday Night Mystery*, NBC, 1994.

Scott Grogan, *The Sunshine Boys* (also known as *Neil Simon's "The Sunshine Boys"*), 1995.

Rick, *Edie & Pen* (also known as *Desert Gamble*), HBO, 1996.

Bill Case, *Casper: A Spirited Beginning*, 1997.

Merle Hammond, *Final Justice*, Lifetime, 1998.

Willie, *The Pass* (also known as *Highway Hitcher*), Showtime, 1998.

William Christy Cabanne, *And Starring Pancho Villa as Himself*, 2003.

Snow Miser, *The Year Without a Santa Claus*, 2006.

Glen Glahm, *The Thick of It*, 2007.

Television Appearances; Episodic:

"Sex Therapy," *The Tomorrow Show* (also known as *Tomorrow* and *Tomorrow Coast to Coast*), 1976.

"Monty Hale," *America 2–Night*, 1978.

Lenny, "Lenny and the Squigtones," *American Bandstand*, 1979.

Lenny Kosnowski, "Fonzie's Funeral: Part 2," *Happy Days*, 1979.

Lenny, *Bandstand* (also known as *AB* and *American Bandstand*), 1979.

Joey, "Internal Injury," *The Goodtime Girls*, ABC, 1980.

Chain Reaction, five episodes, 1980.

Cohost, *Fridays*, 1981.

David St. Hubbins, *The Joe Franklin Show*, 1984.

Musical guest, *Saturday Night Live* (also known as *SNL*), NBC, 1984.

Guest host, *Saturday Night Live* (also known as *SNL*), NBC, 1984.

David St. Hubbins, *Late Night with David Letterman*, NBC, 1984.

"The Borrowing," *George Burns Comedy Week*, 1985.

Mr. Wallace, "Davy Crockett," *Tall Tales & Legends* (also known as *Shelley Duvall's "Tall Tales and Legends"*), Showtime, 1985.

Mac Macintosh, "Johnny Appleseed," *Tall Tales & Legends* (also known as *Shelley Duvall's "Tall Tales and Legends"*), Showtime, 1986.

Gibby Fiske, "Felines ... Nothing More Than Felines," *Dream On*, HBO, 1990.

Dennis, "Mad about the Boy," *Empty Nest*, 1990.

Ross McKay, "The Return of Preston Giles," *Murder, She Wrote*, CBS, 1990.

My Talk Show, 1990.

David St. Hubbins, *MTV News: The Week in Rock*, MTV, 1991.

"And Your Little Dog, Too," *Dream On*, HBO, 1991.

Dr. Mummenschvantz, "The Bride of Mummula," *Morton & Hayes* (also known as *Partners in Life*), CBS, 1991.

Voice of David St. Hubbins, "The Otto Show," *The Simpsons* (animated), Fox, 1992.

Guest host, "Michael McKean," *An Evening at the Improv*, 1992.

David St. Hubbins, *Rockline on MTV*, MTV, 1992.

David St. Hubbins, *Headbangers Ball* (also known as *MTV Headbangers Ball*), MTV, 1992.

David St. Hubbins, *The Arsenio Hall Show*, two episodes, 1992.

Voice of Battleheim, guy in the lab coat, Kyle, and Myman, *Dinosaurs* (animated), various episodes, beginning c. 1992.

David St. Hubbins, *Late Night with David Letterman*, 1992.

David St. Hubbins, *Tonight with Jonathan Ross*, two episodes, 1992.

David St. Hubbins, *ABC in Concert*, 1992.

Mr. Gordon, "Winter, Spring, Summer, or Fall, All You Gotta Do Is Call ...," *Family Album*, 1993.

David St. Hubbins, "Stewart's House," *Beavis and Butt–Head*, 1993.

Voice of Spink, "King Yakko," *Animaniacs* (animated), 1993.

Voice, "A Civil War," *Duckman* (animated), USA Network, 1994.

Dr. Fabian Leek, "Vatman," *Lois & Clark: The New Adventures of Superman,* ABC, 1994.

Voices of Dr. Herder Bryant, Ed, Parish, guy in lab coat, Ansel, and parent patrol officer, *Dinosaurs* (animated), ABC, various episodes, beginning c. 1994.

Dirk Clearfield, "Sell It Like It Is," *Getting By,* 1994.

Voice of Jake/cowboy number one, "Gold Rush/A Gift of Gold/Dot's Quiet Time," *Animaniacs* (animated; also known as *Steven Spielberg Presents Animaniacs*), 1994.

Noel Babcock, Ph.D., "Nanny and the Professor," *The Nanny,* CBS, 1995.

Mr. Rastatter, "The One with the List," *Friends,* NBC, 1995.

Father Damian, "Caroline and the Wedding," *Caroline in the City,* NBC, 1995.

The clown, "The Thaw," *Star Trek: Voyager,* 1996.

Voice of Cecil, *Disney's Jungle Cubs* (animated; also known as *Jungle Cubs*), ABC, 1996.

"All about Louie," *Dream On,* HBO, 1996.

Voice of toll collector, "The Mummy/Robin Brain," *Pinky and the Brain,* 1996.

Voice of Dr. Jeffrey Otitus, "Reigning Cats and Dogs," *Road Rovers* (animated), The WB, 1996.

Barrington "Barry" LeTissier, "Family," *Tracey Takes On ...,* HBO, 1996.

Later with Greg Kinnear, 1996.

Barrington "Barry" LeTissier, "Food," *Tracey Takes On ...,* HBO, 1997.

Miner, "Mining Accident," *The Weird Al Show,* 1997.

Himself, "BooBooKitty," *Space Ghost Coast to Coast,* Cartoon Network, 1997.

Voice of Jasper Badum, *Disney's 101 Dalmatians: The Series* (animated), ABC, syndicated, and The Disney Channel, 1997.

Voices of Raymond and Rupert, "Mr. Monkeyman," *Johnny Bravo* (animated), Cartoon Network, 1997.

Dennis Page, "Second Time Around," *Murphy Brown,* CBS, 1997.

Voice of Ponytail, "Mice Don't Dance/Brain Drained," *Pinky and the Brain,* 1997.

Arthur Willhaven, "Morality Bites," *The Closer,* CBS, 1998.

Dave Whitby, "Veronica's Cheating Partners," *Veronica's Closet,* 1998.

Voice of Mr. Bream, "Yes, Mikey, Santa Does Shave: Parts 1 & 2," *Recess,* 1998.

Obermeyer, "Pearce's New Buddy," *LateLine,* ABC, 1998.

Morris Fletcher, "Dreamland," *The X–Files,* Fox, 1998.

Morris Fletcher, "Dreamland II," *The X–Files,* Fox, 1998.

Voice of Schneiderlander, "Broadway Malady," *Pinky and the Brain* (animated), 1998.

Voice of Mel Anoma, "Inherit the Wheeze," *Pinky and the Brain* (animated), 1998.

Voice of Nevel Nosenest, "Music Lesson," *Animaniacs* (animated), 1998.

Professor Peens, "Life Is Precious and God and the Bible," *Mr. Show,* HBO, 1998.

Voice of Insaniac/Freakenstein, "'Small Soldiers': Size Doesn't Matter," *HBO First Look,* HBO, 1998.

Lewis Stickley, "Maggie's Master Plan," *Maggie Winters,* CBS, 1998.

Dick Obermeyer, "Pearce's New Buddy," *LateLine,* 1998.

"Spinal Tap/Tonic," *My Generation,* 1998.

Voice of L. G. Algae, "The Mighty Knothead/Pond Scum," *The Angry Beavers,* 1998.

Voice of 50's Joker, "Legends of the Dark Knight," *The New Batman Adventures* (animated), 1998.

Lewis Stickley, "You'll Never Walk Alone in This Town Again," *Maggie Winters,* CBS, 1999.

Sherman Smith, "Blind Faith," *Providence,* NBC, 1999.

Voices of Arthur Fortune and Jerry Rude, "Monty Can't Buy Me Love," *The Simpsons* (animated), Fox, 1999.

Morris Fletcher, "Three of a Kind," *The X–Files,* Fox, 1999.

Jedediah Lawrence, "State of the Unions," *Boy Meets World,* ABC, 1999.

Voice of Johnny Stitches, "It Girl," *Hey Arnold!,* Nickelodeon, 1999.

Sin City Spectacular (also known as *Penn & Teller's Sin City Spectacular*), FX Network, c. 1999.

"The Films of Rob Reiner," *The Directors,* 1999.

Voice of Ian Peek, "Sneak Peek," *Batman Beyond* (animated), The WB, 2000.

Elias Grace, "Meta," *Law & Order,* NBC, 2000.

Lieutenant Praeger, "Springing Tiny," *The Huntress,* USA Network, 2000.

The List, VH1, 2000.

Host, "Trial and Error," *Comedy Central Canned Ham,* Comedy Central, 2000.

Host, "Canned Hamm: Little Nicky," *Comedy Central Canned Ham,* Comedy Central, 2000.

David St. Hubbins, "This Is Spinal Tap," *VH–1 Where Are They Now?,* VH1, 2000.

Rock & Roll Jeopardy, two episodes, 2000.

David St. Hubbins, "The Two Mrs. Thorsons: Part 1," *The Huntress,* USA Network, 2001.

Psycho–Vivor host, "Barry Boinks Caroline," *Strip Mall,* Comedy Central, 2001.

Psycho–Vivor host, "Psycho–Vivor," *Strip Mall,* Comedy Central, 2001.

Voice of Pengrove Pig, "European Road Show," *Family Guy* (animated), Fox, 2001.

Morris Fletcher, "All about Yves," *The Lone Gunmen,* Fox, 2001.

Voice of Ralph Thorson, "The Quest: Parts 1 & 2," *The Huntress,* USA Network, 2001.

"Laverne & Shirley," *TVography,* 2001.

"The Films of Garry Marshall," *The Directors,* 2001.

Voice of Maestro Bingo Bunny, "Daisy Wants to Play an Instrument/Ball of Yarn," *Oswald* (animated), 2001.

Voice of cousin Louie, "Odd One Out/Goodbye Best Friend," *Oswald* (animated), 2002.

Voice of Maestro Bingo Bunny, "Fixing the Piano/ Oswald Makes a Date," *Oswald* (animated), 2002.

Morris Fletcher, "Jump the Shark," *The X–Files,* Fox, 2002.

Voice of the sportsman, "Legends: Parts 1 & 2," *Justice League* (animated), Cartoon Network, 2002.

"Show 22," *Pyramid,* 2002.

Saturday Night Live: TV Tales, E! Entertainment Television, 2002.

Bobby Lightfoot, "Family Therapy," *As Told by Ginger,* 2002.

Voice of Spyro, "Shaggy Busted," *Harvey Birdman: Attorney at Law,* 2002.

Voice of Spyro, "The Dabba Don," *Harvey Birdman: Attorney at Law,* 2002.

Dr. Edmund, "The Hologram Man," *The Zeta Project,* 2002.

Voice of Lo–Fi, "The Chief's New Groove," *Teamo Supremo,* 2002.

Pyramid (also known as *The $100,000 Pyramid*), syndicated, 2002 and 2003.

Life & Times (also known as *Life and Times Tonight*), 2002.

"The Simpsons," *Inside the Actors Studio,* Bravo, 2003.

Jerry Palter, *MADtv,* Fox, 2003.

Voice of Pinkerton/Earthflower, "Simmons' Documentary/Big Bob's Crisis," *Hey Arnold!,* Nickelodeon, 2003.

CBS News Sunday Morning, CBS, 2003.

At the Angelika (also known as *At the IFC Center*), Independent Film Channel, 2003.

Fox and Friends (also known as *Fox and Friends First* and *Fox and Friends Weekend*), Fox News, 2003.

"Bernard Goldberg, Michael McKean," *Fox News,* 2003.

Adrien Van Voorhees, *Star CloseUp,* 2003.

The Panel, Ten Network, 2003.

Micallef Tonight, Nine Network, 2003.

In Entertainment, Ten Network, 2003.

"Penny Marshall," *Intimate Portrait,* Lifetime, 2003.

David St. Hubbins, *Just for Laughs* (also known as *Ed Byrne's "Just for Laughs," Just for Laughs Comedy Festival,* and *Just for Laughs Montreal Comedy Festival*), CBC, two episodes, 2003.

Perry White, "Perry," *Smallville* (also known as *Smallville Beginnings*), 2003.

Voice of Spyro, "Deadomutt: Part 2," *Harvey Birdman: Attorney at Law* (animated), 2003.

Music News, 2004.

ABC Evening News (also known as *ABC World News Tonight* and *World News Tonight*), ABC, 2004.

CW 11 Morning News (also known as *The WB 11 Morning News*), The CW, 2004, 2005, 2006, and 2008.

Entertainment Tonight (also known as *E.T.* and *This Week in Entertainment*), syndicated, 2004, 2009.

Extra (also known as *Extra: The Entertainment Magazine*), syndicated, 2004.

Dinner for Five, Independent Film Channel, 2004.

Today (also known as *NBC News Today* and *The Today Show*), NBC, 2004.

The Biz, Cable News Network, 2004.

"Music Special," *McEnroe,* CNBC, 2004.

"Humor in Performance," *Working in the Theatre,* 2004.

"Top 10 TV Dads," *TV Land's Top Ten,* TV Land, 2004.

"The Andy Griffith Show Episodes," *TV Land's Top Ten,* TV Land, 2004.

KTLA Morning News (also known as *KTLA Morning Show*), NBC, 2004 and 2007.

"Spinal Tap and Beyond/Fit and Fat," *Nitebeat,* 2005.

"Wacky Neighbors," *TV Land's Top Ten,* TV Land, 2005.

"Fish Fry," *The Barry Z Show* (also known as *Z–TV*), 2005.

Voice of Spyro, "Mindless," *Harvey Birdman: Attorney at Law* (animated), 2005.

CBS 2 News This Morning, CBS, 2005, 2008, and 2009.

Dr. Atticus Liddell, "A Clean Conscience," *Alias,* ABC, 2005.

Dr. Atticus Liddell, "Mirage," *Alias,* ABC, 2005.

Dwight Biddle, "Truly, Madly, Deeply," *Boston Legal,* 2005.

Voice of Groink, "Blikmail/Love Jackal," *Catscratch,* Nickelodeon, 2006.

Dr. Howard "J." Hubbins, "Pink Freud," *Help Me Help You,* 2006.

Theater Talk, 2006.

Breakfast with the Arts, Arts & Entertainment, two episodes, 2006.

"Teenage Wasteland," *The Drug Years,* VH1, 2006.

MTV News, MTV, 2006.

London Tonight, 2006.

Narrator, "The Best of Nature: 25 Years," *Nature,* PBS, 2007.

Leonard "Lenny" Kosnowski, "Oddballs & Original Characters," *TV Land Confidential,* TV Land, 2007.

Voice of Kalgoron, "Wrath of the Spider Queen," *Grim & Evil* (animated; also known as *The Grim Adventures of Billy & Mandy*), Cartoon Network, 2007.

CNN Newsroom, Cable News Network, 2007.

Matt Tessler, "The Bat Mitzvah," *Curb Your Enthusiasm,* 2007.

Bill Nolan, "Called Home," *Law & Order,* NBC, 2008.

Dr. Donald Metz, "Misled and Misguided," *The Unit,* 2008.

Dr. Donald Metz, "Switchblade," *The Unit,* 2008.

David St. Hubbins, *The Comedy Map of Britain,* BBC, 2008.

"2008 Tony Awards Prevue," *Broadway Beat,* 2008.

Theater Talk, 2008, 2009.

WUSA Eyewitness News (also known as *The 11 PM Report, WDVM Eyewitness News, WTOP Eyewitness News,* and *WUSA 9 News*), 2009.

Eyewitness News, 2010.

Perry White, "Hostage," *Smallville* (also known as *Smallville Beginnings*), 2010.

Voice of David St. Hubbins, "Money Can't Buy Everything," *Mega Man;* also provided the voices of Jake and Spink, *Animaniacs* (animated); appeared as Dick Clearfield, *Getting By.*

Television Talk Show Guest Appearances; Episodic:
Dinah!, 1976.
The Peter Marshall Variety Show, 1977.
The Merv Griffin Show, 1977.
The Mike Douglas Show, 1977.
The Hollywood Squares, 1978.
Late Night with David Letterman, 1990, 1991, and 1993.
The Dennis Miller Show, 1992.
Good Morning America (also known as *G.M.A.*), 1992, 1999.
Later with Bob Costas, 1993.
Late Night with Conan O'Brien, NBC, 1993, 1994, 1995, 2003.
Late Show with David Letterman (also known as *Letterman* and *The Late Show*), CBS, 1994, 1995, 2000, 2003.
The Jon Stewart Show, 1995.
The Rosie O'Donnell Show, syndicated, 1999.
Good Morning America (also known as *G.M.A.*), 1999.
The Martin Short Show, 2000.
The Early Show, 2000.
Showbiz Today, 2000.
The Howard Stern Radio Show, 2000.
The Daily Show (also known as *A Daily Show with Jon Stewart,* *The Daily Show with Jon Stewart,* and *The Daily Show with Jon Stewart Global Edition*), Comedy Central, 2000 and 2009.
The Tonight Show with Jay Leno, NBC, 2000, 2009.
The Charlie Rose Show, PBS, 2003.
Today, NBC, 2003.
The View, ABC, 2003.
The Tony Danza Show, syndicated, 2004 and 2006.
Jimmy Kimmel Live!, ABC, 2005.
Real Time with Bill Maher (also known as *Real Time with Bill Maher: Electile Dysfunction '08*), HBO, 2005 and 2006.
Tavis Smiley, PBS, 2005 and 2009.
Breakfast, BBC, 2007.
Countdown w/Keith Olbermann, MSNBC, 2009.
Breakfast Television, two episodes, 2009.
The Joy Behar Show, HLN, 2009.
The Tonight Show with Conan O'Brien, NBC, 2009.
Late Night with Jimmy Fallon, NBC, 2009.

Television Appearances; Specials:
Economic Love–In, 1973.
The Riddlers, 1977.
David Letterman's Holiday Film Festival, 1985.
Principal Ford, *The American Film Institute Presents: TV or Not TV?,* 1990.

David St. Hubbins, *A Spinal Tap Reunion: The 25th Anniversary London Sell–Out* (also known as *The Return of Spinal Tap*), NBC, 1992.
David St. Hubbins, *The Freddie Mercury Tribute: Concert for AIDS Awareness,* 1992.
David St. Hubbins, *American Bandstand's 40th Anniversary Special,* 1992.
David St. Hubbins, *Halloween Jam at Universal Studios,* 1992.
Segment host, *A 70's Celebration: The Beat Is Back,* NBC, 1993.
The Laverne & Shirley Reunion, ABC, 1995.
Barry, *The Best of Tracey Takes On ...,* HBO, 1996.
Host, *Canned Ham: Trial and Error,* Comedy Central, 1997.
Host, *Totally Ridiculous! The World's Funniest True Stories,* UPN, 1998.
The devil in "Little Women," *Saturday Night Live: The Best of Chris Farley,* NBC, 1998.
Restaurant manager, *Saturday Night Live: The Best of Dana Carvey,* NBC, 1998.
David St. Hubbins, *SNL: 25 Years of Music,* 1999.
David St. Hubbins, *Just for Laughs: Montreal Comedy Festival,* 1999.
Voice of drummer, *Snowden's Christmas* (animated), CBS, 1999.
The Comedy Central Presents the New York Friars Club Roast of Jerry Stiller, Comedy Central, 1999.
Host, *Uncomfortably Close with Michael McKean: Jason Alexander,* Comedy Central, 1999.
Host, *Uncomfortably Close with Michael McKean: Jerry Stiller,* Comedy Central, 1999.
Host, *Uncomfortably Close with Michael McKean: Jonathan Winters,* Comedy Central, 2000.
Host, *Uncomfortably Close with Michael McKean: Rob Reiner,* Comedy Central, 2000.
Roast master, *The Comedy Central Presents the New York Friars Club Roast of Rob Reiner,* Comedy Central, 2000.
David St. Hubbins, *AFI's 100 Years ... 100 Laughs: America's Funniest Movies,* 2000.
David St. Hubbins, *100 Greatest Artists of Hard Rock,* 2000.
The Mark Twain Prize: Jonathan Winters, 2000.
Host, *Uncomfortably Close with Michael McKean: George Carlin,* Comedy Central, 2001.
Host, *Uncomfortably Close with Michael McKean: Harold Ramis,* Comedy Central, 2001.
Laverne & Shirley, Arts and Entertainment, 2001.
Narrator, *Intimate Portrait: Cindy Williams,* Lifetime, 2001.
Narrator, *Australia's Little Assassins,* PBS, 2001.
Narrator, *Condition Black,* PBS, 2002.
Entertainment Tonight Presents: Laverne and Shirley Together Again, ABC, 2002.
Saturday Night Live: TV Tales, 2002.
David St. Hubbins, American Bandstand's 50th Anniversary Celebration, 2002.
ABC's 50th Anniversary Celebration, ABC, 2003.

Live from the Red Carpet: The 2004 Grammy Awards, 2004.

Live from the Academy Awards, 2004.

2004 IFP/West Independent Spirit Awards Pre–Show, 2004.

Live from the Red Carpet: The 2004 Academy Awards, 2004.

All Access Pass: The TV Land Awards, TV Land, 2004.

101 Most Unforgettable SNL Moments, E! Entertainment Television, 2004.

David St. Hubbins, *Spinal Tap Goes 20,* Independent Film Channel, 2004.

TV Guide CloseUp: Behind the Scenes of "Smallville," TV Guide, 2004.

Broadway on Broadway, NBC, 2004.

Saturday Night Live in the '80s: Lost & Found, NBC, 2005.

David St. Hubbins, *VH1's Heavy: The Story of Metal,* VH1, 2006.

The 50 Greatest Comedy Films, Channel 4, 2006.

Hooray for Broadway: A Springtime Celebration, 2006.

Jerry Palter/David St. Hubbins/Lane Iverson, *Ricky Gervais Meets ... Christopher Guest,* 2006.

Live Earth (also known as *Live Earth 7.7.07, Live Earth: The Concerts for a Climate in Crisis,* and *SOS: The Movement for a Climate in Crisis*), NBC, 2007.

"Would Ya Hit a Guy with Glasses?: Nerds, Jerks & Oddballs," *Make 'Em Laugh: The Funny Business of America,* PBS, 2009.

"Slip on a Banana Peel: The Knockabouts," *Make 'Em Laugh: The Funny Business of America,* PBS, 2009.

"Sock it to Me? Satire and Parody," *Make 'Em Laugh: The Funny Business of America,* PBS, 2009.

The Thanksgiving Day Parade on CBS, CBS, 2009.

Television Appearances; Pilots:

The TV Show, ABC, 1979.

Howard Bender, *The Bounder,* CBS, 1984.

Harvey Baines, *Heaven Will Wait,* CBS, 1997.

Arthur Willhaven, *The Closer,* CBS, 1998.

Will Masters, *Masters of Horror and Suspense,* NBC, 1999.

Nathan Pugh, *Legal Aid,* CBS, 1999.

Host, *The Whitey Show,* 1999.

Voice, *Doomsday,* UPN, 2001.

The 'Burbs, FX Network, 2002.

Television Appearances; Awards Presentations:

Presenter, *The 28th Annual Primetime Emmy Awards,* 1976.

The 34th Annual Golden Globe Awards, 1977.

Presenter, *MTV Video Music Awards,* MTV, 1991.

The 6th Annual American Comedy Awards, ABC, 1992.

Presenter, *The 19th Annual American Music Awards,* 1992.

The ... Annual CableACE Awards, 1992, 1993.

Presenter, *The ... Annual CableACE Awards,* TNT, 1994, 1996.

Presenter, *Cybermania '94: Ultimate Gamers Awards,* 1994.

The 23rd Annual People's Choice Awards, 1997.

Presenter, *1998 Creative Arts Emmy Awards,* TV Land, 1998.

Presenter, *Brit Awards 1998,* 1998.

TV Land Awards: A Celebration of Classic TV, TV Land, Nickelodeon, 2004.

The 2004 IFP/West Independent Spirit Awards, Independent Film Channel, 2004.

Presenter, *49th Annual Drama Desk Awards,* 2004.

The 76th Annual Academy Awards, ABC, 2004.

The 2nd Annual TV Land Awards, TV Land, 2004.

The 20th Anniversary Independent Spirit Awards Special, Independent Film Channel, 2005.

Presenter, *The 60th Annual Tony Awards,* CBS, 2006.

The 52nd Annual Grammy Awards, CBS, 2010.

Television Appearances; Other:

VH1 Presents the 70's (miniseries), 1996.

Television Director; Episodic:

"The Playboy Show," *Laverne & Shirley* (also known as *Laverne & Shirley & Company* and *Laverne & Shirley & Friends*), ABC, 1982.

"Home Buddies," *Morton & Hayes* (also known as *Partners in Life*), CBS, 1991.

"B. S. Elliot," *Dream On,* HBO, 1992.

"Felines ... Nothing More Than Felines," *Dream On,* HBO, 1994.

"Significant Author," *Dream On,* HBO, 1995.

"All About Louie," *Dream On,* HBO, 1996.

"Politics," *Tracey Takes On ...,* HBO, 1997.

"Mothers," *Tracey Takes On ...,* HBO, 1997.

"Money," *Tracey Takes On ...,* HBO, 1997.

"Race Relations," *Tracey Takes On ...,* HBO, 1997.

"Supernatural," *Tracey Takes On ...,* HBO, 1997.

Television Producer; Specials:

(With others) *A Spinal Tap Reunion: The 25th Anniversary London Sell–Out* (also known as *The Return of Spinal Tap*), NBC, 1992.

Uncomfortably Close with Michael McKean: Jason Alexander, Comedy Central, 1999.

Uncomfortably Close with Michael McKean: Jerry Stiller, Comedy Central, 1999.

Uncomfortably Close with Michael McKean: Jonathan Winters, Comedy Central, 2000.

Uncomfortably Close with Michael McKean: Rob Reiner, Comedy Central, 2000.

Uncomfortably Close with Michael McKean: George Carlin, Comedy Central, 2001.

Television Work; Specials:

Director, "The Rich Hall Show," *Showtime Comedy Spotlight,* Showtime, 1987.

Film Appearances:

Cracking Up, 1977.

Willy, *1941,* Universal, 1979.

Eddie Winslow, *Used Cars,* Columbia, 1980.

Dr. Simon August, *Young Doctors in Love,* Twentieth Century–Fox, 1982.

David St. Hubbins, *This Is Spinal Tap,* Embassy, 1984.

Andy Richardson, *D.A.R.Y.L.,* Paramount, 1985.

Mr. Green, *Clue* (also known as *Clue: The Movie*), Paramount, 1985.

British party guest, *Jumpin' Jack Flash,* Twentieth Century–Fox, 1986.

Bu Montgomery of the Barbusters, *Light of Day,* TriStar, 1987.

State trooper, *Planes, Trains, and Automobiles,* Paramount, 1987.

Fred Ritter, *Short Circuit 2,* TriStar, 1988.

Reverend Prufrock, *Portrait of a White Marriage,* 1988.

Phil Dreyer, *Hider in the House,* 1989.

Emmet Sumner, *The Big Picture,* Columbia, 1989.

Woody, the pool boy, *Earth Girls Are Easy,* Vestron, 1989.

Hal, *Flashback,* Paramount, 1990.

Adult Jack Twiller, *Book of Love,* New Line Cinema, 1991.

Harvey Cooper, *True Identity,* Buena Vista, 1991.

Eddy Revere, *Man Trouble,* Twentieth Century–Fox, 1992.

George Talbot, *Memoirs of an Invisible Man* (also known as *Les aventures d'un homme invisible*), Warner Bros., 1992.

David St. Hubbins, *Spinal Tap: Break Like the Wind— The Videos,* 1992.

Immigration Agent Gordon Seedling, *Coneheads,* Paramount, 1993.

Mojo Flats, 1993.

Rick Rochester, *Radioland Murders,* Universal, 1994.

Milo, *Airheads,* Twentieth Century–Fox, 1994.

Frank, *Across the Moon* (also known as *Tehachapi*), Hemdale, 1994.

Mr. Larry Dittmeyer, *The Brady Bunch Movie,* Paramount, 1995.

Voice of Rupert, *Johnny Bravo,* 1995.

Frank, *Across the Moon* (also known as *Mojo Flats*), 1995.

Rick, *Edie & Pen,* 1996.

Sitcom star, *The Pompatus of Love,* 1996.

Willy, *The Making of "1941,"* 1996.

Paulie, *Jack,* Buena Vista, 1996.

Elliot Lewis, *No Strings Attached,* 1997.

Peter Randall, *That Darn Cat,* Buena Vista, 1997.

Phillip Barrow, *Nothing to Lose,* Buena Vista, 1997.

Bill Case, *Casper: A Spirited Beginning,* Twentieth Century–Fox Home Entertainment, 1997.

New Mark, *Still Breathing,* October Films, 1997.

John Tesh, Entertainment Tonight anchor, *Saturday Night Live: The Best of Mike Meyers,* NBC, 1998.

Dr. Maxwell Hersh, *With Friends Like These …,* Miramax, 1998.

J. P., *Archibald the Rainbow Painter* (also known as *The Homefront*), Empty Box Productions, 1998.

Voices of Insaniac and Freakenstein, *Small Soldiers* (animated and live–action), DreamWorks/Red Feather Photoplays, 1998.

Reverend Hooper, *The Man Who Counted,* Cumberland Films, 1998.

David St. Hubbins, *Spinal Tap: The Final Tour,* 1998.

Willie L., *The Pass* (also known as *Highway Hitcher*), 1998.

Will Masters, *Masters of Horror and Suspense,* 1999.

Principal Potter, *Teaching Mrs. Tingle,* Miramax/ Dimension Films, 1999.

Mr. Walsh, *Mystery, Alaska,* Buena Vista, 1999.

Sugar: The Fall of the West, Next Generation, 1999.

Mr. Livingston, *Kill the Man,* Fresh Produce/Seattle Pacific Investments/Summit Entertainment, 1999.

Reverend Shillerman, *True Crime,* Warner Bros., 1999.

Stefan Vanderhoof, *Best in Show* (also known as *Dog Show!*), Warner Bros., 2000.

Lance DeSalvo, *Beautiful,* Destination Films, 2000.

David St. Hubbins, *100 Greatest Artists of Hard Rock,* 2000.

Chief of police, *Little Nicky,* 2000.

David St. Hubbins, *Catching Up with Marty DiBergi,* 2000.

Bob Benson, *My First Mister,* 2001.

Voice of bird, *Dr. Dolittle 2* (also known as *DR2*), Twentieth Century–Fox, 2001.

Panelist, *Wild Desk Ride* (also known as *Conan O'Brien's Wild Desk Ride*), 2001.

Voice of Mr. Bream, *Recess Christmas: Miracle on Third Street,* 2001.

Award presenter, *On the Edge,* 2001.

Alex, *Never Again,* USA Films, 2002.

Monsieur Duke, *Slap Her … She's French* (also known as *Freche Biester!*), Premiere Marketing and Distribution Group, 2002.

Himself, *Gigantic: A Tale of Two Johns,* Bonfire Films of America, 2002.

Voice of Sarousch, *The Hunchback of Notre Dame II* (animated), Buena Vista Home Video/Walt Disney Home Video, 2002.

Porterfield "Porty" Pendleton, *Teddy Bears' Picnic,* Magnolia Pictures, 2002.

Dwain, *The Guru* (also known as *Le gourou et les femmes*), MCA/Universal, 2002.

Video executive, *Auto Focus,* Sony Pictures Classics, 2002.

Howard, *100 Mile Rule,* Honeydo/Road Rules Productions, 2002.

Gigantic (A Tale of Two Johns), 2002.

Jerry Palter, *A Mighty Wind,* Warner Bros., 2003.

Captain Van Legge, *Haunted Lighthouse* (also known as *R. L. Stein's "Haunted Lighthouse"*), Lookout Entertainment, 2003.

Patient, *Candor City Hospital,* HelloBox Films, 2003.

Adult Jack Twiller, *Meet Bob Shaye,* New Line Home Video, 2004.

David St. Hubbins, *The Secret Policeman's Ball: The Music Edition,* 2004.

The Aristocrats (also known as *The @r!$t*(r@t$)*, Lions Gate Films, 2005.

Voice of narrator/Arnie the Doughnut, *Arnie the Doughnut,* Weston Woods Studios, 2005.

Prison trustee, *The Producers,* Columbia, 2005.

David St. Hubbins, *The 100 Funniest Movies,* 2006.

Comedy Club Shoot–Out: Vol. 2, Lions Gate Films, 2006.

Dr. Flossman, *Open Wide: Tooth School Inside,* Scholastic, 2006.

Jerry Palter, *The Harry Smith Project Live,* Shout! Factory, 2006.

Ken Hyman, *Relative Strangers,* First Look, 2006.

Lane Iverson, *For Your Consideration,* Warner Bros., 2006.

Chester Jenkins, *Joshua,* Twentieth Century–Fox, 2007.

Voice of Rock, *Surf's Up,* Sony, 2007.

Billionaire Steve Lavisch, *The Grand,* Anchor Bay Entertainment, 2007.

David St. Hubbins, *It Might Get Loud,* Sony, 2008.

Harlan, *Adventures of Power,* Variance Films, 2008.

Fritz number two, *Imps*,* Monterey Media, 2009.

Boris' friend, *Whatever Works,* Sony Pictures Classics, 2009.

David St. Hubbins, *Stonehenge: 'Tis a Magic Place,* iTunes, 2009.

David St. Hubbins, *Spinal Tap: Back from the Dead,* Artist 2 Market, 2009.

Stage Appearances:

Accomplice, Pasadena Playhouse, Pasadena, CA, 1989, then Richard Rodgers Theatre, New York City, 1990.

Edna Turnblad, *Hairspray,* Neil Simon Theatre, New York City, 2002–2009.

Sam, *Hair,* New Amsterdam Theatre, New York City, 2004.

Phil Wellman, *A Second Hand Memory,* Linda Gross Theatre, New York City, 2004–2005.

Hines, *The Pajama Game,* American Airlines Theatre, New York City, 2006.

Th Homecoming, Cort Theatre, New York City, 2007–2008.

Arthur Przybyszewski, *Superior Donuts,* Music Box Theatre, New York City, 2009–10.

RECORDINGS

Albums:

(With Credibility Gap) *A Great Gift Idea* (comedy album), 1974.

(With David Lander) *Lenny and the Squigtones,* Casablanca Record and FilmWorks, 1979.

Break Like the Wind, c. 1992.

Other albums include *This Is Spinal Tap* and (with Credibility Gap) *Woodshtick.*

Videos:

David St. Hubbins, *A Year and a Half in the Life of Metallica,* 1992.

Short 3: Authority, 2000.

Adam Sandler Goes to Hell, 2001.

Panelist, *Wild Desk Ride* (also known as *Conan O'Brien's Wild Desk Ride*), 2001.

Performer, *Standing Ovations 2,* 2004 BroadwayWorld.com, 2004.

Threads of Mythology, Part 2, Twentieth Century–Fox, 2005.

Unwigged & Unplugged Live Concert DVD: An Evening with Christopher Guest, Michael McKean and Harry Shearer, 2009.

Video Games:

Voice of Dungeon Master Dalboz of Gurth, *Zork: Grand Inquisitor,* 1997.

WRITINGS

Television Episodes:

(With David L. Lander and Harry Shearer) "Hi, Neighbor," *Laverne & Shirley* (also known as *Laverne & Shirley & Company* and *Laverne & Shirley & Friends*), ABC, 1976.

(With Lander) "Hi, Neighbor, Book 2," *Laverne & Shirley* (also known as *Laverne & Shirley & Company* and *Laverne & Shirley & Friends*), ABC, 1977.

"Michael McKean/Chaka Khan/The Folksmen," *Saturday Night Live* (also known as *SNL*), NBC, 1984.

(With Christopher Guest) "The Bride of Mummula," *Morton & Hayes* (also known as *Partners in Life*), CBS, 1991.

"Springing Tiny," *The Huntress,* USA Network, 2000.

Television Specials:

Economic Love–In, 1973.

A Spinal Tap Reunion: The 25th Anniversary London Sell–Out (also known as *The Return of Spinal Tap*), NBC, 1992.

Uncomfortably Close with Michael McKean: Jason Alexander, Comedy Central, 1999.

Uncomfortably Close with Michael McKean: Jerry Stiller, Comedy Central, 1999.

Uncomfortably Close with Michael McKean: Jonathan Winters, Comedy Central, 2000.

Uncomfortably Close with Michael McKean: Rob Reiner, Comedy Central, 2000.

Uncomfortably Close with Michael McKean: George Carlin, Comedy Central, 2001.

Uncomfortably Close with Michael McKean: Harold Ramis, Comedy Central, 2001.

Television Music; Episodic:

Song "Creature without a Head," "Monty Hale," *America 2–Night,* 1978.

"Love Is A Terrible Thing," *Bandstand* (also known as *AB* and *American Bandstand*), 1979.

Song "If Only I Had Listened To Mama," "The Fourth Annual Shotz Talent Show," *Laverne & Shirley* (also known as *Laverne & Shirley & Company* and *Laverne & Shirley & Friends*), ABC, 1979.

Song "The Look," "Sing, Sing, Sing," *Laverne & Shirley* (also known as *Laverne & Shirley & Company* and *Laverne & Shirley & Friends*), ABC, 1981.

Songs "Christmas with the Devil" and "Big Bottom," "Barry Bostwick/Spinal Tap," *Saturday Night Live* (also known as *SNL* Night), NBC, 1984.

Songs "Blood on The Coal" and "Old Joe's Place," "Michael McKean/Chaka Khan/The Folksmen," *Saturday Night Live* (also known as *SNL*), NBC, 1984.

Song "The Majesty of Rock," "Stewart's House," *Beavis and Butt–Head* (animated), 1993.

Song "Death Lies Awaitin," *McEnroe,* 2004.

Song "Stonehenge," "Simon Said," *Supernatural,* 2006.

Television Music; Other:

Composer, *The T.V. Show,* 1979.

Composer, *Morton & Heyes,* 1991.

Composer, *A Spinal Tap Reunion: The 25th Anniversary London Sell–Out* (special; also known as *The Return of Spinal Tap*), NBC, 1992.

Song composer, "Too Many Nights," *Attack of the 50 Ft. Woman* (movie), HBO, 1993.

Uncomfortably Close with Michael McKean (specials), 1999–2001.

Song composer, "A Kiss at the End of the Rainbow," *The 76th Annual Academy Awards,* ABC, 2004.

Screenplays:

(With Rob Reiner, Christopher Guest, and Harry Shearer) *This Is Spinal Tap,* Embassy, 1984.

(With Guest and Michael Varhol) *The Big Picture* (based on a story by Varhol and Guest), Columbia, 1989.

Spinal Tap: Break Like the Wind—The Videos, 1992.

Film Music:

Composer and lyricist, *This Is Spinal Tap,* Embassy, 1984.

Songwriter, "The Whites of Their Eyes," *The Big Picture,* Columbia, 1989.

Songwriter, "Big Bottom," "Earache My Eye," *Soundgarden: Louder Than Live,* 1990.

Songwriter, "Gimme Some Money," *Don't Tell Mom the Babysitter's Dead,* 1991.

Composer, *Spinal Tap: Break Like the Wind—The Videos,* 1992.

Composer and lyricist for the songs "Covered Wagons, Open–Toed Shoes" and "A Penny for Your Thoughts," *Waiting for Guffman,* Sony Pictures Classics, 1996.

Song composer, "Louisiana Nights," *Best in Show* (also known as *Dog Show!*), Warner Bros., 2000.

Songwriter, "Old Joe's Place," "The Good Book Song," "A Kiss at the End of the Rainbow," "Just That Kinda Day," "Never Did No Wanderin," "Fare Away," "Potato's in the Paddy Wagon," and "A Mighty Wind," *A Mighty Wind,* 2003.

Songwriter, "Banjo Daddy," *Standing Ovations,* BroadwayWorld.com, 2004.

Songwriter, "Big Bottom," *It Might Get Loud,* Sony Pictures Classics, 2009.

Video Game Music:

Songwriter, "Tonight I'm Gonna Rock You Tonight," *Guitar Hero II,* Activision, 2006.

MENDLER, Bridgit 1992–

PERSONAL

Born December 18, 1992, in Washington, DC.

Addresses: *Agent*—The Gersh Agency, 9465 Wilshire Blvd., 6th Floor, Beverly Hills, CA 90212. *Manager*—LA Entertainment, 9420 Reseda Blvd., Suite 838, Northridge, CA 91316.

Career: Actress.

CREDITS

Television Appearances; Series:

Juliet Van Heusen, *Wizards of Waverly Place,* The Disney Channel, 2009–10.

Teddy Duncan, *Good Luck Charlie,* The Disney Channel, 2010.

Television Appearances; Episodic:

Lulu's dream daughter, *General Hospital,* ABC, 2006.

The Tyra Banks Show, The CW, two episodes, 2008.

Penny, "Wrong Song," *Jonas,* 2009.

Film Appearances:

The Legend of Buddha, 2004.

Pamela, *Alice Upside Down,* Anchor Bay Entertainment, 2007.

Kristen Gregory, *The Clique,* Warner Home Video, 2008.

Emma Clayhill, *Labor Pains,* First Look Pictures Releasing, 2009.

Becca, *Alvin and the Chipmunks: The Squeakquel* (also known as *Alvin 2*), Twentieth Century–Fox, 2009.

RECORDINGS

Video Games:
Voice of Thorn, *Bone: The Great Cow Race,* Telltale Games, 2006.

MENKE, Sally 1953–2010
(Sally Jo Menke)

PERSONAL

Full name, Sally JoAnne Menke; born December 17, 1953, in Mineola, NY; died September 27, 2010, in Los Angeles, CA. Editor. Known for her seventeen-year collaboration with Quentin Tarantino, Menke received numerous nominations for Academy Awards, American Cinema Editors Awards, and British Academy of Film and Television Arts Awards. She began by editing television documentaries and progressed to full-length films, hitting her stride in the early 1990s with *Teenage Mutant Ninja Turtles; The Search for Signs of Intelligent Life in the Universe,* starring Lily Tomlin; and her first Tarantino production, the crime cult film *Reservoir Dogs.* Director Oliver Stone worked with Menke on the last of his Vietnam War trilogy, the 1993 film *Heaven and Earth.* In 1994 she teamed up with Tarantino again to make the stylized crime thriller *Pulp Fiction,* for which she earned her first Academy Award nomination. She edited the neo-noir crime film *Mulholland Falls* in 1996 and Tarantino's *Jackie Brown,* a tribute to 1970s blaxploitation films, in 1997. *Kill Bill* Volumes 1 and 2, her 2003 to 2004 collaboration with Tarantino, also paid tribute to earlier film genres and used extensive pop music and culture references. It was nominated for several editing awards, winning two from film critics societies in Las Vegas and San Diego. Her last Tarantino work, *Inglorious Basterds* (2009), was also nominated for an Academy Award, among other best-editing nominations. In 2010 Menke edited her last film, the thriller *Peacock,* directed by Michael Lander.

PERIODICALS

Los Angeles Times, September 29, 2010.
New York Times, September 29, 2010.

MOYNAHAN, Bridget 1971–

PERSONAL

Full name, Kathryn Bridget Moynahan; born April 28, 1971, in Binghamton, NY; daughter of Brad Moynahan (a scientist and college administrator); mother, a former schoolteacher; children: (with Tom Brady, a professional football player) John Edward Thomas. *Education:* Studied acting at the Caymichael Patten Studio.

Addresses: *Agent*—Innovative Artists, 1505 10th St., Santa Monica, CA 90401; WME Entertainment, One William Morris Pl., Beverly Hills, CA 90212. *Manager*—Brillstein Entertainment Partners, 9150 Wilshire Blvd., Suite 350, Beverly Hills, CA 90212. *Publicist*—Baker, Winokur, Ryder, 825 Eighth Ave., Worldwide Plaza, New York, NY 10019.

Career: Actress. Previously worked as a model. Appeared in television and radio commercials for Comcast, 2005; Garnier Nutritioniste, spokesmodel, 2009—.

CREDITS

Film Appearances:
Apartment owner, *Row Your Boat,* Guallane Pictures, 1999.
Amy, *In the Weeds,* Moonstone Entertainment, 2000.
Fame, *Trifling with Fate,* 2000.
Rachel, *Coyote Ugly,* Buena Vista, 2000.
Marie, *Whipped,* Destination Films, 2000.
Halley Buchanan, *Serendipity,* Miramax, 2001.
Dr. Caroline "Cathy" Muller, *The Sum of All Fears* (also known as *Total Fears*), Paramount, 2002.
Layla Moore, *The Recruit,* Buena Vista, 2003.
Susan Calvin, *I, Robot,* Twentieth Century–Fox, 2004.
Herself, *Day Out of Days: The "I, Robot" Production Diaries* (documentary), Twentieth Century–Fox, 2004.
Charlie Kelsey, *Gray Matters,* Yari Film Group Releasing, 2006.
Eliza Coles, *Unknown,* IFC First Take, 2006.
Amy Newman, *Prey,* Weinstein Company, 2007.
Helen Owen, *Noise,* THINKFilm, 2007.
Herself, *Journey into the Unknown* (short film), Weinstein Company, 2007.
Dorothy Quimby, *Ramona and Beezus,* Twentieth Century–Fox, 2010.

Television Appearances; Series:
Natasha, *Sex and the City,* HBO, 1999–2000.
Whitney Crane, *Six Degrees,* ABC, 2006–2007.
Erin Reagan-Boyle, *Blue Bloods,* CBS, 2010—.

Television Appearances; Specials:
Herself and Hally, *On the Set: "Serendipity,"* 2001.
Presenter, *The 2002 MTV Movie Awards,* MTV, 2002.
The 2004 ESPY Awards, ESPN, 2004.
The 20th IFC Independent Spirit Awards, Independent Film Channel and Bravo, 2005.
Moving Images Salutes Will Smith, Bravo, 2007.

Television Appearances; Pilots:
Erin Moriarty, *Bunker Hill,* TNT, 2009.
Erin Reagan–Boyle, *Blue Bloods,* CBS, 2010.

Television Appearances; Episodic:
Lily, "Lily of the Field," *Going to California,* Showtime, 2001.
The Tonight Show with Jay Leno, NBC, 2002.
Late Night with Conan O'Brien, NBC, 2003.
"The Making of 'I, Robot,'" *HBO First Look,* HBO, 2004.
The Late Late Show with Craig Kilborn (also known as *The Late, Late Show*), CBS, 2004.
Good Morning America (also known as *G.M.A.*), ABC, 2005.
The View, ABC, 2006.
Ashley Cardiff, "Help!," *Eli Stone,* ABC, 2008.
Ashley Cardiff, "Owner of a Lonely Heart," *Eli Stone,* ABC, 2008.

OTHER SOURCES

Periodicals:
Harper's Bazaar, July, 2008, p. 138.
People Weekly, April 20, 2009, p. 60.
USA Today, July 23, 2010, p. 9D.

MYHRE, John

PERSONAL

Addresses: *Agent*—Sandra Marsh and Associates, 9150 Wilshire Blvd., Suite 220, Beverly Hills, CA 90212.

Career: Production designer and art director.

Awards, Honors: Academy Award nomination (with Peter Howitt), best art direction—set decoration, Film Award nomination, best production design, British Academy of Film and Television Arts, Excellence in Production Design Award nomination (with others), Art Directors Guild, Golden Satellite Award nomination, best motion picture art direction, International Press Academy, 1999, all for *Elizabeth;* Academy Award (with Gordon Sim), best art direction–set decoration, Film Award nomination, production design, British Academy of Film and Television Arts, Excellence in Production Design Award nomination (with others), feature film—period or fantasy films, Art Directors Guild, 2003, all for *Chicago;* Satellite Award nomination, outstanding art direction and production design, 2005, Academy Award (with Gretchen Rau), best art direction–set decoration, Film Award nomination, best

production design, British Academy of Film and Television Arts, Excellence in Production Design Award (with others), feature film—period or fantasy film, Art Directors Guild, 2006, all for *Memoirs of a Geisha;* Satellite Award nomination (with others), best art direction and production design, 2006, Academy Award nomination (with Nancy Haigh), best achievement in art direction, Excellence in Production Design Award nomination (with others), feature film—period film, Art Directors Guild, 2007, all for *Dreamgirls;* Hollywood Film Award, production designer of the year, Hollywood Film Festival, 2006; Emmy Award (with others), outstanding art direction for a variety, music, or nonfiction programming, Excellence in Production Design Award nomination (with others), television—variety or awards show, musical special, or documentary, Art Directors Guild, 2007, all for *Tony Bennett: An American Classic;* Academy Award nomination (with Gordon Sim), best achievement in art direction, 2010, for *Nine.*

CREDITS

Film Art Director:
Amazing Grace and Chuck, TriStar, 1987.
Russkies, New Century Vista Film Company, 1987.
Deadly Weapon, Empire Pictures, 1989.
Blind Fury, TriStar, 1989.
Welcome Home, Roxy Carmichael, Paramount, 1990.
Popcorn (also known as *Phantom of the Cinema*), Studio Three, 1991.
Salmonberries, Roxie Releasing, 1991.
Hear No Evil (also known as *Danger Sign*), Twentieth Century–Fox, 1993.
What's Eating Gilbert Grape, Paramount, 1993.
It Runs in the Family, Metro–Goldwyn–Mayer, 1994.

Film Production Designer:
Puppetmaster (also known as *Puppet Master I*), Paramount, 1989.
The Silencer, Academy, 1992.
Airborne, Warner Bros., 1993.
Foxfire, Samuel Goldwyn Company, 1996.
Leo Tolstoy's "Anna Karenina" (also known as *Anna Karenina*), Warner Bros., 1997.
Lawn Dogs, Strand Releasing, 1997.
Elizabeth (also known as *Elizabeth: The Virgin Queen*), Gramercy, 1998.
X–Men (also known as *X–Men 1.5*), Twentieth Century–Fox, 2000.
Ali, Columbia, 2001.
Chicago, Miramax, 2002.
The Haunted Mansion (also known as *Disney's "The Haunted Mansion"*), Buena Vista, 2003.
Memoirs of a Geisha, Columbia, 2006.
Dreamgirls, DreamWorks, 2006.
Wanted, Universal, 2008.
Nine, Weinstein Company, 2009.

Film Work; Other:
Assistant property master, *Night of the Comet,* Atlantic Releasing Corp., 1984.
Property master, *Creature* (also known as *Titan Find*), Metro–Goldwyn–Mayer, 1985.
Property master, *Student Confidential,* Troma Entertainment, 1987.
Set decorator, *18 Again!,* New World, 1988.
Supervising art director, *Immortal Beloved,* Columbia, 1994.

Film Appearances:
Himself, *"X–Men" Production Scrapbook* (documentary), Twentieth Century–Fox Home Entertainment, 2003.

Television Set Decorator; Series:
Lifestories, NBC, 1990.

Television Art Director; Movies:
Out on the Edge, CBS, 1989.

Television Production Designer; Movies:
One Woman's Courage, NBC, 1994.
Vanishing Point, Fox, 1997.

Television Work; Specials:
Art director, *The Sunset Gang,* PBS, 1991.
Production designer, *Tony Bennett: An American Classic,* NBC, 2006.

Television Appearances; Specials:
The Making of "Ali," 2001.
The 75th Annual Academy Awards, ABC, 2003.
MovieReal: Memoirs of a Geisha, Arts and Entertainment, 2005.
The 78th Annual Academy Awards, ABC, 2008.

Television Appearances; Episodic:
"Ali," *HBO First Look,* HBO, 2001.
"The Making of 'Dreamgirls,'" *HBO First Look,* HBO, 2006.

N

NICASTRO, Michelle 1960–2010

PERSONAL

Born March 31, 1960, in Washington, DC; died of breast cancer, November 4, 2010, in Toluca Lake, CA. Actress and singer. Nicastros varied career included appearances in Broadway shows, on television, and in Hollywood films. Placido Domingo helped establish her singing career, presenting her as a soloist at the Hollywood Bowl. Her first stage appearance was as Ariadne in *Merlin,* the 1983 Broadway musical. A 1984 role on the series *Airwolf* introduced her to television audiences and was followed by guest-star roles on *Who's the Boss?, Charles in Charge, Knight Rider, Wings,* and *Coach.* In 1984 she also began appearing in films, first in *Body Rock* and then in *Bad Guys* (1986) and, most memorably, in the 1989 romantic comedy *When Harry Met Sally.* Nicostas portrayal of the character Eponine in the 1988 Los Angeles stage production of *Les Miserables* won her both Drama-Logue and Robby Awards. From 1989 to 1990 she played a torch singer on the Daytime Emmy Award-winning series *Santa Barbara,* and she costarred in Barry Manilow's worldwide *Showstoppers* tour in 1992. Her voice talents made her familiar in the role of Princess Odette in the animated 1994 film *The Swan Princess,* as well as in its 1997 and 1998 sequels. Nicosta recorded four record albums of songs from contemporary musicals and classic cartoons.

PERIODICALS

Epoch Times, November 10, 2010.
Los Angeles Times, November 10, 2010.
Mercury News, November 9, 2010.
Variety, November 10, 2010.

NICOTERO, Gregory 1963–
(Greg Nicotero)

PERSONAL

Born March 15, 1963, in Pittsburgh, PA; father, a physician; married Shari (an assistant director); children: Deven, Alyssa. *Education:* Attended college. *Avocational Interests:* Playing guitar.

Addresses: *Office*—KNB EFX Group, Inc., 7535 Woodman Pl., Van Nuys, CA 91405. *Agent*—United Talent Agency, 9560 Wilshire Blvd., Suite 500, Beverly Hills, CA 90212.

Career: Special effects makeup artist, special effects makeup designer, special effects makeup supervisor, makeup effects supervisor, puppeteer, producer, second unit director, and actor. KNB EFX Group, Inc., Van Nuys, CA, cofounder and principal, 1988—.

Awards, Honors: CableACE Award nomination (with others), make–up, 1994, for *Body Bags;* CableACE Award nomination (with others), make–up, 1995, for *State of Emergency;* Saturn Award (with others), best make–up, Academy of Science Fiction, Fantasy, and Horror Films, 1999, for *Vampire$;* Emmy Award (with others), outstanding special visual effects for a miniseries, movie or a special, 2001, for *Dune;* Best Make–Up (with others), Sitges–Catalonian International Film Festival, 2002, for *Cabin Fever;* Golden Satellite Award nomination (with Howard Berger), best visual effects, International Press Academy, Phoenix Film Critics Society Award nomination (with Berger), best visual effects, 2004, both for *Kill Bill: Vol. 1;* Hollywood Film Award, makeup of the year, Hollywood Film Festival, 2005; Time–Machine Honorary Award, Sitges–Catalonian International Film Festival, 2005; Film

Award (with Berger and Nikki Gooley), best makeup/hair, British Academy of Film and Television Arts, Saturn Award (with Berger and Gooley), best make–up, Academy of Science Fiction, Fantasy, and Horror Films, 2006, all for *The Chronicles of Narnia: The Lion, the Witch and the Wardrobe;* Saturn Award nomination (with Berger), best make–up, Academy of Science Fiction, Fantasy, and Horror Films, 2006, for *Sin City;* Saturn Award nomination (with Berger), best make–up, Academy of Science Fiction, Fantasy, and Horror Films, 2006, for *Land of the Dead;* Saturn Award nomination (with others), best make–up, Academy of Science Fiction, Fantasy, and Horror Films, 2007, for *The Hills Have Eyes;* Saturn Award nomination (with Scott Patton), best make–up, Academy of Science Fiction, Fantasy, and Horror Films, 2007, for *The Texas Chainsaw Massacre: The Beginning;* Saturn Award nomination (with others), best make–up, Academy of Science Fiction, Fantasy, and Horror Films, 2008, for *Planet Terror;* Saturn Award nomination (with Paul Engelen), best make–up, Academy of Science Fiction, Fantasy, and Horror Films, 2009, for *The Chronicles of Narnia: Prince Caspian;* Sewickley Academy Arts Hall of Fame, inductee, 2009; Emmy Award (with others), outstanding prosthetic makeup for a series, miniseries, movie or a special, 2010, for *The Pacific;* Saturn Award nomination (with Berger), best make–up, Academy of Science Fiction, Fantasy, and Horror Films, 2010, for *The Book of Eli;* Saturn Award nomination (with Berger), best make–up, Academy of Science Fiction, Fantasy, and Horror Films, 2010, for *Drag Me To Hell.*

CREDITS

Film Work:

Assistant to Tom Savini and special makeup effects artist, *Day of the Dead* (also known as *George A. Romero's "Day of the Dead"*), United Film Distribution Company, 1985.

(As Greg Nicotero) Additional special effects makeup, *Invasion U.S.A.,* Cannon, 1985.

Effects technician, *From Beyond* (also known as *H. P. Lovecraft's "From Beyond"*), 1986.

Special makeup effects unit crew and (uncredited) special effects technician, *Evil Dead II,* Rosebud Releasing Corp., 1987.

Special effects and makeup effects, *Creepshow 2* (also known as *Dead and Undead: Creepshow 2*), New World Pictures, 1987.

(Uncredited) Creature effects crew, *Predator,* 1987.

Special effects crew and special makeup effects constructor, *Phantasm II,* Universal, 1988.

Special makeup effects artist, *Monkey Shines* (also known as *Monkey Shines: An Experiment in Fear*), Orion, 1988.

Special makeup effects artist, *Intruder* (also known as *Night Crew: The Final Checkout*), Empire Pictures, 1989.

Special makeup effects artist, *The Horror Show,* United Artists, 1989.

Special effects, *Nightwish,* 1989.

Cadaver consultant, *Gross Anatomy,* Walt Disney Studios Distribution, 1989.

Creature supervisor, *DeepStar Six,* TriStar, 1989.

Special effects, *The Horror Show,* United Artists, 1989.

Special makeup effects artist and supervisor, *A Nightmare on Elm Street: The Dream Child* (also known as *A Nightmare on Elm Street 5: The Dream Child* and *Nightmare on Elm Street 5*), 1989.

Special makeup effects artist, and special makeup effects and bride effects creator, *Bride of Re–Animator,* 50th Street Films, 1990.

Additional makeup effects supervisor, *Night Angel,* 1990.

(As Greg Nicotero) Buffalo effects supervisor, *Dances with Wolves,* 1990.

Makeup artist, *Texas Chainsaw Massacre 3* (also known as *Leatherface: Texas Chainsaw Massacre III, Leatherface,* and *Leatherface: The Texas Chainsaw Massacre III*), New Line Cinema, 1990.

(As Greg Nicotero) Special makeup effects supervisor, *Tales from the Darkside: The Movie* (also known as *Creepshow 3, Darkside Movie,* and *Tales from the Darkside*), Paramount, 1990.

(As Greg Nicotero) Special makeup effects artist, *Sibling Rivalry,* Columbia, 1990.

(As Greg Nicotero) Special makeup effects artist, *Misery,* Columbia, 1990.

Special makeup effects artist, *Children of the Night,* Columbia, 1991.

Special makeup effects supervisor, *The People Under the Stairs,* Universal, 1991.

Special makeup effects supervisor, *The Nutt House* (also known as *The Nutty Nutt*), Triboro Entertainment Group, 1992.

Mechanical animal effects, *City Slickers,* Columbia, 1991.

(As Greg Nicotero) Designer, *Mindwarp* (also known as *Brain Slasher*), 1992.

Special makeup effects and special makeup effects supervisor, *Army of Darkness* (also known as *Army of Darkness: The Ultimate Experience in Medieval Horror* and *Bruce Campbell vs. Army of Darkness*), Universal, 1992.

Special makeup effects supervisor, *Dr. Giggles,* Universal, 1992.

Second unit director, *Severed Ties,* Columbia, 1992.

Second unit director, *The Nutt House* (also known as *The Nutty Nut*), Triboro Entertainment Group, 1992.

Effects supervisor and special makeup effects artist, *Jason Goes to Hell: The Final Friday* (also known as *Jason Goes to Hell*), 1993.

Special effects supervisor, *Skinner,* A–Pix Entertainment, 1993.

Special makeup effects, *Doppelganger* (also known as *Doppelanger: The Evil Within*), CBS/Fox, 1993.

Special makeup effects supervisor, *Maniac Cop 3: Badge of Silence* (also known as *MC3: Maniac Cop 3* and *Maniac Cop III: Badge of Silence*), Academy Home Entertainment, 1993.

Special makeup effects supervisor for second unit, *Infested* (also known as *Ticks*), Republic Pictures Home Video, 1993.

Special makeup effects artist, *Skinner,* A–Pix Entertainment, 1993.

Special makeup effects, *Ed and His Dead Mother,* IRS Media, 1993.

Special makeup effects supervisor, *Pumpkinhead II: Blood Wings* (also known as *Pumpkinhead II*), 1994.

(Uncredited) Special makeup supervisor, *Pulp Fiction,* Miramax, 1994.

Special makeup effects, *New Nightmare* (also known as *Wes Craven's "New Nightmare"*), New Line Cinema, 1994.

Special makeup effects and puppeteer, *Vampire in Brooklyn* (also known as *Wes Craven's "Vampire in Brooklyn"*), Paramount, 1995.

Special makeup effects, *In the Mouth of Madness* (also known as *John Carpenter's "In the Mouth of Madness"*), New Line Cinema, 1995.

Special makeup effects supervisor, *The Walking Dead,* Savoy Pictures, 1995.

Special makeup effects supervisor, *Galaxis,* Prism Entertainment Corp., 1995.

Special makeup effects, *Lord of Illusions,* United Artists, 1995.

(As Greg Nicotero) Special effects prosthetics, *Never Talk to Strangers,* TriStar, 1995.

Supervisor, *Darkman II: The Return of Durant,* 1995.

Special makeup effects supervisor, *Lord of Illusions,* 1995.

(As Greg Nicotero) Co–executive producer, *Black Velvet Pantsuit,* 1995.

Special effects supervisor, *Village of the Damned,* Universal, 1995.

(As Greg Nicotero) Stunts and makeup effects supervisor, *From Dusk Till Dawn,* Dimension Films, 1996.

Puppeteer, *Black Sheep,* Paramount, 1996.

(As Greg Nicotero) Supervisor for turboman suit, *Jingle All the Way,* Twentieth Century–Fox, 1996.

(As Greg Nicotero) Animatronic crocodiles supervisor, *Eraser,* 1996.

(As Greg Nicotero) Special makeup effects supervisor, *Scream,* Dimension Films, 1996.

Special makeup supervisor, *DNA* (also known as *Genetic Code*), Astra Cinema, 1997.

Special makeup effects supervisor, *The Night Flier* (also known as *Stephen King's "The Night Flier"*), New Line Cinema, 1997.

Animatronic creature effects and special makeup effects, *Spawn,* New Line Cinema, 1997.

Special makeup effects supervisor, *Boogie Nights,* New Line Cinema, 1997.

(As Greg Nicotero) Special makeup effects supervisor, *Scream 2,* Dimension Films, 1997.

Special makeup effects and second unit director, *Wishmaster* (also known as *Wes Craven Presents "Wishmaster"*), Imperial Entertainment, 1997.

Supervisor, *Jungle2jungle,* Walt Disney Studios Distribution, 1997.

Makeup effects supervisor, *Phantoms* (also known as *Dean Koontz's "Phantoms"* and *Phantom*), Dimension Films, 1998.

Special makeup effects, *Vampire$* (also known as *Vampires* and *John Carpenter's "Vampires"*), Columbia, 1998.

(As Greg Nicotero) Supervisor, *Very Bad Things,* Polygram Filmed Entertainment, 1998.

Special makeup and creature effects and puppeteer, *The Faculty* (also known as *Parasite*), Dimension Films, 1998.

Special makeup effects supervisor, *From Dusk Till Dawn 2: Texas Blood Money,* Amuse Pictures, 1999.

(As Greg Nicotero) Puppeteer and special makeup effects supervisor, *The Haunting* (also known as *La maldicion*), DreamWorks, 1999.

(As Greg Nicotero) Special makeup effects, supervisor, and director of blue screen unit, *From Dusk Till Dawn 3: The Hangman's Daughter* (also known as *The Hangman's Daughter*), 1999.

Makeup effects supervisor and (as Greg Nicotero) puppeteer, *Bats,* Columbia, 1999.

Special makeup effects, *House on Haunted Hill,* Warner Bros., 1999.

(As Greg Nicotero) Special makeup effects supervisor, *The Green Mile* (also known as *Stephen King's "The Green Mile"*), Warner Bros., 1999.

Special creature effects, *Spiders,* 2000.

Special creature effects, *Crocodile,* 2000.

(As Greg Nicotero) Puppeteer, *Ghost of Mars* (also known as *John Carpenter's "Ghost of Mars"*), 2000.

Special makeup and creature effects supervisor, *Little Nicky,* 2000.

(As Greg Nicotero) Behind–the–scenes video, *The Making of "Evil Dead II" or the Gore the Merrier,* 2000.

(As Greg Nicotero) Puppeteer, *What Lies Beneath,* DreamWorks, 2000.

Special makeup effects artist, *The Crow: Salvation,* Dimension Films, 2000.

(As Greg Nicotero) Special makeup effects supervisor, *Picking Up the Pieces* (also known as *Virgin Hand*), WMA Independent, 2000.

(As Greg Nicotero) Special makeup effects, *Mission to Mars* (also known as *M2M*), Buena Vista, 2000.

Prosthetics supervisor and special makeup effects supervisor, *The Cell* (also known as *Lethal Cell*), New Line Cinema, 2000.

(As Greg Nicotero) Special makeup effects supervisor, *Unbreakable,* Buena Vista, 2000.

Supervisor of special makeup effects, *The Adventures of Rocky and Bullwinkle,* Universal, 2000.

Supervisor of special makeup and creature effects, *Little Nicky,* New Line Cinema, 2000.

Special makeup effects supervisor, special makeup and creature effects, and puppeteer, *Spy Kids,* Dimension Films, 2001.

(As Greg Nicotero) Special makeup effects artist, *The Animal* (also known as *Animal Man*), Columbia, 2001.

(As Greg Nicotero) Special makeup effects artist, *Mulholland Dr.* (also known as *Mulholland Drive*), Universal, 2001.

Special makeup effects artist, *Ghost of Mars* (also known as *John Carpenter's "Ghost of Mars"*), Screen Gems, 2001.

Special makeup effects supervisor, *Thir13en Ghosts,* Warner Bros., 2001.

Special makeup effects supervisor, *Vanilla Sky,* Paramount, 2001.

(As Greg Nicotero) Puppeteer, *Rat Race,* Paramount, 2001.

Special makeup and creature effects, *Soulkeeper,* 2001.

Supervisor of special creature effects, *Evolution,* 2001.

(As Greg Nicotero) Supervisor of special makeup and animatronic effects, *The Salton Sea,* 2002.

(As Greg Nicotero) Supervisor, *Murder by Numbers* (also known as *Murd3r 8y Num8ers*), 2002.

(As Greg Nicotero) Special effects makeup supervisor, *Bubba Ho–tep,* 2002.

Special makeup effects supervisor, *Cabin Fever,* 2002.

Special effects makeup supervisor, *feardotcom,* Warner Bros., 2002.

(As Greg Nicotero) Puppeteer and supervisor, *The Time Machine* (also known as *Time Machine*), DreamWorks, 2002.

(Uncredited) Special makeup effects artist, *Minority Report,* Twentieth Century–Fox, 2002.

Character prosthetics supervisor and (as Greg Nicotero) special makeup effects artist, *Austin Powers in Goldmember* (also known as *Austin Powers: Goldmember*), New Line Cinema, 2002.

Special makeup effects supervisor, *Spy Kids 2: Island of Lost Dreams* (also known as *Spy Kids 2: The Island of Lost Dreams*), Dimension Films, 2002.

Special makeup effects supervisor, *Vampires: Los Muertos* (also known as *John Carpenter's "Vampires: Los Muertos"* and *John Carpenter Presents "Vampires 2: Los Muertos"*), Screen Gems, 2002.

(As Greg Nicotero) Special makeup effects artist, *The Rules of Attraction,* Lions Gate Films, 2002.

Special makeup effects supervisor and puppeteer, *Identity,* Columbia, 2003.

(As Greg Nicotero) Animatronics effects supervisor and puppeteer, *Hulk,* 2003.

Special effects makeup, *Spy Kids 3–D: Game Over* (also known as *Spy Kids 3: Game Over*), 2003.

Special makeup effects, *The Texas Chainsaw Massacre* (also known as *Texas Chainsaw*), 2003.

(As Greg Nicotero) Special makeup effects, *Once Upon a Time in Mexico* (also known as *Legend of Mexico*), Columbia, 2003.

Special makeup effects supervisor and (as Greg Nicotero) special makeup effects artist, *Kill Bill: Vol. 1* (also known as *Kill Bill, Kill Bill Part 1, Quentin Tarantino's "Kill Bill: Volume One,"* and *Kiru Biru*), Miramax, 2003.

Special creature effects supervisor, *Tremors 4: The Legend Begins,* 2004.

Special makeup effects, *Ginger Snaps: Unleashed* (also known as *Ginger Snaps 2* and *Werewolf: Gingersnapsu*), 2004.

Special effects supervisor, *Blind,* 2004.

(As Greg Nicotero) Designer of special makeup effects and werewolf animatronics, *Ginger Snaps Back: The Beginning* (also known as *Hellwolf: You Will Be Eaten Alive*), 2004.

Special makeup effects supervisor, *Riding the Bullet* (also known as *Stephen King's "Riding the Bullet"*), 2004.

(As Greg Nicotero) Special effects supervisor, *Lemony Snicket's A Series of Unfortunate Events,* 2004.

Additional still photographer and additional videographer, *The Dead Will Walk* (documentary), Anchor Bay Entertainment, 2004.

(As Greg Nicotero) Still photographer of behind–the–scenes and behind–the–scenes video, *Nightmares in Foam Rubber* (short documentary; also known as *The Making of Creepshow 2*), Anchor Bay Entertainment, 2004.

Supervisor, *Employee of the Month,* DEJ Productions, 2004.

(As Greg Nicotero) Special makeup supervisor, *Kill Bill: Vol. 2* (also known as *Kill Bill, Kill Bill Part 2,* and *Vol. 2*), Miramax, 2004.

(As Greg Nicotero) Special makeup effects supervisor, *Ray,* Universal, 2004.

Animatronics, *Johnson Family Vacation,* Fox Searchlight, 2004.

(As Greg Nicotero) Additional werewolf effects creator and additional special makeup effects supervisor, *Cursed* (also known as *Wes Craven's "Cursed"*), Miramax, 2005.

Second unit director, *Land of the Dead* (also known as *George A. Romero's "Land of the Dead"*), 2005.

(As Greg Nicotero) Special makeup effects designer, *Dominion: Prequel to the Exorcist* (also known as *Paul Schrader's "Exorcist: The Original Prequel"*), Warner Bros., 2005.

(As Greg Nicotero) Special makeup effects supervisor, *Sin City* (also known as *Frank Miller's "Sin City"*), Dimension Films, 2005.

(As Greg Nicotero) Special makeup effects artist and special makeup effects designer and creator, *The Amityville Horror,* Metro–Goldwyn–Mayer, 2005.

(As Greg Nicotero) Special makeup effects artist, *The Adventures of Sharkboy and Lavagirl 3–D,* Dimension Films, 2005.

(As Greg Nicotero) Special makeup effects supervisor, *Land of the Dead* (also known as *George A. Romero's "Land of the Dead"*), Universal, 2005.

Project supervisor, *The Island,* DreamWorks, 2005.

(As Greg Nicotero) Supervisor, *Serenity,* Universal, 2005.

Special makeup effects designer and creator, *Hostel,* Lions Gate Films, 2005.

Special makeup and creatures, *The Chronicles of Narnia: The Lion, the Witch and the Wardrobe* (also known as *The Chronicles of Narnia*), Buena Vista, 2005.

(As Greg Nicotero) Special makeup effects designer, *The Hills Have Eyes,* Fox Searchlight, 2006.

Makeup effects supervisor, *Poseidon* (also known as *Poseidon: The IMAX Experience*), Warner Bros., 2006.

(As Greg Nicotero) Puppetry supervisor and effects supervisor, *Casino Royale* (also known as *007 Casino Royale*), Metro–Goldwyn–Mayer, 2006.

(As Greg Nicotero) Materials, *Miracles and Mystery: Creating "The Green Mile,"* 2006.

Special makeup effects supervisor and makeup supervisor, *Comedy Hell,* 2006.

(As Greg Nicotero) Special makeup supervisor, *The Texas Chainsaw Massacre: The Beginning* (also known as *Texas Chainsaw: Beginning*), New Line Cinema, 2006.

(As Greg Nicotero) Special effects makeup, *The Return,* Rogue Pictures, 2006.

Special makeup effects artist, *Deja Vu,* Buena Vista, 2006.

Special makeup effects artist, *Primeval* (also known as *Kiss*), Buena Vista, 2007.

(As Greg Nicotero) Special makeup effects designer and creator, *The Hitcher,* Rogue Pictures, 2007.

Special makeup effects designer, *The Hills Have Eyes II,* Fox Atomic, 2007.

Special makeup effects supervisor, *Disturbia,* Paramount, 2007.

Special makeup effects designer, *Death Proof* (also known as *Grindhouse Presents: Quentin Tarantino's "Death Proof," Grindhouse: "Death Proof," Quentin Tarantino's "Death Proof,"* and *Quentin Tarantino's "Thunder Bolt"*), Genius Products, 2007.

Special makeup effects designer and creator, *Hostel: Part II,* Lions Gate Films, 2007.

(As Greg Nicotero) Special makeup effects show supervisor, *Transformers* (also known as *Transformers: The IMAX Experience*), Paramount, 2007.

Special makeup effects designer, *Planet Terror* (also known as *Grindhouse Presents: Robert Rodriguez's "Planet Terror"* and *Robert Rodriguez's "Planet Terror"*), 2007.

(As Greg Nicotero) Special makeup effects producer, *Diary of the Dead* (also known as *George A. Romero's "Diary of the Dead"* and *The Death of Death*), Third Rail Releasing, 2007.

Second unit director, *The Haunting Hour: Don't Think About It* (also known as *R. L. Stine's "The Haunting Hour: Don't Think About It"*), Universal Studios Home Entertainment, 2007.

Creature designer, creature makeup effects, creature effects, puppeteer, and second unit director, *The Mist* (also known as *Stephen King's "The Mist"*), Metro–Goldwyn–Mayer, 2007.

(As Greg Nicotero) Puppeteer and special makeup effects artist, *The Great Debaters,* Weinstein Company, 2007.

Supervisor, *The Reaping* (also known as *Reaping*), 2007.

Special effects of dog puppet, *Spider–Man 3* (also known as *Spider–Man 3: The IMAX Experience*), 2007.

(As Greg Nicotero) Animatronics supervisor and puppeteer, *Transformers* (also known as *Transformers: The IMAX Experience*), 2007.

Supervisor, *Underdog* (also known as *Iron–Puppy Underdog*), 2007.

Special effects, *Wretched,* 2007.

(As Greg Nicotero) Special effects makeup, *Borderland,* After Dark Films, 2007.

(As Greg Nicotero) Special effects, *X,* 2008.

Special makeup effects supervisor and special makeup effects show supervisor, *The Chronicles of Narnia: Prince Caspian* (also known as *Prince Caspian*), Walt Disney Studios Motion Pictures, 2008.

Special makeup effects designer, *Mirrors,* Twentieth Century–Fox, 2008.

Makeup designer, *Milk,* Focus Features, 2008.

Key special makeup effects supervisor, *Seven Pounds,* Columbia, 2008.

(As Greg Nicotero) Project consultant, *Lost Boys: The Tribe,* Warner Home Video, 2008.

(Uncredited) Special effects makeup, *Indiana Jones and the Kingdom of the Crystal Skull,* 2008.

Special effects animatronics supervisor, *Transformers: Revenge of the Fallen* (also known as *Transformers: Revenge of the Fallen—The IMAX Experience* and *Transformers: Revenge*), 2009.

Special effects makeup, *Splice,* 2009.

Executive producer, *Bob Burns' Hollywood Halloween* (documentary), 2009.

(As Greg Nicotero) Special makeup effects designer and creator, *The Unborn,* Rogue Pictures, 2009.

(As Greg Nicotero) Puppeteer and special makeup effects producer, *The Last House on the Left,* Rogue Pictures, 2009.

(As Greg Nicotero) Key special makeup effects supervisor, *Drag Me to Hell* (also known as *Spell*), Universal, 2009.

Special makeup effects supervisor, *Inglourious Basterds,* Weinstein Company, 2009.

(As Greg Nicotero) Special makeup effects, *Public Enemies,* Universal, 2009.

(As Greg Nicotero) Key special makeup effects supervisor, *Shorts* (also known as *Shorts: The Adventures of the Wishing Rock*), Warner Bros., 2009.

Key special makeup effects supervisor and special makeup effects, *The Final Destination* (also known as *The Final Destination in 3–D* and *Final Dead Circuit 3–D*), Warner Bros., 2009.

Special makeup effects producer, *Survival of the Dead* (also known as *George A. Romero's "Survival of the Dead"*), Magnet Releasing, 2009.

(As Greg Nicotero) Special makeup effects supervisor, *Jennifer's Body,* Twentieth Century–Fox, 2009.

Key special makeup effects supervisor, *Surrogates* (also known as *Vicarious*), Walt Disney Studios Motion Pictures, 2009.

Key special makeup effects supervisor, *The Book of Eli* (also known as *The Walker*), Warner Bros., 2010.

Prosthetics supervisor and (as Greg Nicotero) special makeup effects, *Edge of Darkness,* Warner Bros., 2010.

Puppeteer, creature effects supervisor, and (as Greg Nicotero) special makeup and creature effects, *Predators,* 2010.

Key special makeup effects supervisor, *Piranha* (also known as *Piranha 3D*), Dimension Films, 2010.

Practical elements, *The Sorcerer's Apprentice,* Walt Disney Studios Distribution, 2010.

Special effects makeup, *The Last Exorcism,* Lions Gate Films, 2010.

Also worked as (as Greg Nicotero) special effects make–up, *The Onion Movie.*

Film Appearances:

Private Johnson, *Day of the Dead* (also known as *George A. Romero's "Day of the Dead"*), United Film Distribution Company, 1985.

(Uncredited) Extra, *Night of the Creeps,* TriStar, 1986.

Himself, *Scream Greats, Vol. 1: Tom Savini Master of Horror Effects* (documentary; also known as *Scream Greats, Vol. 1*), Paramount Home Video, 1986.

Townie in car, *Intruder* (also known as *Night Crew: The Final Checkout*), Empire Pictures, 1989.

(Uncredited) Guy in gas station, *Halloween 5* (also known as *Halloween 5: The Revenge of Michael Myers*), Galaxy International Releasing, 1989.

Elevator punk, *The Demolionist,* 1995.

Sex machine's buddy, *From Dusk Till Dawn,* Dimension Films, 1996.

(As Greg Nicotero) Himself, the special makeup effects guy, *Full Tilt Boogie* (documentary), Miramax, 1997.

(Uncredited) Rollercoaster technician, *House on Haunted Hill,* Warner Bros., 1999.

(As Greg Nicotero) Himself, *The Men Behind the Army* (short documentary), Anchor Bay Entertainment, 1999.

(As Greg Nicotero) Himself, *The Making of "Evil Dead II" or the Gore the Merrier* (short documentary), Anchor Bay Entertainment, 2000.

(As Greg Nicotero) Himself, *Pulp Fiction: The Facts* (short documentary), Buena Vista Home Entertainment, 2002.

Himself, *We Knows What to Do With Them Parts ...* (short documentary), New Line Home Video, 2003.

Himself, *The Saw Is Family: Making "Leatherface"* (short documentary), New Line Home Video, 2003.

Himself, *The Many Days of "Day of the Dead"* (short documentary), Anchor Bay Entertainment, 2003.

Himself, *Dirt Dragons: "Tremors 4: The Legend Begins"* (short documentary), Universal Studios Home Video, 2004.

(As Greg Nicotero) Himself, special makeup effects supervisor, *The Good, the Bad & the Bloody: Inside KNB EFX* (short documentary), Columbia TriStar Home Entertainment, 2004.

(As Greg Nicotero) Himself, *Comic Book: The Movie,* Miramax Home Entertainment, 2004.

Himself, *John Carpenter: Fear Is Just the Beginning ... The Man and His Movies,* 2004.

Himself, *Nightmares in Foam Rubber* (short documentary; also known as *The Making of Creepshow 2*), Anchor Bay Entertainment, 2004.

(Uncredited) Man pushing Dracula's coffin, *Cursed* (also known as *Wes Craven's "Cursed"*), Miramax, 2005.

(As Greg Nicotero) Bridgekeeper zombie, *Land of the Dead* (also known as *George A. Romero's "Land of the Dead"*), Universal, 2005.

Himself, *The Cursed Effects* (short documentary), Dimension Home Video, 2005.

Himself, *Fangoria: Blood Drive II,* Koch Vision, 2005.

Himself, *"Land of the Dead": Bringing the Dead to Life* (short documentary), Universal Studios Home Video, 2005.

Himself, *Undead Again: The Making of "Land of the Dead"* (short documentary), Universal Studios Home Video, 2005.

Himself, *"Land of the Dead": A Day with the Living Dead* (short documentary), Universal Studios Home Video 2005.

(As Greg Nicotero) Cyst, *The Hills Have Eyes,* Fox Searchlight, 2006.

Stoner dude Michael, *Cemetery Gates,* 2006.

Himself, *The Shark Is Still Working* (documentary), 2006.

Himself, *Working with a Master: John Carpenter* (short documentary), Anchor Bay Entertainment, 2006.

(As Greg Nicotero) Himself, *Surviving the Hills: Making of "The Hills Have Eyes"* (short documentary), Twentieth Century–Fox, 2006.

Himself, *"Halloween": 25 Years of Terror* (documentary), Anchor Bay Entertainment, 2006.

(As Greg Nicotero) Himself, *Miracles and Mystery: Creating "The Green Mile"* (documentary), Warner Home Video, 2006.

(As Greg Nicotero) Zombie surgeon, *Diary of the Dead* (also known as *George A. Romero's "Diary of the Dead"* and *The Death of Death*), Third Rail Releasing, 2007.

Himself, *Wigs, Teeth and Powder!: The Makeup Effects of "The Washingtonians"* (short film), Anchor Bay Entertainment, 2007.

(As Greg Nicotero) Himself, *Down to the Bone: Anatomy of a Prequel* (documentary), New Line Home Video, 2007.

Third makeup effects guy, *Gingerdead Man 2: Passion of the Crust,* Full Moon Entertainment, 2008.

Himself, *Monsters Among Us: The Creature FX of "The Mist"* (short documentary), Genius Products, 2008.

Himself, *"The Mist": Taming the Beast—The Making of Scene 35* (short documentary), Genius Products 2008.

Himself, *The Horror Of It All: The Visual FX of "The Mist"* (short documentary), Genius Products, 2008.

Himself, *He Who Made Monsters: The Life and Art of Jack Pierce* (short film), Universal Studios Home Entertainment, 2008.

(Uncredited) Gestapo major, *Inglourious Basterds,* Weinstein Company, 2009.

Himself, *Bob Burns' Hollywood Halloween* (documentary), 2009.

Boat captain, *Piranha* (also known as *Piranha 3D*), Dimension Films, 2010.

Also appeared as (as Greg Nicotero) on–camera interview, *Going to Pieces: The Rise and Fall of the Slasher Film.*

Television Work; Series:

Effects supervisor, *Tremors: The Series,* Sci–Fi Channel, 2002.

(As Greg Nicotero) Prosthetics effects supervisor, *Deadwood,* HBO, 2004–2006.

Special effects makeup, *Masters of Horror,* Showtime, 2005–2007.

(As Greg Nicotero) Special makeup effects artist, *Fear Itself,* NBC, 2008.

Television Work; Miniseries:

Lead special effects supervisor, *Dune* (also known as *Frank Herbert's "Dune"*), Sci–Fi Channel, 2000.

Special makeup effects supervisor and animatronic effects, *Desperation* (also known as *Stephen King's "Desperation"*), ABC, 2006.

Key special makeup effects supervisor, *The Pacific,* HBO, 2010.

Television Work; Movies:

Special makeup supervisor, *Attack of the 50 Ft Woman,* HBO, 1993.

(As Greg Nicotero) Special makeup effects, *Body Bags* (also known as *John Carpenter Presents "Mind Games"*), Showtime, 1993.

Supervisor, *Hercules and the Amazon Women,* syndicated, 1994.

Special makeup effects, *Citizen X,* HBO, 1995.

Television Work; Specials:

Executive producer, *Starz Inside: Fantastic Flesh* (documentary), Starz!, 2008.

Television Work; Episodic:

Special effects, "Halloween Candy," *Tales from the Darkside,* 1985.

(As Greg Nicotero) Puppeteer, "Sandkings," *The Outer Limits* (also known as *The New Outer Limits*), Showtime, 1995.

(As Greg Nicotero) Puppeteer, "M. Premie Unplugged," *The Practice,* ABC, 2002.

Special effects, "Incident On and Off a Mountain Road," *Masters of Horror,* Showtime, 2005.

Special makeup effects artist, "Dreams in the Witch–House," *Masters of Horror,* Showtime, 2005.

Special makeup effects artist, "Valerie on the Stairs," *Masters of Horror,* Showtime, 2006.

Television Appearances; Movies:

(As Greg Nicotero) Man with dog, "Hair," *Body Bags* (also known as *John Carpenter Presents "Mind Games"*), Showtime, 1993.

Television Appearances; Specials:

Masters of Fantasy: John Carpenter, Sci–Fi Channel, 1998.

Monsterama: KNB EFX, 2004.

"Reservoir Dogs" Revisited, Independent Film Channel, 2005.

Dream of the Dead, Independent Film Channel, 2005.

30 Even Scarier Movie Moments, Bravo, 2006.

Bloodsucking Cinema, Starz, 2007.

Zombiemania, 2008.

Starz Inside: Fantastic Flesh, Starz!, 2008.

His Name Was Jason: 30 Years of "Friday the 13th," 2009.

Monsterland, 2009.

Television Appearances; Episodic:

The Sharon Osbourne Show (also known as *Sharon*), syndicated, 2003.

(As Greg Nicotero) *The Late Late Show with Craig Ferguson,* CBS, 2005.

OTHER SOURCES

Periodicals:

Entertainment Weekly, June 17, 2005, p. 38.

O–P

O'HARA, Conchita
    See RIVERA, Chita

O'HARA, Conchita
    See RIVERA, Chita

OLMOS, Bodie 1975–

PERSONAL

Full name, Bodie James Olmos; born August 27, 1975, in Los Angeles, CA; son of Edward James Olmos (an actor) and Kaija Keel; grandson of Howard Keel (an actor); brother of Mico Olmos (an actor). *Education:* University of California, Los Angeles, graduated, 2000; also graduate of Sanford Meisner Center, North Hollywood, CA. *Avocational Interests:* Running, surfing, playing drums.

Addresses: *Agent*—Leavitt Talent Group, 11500 West Olympic Blvd., Suite 400, Los Angeles, CA 90064.

Career: Actor. Olmos Productions, vice president for development; also worked as production coordinator.

CREDITS

Film Appearances:
Fernando Escalante, *Stand and Deliver,* Warner Bros., 1988.
The Wonderful Ice Cream Suit, Buena Vista/Walt Disney, 1998.
The Last Winter (short film), Olmos Productions, 2002.
Daniel, *Manejar* (short film), Annex Film Group, 2005.
Al, *Resilience,* Lost Battalion Films, 2006.
Forensics officer, *Splinter,* Magic Lamp Releasing, 2007.

Television Appearances; Series:
Brendan "Hot Dog" Constanza, *Battlestar Galactica* (also known as *BSG*), Sci–Fi Channel, 2004–2009.

Television Appearances; Movies:
(Uncredited) Ranger's son, *The Ballad of Gregorio Cortez,* PBS, 1982.
Moctesuma Esparza, *Walkout,* HBO, 2006.

Television Appearances; Specials:
This Is Your Life, NBC, 1987.
Battlestar Galactica: The Last Frakkin' Special, Sci–Fi Channel, 2009.

Television Appearances; Episodic:
Young Jess Gonzales, "The Forgotten War," *American Family* (also known as *American Family: Journey of Dreams*), PBS, 2002.
Young Jess Gonzales, "La Cama," *American Family* (also known as *American Family: Journey of Dreams*), PBS, 2002.
Young Jess Gonzales, "The Fighting Fridas," *American Family* (also known as *American Family: Journey of Dreams*), PBS, 2002.
Young Jess Gonzales, "La Casa," *American Family* (also known as *American Family: Journey of Dreams*), PBS, 2002.

Stage Appearances:
Appeared in *War,* Latino Theatre Company, Los Angeles Theatre Center, Los Angeles; also appeared in a production of *Zoot Suit.*

RECORDINGS

Videos:
Battlestar Galactica: The Journey, Universal Studios Home Entertainment, 2009.
Battlestar Galactica: The Journey Ends—The Arrival, Universal Studios Home Entertainment, 2009.

OTHER SOURCES

Periodicals:
Starburst, April, 2008, pp. 64–68.

ORCI, Roberto 1973–
(Roberto Gaston Orci)

PERSONAL

Born July 20, 1973, in Mexico City, Mexico; brother of J. R. Orci (a writer); married Melissa Blake (a writer).

Addresses: *Agent*—Creative Artists Agency, 2000 Avenue of the Stars, Los Angeles, CA 90067. *Publicist*—I/D Public Relations, 8409 Santa Monica Blvd., West Hollywood, CA 90069.

Career: Producer and writer. Kurtzman/Orci (a production company), Universal City, CA, principal.

Awards, Honors: WGA Television Award nominations (with others), new series and long form—original, Writers Guild of America, 2009, both for *Fringe*; Saturn Award nomination (with Alex Kurtzman), best writing, Academy of Science Fiction, Fantasy, and Horror Films, WGA Screen Award nomination (with Alex Kurtzman), best adapted screenplay, Writers Guild of America, 2010, both for *Star Trek*.

CREDITS

Film Work:
Executive producer, *Denial* (short film), 2006.
Producer, *Eagle Eye* (also known as *Eagle Eye: The IMAX Experience*), DreamWorks, 2008.
Executive producer, *Star Trek* (also known as *Star Trek: The Future Begins* and *Star Trek: The IMAX Experience*), Paramount, 2009.
Executive producer, *The Proposal*, Walt Disney Studios Motion Pictures, 2009.

Film Appearances:
Himself, *The Dialogue: An Interview with Screenwriters Alex Kurtzman and Roberto Orci*, 2007.
Himself, *From Script to Sand: The Skorponok Desert Attack* (short documentary), DreamWorks Home Entertainment, 2007.
Himself, *Our World* (documentary), DreamWorks Home Entertainment, 2007.
Himself, *Their War* (documentary), DreamWorks Home Entertainment, 2007.
Himself, *Villains of "Star Trek"* (short documentary), Paramount Home Entertainment, 2009.
Himself, *The Human Factor: Exacting Revenge of the Fallen* (documentary), Paramount Home Entertainment, 2009.

Television Work; Series:
Executive producer, *Jack of All Trades,* syndicated, 2000.
Supervising producer, *Alias,* ABC, 2001–2002.
Co–executive producer, *Alias,* ABC, 2002–2003.
Executive producer, *Alias,* ABC, 2003–2004.
Executive producer, *Fringe,* Fox, 2008–2009.
Creator, *Fringe,* Fox, 2008—.
Consulting producer, *Fringe,* Fox, 2009–10.

Television Work; Movies:
Executive producer, *The Secret Service,* 2004.

Television Executive Producer; Pilots:
Hawaii Five–O, CBS, 2010.
Locke & Key, Fox, 2010.

Television Work; Episodic:
(As Roberto Gaston Orci) Co–executive producer, "City of the Dead," *Hercules: The Legendary Journey,* 1999.
(As Roberto Gaston Orci) Creative consultant, "Punch Lines," *Xena: Warrior Princess,* syndicated, 2000.
Co–executive producer, *Xena: Warrior Princess,* syndicated, 2000.

Television Appearances; Episodic:
Himself, "'Transformers': Their War. Our World," *HBO First Look,* HBO, 2007.
Himself, "The Making of 'Eagle Eye,'" *HBO First Look,* HBO, 2008.
Himself, "Eagle Eye," *HBO First Look,* HBO, 2008.

WRITINGS

Screenplays:
The Island, DreamWorks, 2005.
The Legend of Zorro (also known as *Z*), Columbia, 2005.
Mission: Impossible III (also known as *M:i:III*), Paramount, 2006.
Transformers (also known as *Transformers: The IMAX Experience*), Paramount, 2007.
Star Trek (also known as *Star Trek: The Future Begins* and *Star Trek: The IMAX Experience*), Paramount, 2009.
Transformers: Revenge of the Fallen (also known as *Transformers: Revenge of the Fallen—The IMAX Experience* and *Transformer: Revenge*), Paramount, 2009.

Film Stories:
The Legend of Zorro (also known as *Z*), 2005.
Transformers (also known as *Transformers: The IMAX Experience*), 2007.

Television Movies:
The Secret Service, 2004.

Television Pilot Stories:
Hawaii Five–O, CBS, 2010.

Television Episodes:
Xena: Warrior Princess, syndicated, 1995.
Hercules: The Legendary Journeys, syndicated, 1997–99.
Jack of All Trades, syndicated, 2000.
Alias, ABC, 2001–2003.
"Lanakila," *Hawaii Five–O,* CBS, 2010.

ORISTANO, Stacey 1980–

PERSONAL

Born May 6, 1980, in Arlington, TX. *Education:* Graduate of Rose Bruford Training College of Speech and Drama (now Rose Bruford College of Theatre and Performance), London.

Addresses: *Manager*—Justice and Ponder, PO Box 480033, Los Angeles, CA 90048. *Publicist*—Mona Loring, MLC Public Relations, 5030 Cheseboro Rd., Suite 202, Agoura Hills, CA 91301.

Career: Actress and voice performer. Concert vocalist, with performances in London, New York City, and Dallas, TX.

CREDITS

Television Appearances; Series:
Mindy Collette/Mindy Riggins, *Friday Night Lights* (also known as *F.N.L.*), NBC, 2006–2008, DirecTV, 2009, NBC, 2009–10.
(English–language version) Voice of Miss Noriti, *Shin Chan* (animated; also known as *Kureyon Shin–chan;* originally released in Japan in Japanese), Cartoon Network, 2007.

Also provided English–language voices for dubbed versions of animated series, originally broadcast in Japan in Japanese, including voice of Toikio for *School Rumble: Second Semester;* voice of dream girl, girl students A and B, and a woman, *Ghost Hunt,* broadcast in North America by FUNimation; and voice of Honoka Iwakura, *Sasami maho shojo kurabu* (also known as *Sasami: Magical Girls Club*), FUNimation.

Television Appearances; Episodic:
Girlfriend, *Chappelle's Show* (also known as *Chappelle's Show: The Lost Episodes*), Comedy Central, 2003 and French girl, *Tough Crowd with Colin Quinn,* Comedy Central, 2004.

Film Appearances:
Zuzmen, *Dragonball: Evolution* (also known as *D.B.E.*), Twentieth Century–Fox, 2009.

RECORDINGS

Videos:
(English–language version) Voice of high school girl, *XXXHOLiC* (originally broadcast in Japan in Japanese as a television series), FUNimation Entertainment, 2007.

OUTERBRIDGE, Peter 1966–

PERSONAL

Born June 30, 1966, in Toronto, Ontario, Canada; father, a lawyer; married Tammy Isbell (an actress), May, 2000. *Education:* University of Victoria, B.F.A.

Addresses: *Agent*—Silver, Massetti, and Szatmary, 8730 West Sunset Blvd., Suite 440, West Hollywood, CA 90069.

Career: Actor.

Awards, Honors: Gemini Award nomination, best actor in a dramatic program or miniseries, Academy of Canadian Cinema and Television, 1996, for "Sand Kings," *The Outer Limits;* Genie Award nomination, best actor in a leading role, Academy of Canadian Cinema and Television, 1997, for *Kissed;* Gemini Award nomination, best featured supporting actor in a dramatic program, 1997, for *Captive Heart: The James Mink Story;* Gemini Award nomination, best actor in a dramatic program or miniseries, 2001, for *Chasing Cain;* Genie Award nominations, best actor, 2001, 2003, for Marine Life; Gemini Award nomination, best guest actor in a dramatic series, 2004, for *This Is Wonderland;* Gemini Award nominations, best actor in a continuing leading dramatic role, 2005, 2006, 2007, 2008, all for *ReGenesis.*

CREDITS

Film Appearances:
Randal, *Hate Mail* (short film), 1992.
Josef Grool, *Cool Runnings,* Buena Vista, 1993.

Johnny, *For the Moment,* 1993, John Aaron Productions, 1996.

John Cheever, *Replikator,* Producers Network Associates, 1994.

Sloan, *Paris, France,* Alliance, 1994.

Jules, *The Michelle Apts.,* ARTOpelli Motion Pictures, 1995.

Matt, *Kissed,* Samuel Goldwyn, 1997.

Jeremy/Judy, *Better than Chocolate,* Trimark Pictures, 1999.

Eddie, *Fools Die Fast,* 2000.

Robert Kiely, *Marine Life,* Crescent Releasing, 2000.

Sergei Kirov, *Mission to Mars* (also known as *M2M*), Buena Vista, 2000.

Special Agent Sean Donahue, *Double Frame,* Eagle Pictures, 2000.

Everette Hatch, *The Bay of Love and Sorrows,* Odeon Films, 2002.

James Lennox, *Men with Brooms,* Artisan Entertainment, 2002.

Dave Miller, *Cold Creek Manor,* Buena Vista, 2003.

Orlando, *June & Orlando* (short film), 2003.

Curt Bonner, *Chicks with Sticks* (also known as *Anyone's Game* and *Hockey Mom*), Monarch Home Video, 2005.

Earl, *Ill Fated,* Ocule Films, 2005.

Styles, *Land of the Dead* (also known as *George Romero's "Land of the Dead"*), Universal, 2005.

Dumbrowski, *Lucky Number Slevin* (also known as *Lucky Number S7evin*), Metro–Goldwyn–Mayer, 2006.

Deputy Christian Hecker, *Population 436,* Sony Pictures Home Entertainment, 2006.

Detective Ryan Johnson, *Burning Mussolini,* F.A.T. Productions/Reel Entertainment, 2009.

William Easton, *Saw VI,* Lions Gate Films, 2009.

Television Appearances; Series:

Officer Jeff Hartley, a recurring role, *The Commish,* ABC, between 1991 and 1993.

John Henry Manning, *Michael Hayes,* CBS, 1997–98.

Barry Baldwin, a recurring role, *Millennium,* Fox, 1998–99.

David Sandstrom, *ReGenesis,* The Movie Network, 2004–2008.

Handsome Dan Farmer, *Happy Town,* ABC, 2010.

Narrator, *Beast Legends,* Syfy, 2010.

Television Appearances; Movies:

Dylan Wiatt, *Drop Dead Gorgeous* (also known as *Victim of Beauty*), USA Network, 1991.

Barry Donovan, *Diagnosis of Murder* (also known as *Diagnosis Murder*), CBS, 1992.

Paul Temple, *Another Woman,* CBS, 1994.

Greg, *Falling for You,* CBS, 1995.

Thomas Benti, *The Android Affair,* USA Network, 1995.

Jim O'Neil, *Giant Mine,* CBC, 1996.

Sergei, *Jack Reed: Death and Vengeance,* NBC, 1996.

William Johnson, *Captive Heart: The James Mink Story,* CBS, 1996.

Adam, *Closer and Closer,* Lifetime, 1996.

Jack Bolinas, *Murder in My Mind,* CBS, 1997.

Felder, *The Time Shifters* (also known as *Thrill Seekers*), TBS, 1999.

John Rank, *Escape from Mars,* UPN, 1999.

Lee Nash/Carter, *Escape Velocity,* Sci–Fi Channel, 1999.

Roger Deacon, *Out of Sync* (also known as *Lip Service*), VH1, 2000.

(Uncredited) *Killing Moon,* 2000.

Alex, *The Pretender 2001* (also known as *The Pretender*), TNT, 2001.

Detective Bob Kozlowski, *Chasing Cain: Face,* CBC, 2002.

Theodore Gray, *The Rendering* (also known as *Portrait of a Murder*), The WB, 2002.

Gord Black, *100 Days in the Jungle,* 2002.

Nick Simms, *The Risen,* The Movie Network, 2003.

Gordon Wintrob, *Murder in the Hamptons,* Lifetime, 2005.

Denis Teague, *Intimate Stranger,* Lifetime, 2006.

Officer Wayne, *In God's Country,* Lifetime, 2007.

Charlie Manning, *My Name Is Sarah,* Lifetime, 2007.

Captain Colvin, *The Deadliest Sea,* The Discovery Channel, 2009.

Television Appearances; Specials:

Rodney, *Dinner Along the Amazon,* 1996.

(In archive footage) Matt, Weird Sex and Snowshoes: A Trek through the Canadian Cinematic Psyche, 2004.

Al Burton, *Behind the Camera: The Unauthorized Story of "Diff'rent Strokes,"* NBC, 2007.

Narrator, *The Real Superhumans and the Quest for the Future Fantastic,* The Discovery Channel, 2007.

Television Appearances; Miniseries:

Jim Coutts, *Trudeau,* CBC, 2002.

Alec Becker, *10.5: Apocalypse* (also known as *10.5*), NBC, 2006.

Television Appearances; Pilots:

Dr. Reyes, *Fringe,* Fox, 2008.

Television Appearances; Episodic:

Jeff Chandler, "Just Say No! High," *21 Jump Street,* syndicated, 1990.

Rick, "Wasting Away," *The Hidden Room,* Lifetime, 1991.

Talbot, "Programmer/Child's Play," *Secret Service,* NBC, 1992.

Jesse, "Fay & Ivy," *Nightmare Cafe,* NBC, 1992.

Young Thomas Constantine, "Father's Day," *Forever Knight,* syndicated, 1994.

Translation voice, "Romeo and Juliet in Sarajevo," *Frontline,* PBS, 1994.

Count Marek, "What a Tangled Web We Weave," *Avonlea* (also known as *Road to Avonlea* and *Tales from Avonlea*), The Disney Channel, 1995.

Dr. Andy Groenig, "Caught in the Act," *The Outer Limits* (also known as *The New Outer Limits*), Showtime, 1995.

Dr. Andy Groenig, "The New Breed," *The Outer Limits* (also known as *The New Outer Limits*), Showtime, 1995.

Paul Kinman, "Reluctant Heroes," *Highlander* (also known as *Highlander: The Series*), syndicated, 1995.

"Sand Kings," *The Outer Limits* (also known as *The New Outer Limits*), Showtime, c. 1995.

Ned, "Betrayal," *Lonesome Dove: The Outlaw Years,* syndicated, 1996.

Roger, "Treason," *La Femme Nikita* (also known as *Nikita*), USA Network, 1997.

Ned Bailey, "What Will the Neighbors Think?," *The Outer Limits* (also known as *The New Outer Limits*), Showtime, 1999.

Joe, "Subterra," *Earth: Final Conflict* (also known as *Gene Roddenberry's ''Earth: Final Conflict''*), syndicated, 2001.

Tyrone Fox, "Goodbye, Tyrone," *Paradise Falls,* Showcase, 2001.

Tyrone Fox, "Jessica Fights Back," *Paradise Falls,* Showcase, 2001.

Zach Griffiths, "Replica," *The Outer Limits* (also known as *The New Outer Limits*), Showtime, 2001.

Trevor McDowell, "Mr. Monk and the Marathon Man," *Monk,* USA Network, 2002.

Dr. Milton Bradshaw, "A Matter of Time: Parts 1 & 2," *Mentors,* The Family Channel (Canada), 2002.

Dr. Milton Bradshaw, "Secrets and Lies," *Mentors,* The Family Channel (Canada), 2002.

Ronnie Stark, "Day 2: 2:00 a.m.–3:00 a.m.," *24,* Fox, 2003.

Ronnie Stark, "Day 3: 3:00 a.m.–4:00 a.m.," *24,* Fox, 2003.

Jason Herlock, "Paul Is Dead," *Miracles,* ABC, 2003.

Jerry Weicker, "The People vs. Achmed Abbas," *The D.A.,* ABC, 2004.

Jerry Weicker, "The People vs. Oliver C. Handley," *The D.A.,* ABC, 2004.

Jerry Weicker, "The People vs. Patricia Henry," *The D.A.,* ABC, 2004.

Jerry Weicker, "The People vs. Sergius Kovinsky," *The D.A.,* ABC, 2004.

Dale Robertson, *This Is Wonderland,* CBC, 2004.

Clark White, "Progeny," *Medical Investigation,* NBC, 2004.

Detective William Murdoch, "Except the Dying," *The Murdoch Mysteries,* Bravo!Canada, 2004.

Detective William Murdoch, "Poor Tom Is Cold," *The Murdoch Mysteries,* Bravo!Canada, 2004.

Detective William Murdoch, "Under the Dragon's Tail," *The Murdoch Mysteries,* Bravo!Canada, 2005.

Randy Cioffi, "Gentleman Jim," *Tilt,* ESPN, 2005.

Randy Cioffi, "Shuffle Up and Deal," *Tilt,* ESPN, 2005.

Phil Goody, "The Rival House," *Puppets Who Kill,* Comedy Central, 2006.

Peter Varland, "The Rules of Attachment: Parts 1 & 2," *Whistler,* The N, 2007.

"Last Run," *Whistler,* The N, 2007.

Malcolm Dawkins, "Folding Man," *Sanctuary,* Sci–Fi Channel, 2008.

Brad Borden, "Summer's End," *Heartland,* 2008.

Walter Volcek, "Clean Hands," *Flashpoint,* CBS, 2009.

OTHER SOURCES

Periodicals:
Toronto Sun, September 15, 2000.

PADALECKI, Jared 1982–

PERSONAL

Full name, Jared Tristan Padalecki; born July 19, 1982, in San Antonio, TX; son of Gerald R. (an accountant and tax supervisor) and Sharon L. (a high school English teacher) Padalecki; married Genevieve Cortese (an actress), February 27, 2010. *Education:* Attended high school in San Antonio, TX. *Avocational Interests:* Sports, reading.

Addresses: *Agent*—Jason Heyman, Creative Artists Agency, 2000 Avenue of the Stars, Los Angeles, CA 90067. *Manager*—Daniel Spilo, Industry Entertainment, 955 South Carrillo Dr., 3rd Floor, Los Angeles, CA 90048.

Career: Actor.

Awards, Honors: Teen Choice Award nomination, choice actor in a television drama, 2002, for *Gilmore Girls;* Teen Choice Award nomination, choice male movie breakout performance, 2005, for *House of Wax;* Teen Choice Award nomination, choice actor in a television drama, 2007, for Supernatural.

CREDITS

Television Appearances; Series:
Dean Forester, a recurring character, *Gilmore Girls* (also known as *Gilmore Girls: Beginnings*), The WB, 2000–2005.

Sam Winchester, *Supernatural,* The WB, 2005–2006, The CW, 2006—.

Host, *Room 401,* MTV, 2007.

Television Appearances; Movies:
Zachery Gray, *A Ring of Endless Light,* The Disney Channel, 2002.

Television Appearances; Pilots:
Sam, *Silent Witness,* NBC, 2000.
Dean Forester, *Gilmore Girls* (also known as *Gilmore Girls: Beginnings*), The WB, 2000.
Close to Home, Fox, 2001.
Clay MacGyver, *Young MacGyver,* The WB, 2003.
Sam Winchester, *Supernatural,* The WB, 2005.

Television Appearances; Specials:
Contestant, *Claim to Fame,* Fox, 1999.
Supernatural File, 2007.

Television Appearances; Episodic:
Paul Harris, "Piece of Mind," *ER,* NBC, 2001.
Movie Life: House of Wax, MTV, 2005.
Total Request Live (also known as *Total Request with Carson Daly, TRL,* and *TRL Weekend*), MTV, 2005.
Ellen: The Ellen DeGeneres Show, syndicated, 2005.
"The Girl Who Punk'd Ashton," *America's Next Top Model* (also known as *America's Next Top Model 2, America's Next Top Model with Tyra Banks, ANTM,* and *Top Model*), The CW, 2006.
Extra (also known as *Extra: The Entertainment Magazine*), syndicated, 2006.
HypaSpace (also known as *HypaSpace Daily* and *HypaSpace Weekly*), SPACE, 2008.
KTLA Morning News (also known as *KTLA Morning Show*), KTLA, 2009.
The Bonnie Hunt Show, NBC, 2009.
Project: Comic-Con, 2010.

Television Appearances; Miniseries:
I Love the '90s, VH1, 2004.

Television Appearances; Awards Presentations:
The ... Teen Choice Awards, Fox, 1999, 2001, 2003, 2004.
Presenter, *The 11th Annual Critics' Choice Awards,* The WB, 2006.
Presenter, *The ... Teen Choice Awards,* Fox, 2007.
Scream Awards, Spike TV, 2008.

Film Appearances:
Matt Nelson, *A Little Inside* (also known as *Me and Dad*), Monarch Home Video, 2001.
(Uncredited) High school bully, *Cheaper by the Dozen,* Twentieth Century–Fox, 2003.
Trey Lipton, *New York Minute,* Warner Bros., 2004.
John Davis, *Flight of the Phoenix,* Twentieth Century–Fox, 2004.
Wade, *House of Wax,* Warner Bros., 2005.
Tom, *Cry Wolf,* Rogue Pictures, 2005.

(Uncredited) J. P., *House of Fears,* Your Indie Films, 2007.
Thomas Kinkade, *Christmas Cottage* (also known as *Thomas Kinkade's "Christmas Cottage"*), Lions Gate Films, 2008.
Clay Miller, *Friday the 13th,* New Line Cinema, 2009.

OTHER SOURCES

Periodicals:
Movieline's Hollywood Life, May, 2004, p. 26.
Starlog, November, 2008, pp. 46–49.
TV Guide, May 5, 2008, pp. 64–65.

PALTROW, Gwyneth 1972–

PERSONAL

Full name, Gwyneth Kate Paltrow; born September 27 (some sources cite September 28), 1972, in Los Angeles, CA; daughter of Bruce Paltrow (a television writer and producer) and Blythe Danner (an actress); sister of Jake Paltrow (an actor and director); married Chris Martin (a singer, songwriter, and recording artist), December 5, 2003; children: Apple Blythe Alison, Moses Bruce Anthony. *Education:* Briefly attended University of California, Santa Barbara, c. 1990–91. *Politics:* Democrat. *Religion:* Jewish.

Addresses: *Agent*—United Talent Agency, 9560 Wilshire Blvd., Suite 500, Beverly Hills, CA 90212. *Manager*—Aleen Keshishian, Brillstein Entertainment Partners, 9150 Wilshire Blvd., Suite 350, Beverly Hills, CA 90212. *Publicist*—Stephen Huvane, Slate Public Relations, 8322 Beverly Blvd., Suite 201, Los Angeles, CA 90048.

Career: Actress. Appeared in print ads for Esprit, Christian Dior, Estee Lauder, and others, and in commercials for Martini Rosso and other products. Designer of a collection of greeting cards for Tiny Prints, 2009; Robin Hood (charitable organization), board member; GOOP.com, creator of Web site and writer of regular newsletter.

Awards, Honors: Golden Satellite Award, best actress in a comedy or musical motion picture, International Press Academy, 1996, for *Emma;* Saturn Award nomination, best supporting actress, Academy of Science Fiction, Fantasy, and Horror Films, 1996, for *Seven;* Blockbuster Entertainment Award, favorite actress in a suspense film, 1998, for *A Perfect Murder;* Florida Film Critics Circle Award, best actress, 1998, for *Sliding*

Doors and *Shakespeare in Love;* special award, San Diego Film Critics Society, and Golden Aries, best foreign actress, Russian Guild of Film Critics, both 1998, for *Sliding Doors, Shakespeare in Love,* and consistent acting excellence; Sierra Award, best actress, Las Vegas Film Critics Society, 1998, Golden Globe Award and Golden Satellite Award nomination, both best actress in a comedy or musical motion picture, Academy Award, Screen Actors Guild Award, Film Award nomination, British Academy of Film and Television Arts, Florida Film Critics Circle Award, Chicago Film Critics Association Award nomination, Kansas City Film Critics Circle Award, Online Film Critics Society Award nomination, and MTV Movie Award nomination, all best actress, Blockbuster Entertainment Award nomination, favorite actress in a comedy or romance, Screen Actors Guild Award (with others), outstanding cast performance, MTV Movie Award (with Joseph Fiennes), best kiss, Teen Choice Award nomination, choice actress in a film and sexiest love scene in a film (with Fiennes), all 1999, and Empire Award, best actress, 2000, all for *Shakespeare in Love;* Blockbuster Entertainment Award nomination, favorite actress in a suspense film, 2000, for The *Talented Mr. Ripley;* Blockbuster Entertainment Award, favorite actress in a dramatic or romance film, MTV Movie Award nomination (with Ben Affleck), best kiss, 2001, both for *Bounce;* Golden Satellite Award nomination, best supporting actress in a comedy or musical film, and Phoenix Film Critics Society Award nomination (with others), best acting ensemble, both 2002, for The Royal Tenenbaums; Teen Choice Award nomination, choice actress in a comedy film, 2002, for *Shallow Hal; Evening Standard* Theatre Award nomination, 2002, and Laurence Olivier Award nomination, Society of West End Theatre, 2003, both best actress, for *Proof;* Crystal Award, Women in Film, 2004; Special Award, distinguished decade of achievement in film, ShoWest Convention, National Association of Theatre Owners, 2004; MTV Movie Award nomination (with Jude Law), best kiss, 2005, for Sky Captain and the World of Tomorrow; Golden Globe Award nomination, best actress in a motion picture drama, 2006, for *Proof;* Grammy Award nomination, best spoken–word album, National Academy of Recording Arts and Sciences, 2008, for *Brown Bear and Friends;* Teen Choice Award nomination, choice actress in an action–adventure movie, 2008, and Saturn Award nomination, best actress, 2009, both for *Iron Man;* Independent Spirit Award nomination, best female lead, Independent Features Project/West, 2010, for *Two Lovers.*

CREDITS

Film Appearances:
Rebecca, *Shout,* Universal, 1991.
Young Wendy, *Hook,* TriStar, 1991.
Ginnie, *Flesh and Bone,* Paramount, 1993.
Paula Bell, *Malice,* Columbia, 1993.

Paula Hunt, *Mrs. Parker and the Vicious Circle* (also known as *Mrs. Parker and the Round Table*), Fine Line, 1994.
Lucy Trager, *Moonlight and Valentino,* Gramercy, 1995.
Patsy Jefferson, *Jefferson in Paris,* Buena Vista, 1995.
Tracy Mills, *Seven* (also known as *Se7en*), New Line Cinema, 1995.
(Uncredited) Student, *Higher Learning,* 1995.
Emma Woodhouse (title role), *Emma,* Miramax, 1996.
Julie DeMarco, *The Pallbearer* (also known as *Happy Blue*), Miramax, 1996.
Clementine, *Sydney* (also known as *Hard Eight*), Samuel Goldwyn, 1997.
Emily Bradford Taylor, *A Perfect Murder* (also known as *Dial M*), Warner Bros., 1998.
Estella, *Great Expectations,* Twentieth Century–Fox, 1998.
Helen Baring, *Hush,* TriStar, 1998.
Helen Quilley, *Sliding Doors,* Miramax, 1998.
Viola De Lesseps/Thomas Kent, *Shakespeare in Love,* Miramax, 1998.
Voice of Sarah Orne Jewett, *Out of the Past,* Zeitgeist Films/Unapix Films, 1998.
Marge Sherwood, *The Talented Mr. Ripley* (also known as *Eclipse* and The Mysterious Yearning Secretive Sad Lonely Troubled Confused Loving Musical Gifted Intelligent Beautiful Tender Sensitive Haunted Passionate Talented Mr. Ripley), Paramount, 1999.
Abby Janello, *Bounce,* Miramax, 2000.
(Uncredited) Herself, *The Intern* (also known as *Intern*), York Entertainment, 2000.
Liv, *Duets,* Buena Vista, 2000.
(Uncredited; in archive footage) Herself, *Pootie Tang,* Paramount, 2001.
Margot Tenenbaum, *The Royal Tenenbaums,* Buena Vista, 2001.
Rosemary Shanahan, *Shallow Hal* (also known as *My Sweet Rosemary*), Twentieth Century–Fox, 2001.
Skye Davidson, *The Anniversary Party,* Fine Line, 2001.
Herself and Dixie Normous, *Austin Powers in Goldmember* (also known as *Austin Powers: Goldmember*), New Line Cinema, 2002.
Maud Bailey, *Possession,* Warner Bros., 2002.
Donna Jensen, *View from the Top* (also known as *Flight Girls*), Miramax, 2003.
Herself, *Ashtanga, NY* (short film), Americas in Transition, 2003.
Sylvia Plath (title role), *Sylvia* (also known as *The Beekeeper's Daughter* and *Ted and Sylvia*), Focus Features, 2003.
Catherine, *Proof* (also known as *Proof of My Life*), Miramax, 2004.
Polly Perkins, *Sky Captain and the World of Tomorrow* (also known as *The World of Tomorrow*), Paramount, 2004.
Kitty Dean, *Infamous,* Warner Independent Pictures, 2006.
Hollywood Jacks, *Love and Other Disasters,* Eurocorp, 2006, Image Entertainment, 2008.

Hope Finch, *Running with Scissors,* TriStar, 2006.
Dora Shaller, *The Good Night,* Yari Film Group, 2007.
Pepper Potts, *Iron Man,* Paramount, 2008.
Michelle Rausch, *Two Lovers,* Magnolia Pictures, 2008.
Valentino: The Last Emperor (documentary), Truly Indie/Vitagraph Films, 2008.
Pepper Potts, *Iron Man 2* (also known as *Iron Man 2: The IMAX Experience* and *Iron 2 Man*), Paramount, 2010.
Kelly Canter, *Country Strong,* Screen Gems, 2010.

Film Work:
Coproducer, *View from the Top* (also known as *Flight Girls*), Miramax, 2003.
Director, *Dealbreaker* (short film), Glamour Magazine, 2005.

Television Appearances; Miniseries:
Angela Pritchard, *Cruel Doubt,* NBC, 1992.
Voice of Jefferson's granddaughter, *Thomas Jefferson,* 1997.

Television Appearances; Movies:
Carol Fagot Applegarth Holland, *Deadly Relations,* ABC, 1993.

Television Appearances; Series:
Host, *Spain ... On the Road Again,* PBS, 2008.

Television Appearances; Specials:
Spotlight: David Schwimmer, Comedy Central, 1996.
Shakespeare in Love and on Film, 1999.
We All Dream of Oz, TNT, 2000.
Reel Comedy: Shallow Hal (also known as *Comedy Central Canned Ham*), Comedy Central, 2001.
The Concert for New York City, VH1, 2001.
Holiday with the Stars, E! Entertainment Television, 2001.
Herself, *Searching for Debra Winger,* Showtime, 2002.
Behind the Scenes of "Possession," 2002.
(In archive footage) *101 Most Shocking Moments in Entertainment,* E! Entertainment Television, 2003.
(Uncredited; in archive footage) Sharon Stone, *Saturday Night Live: The Best of Chris Kattan,* NBC, 2003.
(In archive footage) *101 Biggest Celebrity Oops,* E! Entertainment Television, 2004.
(In archive footage) *101 Most Unforgettable SNL Moments,* E! Entertainment Television, 2004.
I'm Going to Tell You a Secret, VH1, 2005.
Jay Z: Live at the Royal Albert Hall, 2006.
(Uncredited; in archive footage) Viola De Lesseps, *Boffo! Tinseltown's Bombs and Blockbusters,* HBO, 2006.
La Marato, 2006.
(In archive footage) *Camara negra. Teatro Victoria Eugenia,* 2007.
Presenter, *Swarovski Style Rocks,* Bravo, 2008.

Voice, *Classical Baby (I'm Grown Up Now): The Poetry Show,* HBO, 2008.
The Victoria's Secret Fashion Show, CBS, 2008.
(Uncredited; in archive footage) *Del corto a Hollywood,* 2008.
(In archive footage) *Oscar, que empiece el espectaculo,* Canal+ Espana, 2008.
Stand Up to Cancer, multiple networks, 2010.

Television Appearances; Episodic:
Nyhetsmorgon, 1995, 1998.
Lo + plus, 1996.
Corazon, corazon, 1996.
Cinema 3, 1996, 1999, 2008, 2010.
Saturday Night Live (also known as *SNL*), NBC, 1999, 2000, 2001, 2011.
Voice, "The Clips Show Wherein Dante and Randal are Locked in the Freezer and Remember Some of the Great Moments of Their Lives," *Clerks* (animated; also known as Clerks: The Animated Series and Clerks: Uncensored), ABC, 2000.
"The Scene," *Gary & Mike,* UPN, 2001.
Inside the Actors Studio (also known as *Actors Interview* and Inside the Actors Studio: The Craft of Theatre and Film), Bravo, 2001.
"Being 'Shallow Hal,'" *HBO First Look,* HBO, 2001.
(In archive footage) "Gwyneth Paltrow," *Love Chain,* E! Entertainment Television, 2003.
"Stella's Story," *Imagine,* BBC, 2003.
(In archive footage) *Celebrities Uncensored,* 2003, 2004, 2005.
Entertainment Tonight (also known as *ET*), syndicated, numerous appearances, beginning 2003.
(In archive footage) "Awesomely Wacky Celebrity Baby Names," *VH1: All Access,* VH1, 2003.
Film '72, BBC, 2004, 2006.
CBS News Sunday Morning, CBS, 2005.
(Uncredited; in archive footage) *Troldspejlet,* 2005.
Corazon de ..., 2005, 2006.
"Gwyneth Paltrow," *What It Takes,* 2006.
The Culture Show, BBC, 2006.
(In archive footage) *La imagen de tu vida,* 2006.
"Idol Gives Back: Part Two," *American Idol* (also known as *American Idol: The Search for a Superstar* and *Idol*), Fox, 2007.
(Uncredited; in archive footage) "Old Hollywood: Silent Stars, Deadly Secrets," *City Confidential,* Arts and Entertainment, 2007.
(Uncredited; in archive footage) Helen Quilley, "Parallel Worlds: A User's Guide," *Time Shift,* BBC, 2007.
(Uncredited; in archive footage) Viola De Lesseps, "Shakespeare in Love," *Movie Connections,* 2007.
(In archive footage) *Vinte na Galega,* 2007.
(In archive footage) *The O'Reilly Factor,* Fox News Channel, 2008.
(In archive footage) Viola De Lesseps, *60/90,* 2008.
Live from Studio Five, Channel 5, 2010.
Panelist, *The Marriage Ref,* NBC, 2010.
Made in Hollywood, 2010.

Mark at the Movies, The CW, 2010.

(In archive footage) *Breakfast,* 2010.

Holly Holliday, ''The Substitute,'' *Glee,* Fox, 2010.

Holly Holliday, ''Original Song,'' *Glee,* Fox, 2011.

Holly Holliday, ''Sexy,'' *Glee,* Fox, 2011.

Who Do You Think You Are?, 2011.

Television Talk Show Guest Appearances; Episodic:

Late Night with Conan O'Brien, NBC, multiple appearances, between 1993 and 2005.

Charlie Rose (also known as *The Charlie Rose Show),* 1996.

The Rosie O'Donnell Show, syndicated, between 1996 and 2001.

The Late Show with David Letterman (also known as *The Late Show* and *Letterman),* CBS, 1996, 2005, 2008, 2010.

''Madonna Meets Not Us,'' *Late Lunch,* 1998.

The Tonight Show with Jay Leno, NBC, 1998, 2001, 2003.

Last Call with Carson Daly, NBC, 2002.

Revealed with Jules Asner, E! Entertainment Television, 2002.

Ellen: The Ellen DeGeneres Show, syndicated, 2003.

Parkinson, BBC, 2003.

The Daily Show with Jon Stewart (also known as *The Daily Show* and *The Daily Show with Jon Stewart Global Edition),* Comedy Central, 2004, 2005.

The Oprah Winfrey Show (also known as *Oprah),* syndicated, 2004, 2005.

Today (also known as *NBC News Today* and The Today Show), NBC, 2005.

GMTV, ITV, 2005.

The View, ABC, 2005, 2008.

Shootout (also known as *Hollywood Shootout* and Sunday Morning Shootout), AMC, 2006.

Weekend Sunrise, Seven Network, 2006.

Live with Regis and Kelly, syndicated, 2008.

Friday Night with Jonathan Ross, BBC America, 2008, 2010.

The Tonight Show with Conan O'Brien, NBC, 2009.

Late Night with Jimmy Fallon, NBC, 2010.

Conan, TBS, 2010, 2011.

Television Appearances; Awards Presentations:

Audience member, *The 68th Annual Academy Awards,* ABC, 1996.

Presenter, *The ... MTV Video Music Awards,* MTV, 1996, 2004.

Presenter, *The ... Annual Golden Globe Awards,* NBC, 1997, 2000, 2006.

The 70th Annual Academy Awards Presentation, ABC, 1998.

The 56th Annual Golden Globe Awards, 1999.

Presenter, *The ... Annual Academy Awards,* ABC, 1999, 2000, 2002, 2005, 2007.

The 1999 MTV Movie Awards, MTV, 1999.

6th Annual Screen Actors Guild Awards, 1999.

2000 Blockbuster Entertainment Awards, Fox, 2000.

Presenter, *The VH1/Vogue Fashion Awards,* VH1, 2001.

Presenter, *The 55th Annual Tony Awards,* CBS, 2001.

The ELLE Style Awards, 2002.

The Laurence Olivier Awards 2003, 2003.

The WIN Awards, PAX, 2005.

Presenter, *The 51st Annual Grammy Awards,* CBS, 2009.

National Movie Awards, 2010.

Performer, *The 53rd Annual Grammy Awards,* 2011.

(Uncredited) Performer, *The 68th Annual Golden Globe Awards,* 2011.

Television Work; Episodic:

Song performer, ''It's Only Love,'' ''The First Cut Is the Deepest,'' *One Tree Hill,* The WB, 2004.

Stage Appearances:

The Adventures of Huck Finn, Williamstown Theatre Festival, Williamstown, MA, 1990.

Picnic, Williamstown Theatre Festival, 1991.

The Sweet Bye and Bye, 1992.

Nina, *The Seagull,* Williamstown Theatre Festival, 1994.

Rosalind, *As You Like It,* Williamstown Theatre Festival, 1999.

Catherine, *Proof,* Donmar Warehouse Theatre, London, 2002.

RECORDINGS

Albums:

Reader, *Brown Bear and Friends,* c. 2008.

Recorded ''Forget You'' with the cast of *Glee* for the soundtrack album *Glee: The Music, Volume 4,* 2010; recorded (with Huey Lewis) ''Cruisin''' for the soundtrack of *Duets,* 2000; contributed to the song ''It's Only Love'' by Sheryl Crow.

Videos:

Inside "The Talented Mr. Ripley," Ardustry Home Entertainment, 1999.

Reflections on "The Talented Mr. Ripley," 2000.

Playboy Exposed: Playboy Mansion Parties Uncensored, 2001.

(From archive footage) Voice of Polly Perkins, *The Flying Legion Air Combat Challenge* (video game), 2004.

Brave New World, Paramount, 2005.

The White Shadow: The Shadow of Bruce Paltrow, Twentieth Century–Fox Home Entertainment, 2006.

The Making of "Anton," EastWest Distribution, 2009.

Appeared in the music videos ''Cruisin''' by Huey Lewis, 2000; and ''I Wanna Come Over'' by Melissa Etheridge.

WRITINGS

Books:
(With Mario Batali) *Spain: A Culinary Road Trip,* 2008.

Film Scripts:
Dealbreaker (short film), Glamour Magazine, 2005.

OTHER SOURCES

Books:
Hill, Anne E., *Gwyneth Paltrow,* Chelsea House Publishers, 2002.
Milano, Valerie, *Gwyneth Paltrow,* ECW Press, 2000.
Newsmakers 1997, Issue 4, Gale, 1997.

Periodicals:
Biography, spring, 2004.
Current Biography, January, 2005, pp. 57–61.
Daily Mail (London), June 26, 2010; July 24, 2010.
Daily Telegraph (London), April 30, 2008.
Entertainment Weekly, January 8, 1999, p. 26; March 1, 1999, p. 38; June 21, 2002, p. 90; November 28, 2003, pp. 42–43; September 17, 2004; February 2, 2007.
Harper's Bazaar, April, 1996, p. 188.
House and Garden, November, 2007, pp. 108–19.
In Style, January, 1999, p. 128.
Life, May 1, 1999, p. 60.
Newsweek, July 29, 1996, pp. 66–68.
New York, July 29, 1996.
New York Times, August 13, 1994; July 28, 1996, p. H11; August 10, 2005.
People Weekly, May 10, 1999, p. 169; December 17, 2001, pp. 71–72; October 14, 2002, pp. 68–69; January 27, 2003, p. 69; December 8, 2003, p. 21; December 22, 2003, p. 78; September 20, 1008, p. B9.
Time, December 15, 2003, p. 91; September 5, 2005.
Times (London), November 21, 2005.
TV Guide, October 13, 2008, pp. 36–37.
USA Today, January 7, 2009.
Variety, June 28, 1999, p. 75; June 3, 2002, p. 45.
Women's Wear Daily, December 14, 1998, p. 4.

PARKER, Mary–Louise 1964–
   (Mary Louise Parker)

PERSONAL

Born August 2, 1964, in Fort Jackson, SC; father, a military officer and a judge; children: (with actor Billy Crudup) William Atticus; (adopted) Caroline Aberash.

Education: Attended North Carolina School of the Arts; attended Bard College, 1990. *Avocational Interests:* Reading poetry, knitting, cooking.

Addresses: *Agent*—Scott Henderson, WME Entertainment, 9601 Wilshire Blvd., 3rd Floor, Beverly Hills, CA 90210; (voice work and commercials) Alix Gucovsky, Special Artists Agency, 9465 Wilshire Blvd., Suite 470, Beverly Hills, CA 90212.

Career: Actress. Cofounder of a theatre company; appeared in public service announcements. Formerly worked as a waitress, telemarketer, shoe salesperson, and cashier.

Awards, Honors: Theatre World Award, outstanding new performer, Clarence Derwent Award, Actors' Equity Association, Antoinette Perry Award nomination, best leading actress in a play, and Drama Desk Award nomination, all 1990, for *Prelude to a Kiss;* named one of the most "promising new actors of 1990," *John Willis' Screen World,* 1990; Obie Award, best performance, *Village Voice,* Lucille Lortel Award, outstanding actress in a play or musical, League of Off–Broadway Theatres and Producers, and Outer Critics Circle Award nomination, all 1997, for *How I Learned to Drive;* Genie Award nomination, best actress, Academy of Canadian Cinema and Television, 2000, for *The Five Senses;* Obie Award, best performance, Antoinette Perry Award, best leading actress in a play, Outer Critics Circle Award and Drama Desk Award, outstanding actress in a play, Lucille Lortel Award, outstanding actress, Drama League Award, distinguished performance, and Life in Theatre Award, T. Schreiber Studio, all 2001, for *Proof;* Emmy Award nomination, outstanding supporting actress in a drama series, 2002, and Screen Actors Guild Award nomination (with others), outstanding performance by an ensemble in a drama series, 2003, both for *The West Wing;* Emmy Award, Golden Globe Award, and Golden Satellite Award nomination, International Press Academy, all best supporting actress in a television series, miniseries, or movie, and Screen Actors Guild Award nomination, best actress in a television movie or miniseries, all 2004, for *Angels in America;* Artistic Achievement Award, Philadelphia Film Festival, 2004; Satellite Award, 2005, and Satellite Award nominations, 2006, 2008, 2009, Screen Actors Guild Award nominations, outstanding actress in a comedy series, 2006, 2007, 2008, 2009, Golden Globe Award, 2006, and Golden Globe Award nominations, 2007, 2008, 2009, and Emmy Award nominations, 2007, 2008, 2009, all best actress in a musical or comedy television series, Screen Actors Guild Award nominations (with others), outstanding ensemble in a comedy series, 2007, 2009, and People Choice Award nomination, favorite television drama diva, 2009, all for *Weeds;* Emmy Award nomination and Gemini Award, both best actress in a dramatic program or miniseries, 2007, for *The Robber Bride.*

CREDITS

Film Appearances:

(As Mary Louise Parker) Charlotte, *Signs of Life* (also known as *One for Sorrow, Two for Joy*), Avenue, 1989.

Lisa, *Longtime Companion*, Samuel Goldwyn, 1989.

Dee, *Grand Canyon*, Twentieth Century–Fox, 1991.

Ruth Jamison, *Fried Green Tomatoes* (also known as *Fried Green Tomatoes at the Whistle Stop Cafe*), Universal, 1991.

Rita, *Mr. Wonderful,* Warner Bros., 1993.

Dianne Sway, *The Client,* Warner Bros., 1994.

Ellen, *Bullets over Broadway,* Miramax, 1994.

Joanne White, *Naked in New York,* Fine Line, 1994.

Pooty, *Reckless,* Samuel Goldwyn, 1995.

Robin Nickerson, *Boys on the Side,* Warner Bros., 1995.

Henrietta Stackpole, *Portrait of a Lady,* Gramercy, 1996.

Julia Hirsch, *Let the Devil Wear Black,* Trimark Pictures, 1999.

Peggy Blane, *Goodbye Lover* (also known as *Patricia Arquette's "Goodbye Lover"*), Warner Bros., 1999.

Rona, *The Five Senses,* Fine Line, 1999.

Molly Graham, *Red Dragon,* Metro–Goldwyn–Mayer, 2002.

Sarah Richardson, *The Quality of Mercy,* 2002.

Toni Edelman, *Pipe Dream,* Castle Hill, 2002.

Lillian, *Saved!,* Metro–Goldwyn–Mayer/United Artists, 2004.

Constance, *Romance & Cigarettes,* Metro–Goldwyn–Mayer, 2005.

(In archive footage) Harper Pitt, *Wrestling with Angels: Playwright Tony Kushner* (documentary), Balcony Releasing, 2006.

Zee James, *The Assassination of Jesse James by the Coward Robert Ford* (also known as *The Assassination of Jesse James*), Warner Bros., 2007.

Helen Grace, *The Spiderwick Chronicles* (also released as *The Spiderwick Chronicles: The IMAX Experience*), Paramount, 2008.

Jordan Karsch, *Solitary Man,* Anchor Bay Films, 2010.

Gail Potter, *Howl,* Oscilloscope Pictures, 2010.

Sarah, *Red,* Summit Entertainment, 2010.

Katharine, *Les passages,* Arcades Project, 2010.

Television Appearances; Series:

Amy Gardner, a recurring role, *The West Wing,* NBC, 2001–2003, 2005–2006.

Nancy Botwin, *Weeds,* Showtime, 2005—.

Also appeared in a recurring role in *Ryan's Hope,* ABC.

Television Appearances; Miniseries:

Bonnie Hanssen, *Master Spy: The Robert Hanssen Story,* CBS, 2002.

Harper Pitt, *Angels in America,* HBO, 2003.

Television Appearances; Movies:

Pearl Spencer, *Too Young the Hero,* CBS, 1988.

Phyllis McGuire, *Sugartime,* HBO, 1995.

(As Mary Louise Parker) Caroline Walker, *Murder in Mind,* HBO, 1997.

Officer Emily Peck, *The Maker,* HBO, 1997.

Rica Martin, *Legalese* (also known as *Scandal*), TNT, 1998.

Dr. Valerie Crane, *The Simple Life of Noah Dearborn,* CBS, 1999.

Sue Zaidman, *The Best Thief in the World,* Showtime, 2004.

Corrine Morgan–Thomas, *Miracle Run,* Lifetime, 2004.

Ellen Grier, *Vinegar Hill,* CBS, 2005.

Zenia Arden, *The Robber Bride,* Oxygen, 2007.

Television Appearances; Specials:

Linda, "A Place for Annie," *Hallmark Hall of Fame,* ABC, 1994.

Lucy Ann Deen Dulcimer Bedloe, "Saint Maybe" (also known as Anne Tyler's "Saint Maybe"), *Hallmark Hall of Fame,* CBS, 1998.

Cate DeAngelo, "Cupid & Cate," *Hallmark Hall of Fame,* CBS, 2000.

Herself, *Inside "Red Dragon,"* 2002.

AFI Life Achievement Award: A Tribute to Meryl Streep, 2004.

Weeds: Suburban Shakedown, 2005.

Presenter, *The (28th Annual) Kennedy Center Honors: A Celebration of the Performing Arts,* CBS, 2005.

(Uncredited; in archive footage) Rita, *Premio Donostia a Matt Dillon,* 2006.

Reinventando Hollywood, 2008.

(In archive footage) Nancy Botwin, *Sexo en serie,* Canal+ Espana, 2008.

AFI Life Achievement Award: A Tribute to Mike Nichols, TV Land, 2010.

Television Appearances; Episodic:

Entertainment Tonight (also known as *E.T.* and *This Week in Entertainment*), syndicated, 2009.

Guest host, "Elvis Costello Interviewed by Mary–Louise Parker," *Spectacle: Elvis Costello With ...,* Sundance Channel, 2010.

America in Primetime, 2010.

Television Talk Show Guest Appearances; Episodic:

The Late Show with David Letterman (also known as *The Late Show* and *Letterman*), CBS, 1995, 2008, 2009.

The Rosie O'Donnell Show, syndicated, between 1997 and 2002.

Today (also known as *NBC News Today* and *The Today Show*), NBC, 2005.

GMTV, ITV, 2008.

Rachael Ray, syndicated, 2008.

Live with Regis and Kelly, syndicated, 2009.

The Late Late Show with Craig Ferguson, CBS, 2009.

The Bonnie Hunt Show, NBC, 2009.
Chelsea Lately, E! Entertainment Television, 2009.

Also appeared in *The Isaac Mizrahi Show,* Oxygen.

Television Appearances; Awards Presentations:
The ... Annual Tony Awards, 1990, CBS and PBS, 2001, CBS, 2005.
The 20th Annual People's Choice Awards, 1994.
Presenter, *The ... Annual Tony Awards,* CBS, 2002, 2008.
The ... Primetime Emmy Awards, NBC, 2002, ABC, 2004, ABC, 2008, CBS, 2009.
The ... Annual Golden Globe Awards, NBC, 2004, 2006, 2007, 2009.
Presenter, *The ... Primetime Emmy Awards,* Fox, 2007.
Presenter, *The 2007 Screen Actors Guild Awards,* TBS and TNT, 2007.

Stage Appearances:
The Girl in Pink, Quaigh Theatre, New York City, 1986.
Jackie, *Hay Fever,* Studio Arena Theatre, Buffalo, NY, 1986–87.
Marianne, *The Miser,* Syracuse Stage, Syracuse, NY, 1987–88.
Cecily Cardew, *The Importance of Being Earnest,* Hartford Stage Company, Hartford, CT, 1989–90.
Jane Hogarth, *The Art of Success,* Manhattan Theatre Club Stage I, New York City, 1989–90.
Rita, *Prelude to a Kiss,* Berkeley Repertory Theatre, Berkeley, CA, then Circle Repertory Theatre, New York City, 1990, then Helen Hayes Theatre, New York City, 1990–91.
Jean, *Babylon Gardens,* Circle Repertory Theatre, 1991.
Brenda, *Four Dogs and a Bone,* Manhattan Theatre Club Stage II, New York City, 1993.
Cherie, *Bus Stop,* Circle in the Square, New York City, 1996.
L'il Bit, *How I Learned to Drive,* Vineyard Theatre, New York City, 1997–98.
Poopay, *Communicating Doors,* Variety Arts Theatre, New York City, 1998–99.
Catherine, *Proof,* Manhattan Theatre Club Stage II, 2000, then Walter Kerr Theatre, New York City, 2000–2001.
Rachel, *Reckless,* Manhattan Theatre Club and Second Stage Theatre, Biltmore Theatre (now Samuel J. Friedman Theatre), New York City, 2004.
Escape: 6 Ways to Get Away (one–act; benefit), Circle in the Square, 2005.
Jean, *Dead Man's Cell Phone,* Playwrights Horizons Theatre, New York City, 2008.
Hedda Tesman, *Hedda Gabler,* Roundabout Theatre Company, American Airlines Theatre, New York City, 2009.

Also appeared in *The Age of Pie, The Little Foxes, The Night of the Iguana, Throwing Your Voice,* and *Up in Saratoga.*

RECORDINGS

Videos:
"Fried Green Tomatoes": The Moments of Discovery, 1998.
No Apologies: "Sorry, Haters" Roundtable (also known as *No Apologies*), IFC in Theatres, 2006.
The Assassination of Jesse James: Death of an Outlaw, Warner Bros. Home Video, 2008.

Appeared in the music video "You Got It" by Bonnie Raitt.

OTHER SOURCES

Books:
Newsmakers, Issue 2, Gale, 2002.

Periodicals:
Entertainment Weekly, February 10, 1995, pp. 40–41.
Jane, May, 1999, pp. 88–89.
Los Angeles Times, June 8, 2008.
Newsweek, October 7, 2002, p. 66.
New York Times, March 3, 2008, pp. E1, E6.
People Weekly, December 8, 2003, p. 99.
Time, April 18, 1994, p. 85.
TV Guide, November 19, 2007, p. 73; May 5, 2008, pp. 62–63.

PELLETIER, Bronson 1986–

PERSONAL

Born December 31, 1986.

Career: Actor. Also performed as traditional Native American dancer at pow wow gatherings.

Awards, Honors: Leo Award nominations, best performance in a youth or children's program or series, Motion Picture Arts and Sciences Foundation of British Columbia, 2006, 2007, and Gemini Award nomination, best performance in a children's or youth program or series, Academy of Canadian Cinema and Television, 2007, all for *Renegadepress.com.*

CREDITS

Film Appearances:
Jared, *New Moon* (also known as *New Moon: Twilight Saga, Twilight: New Moon, The Twilight Saga: New Moon,* and *Twilight 2*), Summit Entertainment, 2009.

Jared, *Eclipse* (also known as *Twilight: Eclipse, The Twilight Saga: Eclipse, The Twilight Saga: Eclipse—The IMAX Experience,* and *Twilight 3*), Summit Entertainment, 2010.

Television Appearances; Series:

Jack Sinclair, a recurring role, *Renegadepress.com,* Aboriginal Peoples Television Network, 2005–2008.
Kit Whitefeather, *Dinosapien,* Discovery Kids, 2007.

Television Appearances; Specials:

Teen Choice Awards, Fox, 2010.

Television Appearances; Episodic:

Made in Hollywood, 2009.
Up Close with Carrie Keagan, ABC, 2009.
(In archive footage) *The Tonight Show with Conan O'Brien,* NBC, 2009.

PESSOA, Andy 1996(?)–

PERSONAL

Full name, Andrew Stephan Pessoa; born October 30, 1996 (some sources cite 1995), in Kearney, NE; son of David and Stephanie Pessoa.

Career: Actor and voice performer.

CREDITS

Film Appearances:

Billy, *Fishy* (short film), Common Law Cousins, 2006.
Second gifted kid, *If I Had Known I Was a Genius* (also known as *Genius: If Only I Had Known*), Gibraltar Entertainment, 2006.
Jimmy, *Let's Play* (short film), Grass Graphics Films, 2007.
Noah, *Wish* (short film), Market Street Films, 2008.
Walter, *Lower Learning,* Anchor Bay Entertainment, 2008.

Television Appearances; Series:

Garrett Delfino and Stinky Cast, recurring roles, *Zeke and Luther,* The Disney Channel, 2009, 2010.

Television Appearances; Pilots:

Young Kenny, *My Name Is Earl,* NBC, 2005.

Television Appearances; Episodic:

Kid on Duck's team, "The Gang Gives Back," *It's Always Sunny in Philadelphia* (also known as *It's Always Sunny*), FX Network, 2006.
Andy, "Apologies for the Frivolity," *Two and a Half Men,* CBS, 2006.
Ian Bankova, "Four Dreams: Parts 1 & 2," *Medium,* NBC, 2006.
Young Oliver, "Oh Say, Can You Remember the Words?," *Hannah Montana* (also known as *Hannah Montana Forever* and *Secret Idol Hannah Montana*), The Disney Channel, 2006.
Young Oliver, "Money for Nothing, Guilt for Free," *Hannah Montana* (also known as *Hannah Montana Forever* and *Secret Idol Hannah Montana*), The Disney Channel, 2006.
Young Kenny, "Dad's Car," *My Name Is Earl,* NBC, 2006.
Bobby, "My Friend with Money," *Scrubs* (also known as *Scrubs: Med School*), NBC, 2007.
Young Kenny, "The Magic Hour," *My Name Is Earl,* NBC, 2008.
Young Kenny, "We've Got Spirit," *My Name Is Earl,* NBC, 2008.
Alfred, "Smarty Pants," *Wizards of Waverly Place,* The Disney Channel, 2008.
Alfred, "Beware Wolf," *Wizards of Waverly Place,* The Disney Channel, 2008.
Young Morgan, "Chuck versus the Best Friend," *Chuck,* NBC, 2009.

Radio Appearances; Episodic:

Voice of Barrett Jones, "Game for a Mystery," *Adventures in Odyssey,* 2010.
Voice of Barrett Jones, "When You're Right, You're Right," *Adventures in Odyssey,* 2010.

RECORDINGS

Videos:

(In archive footage) Alfred, *Wizards of Waverly Place: Fashionista Presto Chango,* Walt Disney Studios Home Entertainment, 2009.
Voice of Merry Gamgee, *The Lord of the Rings: Aragorn's Quest* (video game), 2010.

PHELAN, Walter
(Walter T. Phelan, Jr.)

PERSONAL

Career: Actor, stunt performer, and special makeup effects artist.

CREDITS

Film Appearances:
Monster, *From Dusk Till Dawn,* Dimension Films, 1996.
Creature stage number two, *Wishmaster* (also known as *Wes Craven Presents "Wishmaster"*), Live Entertainment, 1997.
Dr. Satan, *House of 1000 Corpses,* Lions Gate Films, 2003.
Himself and Dr. Satan, *30 Days in Hell: The Making of "The Devil's Rejects"* (documentary), Lions Gate Films Home Entertainment, 2005.
Himself, *The Horrorhound* (documentary), 2007.
The creature, *Eyes of the Woods,* Central Film Company, 2009.
Windigo, *Maneater,* Lightning Media, 2009.

Film Work:
Makeup effects technician, *Necronomicon: Book of Dead* (also known as *Necronomicon* and *H. P. Lovecraft's "Necronomicon, Book of the Dead"*), New Line Home Video, 1993.
(As Walter T. Phelan, Jr.) Stunts and makeup effects project head, *Tales from the Crypt: Demon Knight* (also known as *Tales from the Crypt Presents: "Demon Knight"*), MCA/Universal, 1995.
Effects crew, *Bordello of Blood,* Universal, 1996.
Foam department, *Fantastic Four,* Twentieth Century–Fox, 2005.
Stunts, *Hallowed Ground,* 2007.
Special makeup effects assistant, *Night Skies,* Sony Pictures Home Entertainment, 2007.
Prosthetic foam department (spectral motion), *Hellboy II: The Golden Army,* Universal, 2008.
Special makeup effects technician, *Watchmen* (also known as *Watchmen: The IMAX Experience*), Warner Bros., 2009.
Foam department, *Race to Witch Mountain,* Walt Disney Studios Motion Pictures, 2009.
Foam department, *Cirque Du Freak: The Vampire's Assistant,* Universal, 2009.

Television Appearances; Movies:
Scarecrow, *Hallowed Ground,* Sci–Fi Channel, 2007.

Television Appearances; Episodic:
(As Walter T. Phelan, Jr.) Alien, "The Unnatural," *The X–Files,* Fox, 1999.
Abraxas, "Witch Trial," *Charmed,* The WB, 1999.
Johnny Thing, "The Fair Haired Child," *Masters of Horror,* Showtime, 2006.
The creature, "The Sacrifice," *Fear Itself,* NBC, 2008.

Television Work; Movies:
Makeup effects project head, *Tales from the Crypt: Demon Knight* (also known as *Tales from the Crypt Presents: Demon Knight*), 1995.

Television Work; Pilots:
Special makeup and creature effects, *Tarzan's Return* (movie), syndicated, 1996.

Television Work; Episodic:
Special makeup effects artist, "House of Horror," *Tales from the Crypt,* HBO, 1993.
Special effects technician, *Punk'd,* MTV, 2006.

RECORDINGS

Video Games:
Mummy and zombie, *Goosebumps: Escape from Horrorland,* 1996.

PHILLIPS, Derek 1976–

PERSONAL

Born April 18, 1976, in Miami, FL. *Education:* Baylor University, B.F.A.

Addresses: *Agent*—Pantheon Talent Group, 1900 Avenue of the Stars, 28th Floor, Los Angeles, CA 90067. *Manager*—Laina Cohn, Laina Cohn Management, 15066 Sutton St., Sherman Oaks, Ca 91403.

Career: Actor, producer, and director. Second Thought Theatre, assistant director, associate producer, and resident actor.

CREDITS

Television Appearances; Series:
Billy Riggins, *Friday Night Lights* (also known as *F.N. L.*), NBC, 2006–2008, DirecTV, 2009, NBC, 2009–10.

Television Appearances; Pilots:
Billy Riggins, *Friday Night Lights,* NBC, 2006.

Television Appearances; Episodic:
Keevan, *The Guiding Light,* CBS, 2002.
Field cop, "Dead Fall," *Prison Break,* Fox, 2006.
Dale, "Testing 1–2–3," *Grey's Anatomy,* ABC, 2007.
Dale, "Didn't We Almost Have It?," *Grey's Anatomy,* ABC, 2007.
Ryan Ferraro, "End Game," *Numb3rs* (also known as *Num3ers*), CBS, 2008.
Stomper, "Strike Three," *The Closer,* TNT, 2009.

Sean Riley, "How to Beat a Bad Guy," *Medium,* CBS, 2010.
Jason, "Tunnel Vision," *Trauma,* NBC, 2010.
Eddie Lindy, "Triangles," *Private Practice,* ABC, 2010.
Eddie Lindy, "Pulling the Plug," *Private Practice,* ABC, 2010.
Eddie Lindy, "Eyes Wide Open," *Private Practice,* ABC, 2010.

Also appeared in episodes of *All My Children* and *As the World Turns.*

Film Appearances:
Eddie, *Serum,* Arrival Pictures, 2007.
Skyler, *Son of Morning,* Hothead Entertainment/Synesthesia Productions, 2010.

Stage Appearances:
Appeared in productions of *The Glass Menagerie,* Virginia Stage Company; *Humpty Dumpty,* Second Thought Theatre; *King o' the Moon,* Capital Repertory Theatre; *Of Mice and Men,* Dallas Theatre Center, Dallas, TX; *Pluck the Day,* Second Thought Theatre; and *The Winter's Tale,* Center Stage, Baltimore, MD.

PHILLIPS, Stone 1954–

PERSONAL

Full name, Stone Stockton Phillips; born December 2, 1954, in Texas City, TX; son of Victor (a chemical engineer) and Grace (a schoolteacher) Phillips; married Debra, c. 1986; children: Daniel Streeter. *Education:* Yale University, B.A. (cum laude), philosophy, 1977.

Addresses: *Office*—c/o Dateline NBC, NBC News, 30 Rockefeller Plaza, New York, NY 10112.

Career: News reporter and anchor. WXIA–TV, Atlanta, GA, worked as reporter and producer, beginning in 1977; ABC News, affiliated with documentary unit, then assignment editor in Washington, DC, 1979–81; general assignment news correspondent, 1982–86; contributing correspondent for MSNBC, beginning 1996; left NBC, 2007. Previously worked as a remedial reading teacher in Atlanta, GA.

Member: Scroll and Keys.

Awards, Honors: F. Gordon Brown Award, Yale University, 1976; Emmy Award nomination (with others), coverage of a single breaking news story, 1986–87, for "The Challenger Explosion," *World News Tonight with Peter Jennings;* Emmy Award nomination (with producer Ene Riisna), background/analysis of a single current story, 1987–88, for "To Bring His Daughter Home," *20/20;* three National Headliner Awards, outstanding journalism; Overseas Press Club of America Award; National Association of Black Journalists Award; American Medical Association Award; American Psychological Association Award; B'nai B'rith Award; National Collegiate Athletic Association Post–Graduate Scholar; inductee, Scholar Athlete Hall of Fame, National Football Foundation.

CREDITS

Television Appearances; Series:
Reporter, *20/20* (also known as *ABC News 20/20*), ABC, 1986–91.
NBC Nightly News, NBC, 1992–2005.
Anchor and correspondent, *Dateline NBC,* NBC, 1992–2006.
Weekend Magazine with Stone Phillips, 1993.

Television Appearances; Specials:
The Opening Ceremonies of the 1995 Special Olympics World Games, 1995.
Presenter, *The 32nd Annual Academy of Country Music Awards,* 1997.
Anchor (*Dateline NBC*), *The Greatest Generation* (also known as *Tom Brokaw Reports: The Greatest Generation*), NBC, 1999.
Host (*Dateline NBC*), *Witness to an Execution,* NBC, 2001.
Host, *MSNBC Investigates: Black Hawk Down—The Somali Connection,* MSNBC, 2001.
NBC 75th Anniversary Special (also known as *NBC 75th Anniversary Celebration*), NBC, 2002.
Anchor, *Michael Jackson Unmasked,* NBC, 2003.
Host, *ER 200: A "Dateline" Special,* NBC, 2003.
Host, *Ben & Jen: A "Dateline" Special,* NBC, 2003.
Host, *Deadline,* NBC, 2004.
Host, *Behind "The Apprentice": "Dateline" with Stone Phillips,* NBC, 2004.
Host, *Jane Pauley: Out of the Blue,* NBC, 2004.
Anchor, *John Paul II: An NBC News Special,* NBC, 2005.
The 16th Annual American Century Championship, 2005.
The 17th Annual American Century Championship, 2006.

Television Appearances; Episodic:
World News Tonight with Peter Jennings, ABC, c. 1986.
Substitute host, *Good Morning America,* ABC, 1986.
Guest sports anchor, *World News Sunday,* ABC, 1986.
The Tonight Show Starring Johnny Carson, NBC, 1992.
Late Night with Conan O'Brien, NBC, 1994.

The Rosie O'Donnell Show, syndicated, 1999, 2000, 2001, 2002.

(Uncredited) Himself, "He's Come Undone," *Will & Grace,* NBC, 2000.

Host, "Scott Peterson," *Headliners & Legends,* NBC, 2005.

The Colbert Report, Comedy Central, 2005, 2006.

Himself, "Charity Season," *Open Access,* The Tennis Channel, 2006.

Also appeared as substitute anchor, *Meet the Press,* NBC; substitute anchor, *Today,* NBC.

OTHER SOURCES

Periodicals:
Broadcasting & Cable, June 29, 1998, p. 68.
People Weekly, April 1, 1996, pp. 65–66.
Texas Monthly, July, 1996, p. 20.
USA Today, May 23, 2007.

PICKETT, Jay 1961–

PERSONAL

Born February 10, 1961, in Spokane, WA; married; wife's name, Elena, 1986; children: two.

Career: Actor, producer, and writer.

CREDITS

Film Appearances:
Man in Jeep, *Eve of Destruction,* Orion, 1991.
Parker, *Rush Week,* Alpine Releasing, 1991.
Russell Stewart, *Rumpelstiltskin,* Spelling Films International, 1995.
Bobby, *The Clear Horizon* (short film), ShadowDance Pictures, 2008.
Ross Davis, *Bundy: An American Icon* (also known as *Bundy: A Legacy of Evil*), Barnholtz Entertainment, 2008.
Detective Donovan, *Boston Strangler: The Untold Story,* Weinstein Company, 2008.
Officer Dollinger, *Drifter: Henry Lee Lucas,* Barnholtz Entertainment, 2009.
Grant Mussendon, *The Real Deal,* Loyola Productions, 2009.
Detective Franklin, *Abandoned,* Anchor Bay Entertainment, 2010.
John, *The Perfect Student,* Hybrid, 2010.
Eden, *Soda Springs,* 2C Entertainment, 2011.

Film Producer:
Soda Springs, 2C Entertainment, 2011.

Television Appearances; Series:
Dr. Chip Lakin, *Days of Our Lives* (also known as *Days* and *DOOL*), NBC, 1991–92.
Frank Scanlon, *Port Charles,* ABC, 1997–2003.
Detective David Harper, *General Hospital,* ABC, 1997–2008.

Television Appearances; Movies:
Steve, *A Perry Mason Mystery: The Case of the Jealous Jokester,* NBC, 1995.
Stewart Hancock, *Landslide* (also known as *Buried Alive*), 2004, Hallmark Channel, 2006.

Television Appearances; Specials:
Sex with Cindy Crawford, ABC, 1998.
The 67th Annual Hollywood Christmas Parade, UPN, 1998.

Television Appearances; Episodic:
Alex Leskov, "Russian Holiday," *Rags to Riches,* NBC, 1987.
Filmore Cross, "Waiting for Beckett," *China Beach,* ABC, 1988.
Keith Elliot, "Homecoming," *Mr. Belvedere,* ABC, 1989.
"Let's Call the Whole Thing Off," *Jake and the Fatman,* CBS, 1991.
Gary Andler, "The Witness Killings: Parts 1 & 2," *Matlock,* NBC, 1991.
J. M., "The Gardener," *Hot Line,* 1996.
Eddie, "Would You Want me to Tell You?," *Saving Grace,* TNT, 2007.
Warren, "All in the Family," *Dexter,* Showtime, 2008.
Hit man, "If It's Only in Your Head," *Desperate Housewives,* ABC, 2009.

WRITINGS

Screenplays:
Soda Springs, 2C Entertainment, 2011.

PLEMONS, Jesse 1988–

PERSONAL

Born April 2, 1988, in Dallas, TX. *Education:* Attended high school in Texas. *Avocational Interests:* Playing sports, writing, and playing music.

Addresses: *Agent*—TalentWorks, 3500 West Olive Ave., Suite 1400, Burbank, CA 91505. *Manager*—Simmons and Scott Entertainment, 7942 Mulholland Dr., Los Angeles, CA 90046.

Career: Actor. Appeared in a commercial for Coca–Cola soft drinks at age three.

Awards, Honors: Young Artist Award nomination, best guest–starring young actor in a television drama series, 2002, for *The Guardian.*

CREDITS

Film Appearances:
Hobo, *Finding North,* Cowboy Booking International, 1999.
Tommy Harbor, *Varsity Blues,* Paramount, 1999.
Young Grady, *All the Pretty Horses,* Miramax, 2000.
Ox, *Like Mike,* Twentieth Century–Fox, 2002.
Preacher Star, *Children on Their Birthdays,* Artisan Entertainment/Crusader Entertainment/Moonstone Entertainment, 2002.
Boe, *The Failures,* Plus Entertainment, 2003.
Jay, *When Zachary Beaver Came to Town,* Echo Bridge Entertainment, 2003.
First bully, *The Flyboys* (also known as *Sky Kids*), Halcyon Pictures, 2008.
Jesus, *Shrink,* Roadside Attractions, 2009.
Charles, *Observe and Report,* Warner Bros., 2009.
Spencer West, *Meeting Spencer,* George G. Braunstein Productions, 2010.
Chad, *Happiness Runs,* Strand Releasing, 2010.
Jake, *Paul,* Universal, 2010.

Television Appearances; Series:
Landry Clarke, *Friday Night Lights* (also known as *F.N.L.*), NBC, 2006–2008, DirecTV, 2009, NBC, 2009–10.

Television Appearances; Pilots:
Duran Beck, *Expert Witness,* CBS, 2003.
Landry Clarke, *Friday Night Lights,* NBC, 2006.

Television Appearances; Episodic:
Russell, Jr., "The General's Return," *Walker, Texas Ranger,* CBS, 2000.
Bigger kid, "Really Big Season Opener," *Sabrina, the Teenage Witch* (also known as *Sabrina* and *Sabrina Goes to College*), The WB, 2001.
Lawrence Neal, "Paternity," *The Guardian* (also known as *Ochita bengoshi Nick Fallin*), CBS, 2001.
James Franklin, "Marry, Marry Quite Contrary," *Judging Amy,* CBS, 2003.
Ray Ferris, "The Other Side of Caution," *The Lyon's Den,* NBC, 2003.
Owen Durbin, "Down the Drain," *CSI: Crime Scene Investigation* (also known as *C.S.I.* and *CSI: Las Vegas*), CBS, 2004.
Dawson James, "Cold Day in Shanghai," *Huff,* Showtime, 2004.

Jason Geckler, "Deception," *NCIS: Naval Criminal Investigative Service* (also known as *Navy NCIS: Naval Criminal Investigative Service* and *NCIS*), CBS, 2006.
Jake Burton, "Yesterday," *Grey's Anatomy,* ABC, 2006.
Lemmon, "The Sacrifice," *Fear Itself,* NBC, 2008.
Ryan Stewart, "The Long Blue Line," *Cold Case,* CBS, 2009.
Ryan Stewart, "Into the Blue," *Cold Case,* CBS, 2009.
"Observe and Report," *Reel Comedy,* Comedy Central, 2009.

PROCACCI, Domenico 1960–

PERSONAL

Born 1960, in Bari, Italy.

Addresses: *Office*—Works Media Group, Portland House, 4th Floor, 4 Great Portland St., London W1W 0QJ, England.

Career: Producer, executive, and actor. Fandango (film company), founder, principal, and producer, c. 1989—; Fandango Australia, founder, 2002; Works Media Group, London, board member and film director, 2004—; Fandango Libre (book publisher), founder, 2005; Fandango Portobello Sales, founder and partner, 2007—. Also founder of the film school Fandango Lab; affiliate of Civilian Content, 2004.

Awards, Honors: David di Donatello Award nomination, best producer, 1991, for *The Station;* Australian Film Institute Award nomination (with others), best film, 1994, for *Bad Boy Bubby;* David di Donatello Award nomination, best producer, 1999, for *Radiofreccia;* David di Donatello Award nomination, best producer, 2000, for *But Forever in My Mind;* David di Donatello Award, best producer, 2001, for *The Last Kiss;* nomination for Silver Ribbon, best producer, Italian National Syndicate of Film Journalists, 2001, for *Johnny the Partisan* and *The Last Kiss;* David di Donatello Award, best producer, and David di Donatello Award nomination (with others), best film, both 2003, for *Respiro;* David di Donatello Award nominations, best producer and best film (with others), 2003, for *Remember Me, My Love;* David di Donatello Award nominations, best producer and best film (with others), 2003, for *The Embalmer;* Australian Film Institute Award nomination (with others), best film, 2003, for *Alexandra's Project;* David di Donatello Award nomination, best producer, 2004, for *First Love;* nomination for Silver Ribbon, best producer, Italian National Syndicate of Film Journalists, 2004, for *Secret File, Ora o mai piu,* and other films;

David di Donatello Award, best film, and David di Donatello Award nomination, best producer, both (with others), 2005, for *The Consequences of Love;* nomination for Silver Ribbon, best producer, Italian National Syndicate of Film Journalists, 2005, for *First Love, The Consequences of Love,* and *Working Slowly (Radio Alice);* David di Donatello Award nomination (with others), best producer, 2006, for *Mario's War;* David di Donatello Award nomination (with others), best film, 2006, for *Our Land;* David di Donatello Award nominations, best producer and best film (with others), both 2008, for *Quiet Chaos;* Silver Ribbon, best producer, Italian National Syndicate of Film Journalists, 2008, for *Quiet Chaos, The Right Distance,* and other films; Film Award nomination (with others), best film not in the English language, British Academy of Film and Television Arts, and David di Donatello Awards (with others), best film and best producer, all 2009, for *Gomorrah;* Special Jury Award, Italian Golden Globe Awards, 2009.

CREDITS

Film Producer:
Il grande Blek, Vertigo Film, 1987.
Nulla ci puo fermare, Vertigo Film, 1988.
The Station (also known as *La stazione*), Federal Films, 1990, subtitled version, Aries Film, 1992.
La bionda, 1992.
The Flight of the Innocent (also known as *La corsa dell'innocente*), subtitled version, Metro–Goldwyn–Mayer, 1993.
Bad Boy Bubby, 1993, P & B, 1997.
Come due coccodrilli (also known as *Like Two Crocodiles*), MC4 Distribution, 1994.
Il cielo e sempre piu blu, Fandango/Colorado Film Production, 1995.
Correre contro (also known as *Running Against*), Radiotelevisione Italiana, 1996.
The Quiet Room, Fine Line, 1997.
Epsilon, Miramax/Roadshow Entertainment, 1997.
Le mani forti, Mikado, 1997.
The Room of the Scirocco (also known as *La stanza dello scirocco*), Warner Bros., 1998.
Dance Me to My Song, Palace Entertainment, 1998.
Radiofreccia (also known as *Radio Nights*), Medusa Distribuzione, 1998.
Ecco fatto (also known as *That's It*), Mikado, 1998.
Pereira Declares, 1998.
But Forever in My Mind (also known as *Come te nessuno mai*), Mikado, 1999, subtitled version, Intra Films, 2000.
Johnny the Partisan (also known as *Il partigiano Johnny*), Fandango/Media Trade, 2000.
Lupo mannaro, Fandango, 2000.
Fughe da fermo, Fandango, 2001.
The Last Kiss (also known as *L'ultimo bacio*), Medusa Distribuzione, 2001, subtitled version, THINKFilm, 2002.
Dust, Medusa Distribuzione, 2001, Lions Gate Films, 2003.
He Died with a Falafel in His Hand, Roadshow Entertainment/Village Roadshow Entertainment, 2001.
From Zero to Ten (also known as *Da zero a dieci*), 2002, Antiprod, 2006.
Respiro (also known as *Grazia's Island*), Medusa Distribuzione, 2002, subtitled version, Sony Pictures Classics, 2003.
The Embalmer (also known as *The Taxidermist* and *L'imbalsamatore*), Fandango, 2002, subtitled version, First Run Features, 2003.
Maximum Velocity (also known as *Velocita massima*), Medusa Distribuzione, 2002.
Remember Me, My Love (also known as *Remember Me* and *Ricordati di me*), Medusa Distribuzione, 2003, subtitled version, Roadside Attractions, 2004.
Alexandra's Project, Fandango, 2003, Film Movement, 2004.
B. B. and the Cormorant (also known as *B. B. e il cormorano*), Medusa Distribuzione, 2003.
Ora o mai piu (also known as *Now or Never*), 01 Distribuzione, 2003.
Secret File (also known as *Segreti di stato*), Fandango, 2003.
Break Free (also known as *Liberi*), Fandango, 2003.
First Love (also known as *Primo amore*), Fandango, 2004, subtitled version, Strand Releasing, 2005.
The Consequences of Love (also known as *Le conseguenze dell'amore*), Medusa Distribuzione, 2004, Artificial Eye, 2005.
Nemmeno il destino, Fandango, 2004.
"The Dangerous Thread of Things" segment, *Eros,* Fandango, 2004, Earner Independent Pictures, 2005.
Ogni volta che te ne vai, Fandango, 2004.
Achille e la targaruga (short film), Fandango, 2005.
Tickets, Artificial Eye, 2005.
L'orizzonte degli eventi, Medusa Distribuzione, 2005.
Mario's War (also known as *La guerra di Mario*), Medusa Distribuzione, 2005.
La fondue (short film), Fandango, 2005.
Karma (short film), Fandango, 2005.
Our Land (also known as *The Earth* and *La terra*), Medusa Distribuzione, 2006.
L'amico di famiglia (also known as *Friend of the Family*), Wild Bunch, 2006.
Fascisti su Marte, Fandango, 2006.
La ragioni dell'aragosta (documentary), Istituto Luce, 2007.
Silk, Picturehouse Entertainment, 2007.
The Right Distance (also known as *La giusta distanza*), 01 Distribuzione, 2007.
Parole sante (documentary), Fandango, 2007.
Lascia perdere, Johnny!, Medusa Distribuzione, 2007.
Producer of restored version, *Throw of the Dice* (also known as *Prapancha Pas;* original version released in 1929, Fandango, 2007, Kino International, 2008.

Quiet Chaos (also known as *Caos calmo*), 01 Distribuzione, 2008, subtitled version, IFC Films, 2009.

Treni strettamente riservati (short film), Fandango, 2008.

Gomorrah (also known as *Gomorra*), IFC Films, 2008.

Five Stories (documentary; also known as *Gomorra, cinque storie brevi*), 01 Distribuzione, 2008.

Lesson 21 (also known as *Lezione 21*), RAI Cinema, 2008.

A Perfect Day (also known as *Un giorno perfetto*), 01 Distribuzione, 2008.

The Past Is a Foreign Land (also known as *Il passato e una terra straniera*), 01 Distribuzione, 2008.

Cosmonaut (also known as *Cosmonauta*), 01 Distribuzione, 2009.

Lo spazio bianco (also known as *The White Space*), 01 Distribuzione, 2009.

Baciami ancora (also known as *Kiss Me Again*), Medusa Distribuzione, 2010.

Loose Cannons (also known as *Mine vaganti*), Peccadillo Pictures, 2010.

The Passion (also known as *La passione*), 01 Distribuzione, 2010.

Film Executive Producer:

Spank, Palace Films/Australian Film Finance Corp., 1999.

Super 8 Stories (documentary), Fandango, 2001.

Tre per sempre, Fandango/Vertigo Productions, 2002.

The Tracker, Fandango, 2002, ArtManhattan Productions, 2004.

Tom White, Cinemavault Releasing, 2004.

Working Slowly (Radio Alice) (also known as *Lavorare con lentezza*), Fandango, 2004.

Ten Canoes, Palm Pictures, 2007.

Dr. Plonk, Fandango, 2007.

Seven Pounds, Columbia, 2008.

Film Coproducer:

Zivot a neobycejna dobrodruzstvi vojaka Ivana Conkina (also known as *The Extraordinary Adventures of Ivan Chonkin*), multiple distributors, including Fandango, Channel Four Films, MK2 Productions, Portobello Pictures, and Studio Trite, 1994.

Guiltrip, 1995.

Le monde a l'envers, Eurozoom/Gaia Films, 1998.

The Ice Rink (also known as *La patinoire*), Les Films des Tournelles, 1998, subtitled version, Kino Video, 2001.

The War Zone (also known as Tim Roth's "The War Zone"), Lot 47 Films, 1999.

Calle 54 (concert documentary), subtitled version, Miramax, 2000.

The Monkey's Mask (also known as *Poetry, Sex*), Strand Releasing, 2001.

Dark Blue World (also known as *Tmavomodry svet*), subtitled version, Sony Pictures Classics, 2001.

The Bank, Fandango, 2001, Cinema Guild, 2002.

Samsara, Miramax, 2002.

In Prison My Whole Life (documentary), Fandango/Nana, 2007.

Barney's Version, Serendipity Point Films/Harold Greenberg Fund, 2010.

Film Associate Producer:

Just Run! (also known as *Tu que harias por amor?*), 2001, Maverick Entertainment Group, 2003.

Film Appearances:

Himself, *The Bet,* Dreamages Films, 2005.

Ambassador, *Silk,* Picturehouse Entertainment, 2007.

Television Appearances; Specials:

The 21st European Film Awards (also known as *The 2008 European Film Awards*), 2008.

Television Appearances; Episodic:

Quelli che ... il calcio, 2009.

OTHER SOURCES

Periodicals:

Variety, January 12, 2004, p. 12; May 10, 2004, p. 18; December 25, 2006, p. 7; May 11, 2009, p. A57.

PRUCHA, Jackie

PERSONAL

Career: Actress.

CREDITS

Film Appearances:

Party guest, *Petunia* (short film), 2002.

Elena Porcini, *Battaglia* (short film), 2005.

Cohen, *Death of Seasons,* 2006.

Ultimate fan's mother, *Return of the Jackalope,* 2006.

Janice, *The Last Adam,* Urban Home Entertainment, 2006.

Miss Pat Hinton, *Dangerous Calling,* Cloud Ten Pictures, 2008.

Officer worker, *Julie & Julia,* Columbia, 2009.

Mary Simpkins, *The Way Home,* Lions Gate Films, 2010.

Nurse, *For Colored Girls Who Have Considered Suicide When the Rainbow Enuf,* Lions Gate Films, 2010.

Television Appearances; Movies:
Polly, *Miss Lettie and Me,* TNT, 2002.

Television Appearances; Pilots:
Judge, *Hollis & Rae,* ABC, 2006.

PRUNER, Karl
(Carl Pruner, Karl Prunner, Karl Purner)

PERSONAL

Born in Toronto, Ontario, Canada; married Sharon Jackson; children: Jordan, Cassidy. *Education:* Attended Carleton University, Ottawa, Ontario, Canada.

Addresses: *Agent*—Edna Talent Management Ltd., 318 Dundas St. W., Toronto, Ontario M5T 1G5, Canada.

Career: Actor. National Arts Centre, member of English Theatre Company, beginning 1977; appeared in commercials.

Member: Alliance of Canadian Cinema, Television, and Radio Artists (president of Toronto chapter, 2005).

Awards, Honors: Gemini Award nomination, best supporting actor, Academy of Canadian Cinema and Television, 1990, for *E.N.G.;* Canadian Comedy Award nomination (with others), pretty fun writing in a film, 2004, for *Expecting.*

CREDITS

Television Appearances; Miniseries:
The voice, *Thanks of a Grateful Nation* (also known as *The Gulf War*), Showtime, 1998.
Issaac Brock, *War of 1812,* 1999.
Clinton Hill, *Jackie, Ethel, Joan: The Women of Camelot* (also known as *Jackie, Ethel, Joan: The Kennedy Women*), NBC, 2001.
Julian, *I Was a Rat,* BBC, 2001.
Charles Marlow, *L'or,* CBC, 2001.
John Turner, *Trudeau,* CBC, 2002.
Frank Scott, *Trudeau II: Maverick in the Making,* CBC, 2005.
Supervisor from Federal Aviation Administration, *The Path to 9/11,* ABC, 2006.
Charles Preston, *The Trojan Horse,* CBC, 2008.

Television Appearances; Movies:
(As Karl Prunner) Simon, *Bluffing It,* ABC, 1987.

(As Karl Purner) Alex, *Hostile Advances: The Kerry Ellison Story,* Lifetime, 1996.
John Gleeson, *Gotti* (also known as *Gotti: The Rise and Fall of a Real Life Mafia Don*), HBO, 1996.
Marcus Hayworth, *A Prayer in the Dark,* USA Network, 1997.
Dennis Bell, *When Husbands Cheat,* Lifetime, 1998.
Todd Stanfford, *This Matter of Marriage* (also known as *Harlequin's "This Matter of Marriage"*), The Movie Channel, 1998.
David Corliss, *The Fixer,* Showtime, 1998.
Paul Klondike, *My Date with the President's Daughter,* ABC, 1998.
First congressman, *The Long Island Incident,* NBC, 1998.
Jack Marko, *In the Company of Spies,* Showtime, 1999.
General Sullivan, *The Crossing,* Arts and Entertainment, 2000.
Dick Baker, *Catch a Falling Star,* CBS, 2000.
Mr. Ross, *Finding Buck McHenry,* Showtime, 2000.
Count Krelski, *Mom's Got a Date with a Vampire,* The Disney Channel, 2000.
Phil Davis, *One True Love,* CBS, 2000.
Douglas Weiss, *Sex, Lies & Obsession,* Lifetime, 2001.
Henry Quinn, *Crossed Over,* CBS, 2002.
Detective Baker, *The Interrogation of Michael Crowe,* Court TV, 2002.
Chasing Cain: Face, CBC, 2002.
Quidd, *Threshold,* Sci–Fi Channel, 2003.
Ed Zuterman, *Burn: The Robert Wraight Story,* CTV, 2003.
Victor Petronovich, *Bugs,* Sci–Fi Channel, 2003.
Detective Richard Klassen, *The Elizabeth Smart Story* (also known as *Kidnapped: The Elizabeth Smart Story*), CBS, 2003.
Maracek, *Thoughtcrimes,* USA Network, 2003.
Professor, *Brave New Girl,* ABC Family, 2004.
Dale Wyman, *Open Heart,* 2004.
Detective Hank Girardin, *Tripping the Wire: A Stephen Tree Mystery,* Lifetime, 2005.
Judge, *The Wives He Forgot,* Lifetime, 2006.
Bill Strand, *Tipping Point,* Lifetime, 2007.

Television Appearances; Series:
Dan Watson, *E.N.G.,* Lifetime, 1989–c. 1994.
Stephen Bennett, *Ready or Not,* Global, then Showtime, 1996–97.
Ian Farve, *Total Recall 2070* (also known as *Total Recall: The Series*), Showtime, 1999.

Television Appearances; Specials:
Sir Isaac Newton, *Newton: A Tale of Two Isaacs,* HBO, 1998.
John Knox, *Empire of the Bay,* PBS, 2000.

Television Appearances; Pilots:
Ian Farve, *Total Recall 2070* (also known as *Total Recall 2070: Machine Dreams*), Showtime, 1998.

Television Appearances; Episodic:

Steve, "Duddleman and the Diamond Ring," *The Littlest Hobo,* syndicated, 1980.

Martin Glazer, "There Was an Old Woman," *The Twilight Zone,* 1988.

Michael Abbott, "State of Mind," *Street Legal,* CBC, 1988.

Russian guard, "Covert Agenda," *Adderly,* CBS, 1988.

Paul, "Dream Child," *The Hidden Room,* Lifetime, 1991.

Matthew, "Faithful Followers," *Forever Knight,* syndicated, 1994.

Anton Calvin, "Citizen Caine," *Kung Fu: The Legend Continues,* syndicated, 1995.

Malcolm MacEwan, "Secrets and Sacrifices," *Road to Avonlea* (also known as *Avonlea* and *Tales from Avonlea*), CBC, 1996.

Artie Collins, "Rust Proof," *Side Effects,* CBC, 1996.

John Taylor, "One Good Man," *Due South* (also known as *Direction: Sud*), CBS, 1996.

Julian Lambert, "Betrayal," *TekWar* (also known as *TekWar: The Series*), USA Network, 1996.

Percy Ardley, "Moonshine Struck," *Wind at My Back,* CBC, 1996, then Odyssey, 2000.

"Proofs for the Existence of God," *Nothing Sacred,* ABC, 1997.

David Vancha, "Kiss of the Tiger," *Psi Factor: Chronicles of the Paranormal,* syndicated, 1998.

Voice of Beta Ray Bill, "Innervisions," *The Silver Surfer* (animated), Fox, 1998.

Voice of Chiron, "Jason and Medea," *Mythic Warriors: Guardians of the Legend,* CBS, 1999.

Voice of Chiron, "The Hounds of Actaeon," *Mythic Warriors: Guardians of the Legend,* CBS, 1999.

(As Carl Pruner) Barry Lewis, "Old Flames," *Twice in a Lifetime,* PAX, 2000.

Martin Halford, "Care & Control," *The Associates,* CTV, 2001.

Michael Black, "Busy Man," *Doc,* PAX, 2002.

Simon Fletcher, "One Step Closer," *Mutant X,* syndicated, 2003.

Bretts Ravenwood, "Section 24," *Snakes & Ladders,* CBC, 2004.

Dallas Macon, "The Holocaust Survivor," *Sue Thomas: F.B.Eye,* PAX, 2004.

Colonel Grant, "Cuddles the Manchurian Candidate," *Puppets Who Kill,* Comedy Central, 2005.

Congressman Wade Keene, "Political Eyes," *Angela's Eyes,* Lifetime, 2006.

Quebec Premiere Belanger, "Nothing to Declare," *The Border,* CBC, 2008.

Principal, "Chapter Five," *Living in Your Car,* HBO Canada, 2010.

Priest, "Dallas Alice Doesn't Live Here Anymore," *Happy Town,* ABC, 2010.

Appeared in an episode of *Tilt,* ESPN.

Film Appearances:

William, *The Good Mother* (also known as *The Price of Passion*), Buena Vista, 1988.

Hal, *Thick As Thieves,* 1991.

Frank Jobs, *Dick,* Columbia, 1999.

Keith Taylor, *Fall* (also known as *Fall: The Price of Silence*), Annex Entertainment, 2000.

Jack, *Expecting,* Corus, 2002.

Voice of Edward Weston, *Tina in Mexico,* 2002.

Dennis Slayne, *The Recruit,* Buena Vista, 2003.

Dyer, *Welcome to Mooseport,* Twentieth Century–Fox, 2004.

Martin Brooks, *The Skulls III,* Universal Home Entertainment, 2004.

Rex Ventura, *Zeyda and the Hitman* (also known as *Running with the Hitman*), 2004, Marvista Entertainment, 2006.

Walter Pierce, *The River King,* Momentum Pictures, 2005.

Pete, *Flash of Genius,* Universal, 2008.

Mr. Jaffe, *The Cry of the Owl,* Myriad Pictures, 2009.

Zach Emmett, *Die,* Caramel Film, 2010.

Stage Appearances:

Appeared as commander, *Don Juan;* Nugget and horseman, *Equus;* Lucianus, *Hamlet;* constable of France, *Henry V;* Antony's servant, first citizen, and Claudius, *Julius Caesar;* Karl, *Just a Job;* guard, *Mary Steward,* Stratford Festival, Stratford, Ontario, Canada; soldier and peasant, *Mother Courage;* and Darcy, *Pride and Prejudice,* Royal Alexandra Theatre; and chief, *Savages.*

WRITINGS

Screenplays:

(Contributor of dialogue) *Expecting,* Corus, 2002.

OTHER SOURCES

Periodicals:

TV Zone, November, 1999, pp. 54–59.

R

RABEN, Alexis 1980–
(Alex Raben)

PERSONAL

Born August 25, 1980, in Moscow, U.S.S.R. (now Russia); married Miguel Sapochnik (a director and writer), 2006. *Education:* Wesleyan University, B.A. (with honors); trained with Bill Esper, Maggie Flanigan Studios, New York City.

Addresses: *Agent*—Innovative Artists Talent and Literary Agency, 1505 10th St., Santa Monica, CA 90401. *Manager*—Commonwealth Talent Group, 5225 Wilshire Blvd., Suite 509, Los Angeles, CA 90036. *Publicist*—Mona Loring, MLC Public Relations, 5030 Cheseboro Rd., Suite 202, Agoura Hills, CA 91301.

Career: Actress. Anouk (clothing label), former owner and designer.

CREDITS

Film Appearances:
June, *Up to the Roof* (short film), Backhouse Productions/Hook Line Sinker Films, 2002.
Woman, *The Therapy Session* (short film), Rusty Nail, 2003.
(As Alex Raben) Woman, *Mindcrime* (short film), Hypnotic, 2003.
Natasha, *Sweet Judy Blue Eyes* (short film), Blue Engine Pictures, 2004.
Belicec's aide, *The Invasion,* Warner Bros., 2007.
Anna, *Outlanders,* Jinga Films, 2007.
Marie, *Love from the Machine,* Gruve Digital Productions, 2008.
Katja, *Miss March,* Fox Searchlight, 2009.

Betsy, *D.A.I.Sy* (short film), 2009.
Amanda, *Jeffie Was Here,* Blue Yonder Films, 2010.

Also appeared in the short film *Absolute Pitch.*

Stage Appearances:
Appeared in multiple roles, *All in the Timing* and *Feiffer's People,* both Arthur Seleen Theatre New York City; as Theresa, *Dopes,* and as Catherine, *First Night,* both Provincetown Repertory Theatre, Provincetown, MA; Julia Howards and Susan, *Hello Herman,* Grove Street Playhouse; Nastassya, *The Idiot,* Theatre for the New City, New York City; and Nicole and Anna, *We Had a Very Good Time,* Arthur Seleen Theatre.

OTHER SOURCES

Periodicals:
Moviehole, March 15, 2009.

Electronic:
Alexis Raben Official Site, http://web.me.com/alexisraben, September 8, 2010.

RAFTER, Brogan
See LEET, Scott Anthony

REEDER, Ana

PERSONAL

Education: Middlebury College, B.A.; New York University, M.F.A.

Addresses: *Agent*—Cornerstone Talent Agency, 37 West 20th St., Suite 1108, New York, NY 10011; Mitchell K. Stubbs and Associates, 8675 West Washington Blvd., Suite 203, Culver City, CA 90232.

Career: Actress.

Member: Actors' Equity Association.

Awards, Honors: Jury Award, best actress, Santa Barbara International Film Festival, 2001, and Independent Spirit Award nomination, best debut performance, Independent Features Project/West, 2002, both for *Acts of Worship;* Obie Award (with others), outstanding ensemble, *Village Voice,* 2004, for *Small Tragedy.*

CREDITS

Stage Appearances:

Patience and queen's waiting woman, *Henry VIII,* New York Shakespeare Festival, Delacorte Theatre, Public Theatre, New York City, 1997.

Third witch, *Macbeth,* New York Shakespeare Festival, Martinson Hall, Public Theatre, New York City, 1998.

Laura, *Some Voices,* New Group, Theatre at St. Clement's, New York City, 1999.

Harriet Fenwick and Kate, *An Experiment with an Air Pump,* Manhattan Theatre Club Stage I, New York City, 1999.

Jane Yeager, *The Time of the Cuckoo,* Mitzi E. Newhouse Theatre, New York City, 2000.

Shari, *The Distance from Here,* Almeida Theatre, London, 2002.

Rosie Pye, *Humble Boy,* Manhattan Theatre Club Stage I, 2003.

Grete, *Sight Unseen,* Manhattan Theatre Club, Biltmore Theatre (now Samuel J. Friedman Theatre), New York City, 2004.

Jen, *Small Tragedy,* Playwrights Horizons Theatre, New York City, 2004.

Thea Elvsted, *Hedda Gabler,* New York Theatre Workshop, New York City, 2004.

Title role, *Carol Mulroney,* Huntington Theatre Company, Virginia Wimberly Theatre, Boston Center for the Arts, Boston, MA, 2005.

Hetty Grigs and Anna Livia Spoon, *The Wooden Breeks,* Manhattan Class Company, Lucille Lortel Theatre, New York City, 2006.

Dull Gret and Nell, *Top Girls,* Manhattan Theatre Club, Biltmore Theatre, 2008.

Thea Elvsted, *Hedda Gabler,* Roundabout Theatre Company, American Airlines Theatre, New York City, 2009.

Also appeared in New York City productions of *Fire Eater,* New York Stage and Film Theatre; *Killers and Other Family,* Rattlestick Theatre; *Living Room in Af-* *rica;* and *Maid,* Lincoln Center Theatre; appeared in regional productions, including *The Lady in Question; Night Season,* Bay Street Theatre; and *The Tempest,* Shakespeare Theatre, Washington, DC.

Film Appearances:

St. Therese, *Diary of a City Priest,* Heartland Film Festival, 2001.

Alix, *Acts of Worship,* 2001, Manifesto Films, 2003.

Michelle, *The Paper Boy* (short film), 2003.

Jess Walton, *The Return of the Muskrats* (short film), Cheshire Project, 2006.

Pool–side woman, *No Country for Old Men,* Miramax, 2007.

Lucy, *The Assastant* [sic] (short film), Small Motor Skills, 2008.

Gladys Riggs, *The Getaway* (short film), Marigold Films, 2010.

Margo, *The Locksmith* (also known as *Homewrecker*), First Look International, 2010.

Other films include *Marie and Bruce.*

Film Costume Designer:

The Return of the Muskrats (short film), Cheshire Project, 2006.

Television Appearances; Movies:

Lynn Mills, *You Don't Know Jack,* HBO, 2010.

Television Appearances; Series:

Liz Berlin, *Katie Joplin,* The WB, 1999.

Carol Tobin, a recurring role, *Damages,* FX Network, 2010.

Television Appearances; Episodic:

Annette Perry, "Hubris," *Law & Order,* NBC, 2001.

Mrs. McCorkle, "Raw," *Law & Order: Special Victims Unit* (also known as *Law & Order: SVU* and *Special Victims Unit*), NBC, 2005.

Kelly Devere, "Burn, Baby, Burn," *Kidnapped* (also known as *Kidnap*), NBC, 2006.

Television Appearances; Pilots:

Ellen Hinske, *The Jury,* Fox, 2004.

RICHARDS, Steve

PERSONAL

Born in PA. *Education:* Temple University, graduated (with honors); University of California, Los Angeles, M.B.A.

Addresses: *Office*—Dark Castle Entertainment/Silver Pictures, 4000 Warner Blvd., Building 90, Burbank, CA 91522.

Career: Producer and executive. International Movie Group, worked in film distribution; Scott Free, worked in film production; Silver Pictures, Burbank, CA, chief operation officer, 1996—; Dark Castle Entertainment, Burbank, CA, copresident and executive producer of all films, 1999—.

CREDITS

Film Executive Producer:
House on Haunted Hill, Warner Bros., 1999.
Thir13en Ghosts, Warner Bros., 2001.
Ghost Ship, Warner Bros., 2002.
Gothika, Warner Bros., 2003.
House of Wax, Warner Bros., 2005.
Kiss Kiss Bang Bang, Warner Bros., 2005.
The Reaping, Warner Bros., 2007.
The Invasion, Warner Bros., 2007.
RocknRolla, Warner Bros., 2008.
The Hills Run Red, Warner Bros., 2009.
Orphan (also known as *Esther*), Warner Bros., 2009.
Whiteout, Warner Bros., 2009.
Ninja Assassin, Warner Bros., 2009.
The Losers, Warner Bros., 2010.
The Book of Eli (also known as *The Walker*), Warner Bros., 2010.
Unknown White Male, Warner Bros., 2011.

Film Producer:
Coproducer, *Dungeons & Dragons,* New Line Cinema, 2000.
Coproducer, *The Animatrix* (animated), Warner Home Video, 2003.
Body Armour, Darclight Films International, 2007.
Botched, Optimum Releasing, 2007.
Return to House on Haunted Hill, Warner Bros., 2007.
Echelon Conspiracy (also known as *The Conspiracy* and *The Gift*), After Dark Films, 2009.

Film Associate Producer:
The Matrix Reloaded (also known as *The Matrix Reloaded: The IMAX Experience*), Warner Bros., 2003.
The Matrix Revolutions (also known as *The Matrix Revolutions: The IMAX Experience*), Warner Bros., 2003.

Television Executive Producer; Movies:
Made Men, HBO, 1999.
Proximity, Cinemax, 2001.

Dungeons & Dragons: Wrath of the Dragon God (also known as *Dungeons & Dragons 2: The Elemental Might*), Sci–Fi Channel, 2005.

Television Producer; Movies:
Jane Doe (also known as *Runaway Jane*), USA Network, 2001.
Bet Your Life (also known as *time Limit 24* and *24 Escape*), NBC, 2004.

Television Associate Producer; Movies:
Double Tap, HBO, 1997.

Television Work; Series:
Co–executive producer, *Next Action Star,* NBC, 2004.

RILEY, Tom 1981–

PERSONAL

Born April 5, 1981, in Maidstone, England. *Education:* Birmingham University, degree in English literature and drama (first class honors), 2002; studied acting at the London Academy of Music and Dramatic Arts, 2002–05.

Addresses: *Agent*—International Creative Management, 10250 Constellation Blvd., 9th Floor, Los Angeles, CA 90067; Conway van Gelder Grant, 18–21 Jermyn St., London SW1 6HP, England. *Manager*—The Collective, 9100 Wilshire Blvd., 700W Beverly Hills, Los Angeles, CA 90212.

Career: Actor.

CREDITS

Film Appearances:
David, *A Few Days in September* (also known as *Quelques jours en septembre*), Koch Lorber Films, 2006.
Joe Clarke, *I Want Candy,* Magnolia Home Entertainment, 2007.
Paul, *Return to the House on Haunted Hill,* Warner Premiere, 2007.
Rob, *Close* (short film), 2008.
Mike, *Curiosity* (short film), Shorts International, 2009.
Freddie, *Happy Ever After,* 2009.
Romeo, *St Trinian's II: The Legend of Fritton's Gold* (also known as *St Trinian's 2: The Legend of Fritton's Gold* and *St Trinian's II*), 2009.

Television Appearances; Miniseries:
Mr. Wickham, *Lost in Austen,* ITV, 2008.
Gavin Sorenson, *Bouquet of Barbed Wire,* 2010.

Television Appearances; Movies:
Dr. James Walton, *Casualty 1906,* 2006.
Bobby Argyle, *Marple: Ordeal by Innocence* (also known as *Miss Marple Series III*), ITV and PBS, 2007.

Television Appearances; Specials:
Himself, *Lost in Austen: Behind the Scenes* (documentary), ITV, 2008.

Television Appearances; Pilots:
Nigel and Brainstorm, *No Heroics,* ABC, 2009.

Television Appearances; Episodic:
Dave Beethoven, *Freezing,* BBC2, 2007, 2008.
Philip Horton, "And the Moonbeams Kiss the Sea," *Inspector Lewis* (also known as *Lewis*), ITV and PBS, 2008.
Dr. James Walton, *Casualty 1907,* BBC, 2008.
Raymond, "Appointment with Death," *Agatha Christie: Poirot,* ITV and Arts and Entertainment, 2008.
Xpose, TV3, 2009.

Stage Appearances:
Dahling You Were Marvellous, Edinburgh Fringe Festival, Edinburgh, Scotland, 2001.
Andi, *The Woman Before,* Royal Court Theatre, London, 2005.
Flight 5065, 2005.
Censorship, Royal Court Theatre, 2006.
Victory (a reading), Royal Court Theatre, 2006.
Posh (a reading), Royal Court Theatre, 2007.
Shuffle, Latitude Festival, Royal Court Theatre, 2007.
The Entertainer (a reading), Royal Court Theatre, 2007.
Philip, *The Vertical Hour,* Royal Court Theatre, 2008.
Light Shining in Buckinghamshire (a reading), Royal Court Theatre, 2008.
Tom, *Paradise Regained,* Royal Court Theatre, 2008.
Charlie McCorkle, *A House Not Meant to Stand,* 2009.
Bach, *Hurts Given and Received,* 2010.

Also appeared in *Clockwork Orange; North Greenwich,* London Academy of Music and Dramatic Arts, London; *The Peoples' Temple,* London Academy of Music and Dramatic Arts.

Radio Appearances:
Philip, *The Vertical Hour,* BBC Radio 3, 2008.
Adult Thomas, *Coram Boy,* BBC Radio 4, 2008.

OTHER SOURCES

Electronic:
Tom Riley Official Site, http://www.tom-riley.com, September 3, 2010.

RIMES, LeAnn 1982–

PERSONAL

Full name, Margaret LeAnn Rimes; born August 28, 1982, in Jackson, MS (some sources say Pearl, MS); daughter of Wilbur (a salesman, personal manager, and producer) and Belinda (maiden name, Butler) Rimes; married Dean Allen Sheremet (a dancer, songwriter, and actor), February 23, 2002 (divorced June 19, 2010); married Eddie Cibrian (an actor), April 22, 2011. *Avocational Interests:* Yoga, bicycling.

Addresses: *Agent*—Creative Artists Agency, 2000 Avenue of the Stars, Los Angeles, CA 90067; 3310 West End Ave., Nashville, TN 37203. *Manager*—Fitzgerald–Hartley, 34 N. Palms St., Suite 100, Ventura, CA 93001.

Career: Actress and singer. Won junior vocalist competition on *Star Search,* 1990; regularly appeared on Johnnie High Country Musical Revue, early to mid–1990s; signed with Curb Records, 1995; performed national anthem before numerous events as a child. Appeared in television commercials, including Tweety for Target, 1995, Samsung phones, 1997, and Dr. Pepper beverages, 2004; appeared in print ads for National Fluid Milk Processing Board, 1998; appeared in infomercials, including Leeza's Sheer Cover cosmetics, 2008.

Awards, Honors: Grammy Award, best new artist, 1996; Academy of Country Music Award, song of the year, 1996; Academy of Country Music Award, top new female vocalist, 1996; Academy of Country Music Award, single of the year, Grammy Award, best female country vocal performance, 1996, both for "Blue"; American Music Award, favorite new artist, 1997; Horizon Award, Country Music Association, 1997; Female Star of Tomorrow, The Nashville Network/Music City News, 1997; Female Rising Star of the Years, Country Music Television, 1997; Country Single Sale Artist of the Year, *Billboard,* 1998; Female Country Artist of the Year, *Billboard,* 1998; Contemporary Christian Artist of the Year, *Billboard,* 1998; Lone Star Film and Television Special Award, rising star actress, 1998; Blockbuster Entertainment Award, favorite song from a movie—internet only, 2001, for *Coyote Ugly;* BPI Award, best album, 2004, for *The Best of LeAnn Rimes;*

Country Music Television Award (with Bon Jovi), collaborative video of the year, 2008, for "Till We Ain't Strangers Anymore"; Home Depot Humanitarian Award, Academy of Country Music, 2009; American Music Award; New Country Act of the Years, International Touring Talent Publication; International Rising Star of the Year, British Country Music Awards; Artist of the Year, North Texas Music Festival; other awards include Academy of Country Music Awards.

CREDITS

Film Appearances:
Herself, *Christmas Time with Eddy Arnold,* Spring House, Inc., 1997.
Herself, *Dill Scallion,* The Asylum, 1999.
Singing voice of herself and singing voice of Piper Perabo, *Coyote Ugly,* Buena Vista, 2000.
Herself, *Thank You Billy Graham* (short film), Pat's Gold, 2006.
Voice of Kelly Deegan, *Holly Hobbie and Friends: Christmas Wishes* (short animated film), Paramount, 2006.
Pam, *Good Intentions,* 2010.

Television Appearances; Series:
Host, *Nashville Star,* USA Network, 2003.

Television Appearances; Movies:
LeAnn, *Holiday in Your Heart,* ABC, 1997.
Meg Galligan, *Northern Lights* (also known as *Nora Roberts' "Northern Lights"*), Lifetime, 2009.

Television Appearances; Awards Presentations:
Performer, *The 30th Annual Country Music Association Awards,* CBS, 1996.
The ... Annual Grammy Awards, CBS, 1997, 1998.
The ... Annual Academy of Country Music Awards, NBC, 1997, CBS, 1998, 1999.
The 24th Annual Daytime Emmy Awards, ABC, 1997.
The ... Annual American Music Awards, ABC, 1997, 1998.
Host, *TNN Music City News Country Awards,* The Nashville Network, 1997.
The ... Annual Country Music Association Awards, CBS, 1997, 1998, 2000, ABC, 2006, 2007, Country Music Television, 2009.
The ... Billboard Music Awards, Fox, 1997, 1998, 1999.
Presenter, *The ... Annual American Music Awards,* ABC, 1998, 1999, 2001, 2002, 2005.
The 1998 World Music Awards, ABC, 1998.
Presenter, *The 14th Annual Soap Opera Awards,* NBC, 1998.
TNN Music City News Country Awards, The Nashville Network, 1998.
The 25th Annual People's Choice Awards, CBS, 1999.

Presenter, *The WB Radio Music Awards,* The WB, 1999.
The ... Blockbuster Entertainment Awards, Fox, 2000, 2001.
Host, *The 36th Annual Academy of Country Music Awards,* CBS, 2001.
Presenter, *The ... Annual CMA Awards,* CBS, 2003, ABC, 2010.
Host, *The BRICK Awards,* The CW, 2007.
The ... CMT Music Awards, Country Music Television, 2007, 2010.
Performer, *The ... Annual Academy of Country Music Awards,* CBS, 2008, 2010.
Presenter, *The 51st Annual Grammy Awards,* CBS, 2009.
The 2009 MTV Movie Awards, MTV, 2009.

Television Appearances; Specials:
Opryland's Country Christmas, CBS, 1996.
LeAnn Rimes in Concert, The Disney Channel, 1997.
Intimate Portrait: Wynonna, Lifetime, 1997.
Host, *Fan Fair Phenomenon,* The Nashville Network, 1997.
Host, *Countryfest '97,* CBS, 1997.
CMT Labor Day Top 100, Country Music Television, 1997.
Barbara Walters Presents: 6 to Watch, ABC, 1997.
Host (Nashville), *The All–American Thanksgiving Parade,* CBS, 1997.
Christmas Time with Eddy Arnold, The Nashville Network, 1997.
Cohost, *The Sound of the Grammys '98,* E! Entertainment Television, 1998.
CMA 40th: A Celebration, CBS, 1998.
The 21 Hottest Stars Under 21, ABC, 1999.
Performer, *VH1 Divas Live 2,* VH1, 1999.
Elton John: With a Little Help from My Friends, 1999.
Performer, *A Home for the Holidays,* CBS, 1999.
Teen People's 21 Hottest Stars Under 21, ABC, 1999.
Intimate Portrait: Barbara Mandrell, Lifetime, 1999.
Pixelon's I–Bash!, PAX, 1999.
All Access: LeAnn Rimes, Country Music Television, 1999.
A Home for the Holidays, CBS, 1999.
Host, *Class of 2000,* 2000.
Diane Warren: How Do I Live?, 2000.
Elvis Lives, NBC, 2002.
Performer, *XIX Winter Olympics Opening Ceremony,* NBC, 2002.
I Love the '80s, VH1, 2002.
Maxim Hot 100, NBC, 2003.
Song performer, *Boston Pop Fireworks Spectacular,* CBS, 2003.
Host, *Daytona 500: The Great American Race Pre–Race Show,* 2003.
100 Years of Hope and Humor, NBC, 2003.
Host, *CMT 100 Greatest Songs of Country Music Concert,* Country Music Television, 2003.
CMA Awards Red Carpet Preview, 2003.

Intimate Portrait: LeAnn Rimes, Lifetime, 2003.

LeAnn Rimes Live, Country Music Television, 2003.

A Kid Rock Christmas, VH1, 2003.

Performer, *LeAnn Rimes: Custom Concert,* 2004.

Christmas in Washington, TNT, 2004.

Performer, *CMA Music Festival,* CBS, 2004.

CMA Red Carpet Live from NYC, Country Music Television, 2005.

CMT: The Greatest—20 Sexiest Women, Country Music Television, 2006.

Trail Mix, Animal Planet, 2006.

CMT: The Greatest—Sexiest Southern Women, Country Music Television, 2006.

CMT: The Greatest—40 Days That Shaped Country Music, Country Music Television, 2006.

CMA Red Carpet 2006, Country Music Television, 2006.

InStyle Celebrity Weddings, ABC, 2006.

CMA Music Festival: Country Music's Biggest Party, ABC, 2006.

MTV Unplugged: Bon Jovi, MTV, VH1, and Country Music Television, 2007.

An Evening with Amy Grant, Featuring the Nashville Symphony, 2007.

Presenter, *Fashion Rocks,* CBS, 2007.

CMT 100 Greatest Videos, Country Music Television, 2008.

Stand Up to Cancer, CBS, ABC, and NBC, 2008.

George Strait: ACM Artist of the Decade All Star Concert, 2009.

I Get That a Lot, CBS, 2009.

CMT Star: Nashville Mansions, Country Music Television, 2009.

George Strait: ACM Artist of the Decade All Star Concert, CBS, 2009.

Gordon Ramsay: Cookalong Live, Fox, 2009.

Performer, *Macy's 4th of July Fireworks Spectacular 2010,* NBC, 2010.

Television Appearances; Episodic:

Star Search, syndicated, 1990.

The Rosie O'Donnell Show, syndicated, 1996, 1997, 1999.

Late Show with David Letterman (also known as *Letterman* and *The Late Show*), CBS, 1996, 2007.

Madison, *Days of Our Lives* (also known as *DOOL* and *Days*), NBC, 1998.

Herself, "Ohmigod, Fanatic," *Moesha,* UPN, 1999.

MADtv, Fox, 2000.

Connie Francis, "Where the Boys Are," *American Dreams* (also known as *Our Generation*), NBC, 2003.

Star Search, CBS, 2003.

"Sara Evans," *Inside Fame,* 2003.

Tinseltown TV, International Channel, 2003.

Today, Nine Network, 2003.

Good Morning Australia, Ten Network, 2003.

Rove Live, Ten Network, 2003.

The Late Late Show with Craig Kilborn (also known as *The Late Late Show*), CBS, 2003.

The Sharon Osbourne Show (also known as *Sharon*), syndicated, 2003.

Jimmy Kimmel Live!, ABC, 2003, 2005, 2007, 2009.

The Tonight Show with Jay Leno, NBC, 2003, 2004, 2005, 2006, 2007.

Today with Des and Mel, ITV, 2004.

The Terry and Gaby Show, 2004.

Breakfast, BBC, 2004.

Kelly, UTV, 2004.

Musical guest, "Lippe blofft," *Lippe blofft,* 2004.

"The Cox Family," *Extreme Makeover: Home Edition,* ABC, 2004.

Performer, *The Late Late Show,* CBS, 2004.

Parkinson, BBC, 2004.

GMTV, ITV, 2004.

CD:UK, ITV, 2004.

This Morning, ITV, 2004.

"It's a Big Country," *48 Hours* (also known as *48 Hours Investigates* and *48 Hours Mystery*), CBS, 2004.

The View, ABC, 2004.

"Human Body," *Blue Collar TV,* Comedy Central, 2004.

The Tony Danza Show, syndicated, 2004, 2005.

Today (also known as *NBC News Today* and *The Today Show*), NBC, 2005, 2007, 2008, 2009.

Hannity & Colmes, Fox News, 2005.

Tavis Smiley, PBS, 2005.

The Late Late Show with Craig Ferguson, CBS, 2005.

20/20 (also known as *ABC News 20/20*), ABC, 2005.

Cribs (also known as *MTV Cribs*), MTV, 2005.

Herself, "Christmas Wish," *Three Wishes,* NBC, 2005.

Herself, "Nice Package," *Love Monkey,* CBS, 2006.

"Hairdos and Heartache: The Women of Country Music," *Biography,* Arts and Entertainment, 2006.

Loose @ 5.30, 2006.

Top of the Pops, BBC, 2006.

"Annette Benning & Warren Beatty Get Honored by St. Johns, Chris Brown & Neo on a Soundcheck & CMT Honors Reba," *In the Cutz* (also known as *In the Mix*), Urban America, 2006.

Performer, "Reba," *CMT Giants,* Country Music Television, 2006.

Entertainment Tonight (also known as *E.T.*), syndicated, 2006, 2009, 2010.

Performer, *Live from Abbey Road,* Sundance Channel, 2007.

Musical guest, "Round 7 Results," *Dancing with the Stars* (also known as *D.W.T.S.*), ABC, 2007.

"LeAnn Rimes," *Sidewalks Entertainment,* 2007.

Headline Country (also known as *Country Music Across America*), 2007, 2008.

"Joss Stone & LeAnn Rimes," *CMT Crossroads,* Country Music Television, 2008.

CMT Insider, Country Music Television, 2008, 2009, 2010.

Also appeared in *Austin City Limits,* PBS.

Stage Appearances:
Made stage debut in *A Christmas Carol,* Dallas, TX.

RECORDINGS

Albums:
Everybody's Sweetheart, 1991.
From My Hear to Yours, 1992.
All That, 1994.
After All, Nor Va Jak, 1994.
Blue, Curb, 1996.
You Light Up My Life: Inspirational Songs, Curb Records, 1997.
Unchained Melody: The Early Years, Curb, 1997.
Sittin' on Top of the World, Curb, 1998.
LeAnn Rimes, Curb, 1999.
I Need You, Curb, 2001.
Twisted Angel, Curb, 2002.
Greatest Hits, Curb, 2003.
What a Wonderful World, Curb, 2004.
This Woman, Curb, 2005.
Family, 2007.
Lady and Gentlemen, 2010.

WRITINGS

Novels:
(With Tom Carter) *Holiday in Your Heart: A Novel,* Doubleday, 1997.

Children's Books:
Jag, Dutton Children's Books, 2003.
Jag's New Friend, Dutton Children's Books, 2004.

Nonfiction:
(With Darrel Brown) *What I Cannot Change,* 2009.

OTHER SOURCES

Books:
Alter Zymet, Cathy, *LeAnn Rimes,* 1999.
Contemporary Authors Online, Thomson Gale, 2005.
Contemporary Musicians, Vol. 46, Gale Group, 2004.
Newsmakers, Issue 4, Gale Research, 1997.

Periodicals:
Billboard, December 6, 1997, p. 43; September 19, 1998, p. 6; May 20, 2000, p. 110.
Good Housekeeping, November, 1997, p. 210.
People Weekly, June 14, 2010, p. 142.
Redbook, October, 2007, p. 142.
Teen People, September 1, 2002, p. 112.

RIVERA, Chita 1933–
   (Conchita del Rivero, Conchita O'Hara)

PERSONAL

Full name, Dolores Conchita Figueroa del Rivero; born January 23, 1933, in Washington, DC; daughter of Pedro Julio Figueroa (a musician) and Katherine (a government clerk; maiden name, Anderson) del Rivero; married Anthony Mordente (a dancer and director), December 1, 1957 (divorced, 1966); children: Lisa (a director and choreographer). *Education:* Trained at American School of Ballet, 1950–51. *Avocational Interests:* Cooking, bowling, horseback riding, tennis, swimming.

Addresses: *Agent*—Tim Curtis, WME Entertainment, 9601 Wilshire Blvd., 3rd Floor, Beverly Hills, CA 90210.

Career: Actress, singer, and dancer. Performer in nightclubs and cabarets throughout the world, including the Grand Finale, New York City, and Studio One, Los Angeles, both 1975, and Feinstein's at the Regency Hotel, New York City, 2005; performer on tours for the Oldsmobile Industrial Show.

Member: American Federation of Television and Radio Artists, Actors' Equity Association, Screen Actors Guild.

Awards, Honors: Antoinette Perry Award nomination, best supporting or featured actress in a musical, 1961, for *Bye Bye Birdie;* Antoinette Perry Award nomination, best actress in a musical, 1976, for *Chicago;* National Academy of Concert and Cabaret Arts Award, best variety performance, 1980; Antoinette Perry Award nomination, best actress in a musical, 1981, for *Bring Back Birdie;* Antoinette Perry Award nomination, best actress in a musical, 1983, for *Merlin;* Antoinette Perry Award and Drama Desk Award, both best actress in a musical, 1984, for *The Rink;* inducted into Television Academy Hall of Fame, 1985; Antoinette Perry Award nomination, best actress in a musical, 1986, for *Jerry's Girls;* Antoinette Perry Award and Drama Desk Award, both outstanding actress in a musical, and Drama League Award, distinguished achievement in musical theater, all 1993, and Outer Critics Circle Award, best actress in a musical, 1994, all for *Kiss of the Spider Woman;* ALMA Award nomination, outstanding performance by an individual or act in a variety or comedy special, American Latin Media Arts Awards, National Council of La Raza, 1999, for *Great Performances;* Ellis Island Medal of Honor, 2000; Sarah Siddons Award, outstanding performance in a Chicago theatrical production, Sarah Siddons Society, c. 2001, for *The*

Visit; Kennedy Center Honors, John F. Kennedy Center for the Performing Arts, Washington, DC, 2002; Antoinette Perry Award nomination, best featured actress in a musical, and Outer Critics Circle Award nomination, outstanding actress in a musical, both 2003, for *Nine;* Lifetime Achievement Award, Astaire Awards, Theatre Development Fund, 2003; Career Award, New Dramatists, 2006; Rolex Dance Award, Career Transition for Dancers, 2006; Presidential Medal of Freedom, 2009.

CREDITS

Stage Appearances; Musicals:

(Broadway debut) Dancer, *Guys and Dolls,* Forty–Sixth Street Theatre, New York City, 1950.

(As Conchita del Rivero) Dancer, *Call Me Madam,* Imperial Theatre, New York City, 1952.

Dancer, *Can–Can,* Shubert Theatre, New York City, 1953.

(Originally cast as Chita O'Hara, then as Rivera) Member of ensemble, *Shoestring Revue,* President Theatre, New York City, 1955.

Fifi, *Seventh Heaven,* American National Theatre and Academy Theatre, New York City, 1955.

Rita Romano, *Mr. Wonderful,* Broadway Theatre, New York City, 1956–57.

Anita, *West Side Story,* Winter Garden Theatre, New York City, 1957, then (London debut) Her Majesty's Theatre, 1958.

Standby for Mehitabel, *Shinbone Alley,* Broadway Theatre, 1957.

Rosie Grant, *Bye Bye Birdie,* Martin Beck Theatre, New York City, 1960, then Her Majesty's Theatre, 1961.

Athena Constantine, *Zenda,* Curran Theatre, San Francisco, CA, then Pasadena Civic Auditorium, Pasadena, CA, both 1963.

Anyanka, *Bajour,* Shubert Theatre, 1964, then Lunt–Fontanne Theatre, New York City, 1965.

Jenny, *The Threepenny Opera,* Mineola Theatre, Mineola, NY, 1966.

Flower Drum Song, Melody Top Theatre, Milwaukee, WI, 1966.

Beatriz, *1491,* Dorothy Chandler Pavilion, Los Angeles, 1969.

Zorba, Westbury Music Fair, Westbury NY, 1970.

Milliken Breakfast Show, Waldorf–Astoria Hotel, New York City, 1972.

Sondheim: A Musical Tribute (revue; benefit performance), Shubert Theatre, 1973.

Velma Kelly, *Chicago,* Forty–Sixth Street Theatre, 1975.

Sing Happy! (revue), Avery Fisher Hall, Lincoln Center, New York City, 1978.

V.I.P. Night on Broadway (revue; benefit performance), Shubert Theatre, 1979.

Rose, *Bring Back Birdie,* Martin Beck Theatre, 1981.

Hey Look Me Over, Avery Fisher Hall, Lincoln Center, 1981.

The queen, *Merlin,* Mark Hellinger Theatre, New York City, 1983.

Anna, *The Rink,* Martin Beck Theatre, 1984.

Member of ensemble, *Jerry's Girls* (revue), St. James Theatre, New York City, 1985–86.

Happy Birthday, Mr. Abbott! Or Night of 100 Years, Palace Theatre, New York City, 1987.

La Mome Pistache, *Can–Can,* Chicago Theatre, Chicago, IL, 1988.

Aurora (title role), *Kiss of the Spider Woman,* London performance, then St. Lawrence Centre, Toronto, Canada, then Broadhurst Theatre, New York City, 1993–95.

Angela Lansbury—A Celebration (benefit performance), Majestic Theatre, New York City, 1996.

Two Broadway Legends, Together at Last!, North Shore Music Theatre, Beverly, MA, 1997.

Roxie Hart, *Chicago,* Las Vegas, NV, 2000.

Reno Sweeney, *Anything Goes,* Paper Mill Playhouse, Millburn, NJ, 2000.

Magdalena Monteverde, *Casper: The Musical,* Bendem Center, Pittsburgh, PA, 2001.

Liliane La Fleur, *Nine,* Roundabout Theatre Company, Eugene O'Neill Theatre, New York City, 2003.

Chita Rivera: The Dancer's Life, Old Globe Theatre, San Diego, CA, 2005, then Gerald Schoenfeld Theatre, New York City, 2005–2006.

Chance & Chemistry: A Centennial Celebration of Frank Loesser (benefit), Minskoff Theatre, New York City, 2009.

Stage Appearances; Other:

Billie Dawn, *Born Yesterday,* Walnut Street Theatre, Philadelphia, PA, 1972.

Father's Day, Ivanhoe Theatre, Chicago, IL, 1974.

La vieja, *Venecia,* George Street Playhouse, New Brunswick, NJ, 2001.

The Visit, Goodman Theatre, Chicago, 2001.

Title role, *The House of Bernarda Alba,* Mark Taper Forum, Los Angeles, 2002.

Major Tours:

(As Conchita del Rivero) Principal dancer, *Call Me Madam,* U.S. cities, 1952.

Rosie Grant, *Bye Bye Birdie,* U.S. cities, 1962.

Title role, *Sweet Charity,* U.S. and Canadian cities, 1967–68.

Leader, *Zorba,* U.S. cities, 1969.

Jacques Brel Is Alive and Well and Living in Paris, U.S. cities, 1972.

Lilli Vanessi/Katherine, *Kiss Me Kate,* U.S. cities, 1974.

Velma Kelly, *Chicago,* U.S. cities, 1977–78.

Chita and All That Jazz (nightclub act), U.S. cities, beginning 1997.

Chita Rivera: The Dancer's Life, U.S. cities, beginning 2007.

Film Appearances:

Nickie, *Sweet Charity* (also known as *Sweet Charity: The Adventures of a Girl Who Wanted to Be Loved*), Universal, 1969.

Guest at Heartland, *Sgt, Pepper's Lonely Hearts Club Band* (also known as *Banda de los corazones*), Universal, 1978.

(Uncredited) Herself, *He Makes Me Feel Like Dancin'*, 1983.

(In archive footage) *That's Dancing!*, 1985.

Nickie, *Chicago*, Miramax, 2002.

Giannina, *Kalamazoo?*, Reel Source, 2006.

Move (documentary), Soderling Productions, 2010.

Broadway: Beyond the Golden Age (documentary), Second Act Productions, 2010.

Other films include *Stonewall 25: Voices of Pride and Protest* and *That's Singing: The Best of Broadway*.

Television Appearances; Specials:

"Maurice Chevalier: The Show," *Max Liebman Presents*, NBC, 1956.

The General Motors 50th Anniversary Show, NBC, 1957.

Arthur Godfrey and the Sounds of New York, CBS, 1963.

The George Burns Special, CBS, 1976.

The Stars and Stripes Show, NBC, 1976.

Gingerbread lady, "Hansel and Gretel," *Once Upon a Brothers Grimm*, CBS, 1977.

The Kennedy Center Honors: A Celebration of the Performing Arts, CBS, 1979, 1994, 1998, 2002, 2003.

Macy's Thanksgiving Day Parade, 1980, NBC, 1985.

Fastrada, *Pippin: His Life and Times*, 1981.

Broadway Plays Washington: Kennedy Center Tonight (also known as *Broadway Plays Washington*), PBS, 1982.

Gala of Stars, 1984.

The Night of 100 Stars II, ABC, 1985.

"The Best of Broadway," *Great Performances*, PBS, 1985.

"Broadway Sings: The Music of Jule Styne," *Great Performances*, PBS, 1987.

"Celebrating Gershwin: 'S Wonderful," *Great Performances*, PBS, 1987.

This Is Your Life, 1987.

Sammy Davis, Jr.'s 60th Anniversary Celebration, ABC, 1990.

Night of 100 Stars III, NBC, 1990.

(In archive footage) "The Music of Kander and Ebb: Razzle Dazzle," *Great Performances*, PBS, 1997.

Broadway '97: Launching the Tonys, PBS, 1997.

A Walk Down 42nd Street with David Hartman, PBS, 1998.

"The New Jersey Performing Arts Center Opening," *Great Performances*, PBS, 1998.

"Sammy Davis, Jr.: Mr. Entertainment," *Biography*, Arts and Entertainment, 1999.

Bob Fosse: The E! True Hollywood Story, E! Entertainment Television, 1999.

"Shirley Maclaine: This Time Around," *Biography*, Arts and Entertainment, 2000.

"Dick Van Dyke: Put On a Happy Face," *Biography*, Arts and Entertainment, 2000.

"My Favorite Broadway: The Love Songs," *Great Performances*, PBS, 2001.

Liza Minelli: The E! True Hollywood Story, E! Entertainment Television, 2002.

The 100 Greatest Musicals, Channel 4, 2003.

Broadway: The Golden Age, by the Legends Who Were There (also known as *Broadway, Broadway: The Golden Age*, and *Broadway: The Movie*), PBS, 2003.

"Broadway's Lost Treasures," *Great Performances*, PBS, 2003.

"Broadway's Lost Treasures II," *Great Performances*, PBS, 2004.

(In archive footage) "Judy Garland: By Myself," *American Masters*, PBS, 2004.

(In archive footage) "Broadway's Lost Treasures III: The Best of the Tony Awards," *Great Performances*, PBS, 2005.

(In archive footage) *El camino de Antonio Banderas*, 2006.

(In archive footage) *Vanessa Williams: The E! True Hollywood Story*, E! Entertainment Television, 2007.

Mr. Prince, Ovation, 2009.

"Jerome Robbins: Something to Dance About," *American Masters*, PBS, 2009.

Television Appearances; Series:

Connie Richardson, a recurring role, *The New Dick Van Dyke Show*, CBS, 1973–74.

Melody Rambo, *One Life to Live*, 1982.

Television Appearances; Episodic:

The Imogene Coca Show, NBC, 1954.

Frankie Laine Time, 1955.

Caesar's Hour, NBC, 1956.

Tonight! (also known as *The Knickerbocker Beer Presents the Steve Allen Show*, *Knickerbocker Beer Show*, *The Steve Allen Show*, and *Tonight Starring Steve Allen*), 1956.

The Dinah Shore Chevy Show (also known as *The Dinah Shore Show*), NBC, 1958.

The Voice of Firestone, 1958.

"Tiptoe through TV," *The Revlon Revue*, CBS, 1960.

"Variety: The World of Show Biz," *The Revlon Revue*, CBS, 1960.

The Ed Sullivan Show (also known as *Toast of the Town*), CBS, 1960, 1962.
The Garry Moore Show, CBS, 1960, 1963, 1964.
Mrs. Dame, "The Bellero Shield," *The Outer Limits,* ABC, 1964.
The Judy Garland Show, 1964.
Big Night Out, 1964.
The Entertainers, 1965.
ABC's Nightlife (also known as *The Les Crane Show*), ABC, 1965.
The Hollywood Palace, 1965, 1966, 1968.
The Dean Martin Comedy Hour (also known as *The Dean Martin Show*), 1966.
The Jonathan Winters Show, 1968.
The Woody Woodbury Show, 1968.
The Mike Douglas Show, 1968, 1972, 1976.
The Carol Burnett Show (also known as *Carol Burnett and Friends*), 1969, 1971.
Herself, "Gloria Does Her Thing," *That's Life,* 1969.
Playboy after Dark, 1970.
Saturday Night Live with Howard Cosell, 1975.
Sammy and Company, 1975.
Dinah!, 1975.
Captain Kangaroo, 1976.
The Chuck Barris Rah–Rah Show, 1978.
The Merv Griffin Show, 1978.
The Bobby Vinton Show, 1978.
Good Morning America (also known as *G.M.A.*), 1978, 1984.
De Mike Burstyn Show, 1979.
Horas doradas, 1980.
Barrymore, 1997.
The Rosie O'Donnell Show, syndicated, 1997, 2000, 2002.
America (also known as *Paul O'Grady's America*), 2001.
Lenore, "Dance Cards & Greeting Cards," *Will & Grace,* NBC, 2005.
Character Studies, PBS, 2005.
"Broadway Legends Soiree," *Party Planner with David Tutera,* The Discovery Channel, 2005.
Today (also known as *NBC News Today* and *The Today Show*), NBC, 2005.
(In archive footage) *De par en par,* 2007.
The Alan Titchmarsh Show, ITV, 2008.

Also appeared in episodes of *The Arthur Godfrey Show,* CBS; *The Electric Company;* as voice of insect, *Happily Ever After: Fairy Tales for Every Child,* HBO.

Television Appearances; Awards Presentations:

Presenter, *The ... Annual Tony Awards,* CBS, annually, 1984–88, 1997, 1999, then 2004–06.
The Golden Eagle Awards, syndicated, 1987.
America's Dance Honors, ABC, 1990.
The ... Annual Tony Awards, CBS, 1993, 2003.

Television Appearances; Other:

Josie Hopper, *The Marcus–Nelson Murders* (pilot; also known as *Kojak and the Marcus–Nelson Murders* and *Kojak: The Marcus–Nelson Murders*), CBS, 1973.
Risa Dickstein, *The Mayflower Madam* (movie), CBS, 1987.
Broadway: The American Musical (miniseries), PBS, 2004.

RECORDINGS

Albums; Original Cast Recordings:

Seventh Heaven, 1955.
Mr. Wonderful, 1956.
West Side Story, 1957.
Bye Bye Birdie, 1960.
(London cast recording) *Bye Bye Birdie,* 1961.
Zenda, 1963.
Bajour, 1964.
Sweet Charity, 1969.
Sondheim: A Musical Tribute, 1973.
Chicago, 1975.
Bring Back Birdie, 1981.
The Rink, 1984.
(London cast recording) *Kiss of the Spider Woman,* 1992.
Nine, 2003.

Videos:

Kiss of the Spider Woman—Making the Musical, 2008.

OTHER SOURCES

Books:

Dictionary of Hispanic Biography, Gale, 1996.

Periodicals:

Advocate, February 14, 2006, p. 29.
American Theatre, November, 2003, p. 3.
Dance, February, 2004, p. 38; December, 2005, p. 108; April, 2007, p. 16.
New York Observer, January 10, 2005, p. 3.
Playbill, July 31, 2003, p. 8.
Washington Post, December 8, 2002, pp. G1–G10.

Electronic:

Chita Rivera Official Site, http://www.chitarivera.com, August 24, 2010.

ROSE, Earl 1946–

PERSONAL

Full name, Earl Alexander Rose; born September 5, 1946, in New York, NY; son of Irving and Irene Rose; married; wife's name, Pamela. *Education:* Attended Vienna Academy of Music, 1967–68; Mannes College of Music, B.S., 1970. *Avocational Interests:* Swimming, movies.

Addresses: *Agent*—International Creative Management, 10250 Constellation Way, 9th Floor, Los Angeles, CA 90067.

Career: Composer, conductor, musician, and recording artist. Concert pianist with symphony orchestras; musician appearing on television, radio, and stage throughout North America; assistant music coordinator for television talk shows hosted by Dick Cavett, 1968, and Johnny Carson, 1973–88.

Member: National Academy of Recording Arts and Sciences, American Society of Authors, Composers, and Publishers, American Guild of Authors and Composers, Songwriters Guild of America, Friars Club.

Awards, Honors: Daytime Emmy Award nominations (with Sybil Weinberger), outstanding music direction and composition for a drama series, 1986, 1988, 1989, all for *Ryan's Hope;* Daytime Emmy Award nomination, outstanding music direction and composition, 1990, for "My Dad Can't Be Crazy ... Can He?," *ABC Afterschool Specials;* ASCAP Film and Television Music Awards, most performed underscore, American Society of Composers, Authors, and Publishers, 1992, 1993, 1994; Daytime Emmy Award nomination (with Victoria Shaw0, outstanding original song, 1997, for *As the World Turns;* Daytime Emmy Award nominations, outstanding musical direction and composition for a drama series (with others), 1998, 1999, and 2000, all for *As the World Turns;* Daytime Emmy Award (with others), outstanding original song, 1999, for "This Is our Moment," *As the World Turns;* Daytime Emmy Award nomination (with others), outstanding original song, 1999, for "You Are (Where I Belong)," *As the World Turns;* News and Documentary Emmy Award nomination (with Mike Fennell), outstanding music and sound, 2004, for *Wake Island: Alamo of the Pacific.*

CREDITS

Television Appearances; Specials:
Pianist, *A Colbert Christmas: The Greatest Gift of All!,* Comedy Central, 2008.

Television Appearances; Episodic:
Pianist, "Not Just a River in Egypt," *Jack & Jill,* 1999.

Television Work; Specials:
Music arranger, *Ballyhoo: The Hollywood Sideshow!,* AMC, 1996.
Pianist and score producer, *Stardust: The Bette Davis Story,* TCM, 2006.

Film Work:
Music orchestrator, *Mad Dog Time* (also known as *Trigger Happy*), United Artists, 1996.
(Uncredited) Song arranger, *The Object of My Affection,* Twentieth Century–Fox, 1998.
Song performer, "Melissa's Dream," *White Oleander,* Warner Bros., 2002.

WRITINGS

Television Music; Series:
Ryan's Hope, ABC, 1985–89.
Dick Cavett Show, ABC, 1986–87.
(With others) *Another World,* NBC, 1990.
All My Children, ABC, 1990–94.
Sesame Street (also known as *The New Sesame Street, Open Sesame,* and *Sesame Street Unpaved*), PBS, several episodes, 2007.

Television Music; Specials:
Underscore and title song, "My Dad Can't Be Crazy, Can He?," *ABC Afterschool Specials,* ABC, 1989.
Ballyhoo: The Hollywood Sideshow!, AMC, 1996.
Masada, History Channel, 2002.
Wake Island: Alamo of the Pacific, History Channel, 2003.
"Convertibles," *Modern Marvels,* History Channel, 2003.
Nostradamus: 500 Years Later, 2003.
Remember the Alamo, History Channel, 2003.
In the Shadow of "Cold Mountain," 2003.
Nazi Spies in America, 2004.
Rescue at Dawn: The Los Banos Raid, History Channel, 2004.
Countdown to Armageddon, History Channel, 2004.
The Presidents, History Channel, 2005.
Secret Missions of the Civil War, History Channel, 2005.
Stardust: The Bette Davis Story, TCM, 2006.
"James Woods," *Biography,* Arts and Entertainment, 2007.
70's Fever, History Channel, 2008.
Inventing L.A.: The Chandlers and Their Times, PBS, 2009.

Hard Times for an American Girl: The Great Depression, HBO, 2009.

Television Music; Movies:
Underscore and song "I Want to Share Today with You," *Thin Ice,* CBS, 1981.
Additional music, *Gunshy,* Cinemax, 1998.

Television Music; Miniseries:
Sex in World War II, 2002.

Film Scores:
How to Score with Girls, 1980.
Mad Dog Time (also known as *Trigger Happy*), United Artists, 1996.

Songs Featured in Films:
"I'm a Zoo," *Breakfast of Aliens,* Hemdale Releasing, 1993.
"Melissa's Dream," *White Oleander,* Warner Bros., 2002.

Songwriter; Other:
Captain Kangaroo (television series), CBS, between 1977 and 1980.
"Tuesday at Nola," *Joe and Max* (television movie), Starz!, 2002.

Songwriter, "This Is Our Moment" and "You Are (Where I Belong)," *As the World Turns* (television series), CBS; other songs include "Linnea, My Love," 1975; "Overnight Success," 1978; "Someone, Somewhere," 1978; "I Want to Share Today with You," 1981; "Right from the Heart," 1985; (with Peabo Bryson) "I Found Love;" and "Yes, I Know."

Other:
Composer of orchestral works, including "Contrast for Piano and Orchestra," 1982.

ROSSIO, Terry 1960–

PERSONAL

Born July 2, 1960, in Kalamazoo, MI. *Education:* California State University, Fullerton, B.A., communications.

Addresses: *Office*—Scheherazade Films, 500 South Buena Vista St. Animation Bldg., Suite 1D–2, Burbank, CA 91521. *Agent*—Creative Artists Agency, 2000 Avenue of the Stars, Los Angeles, CA 90067. *Manager*—Dodie Gold Management, 9165 Alcott St., Suite 202, Los Angeles, CA 90035.

Career: Writer, producer, and creative consultant. Ted Elliott/Terry Rossio Productions, partner; Scheherazade Productions, Los Angeles, partner with Ted Elliott. Previously worked as a machine parts inspector.

Member: Writers Guild of America West.

Awards, Honors: Apex Award, best original fantasy, science fiction, or horror screenplay, and Fennecus Award nomination, best screenplay, both (with Ted Elliott, John Musker, and Ron Clements) 1992, for *Aladdin;* Annie Award, outstanding individual achievement for writing in an animated feature production, International Animated Film Society, Fennecus Award nomination, best adapted screenplay, Apex Award nomination, best fantasy, science fiction, or horror screenplay, Academy Award nomination, best screenplay adaptation, Film Award, best adapted screenplay, British Academy of Film and Television Arts, Saturn Award nomination, best writing, Academy of Science Fiction, Fantasy, and Horror Films, 2002, Nebula Award nomination, best script, Science Fiction and Fantasy Writers of America, all (with Elliott, Joe Stillman, and Roger S. H. Schulman) for *Shrek;* Bram Stoker Award nomination (with Ted Elliott), screenplay, 2004, for *Pirates of the Caribbean: The Curse of the Black Pearl.*

CREDITS

Film Work:
Creative consultant and story consultant, *Antz* (animated; also known as *Ants Work*), 1998.
Coproducer, *Shrek* (animated), DreamWorks, 2001.
Creative consultant, *Sinbad: Legend of the Seven Seas* (animated), DreamWorks, 2003.
Creative consultant, *Sherk 2* (animated), DreamWorks, 2004.
Executive producer, *Deja Vu,* Buena Vista, 2006.
Executive producer, *Invocation, Kumbha Mela* (documentary), 2008.
Executive producer, *Laundry* (short film), 2009.
Associate producer, *G–Force* (also known as *Spy Animal: G–Force*), Walt Disney Studios Motion Pictures, 2009.
Associate producer, *The Death of Toys,* 2010.

Film Appearances:
Himself, *An Epic at Sea: The Making of "Pirates of the Caribbean: The Curse of the Black Pearl"* (short documentary), Buena Vista Home Entertainment, 2003.

Television Director; Episodic:
"Potion," *Turbo Dates,* 2008.

Also directed "Two–Fr," *Turbo Dates;* "More Special," *Turbo Dates;* "Full Disclosure," *Turbo Dates;* "Apples and Oranges," *Turbo Dates.*

WRITINGS

Screenplays; with Ted Elliott:
Little Monsters (also known as *Little Ghost Fighters*), United Artists, 1989.
(Also with John Musker and Ron Clements) *Aladdin* (animated), Buena Vista, 1992.
(Also with David Goyer) *The Puppet Masters* (also known as *Robert A. Heinlein's "The Puppet Masters"*), Buena Vista, 1994.
(Also with Gavin Scott and Adam Rifkin) *Small Soldiers,* DreamWorks, 1998.
(Also with John Eskow) *The Mask of Zorro,* TriStar, 1998.
The Road to El Dorado (animated), DreamWorks, 2000.
(Also with Joe Stillman and Roger S. H. Schulman) *Shrek* (animated; based on a book by William Steig), DreamWorks, 2001.
(Also with Stuart Beattie and Jay Wolpert) *Pirates of the Caribbean: The Curse of the Black Pearl,* Buena Vista, 2003.
National Treasure, Buena Vista, 2004.
Deja Vu, Buena Vista, 2006.
Pirates of the Caribbean: Dead Man's Chest (also known as *P.O.T.C. 2* and *Pirates 2*), Buena Vista, 2006.
Pirates of the Caribbean: At World's End (also known as *P.O.T.C. 3, Pirates 3,* and *Pirates of Caribbean: World End*), Buena Vista, 2007.
Laundry (short film), 2009.

Film Stories:
Godzilla, 1998.
The Mask of Zorro, TriStar, 1998.
Treasure Planet (animated), 2002.
Diary of a Producer (short film), 2003.
Spirit of the Ride (documentary), 2003.
Pirates of the Caribbean: The Curse of the Black Pearl, Buena Vista, 2003.
The Legend of Zorro (also known as *Z*), Columbia, 2005.
National Treasure: Book of Secrets (also known as *National Treasure 2: Book of Secrets*), Walt Disney Studios Motion Pictures, 2007.

Television Episodes:
Turbo Dates, 2008.

Video Games:
Steven Spielberg's Director's Chair, Microsoft, 1996.

Books:
(With Ted Elliott, James Luceno, and others) *The Mask of Zorro: A Novelization,* Pocket Books, 1998.

OTHER SOURCES

Periodicals:
Starlog, November, 1994.

RUNCORN, James 1974–

PERSONAL

Original name, Jonathan Barr; born May 31, 1974, in Upland, CA; married Tena (worked in casting), December 18, 1993; children: Elijah (an actor), Jonah Jamarri, two additional children.

Addresses: *Agent*—Shirley Wilson and Associates, Los Angeles, CA.

Career: Actor. Appeared in television commercials, including Invisible, and MoveOn.org. Also worked as special education teacher for the Los Angeles Unified School District, 2001. *Military service:* U.S. Army Honor Guard; served at Arlington National Cemetery and as a sentinel at the Tomb of the Unknowns.

Member: Screen Actors Guild.

CREDITS

Film Appearances:
Brody, *Sacrifice,* 2005.
(Uncredited) Old troop commando, *xXx: State of the Union* (also known as *xXx 2: The Next Level, xXx2: The Next Level, Cold Circle & Intersection,* and *xXx: The Next Level,* Columbia, 2005.
Chris, *Fellowship* (short film), 2005.
Limo driver, *Entity: Nine* (short film), 2006.
Castel, *Looking for My Brother* (short film), University of Southern California, 2006.
Jim, *Lonely Caller* (short film), 2007.
Justin, *Love Is,* 2007.
Howard Neumann, *Choose Connor* (also known as *The Politician*), Strand Releasing, 2007.

Second jogger, *Mr. Blue Sky,* 2007.
Incest: A Family Tragedy (documentary), CMV Laservision, 2007.
Bailiff, *InAlienable,* Anchor Bay Entertainment, 2008.
Derrick, *The Last Laugh* (short film), 2009.

Film Work:
Consultant on deafness, *Neighborhood Watch* (also known as *Deadly End*), Cafe Productions, 2005.
Producer, *Love Is,* 2007.
Associate producer, *Choose Connor* (also known as *The Politician*), Strand Releasing, 2007.

Television Appearances; Movies:
Sir James Cantlie, *Sun Yat Sen: In the Mouth of the Dragon,* 2000.

Television Appearances; Episodic:
Bartender, *MADtv,* Fox, 2001.
(Uncredited) Addict, "Rage," *The District,* CBS, 2003.
Himself, "Runcorn/Los Angeles," *Adoption Stories,* 2004.
Audio tech, "Drop," *Vanished,* Fox, 2006.
Himself, the wiggler, "Wipeout Soccer Special," *Wipeout,* ABC, 2010.

WRITINGS

Screenplays:
Love Is, 2007.

RYAN, Amanda 1972–

PERSONAL

Born 1972 in the United Kingdom. *Education:* Studied acting at the Royal Academy of Dramatic Art.

Addresses: *Agent*—Markham, Froggatt, and Irwin, 4 Windmill St., London W1P 1HF, England.

Career: Actress.

CREDITS

Film Appearances:
Gypsy saleswoman, *Jude,* Gramercy, 1996.
Joanna, *Metroland,* Lions Gate Films, 1997.

Sukey Damson, *The Woodlanders,* Buena Vista Home Video, 1997.
Lulu, *The Man Who Held His Breath* (short film), 1998.
Lettice Howard, *Elizabeth* (also known as *Elizabeth: The Virgin Queen*), Universal, 1998.
Sarah, *Simon Magus,* Fireworks Pictures, 1999.
Ann, *Mauvaise passe,* Pathe, 1999.
Mrs. Crevand, *Best,* Optimum Releasing, 2000.
Josie, *Whoosh* (short film), UK Film Council, 2002.
Electra, *Red Mercury,* MTI Home Video, 2005.
Julia, *Christmas Merry* (short film), 2005.
Kate, *Sparkle,* Revolver Entertainment, 2007.

Television Appearances; Series:
Jasmine (navigator), *The Micronots!,* 1993.
Sophie Moore, *Attachments,* BBC2, 2000.
Carrie Rogers, *Shameless,* Channel 4 and BBC America, 2007–2009.

Television Appearances; Miniseries:
Agnes Wickfield, *David Copperfield,* BBC1, 1999, PBS, 2000.
Holly, *The Forsyte Saga,* PBS and BBC2, 2002.
Greta Banham, *Real Men,* BBC, 2003.
Holly Dartie nee Forsyte, *The Forsyte Saga, Series II* (also known as *The Forsyte Saga: To Let*), PBS, 2003.
Ronnie Johnson, *The Amazing Mrs Pritchard,* BBC and PBS, 2006.

Television Appearances; Movies:
Vera Campbell, *Britannic,* Fox Family, 2000.
DC Karen Hearst, *Stealing Lives,* 2004.

Television Appearances; Specials:
"The Hunger": An MTV Sneak Preview, MTV, 1996.

Television Appearances; Pilots:
Cuby Trevanion, *Poldark,* BBC, 1996.

Television Appearances; Episodic:
Jodie, "Bits and Pieces," *The Bill,* ITV1, 1996.
Jane Trethowan, "Last Judgement," *Wycliffe,* ITV, 1996.
Kay Brooks, "The Daughters of Cain," *Inspector Morse,* ITV and PBS, 1996.
"The Birthday Trap," *The New Adventures of Robin Hood,* TNT, 1997.
Musidora, "The Swords," *The Hunger,* Showtime, 1997.
Natasha, "Blood Ties: Parts 1 & 2," *Supply & Demand,* ITV, 1998.
Charlotte Sinclair, "Previous Convictions," *Kavanagh QC,* ITV, 1999.
Deborah St. James, "A Great Deliverance," *The Inspector Lynley Mysteries,* BBC1 and PBS, 2001.

Kate Lowry, "The Unwanted," *Dalziel and Pascoe*, BBC, 2002.

Romy, "Ringers," *Murphy's Law*, BBC1 and BBC America, 2004.

Helen Cousins, *Murder Investigation Team* (also known as *M.I.T.: Murder Investigation Team*), ITV and Arts and Entertainment, 2005.

Verity, *EastEnders*, BBC, 2007.

Martha Filby, "The Creeper," *Midsomer Murders*, ITV and Arts and Entertainment, 2009.

Stage Appearances:

Sonya, *The Wood Demon*, Playhouse Theatre, London, 1997.

Also appeared as Stella, *A Streetcar Named Desire*, Theatre Clwyd; Davina, *Otherwise Engaged*, Criterion Theatre, London; Cathy Earnshaw, *Wuthering Heights*, Birmingham Repertory; Hermione, *A Winter's Tale*, Headlong.

Major Tours:

Alice, *Closer*, U.K. cities, 1999.

Davina, *Otherwise Engaged*, U.K. cities, 2005.

Also toured as Cathy Earnshaw, *Wuthering Heights*.

OTHER SOURCES

Electronic:

Amanda Ryan Official Site, http://www.markham froggattandirwin.com, September 8, 2010.

S

SALVATORE, Richard
(Richie Salvatore)

PERSONAL

Born in the Bronx, New York, NY; son of Steve Salvatore (a theatre producer) and Geraldine Stuart (a singer); married Sarah Ann Schultz (an actress), August 31, 2003; children: one. *Education:* Graduated from Hofstra University.

Addresses: *Office*—Salvatore/Ornston Productions, 5650 Camelia Ave., Los Angeles, CA 90035.

Career: Producer. Salvatore/Ornston Productions, Los Angeles, CA, principal. Poppolini's (a restaurant), New York City, co–owner; also ran bars in New York City.

CREDITS

Film Producer:
Earth Minus Zero, PM Entertainment Group, 1996.
Matter of Trust, VCL Communications, 1997.
Laws of Deception, Eternity Pictures, 1997.
Detour, October Films, 1998.
If You Only Knew, Eternity Pictures, 2000.
Enemies of Laughter, Outrider Pictures, 2000.
Whacked!, THINKFilm, 2000.
Arizona Summer, MTI Home Video, 2003.
Shadow of Fear, Mainline Productions, 2004.
Final Move (also known as *Checkmate*), MTI Home Video, 2006.
End Game, Metro–Goldwyn–Mayer, 2006.
Blonde Ambition (also known as *Working Blonde*), First Look International, 2007.
Hero Wanted, Sony Pictures Entertainment, 2008.

Homeland Security (also known as *My Mom's New Boyfriend* and *My Spy*), Sony Pictures Home Entertainment, 2008.
The Way of War, First Look International, 2009.
Give 'Em Hell, Malone (also known as *Malone*), National Entertainment Media, 2009.
Lies & Illusions, Anchor Bay Films, 2009.
Wrong Turn at Tahoe, Paramount Home Entertainment, 2009.
Finding Bliss, Phase 4 Films, 2010.
The Hit List, 2010.
Lola, 2011.

Also worked as producer, *Rule # One; My Mom's New Boyfriend.*

Film Executive Producer:
The Giving Tree (also known as *Brutal Truth* and *Shaded Places*), A–Pix Entertainment, 2000.
Den of Lions, Millennium Films, 2003.
Joe Killionaire, ITN Distribution, 2004.
7–10 Split (also known as *Strike*), Anchor Bay Entertainment, 2007.
Senior Skip Day (also known as *Sex and the School*), First Look International, 2008.
Falling Up, 2009.
The Big Bang, 2010.

Also worked as executive producer on *Strike; The Brutal Truth.*

Film Coproducer:
(Uncredited) *Deuces Wild,* Metro–Goldwyn–Mayer, 2002.

Film Additional Casting:
The Basket, Metro–Goldwyn–Mayer, 1999.

Film Stunt Performer:
The Hit List, Sony Pictures Entertainment, 2010.

Film Appearances:

Security guard, *Matter of Trust,* 1997.

(As Richie Salvatore) *Whacked!,* THINKFilm, 2002.

Spec house dad, *Blonde Ambition* (also known as *Working Blonde*), 2007.

Television Work; Movies:

Producer, *Mel,* HBO, 1998.

Casting director, *Partners,* CBS, 2000.

Producer, *Skeleton Man,* Sci–Fi Channel, 2004.

Executive producer, *MorphMan* (also known as *Larva*), 2005.

SCHULTZ, Sarah Ann

PERSONAL

Married Richard Salvatore (a producer), August 31, 2003.

Career: Actress. Also worked as a model. Sarahbella (a vintage baby apparel line), owner, 2005—.

CREDITS

Film Appearances:

Waitress, *Waitin' to Live,* Anthem Pictures, 2002.

Anna Nazarova, *Den of Lions,* Millennium Films, 2003.

Saran Wrapps, *Joe Killionaire,* ITN Distribution, 2004.

Sister Anja, *The First Vampire: Don't Fall for the Devil's Illusions* (short film), 2004.

Genie Bloom, *Shadow of Fear,* Mainline Productions, 2004.

Nikki Zeale, *Final Move* (also known as *Checkmate*), MTI Home Video, 2006.

Janice Frost, *End Game,* Metro–Goldwyn–Mayer, 2006.

Mrs. Bailey, *7–10 Split* (also known as *Strike*), Cameo FJ Entertainment, 2007.

Reporter Paula Felton, *Cleaner,* Screen Gems, 2007.

Claudette French, *Blonde Ambition* (also known as *Working Blonde*), First Look International, 2007.

Eleven, *The Way of War,* First Look International, 2009.

Sam and Alicia, *Lies & Illusions,* Anchor Bay Films, 2009.

Gwen, *Locked Down,* Lions Gate Films, 2010.

News anchor Jenny Rawlins, *The Hit List,* Sony Pictures Entertainment, 2010.

Malia, *Abelar: Tales of an Ancient Empire* (also known as *Tales of an Ancient Empire*), KIPPJK, 2010.

Magda, *Soldiers of Fortune,* Metro–Goldwyn–Mayer, 2011.

Film Work:

Stunt performer, *The Hit List,* Sony Pictures Entertainment, 2010.

Executive producer, *Lola,* 2011.

Also worked as stunts, *My Mom's New Boyfriend.*

Television Appearances; Movies:

Lieutenant Scott, *Skeleton Man,* Sci–Fi Channel, 2004.

Barbara, *MorphMan* (also known as *Larva*), Sci–Fi Channel, 2005.

Xandrea, *Wolvesbayne,* Sci–Fi Channel, 2009.

Television Appearances; Episodic:

Maria Semov, "The Woman in the Car," *Bones,* Fox, 2006.

Herself, *Mission Hollywood,* 2009.

Herself, *E–Explosiv—Das Magazin,* 2009.

SEDA, Jon 1970–
(Jonathan Seda)

PERSONAL

Born October 14, 1970, in New York, NY; raised in Clifton, NJ; married Elisabeth Gomez, July 4, 2000; children: four, including Jonathan and a stepdaughter. *Education:* Attended Weist–Barron Acting School, New York City. *Avocational Interests:* Music, playing drums and piano, writing.

Addresses: *Agent*—International Creative Management, 10250 Constellation Way, 9th Floor, Los Angeles, CA 90067. *Manager*—Abe Hoch, A Management, 500 South Buena Vista St., Suite 1C–12, Burbank, CA 91521.

Career: Actor. Appeared in commercials, including Spanish–language television commercials. Also worked as a boxer.

Awards, Honors: Independent Spirit Award nomination, best male lead, Independent Features Project/West, 1995, for *I Like It Like That;* nomination for Palm d'Or, Cannes International Film Festival, 1996, for *The Sunchaser;* ALMA Award nominations, outstanding performance in a crossover role in a television series, American Latin Media Arts Awards, National Council of La Raza, 1998 and 1999, both for *Homicide: Life on the Street;* ALMA Award nomination, outstanding actor in a feature film, 1998, for *Selena;* Margo Albert Award, most promising actor, Nosotros Golden Eagle Awards, 2000.

CREDITS

Film Appearances:

Vinnie, *Zebrahead* (also known as *The Colour of Love*), Triumph Releasing, 1992.

Romano, *Gladiator,* Columbia, 1992.

Dominican, *Carlito's Way,* Universal, 1993.

Mario, *New York Cop,* Toei, 1993, Overseas Film-Group, 1996.

Chino Linares, *I Like It Like That* (also known as *Black Out*), Columbia, 1994.

Jose, *Twelve Monkeys,* Universal, 1995.

(As Jonathan Seda) Pete, *Boys on the Side,* 1995.

Alex, *Primal Fear,* Paramount, 1996.

Brandon "Blue" Monroe, *The Sunchaser,* Warner Bros., 1996.

Handsome, *Dear God,* Paramount, 1996.

Billy, *The Price of Kissing,* 1997.

Chris Perez, *Selena,* Warner Bros., 1997.

Sonny Ortega, *Price of Glory,* New Line Cinema, 2000.

Kyle, *Little Pieces,* 2000.

Charlie, *Love the Hard Way,* 2001, Kino International, 2003.

Rikki Ortega, *King Rikki* (also known as *The Street King*), Dream Rock/Moonstone Entertainment, 2002.

Jesus "Chuy" Campos, *Undisputed* (also known as *Dead Lock*), Miramax, 2002.

Roberto, *Bad Boys II* (also known as *Bad Boys 2: Bad* and *Good Cops: Bad Boys II*), Columbia, 2003.

Richard, *One Long Night,* Polychrome Pictures/Vivendi Entertainment, 2007.

Television Appearances; Series:

Under Fire, 1995.

Detective Paul Falsone, *Homicide: Life on the Street* (also known as *Homicide*), NBC, 1997–99.

Matty Caffey, a recurring role, *Third Watch,* NBC, 1999–2000.

Jake Shaw, *UC: Undercover,* NBC, 2001–2002.

Damian "Dame" Ruiz, *Kevin Hill,* UPN, 2004–2005.

Ray Blackwell, *Close to Home,* CBS, 2006–2007.

Nelson Hidalgo, *Treme,* HBO, 2011—.

Television Appearances; Movies:

Payne, *Daybreak,* HBO, 1993.

Eddie Rios, *Mistrial,* HBO, 1996.

Detective Paul Falsone, *Homicide: The Movie,* NBC, 2000.

Luis DeLeon, *Thin Air* (also known as *Robert B. Parker's "Thin Air"* and *Thin Air: A Spenser Mystery*), Arts and Entertainment, 2000.

Sally "Fish" Pescatore, *Double Bang,* HBO, 2001.

Ariel Silva, *One Hot Summer,* Lifetime, 2009.

Television Appearances; Miniseries:

Sergeant John Basilone, *The Pacific,* HBO, 2010.

Television Appearances; Pilots:

Alonzo, *Good Guys, Bad Guys,* NBC, 2000.

Damian "Dame" Ruiz, *Kevin Hill,* UPN, 2004.

Joe Matty, *Legally Mad,* NBC, 2010.

Frankie, *Cutthroat,* ABC, 2010.

Television Appearances; Episodic:

Sal Medina, "You Bet Your Life," *NYPD Blue* (also known as *N.Y.P.D.*), ABC, 1994.

Bobby Lunas, "Knock You Out" (also known as "Mama Said Knock You Out"), *New York Undercover,* Fox, 1995.

Bobby Lunas, "Innocent Bystander," *New York Undercover,* Fox, 1995.

Dino Ortolani (Prisoner 96C382), "The Routine," *Oz,* HBO, 1997.

Dino Ortolani, "A Game of Checkers," *Oz,* HBO, 1997.

Detective Paul Falsone, "Baby, It's You: Part 1," *Law & Order,* NBC, 1997.

Dino Ortolani, "A Day in the Death …," *Oz,* HBO, 2003.

Nick Duarte, "Dial 'O' for Murder," *Hack,* CBS, 2003.

Junior Gomez, "Die Fast, Die Furious," *Las Vegas,* NBC, 2004.

Victor Torres, "Last Rites," *The Jury,* Fox, 2004.

John Gregory, "Free Fall," *Ghost Whisperer,* CBS, 2006.

John Gregory, "The One," *Ghost Whisperer,* CBS, 2006.

Hector Salazar, "Tipping Point," *CSI: Miami,* CBS, 2008.

Donny, "Brave Heart," *House M.D.* (also known as *House*), Fox, 2009.

Lonnie Moses, "Arm in Arms," *Numb3rs* (also known as *Num3ers*), CBS, 2010.

Cole, "Center of the Storm," *Burn Notice,* USA Network, 2010.

Detective Frank Verico, "Off the Hook," *The Closer,* TNT, 2010.

Sergeant Cage, "Mana'o," *Hawaii Five–O,* CBS, 2010.

Appeared as Victor Ventana in an episode of *Walker, Texas Ranger.*

Television Appearances; Specials:

(In archive footage) Detective Paul Falsone, *Anatomy of a "Homicide: Life on the Street,"* NBC, 1998.

Intimate Portrait: Jennifer Lopez, Lifetime, 2002.

Television Appearances; Awards Presentations:

The … NCLR Bravo Awards, Fox, 1995, 1996.

The … ALMA Awards, ABC, 1998, 1999.

Presenter, *The 5th Annual ALMA Awards,* ABC, 2000.

RECORDINGS

Videos:

Making of Selena: 10 Years Later, Warner Home Video, 2007.

OTHER SOURCES

Periodicals:
Teen, July, 1998, p. 38.

SHAFFER, Atticus 1998–

PERSONAL

Born June 19, 1998, in Santa Clarita, CA.

Addresses: *Agent*—Cindy Osbrink, Osbrink Agency, 4343 Lankershim Blvd., Suite 100, Universal City, CA 91602; (voice work), Melissa Berger, Cunningham, Escott, Slevin, and Doherty Talent Agency, 10635 Santa Monica Blvd., Suite 140, Los Angeles, CA 90025. *Manager*—Linda Defillipo, DC Talent, Santa Clarita, CA.

Career: Actor. Appeared in commercials.

Member: American Federation of Television and Radio Artists, Screen Actors Guild.

CREDITS

Film Appearances:
Little boy on bus, *Leaving Barstow,* Osiris Entertainment, 2008.
Boy at bus bench, *Hancock* (also known as *Hidden from Earth*), Columbia, 2008.
Timmy/Atticus, *An American Carol* (also known as *Big Fat Important Movie*), Vivendi Entertainment, 2008.
Matty Newton, *The Unborn,* Rogue Pictures, 2009.
Voice of animal boy, *Ice Age: Dawn of the Dinosaurs* (animated), Twentieth Century–Fox, 2009.
Second kid detective, *Opposite Day,* TVA Films, 2009, Anchor Bay Entertainment, 2010.
Voice of Tommy, *Subject: I Love You,* Radiant Studios, 2010.

Film Work:
Automated dialogue replacement (ADR), *Year One,* Columbia, 2009.

Television Appearances; Series:
Brick Heck, *The Middle,* ABC, 2009—.

Television Appearances; Pilots:
Brick Heck, *The Middle,* ABC, 2009.

Television Appearances; Episodic:
Jonah, "The Class Rides a Bull," *The Class,* CBS, 2007.
Irish boy, *Days of Our Lives* (also known as *Days* and *DOOL*), NBC, 2007.
Boy, "Take Your Daughter to Work Day," *Carpoolers,* ABC, 2008.
Voice of Aaron, "Bad Fad," *Out of Jimmy's Head* (animated), Cartoon Network, 2008.
Space camper, "Chaz Dalton's Space Academy," *My Name Is Earl,* NBC, 2009.
Jimmy Kimmel Live!, ABC, 2009, 2010.
Voice, *Fish Hooks,* The Disney Channel, 2010.
The View, ABC, 2010.
The Bonnie Hunt Show, NBC, 2010.
Entertainment Tonight (also known as *E.T.* and *This Week in Entertainment*), syndicated, 2010.

SHANKAR, Ravi 1920–

PERSONAL

Original name, Rabendra Shankar; born April 7, 1920, in Benares (now Varanasi), India; son of Shyama (an attorney) and Hemangini Shankar; married Annapurna Dvi Allauddin, May, 1941 (divorced, 1961); married Sukanya Rajan, 1988; children: (first marriage) Shubendra, Geetalil; (second marriage) Anoushka (a sitarist); (with Sue Jones) Norah Jones (a singer). *Education:* Studied with brother Uday Shankar in Paris, 1930, and with Ustad Allaudin Khan in Maihar, 1938. *Avocational Interests:* Films, music, people theatre.

Addresses: *Contact*—c/o Sullivan Sweetland, 28 Albion St., London W2 2AX, England.

Career: Composer, musician, and actor. MP, member of Rajya Sabha since 1986. Uday Shan–Kar Company, dancer, 1930–c. 1936; India Renaissance Artists, founder, 1947–?; All–India Radio, music director, 1949–56; music choreography for ASIAD 82 (Asian Games, New Delhi, 1982); Ravi Shankar Centre, New Delhi, India, opened 2001; University of California at San Diego, Regents Professor of Music.

Member: National Academy of Arts and Sciences.

Awards, Honors: Filmfare Award, best music director, 1957, for *Chori, Chori;* Silver Berlin Bear, special prize for best film music, Berlin International Film Festival, 1957, for *Kabuliawawa;* Filmfare Award, best music director, 1960, for *Anari;* Filmfare Award, best music director, 1961, for *Dil Apna Aur Preet Parai;* Sangeet Natak Akademi, President's award, 1962, and fellow, 1977; Filmfare Award, best music director, 1963, for

Professor; Grammy Award nomination, best folk recording, National Academy of Recording Arts and Sciences, 1966, for *Sound of the Sitar;* Grammy Award (with Yehudi Menuhin), best chamber music performance, 1967, for *West Meets East;* Filmfare Award, best music director, 1967, for *Suraj;* Artist of the Year, *Billboard* magazine, 1968; Filmfare Award, best music director, 1969, for *Brahmachari;* Filmfare Award, best music director, 1971, for *Pehchan;* Grammy Award (with others), album of the year, 1972, for *The Concert for Bangladesh;* Filmfare Award, best music director, 1972, for *Mera Naam Joker;* Filmfare Award, best music director, 1973 for *Be–Imaan;* International Music Council Music Prize, UNESCO, 1975; Grammy Award nomination (with others), best chamber music performance, 1977, for *Improvisations–East Meets West–Album 3;* Presidential Padma Vibhushan Award, 1980; Benares Hindu University Deshikottam Award, 1982; Grammy Award nomination (with Ali Akbar Khan), best ethnic or traditional recording, 1983, for *Raga Mishra Piloo;* Grammy Award nomination (with George Fenton and others), best original score for motion picture or television special, 1983, for *Gandhi;* Academy Award nomination (with Fenton), best original music score, 1982, Film Award nomination (with Fenton), best score, British Academy of Film and Television Arts, 1983, both for *Gandhi;* Grand Prize, Fukuoka Asian Cultural Prizes, Japan, 1991; Ramon Magsaysay Award, 1992; Bharatiya Vidya Bhavan Mahatma Gandhi Award, 1992; House of Commons Shield, 1995; Crystal Award, 1995; Premium Imperial Arts Award, 1997; Light of Asia Award, 1997; Juliet Hollister Award, 1998; Polar Music Prize, 1998; Bharat Ratna, 1999; Honorary Award, International Biennial for Film Music, 1999; Commander of Legion of Honour, 2000; made Honorary Knight Commander of the Order of the British Empire, 2001; Grammy Award, best world music album, 2002, for *Full Circle: Carnegie Hall 2000;* awarded Padma Visbushan, India's highest civilian honor.

CREDITS

Stage Work:
Musical supervisor, *The Guide,* Hudson Theatre, Los Angeles, 1968.

Film Work:
Music director, *Chappaqua,* Rooks/Regional, 1967.

Film Appearances:
Mastera Indiiskogo iskusstva (also known as *Indian Artists in the U.S.S.R.*), 1954.
Ustad Aluddin Khan, 1963.
Sun God, *Chappaqua,* 1966.
Himself, *Monterey Pop,* 1968.
Himself, *Ravi Shankar,* 1970.

Raga, 1971.
Himself, *The Concert for Bangladesh,* 1972.
Himself, *Ravi Shankar: Between Two Worlds,* 2001.
The Song of the Little Road, NEHST OUT, 2003.
Concert for George, Warner Home Video, 2003.
Trinidad and Tobago cricketer, *Hit for Six,* Blue Waters, 2007.
Glass: A Portrait of Philip in Twelve Parts, Koch Lorber Films, LLC, 2007.

Also appeared in *Song of the Little Road* and *Reaching Silence.*

Television Appearances; Series:
Sixties Summer Songs, 1999.

Television Appearances; Miniseries:
Himself, *Rock & Roll,* PBS, 1995.

Television Appearances; Specials:
The Best on Record, 1968.
Unterwegs nach Kathmandu, 1971.
The Night of Music: A Global Celebration, PBS, 1986.
Menuhin: A Family Portrait, PBS, 1991.
Woodstock Diary, 1994.
Stand and Be Counted, The Learning Channel, 2000.
George Harrison–Der sanfte Beatle, 2001.
Concert for Bangladesh Revisited with George Harrison and Friends, Apple Corps, 2005.
Ravi Shankar, l'extraordinaire lecon, Arte, 2010.

Television Appearances; Episodic:
A Whole Scene Going, 1966.
The Hollywood Palace, 1967.
American Bandstand, 1967.
The Smothers Brothers Comedy Hour, 1968.
The David Frost Show, two episodes 1969.
The Ed Sullivan Show, 1970.
The Midnight Special, 1973, 1974, 1975.
"Ravi Shankar," *The South Bank Show,* ITV, 2001.
Through the Keyhole, ITV, BBC, 2004.
"Ravi Shankar," *HARDtalk Extra,* BBC, 2005.

Also appeared in "Mighty Good: The Beatles," *All You Need Is Love.*

RECORDINGS

Albums:
Three Ragas, EMI Angel, 1956.
Ravi Shankar, India's Master Musician, World–Pacific, 1958.
Improvisations, World–Pacific, 1962.
Indian's Most Distinguished Musician in Concert, EMI Angel, 1962.

India's Master Musician, EMI Angel, 1963.

Ravi Shankar, Portrait of a Genius, Angel, 1964.

India's Master Musician: Ravi Shankar, EMI, 1964.

Ragas and Talas, Angel, 1964.

In London, EMI Angel, 1964.

Menuhin Meets Shankar, Angel, 1966.

The Sound of the Sitar, World–Pacific, BGO, 1966.

The Sounds of India: Ravi Shankar, Columbia, 1966.

Three Ragas, Capitol, 1966.

Exotic Sitar and Sarod, Capitol, 1967.

Ravi Shankar in San Francisco, EMI Angel, 1967.

Ravi Shankar at the Monterey International Festival, Angel, 1967.

Two Raga Moods, Capitol, 1967.

West Meets East (two volumes), Angel, 1967.

A Morning Raga, An Evening Raga, Angel, 1968.

Chappaqua (soundtrack), Columbia, 1968.

Charly (soundtrack), World–Pacific, 1968.

Ravi Shankar in New York, World–Pacific, 1968.

Ravi Shankar, Capitol, 1968.

Six Ragas, Capitol, 1968.

The Sounds of India, Columbia, 1968.

Ravi Shankar at the Woodstock Festival, World–Pacific, 1970.

Raga (soundtrack), Apple, 1971.

Shankar: Concerto #1 for Sitar and Orchestra, Angel, 1971.

(With others) *The Concert for Bangladesh,* 1972.

In Concert, Apple, 1972.

Transmigration Macabre, Spark, 1973.

Ragas, Fantasy, 1973.

Shankar Family and Friends, Dark Horse/A&M, 1974.

Raga Parameshwari, Capitol, 1976.

Ravi Shankar's Festival from India, Dark Horse/A&M, 1976.

East Greets East, Deutsche Grammophon, 1978.

Ragas Hameer and Gara, Deutsche Grammophon, 1979.

Recorded in Concert, Royce Hall UCLA, 1979.

Homage to Mahatma Ghandi and Baba Allauddin, Deutsche Grammophon, 1981.

Ghandi (soundtrack), RCA, 1982.

Raga–Mala (Sitar Concerto No. 2), Angel, 1982.

Improvisations–East Meets West–Album 3, 1983.

Raga Mishra Piloo, 1983.

Tana Mana, Private, 1987.

Sitar, 1989.

Inside the Kremlin, Private Music, 1989.

(With Philip Glass) *Passages,* Private Music, 1990.

Golden Jubilee Concert, Chhanda Dhara, 1990.

The Genius of Ravi Shankar, Scorpio, 1990.

Maestro's Choice, D D D, 1991.

Megh Malhar, Vol. 1, Music Today, 1991.

(With others) *The Tiger and the Brahmin,* Kid Rhino, 1992.

Farewell, My Friend, EMI India, 1992.

Ravi Shankar, Deutsche Grammphon, 1993.

Sitar, Music Today, 1994.

Concert for Peace: Royal Albert Hall, Moment, 1995.

Ravi Shankar in Venice: Raga Gurjari Todi, Manj–Khamaj, Shailangi, Discovery, 1995.

Doyen of Hinustani Music, Oriental, 1995.

In Celebration, Angel, 1995.

Shankar: In Celebration, EMI Angel, 1995.

Genesis (soundtrack), Milan, 1995.

Sublime Sounds of Sitar, Oriental, 1996.

Towards the Rising Sun, DG Deutsche Grammophon, 1996.

Chants of India, Angel, 1997.

Raga Mala, Angel/Genesis, 1997.

Mantram: Chant of India, EMI Angel, 1997.

Raga Tala, Movie Play, 1997.

From India, A World of Music, 1997.

Raga Jogeshwari, Interra, 1998.

Ragas Varanasi, Ex Works, 1998.

Flue & Sitar Music of India, Laserlight, 1999.

Legends, Vol. 1, Gramophone, 1999.

Legends, Vol. 2, Gramophone, 1999.

Legends, Vol. 3, Gramophone, 1999.

Golden Jubilee Concert, Vol. 1, Chhandra Dhara, 1999.

Golden Jubilee Concert, Vol. 2, Chhandra Dhara, 1999.

The Master Musicians of India, Prestige, 1999.

Flute and Sitar Music of India, Empire, 1999.

Native Flute Music of India, Legacy, 1999.

Spirit of India: Flute & Tabla, Legacy, 1999.

Sitar Master, 2000.

Four Ragas, Movie Play, 2000.

Master Drummers of India, Legacy, 2001.

Master of Sitar, Nascente, 2001.

Full Circle: Carnegie Hall 2000, EMI Angel, 2001.

Bridges: Best of Private Music Recordings, 2001.

Vision of Peace: The Art of Ravi Shankar, DG Deutsche Grammophon, 2001.

Collected, Music Club, 2001.

Pandit Ravi Shankar, EMI, 2001.

Inde du Nord, Ocora, 2001.

Festival from India, Beat Goes On, 2002.

The Teacher, Manteca, 2002.

East Meets West, Vol. 2, Beat Goes On, 2002.

From Dusk to Dawn: The Raga Collection, 2002.

Music from India, Music Digital, 2002.

The Best of Ravi Shankar, Music Today, 2003.

Spiritual Music of India: Ragas for Meditation, Proper Sales & Dist., 2003.

Sitar, Saregama, 2003.

Legends, Saregama, 2003.

Unique: Indian Night Live Stuttgart '88, Chhanda Dhara, 2004.

The Rough Guid to Ravi Shankar, World Music Network, 2004.

Traditional: The Spirt of India, DG Deutsche Grammophon, 2004.

Alap, Pt. 1/Jod, Pt. 2/Gat, Pt. 3, Saregama, 2004.

Raga Jog: Alp, Jod, Jhala and Gat in Teentaal, Saregama, 2004.

Raga Mishra Bhairavi: Dhun in Ardha Taal (8 Beets)/ Drut Teentaal, Saregama, 2004.

Homage to Mahatma Ghandi, UNI, 2004.

Three Ragas, Rremark, 2004.

Digital Collection, Vol. 1, Saregama, 2004.
Digital Collection, Vol. 3, Saregama, 2004.
Digital Collection, Vol. 4, Saregama, 2004.
Eternal Ragas, Saregama, 2004.
Timeless Classics: Hindustani Classical, Saregama, 2004.
Jugalbandi: Palas Kafi & Bilaskhani Todi, Saregama, 2004.
Sangeet Sartaj, Vols. 1 & 2, Music Today, 2005.
Sur Saaz Aur Taal, Vol. 2, Music Today, 2005.
Jazz et Ragas, Beat Goes On, 2005.
Shankar: Sitar Concertos and Other Works, EMI, 2005.
Spirit of India, Chhanda Dhara, 2005.
Raga Charukauns, Chhanda Dhara, 2005.
Saaz Sitar, Vol. 1, Music Today, 2005.
Saaz Sitar, Vol. 2, Music Today, 2005.
The Man and His Music, SBMC, 2006.
The Golden Collection, Saregama, 2006.
Journey through His Music, Membran, 2006.
Raga Jogeshwari, Fontana, 2006.
Homage to Mahatma Ghandi, Fontana, 2006.
First LP Record, Saregama, 2006.
Sitar Soul, Music Today, 2007.
Traditional Ragas, Deja Vu, 2007.
Flowers of India, EI, 2007.
Best of Ravi Shankar, Arc, 2008.
More Flowers of India, EI, 2008.
Film India: The Cinema of Ravi Shankar, EI, 2009.
The Master, Deutsche Grammophon, 2010.
Rare and Glorious, Times Square, 2010.
Masters of Indian Classical Music, Volume II, Arc, 2010.
Nine Decades, Vol. 1: 1967–1968, East Meets West, 2010.

Videos:

Raga, Capitol, 1964.
Raga, Mystic Fire, 1998.
In Portrait, BBC, 2002.
Wisdom, Late Night and Weekends, 2008.
In Portrait: Between Two Worlds/Live in Concert, Kultur, 2009.

WRITINGS

Film Scores:

Neecha Nagar (also known as *Lowly City*), 1946.
Dharti Ke Lal (also known as *Children of the Earth*), 1946.
Kabuliwala, 1956.
Aparajito (also known as *The Unvanquished*), 1956.
En Djungelsaga (also known as *The Flute and the Arrow*), 1957.
A Chairy Tale (also known as *Il etait une chaise*), 1957.
Pather Panchali (also known as *The Lament of the Path, The Saga of the Road,* and *Song of the Road*), Government/Edward Harrison, 1958.

Parash Pathar (also known as *Paras–Pathar* and *The Philosopher's Stone*), 1958.
The Sword and the Flute, 1959.
Apur Sansar (also known as *The World of Apu*), Satyajit Ray/Edward Harrison, 1959.
Aparajito (also known as *The Unvanquished*), Epic Aurora, 1959.
Anduradha (also known as *Love of Anuradha*), 1960.
Dheuer Pare Dheu (also known as *Waves After Waves*), 1962.
Tarzan Goes to India, Metro–Goldwyn–Mayer, 1962.
Godaan, 1963.
The Psychedelics, 1966.
Chappaqua, Rooks/Regional, 1967.
My Music My Life, 1968.
Charly, Selmur/Cinema Releasing Corp., 1968.
Niet genoeg (also known as *Not Enough*), 1968.
Sex and the Animals, 1969.
Raga, 1971.
Meera, 1979.
Pasi, 1980.
(With George Fenton) *Gandhi,* Columbia, 1982.
Genesis, Cactus, 1986.
Yehudi Menuhin: The Violin of the Century, 1996.
Zakir and His Friends, 1997.
Tenussian Vacuvasco, 2000.
Ravi Shankar: Between Two Worlds, 2001.
Partition, Myriad, 2009.

Film Songs:

"Chanda Mam Door Ke," *Vachan,* 1955.
"Piece pour sitar," *Wow,* 1970.
"Jai Bolo Be–Imaan Ki," "Yeh Raakhi Bandhan Hai Aesa," "Dekho Ji Raat Ko Julam Ho Gaya," "Main to Chali Hoon," "Patla Patla Reshmi Kurta," "Hum Do Mast Malang," *Be–Imaan,* 1972.
"Tala Rasa Ranga," "Tabla Dhwani," *Merton* (also known as *Merton: A Film Biography*), 1984.
"The Trembler," *Natural Born Killers,* 1994.
"Shuddia Sarang," *America's Sweetheart* (also known as *American Sweetheart*), 2001.
"Gat I," *Anything Else,* DreamWorks, 2003.
"Raga Madhuvanti," *Catch and Release* (also known as *Catch & Release*), Columbia, 2006.
"Ghanashyam," "Raga Rajya–Kalyan," *Music and Lyrics,* Warner Bros., 2007.
"Music," *The Darjeeling Limited,* Twentieth Century–Fox, 2007.
"Raga Manj Khamaj," *Taking Woodstock,* Focus Features, 2009.

Television Scores; Movies:

Alice in Wonderland, 1967.

Television Scores; Specials:

Unterwegs nach Kathmandu, 1971.
The Tiger and the Brahmin (animated), Showtime, 1991.

Television Songs; Miniseries:
The Beatles Anthology, 1995.

Autobiographies:
My Music, My Life, 1968.
Raga Mala: The Autobiography of Ravi Shankar, 1999.

Also wrote *Rag Anurag.*

OTHER SOURCES

Books:
Baker's Biographical Dictionary of Musicians, Schirmer, 2001.
Contemporary Musicians, Volume 38, Gale Group, 2003.
Encyclopedia of World Biography Supplement, Volume 22, Gale Group, 2002.
International Dictionary of Films and Filmmakers, Volume 4: *Writers and Production Artists,* St. James Press, 1996.

Periodicals:
Billboard, March 18, 1995, p. 1; December 23, 1995, p. 17; May 3, 1997, p. 11; June 28, 1997, p. 52; October 16, 1999, p. 13; March 17, 2001, p. 11.
Down Beat, March, 2002, p. 44.
New Statesman, March 21, 1997, p. 50; April 24, 2000, p. 47.

Electronic:
Ravi Shankar Web Site, http://www.ravishankar.org, May 8, 2003.

SHAWN, Wallace 1943–
    (Wally Shawn)

PERSONAL

Born November 12, 1943, in New York, NY; son of William (a magazine editor) and Cecille (a journalist; maiden name, Lyon) Shawn; brother of Allen Shawn (a composer); companion of Deborah Eisenberg (a playwright and fiction writer). *Education:* Harvard University, B.A., history, 1965; Magdalen College, Oxford, B.A. (philosophy, politics, and economics), 1968, M.A., 1975; studied acting with Katharine Sergava at HB Studio in New York City, 1971.

Addresses: *Agent*—Cary Berman, William Morris Agency, 151 El Camino Dr., Beverly Hills, CA 90212.

Manager—Christopher Black, Ensemble Entertainment, 10474 Santa Monica Blvd., Suite 380, Los Angeles, CA 90025.

Career: Writer and actor. Indore Christian College, Indore, India, English teacher, 1965–66; Church of Heavenly Rest Day School, New York City, teacher of English, Latin, and drama, 1968–70; Laurie Love, Ltd., New York City, shipping clerk, 1974–75; Hamilton Copy Center, New York City, copying machine operator, 1975–76.

Member: Screen Actors Guild, Actors' Equity Association, Dramatists Guild, Writers Guild East.

Awards, Honors: Fulbright scholar in India, 1965–66; Obie Award, distinguished playwriting, *Village Voice,* 1975, for *Our Late Night;* Guggenheim fellowship, 1978; Boston Society of Film Critics Award (with Andre Gregory), best screenplay, 1982, for *My Dinner with Andre;* Obie Award, distinguished playwriting, 1986, for *Aunt Dan and Lemon;* Obie Award, best play, 1991, for *The Fever;* Award in Literature, American Academy of Arts and Letters, 1997.

CREDITS

Film Appearances:
Assistant insurance man, *All That Jazz,* Twentieth Century–Fox, 1979.
Jeremiah, *Manhattan,* United Artists, 1979.
Workshop member, *Starting Over,* Paramount, 1979.
Strong Medicine, 1979.
Eric Van Dongen, *Simon,* Warner Bros., 1980.
Mugger, *Cheaper to Keep Her,* American Cinema, 1980.
(As Wally Shawn) Waiter, *Atlantic City* (also known as *Atlantic City, U.S.A.*), Paramount, 1981.
Wallace, *My Dinner with Andre,* New Yorker, 1981.
Oliver, *A Little Sex,* Universal, 1982.
Earl, *Strange Invaders,* Orion, 1983.
Frank Judd, *Saigon–Year of the Cat,* Warner Bros., 1983.
Harold DeVoto, *Deal of the Century,* Warner Bros., 1983.
Otto Jaffe, *Lovesick,* Warner Bros., 1983.
Professor Jules Goldfarb, *The First Time* (also known as *Doin' It*), New Line Cinema, 1983.
Dr. Elliot Fibel, *Micki + Maude,* Columbia, 1984.
Freud, *The Hotel New Hampshire,* Orion, 1984.
Mr. Pardon, *The Bostonians,* Almi, 1984.
Turtle, *Crackers,* Universal, 1984.
Father Abruzzi, *Heaven Help Us* (also known as *Catholic Boys*), TriStar, 1985.
Mike Hoover, *Head Office,* TriStar, 1986.
Defense attorney, *The Bedroom Window,* De Laurentiis Entertainment Group, 1987.

Ellen, *Nice Girls Don't Explode,* New World, 1987.

John Lahr, *Prick Up Your Ears,* Samuel Goldwyn, 1987.

Masked Avenger, *Radio Days,* Orion, 1987.

Vizzini, *The Princess Bride,* Twentieth Century–Fox, 1987.

Oiseau, *The Moderns,* Island Alive, 1988.

Dr. Fishbinder, *She's Out of Control,* Columbia, 1989.

Howard Saravian, *Scenes from the Class Struggle in Beverly Hills,* Cinecom, 1989.

Translator, *We're No Angels,* Paramount, 1989.

Dr. Block, *Unbecoming Age* (also known as *The Magic Bubble*), 1992.

Everett Willis, *Nickel & Dime,* Columbia/TriStar Home Video, 1992.

Sibor, *Mom and Dad Save the World,* Warner Bros., 1992.

Simon Carr, *Shadows and Fog,* Orion, 1992.

Cashpot, *The Double 0 Kid,* Prism Pictures, 1993.

Larry, *The Cemetery Club* (also known as *Looking for a Live One*), Buena Vista, 1993.

Mr. Little, *The Meteor Man,* Metro–Goldwyn–Mayer, 1993.

Canadian prime minister Clark MacDonald, *Canadian Bacon,* Gramercy, 1994.

Horatio Byrd, *Mrs. Parker and the Vicious Circle* (also known as *Mrs. Parker and the Round Table*), Miramax, 1994.

Vanya, *Vanya on 42nd Street,* Mayfair, 1994.

Kalamazoo, No. 9 Films, 1994.

Cosmo, *The Wife,* Artistic License Films, 1995.

Mr. Alphonse (some sources cite Wendell) Hall, *Clueless* (also known as *I Was a Teenage Teenager* and *No Worries*), Paramount, 1995.

Voice of Principal Mazur, *A Goofy Movie* (animated), Buena Vista, 1995.

Voice of Rex, *Toy Story* (animated), Buena Vista, 1995.

Echidna, *Napoleon,* 1995.

Victor "Vic" Finley, *House Arrest,* Metro–Goldwyn–Mayer, 1996.

Voice of Labrador, *All Dogs Go to Heaven 2* (animated), Metro–Goldwyn–Mayer, 1996.

Arthur Blake, *Just Write,* Curb Entertainment/Heartland Film Releasing, 1997.

Furnace man, *Critical Care,* Live Film and Mediaworks, 1997.

Marty, *Vegas Vacation* (also known as *National Lampoon's Vegas Vacation*), Warner Bros., 1997.

Voice of Tarzan the chimp, *The Jungle Book: Mowgli's Story* (animated), 1998.

Die Wholesale, 1998.

Dr. Edward (some sources cite Elliott) Coleye, *My Favorite Martian* (also known as *My Favourite Martian*), Buena Vista, 1999.

Voice of Rex, *Toy Story 2* (animated), Buena Vista, 1999.

A Tekerolantos naploja (also known as *The Diary of the Hurdy–Gurdy Man*), 1999.

Gene, *The Prime Gig,* New Line Cinema/Fine Line, 2000.

Voice of Rex, *Buzz Lightyear of Star Command: The Adventure Begins* (animated), 2000.

George Bond, *The Curse of the Jade Scorpion* (also known as *Im Bann des Jade Skorpions*), DreamWorks, 2001.

(Uncredited) Voice of Rex, *Monsters, Inc.* (animated), Buena Vista, 2001.

Doctor, *Love Thy Neighbor,* Tribeca Rules Productions, 2002.

Mr. Gelb, "Greta," *Personal Velocity: Three Portraits* (also known as *Personal Velocity*), Metro–Goldwyn–Mayer/United Artists, 2002.

Ezra, *The Haunted Mansion* (also known as *Disney's The Haunted Mansion*), Buena Vista, 2003.

Voice Principal Strickler, *Teacher's Pet: The Movie* (animated), Buena Vista, 2003.

Duplex, Miramax, 2003.

Sy, *Melinda and Melinda,* Twentieth Century–Fox, 2004.

Voice of Gilbert Huph, *The Incredibles* (animated; also known as *Mr. Incredible*), Buena Vista, 2004.

Voice of Principal Fetchit, *Chicken Little* (animated), Buena Vista, 2005.

Voice of purple pirate Paul/narrator, *Tom and Jerry in Shiver Me Whiskers,* Warner Home Video, 2006.

Voice of Billy, *Air Buddies,* Buena Vista, 2006.

Baron Von Westphalen, *Southland Tales,* United International, 2006.

Voice of Munk, *Happily N'Ever After,* Lions Gate Films, 2006.

Math teacher, *I Could Never Be Your Woman,* Eagle Films, 2007.

Wallace Shawn, *New York City Serenade* (also known as *NYC Serenade*), Anchor Bay, 2007.

Strange Culture, Videorama, 2007.

Mr. Gibson, *Kit Kittredge: An American Girl,* New Line Cinema, 2008.

Voice of Mr. Gibbles, *Scooby–doo and the Goblin King* (animated), Warner Bros., 2008.

The Windmill Movie, HBO, 2008.

Capitalism: A Love Story (also known as *The New Movie*), Alliance, 2009.

MindFlux: A Film About Richard Foreman, Rides Media, 2009.

Booker/broker/Lancealot Squarejaw, *Jack and the Beanstalk,* Avalon Family, 2010.

Dr. Christian Burr, *Furry Vengeance,* Pioneer, 2010.

Voice of Rex the green dinosaur, *Toy Story 3* (also known as *3* and *Toy Story 3: An IMAX 3D Experience*), Walt Disney, 2010.

Voice of Calico, *Cats & Dogs: The Revenge of Kitty Galore,* Warner Bros., 2010.

Sandy, *The Speed of Thought,* Highland Film Group, 2011.

Television Appearances; Series:

Professor Marvel, *One Life to Live,* 1992.

Mr. Alphonse Hall, *Clueless,* UPN, 1996–97.

Voice of Freddy, *The Lionhearts* (animated), syndicated, 1998.

Voice of Principal Strickler, *Teacher's Pet* (animated; also known as *Disney's Teacher's Pet*), ABC, 2000–2002.

Cyrus Rose, a recurring role, *Gossip Girl,* 2008–10.

Voice of Taotie, *Kung Fu Panda: Legends of Awesomeness* (animated), 2011.

Television Appearances; Miniseries:

I. E. Shinn, *Blonde* (also known as *Marilyn Monroe*), CBC, 2001.

Television Appearances; Movies:

Frank Judd, *Saigon: Year of the Cat,* 1983.

Eligible Dentist, 1993.

Stan Spiegel (Charlie's father), *Just Like Dad,* The Disney Channel, 1995.

Zack, *Noah,* ABC, 1998.

Gene, *The Prime Gig,* Independent Film Channel, 2001.

Mimir, *Mr. St. Nick,* ABC, 2002.

Spaulding, *Sun Gods,* 2002.

Colonel Wilson, *Monte Walsh,* TNT, 2003.

Zeb Rosecog, *Karroll's Christmas,* 2004.

Marty, *The 12th Man,* 2006.

Television Appearances; Episodic:

Arnie Ross, "The Schloogel Show," *Taxi,* ABC, 1982.

Arnie Ross, "Arnie Meets the Kids," *Taxi,* ABC, 1983.

Jeffrey Engels, "Cliff's Mistake," *The Cosby Show,* NBC, 1987.

Jeffrey Engels, "The Day the Spores Landed," *The Cosby Show,* NBC, 1989.

Jeffrey Engels, "Cliff's Nightmare," *The Cosby Show,* NBC, 1990.

Jeffrey Engels, "The Moves," *The Cosby Show,* NBC, 1990.

Narrator, "Bad Sausage Sandwich," *The Cosby Show,* NBC, 1990.

Howard Buckley, *Davis Rules,* ABC, 1991.

Jeffrey Engels, "Olivia's Field Trip," *The Cosby Show,* NBC, 1991.

Riley Baker, "A Bus Named Desire," *Civil Wars,* ABC, 1992.

Grand Nagus Zek, "The Nagus" (also known as "Friends and Foes"), *Star Trek: Deep Space Nine* (also known as *Deep Space Nine, DS9,* and *Star Trek: DS9*), syndicated, 1993.

Grand Nagus Zek, "Rules of Acquisition," *Star Trek: Deep Space Nine* (also known as *Deep Space Nine, DS9,* and *Star Trek: DS9*), syndicated, 1993.

Mr. Gonley, "Lapses in Memory," *Matrix,* USA Network, 1993.

Voice of the little man, "Ice Blue Pink," *The Pink Panther,* 1993.

Charles Haste, "Pinske Business," *The Nanny,* CBS, 1994.

Marvin, *Something Wilder,* NBC, 1994.

Stuart Best, "The Best and Not–So–Brightest," *Murphy Brown,* CBS, 1994.

Stuart Best, "The Fifty Anchor," *Murphy Brown,* CBS, 1994.

Grand Nagus Zek, "Prophet Motive," *Star Trek: Deep Space Nine* (also known as *Deep Space Nine, DS9,* and *Star Trek: DS9*), syndicated, 1995.

The Charlie Rose Show (also known as *Charlie Rose*), 1995.

Showbiz Today, 1995.

Stuart Best, "Up in Smoke," *Murphy Brown,* CBS, 1996.

Voice characterization, "The Third Pig," *Tales from the Crypt,* HBO, 1996.

Grand Nagus Zek, "Ferengi Love Songs" (also known as "Of Love and Profit"), *Star Trek: Deep Space Nine* (also known as *Deep Space Nine, DS9,* and *Star Trek: DS9*), syndicated, 1997.

Stuart Best, "Hero Today, Gone Tomorrow," *Murphy Brown,* CBS, 1997.

Voice of rifle shooting instructor, "How to Fire a Rifle without Even Trying," *King of the Hill* (animated), Fox, 1997.

Grand Nagus Zek, "Profit and Lace," *Star Trek: Deep Space Nine* (also known as *Deep Space Nine, DS9,* and *Star Trek: DS9*), syndicated, 1998.

Jeffrey Haven, "The Mother Meets the Parents," *Reunited,* UPN, 1998.

Voice of Philip Ny, "Nine Pretty Darn Angry Men," *King of the Hill* (animated), Fox, 1998.

Frank Hopper, "A Case of Do or Die," *Homicide: Life on the Street* (also known as *Homicide* and *H: LOTS*), NBC, 1999.

Grand Nagus Zek, "The Dogs of War," *Star Trek: Deep Space Nine* (also known as *Deep Space Nine, DS9,* and *Star Trek: DS9*), syndicated, 1999.

Grand Nagus Zek, "The Emperor's New Cloak," *Star Trek: Deep Space Nine* (also known as *Deep Space Nine, DS9,* and *Star Trek: DS9*), syndicated, 1999.

Mr. Fleming, "Book 'em, Griff," *Cosby,* CBS, 1999.

Mr. Fleming, "The Vesey Method," *Cosby,* CBS, 1999.

Dean Spencer Webb, "Don't Be Thrown," *Three Sisters,* NBC, 2001.

Dr. Howard Stiles, "Sight Unseen," *Crossing Jordan,* NBC, 2001.

"Clueless," *E! True Hollywood Story,* E! Entertainment Television, 2001.

Mr. Dune, "Falling Up," *Ally McBeal,* Fox, 2001.

Voice of Bertram, "Emission Impossible," *Family Guy* (animated), Fox, 2001.

Dr. Howard Stiles, "Crime & Punishment," *Crossing Jordan,* NBC, 2002.

Dr. Howard Stiles, "Scared Straight," *Crossing Jordan,* NBC, 2002.

Dr. Howard Stiles, "Secrets & Lies: Part 2," *Crossing Jordan,* NBC, 2002.

Voice of gauntlet, "Running the Gauntlet!," *TeamoSupremo* (animated), ABC and Toon Disney, 2002.

Dr. Howard Stiles, "Cruel and Unusual," *Crossing Jordan,* NBC, 2003.

Dr. Howard Stiles, "Fire and Ice," *Crossing Jordan*, NBC, 2003.

Dr. Howard Stiles, "Intruded," *Crossing Jordan*, NBC, 2003.

Dr. Howard Stiles, "Death Toll," *Crossing Jordan*, NBC, 2003.

Voice of Mr. Goldberg, "Going–Away Goose/Time to Clomb!," 2003.

Martin Grable, "Splat!," *Sex and the City* (also known as *S.A.T.C.* and *Sex and the Big City*), HBO, 2004.

Dr. Sigmund Von Oy, "Hold This," *Fat Actress*, 2005.

Dr. Sigmund Von Oy, "The Koi Effect," *Fat Actress*, 2005.

Now with Bill Moyers (also known as *Now*), PBS, 2005.

Arlos, "The Ties That Bind," *Stargate SG–1*, 2005.

Lonny Moon, "They Asked Me Why I Believe in You," *Desperate Housewives*, ABC, 2005.

Voice of Bertram, "Sibling Rivalry," *Family Guy* (animated), Fox, 2006.

Film professor, "Weeping Willow," *Law & Order: Criminal Intent* (also known as *Law & Order: CI*), CBS, 2006.

Garson Leeds, "I'm with Blank," *The Return of Jezebel James*, 2006.

Up Close with Carrie Keagan, 2007.

Animal handler, "Dog Eat Dog," *Cashmere Mafia*, 2008.

William Halsey, "LGB Tease," *The L Word*, 2008.

William Halsey, "Look Out, Hear They Come!," *The L Word*, 2008.

William Halsey, "Lights! Camera! Action!," *The L Word*, 2008.

Professor Roy Batters, "Snatched," *Law & Order: Special Victims Unit* (also known as *Law & Order: SVU* and *Special Victims Unit*), NBC, 2009.

The Sorcerer, "Let All the Children Boogie," *Life on Mars*, ABC, 2009.

Teddy Lempell, "The Beginning of the End," *ER*, NBC, 2009.

Made in Hollywood, 2009.

William Halsey, "Long Night's Journey Into Day," *The L Word*, 2009.

William Halsey, "Litmus Test," *The L Word*, 2009.

Dr. Alan Rubin, *The Daily Show* (also known as *The Daily Show with Jon Stewart*, *A Daily Show with Jon Stewart*, and *The Daily Show with Jon Stewart Global Edition*), 2010.

Sterling Biddle, "Don't Forget to Thank Mr. Zedeck," *Damages*, FX Network, 2010.

Television Appearances; Pilots:

Mr. Wendell Hall, *Clueless*, UPN, 1995.

Stop and Go, CBS, 1998.

Television Appearances; Specials:

Professor Silversmith, *How to Be a Perfect Person in Just Three Days*, PBS, 1984.

Blind Men, 1998.

A tekeroelantos naploja (also known as *The Diary of the Hurdy–Gurdy Man*), Magyar Televizio, 1999.

Stage Appearances:

Alice in Wonderland, New York City, 1974.

Siro and narrator of prologue, *The Mandrake*, New York Shakespeare Festival, Public Theatre, New York City, 1977.

Behemoth the cat, *The Master and Margarita*, New York Shakespeare Festival, Public Theatre, 1978.

Ilya, *Chinchilla*, Phoenix Theatre Company, Marymount Manhattan Theatre, New York City, 1979.

My Dinner with Andre, London production, 1980.

Julius Goldfarb, *The First Time*, New York City, 1983.

Speaker, *Schoenberg's Ode to Napoleon*, Symphony Space Theatre, New York City, 1984.

Father, Freddie, and Jasper, *Aunt Dan and Lemon*, New York Shakespeare Festival, Public Theatre, 1985.

The Fever (monologue), Public Theatre, 1990, then Second Stage Theatre, New York City, 1991, later La MaMa Experimental Theatre Club, New York City, 1991, then Lincoln Center Theatre, New York City, 1991.

Stage Work:

Director, *In the Dark* (opera), Lenox Arts Center, Lenox, MA, 1976.

RECORDINGS

Videos:

Himself, *As You Wish: The Story of the Princess Bride* (short documentary), Metro–Goldwyn–Mayer/United Artists Home Entertainment, 2001.

"Clueless": The Class of '95, Paramount Home Video, 2005.

USIDent TV: Surveilling the Southland, Sony, 2008.

Video Games:

Voice of Rex, *Toy Story*, 1996.

Voice of Rex, *Toy Story Activity Center*, 1996.

Voice of Gilbert Huph, *The Incredibles*, 2004.

Voice of Vizzini, *The Princess Bride Game*, Worldwide Biggies, 2008.

WRITINGS

Stage Plays:

Four Meals in May, 1967.

Our Late Night, New York Shakespeare Festival, Public Theatre, New York City, 1975, published by Targ Editions, 1984.

Librettist, *In the Dark* (opera; music Allen Shawn), Lenox Arts Center, Lenox, MA, 1976.

Three Short Plays (also known as *A Thought in Three Parts;* contains "Summer Evening," "The Youth Hostel," and "Mr. Frivolous"), New York Shakespeare Festival, Public Theatre, 1976, published in *Wordplays,* Volume 2, Performing Arts Journal Publications, 1982.

The Mandrake (translation of *La mandragola* by Niccolo Machiavelli), New York Shakespeare Festival, Public Theatre, 1977, published by Dramatists Play Service, c. 1978.

The Family Play, New York City, 1978.

Marie and Bruce, London production, 1979, then New York Shakespeare Festival, Public Theatre, 1980, published by Grove, 1980.

(With Andre Gregory) *My Dinner with Andre,* London production, 1980.

The Hotel Play, La MaMa Experimental Theatre Club, New York City, 1981, published by Dramatists Play Service, c. 1982.

Mandragola (musical adaptation of his earlier adaptation, *The Mandrake;* music and lyrics by Howard Goodall), London production, 1984.

Aunt Dan and Lemon, New York Shakespeare Festival, Public Theatre, 1985, published by Grove, 1985.

The Fever (monologue), Public Theatre, 1990, then Second Stage Theatre, New York City, 1991, later La MaMa Experimental Theatre Club, New York City, 1991, then Lincoln Center Theatre, New York City, 1991, published by Noonday, 1991.

The Designated Mourner, Royal National Theatre, London, c. 1996, later New York City, 2000, published by Faber & Faber, 1996.

The libretto *The Music Teacher* (music by Allen Shawn), Minetta Lane Theatre, New York City, 2006.

Also author of *The Hospital Play; Our Late Night,* Joseph Papp Public Theatre, New York City; *Aunt Dan and Lemon, Night,* Joseph Papp Public Theatre; and *The Old Man.*

Screenplays:

(With Andre Gregory) *My Dinner with Andre* (based on his play), New Yorker, 1981, published by Grove, 1981.

The Designated Mourner (based on his play), First Look Pictures, 1997.

Marie and Bruce (also known as *Marie & Bruce* and *Wallace Shawn's Marie & Bruce*), New Films International, 2004.

The Fever, HBO, 2004.

Teleplays; Movies:

The Fever (based on his play), HBO, 2003.

Anthologies:

Four Plays, Noonday, 1997.

Plays One, Faber & Faber, 1997.

Contributor of articles to periodicals.

OTHER SOURCES

Books:

Contemporary Dramatists, Sixth edition, St. James Press, 1999.

Periodicals:

American Theatre, September, 1997, p. 12.

Interview, March, 1989, pp. 72–75, 124, 126.

National Review, June 16, 1997, p. 56.

SHEFFER, Craig 1960–

PERSONAL

Born April 23, 1960, in York, PA; father, a prison guard and scriptwriter; mother, a worker in a nursing home; children: (with Gabrielle Anwar) Willow. *Education:* Studied drama at East Stroudsburg State College. *Avocational Interests:* Motorcycle riding, rodeos, boxing, writing fiction and poetry, playing guitar and harmonica, photography.

Addresses: *Agent*—The Gersh Agency, 232 North Canon Dr., Beverly Hills, CA 90210. *Manager*—Kramer Management, 5699 Kahan Rd., 275, Agoura Hills, CA 91301.

Career: Actor and producer. Desert Wind Films, cofounder. Appeared in television commercials. Also worked as a waiter, bus person, steel mill worker, and a garbage collector, and as a valet to Count Basie.

Member: Screen Actors Guild, SANE (formerly National Committee for a Sane Nuclear Policy).

Awards, Honors: DramaLogue Award, 1988, for *G. R. Point.*

CREDITS

Film Appearances:

Bryon Douglas, *That Was Then ... This Is Now,* Paramount, 1985.

Frankie, *Voyage of the Rock Aliens,* Prism Entertainment, 1985.

Joe Fisk, *Fire with Fire* (also known as *Captive Hearts*), Paramount, 1986.

Hardy Jenns, *Some Kind of Wonderful,* Paramount, 1987.

Eddie McGuinn, *Split Decisions,* New Century/Vista, 1988.

Aaron Boone/Cabal, *Nightbreed* (also known as *Clive Barker's "Nightbreed"* and *Night Breed*), Twentieth Century–Fox, 1990.

Randall Atkins, *Blue Desert* (also known as *Silent Victim*), Academy Home Entertainment, 1991.

Zane, *Instant Karma,* Metro–Goldwyn–Mayer/United Artists, 1991.

Norman Maclean, *A River Runs Through It,* Columbia, 1992.

Rau, *Eye of the Storm* (also known as *Jack Higgins: Die Krieger*), New Line Home Video, 1992.

Allan Dallis, *Fire in the Sky,* Paramount, 1993.

Joe Kane, *The Program,* Buena Vista, 1993.

R. J., *Fire on the Amazon* (also known as *Lost Paradise*), 1993.

Cliff, *The Road Killers* (also known as *Roadflower*), Miramax, 1994.

Frank, *Sleep with Me,* Metro–Goldwyn–Mayer/United Artists, 1994.

Henri Guillaumet, *Wings of Courage* (also known as *Guillaumet, les ailes du courage*), Sony Pictures Classics, 1995.

Jack Cooper, *The Desperate Trail,* 1995.

King, *The Grave,* 1996.

Lance, *Head Above Water,* 1996.

Nick Seger, *Executive Power,* 1997.

Bobby Ray, *Flypaper,* 1997.

Connor Mcewen, *Double Take,* Twice Removed Productions, 1997.

Joseph, *Bliss,* Sony Pictures Entertainment, 1997.

Nick Seger, *Executive Power,* Naegele–Derrick Productions, 1997.

Adam Ellis, *The Fall,* Movie Screen Entertainment, 1998.

Laird Atkins, *Shadow of Doubt,* 1998.

Martin, *Fear of Flying* (also known as *Turbulence II: Fear of Flying*), 1999.

Mordred, *Merlin: The Return,* Peakviewing Transatlantic, 1999.

The Pavilion, Quantum Entertainment, 1999.

Quest for Atlantis, 1999.

Brian Goodman, *Deep Core* (also known as *Deep Core 2000*), Paramount/New City Releasing, 2000.

Detective Joseph Thorne, *Hellraiser: Inferno* (also known as *Hellraiser V: Inferno*), Dimension Films, 2000.

Woody Miller, *Net Worth,* Curb Entertainment, 2000.

Mike, *Maze* (also known as *Touched*), 2000.

Nick Watts, *Turbulence 3: Heavy Metal,* 2001.

Gordon Childs, *Deadly Little Secrets,* Mainline Releasing/ThinkFilm/Velocity Home Entertainment, 2001.

Marco, *Save It for Later,* Ananda Films, 2001.

Marty Bauer, *Flying Virus,* American Cinema International, 2001.

Wesley Clayborne, *Ritual* (also known as *Tales from the Crypt Presents: Revelation* and *Tales from the Crypt Presents: Voodoo*), Miramax/Dimension/RKO Radio Pictures, 2001.

Berserker, Peakviewing Transatlantic, 2001.

Detective Stratten, *Final Breakdown* (also known as *Turnaround*), Niko Filmworks, 2002.

From Russia to Hollywood: The 100–Year Odyssey of Chekhov and Shdanoff (documentary), 2002.

Lowell, *Dracula II: Ascension,* Buena Vista Home Video, 2003.

Shamus, *Mob Dot Com,* Regent Entertainment, 2003.

Lowell, *Dracula II: Ascension* (also known as *Wes Craven Presents "Dracula II: Ascension"*), Dimension Films, 2003.

Retrosexual: The 80's, VH1, 2004.

Alan, *Prodigal Son,* 2004.

Tom Mitchell, *Tom's Nu Heaven,* 2005.

Frank Hossom, *The Second Front,* MTI Home Video, 2005.

Interviewer, *Find Love,* 2006.

Morton, *Love Lies Bleeding,* Sony, 2008.

Kenneth, *While She Was Out* (also known as *Alive*), Anchor Bay, 2008.

Bill, *Ashley's Ashes,* FKF Media, 2010.

Film Executive Producer:

Instant Karma, Metro–Goldwyn–Mayer/United Artists, 1991.

Demolition Man, Warner Bros., 1993.

Film Director:

Prodigal Son, 2004.

(And producer) *American Crude,* Sony, 2008.

Television Appearances; Series:

Ian Hayden, *One Life to Live,* ABC, c. 1980.

Brian Chadway, *The Hamptons,* ABC, 1983.

Voice of Mick, *Teen Wolf,* 1986–88.

Keith Scott, *One Tree Hill,* The WB, 2003–2008.

Television Appearances; Miniseries:

Voice, *500 Nations,* CBS, 1995.

Constant Bradley, *A Season in Purgatory,* CBS, 1996.

Television Appearances; Movies:

Rob Harrison, *Babycakes* (also known as *Big Girls Don't Cry* and *Sugarbaby*), CBS, 1989.

First lieutenant Marshall Buxton, *In Pursuit of Honor,* HBO, 1995.

Jack Cooper, *The Desperate Trail,* TNT, 1995.

Mike, *Bloodknot,* 1995.

Henry (some sources cite Lance), *Head above Water,* HBO, 1996.

King, *The Grave,* HBO, 1996.

Dr. Douglas, *Miss Evers' Boys,* HBO, 1997.

Jack Safrenek, *Rhapsody in Bloom,* Starz!, 1998.

Laird Atkins, *Shadow of Doubt* (also known as *Reasonable Doubt*), Cinemax, 1998.
Martin Messerman, *Turbulence 2: Fear of Flying* (also known as *Fear of Flying*), Cinemax, 1999.
Dr. Paul Venters, *Without Malice*, 2000.
Mike, *Maze* (also known as *Touched*), Starz!, 2001.
Nick Watts, *Turbulence 3: Heavy Metal* (also known as *Turbulence 3: Metal hurlant*), Cinemax, 2001.
Cabin Pressure, 2001.
Quinn Halloran/John Williams, *Long Lost Son*, 2006.
Sheriff, *Lies Between Friends*, Hallmark Channel, 2010.

Television Appearances; Specials:
Ernie Bishop, Ed, and the bridge keeper, *Merry Christmas, George Bailey*, PBS, 1997.
Himself, *The Reality Trip*, 1997.

Television Appearances; Episodic:
Norman Maclean, "Floden som rinner fram," *Nyhetsmorgon*, 1993.
Alternative prize to Budd, "You Can't Miss," *Married with Children* (also known as *Married ... with Children*), Fox, 1993.
Martin Antonelli, "Separation," *Family Law*, CBS, 2001.
Headliners and Legends: Cameron Diaz, MSNBC, 2001.
Andrew Kane, "Get Your Mack On," *Fastlane*, Fox, 2002.
Older Robert Wheeler, "Ghost Dance," *Into the West*, TNT, 2005.
Federal Marshal Daniel Wayne, "A Very Juliet Episode," *Psych*, USA Network, 2010.

Stage Appearances:
Alan, *Torch Song Trilogy*, Little Theatre, New York City, 1983.
Billy Dukes, *Punchy*, Westside Mainstage Theatre, New York City, 1983.
Larkin, *Fresh Horses*, Workshop of the Players Art Theatre, New York City, 1986.

Appeared in *G. R. Point*, Los Angeles production; also appeared in productions of *The American Dream*, *Death of a Salesman*, *The Glass Menagerie*, and *The Tempest*.

RECORDINGS

Videos:
Deep Currents: Making "A River Runs Through It," Sony, 2009.

WRITINGS

Film Songs:
"Oh Daddy Oh," and "Mano A Mano," *American Crude*, Sony, 2008.

Screenplays:
American Crude, Sony, 2008.

OTHER SOURCES

Periodicals:
Detour, April, 1997, pp. 62–66.
Vanity Fair, May, 1996, p. 429.

SHERIDAN, Jim 1949–

PERSONAL

Born February 6, 1949, in Dublin, Ireland; emigrated to Canada then New York City, 1981, returned to Ireland, 1989; son of Peter (a railroad worker and actor) and Anna Sheridan; married Fran, 1972; children: Naomi (an author), Kristen (an author), Tess. *Education:* Graduated from University College, Dublin, Ireland; also attended New York University's Institute of Film and Television.

Addresses: *Office*—Hell's Kitchen, Inc., 92 Merion Rd., Ballsbridge, Dublin 4, Ireland. *Agent*—Creative Artists Agency, 2000 Avenue of the Stars, Los Angeles, CA 90067.

Career: Director, producer, writer, and actor. Hell's Kitchen Productions (a production company), partner, 1989. Project Arts Theatre, Dublin, Ireland, director, 1976–80; New York Irish Arts Center, New York City, artistic director, 1982–87; Children's Theatre Company, Dublin, Ireland, founder; worked at the Lyric Theatre, Belfast, Northern Ireland, the Abbey Theatre, Dublin, Ireland, and the English 7:84 Company; Mr. Pussy's Cafe de Luxe, Dublin, Ireland, cofounder (with singers Bono and Gavin Friday), 1994; previously worked as a cab driver and club manager.

Awards, Honors: Fringe Award, best play, Edinburgh Fringe Festival, 1983, for *Spike in the First World War;* Academy Award nominations, best adapted screenplay (with Shane Connaughton) and best director, WGA Screen Award nomination (with Connaughton), best screenplay based on material from another medium, Writers Guild of America, Prize of the Ecumenical Jury—Special Mention, Montreal World Film Festival, 1989, Independent Spirit Award, best foreign film, Film Award nominations, best film (with Noel Pearson) and best adapted screenplay (with Connaughton), British Academy of Film and Television Arts, Audience Award, feature, Angers European First Film Festival, 1990, Guild Film Award—Silver, foreign film, 1991, all for

My Left Foot; Academy Award nominations, best director, best picture, and best adapted screenplay (with Terry George), WGA Screen Award nomination (with George), best screenplay based on material previously produced or published, Writers Guild of America, 1993, Golden Berlin Bear, Berlin International Film Festival, Film Award nomination (with George), best adapted screenplay, British Academy of Film and Television Arts, 1994, *Evening Standard* British Film Award, best film, 1995, all for *In the Name of the Father;* Reader Jury Award, *Berlin Morgenpost,* Golden Berlin Bear nomination, Golden Globe Award nomination, best director of a motion picture, 1998, Goya Award, best European film, 1999, all for *The Boxer;* Excellence Award, Boston Irish Film Festival, 2003; Audience Award, best feature film, AFI Fest, Audience Award, best feature, High Falls Film Festival, British Independent Film Award nomination, best director, Grand Prix, Ghent International Film Festival, Humanitas Prize (with others), Sundance Film Company, National Board of Review Award (with others), best screenplay—original, 2003, Academy Award nomination (with others), best writing—original screenplay, Critics Choice Award (with others), best writer, Broadcast Film Critics Association, Critics Choice Award nomination, best director, Golden Globe Award nomination (with others), best screenplay—motion picture, Golden Kinnaree Award, best director, Bangkok International Film Festival, Golden Kinnaree Award nomination, best film, Golden Satellite Award, best director, International Press Academy, Independent Spirit Award nominations, best director, and best feature (with Arthur Lappin), Online Film Critics Society Award nomination (with others), Phoenix Film Critics Society Award (with others), best screenplay—original, Phoenix Film Critics Society Award nomination, best director, WGA Screen Award nomination (with others), best original screenplay, Writers Guild of America, 2004, all for *In America;* Distinguished Achievement Award, Palm Springs International Film Festival, 2004; Britannia Award, artistic excellence, BAFTA/LA Britannia Awards, Irish Film and Television Award, best director for film, 2010, for *Brothers.*

CREDITS

Film Work:

Director, *My Left Foot* (also known as *My Left Foot: The Story of Christy Brown*), Miramax, 1989.

Director and (with Noel Pearson) producer, *The Field,* Avenue Pictures, 1990.

Producer and director, *In the Name of the Father,* Universal, 1993.

Producer, *Some Mother's Son,* Columbia, 1996.

Producer and director, *The Boxer,* Universal, 1997.

Producer, *Agnes Browne* (also known as *The Mammy*), October Films, 1999.

Executive producer, *Borstal Boy,* Strand Releasing, 2000.

Producer, *On the Edge,* Universal, 2000.

Executive producer, *Bloody Sunday,* Paramount Classics, 2002.

Director and producer, *In America,* Twentieth Century–Fox, 2002.

Producer and director, *Get Rich or Die Tryin',* Paramount, 2005.

Producer, *A Portrait of an Artist: The Making of "Get Rich or Die Tryin'"* (short documentary), Paramount, 2006.

Director, *Brothers* (also known as *My Brother*), Lions Gate Films, 2009.

Film Appearances:

Jonathan Swift/Dean Swift, *Words Upon the Window Pane,* 1994.

Himself, *Irish Cinema: Ourselves Alone?,* 1995.

C.P.A.D. leader, *The General* (also known as *I Once Had a Life*), Sony Pictures Classics, 1998.

Himself, *Fighting for Peace: Inside "The Boxer,"* 1998.

Bob Bishop, *Best,* 2001.

Himself, *Bloody Sunday: History Retold* (short documentary), Paramount Home Video, 2003.

Narrator, *The Carpenter and His Clumsy Wife,* 2004.

King Philip V of Spain, *The Bridge of San Luis Rey,* Fine Line. 2004.

Himself, *A Portrait of an Artist: The Making of "Get Rich or Die Tryin'"* (short documentary), Paramount, 2006.

Himself, *The Making of "Anton"* (documentary), East-West Distribution, 2009.

Himself, *Re–Made in the USA: How Brodre Became Brothers* (short film), Lions Gate Films Home Entertainment, 2010.

Himself, *Jim Sheridan: Film and Family,* Lions Gate Films Home Entertainment, 2010.

Stage Work:

Director, *Shadow of a Gunman,* Abbey Theatre, Dublin, Ireland, 1981, then Actors Playhouse, New York Irish Arts Center, New York City, 1984.

Television Appearances; Specials:

The 62nd Annual Academy Awards, ABC, 1992.

Presenter, *The 66th Annual Academy Awards Presentation,* ABC, 1994.

The 2004 IFP/West Independent Spirit Awards, Independent Film Channel and Bravo, 2004.

Happy Birthday Oscar Wilde, BBC, 2004.

What If, 2006.

Presenter, *The 4th Irish Film and Television Awards,* 2007.

The 6th Annual Irish Film and Television Awards, 2009.

Music of Ireland: Welcome Home, 2010.

Music of Ireland: Welcome to America, 2010.

Television Appearances; Episodic:

Himself, "Om filmen 'I faderns namn,'" *Nyhetsmorgon,* 1994.

Charlie Rose (also known as *The Charlie Rose Show*), PBS, 1997.
The Late Late Show, CBS, 2003.
The Late Late Show with Craig Ferguson, CBS, 2005.
Xpose, 2008.
Made in Hollywood, 2009.

WRITINGS

Screenplays:
(With Shane Connaughton) *My Left Foot* (also known as *My Left Foot: The Story of Christy Brown;* based on the writings of Christy Brown), Miramax, 1989.
(With Noel Pearson) *The Field* (based on a play by J. B. Keane), Avenue Pictures, 1990.
Into the West, Miramax, 1992.
(With Terry George) *In the Name of the Father,* Universal, 1993.
Some Mother's Son, Columbia, 1996.
The Boxer, Universal, 1997.
(With Naomi Sheridan and Kirsten Sheridan) *In America,* Twentieth Century–Fox, 2002.

Plays:
Mobile Homes, produced at Project Arts Center, Dublin, Ireland, published by Co–Op Books, 1978.
Spike in the First World War, produced 1983.

Also wrote other plays.

OTHER SOURCES

Books:
International Dictionary of Films and Filmmakers, Volume 2: *Directors,* St. James Press, 1996.

Periodicals:
Cineaste, summer, 1998, p. 13.
Entertainment Weekly, March, 1994, p. 100.
New Yorker, March 21, 1994, p. 218.
USA Today, November 1, 2005.

SHERMAN, Howard
    See HOWARD, Sherman

SHOR, Miriam 1971–

PERSONAL

Born July 25, 1971, in Minneapolis, MN; daughter of Francis Shor (a scholar and university professor); children: one. *Education:* University of Michigan, B.A., English, and some sources cite B.F.A., English and theatre.

Addresses: *Agent*—William Morris Agency, 151 South El Camino Dr., Beverly Hills, CA 90212.

Career: Actress.

Member: Actors' Equity Association.

Awards, Honors: Screen Idol Award, best supporting actress, Los Angeles Outfest, and Golden Satellite Award nomination, best supporting actress in a comedy or musical, International Press Academy, both 2002, for *Hedwig and the Angry Inch.*

CREDITS

Stage Appearances:
A Man for All Seasons, Connecticut production, c. 1990.
Polly Peachum, *The Threepenny Opera,* Wilma Theatre, Philadelphia, PA, 1997–98.
Yitzhak, *Hedwig and the Angry Inch,* Jane Street Theatre, New York City, 1998–2000.
Hair (musical), City Center Theatre, New York City, 2001.
Mary, *Merrily We Roll Along,* Eisenhower Theatre, John F. Kennedy Center for the Performing Arts, Washington, DC, 2002.
Ruth Hoch, *Book of Days,* Signature Theatre Company, Peter Norton Space, New York City, 2002.
Sh–K–Boom Room Holiday Concert, Village Theatre, New York City, 2002.
Kate, *Worm Day,* DR 2 Theatre, 2003.
Mondo Drama, Drama Department, Greenwich House Theatre, New York City, 2003.
Boy, Primary Stages, New York City, 2004.
Ida Head, *Dedication or The Stuff of Dreams,* 59E59 Theater A, New York City, 2005.
Sandrine/Marvalyn/Marci/Rhonda, *Almost, Maine,* Daryl Roth Theatre, New York City, 2006.
Gloria, *Scarcity,* Linda Gross Theatre, New York City, 2007.

Appeared in *Perversion Incognito,* Catch a Rising Star; *Present Laughter,* Centennial Theatre Festival; in *The Lion in Winter* and *Oleanna.*

Major Tours:
Appeared in a touring production of *Fiddler on the Roof,* U.S. cities.

Film Appearances:

Second blind date, *Entropy,* Interlight/Phoenician Entertainment/Tribeca Productions, 1999.

Stephanie, *Flushed,* First Run Features, 1999.

Beth, *Snow Days,* Curb Entertainment, 1999, released as *Let It Snow,* Artistic License, 2001.

Carol/penthouse hostess, *Bedazzled,* Twentieth Century–Fox, 2000.

Yitzhak, *Hedwig and the Angry Inch,* Fine Line, 2001.

Set Set Spike, 2002.

Laura, *Second Born,* 2003.

Lara Griffin, *Lbs.,* Truly Indie, 2004.

Vanessa, *Pizza,* IFC Films, 2005.

Cheryl, *Shortbus,* A–Film, 2006.

Stephanie, *The Cake Eaters,* Eagle, 2007.

Anne, *Puppy Love,* Intelligent Life, 2008.

Janet Thompson, *The Spirit of '76: The Making of "Swingtown,"* 2008.

Janet Thompson, *Have a Nice Revolution: Sex & Morality in 1970's America,* 2008.

Television Appearances; Series:

Cheryl, *Then Came You,* ABC, 2000.

Julie Hermann, *Inside Schwartz,* NBC, 2001.

Becca, *Big Day,* ABC, 2006–2007.

Carrie Parsons, *Damages,* FX Network, 2007–10.

Janet Thompson, *Swingtown,* CBS, 2008.

Television Appearances; Episodic:

Rosie, "Old Yeller," *Becker,* CBS, 2000.

Rachel Blake, "Just Lie Back," *Deadline,* NBC, 2001.

Justine, "Double Dating," *Married to the Kellys,* ABC, 2004.

Christine, "King Corn," *The West Wing* (also known as *The White House*), NBC, 2005.

Gwen Waters, "BB," *My Name Is Earl,* NBC, 2006.

Rebecca Slater, "30," *Law & Order: Criminal Intent* (also known as *Law & Order: CI*), NBC, 2007.

Entertainment Tonight (also known as *E.T.* and *This Week in Entertainment*), syndicated, 2008.

The Late Late Show with Craig Ferguson, CBS, 2008.

Bonnie, "The Case of the Stolen Sperm," *Bored to Death,* HBO, 2009.

Television Appearances; Movies:

Mary Alice, *The Dan Show,* 2003.

Television Appearances; Other:

Mary Alice, *The Dan Finnerty Comedy Project* (pilot), ABC, 2003.

Appeared in *Invisible Camera Guy* (also known as *ICG*), Lifetime.

RECORDINGS

Albums:

Hedwig and the Angry Inch (original cast recording), Atlantic, 1999.

Videos:

Whether You Like It or Not: The Story of Hedwig, New Line Home Video, 2001.

Video Games:

BioShock, 2007.

OTHER SOURCES

Periodicals:

Detroit Free Press, March 29, 2000.

SHOU, Robin 1960–
 (Robin Chou)

PERSONAL

Born July 17, 1960, in Hong Kong; immigrated to the United States, 1971; father, a tailor. *Education:* California State University, B.S., civil engineering. *Avocational Interests:* Ceramic classes, painting, welding, and woodworking.

Career: Actor, fight choreographer, director, and producer. Worked as a civil engineer for a year and a half.

CREDITS

Film Appearances:

Robin, *Yat goh,* 1987.

(As Robin Chou) Lan Si Han, *Zhan long* (also known as *Death Cage*), 1988.

Hospital assassin, *The Big Heat* (also known as *Cheng shi te jing*), Tai Seng Video Marketing, 1988.

(Uncredited) Bodyguard, *Huang jia shi jie zhi II: Ci xiong da dao* (also known as *In the Line of Duty III* and *In the Line of Duty III: Force of the Dragon*), Universe Laser & Video, 1988.

Killer, *Sing si jin jang* (also known as *City War*), 1988.

Hitman, *Zhi zun wu shang* (also known as *Casino Raiders*), Golden Harvest Company, 1989.

Coffin Rope's man, *Wo zai hei she hui de ri zi* (also known as *My Days Inside the Underworld* and *Tridas: The Inside Story*), 1989.

966, *Sheng gang qi bing di san ji* (also known as *Long Arm of the Law Part 3*), 1989.

Iron Club, *Long zhi zheng ba* (also known as *Burning Ambition*), 1989.

Tomoriki Jiono, *Dong fang lao hu* (also known as *The Cyprus Tigers*), Tai Seng Entertainment, 1989.

Wai Loong, *Chi se da feng bao* (also known as *Death Blow* and *Fatal Termination*), 1990.

Waise Chow, *Tiger Cage 2* (also known as *Sai hak chin, Dirty Money Laundering,* and *Tiger Cage II*), D & B Film Distribution, 1990.

Hawk, *Eastern Heroes,* 1991.

Night–monster, *Hong tian long* (also known as *Fury in Red*), D & B Film Distribution, 1991.

Paul, *Di xia bing gong chang* (also known as *Forbidden Arsenal* and *In the Line of Duty 6*), 1991.

Robin, *Hei mao II* (also known as *Black Cat 2: Assassination of President Yeltsin*), 1992.

A Lung, *Zhi fa wei long* (also known as *Fatal Chase*), 1992.

Co Chi Pang, *Zhi zun te jing,* Dimension Films, 1992.

Dragon Lee, *Honor and Glory* (also known as *Zong heng tian xia* and *Angel the Kickboxer*), 1993.

Gang leader, *Long hu xin feng yun: Zhi tou hao tong ji fan* (also known as *The Most Wanted*), 1994.

Liu Kang, *Mortal Kombat,* New Line Cinema, 1995.

Himself, *"Mortal Kombat": Behind the Scenes* (short film), 1995.

Gobei, *Beverly Hills Ninja,* TriStar, 1997.

Liu Kang, *Mortal Kombat: Annihilation,* New Line Cinema, 1997.

Evan, *Lost Time: The Movie* (short film), 2003.

Evan, narrator, and himself, *Red Trousers: The Life of the Hong Kong Stuntmen* (short documentary), Tai Seng Video Marketing, 2003.

Pirate leader, *DOA: Dead or Alive* (also known as *DOA*), Dimension Films, 2006.

Jackie Chong, *18 Fingers of Death!,* Screen Media Ventures, 2006.

14K, *Death Race,* Universal, 2008.

Himself, *Man of a Thousand Faces* (documentary), 2008.

Gen, *Street Fighter: The Legend of Chun–Li,* Twentieth Century–Fox, 2009.

Film Work:

Fight choreographer: additional action sequences and additional crew, *Mortal Kombat,* New Line Cinema, 1995.

Fight choreographer, *Mortal Kombat: Annihilation,* New Line Cinema, 1997.

(Uncredited) Trainer: Milla Jovovich, *Resident Evil* (also known as *Biohazard*), Screen Gems, 2002.

Producer and director, *Red Trousers: The Life of the Hong Kong Stuntmen* (short documentary), Tai Seng Video Marketing, 2003.

Director, *Lost Time: The Movie* (short film), 2003.

Television Appearances; Movies:

Liang Hong, *Forbidden Nights,* CBS, 1990.

Television Appearances; Episodic:

Ton Siu, "The Red Pole," *Yellowthread Street,* YTV, 1990.

Journalist Feng, "Lost and Found," *Soldier Soldier,* ITV, 1992.

Major Ronald Neguchi, "Nightmare," *The Outer Limits* (also known as *The New Outer Limits*), Showtime, 1998.

Bo–Lin Chen in 1983, "Chinatown," *Cold Case,* CBS, 2009.

WRITINGS

Screenplays:

Red Trousers: The Life of the Hong Kong Stuntmen (short documentary), Tai Seng Video Marketing, 2003.

SHULER–DONNER, Lauren 1949–
(Lauren Shuler)

PERSONAL

Born June 23, 1949, in Cleveland, OH; married Richard Donner (a director, producer, and actor; also known as Richard Schwartzberg), 1985. *Education:* Boston University, B.S., film and communications.

Addresses: *Office*—Donners' Co., 9465 Wilshire Blvd., Suite 420/470, Beverly Hills, CA 90212. *Agent*—Ann Blanchard, William Morris Agency, 151 El Camino Dr., Beverly Hills, CA 90212. *Lawyer*—Hirsch, Wallerstein, Hayum, Matlof, and Fishman, 10100 Santa Monica Blvd., 17th Floor, Los Angeles, CA 90067.

Career: Producer. Worked as an editor of educational films and a television camera operator; Motown Films, began as story editor, became director of creative affairs; Donners' Co., Beverly Hills, CA, principal and producer.

Member: Hollywood Electronic Camera Union.

Awards, Honors: Distinguished Alumni Award, Boston University, 1987; Shaker Heights High School Hall of Fame, 1988; Golden Satellite Award nomination (with Nora Ephron), best motion picture comedy or musical, International Press Academy, 1999, for *You've Got Mail;* Susan B. Anthony "Failure is Impossible" Award, 2006; Women in Film Crystal Award, 2006; Ojai Film Festival Lifetime Achievement Award, 2008.

CREDITS

Film Executive Producer:

Assassins (also known as *Day of Reckoning*), Warner Bros., 1995.

Free Willy 3: The Rescue, Warner Bros., 1997.
Volcano, Twentieth Century–Fox, 1997.
Bulworth, Twentieth Century–Fox, 1998.
Out Cold, Buena Vista, 2001.
Just Married, Twentieth Century–Fox, 2003.

Film Producer:
(As Lauren Shuler; with Lynn Loring) *Mr. Mom* (also known as *Mr. Mum*), Twentieth Century–Fox, 1983.
(As Shuler; with Richard Donner) *Ladyhawke,* Warner Bros., 1985.
(As Shuler) *St. Elmo's Fire,* Columbia, 1985.
(As Shuler) *Pretty in Pink,* Paramount, 1986.
Three Fugitives, Buena Vista, 1989.
Radio Flyer, Columbia, 1992.
Dave (also known as *Mr. President*), Warner Bros., 1993.
Free Willy, Warner Bros., 1993.
The Favor (also known as *The Indecent Favour*), Orion, 1994.
Free Willy 2: The Adventure Home, Warner Bros., 1995.
You've Got Mail (also known as *You Have Mail*), Warner Bros., 1998.
Any Given Sunday (also known as *Gridiron, The League, Monday Night, On Any Given Sunday,* and *Playing Hurt*), Warner Bros., 1999.
X–Men (also known as *X–Men: The Movie* and *X–Men 1.5*), Twentieth Century–Fox, 1999.
Timeline, Paramount, 2003.
X2 (also known as *X–2* and *X–2: X–Men United*), Twentieth Century–Fox, 2003.
Constantine, Warner Bros., 2005.
She's the Man, DreamWorks, 2006.
X–Men: The Last Stand (also known as *X–Men 3, X3,* and *X–Men: Final Decision*), Warner Bros., 2006.
Unaccompanied Minors, Warner Bros., 2006.
The Secret Life of Bees, Twentieth Century–Fox, 2008.
Hotel for Dogs, Paramount, 2009.
X–Men Origins: Wolverine (also known as *Wolverine: X–Men Zero*), Twentieth Century–Fox, 2009.
Cirque du Freak: The Vampire's Assistant (also known as *Circus of the Freak* and *Darren Shan*), Universal, 2009.

Film Appearances:
Nurse, *Lethal Weapon 3,* Warner Bros., 1992.
Bathhouse maid, *Maverick,* Warner Bros., 1994.

Television Work; Series:
Executive producer, *Free Willy* (animated), ABC, beginning 1994.
Producer, *Babes in the Woods,* ITV, beginning 1998.

Television Executive Producer; Pilots:
Brooklyn Princesses, ABC, 2002.
The Thomas Crown Affair, NBC, 2003.

Television Work; Movies:
(As Lauren Shuler) Producer, *Amateur Night at the Dixie Bar and Grill,* NBC, 1979.

Television Work; Specials:
Executive producer, *Cameo by Night,* NBC, 1987.

Television Appearances; Specials:
A Whale of a Business, PBS, 1997.
Signed, Sealed, Delivered, Romance Classics, 1998.
X–Men: The Mutant Watch, Fox, 2000.
Sixteen Candles: The E! True Hollywood Story, E! Entertainment Television, 2001.
X–pose: X2 Mutants Uncovered, Fox, 2003.
Women on Top: Hollywood and Power, AMC, 2003.
The Blockbuster Imperative, Trio, 2003.
Presenter, *Premiere Magazine's 12th Annual Women in Hollywood Awards,* AMC, 2005.
Starz Inside: Unforgettably Evil, Starz!, 2009.

Television Appearances; Episodic:
"The Making of 'You've Got Mail': A Conversation with Nora Ephron," *HBO First Look,* HBO, 1998.
"Constantine: Heaven, Hell and Beyond," *HBO First Look,* HBO, 2005.
The Movie Loft, 2009.

RECORDINGS

Videos:
De Superman a Spider–Man: L'aventure des super–heros, 2002.
X–Men Production Scrapbook, Twentieth Century–Fox, 2003.
The Uncanny Suspects, Twentieth Century–Fox, 2003.
The Second Uncanny Issue of X–Men! Making "X2" (also known as *The Second Uncanny Issue of X–Men*), Twentieth Century–Fox, 2003.
The Secret Origin of X–Men, Twentieth Century–Fox, 2003.
Journey through "Timeline," Paramount, 2004.
The Textures of "Timeline," Paramount, 2004.
X–Men: The Excitement Continues, Twentieth Century–Fox, 2006.
X–Men: Evolution of a Trilogy, Twentieth Century–Fox, 2006.
A Home for Everyone: The Making of "Hotel for Dogs," Paramount Home Video, 2009.
"Hotel for Dogs": K–9 Casting, Paramount Home Video, 2009.
"Hotel for Dogs": That's the Coolest Thing I've Ever Seen!, Paramount Home Video, 2009.

OTHER SOURCES

Periodicals:
People Weekly, August 9, 1993, pp. 40–41.

SILVER, Michael B. 1967–
(Michael Buchman, Michael Silver, Michael Buchman Silver, Mike Silver)

PERSONAL

Full name, Michael Buchman Silver; born July 8, 1967, in New York, NY; brother of Amanda "Mandy" Silver (a writer); grandson of Sidney Buchman (a screenwriter and studio executive); married Katie Mitchell (an actress), October 22, 2000. *Education:* Graduate of Brown University. *Avocational Interests:* Playing tenor saxophone.

Addresses: *Agent*—Pakula, King, and Associates, 9229 West Sunset Blvd., Suite 315, Los Angeles, CA 90069. *Manager*—Charlton Blackburne, A Management, 500 South Buena Vista St., Suite 1C–12, Burbank, CA 91251.

Career: Actor, producer, director, and writer.

CREDITS

Television Appearances; Series:
(Sometimes credited as Michael Buchman Silver) Dr. Paul Myers, a recurring role, *ER*, NBC, between 1995 and 2009.
(As Michael Buchman Silver) Assistant District Attorney Leo Cohen, a recurring role, *NYPD Blue* (also known as *N.Y.P.D.*), ABC, 1996–99, 2001, 2004.
District Attorney Investigator Will Campbell, a recurring role, *For the People* (also known as *Para la gente*), Lifetime, 2002.
Agent Peter Elliott, a recurring role, *CSI: Miami*, CBS, between 2004 and 2006.
David Stein, a recurring role, *Beautiful People*, ABC Family, 2005.

Television Appearances; Movies:
Lieutenant Lonner, *The Enemy Within*, HBO, 1994.
(As Michael Buchman Silver) Tony Lewis, *The Adventures of Young Indiana Jones: Hollywood Follies* (also known as *Young Indiana Jones and the Hollywood Follies*), The Family Channel, 1994.
(As Michael Silver) Trooper, *Bloodhounds*, USA Network, 1996.
Walt Kaplan, *The Big Time*, TNT, 2002.

Television Appearances; Pilots:
The Expendables, NBC, 1999.
David, *Wilder Days*, ABC, 2000.
Baxter, *Day Break*, ABC, 2006.

Charles Difrisco, *Marlowe*, ABC, 2007.
Arnold Heller, *SIS*, Spike TV, 2008.

Television Appearances; Episodic:
Mark, "My Daughter, Myself," *Designing Women*, CBS, 1990.
(As Michael Buchman Silver) Customer, "Teaching with the Enemy," *Cheers*, NBC, 1992.
Dr. Blum, *Civil Wars*, ABC, c. 1992.
(As Michael Buchman Silver) Vinod, "Paradise," *Star Trek: Deep Space Nine* (also known as *Deep Space Nine, DS9*, and *Star Trek: DS9*), syndicated, 1994.
(As Michael Buchman Silver) David, "Mating Rituals," *Blossom*, NBC, 1995.
Scott, "Intern Writer," *The John Larroquette Show* (also known as *Larroquette*), NBC, 1996.
(As Michael Buchman Silver) Fleming Adler, "Guess Who's Coming to Dinner?," *Step by Step*, ABC, 1996.
Public defender, *Moloney*, CBS, c. 1996.
Officer Williams, "The Eyes of the City," *Leaving L.A.*, ABC, 1997.
(As Michael Buchman Silver) Freddy, "Death Song," *The Burning Zone*, UPN, 1997.
(As Michael Buchman Silver) Chris Rockwell, "Jaroldo!," *The Pretender*, 1997.
(As Michael Buchman Silver) Steve, "Dial M for Muffin," *Life with Roger*, The WB, 1997.
(As Michael Buchman Silver) Danny, "Big Brother," *NewsRadio*, NBC, 1998.
(As Michael Buchman Silver) "Holy Words," *Nothing Sacred*, ABC, 1998.
(As Michael Buchman Silver) Doug, "Superfriends," *Fantasy Island*, ABC, 1998.
Howard Grodin, "Dreamland: Parts 1 & 2," *The X–Files*, Fox, 1998.
Michael Dearborn, "Legalese," *Vengeance Unlimited*, ABC, 1999.
(As Michael Buchman Silver) Agent Stern, "Spirit Falls," *Strange World*, ABC, 1999.
(As Michael Buchman Silver) Justin Hopkins, "The Persistence of Tectonics," *Judging Amy*, CBS, 1999.
Paul, "Love's Laborer's Lost," *Once and Again*, ABC, 2001.
Paul, "Forgive Us Our Trespasses," *Once and Again*, ABC, 2001.
Dr. Michael Augustine, "Flesh and Blood," *The Fugitive*, CBS, 2001.
Rich Talridge, "The Waste," *Special Unit 2* (also known as *SU2*), UPN, 2001.
Daniel Michaels, "Moving On," *Family Law*, CBS, 2001.
Ken, "Civil Unrest," *Providence*, NBC, 2001.
Michael, "The Paper Chase," *Felicity*, The WB, 2002.
Prosecuting attorney, "The Accused Is Entitled," *CSI: Crime Scene Investigation* (also known as *C.S.I.* and *CSI: Las Vegas*), CBS, 2002.
U.S. Attorney Raymond Berman, "Hitman," *Law & Order*, NBC, 2002.
Lawyer, "Goodbye, Jenny," *The District*, CBS, 2003.

Lyle Turrow, "Mr. Monk Goes to the Ballgame," *Monk,* USA Network, 2003.

"Amber Synn," *Skin,* Fox, 2003.

"Secrets & Lies," *Skin,* Fox, 2003.

"Endorsement," *Skin,* Fox, 2003.

James, "Love and Games," *Century City,* CBS, 2004.

Emergency medical technician, "Outside Man," *CSI: NY,* CBS, 2004.

Ed Davis, "Code," *Strong Medicine,* Lifetime, 2004.

Rick in 1995, "Ravaged," *Cold Case,* CBS, 2005.

Mandy Baerwitz, "Rhea Reynolds," *Nip/Tuck,* FX Network, 2005.

Dr. Anton Kostov, "The Woman at the Airport," *Bones,* Fox, 2006.

Sam Shapiro, "Riding the Lightning," *Criminal Minds,* CBS, 2006.

Danny Stone, "Coming Out," *Love Monkey,* CBS, 2006.

Baxter, "What if He Lets Her Go?," *Day Break,* ABC, 2006.

Baxter, "What if They're Stuck?," *Day Break,* ABC, 2006.

Professor David Winkler, "President Evil," *Veronica Mars,* The CW, 2006.

Professor David Winkler, "Hi, Infidelity," *Veronica Mars,* The CW, 2006.

Dan Lauter, "Love Triangle," *Shark,* CBS, 2006.

Dan Lauter, "Backfire," *Shark,* CBS, 2006.

Professor David Winkler, "Weevils Wobble but They Don't Go Down," *Veronica Mars,* The CW, 2007.

(Uncredited) Shapiro, "Family Business," *Cane,* CBS, 2007.

Shapiro, "A New Legacy," *Cane,* CBS, 2007.

Dan Lauter, "Eye of the Beholder," *Shark,* CBS, 2007.

Dan Lauter, "In the Crosshairs," *Shark,* CBS, 2007.

Assistant District Attorney Henderson, "Burglary," *Eyes,* ABC, 2007.

Dr. Ron Hillman, "Primed," *Without a Trace* (also known as *W.A.T.*), CBS, 2007.

Martin "Marty", "Hollywood Babylon," *Supernatural,* The CW, 2007.

Steve Levin, "Shrink Rap," *Las Vegas,* NBC, 2007.

Steve Levin, "The Glass Is Always Cleaner," *Las Vegas,* NBC, 2007.

Steve Levin, "Head Games," *Las Vegas,* NBC, 2007.

Steve Levin, "3 Babes, 100 Guns, and a Fat Chick," *Las Vegas,* NBC, 2008.

Arlo Meyers, "Hoosier Daddy," *In Plain Sight,* USA Network, 2008.

Elliott Russell, "Heartbeat," *Eli Stone,* ABC, 2008.

Elliott Russell, "Owner of a Lonely Heart," *Eli Stone,* ABC, 2008.

Stu Orenbacher, "Do You Believe in Magic," *Brothers & Sisters,* ABC, 2008.

Stu Orenbacher, "Owning It," *Brothers & Sisters,* ABC, 2009.

(As Mike Silver) Travis's father, "Hustle and Throw," *The Hustler,* 2009.

(As Mike Silver) Travis's father, "Can't Knock the Hustler," *The Hustler,* 2009.

Personick's attorney, "Depraved Heart," *Lie to Me,* Fox, 2009.

Liam Samuels/Sylar, "Chapter Twelve 'An Invisible Thread,'" *Heroes,* NBC, 2009.

Richard Ranier, "A Beautiful Delusion," *Mental,* Fox, 2009.

Edward Sykes, "Venice Kings," *Dark Blue,* TNT, 2009.

"Happy Ending," *Raising the Bar,* TNT, 2009.

Ken Keller, "The Hankover," *Royal Pains,* USA Network, 2010.

(Uncredited) Ken Keller, "Whole Lotto Love," *Royal Pains,* USA Network, 2010.

Film Appearances:

Luke, *Jason Goes to Hell: The Final Friday* (also known as *Jason Goes to Hell*), New Line Cinema, 1993.

Fraternity member, *Higher Learning,* Columbia, 1995.

(As Michael Buchman) Undercover cop, *Virtuosity,* Paramount, 1995.

(As Michael Buchman Silver) Museum assistant, *Eye for an Eye,* Paramount, 1996.

(As Michael Buchman Silver) Max, *Playing by Heart* (also known as *Dancing about Architecture* and *My Heart, My Love*), Miramax, 1998.

Ben Glazer, *All of It* (also known as *Marriage Material*), 1999.

(As Michael Buchman Silver) Joe, *Seven Girlfriends,* Castle Hill, 1999.

(As Michael Buchman Silver) Marlon, *In the Weeds,* Moonstone Entertainment, 2000.

(As Michael Buchman Silver) Dr. Winslow, *Submerged* (also known as *Destination: Impact* and *Marine Crush*), New City Releasing, 2000.

Bobby, *Legally Blonde* (also known as *Cutie Blonde*), Metro–Goldwyn–Mayer, 2001.

Dr. Jaslow, *I Am Sam,* New Line Cinema, 2001.

Stud, *Chatroom* (short film), Made in Italy Productions, 2003.

Baltimore doctor, *Seabiscuit,* Universal, 2003.

Wanda's father, *Unbeatable Harold,* Lg Entertainment, 2006.

Jerry Sphincter, *Love Shack,* 2010.

Film Work:

Producer and director, *Love Shack,* 2010.

WRITINGS

Screenplays:
Love Shack, 2010.

Television Episodes:

(As Michael Silver) "Black Book," *Medical Investigation,* NBC, 2005.

Also writer for *She Spies.*

SOLOMON, Ed 1960–
(Edward Solomon)

PERSONAL

Born September 15, 1960, in Saratoga, CA; father, an electronics company employee; married Cynthia Cleese (an actress), 1995; children: Olivia, Evan. *Education:* Graduate of University of California, Los Angeles.

Addresses: *Office*—Writers Co–op, 4000 Warner Blvd., Building 1, Burbank, CA 91522. *Agent*—Creative Artists Agency, 2000 Avenue of the Stars, Los Angeles, CA 90067.

Career: Writer, producer, director, and actor. Infinite Monkeys (production company), cofounder; Writers Co–op, Burbank, CA, partner. Also worked as a gag writer, script supervisor, playwright, and standup comedian.

Awards, Honors: Saturn Award nomination, best writer, Academy of Science Fiction, Fantasy, and Horror Films, 1998, for *Men in Black;* Award of Independent Cinema Owners, Mannheim–Heidelberg International Filmfestival, 2003, for *Levity.*

CREDITS

Film Work:
Coproducer, *Bill & Ted's Bogus Journey,* Orion, 1991.
(As Edward Solomon) Associate producer, *Leaving Normal,* Universal, 1992.
Producer and director, *Levity,* Sony Pictures Classics, 2003.
Producer, *Imagine That,* Paramount, 2009.

Film Appearances:
Stupid waiter, *Bill & Ted's Excellent Adventure,* Orion, 1989.
Stupid seance member, *Bill & Ted's Bogus Journey,* Orion, 1991.
Jerk in bar, *Leaving Normal,* Universal, 1992.
Thirteenth destroyer, *Mom and Dad Save the World,* Warner Bros., 1992.
Dreams on Spec (documentary), Indie Rights, 2008.

Television Work; Series:
Executive story editor, *It's Garry Shandling's Show,* c. 1986–89.
Director, *Arresting Behavior,* 1992.

WRITINGS

Screenplays:
(With Chris Matheson) *Bill & Ted's Excellent Adventure,* Orion, 1989.
(With Matheson) *Bill & Ted's Bogus Journey,* Orion, 1991.
(As Edward Solomon) *Leaving Normal,* Universal, 1992.
(With Matheson) *Mom and Dad Save the World,* Warner Bros., 1992.
Super Mario Bros. (also known as *Super Mario Brothers: The Movie*), Buena Vista, 1993.
(Coauthor) *Men in Black* (also known as *MIB*), Columbia, 1997, published in *Men in Black: The Script and the Story behind the Film,* 1997.
(Coauthor) *What Planet Are You From?,* Sony Pictures Entertainment, 2000.
(With others) *Charlie's Angels* (also known as *3 Engel fuer Charlie*), Sony Pictures Entertainment, 2000.
(Uncredited; contributor) *X–Men,* 2000.
Levity, Sony Pictures Classics, 2003.
The In–Laws (also known as *Save the World* and *What a Wedding*), Warner Bros., 2003.
Imagine That, Paramount, 2009.

Also rewriter of scripts by other screenwriters.

Television Writer; Series:
It's Garry Shandling's Show, 1986–89.
The Dave Thomas Comedy Show, CBS, 1990.
Arresting Behavior, 1992.

Television Episodes:
"The Playboy Show," *Laverne and Shirley* (also known as *Laverne & Shirley & Company, Laverne & Shirley & Friends,* and *Laverne DeFazio & Shirley Feeney*), 1982.
(With Jill Gordon) "Of Mice and Men," *Laverne and Shirley* (also known as *Laverne & Shirley & Company, Laverne & Shirley & Friends,* and *Laverne DeFazio & Shirley Feeney*), 1982.
(With Gordon) "The Monastery Show," *Laverne and Shirley* (also known as *Laverne & Shirley & Company, Laverne & Shirley & Friends,* and *Laverne DeFazio & Shirley Feeney*), 1983.

ADAPTATIONS

The characters for the 1992 television series *Bill and Ted's Excellent Adventures,* broadcast by CBS and Fox, were created by Solomon. Several of Solomon's screenplays were adapted by others for publication as "novelizations."

SOMMERS, Stephen 1962–

PERSONAL

Born March 20, 1962, in Indianapolis, IN; married Jana Hydusik (a psychotherapist), July 24, 1993; children: Samantha June, Ashley. *Education:* St. John's University, Collegeville, MN, B.A., 1980; University of Southern California, M.F.A., 1989; also attended University of Seville.

Addresses: *Office*—Sommers Co., 204 Santa Monica Blvd., Suite A, Santa Monica, CA 90401. *Agent*—WME Entertainment, 9601 Wilshire Blvd., 3rd Floor, Beverly Hills, CA 90210.

Career: Executive, director, and writer. Sommers Co., Santa Monica, CA, founder and chief executive officer. Performed with street theatre groups in Europe; also worked as a manager of European rock and roll bands.

Awards, Honors: Chiller–Eyegore Award, Universal Studios, 1999; Saturn Award nominations, best director and best writer, Academy of Science Fiction, Fantasy, and Horror Films, 2000, for *The Mummy.*

CREDITS

Film Director:
Perfect Alibi (short film), 1989.
Catch Me if You Can, Management Company Entertainment Group, 1989.
The Adventures of Huck Finn (also known as *The Adventures of Huckleberry Finn*), Buena Vista, 1993.
The Jungle Book (also known as *Rudyard Kipling's "The Jungle Book"*), Buena Vista, 1994.
Deep Rising (also known as *The Greed*), Buena Vista, 1998.
The Mummy (also known as *Hamunaptra*), Universal, 1999.
The Mummy Returns, Universal, 2001.
(And producer) *Van Helsing,* Universal, 2004.
Revenge of the Mummy: The Ride (short film; also known as *Revenge of the Mummy*), Universal, 2004.
(And producer) *G.I. Joe: The Rise of Cobra* (also known as *G.I. Joe*), Paramount, 2009.

According to some sources, directed the 1989 film *Terror Eyes,* using the name Steve Sommers.

Film Producer:
Executive producer, *Tom and Huck* (also known as *The Adventures of Tom and Huck* and *Tom Sawyer*), Buena Vista, 1995.

The Scorpion King, Universal, 2002.
The Mummy: Tomb of the Dragon Emperor (also known as *The Mummy 3* and *Hamunaptra 3*), Universal, 2008.
The Scorpion King: Rise of a Warrior (also known as *The Scorpion King 2: Rise of a Warrior*), Universal, 2008.

Film Appearances:
(Uncredited) Man sitting in the bathtub at Izzy's place, *The Mummy Returns,* Universal, 2001.
Himself, *Revenge of the Mummy: The Ride* (short film; also known as *Revenge of the Mummy*), Universal, 2004.
The Sci–Fi Boys (documentary), Universal, 2006.

Television Work; Movies:
Co–executive producer, *Oliver Twist,* ABC, 1997.

Television Work; Pilots:
Executive producer, *Transylvania,* NBC, 2004.

Television Appearances; Specials:
The Making of Rudyard Kipling's "The Jungle Book," 1994.
Van Helsing: The Man and the Monsters, Sci–Fi Channel, 2004.
The World of Van Helsing, 2004.
Bloodsucking Cinema, Starz!, 2007.

Television Appearances; Episodic:
"Disasters at Sea: That Sinking Feeling," *Movie Magic,* 1997.
Shootout (also known as *Hollywood Shootout* and *Sunday Morning Shootout*), AMC, 2004.
"The Mummy: Tomb of the Dragon Emperor," *HBO First Look,* HBO, 2008.
The Movie Loft, 2009.

RECORDINGS

Videos:
Building a Better Mummy, 1999.
Spotlight on Location: The Mummy Returns, 2001.
Van Helsing: Behind the Screams, Universal Studios Home Entertainment, 2004.
Executive producer, *Van Helsing: The London Assignment,* Universal Home Video, 2004.
The Making of "The Mummy: Tomb of the Dragon Emperor," Universal Studios Home Entertainment, 2008.
The Big Bang Theory: The Making of "G.I. Joe," Paramount Home Video, 2009.

Albums:
Executive soundtrack producer, *G.I. Joe: The Rise of Cobra* (also known as *G.I. Joe*), 2009.

WRITINGS

Screenplays:
Perfect Alibi (short film), 1989.
Catch Me if You Can, Management Company Entertainment Group, 1989.
The Adventures of Huck Finn (also known as *The Adventures of Huckleberry Finn*), Buena Vista, 1993.
Gunmen, Dimension Films, 1994.
(With others) *The Jungle Book* (also known as *Rudyard Kipling's "The Jungle Book"*), Buena Vista, 1994.
Tom and Huck (also known as *The Adventures of Tom and Huck* and *Tom Sawyer*), Buena Vista, 1995.
Deep Rising (also known as *The Greed*), Buena Vista, 1998.
The Mummy (also known as *Hamunaptra*), Universal, 1999.
The Mummy Returns, Universal, 2001.
(Uncredited) *The Scorpion King* (also based on story by Sommers), Universal, 2002.
Van Helsing, Universal, 2004.
Revenge of the Mummy: The Ride (short film; also known as *Revenge of the Mummy*), Universal, 2004.
(Uncredited) *The Mummy: Tomb of the Dragon Emperor* (also known as *The Mummy 3* and *Hamunaptra 3*), Universal, 2008.
G.I. Joe: The Rise of Cobra (also based on story by Sommers; also known as *G.I. Joe*), Paramount, 2009.

Television Movies:
(Uncredited) *Oliver Twist,* ABC, 1997.

Television Pilots:
Transylvania, NBC, 2004.

ADAPTATIONS

The 2008 film *The Scorpion King: Rise of a Warrior* was based on a story by Sommers.

OTHER SOURCES

Periodicals:
Entertainment Weekly, May 14, 1999, p. 28.
Variety, August 27, 2001, p. 52.

Electronic:
Sommers Company Web Site, http://www.sommerscompany.com, August 18, 2010.
Stephen Sommers Official Site, http://www.stephensommers.com, August 24, 2010.

SPOTTISWOODE, Roger 1945–
(Roger Spottiswood)

PERSONAL

Born January 5, 1945, in Ottawa, Ontario, Canada (some sources cite birthplace as London, England); raised in England; son of Raymond Spottiswoode (a producer and director); married Holly Palance (an actress and screenwriter; divorced, 1998).

Addresses: *Agent*—John Burnham, International Creative Management, 10250 Constellation Way, 9th Floor, Los Angeles, CA 90067.

Career: Director, producer, film editor, and writer. Worked as a film editor for television commercials and documentary films.

Awards, Honors: Special Jury Prize, Cognac Festival du Film Policier, 1982, for *The Pursuit of D. B. Cooper;* Edgar Allan Poe Award nomination (with others), best motion picture, Mystery Writers of America, 1983, for *48 Hrs;* Special Grand Prize of the Jury, Montreal World Film Festival, 1993, Emmy Award nomination, outstanding directing for a miniseries or special, and Directors Guild of America Award nomination, outstanding directorial achievement in dramatic specials, 1994, all for *And the Band Played On;* Gemini Award, best direction in a dramatic program or miniseries, Academy of Canadian Cinema and Television, 1998, for *Hiroshima;* Audience Award, best narrative feature, Hamptons International Film Festival, 2003, for *Spinning Boris;* Audience Award and Best Canadian Film Award, Sudbury Cinefest, 2007, Genie Award, best direction, Academy of Canadian Cinema and Television, 2008, and Jury Award, Beverly Hills Film Festival, 2008, all for *Shake Hands with the Devil.*

CREDITS

Film Director:
Terror Train (also known as *Train of Terror*), Twentieth Century–Fox, 1980.
The Pursuit of D. B. Cooper (also known as *Pursuit*), Universal, 1981.
Under Fire, Orion, 1983.
The Best of Times, Universal, 1986.
Shoot to Kill (also known as *Deadly Pursuit*), Buena Vista, 1988.
Turner & Hooch, Buena Vista, 1989.
Air America, TriStar, 1990.
Stop! Or My Mom Will Shoot, Universal, 1992.
Mesmer, 1994.

Tomorrow Never Dies (also known as *TND*), Metro–Goldwyn–Mayer, 1997.

The 6th Day, Sony Pictures Entertainment, 2000.

Ripley Underground (also known as *White on White*), Fox Searchlight, 2005.

Shake Hands with the Devil, Seville Pictures, 2007, Regent Releasing, 2009.

The Children of Huang Shi (also known as *Escape from Huang Shi*), Sony Pictures Classics, 2008.

(And producer) *The Touch of a Kiss* (short film), 2008.

Forgiveness and Justice, Article 19 Films, 2009.

Film Producer:

Associate producer, *Who'll Stop the Rain?* (also known as *Dog Soldiers*), Metro–Goldwyn–Mayer, 1978.

(As Roger Spottiswood) Executive producer, *Baby: The Secret of the Lost Legend* (also known as *Dinosaur ... Secret of the Lost Legend*), Touchstone, 1985.

Film Editor:

Stamping Ground (also known as *Love and Music*), 1971.

(With others), *Straw Dogs,* Cinerama, 1971.

The Getaway, National General, 1972.

(With others), *Pat Garrett and Billy the Kid,* Metro–Goldwyn–Mayer, 1973.

The Gambler, Paramount, 1974.

Hard Times (also known as *The Streetfighter*), Columbia, 1975.

Television Director; Movies:

The Last Innocent Man, HBO, 1987.

Third Degree Burn, HBO, 1989.

And the Band Played On, HBO, 1993.

Murder Live!, NBC, 1997.

(And executive producer) *Noriega: God's Favorite,* Showtime, 2000.

The Matthew Shepard Story, NBC, 2002.

Ice Bound (also known as *Ice Bound: A Woman's Survival at the South Pole*), CBS, 2003.

Spinning Boris, Showtime, 2003.

Television Director; Pilots:

The Renegades, ABC, 1982.

Turner & Hooch (also known as *The Kid*), NBC, 1990.

Prince Street, NBC, 1997.

Television Director; Other:

"Time Flies When You're Alive" (special), *HBO Showcase,* HBO, 1989.

Hiroshima (miniseries), 1996.

Television Appearances; Specials:

The Secrets of 007: The James Bond Files, CBS, 1997.

James Bond: Shaken and Stirred, ITV, 1997.

Nobody Does It Better: The Music of James Bond, Channel 4, 1998.

28th Annual Genie Awards, 2008.

Television Appearances; Episodic:

"Gene Hackman," *Bravo Profiles,* Bravo, 2000.

RECORDINGS

Videos:

Himself, *Highly Classified: The World of 007,* 1997.

WRITINGS

Screenplays:

(With others) *48 Hours,* Paramount, 1982.

ADAPTATIONS

The 1990 film *Another 48 Hrs.* was based on characters created by Spottiswoode. The television pilot *Turner & Hooch* was based on a story by Spottiswoode.

OTHER SOURCES

Periodicals:

New York Times, November 17, 2000, p. B28.

STAMP, Terence 1938(?)–

PERSONAL

Full name, Terence Henry Stamp; born July 22, 1938 (some sources cite 1939), in London, England; son of Thomas (a tugboat captain) and Ethel Esther (maiden name, Perrott) Stamp; brother of Christopher Stamp (a producer); married Elizabeth O'Rourke (a pharmacist), December 31, 2002 (divorced, 2008). *Education:* Studied drama at Webber–Douglas Academy of Dramatic Art, London.

Addresses: *Agent*—(voice work) Arcieri and Associates, 305 Madison Ave., Suite 2315, New York, NY 10165. *Manager*—Beth Holden–Garland, Untitled Entertainment, 1801 Century Park E., Suite 700, Los Angeles, Ca 90067.

Career: Actor, writer, and director. The Stamp Collection (organic food line), cofounder and partner, beginning 1994. Wanstead Club, worked as assistant professional golfer, c. 1943; also worked as assistant stage manager for British repertory companies.

Member: Brooks's Club.

Awards, Honors: Academy Award nomination, best supporting actor, and Film Award nomination, most promising newcomer to leading film roles, British Academy of Film and Television Arts, both 1963, for *Billy Budd;* Golden Globe Award, new star of the year in films, 1963; Golden Laurel Award nomination, top new male personality, 1965; Cannes International Film Festival Award, best actor, 1965, for *The Collector;* Mystfest Award (with John Hurt and Tim Roth), best actor, 1984, for *The Hit;* Grande Medaille de Vermeil, French government, 1985; honorary D.Arts, University of East London, 1993; Golden Space Needle Award, best actor, Seattle International Film Festival, and Australian Film Institute Award nomination, best actor, both 1994, Golden Globe Award nomination, best actor in a motion picture comedy or musical, Film Award nomination, best leading actor, British Academy of Film and Television Arts, and Chlotrudis Award nomination, best supporting actor, all 1995, all for *The Adventures of Priscilla, Queen of the Desert;* Independent Spirit Award nomination, best male lead, Independent Features Project/West, Golden Satellite Award, best actor in a motion picture drama, International Press Academy, and Sierra Award nomination, best actor, Las Vegas Film Critics Circle, all 2000, for *The Limey.*

CREDITS

Film Appearances:
(Film debut) Title role, *Billy Budd,* United Artists, 1962.
Mitchell, *Term of Trial,* Warner Bros., 1962.
Freddy Clegg, *The Collector* (also known as *The Butterfly Collector*), Columbia, 1965.
Willy Garvin, *Modesty Blaise,* Twentieth Century–Fox, 1966.
Sergeant Francis "Frank" Troy, *Far from the Madding Crowd,* Metro–Goldwyn–Mayer, 1967.
Dave Fuller, *Poor Cow,* National General, 1967.
(Uncredited) *Location: Far from the Madding Crowd* (documentary), 1967.
(Uncredited; in archive footage) Sergeant Francis "Frank" Troy, *Lionpower from MGM,* 1967.
Blue/Azul, *Blue,* Paramount, 1968.
Visitor, *Teorema* (also known as *Theorem*), Continental, 1968.
Toby Dammit, "Never Let the Devil Take Your Head" (also known as "Toby Dammit"), *Spirits of the Dead* (also known as *Tales of Mystery* and *Tales of Mystery and Imagination*), American International Pictures, 1969.
John Soames, *The Mind of Mr. Soames,* Columbia, 1969.
Arthur Rimbaud, *A Season in Hell* (also known as *Una stagione all'inferno*), 1971.
Terence, *Hu–Man,* Romantique–ORTF, 1975.

Daniele "Dany" di Bagnasco, *The Divine Nymph* (also known as *Divine Creature* and *La divina creatura*), Analysis Film Releasing, 1976.
Edgar Poe, *Black–Out,* Avia, 1977.
Alain, *Striptease* (also known as *Insanity*), 1977.
General Zod, *Superman* (also known as *Superman: The Movie*), Warner Bros., 1978.
Prince Lubovedsky, *Meetings with Remarkable Men,* Libra, 1978.
General Zod, *Superman II,* Warner Bros., 1979.
Henry, *Amo non amo* (also known as *I Love You, I Love You Not* and *Together?*), Titanus, 1979.
Licanthropus, il figlio della notte, 1979.
Pope Andreani, *Vatican Conspiracy* (also known as *Death in the Vatican, Morte in Vaticano,* and *Muerte en el Vaticano*), Film International, 1980.
Skinner/Taskinar, *Monster Island* (also known as *Jules Verne's "Mystery on Monster Island," The Mystery of Monster Island,* and *Misterio en la isla de los monstruos*), Fort–Almeda, 1981.
Willie Parker, *The Hit,* Island Alive, 1984.
(Uncredited) Prince of Darkness, *The Company of Wolves,* Cannon, 1985.
Dr. Steven Phillip, *Link,* Cannon, 1985.
Victor Taft, *Legal Eagles,* Universal, 1986.
Edward, *Hud* (also known as *Skin* and *Vilde, the Wild One*), Synchron, 1986.
Prince Borsa, *The Sicilian,* Twentieth Century–Fox, 1986.
Himself, *Directed by William Wyler* (documentary), 1986.
Sir Larry Wildman, *Wall Street,* Twentieth Century–Fox, 1987.
William Harcourt, *Alien Nation,* Twentieth Century–Fox, 1988.
John Tunstall, *Young Guns,* Twentieth Century–Fox, 1988.
Paul Hellwart, *Genuine Risk,* IRS Releasing, 1991.
Darman, *Prince of Shadows* (also known as *Beltenebros*), 1991.
Jack Schmidt, *The Real McCoy,* Universal, 1992.
Bernadette Bassenger/Ralph, *The Adventures of Priscilla, Queen of the Desert,* Gramercy, 1993.
Himself and Bernadette Bassenger/Ralph, *Ladies Please!,* 1995.
Edward Lamb, *Tire a part* (also known as *Limited Edition*), CTV International, 1997.
Baltazar Vincenza, *Bliss* (also known as *Hard Technique*), Triumph, 1997.
Fred Moore, *Love Walked In* (also known as *Ni el tiro del final*), TriStar, 1998.
Chancellor Valorum, *Star Wars: Episode I—The Phantom Menace* (also known as *The Phantom Menace* and *Star Wars I: The Phantom Menace*), Twentieth Century–Fox, 1999.
Wilson, *The Limey,* Artisan Entertainment, 1999.
Terry Strictor, *Bowfinger,* Universal, 1999.
Dr. Bud Chantilas, *Red Planet,* Warner Bros., 2000.
John, *My Wife Is an Actress* (also known as *Ma femme est une actrice*), Sony Pictures Classics, 2001.

Magnus Martel, *Revelation,* First Look Home Entertainment, 2001.

Man on man/himself, *Full Frontal,* Miramax, 2002.

Jack Taylor, *My Boss's Daughter* (also known as *The Guests*), Dimension Films, 2003.

Philip Naudet, *The Kiss,* MTI Home Video, 2003.

Ramsley, *The Haunted Mansion* (also known as *Disney's "The Haunted Mansion"*), Buena Vista, 2003.

Himself and Toby Dammit, *Fellini: I'm a Born Liar* (documentary; also known as *Federico Fellini: I'm a Big Liar, I'm a Born Liar,* and *Fellini: Je suis un grand menteur*), First Look Pictures Releasing, 2003.

Samuel Fish, *Dead Fish,* Mobius International, 2004.

Stick, *Elektra,* Twentieth Century–Fox, 2005.

Baker, *These Foolish Things,* Outsider Pictures, 2006.

(In archive footage) General Zod, *Superman II,* Warner Bros., 2006.

Brigham Young, *September Dawn,* Black Diamond Pictures/Slow Hand Releasing, 2007.

(Uncredited; in archive footage) Bernadette Bassenger, *Here's Looking at You, Boy* (documentary), SND Films, 2007.

Siegfried, *Get Smart,* Warner Bros., 2008.

Storyteller, *Flowers and Weeds* (short film), Live Consciously/Kiros Pictures/Five Island Films, 2008.

Terrence Bundley, *Yes Man,* Warner Bros., 2008.

Ludwig Beck, *Valkyrie* (also known as *Walkuere* and *Walkuere/Valkyrie*), United Artists, 2008.

(In archive footage) *Roman Polanski: Wanted and Desired* (documentary), THINKFilm, 2008.

The Adjustment Bureau, Universal, 2010.

Film Work:
Director, *Stranger in the House,* 1990.

Television Appearances; Series:
David Audley, a recurring role, *Chessgame,* Granada Television, 1983, PBS, 1987.

Host, *The Hunger,* Showtime, multiple episodes, 1997–98.

Voice of Jor–El, *Smallville* (also known as *Smallville Beginnings*), The WB, between 2003 and 2006, then The CW, between 2006 and 2009.

Television Appearances; Movies:
Wazir Jandur, *The Thief of Baghdad* (also known as *Le voleur de Bagdad*), NBC, 1978.

David Audley, *Deadly Recruits,* 1986.

David Audley, *Cold War Killers,* 1986.

David Audley, *The Alamut Ambush,* 1986.

Joe Hartman, *Mindbender* (also known as *Uri Geller*), 1995.

Kozen, *Kiss the Sky,* The Movie Channel, 1999.

Television Appearances; Miniseries:
Hollywood U.K., BBC, 1993.

Narrator, *Jazz Britannia,* BBC, 2005.

Narrator of *The History of Soccer: The Beautiful Game.*

Television Appearances; Specials:
(Uncredited) Himself, *Fade–In* (also known as *Iron Cowboy*), 1968.

The Making of "Superman: The Movie," 1980.

The Making of "Superman II," 1982.

Host, *The Prince's Trust Gala,* TBS, 1989.

Presenter, *The 52nd Annual Golden Globe Awards,* TBS, 1995.

Fame, Fashion and Photography: The Real Blow Up, BBC, 2002.

Hot Buttered Movie Special: Elektra, Spike TV, 2005.

Narrator, *Inside the Twin Towers* (also known as *9/11: The Day the World Changed* and *9/11: The Twin Towers*), The Discovery Channel, 2006.

Live Earth (also known as *Live Earth 7.7.07, Live Earth: The Concerts for a Climate in Crisis,* and *SOS: The Movement for a Climate in Crisis*), NBC, 2007.

Max on Set: Wanted, Cinemax, 2008.

Television Appearances; Episodic:
"Film Night Special: John Schlisinger," *Film Night,* BBC, 1971.

Cinema 3, 1985.

Parkinson One to One, 1988.

Dias de cine, 1992.

V Graham Norton, Channel 4, 2002.

Voices of Dennis and Professor Menace, "Blast from the Past," *Static Shock,* The WB, 2003.

"The Making of 'Elektra'," *HBO First Look,* HBO, 2004.

Film '72, BBC, 2004.

(In archive footage) Bernadette Bassenger/Ralph, "Magnificent Movies," *20 to 1,* Nine Network, 2006.

"Get Smart," *HBO First Look,* HBO, 2008.

Up Close with Carrie Keagan, ABC, 2008.

Stage Appearances:
This Year, Next Year, Vaudeville Theatre, London, 1960.

(Broadway debut) *Alfie,* 1966.

Title role, *Dracula,* Shaftesbury Theatre, London, 1978.

Stranger, *The Lady from the Sea,* Round House Theatre, London, 1979.

Made London debut in a production of *A Trip to the Castle;* also appeared in *Airborne Symphony.*

Major Tours:
Appeared as Whittaker in a touring production of *Long Short and the Tall.*

RECORDINGS

Videos:
(In archive footage) *Making "Superman:" Filming the Legend,* 2001.

(In archive footage) *Taking Flight: The Development of "Superman,"* 2001.

(In archive footage) *The Magic behind the Cape,* 2001.

You Will Believe: The Cinematic Saga of Superman, Warner Home Video, 2006.

Narrator, *The Mythology of Superman,* Warner Home Video, 2006.

Kneel Before Zod, Warner Home Video, 2010.

Also appeared in the music video "At the Bottom of Everything" by Bright Eyes, 2005.

Video Games:

Voice of Manjar Camoran, *The Elder Scrolls IV: Oblivion,* 2K Games/Bethesda Softworks, 2006.

Voice of Prophet of Truth, *Halo 3,* Microsoft Game Studios, 2007.

Voice of Pekwarsky, *Wanted: Weapons of Fate,* Warner Bros., 2009.

WRITINGS

Screenplays:
Stranger in the House, 1990.

Books:
Stamp Album (autobiography), Bloomsbury, 1987.

Coming Attractions (autobiography), 1988.

Double Feature (autobiography), Bloomsbury, 1989.

The Night (novel), Phoenix House, 1991.

(With Elizabeth Buxton) *The Stamp Collection Cookbook* (also published as *The Stamp Collection Healthy Eating Cookbook, The Stamp Collection Natural Cookbook,* and *The Wheat and Dairy–Free Cookbook*), 1997.

OTHER SOURCES

Books:
International Dictionary of Films and Filmmakers, Volume 3: *Actors and Actresses,* St. James Press, 1996.

Stamp, Terence, *Stamp Album,* Bloomsbury, 1987.

Stamp, Terence, *Coming Attractions,* 1988.

Stamp, Terence, *Double Feature,* Bloomsbury, 1989.

Periodicals:
Interview, August, 1994, p. 36.

Premiere, October, 1994, p. 100.

STILES, Julia 1981–
(Julie Stiles)

PERSONAL

Full name, Julia O'Hara Stiles; born March 28, 1981, in New York, NY; daughter of John (an owner and operator of a pottery business) and Judith (a potter) Stiles. *Education:* Graduated from Professional Children's School, New York City, 1999; Columbia University, B.A., English, 2005; also attended Screenwriters Lab at Sundance Institute. *Avocational Interests:* Black and white photography, dancing, listening to music, reading.

Addresses: *Agent*—United Talent Agency, 9560 Wilshire Blvd., Suite 500, Beverly Hills, CA 90212; Creative Artists Agency, 9830 Wilshire Blvd., Beverly Hills, CA 90212. *Manager*—Handprint Entertainment, 1100 Glendon Ave., Suite 1000, Los Angeles, CA 90024. *Publicist*—I/D Public Relations, 8409 Santa Monica Blvd., West Hollywood, CA 90069.

Career: Actress. Smithy's Films, New York City, partner. Appeared in print and television advertisements, including promotions for Apple Jacks cereal, 1993, Calvin Klein jeans, 1999, and Tide detergent. Volunteer with Habitat for Humanity International in Costa Rica.

Awards, Honors: Karlovy Vary International Film Festival Award, best actress, 1998, for *Wicked;* named one of *Teen People* magazine's "21 hottest stars under 21," 1999; YoungStar Award nomination, *Hollywood Reporter,* best young actress in a comedy film, YoungStar Award nomination, best performance by a young actress in a comedy film, Teen Choice Award nominations, film–sexiest love scene and film–breakout performance, 1999, tied for Chicago Film Critics Association Award, most promising actress, 2000, and MTV Movie Award, outstanding breakthrough female performance, 2000, all for *10 Things I Hate about You;* Florida Film Critics Circle Award and Online Film Critics Society Award (both with others), both best ensemble performance, National Board of Review Award (with others), best acting by an ensemble, 2000, for *State and Main;* Teen Choice Award nominations, choice chemistry (with Freddie Prinze Jr.) and choice actress, 2000, for *Down to You;* Teen Choice awards, choice actress in a film, and choice fight scene in a film (with Bianca Lawson), MTV Movie Award, best kiss (with Sean Patrick Thomas), and MTV Movie Award nomination, best female performance, all 2001, for *Save the Last Dance;* Golden Satellite Award nomination, best supporting actress in a drama, International Press Academy, 2002, for *The Business of Strangers;* Obie Award, *Village Voice,* for *Everyday Newt Berman;* Teen Choice Award nomination, choice movie actress—drama or action adventure, 2004, for *The Prince & Me;* Teen Choice Award nomination, choice scream, 2006, for *The Omen.*

CREDITS

Film Appearances:
Young Nana's friend, *I Love You, I Love You Not,* Buena Vista, 1996.

Bridget O'Meara, *The Devil's Own*, Columbia, 1997.

Ellie Christianson, *Wicked*, Frankenstein Entertainment, 1998.

Neena Beal, *Wide Awake*, Miramax, 1998.

Imogen, *Down to You*, Miramax, 1999.

Katarina "Kat" Stratford, *10 Things I Hate about You*, Buena Vista, 1999.

Ophelia, *Hamlet*, Miramax, 1999.

Carla Taylor, *State and Main* (also known as *Sequences et consequences*), Fine Line, 2000.

Desi Brable, *O*, Lions Gate Films, 2001.

Paula Murphy, *The Business of Strangers*, IFC Films, 2001.

Sara Johnson, *Save the Last Dance*, Paramount, 2001.

Nicolette, *The Bourne Identity* (also known as *Die Bourne Identitaet*), Universal, 2002.

Becky, *A Guy Thing*, Metro–Goldwyn–Mayer, 2003.

Title role, *Carolina*, Miramax, 2003.

Joan Brandwyn, *Mona Lisa Smile*, Sony Pictures Classics, 2003.

Paige Morgan, *The Prince & Me* (also known as *The Prince and Me*), Paramount, 2004.

Nicky, *The Bourne Supremacy*, Universal, 2004.

Glenna, *Edmond*, First Independent, 2005.

Isold, *A Little Trip to Heaven*, First Look, 2005.

Katherine Thorn, *The Omen*, Warner Bros., 2006.

Nicky Parsons, *The Bourne Ultimatum* (also known as *Bourne Ultimatum*), United International, 2007.

Rosie, *Gospel Hill*, Twentieth Century–Fox, 2008.

Jenny Thierolf, *The Cry of the Owl*, Paramount, 2009.

Ella, *Passage*, Curious Pie, 2009.

Film Director:

Raving, Sundance Channel, 2007.

Television Appearances; Series:

Lumen Ann Pierce, *Dexter*, Showtime, 2010.

Television Appearances; Miniseries:

Katie Herlihy, *The '60s*, NBC, 1999.

Television Appearances; Movies:

Phoebe Jackson, *Before Women Had Wings* (also known as *Oprah Winfrey Presents: Before Women Had Wings*), ABC, 1997.

Television Appearances; Specials:

Teen People's 21 Hottest Stars under 21, ABC, 1999.

Concert for New York City, VH1, 2001.

MTV Presents Teen People Magazine's 25 Hottest Stars under 25, MTV, 2003.

The Omen: Prophecy Fulfilled, 2006.

The Bourne Ultimatum: T4 Movie Special, 2007.

Television Appearances; Awards Presentations:

2000 MTV Movie Awards, MTV, 2000.

MTV Video Music Awards, MTV, 2001.

2001 MTV Movie Awards, MTV, 2001.

Presenter, *The 73rd Annual Academy Awards*, ABC, 2001.

Ego Trip's Race–O–Rama, VH1, 2004.

Presenter, *The 59th Annual Tony Awards*, CBS, 2005.

The 17th Annual Screen Actors Guild Awards, 2011.

Television Appearances; Episodic:

(As Julie Stiles) Erica, "Who Is Max Mouse?," *Ghostwriter*, PBS, 1993.

Erica, "A Crime of Two Cities," *Ghostwriter*, PBS, 1994.

Megan Walker, "The Secret," *Promised Land*, CBS, 1996.

Corey Sawicki, "Mother, May I?: Part 2," *Chicago Hope*, CBS, 1997.

The Rosie O'Donnell Show, syndicated, 1999, 2001.

The Late Show with David Letterman, CBS, 2001, 2002, 2004, 2007.

The Tonight Show with Jay Leno, NBC, 2001, 2006.

Guest host, *Saturday Night Live* (also known as *SNL*), NBC, 2001.

The Daily Show (also known as *A Daily Show with Jon Stewart*, *The Daily Show with Jon Stewart*, and *The Daily Show with Jon Stewart Global Edition*), Comedy Central, 2001, 2003.

(Uncredited) Jenna Bush, *Saturday Night Live* (also known as *SNL*), NBC, 2001.

RI:SE, 2002.

Total Request Live (also known as *TRL*), MTV, 2003.

Late Night with Conan O'Brien, NBC, 2001, 2003, 2006.

"Julia Stiles," *Diary*, MTV, 2003.

The Oprah Winfrey Show (also known as *Oprah*), syndicated, 2003.

Last Call with Carson Daly, NBC, 2004.

Friday Night with Jonathan Ross, BBC, 2004.

Live with Regis and Kelly, syndicated, 2004, 2007.

Punk'd, MTV, 2004.

Jimmy Kimmel Live!, ABC, 2006, 2010.

HypaSpace (also known as *HypaSpace Daily* and *HypaSpace Weekly*), SPACE, 2006.

The Early Show, CBS, 2006.

eTalk Daily (also known as *eTalk*), CTV, 2007.

The Late Late Show with Craig Ferguson, CBS, 2007.

Entertainment Tonight (also known as *E.T.* and *This Week in Entertainment*), syndicated, 2007.

The View, ABC, 2007.

"Miller Time!," *The O'Reilly Factor*, Fox News, 2008.

"Bourne Ultimatum," *Cinetipp*, Pro 7, 2008.

"I Lost Myself in Us," *The City*, 2009.

Stage Appearances:

The Vagina Monologues, Westside Theatre, New York City, 1999–2003.

Viola, *Twelfth Night*, New York Shakespeare Festival, Delacorte Theatre, Public Theatre, New York City, 2002.

Birdie, *Fran's Bed,* Playwrights Horizon Theatre, New York City, 2005.

Steph, *The 24 Hour Plays 2008,* American Airlines Theatre, New York City, 2008.

Carol, *Oleanna,* John Golden Theatre, New York City, 2009.

Julia, *The 24 Hour Plays 2009,* American Airlines Theatre, 2009.

Appeared in *Hughes* and *Matthew/School of Life,* both with Kitchen Theatre; in *Everyday Newt Berman, Photo Op,* and *The Sandalwood Box,* all La MaMa Experimental Theatre Club, New York City; and in *Jungle Movie,* Ridge Theatre.

RECORDINGS

Music Videos:
Appeared in "Sally's Pigeons," by Cyndi Lauper, 1993 and "Crazy," by K–Ci and Jo–Jo, 2000.

Videos:
Cyndi Lauper: 12 Deadly Cyns ... and Then Some, 1994.
The Making of "Save the Last Dance," 2001.
Groovy Gravy: Making the Scene in "A Guy Thing," Metro–Goldwyn–Mayer, 2003.
Inside "A Guy Thing," Metro–Goldwyn–Mayer, 2003.
Omensims, Twentieth Century–Fox, 2006.
Man on the Move: Jason Bourne, Universal, 2007.
The Evolution of Nicky, Universal, 2007.

WRITINGS

Screenplays:
Raving, Sundance Channel, 2007.

With Bob McGrath and Scott Saunders, author of the unproduced screenplay *The Anarchist's Daughter.* Contributor to the young people's magazine *Zuzu.*

OTHER SOURCES

Books:
Newsmakers, Issue 3, Gale, 2002.

Periodicals:
Allure, May, 1999, pp. 182–89.
Harper's Bazaar, July, 1998, p. 116.
Marie Claire, August, 2002, pp. 118–20.
Movieline, September, 1998, p. 15; July, 2000, pp. 48–53.
Premiere, August, 2002, pp. 74–76.
Rolling Stone, April 12, 2001, pp. 89–95, 152.

Seventeen, December, 1998, p. 107; September, 2002, pp. 266–71.
Teen People, May, 2001, p. 104.
Time, April 12, 1999, p. 96.

STONE, Oliver 1946–

PERSONAL

Full name, Oliver William Stone; born September 15, 1946, in New York, NY; son of Louis (a stockbroker) and Jacqueline (maiden name, Goddet) Stone; married Najwa (some sources cite Majwa) Sarkis (a political attache), May 22, 1971 (divorced, 1977); married Elizabeth Burkit Cox (a film production assistant), c. June 7, 1981 (divorced, 1993); companion of Chong Son Chong (an actress and model); children: (second marriage) Sean (an actor), Michael Jack; (with Chong) Tara Chong. *Education:* Attended Yale University, until 1965; New York University, B.F.A., film, 1971; studied with Martin Scorsese.

Addresses: *Office*—Ixtlan, Inc., 2425 Olympic Blvd., Suite 660, Santa Monica, CA 90404. *Agent*—David Styne, Creative Artists Agency, 9830 Wilshire Blvd., Beverly Hills, CA 90212. *Manager*—Geyer Kosinski, Industry Entertainment, 955 South Carrillo Dr., 3rd Floor, Los Angeles, CA 90048.

Career: Director, producer, writer, and actor. Free Pacific Institute, Cholon, Vietnam, teacher, 1965–66; taxi driver, New York City, 1971; Ixtlan, Inc. (film company), Santa Monica, CA, founder, 1977, partner, 1977—. Also founder of Illusion Entertainment Group; Z.com (Internet entertainment studio), affiliate, 2000. Also known as Minh Duc. *Military service:* U.S. Merchant Marine, 1966. U.S. Army, Infantry, 1967–68; served in Vietnam; became specialist fourth class; received Bronze Star and Purple Heart with oak leaf cluster.

Member: Directors Guild of America, Screen Writers Guild, Writers Guild of America, Academy of Motion Picture Arts and Sciences, Yale Club.

Awards, Honors: Academy Award, Golden Globe Award, and WGA Screen Award, Writers Guild of America, all best adapted screenplay, Grammy Award nomination, best album of original score written for a motion picture of television special, 1979, for *Midnight Express;* Academy Award nomination (with Richard Boyle), best original screenplay, Independent Spirit Award nominations, best feature (with Gerald Green), best director, and best screenplay (with Boyle), Independent Features Project/West, WGA Screen Award nomination (with Boyle), best original screenplay, Writers Guild of America, Kansas City Film Critics Circle Award, best director, all 1987, for *Salvador;* Directors Guild of America Award (with others), outstanding directorial achievement in motion pictures, Independent Spirit Awards, best director and best screenplay, Silver Berlin Bear, Berlin International Film Festival, best director, and nomination for Golden Berlin Bear, Academy Award and Golden Globe Award, both best director, tied for Boston Society of Film Critics Award, best director, Bulgarian Cinematography Diploma, Academy Award nomination, Golden Globe Award nomination, and WGA Screen Award nomination, Writers Guild of America, all best original screenplay (with Boyle), Kansas City Film Critics Circle Award, best director, all 1987, Film Award, best director, British Academy of Film and Television Arts, 1988, and Orson Welles Award for directorial achievement, all for *Platoon;* Independent Spirit Award nomination, best director, and nomination for Golden Berlin Bear, both 1989, for *Talk Radio;* Honorary Golden Berlin Bear, 1990; Academy Award, best director, and Academy Award nominations, best adapted screenplay (with Ron Kovic), and best picture (with A. Kitman Ho), Golden Globe Awards, best director, and best adapted screenplay for a motion picture (with Kovic), Directors Guild of America Award (with others), outstanding direction of a motion picture, WGA Screen Award nomination (with Kovic), best adapted screenplay, Writers Guild of America, nomination for Golden Berlin Bear, Filmmaker of the Year Award, Motion Picture Bookers Club, Bulgarian Cinematography Diploma, and Consider the Alternatives Peace Award, SANE Education Fund/ Consider the Alternative Productions, all 1990, and Film Award nomination (with Kovic), best screenplay adaptation, British Academy of Film and Television Arts, 1991, all for *Born on the Fourth of July;* nomination for Golden St. George Award, Moscow International Film Festival, 1991, for *The Doors;* Special Award, meritorious achievement, ShoWest Convention, 1992; Special Prize, Berlin International Film Festival, c. 1991, Golden Globe Award, best director of a motion picture, Directors Guild of America Award nomination, best director of a motion picture, Academy Award nominations, best director, best picture (with Ho), and best adapted screenplay (with Zachary Sklar), Golden Globe Award nomination (with Sklar), best screenplay, WGA Screen Award nomination (with Sklar), best adapted screenplay, Writers Guild of America, and Edgar Allan Poe Award nomination (with Sklar), best motion picture, Mystery Writers of America, all 1992, Film Award nomination (with Sklar), best screenplay adaptation, British Academy of Film and Television Arts, Blue Ribbon Award, best foreign film, Readers' Choice Awards, Mainichi Film Concours and Kinema Junpo Awards, and Mainichi Film Concours, best foreign language film, 1993, and Movie Masterpiece Award, British Empire Awards, 2000, all for *JFK;* Special Award for meritorious achievement, ShoWest Convention, National Association of Theatre Owners, 1992; Direc-

tor of the Decade Award, Chicago International Film Festival, 1992; Gold Reel Award, Independent Feature Project/West, 1992; Order of Arts and Letters, France, 1992; Career Achievement Award, Writers Guild Foundation, 1993; Special Jury Prize, Venice International Film Festival, 1994, and Golden Globe Award nomination, best director of a motion picture, 1995, both for *Natural Born Killers;* Emmy Award (with Janet Yang, Abby Mann, and Diana Pokorny), outstanding movie made for television, 1995, for *Indictment: The McMartin Trial;* Chicago Film Critics Association Award, best director, and Academy Award nomination (with Stephen J. Rivele and Christopher Wilkinson), best original screenplay, 1996, both for *Nixon;* received star on Hollywood Walk of Fame, 1996; Freedom of Expression Award (with Milos Forman), National Board of Review, 1996, for *The People vs. Larry Flynt;* Film Award nomination (with Alan Parker), best screenplay adaptation, British Academy of Film and Television Arts, 1997, for *Evita;* Hermosa Beach Film Festival Award (with Vince DiPersio), best documentary, 1998, for *The Last Days of Kennedy and King;* Crystal Iris, Brussels International Arts Festival, 1998; nomination for Golden Berlin Bear, 2000, for *Any Given Sunday;* Golden Satellite Award (with others), best miniseries or television movie, International Pres Academy, 2001, for *The Day Reagan Was Shot;* International Filmmaker Award, Palm Springs International Film Festival, 2002; Honorary Award of the Festival, Marrakech International Film Festival, 2003; Golden Kinnaree Career Achievement Award, Bangkok International Film Festival, 2004; Lifetime Achievement Award, Stockholm Film Festival, 2004; Special Award, film direction with unique visual sensitivity, Camerimage, 2004; Hollywood Film Award, director of the year, and Hollywood Movie of the Year, Hollywood Film Festival, 2006; Golden Eye for Lifetime Achievement, Zurich Film Festival, 2007.

CREDITS

Film Director:
Street Scenes (documentary; also known as *Street Scenes 1970*), 1970.
Last Year in Viet Nam (short film), 1971.
Seizure (also known as *Queen of Evil*), American International Pictures, 1974.
Mad Man of Martinique (short film), 1979.
The Hand, Warner Bros., 1981.
Platoon, Orion, 1986.
Salvador, Hemdale, 1986.
Wall Street, Twentieth Century–Fox, 1987.
Talk Radio, Universal, 1988.
Born on the Fourth of July, Universal, 1989.
The Doors, TriStar, 1991.
JFK, Warner Bros., 1991.
Heaven & Earth (also known as *Entre ciel et terre*), Warner Bros., 1993.

Natural Born Killers, Warner Bros., 1994.

Nixon, Buena Vista, 1995.

U Turn (also known as *Stray Dogs* and *U Turn—Ici commence l'enfer*), TriStar, 1996.

Any Given Sunday (also known as *Gridiron, The League, Monday Night, On Any Given Sunday,* and *Playing Hurt*), Warner Bros., 1999.

Alexander (also known as *Alexander Revisited: The Final Cut* and *Alexander: Director's Cut*), Warner Bros., 2004.

World Trade Center, Paramount, 2006.

W. (also known as *Bush*), Lions Gate Films, 2008.

South of the Border, Cinema Libre Studio, 2009.

Wall Street: Money Never Sleeps (also known as *Wall Street*), Twentieth Century–Fox, 2010.

Film Executive Producer:

Iron Maze, Academy Entertainment, 1991.

South Central, Warner Bros., 1992.

Zebrahead (also known as *The Colour of Love*), Columbia, 1992.

The Joy Luck Club, Buena Vista, 1993.

The New Age, Wechsler Productions, 1994.

Killer: A Journal of Murder (also known as *The Killer*), Republic, 1995.

Freeway, August Entertainment, 1996.

Cold Around the Heart, 1997.

The Last Days of Kennedy and King (also known as *Assassinated: The Last Days of Kennedy and King*), 1998.

Any Given Sunday (also known as *Gridiron, The League, Monday Night, On Any Given Sunday,* and *Playing Hurt*), Warner Bros., 1999.

The Corruptor, New Line Cinema, 1999.

Film Producer:

Sugar Cookies, Troma Films, 1973.

(With Gerald Green) *Salvador,* Hemdale, 1986.

(With A. Kitman Ho) *Born on the Fourth of July,* Universal, 1989.

(With Edward R. Pressman and Michael Rauch) *Blue Steel,* Metro–Goldwyn–Mayer/United Artists, 1990.

(With Pressman) *Reversal of Fortune,* Warner Bros., 1990.

(With Ho) *JFK,* Warner Bros., 1991.

(With Ho) *Heaven & Earth* (also known as *Entre ciel et terre*), Warner Bros., 1993.

(With Ho) *Natural Born Killers,* Warner Bros., 1994.

Nixon, Buena Vista, 1995.

The People vs. Larry Flynt, Columbia, 1996.

Savior, Budua Productions, 1998.

S.W.A.T., Sony Pictures Classics, 2003.

Alexander (also known as *Alexander Revisited: The Final Cut* and *Alexander: Director's Cut*), Warner Bros., 2004.

South of the Border, Cinema Libre Studio, 2009.

Wall Street: Money Never Sleeps (also known as *Wall Street*), Twentieth Century–Fox, 2010.

Film Work:

Cinematographer, *Street Scenes* (documentary; also known as *Street Scenes 1970*), 1970.

Cinematographer and editor, *Last Year in Viet Nam* (short film), 1971.

Editor, *Seizure* (also known as *Queen of Evil*), American International Pictures, 1974.

Coeditor, *The Hand,* Warner Bros., 1981.

Film Appearances:

Cliff, *The Battle of Love's Return,* Troma Films, 1971.

Last Year in Viet Nam (short film), 1971.

Bum, *The Hand,* Warner Bros., 1981.

(Uncredited) Army officer in destroyed bunker, *Platoon,* Orion, 1986.

Trader in office, *Wall Street,* Twentieth Century–Fox, 1987.

Reporter, *Born on the Fourth of July,* Universal, 1989.

(Uncredited) Film professor, *The Doors,* TriStar, 1991.

Our Hollywood Education, 1992.

Beyond "JFK": The Question of Conspiracy, 1992.

Himself, *Dave,* Warner Bros., 1993.

Himself, *The Last Party* (documentary), Triton Pictures, 1993.

(Uncredited) Narrator during closing credits, *Nixon,* Buena Vista, 1995.

Cronkite Remembers, 1997.

Himself, *Frank Capra's American Dream,* 1997.

Himself, *One Vision,* 1998.

Tug Kowalski, *Any Given Sunday* (also known as *Gridiron, The League, Monday Night, On Any Given Sunday,* and *Playing Hurt*), Warner Bros., 1999.

John Ford Goes to War, 2002.

Jim Brown: All American, 40 Acres & A Mule, 2002.

The Autograph Hunters, 2005.

Torrente 3: El protector, Amiguetes Entertainment, 2005.

Le mis popote, 2006.

Bienvenue a Cannes (also known as *Cannes: All Access*), Turner Classic Movies, 2007.

Behind the Wheel, 2008.

Pierre Rissient: Man of Cinema, Deep Focus, 2008.

Bandes originales: Georges Delerue (also known as *In the Tracks of Georges Delerue*), 2010.

The Invocation, 2010.

Television Work; Movies:

Executive producer, *From Hollywood to Hanoi,* Cinemax, 1993.

Executive producer (with Janet Yang, Abby Mann, and Diana Pokorny), *Indictment: The McMartin Trial,* HBO, 1995.

Executive producer, *The Day Reagan Was Shot,* Showtime, 2001.

Producer and director, *Comandante,* HBO, 2003.

Producer and director, *Persona non Grata,* HBO, 2003.

Television Work; Miniseries:
Executive producer (with A. Kitman Ho, Michael Rauch, and Bruce Wagner), *Wild Palms,* ABC, 1993.

Television Work; Specials:
Executive producer, *The Last Days of Kennedy and King* (also known as *Assassinated: The Last Days of Kennedy and King*), TBS, 1998.
Producer, "Persona Non Grata," *America Undercover,* HBO, 2003.

Television Work; Episodic:
Director, "Persona Non Grata," *America Undercover,* HBO, 2003.
Director, "Looking for Fidel," *America Undercover,* HBO, 2004.

Television Appearances; Series:
Film School, 2004.
Saturday Night at the Movies, 2007.

Television Appearances; Specials:
Welcome Home, HBO, 1987.
The New Hollywood, NBC, 1990.
Beyond "JFK": The Question of Conspiracy, 1992.
The Kennedy Assassinations: Coincidence or Conspiracy, syndicated, 1992.
Oliver Stone: Inside Out (also known as *Oliver Stone*), Showtime, 1992.
Our Hollywood Education, 1992.
1993: A Year at the Movies, CNBC, 1993.
Together for Our Children—M.U.S.I.C., syndicated, 1993.
Empire of the Censors, 1995.
The First 100 Years: A Celebration of American Movies, HBO, 1995.
Frank Capra's American Dream, 1997.
AFI's 100 Years ... 100 Movies, CBS, 1998.
John Wayne: The Unquiet American, Arts and Entertainment, 1998.
The Warner Bros. Story: No Guts, No Glory: 75 Years of Award Winners, TNT, 1998.
The Warner Bros. Story: No Guts, No Glory—75 Years of Blockbusters, TNT, 1998.
Narrator, *Censored!,* AMC, 1999.
Full Contact: The Making of "Any Given Sunday," 1999.
Our Century, The Learning Channel, 1999.
Hollywood, D.C.: A Tale of Two Cities, Bravo, 2000.
20th Century Fox: The Blockbuster Years, AMC, 2000.
The Inside Reel: Digital Filmmaking, PBS, 2001.
Jim Brown: All American, HBO, 2002.
John Ford Goes to War, Starz!, 2002.
(Uncredited; in archive footage) *Who Is Alan Smithee?,* AMC, 2002.
Anthony Hopkins: A Taste for Hannibal, 2002.
Unseen + Untold: Scarface, Universal Studios, 2003.

AFI's 100 Years ... 100 Heroes and Villains, CBS, 2003.
Hollywood High, 2003.
Peter Jennings Reporting: The Kennedy Assassination—Beyond Conspiracy, ABC, 2003.
Playa's Guide to Scarface, VH1, 2003.
The director, *Charging for Alexander,* BBC, 2004.
The 100 Greatest War Films, Channel 4, 2005.
Albert Iglesias, el muscio fiel, Canal+ Espana, 2006.
Oliver Stone–Hollywoods Lieblingsrebell, 2006.
San Sebastian 2006: Cronica de Carlos Boyero, 2006.
The Boomer Century, 2007.
AFI Life Achievement Award: A Tribute to Al Pacino, 2007.
Ciak Point Torino, 2008.
AFI Life Achievement Award: A Tribute to Michael Douglas, 2009.

Television Appearances; Awards Presentations:
The 44th Annual Golden Globe Awards, 1987.
The 59th Annual Academy Awards, 1987.
The 1990 MTV Video Music Awards, MTV, 1990.
Presenter, *The 48th Annual Golden Globe Awards,* TBS, 1991.
Independent Spirit Awards, Bravo, 1991.
The 64th Annual Academy Awards, 1992.
The ALMA Awards, ABC, 1998.
The British Comedy Awards 2006 Live, ITV, 2006.

Television Appearances; Movies:
Comandante, HBO, 2003.
Persona non Grata, HBO, 2003.

Television Appearances; Episodic:
Cinema 3, 1987 and 1996.
Firstworks, The Movie Channel, 1988.
The Story of Hollywood (also known as *Talking Pictures*), TNT, 1988.
ABC News Nightline (also known as *Nightline*), ABC, 1991.
Naked Hollywood, Arts and Entertainment, 1991.
"Who Killed JFK? On the Trail of the Conspiracies," *Investigative Reports,* Arts and Entertainment, 1992.
Primer plano, 1993.
Gente de primera, 1994.
Movie Watch, 1994.
American Cinema, PBS, 1995.
Narrator, "D. W. Griffiths," *Sex and the Silver Screen,* Showtime, 1996.
Moving Pictures, 1996.
Dias de cine, 1996 and 2009.
The Kennedys: Power, Seduction and Hollywood: The E! True Hollywood Story, E! Entertainment Television, 1998.
"The Naked and the Dead," *Great Books,* The Learning Channel, 1998.
"Full Contact: The Making of 'Any Given Sunday'," *HBO First Look,* HBO, 1999.
"The Films of Oliver Stone," *The Directors,* 2000.

Cliff, "The Debut Episode," *Troma's Edge TV*, 2000.

"Show n204," *Mundo VIP*, 2000.

"Al Pacino: Inside Out," *Biography*, Arts and Entertainment, 2001.

"Charlie Sheen," *Biography*, Arts and Entertainment, 2001.

"Lightning in a Bottle," *Hollywood, Inc.*, 2002.

HARDtalk, BBC, 2003.

"Looking for Fidel," *America Undercover*, HBO, 2004.

"The Making of 'Alexander': Fortune Favors the Bold," *HBO First Look*, HBO, 2004.

Mioch versus Goderie, 2004.

Tout le monde en parle, 2004.

"Johnny Depp: Under His Skin," *Biography*, Arts and Entertainment, 2004.

"Val Kilmer," *Biography*, Arts and Entertainment, 2004.

Cinema mil, Televisio de Catalunya, 2005.

Sunday Morning Shootout (also known as *Hollywood Shootout* and *Shootout*), AMC, 2006.

Canada A.M. (also known as *Canada A.M. Weekend*), CTV, 2006.

Breakfast, BBC, 2006.

Film '72, BBC, 2006.

The Late Late Show, CBS, 2006.

"James Woods," *Biography*, Arts and Entertainment, 2007.

"Anthony Hopkins," *Biography*, Arts and Entertainment, 2007.

"Oliver Stone/David Gergen," *The Colbert Report*, Comedy Central, 2008.

"Josh Brolin/Adele," *Saturday Night Live* (also known as *SNL*), NBC, 2008.

Le grand journal de Canal+, 2008.

Sunday AM, BBC, 2008.

Real Time with Bill Maher (also known as *Real Time with Bill Maher: Electile Dysfunction '08*), 2008 and 2009.

Strada, 2008.

"N.Y. Film School," *Filmania: Eiga no tatsujin*, 2009.

Appeared in *Oliver Stone: The Directors*, Encore; also appeared in episodes of *Backstory* (also known as *AMC Backstory* and *Hollywood Backstories*), AMC; and *McLaughlin*, MSNBC.

Television Appearances; Miniseries:

Himself, *Wild Palms*, ABC, 1993.

Himself, *Der Klang der Bilder*, 1995.

RECORDINGS

Videos:

Himself, *The Road of Excess*, 1997.

Patton: A Tribute to Franklin J. Schaffner, 1997.

The Making of "Scarface," 1998.

Money Never Sleeps, 2000.

Conan Unchained: The Making of "Conan" (also known as *Conan Unchained: The Making of "Conan the Barbarian"*), 2000.

Himself, *Oliver Stone's America*, Warner Home Video, 2001.

A Tour of the Inferno: Revisiting "Platoon," 2001.

Chaos Rising: The Storm Around "Natural Born Killers," 2001.

Into the Valley of Death, 2001.

Scarface: The Rebirth, Universal Studios Home Video, 2003.

Scarface: Recreating, Universal Studios Home Video, 2003.

Five Directors on "The Battle of Algiers," The Criterion Collection, 2004.

On the Set of "Alexander," Warner Home Video, 2004.

Fight Against Time: Oliver Stone's "Alexander," Warner Home Video, 2005.

Make Your Own Damn Movie!, Troma Entertainment, 2005.

Resurrecting "Alexander," Warner Home Video, 2005.

The Death of "Alexander," Warner Home Video, 2005.

Vangelis Scores "Alexander," Warner Home Video, 2005.

Perfect Is the Enemy of Good, Warner Home Video, 2005.

Woodward and Bernstein: Lighting the Fire, Warner Home Video, 2006.

Out of the Shadows: The Man Who Was Deep Throat, Warner Home Video, 2006.

Visual and Special Effects, Paramount, 2006.

The Making of "World Trade Center," Paramount, 2006.

They Live by Night: The Twisted Road, Time Warner, 2007.

Act of Violence: Dealing with the Devil, Time Warner, 2007.

Crime Wave: The City Is Dark, Time Warner, 2007.

Side Street: Where Temptation Lurks, Time Warner, 2007.

Tension: Who's Guilty Now?, Time Warner, 2007.

Influence and Appreciation: Taxi Driver, Sony, 2007.

NBK Evolution: How Would It All Go Down?, Warner Bros., 2009.

WRITINGS

Screenplays:

Last Year in Viet Nam (short film), 1971.

Seizure (also known as *Queen of Evil*), American International Pictures, 1974.

Midnight Express (based on Billy Hayes's autobiography of the same name), Columbia, 1978.

The Hand (adapted from Marc Brandel's novel *The Lizard's Tail*), Warner Bros., 1981.

(With John Milius) *Conan the Barbarian* (based on the works of Robert E. Howard), Universal, 1982.

Scarface (adapted from Howard Hawks's 1932 film of the same name), Universal, 1983.

(With David Lee Henry) *8 Million Ways to Die* (based on the novel of the same name by Lawrence Block), TriStar, 1985.

(With Michael Cimino) *Year of the Dragon* (based on the novel of the same name by Robert Daley), Metro–Goldwyn–Mayer/United Artists, 1986.

(With Richard Boyle) *Platoon,* Orion, 1986, published in *Oliver Stone's Platoon and Salvador: The Screenplays,* Vintage, 1987.

(With Boyle) *Salvador,* Hemdale, 1986, published in *Oliver Stone's Platoon and Salvador: The Screenplays,* Vintage, 1987.

(With Stanley Weiser) *Wall Street,* Twentieth Century–Fox, 1987.

(With Eric Bogosian) *Talk Radio* (based on Bogosian's stage play of the same name and Stephen Singular's book *Talked to Death: The Life and Murder of Alan Berg*), Universal, 1988.

(With Ron Kovic) *Born on the Fourth of July* (based on Kovic's autobiography of the same name), Universal, 1989.

(With J. Randall Johnson and Ralph Thomas) *The Doors* (based on John Densmore's book *Riders on the Storm*), TriStar, 1991.

(With Zachary Sklar) *JFK* (based on the books *On the Trail of the Assassins,* by Jim Garrison and *Crossfire: The Plot That Killed Kennedy,* by Jim Marrs), Warner Bros., 1991, published as *JFK: The Book of the Film; The Documented Screenplay,* Applause Theatre Books, 1992.

Heaven & Earth (also known as *Entre ciel et terre;* based on Le Ly Hayslip's memoirs *When Heaven and Earth Changed Places: A Vietnamese Woman's Journey from War to Peace* and *Child of War, Woman of Peace*), Warner Bros., 1993.

(With Richard Rutowski and David Veloz) *Natural Born Killers* (based on a story by Quentin Tarantino), Warner Bros., 1994.

(With Stephen J. Rivele and Christopher Wilkinson) *Nixon,* Buena Vista, 1995, published as *Nixon: An Oliver Stone Film,* edited by Eric Hamburg, Hyperion, 1995.

(With Alan Parker) *Evita* (based on the musical of the same name by Andrew Lloyd Webber and Tim Rice), Buena Vista, 1996.

(Uncredited) *U Turn* (also known as *Stray Dogs* and *U Turn—Ici commence l'enfer*), TriStar, 1996.

Any Given Sunday (also known as *Gridiron, The League, Monday Night, On Any Given Sunday,* and *Playing Hurt*), Warner Bros., 1999.

Comandante, 2003.

Alexander (also known as *Alexander Revisited: The Final Cut* and *Alexander: Director's Cut*), Warner Bros., 2004.

Singularity, Ixtlan Productions, 2008.

Wall Street: Money Never Sleeps (also known as *Wall Street*), Twentieth Century–Fox, 2010.

Television Miniseries:

(With Bruce Wagner) *Wild Palms* (based on the comic strip by Bruce Wagner and Julian Allen), ABC, 1993.

Television Movies:

Comandante, HBO, 2003.

Television Episodes:

"Looking for Fidel," *America Undercover,* HBO, 2004.

Novels:

A Child's Night Dream, St. Martin's Press, 1997.

Nonfiction:

(With Michael Singer) *Oliver Stone's Heaven and Earth: The Making of an Epic Motion Picture,* Tuttle, 1994.

OTHER SOURCES

Books:

Authors and Artists for Young Adults, Volume 15, Gale, 1995.

Encyclopedia of World Biography, 2nd edition, Gale, 1998.

Kunz, Don, editor, *The Films of Oliver Stone,* Scarecrow Press, 1997.

Riordan, James, *Stone: The Controversies, Excesses, and Exploits of a Radical Filmmaker,* Aurum Press, 1996.

St. James Encyclopedia of Popular Culture, St. James Press, 2000.

Toplin, Robert Brent, editor, *Oliver Stone's USA: Film, History, Controversy,* University Press of Kansas, 2000.

Periodicals:

Atlantic Monthly, July, 1997, pp. 96–100.

Cineaste, fall, 1996, pp. 33–37.

Empire, May, 1998, pp. 64–65.

Entertainment Weekly, August 6, 1999, pp. 26–27; February 16, 2001, p. 77.

Esquire, December, 1997, pp. 38–41.

Flicks, May, 1998, p. 35.

New Yorker, August 8, 1994, pp. 40–55.

New York Times, January 2, 1990, pp. C13, C20.

People Weekly, January 22, 1996, pp. 105–108.

Premiere, December, 1987, pp. 33–34, 37–38; January, 1996, pp. 62–65; January, 2000, pp. 78–81, 1979.

Sight and Sound, Volume 6, number 3, 1996, pp. 6–9.

Time, October 6, 1997, p. 109; November 9, 1998, p. 94.

Vogue, December, 1987, pp. 166, 172.

STRACHAN, Alan 1946–

PERSONAL

Career: Film editor and producer. Also worked as assistant film editor and consulting editor.

CREDITS

Film Editor:

The Human Factor, 1975.

The Greek Tycoon, Universal, 1978.

The Passage, United Artists, 1979.

North Sea Hijack (also known as *Assault Force* and *ffolkes*), Universal, 1980.

The Final Conflict (also known as *Omen III: The Final Conflict*), Twentieth Century–Fox, 1981.

The Sender, Paramount, 1982.

Power Game, 1983.

Supervising film editor, *Sahara,* 1983.

Not Quite Paradise (also known as *Not Quite Jerusalem*), 1986.

Withnail & I, Northern Arts Entertainment, 1987.

How to Get Ahead in Advertising, Warner Bros., 1989.

Return from the River Kwai, TriStar, 1989.

Nostradamus, Orion, 1994.

Additional film editor, *The Disappearance of Finbar,* 1996.

Shooting Fish, Fox Searchlight, 1997.

Waking Ned Devine (also known as *Wake Up! Ned!* and *Waking Ned*), Twentieth Century–Fox, 1998.

History Is Made at Night, (also known as *Spy Games*), Trimark Pictures, 1999.

Shergar, Nu Image, 1999.

Saving Grace, Fine Line, 2000.

The War Bride (also known as *Love and War*), 2001.

FeardotCom (also known as *Fear Dot Com*), Warner Bros., 2002.

Lighthouse Hill, 2002, Carnaby International, 2005.

Baltic Storm, IAC Film, 2003.

American Daylight, Kaleidoscope Entertainment, 2004.

I Am David, Lions Gate Films, 2004.

Tooth, Lakeshore Entertainment, 2004.

Color Me Kubrick (also known as *Colour Me Kubrick: A True ... ish Story*), 2005, Magnolia Pictures, 2007.

The Baker (also known as *Assassin in Love*), Screen Media Ventures, 2007.

Dead Man Running, Phase 4 Films, 2010.

Television Film Editor; Miniseries:

On Wings of Eagles, NBC, 1986.

Supervising film editor, *Noble House* (also known as *James Clavell's "Noble House"*), NBC, 1988.

Magic, 1991.

Television Film Editor; Movies:

The Dirty Dozen: The Next Mission (also known as *Dirty Dozen: Next Mission* and *Dirty Dozen 2*), NBC, 1985.

The Best Man (also known as *Best Man, Worst Friend* and *Unhitched*), ABC Family, 2005.

SUMMERS, Marc 1951–

PERSONAL

Original name, Marc Berkowitz; born November 11, 1951, in Indianapolis, IN; married Alice Filous, June 16, 1974; children: two, including Meredith. *Education:* Attended North Central High School, Indianapolis, IN.

Career: Actor, game show host, producer, and writer. Nickelodeon, worked as programming consultant; also worked as executive consultant for game shows. Previously worked as a magician, disc jockey, comedian, and studio page.

Member: Obsessive–Compulsive Foundation (member and national spokesperson).

CREDITS

Television Appearances; Series; Host:

Double Dare, Nickelodeon, 1986–94.

Family Double Dare (also known as *Double Dare* and *Fox Family Double Dare*), Fox, 1988.

Couch Potatoes, syndicated, 1989.

What Would You Do?, Nickelodeon, 1991.

Our Home, Lifetime, 1994–95.

Biggers & Summers, Lifetime, 1995.

Pick Your Brain, syndicated, 1995.

Majority Rules, 1996.

Great Day America, PAX, 1998–99.

It's a Surprise, Food Network, 2000.

History IQ, History Channel, 2000.

Unwrapped, Food Network, 2001–2009.

WinTuition, Game Show Network, 2002.

Trivia Unwrapped, Food Network, 2003.

Television Appearances; Series; Announcer:

Hot Streak (also known as *Bruce Forsyth's Hot Streak*), ABC, 1986.

I Can't Believe You Said That, Fox Family, 1998.

Also announcer for *$1,000,000 Change of a Lifetime* and sub–announcer for *The Joker's Wild.*

Television Appearances; Movies:

Second reporter, *The Sleepwalker Killing* (also known as *Crimes of Passion: Sleepwalker* and *From the Files of Unsolved Mysteries: The Sleepwalker Killing*), NBC, 1997.

Television Appearances; Specials:
Mystery Magical Special (also known as *Marc Summers' Mystery Magical Tour* and *Marc Summers' Mystery Magical Special*), Nickelodeon, 1988.
Walt Disney World's Fourth of July Spectacular, syndicated, 1988.
It's OK to Say No to Drugs, 1988.
Kids Have Rights Too, 1989.
Host, "The Nova Quiz," *Nova,* PBS, 1990.
Judge, *The 1992 Miss Teen USA Pageant,* CBS, 1992.
Member of chorus, *The Gershwins' "Porgy and Bess,"* PBS, 1993.
Tuning In to Media, 1994.
Host, *The Big Help,* 1994.
Weinerville Chanukah Special, Nickelodeon, 1995.

Television Appearances; Pilots:
Host, *Ultimate Revenge,* 2001.

Television Appearances; Awards Presentations:
Presenter, *Nickelodeon's 6th Annual Kids' Choice Awards,* Nickelodeon, 1992.
Nickelodeon's 7th Annual Kids' Choice Awards, Nickelodeon, 1994.

Television Appearances; Episodic:
Guest host, *Scrabble,* 1987.
Super Password, several appearances, 1988.
Guest, *The New Hollywood Squares,* 1988, 1989.
Host, "Super Slop–a–Mania," *Super Sloppy Double Dare,* Nickelodeon, 1989.
Host, "Super Slop–a–Mania II," *Super Sloppy Double Dare,* Nickelodeon, 1989.
Host, "Marc v. Harvey," *Super Sloppy Double Dare,* Nickelodeon, 1989.
Lou Rawls Parade of Stars, 1989.
"Double Dare vs. Wild & Crazy Kids," *Wild & Crazy Kids,* 1990.
Himself, "Cats Nipped," *Where in the World Is Carmen Sandiego?,* Fox, 1995.
Ultimate Revenge (also known as *TNN's Ultimate Revenge*), The Nashville Network, 2002.
Pyramid (also known as *The $100,00 Pyramid*), syndicated, 2003.
Guest host, "April Fool's Special," *Cram,* Game Show Network, 2003.
"The Reality behind Reality," *Chuck Woolery: Naturally Stoned,* 2003.
"GSN Hosts Edition," *Lingo,* 2003.
Dennis Miller, CNBC, 2004.
The Tony Danza Show, syndicated, 2005.
Host, "Iron Chef Boot Camp," *The Next Food Network Star,* Food Network, 2006.
Host, "Finale," *The Next Food Network Star,* Food Network, 2007.
The View, ABC, 2007, 2008, 2009.
The Oprah Winfrey Show (also known as *Oprah*), syndicated, 2008.

Host, "Burgers," *Ultimate Recipe Showdown,* Food Network, 2009.
Host, "Cakes," *Ultimate Recipe Showdown,* Food Network, 2009.
Host, "Desserts," *Ultimate Recipe Showdown,* Food Network, 2009.
Rachael Ray, syndicated, 2009.
"Pizza," *The Best Thing I Ever Ate,* Food Network, 2009.
"Between Bread," *The Best Thing I Ever Ate,* Food Network, 2009.
Host, "With My Hands," *The Best Thing I Ever Ate,* Food Network, 2009.

Also guest for episodes of *Today* and *The Tonight Show with Jay Leno,* NBC.

Television Executive Producer; Series:
Family Double Dare, Fox, 1988.
Pick Your Brain, syndicated, 1993.
Wild & Crazy Kids, 2002.
Trivia Unwrapped, Food Network, 2003.
Co–executive producer, *Wickedly Perfect,* CBS, 2004.
Dinner: Impossible, Food Network, 2007–10.

Television Producer; Series:
I Can't Believe You Said That, Fox Family, 1998.
Double Dare 2000, Nickelodeon, 2000.
Ultimate Revenge (also known as *TNN's Ultimate Revenge*), The Nashville Network, 2002.

Television Director; Episodic:
"Circus Juggling," *Dinner: Impossible,* Food Network, 2008.

Television Work; Other:
Producer, *Bring Me the Head of Dobie Gillis* (pilot), CBS, 1988.
Executive producer, *The Firestarter* (special), Court TV, 2001.

Internet Appearances; Videos:
(In archive footage) *Double Dare: 20 Years and Still Making a Mess,* YouTube, 2006.

RECORDINGS

Videos:
Producer and (in archive footage) host, *Double Dare: The Messiest Moments,* 1988.

WRITINGS

Television Specials:
Mystery Magical Special (also known as *Marc Summers' Mystery Magical Tour* and *Marc Summers' Mystery Magical Special*), Nickelodeon, 1988.

Videos:
Double Dare: The Messiest Moments, 1988.

Autobiography:
(With Eric Hollander) *Everything In Its Place: My Trials and Triumphs with Obsessive Compulsive Disorder,* J. P. Tarcher, 1999.

OTHER SOURCES

Books:
Summers, Marc, and Eric Hollander, *Everything In Its Place: My Trials and Triumphs with Obsessive Compulsive Disorder,* J. P. Tarcher, 1999.

SUTHERLAND, Donald 1934(?)–

PERSONAL

Full name, Donald McNichol Sutherland; born July 17, 1934 (some sources cite 1935), in St. John, New Brunswick, Canada; son of Frederick McLae (in sales) and Dorothy Isobel (maiden name, McNichol) Sutherland; married Lois May Hardwick (an actress), 1959 (divorced); married Shirley Jean Douglas (an actress), 1966 (divorced, 1970); married Francine Racette (an actress), 1972; children: (second marriage) Kiefer (an actor) and Rachel; (third marriage) Roeg, Rossif, Angus Redford. *Education:* Attended University of Toronto; trained for the stage at London Academy of Music and Dramatic Art, late 1950s. *Avocational Interests:* Political causes.

Addresses: *Agent*—Josh Lieberman, Creative Artists Agency, 9830 Wilshire Blvd., Beverly Hills, CA 90212. *Publicist*—Katherine Olim, PMK/HBH Public Relations, 8500 Wilshire Blvd., Suite 700, Beverly Hills, CA 90211.

Career: Actor and producer. McNichol Pictures, Inc., founder, 1981, president, 1981—. Appeared with Perth Repertory Company, Perth, Scotland, and with repertory companies in Nottingham, Chesterfield, Bromley, and Sheffield, England; UC Follies, Toronto, Ontario, Canada, member of comedy troupe. Voice performer and actor in television and radio commercials. CKBW–Radio, worked as news correspondent; also worked as a radio announcer and disc jockey in Canada. Also worked as a miner in Finland. Affiliated with Canadian Centre for Arms Control and Disarmament, Ottawa, Ontario, Canada.

Awards, Honors: Golden Globe Award nomination, best motion picture actor in a musical or comedy, and nomination for Golden Laurel Award, best male

comedy performance, both 1971, for *M*A*S*H;* two Film Award nominations, British Academy of Film and Television Arts, best actor, both 1974, for *Don't Look Now* and *Steelyard Blues;* Earl Grey Award, best acting performance in television in a leading role, Academy of Canadian Cinema and Television, 1978; Saturn Award nomination, best actor, Academy of Science Fiction, Fantasy, and Horror Films, 1979, for *Invasion of the Body Snatchers;* Golden Globe Award nomination, best motion picture actor in a drama, 1981, for *Ordinary People;* Best Actor Award, Karlovy Vary International Film Festival, 1982, Genie Award, best actor, Academy of Canadian Cinema and Television, 1983, for *Threshold;* Emmy Award, outstanding supporting actor in a miniseries or special, 1995, and Golden Globe Award, best supporting actor in a television series, miniseries, or motion picture, 1996, both for *Citizen X;* Golden Satellite Award, best supporting actor in a motion picture drama, International Press Academy, and Golden Globe Award nomination, best supporting actor in a motion picture, both 1999, for *Without Limits;* Governor General's Award for the Performing Arts, Canada, 2000; Jutra Award nomination, best supporting actor, 2001, for *The Art of War;* Blockbuster Entertainment Award nomination (with Clint Eastwood, James Garner, and Tommy Lee Jones), favorite action team, 2001, for *Space Cowboys;* Lucille Lortel Award nomination, outstanding actor, League of Off–Broadway Theatres and Producers, 2001, for *Ten Unknowns;* Golden Globe Award, best supporting actor in a television series, miniseries, or movie, 2003, for *Path to War;* officer, Order of Arts and Letters, France; officer, Order of Canada; honorary degrees include Ph.D., St. Mary's University, and LL.D., McGill University and University of Toronto; Golden Globe Award nomination, best performance by an actor in a supporting role in a series, miniseries or motion picture made for television, 2006, for *Commander in Chief;* Golden Globe Award nomination, best performance by an actor in a miniseries or a motion picture made to television, Emmy Award nomination, outstanding lead actor in a miniseries or a movie, 2006, for *Human Trafficking;* Jury Award, best supporting actor, Ft. Lauderdale International Film Festival, 2005, Satellite Award nomination, best actor in a supporting role, Jury Prize, best actor, 2006, for *Aurora Borealis;* Camie Award (with others), Chicago Film Critics Association Award, best supporting actor, 2006, for *Pride & Prejudice;* Role Model Award, Young Hollywood Awards, 2008; Golden Globe Award nomination, best performance by an actor in a supporting role in a series, miniseries or motion picture made for television, 2008, for *Dirty Sexy Money.*

CREDITS

Film Appearances:
Sergeant Paul, witch, and old man, *Il castello dei morti vivi* (also known as *Castle of the Living Dead, Crypt of Horror,* and *La chateau des morts vivants*), Malasky, 1964.

Bob Carroll, *Dr. Terror's House of Horrors* (also known as *The Blood Suckers*), Regal, 1965.

Joseph, *Fanatic* (also known as *Die! Die! My Darling*), Columbia, 1965.

Pharmacist's mate Nerney, *The Bedford Incident,* Columbia, 1965.

Pussycat Alley (also known as *The World Ten Times Over*), Goldstone, 1965.

Autograph seeking father, *Promise Her Anything,* 1965.

(Uncredited) Francis, *Promise Her Anything,* Paramount, 1966.

Himself, *Operation Dirty Dozen,* 1967.

Scientist at computer and voice of "brain," *Billion Dollar Brain,* United Artists, 1967.

Vernon L. Pinckley, *The Dirty Dozen,* Metro–Goldwyn–Mayer, 1967.

(Uncredited) Voice, *The Shuttered Room,* 1967.

Ackerman, *Sebastian* (also known as *Mr. Sebastian*), Paramount, 1968.

Chorus leader, *Oedipus the King,* Universal, 1968.

Dave Negli, *The Split,* Metro–Goldwyn–Mayer, 1968.

Lawrence, *Interlude,* Columbia, 1968.

Lord Peter Sanderson, *Joanna,* Twentieth Century–Fox, 1968.

Alex, *Alex in Wonderland,* Metro–Goldwyn–Mayer, 1970.

Captain Benjamin Franklin "Hawkeye" Pierce, *M*A*S*H* (also known as *MASH*), Twentieth Century–Fox, 1970.

Charles/Pierre, *Start the Revolution without Me* (also known as *Two Times Two*), Warner Bros., 1970.

Father Michael Ferrier, *Act of the Heart* (also known as *Acte du coeur*), Universal, 1970.

Sergeant Oddball, *Kelly's Heroes* (also known as *The Warriors*), Metro–Goldwyn–Mayer, 1970.

Christ figure, *Johnny Got His Gun,* Cinemation, 1971.

John Klute (title role), *Klute,* Warner Bros., 1971.

Klute in New York: A Background for Suspense, 1971.

Reverend Dupas, *Little Murders,* Twentieth Century–Fox, 1971.

Himself, *F.T.A.* (also known *Foxtrot Tango Alpha, Free the Army,* and *The FTA Show*), American International Pictures, 1972.

Andy Hammond, *Lady Ice,* National General, 1973.

Dan Candy, *Alien Thunder* (also known as *Dan Candy's Law* and *Le tonnerre rouge*), Cinerama, 1973.

Jesse Veldini, *Steelyard Blues* (also known as *The Final Crash*), Warner Bros., 1973.

John Baxter, *Don't Look Now* (also known as *A Venezia ... un dicembre rosso shocking*), Buena Vista, 1973.

Brulard (some sources cite Bruland), *S*P*Y*S,* Twentieth Century–Fox, 1974.

Corpse of Lieutenant Robert Schmied, *Murder on the Bridge* (also known as *Deception, End of the Game, Getting Away with Murder, Assassinio sul ponte,* and *Der Richter und sein henker*), Twentieth Century–Fox, 1975.

Homer Simpson, *The Day of the Locust,* Twentieth Century–Fox, 1975.

Voice of Edward S. Curtis, *The Shadow Catcher,* 1975.

Bertolucci secondo il cinema (documentary; also known as *The Cinema According to Bertolucci* and *The Making of "1900"*), Bauer International, 1975.

Attila, *1900* (also known as *Nineteen Hundred* and *Novecento*), Paramount, 1976.

Giacomo Casanova, *Casanova* (also known as *Fellini's "Casanova"* and *Il Casanova di Federico Fellini*), Universal, 1976.

Liam Devlin, *The Eagle Has Landed,* Columbia, 1976.

(English–language version) Narrator, *La spirale* (also known as *The Spiral*), 1976.

Clumsy waiter, *Kentucky Fried Movie,* United Film Distribution, 1977.

Inspector Steve Carella, *Blood Relatives* (also known as *Les liens du sang*), SNS, 1977.

Jay Mallory, *The Disappearance,* World Northal, 1977.

Matthew Bennell, *Invasion of the Body Snatchers,* United Artists, 1978.

Professor Dave Jennings, *National Lampoon's "Animal House"* (also known as *Animal House*), Universal, 1978.

Reese Halperin, *A Very Big Withdrawal* (also known as *A Man, a Woman, and a Bank*), Avco–Embassy, 1979.

Robert Agar, *The Great Train Robbery* (also known as *The First Great Train Robbery*), United Artists, 1979.

Robert Lees, *Murder by Decree* (also known as *Sherlock Holmes and Saucy Jack* and *Sherlock Holmes: Murder by Decree*), United Artists, 1979.

Calvin Jarrett, *Ordinary People,* Paramount, 1980.

Frank Lansing, *Bear Island* (also known as *Alistair MacLean's "Bear Island"*), Columbia, 1980.

Narrator, *North China Commune* (documentary), National Film Board of Canada, 1980.

Narrator, *Wuxing People's Commune* (documentary), 1980.

Professor Roger Kelly (some sources cite Keller), *Nothing Personal,* American International Pictures, 1980.

Henry Faber, *Eye of the Needle,* United Artists, 1981.

Nick the Noz, *Gas,* Paramount, 1981.

Brian Costello, *Max Dugan Returns,* Twentieth Century–Fox, 1982.

Narrator of the diary, *A War Story* (documentary), National Film Board of Canada, 1982.

Dr. Thomas Vrain, *Threshold,* Twentieth Century–Fox, 1983.

Dr. Arthur Calgary, *Ordeal by Innocence,* Metro–Goldwyn–Mayer/United Artists, 1984.

John Klute and Matthew Benell (in archive footage), *Terror in the Aisles* (also known as *Time for Terror*), 1984.

Westlake, *Crackers,* Universal, 1984.

Brother Thaddeus, *Heaven Help Us* (also known as *Catholic Boys*), TriStar, 1985.

Sergeant–Major Peasy, *Revolution,* Warner Bros., 1985.

Papa, *Kate Bush: The Whole Story,* 1986.

Appleton Porter, *The Trouble with Spies* (also known as *2 Female Spies with Flowered Panties*), De Laurentiis Entertainment Group, 1987.

Father Bob Koesler, *The Rosary Murders,* Samuel Goldwyn, 1987.

Paul Gauguin, *Oviri* (also known as *The Wolf at the Door* and *Gauguin, le loup dans le soleil*), Manson, 1987.

Give Me Your Answer True, 1987.

John Reese, *Apprentice to Murder,* New World Pictures, 1988.

Ben du Doit, *A Dry White Season,* Metro–Goldwyn–Mayer, 1989.

Dr. Charles Loftis, *Lost Angels* (also known as *The Road Home*), Orion, 1989.

Warden Drumgoole, *Lock Up,* TriStar, 1989.

Ivan, *Cerro Torre: Schrei aus Stein* (documentary; also known as *Cerro Torre Scream of Stone, Scream of Stone,* and *Cerro Torre, le cri de la roche*), Alliance, 1990.

O'Connor, *Buster's Bedroom,* Les Productions du Verseau/NEF 2, 1990.

Colonel (some sources cite role as general), *JFK,* Warner Bros., 1991.

Jozef Burski, *Eminent Domain,* Triumph Releasing, 1991.

Ronald Bartel, *Backdraft,* Universal, 1991.

Henderson, *Shadow of the Wolf* (also known as *Agaguk*), Transfilm/Vision International/Le Studio Canal, 1992.

John Williams, *Rakuyo* (also known as *The Setting Sun*), 1992.

Dr. Norman Bethune, *Bethune: Making of a Hero,* 1992.

Roger Hawthorne, *The Railway Station Man,* 1992.

Narrator, *The Poky Little Puppy's First Christmas,* 1992.

Merrick Jamison–Smythe, *Buffy the Vampire Slayer,* Twentieth Century–Fox, 1992.

Flan Kittredge, *Six Degrees of Separation,* Metro–Goldwyn–Mayer, 1993.

Frank, *Benefit of the Doubt* (also known as *Daddy's Home* and *Im Bann des zweifels*), Miramax, 1993.

Jonathan Younger, *Younger and Younger,* Academy Entertainment, 1993.

Kirov, *Red Hot,* SC Entertainment International, 1993.

Narrator, *People of the Forest: The Chimps of Gombe* (documentary), 1993.

(English–language version) Narrator, *Le fleuve aux grandes eaux* (also known as *The Mighty River*), 1993.

Dr. Norman Bethune, *Dr. Bethune,* Tara, 1993.

Andrew Nivens, *The Puppet Masters* (also known as *Robert A. Heinlein's "The Puppet Masters"*), Buena Vista, 1994.

Bob Garvin, *Disclosure,* Warner Bros., 1994.

Craman, *Punch,* Journal Films, 1994.

Himself, *A Century of Cinema* (documentary), 1994.

Major General Donald McClintock, *Outbreak,* Warner Bros., 1995.

Lucien Wilbanks, *A Time to Kill,* Warner Bros., 1996.

Garrett Lawton, *Hollow Point,* 1996.

Jack Shaw/Henry Fields, *The Assignment* (also known as *Jackal*), Sony Pictures Entertainment, 1997.

Jacob Conrad, *Shadow Conspiracy* (also known as *The Shadow Program*), Buena Vista, 1997.

Bill Bowerman, *Without Limits* (also known as *Pre*), Warner Bros., 1998.

Lieutenant Stanton, *Fallen,* Warner Bros., 1998.

Judge Rolf Rausenberger, *Free Money,* 1998.

Captain Robert Everton, *Virus,* Universal, 1999.

Dr. Ben Hillard, *Instinct* (also known as *Ishmael*), Buena Vista, 1999.

Himself, *Virus: Ghost in the Machine,* Universal Studios Home Video, 1999.

Toscano, 1999.

Jerry O'Neill, *Space Cowboys,* Warner Bros., 2000.

Narrator, *Threads of Hope,* 2000.

United Nations Secretary General Douglas Thomas, *The Art of War* (also known as *L'art de guerre*), Warner Bros., 2000.

Dr. Sid, *Final Fantasy: The Spirits Within* (also known as *Fainaru fantaji*), Columbia, 2001.

Don Tyler, *Da wan* (also known as *Big Shot's Funeral, The Funeral of the Famous Star,* and *Happy Funeral*), Sony Pictures Classics, 2001.

Michael, *Panic,* Roxie Releasing, 2001.

Himself, *Fellini: Je suis un grand menteur* (also known as *Fellini: I'm a Born Liar, I'm a Born Liar,* and *Federico Fellini: Sono un gran bugiardo*), 2001, First Look Pictures Releasing, 2003.

Sex at 24 Frames Per Second, 2003.

Inventing Grace, Touching Glory, Teamsters Local 155, 2003.

General Aldryn, *Baltic Storm,* Top Story Filmproduktion, 2003.

John Bridger, *The Italian Job,* Paramount, 2003.

Monroe, *Cold Mountain,* Metro–Goldwyn–Mayer/Miramax, 2003.

Hating Her, Idiom Films, 2003.

Rosario Sarracino, *Piazza delle cinque lune* (also known as *Five Moons Plaza*), Istituto Luce, 2003.

Don Tyler, *Big Shot's Funeral,* 2003.

The Greatest Canadian, CBC, 2004.

Sir! No Sir!, Balcony Rel., 2005.

Ronald Shorter, *Aurora Borealis,* Regent Releasing, 2005.

Ogden C. Osborne, *Fierce People,* Lions Gate Films, 2005.

Mr. Bennet, *Pride & Prejudice,* Universal, 2005.

Carl Wilk, *American Gun,* IFC Films, 2005.

Voice of Colonel Oliver Southern, *Lord of War,* Twentieth Century–Fox, 2005.

John Bell, *An American Haunting* (also known as *An American Haunting–The Billwitch Story*), Lions Gate Films, 2005.

Thorne, *Land of the Blind,* Nordisk Film, 2006.

Hellfrick, *Ask the Dust,* Paramount Vintage, 2006.

Johann von Wolfhaus, *Beerfest,* Warner Bros., 2006.

Narrator, *Dinosaurs: Giants of Patagonia,* La Geode, 2007.

Trumbo, Samuel Goldwyn, 2007.

Narrator, *Mission Antarctique* (also known as *The Last Continent*), Seville Pic, 2007.

Businessman struck by a taxi, *Sleepwalkers,* 2007.

Judge Raines, *Reign Over Me,* Columbia, 2007.

Lars, *Puffball* (also known as *Puffball: The Devil's Eye*), IFC Films, 2007.

Award show presenter, *L'age des tenebres* (also known as *Days of Darkness* and *The Age of Ignorance*), Alliance Atlantis, 2007.

Odgen C. Osborne, *Fierce People,* Lions Gate Films, 2007.

Dalton Trumbo, *Trumbo,* Samuel Goldwyn, 2008.

Nigel Honeycutt, *Fool's Gold,* Warner Bros., 2008.

Voice of President Stone, *Astro Boy,* Summit Entertainment, 2009.

Kranski, *The Con Artist,* Maple Pictures, 2010.

Uncle Aquila, *The Eagle* (also known as *The Eagle of the Ninth*), Focus Features, 2011.

Harry McKenna, *The Mechanic,* 2011.

Film Work:

Coproducer and codirector, *F.T.A.* (also known as *Foxtrot Tango Alpha, Free the Army,* and *The FTA Show*), American International Pictures, 1972.

Executive producer, *Steelyard Blues* (also known as *The Final Crash*), Warner Bros., 1973.

Television Appearances; Series:

Narrator, *Great Books,* The Learning Channel, 1993–2000.

Nathan Templeton, *Commander in Chief,* 2005–2006.

Patrick "Tripp" Darling III, *Dirty Sexy Money,* 2007–2009.

Father Mapple, *Moby Dick,* 2010.

Television Appearances; Miniseries:

Sim, *A Farewell to Arms,* 1966.

Narrator, *The Prize: The Epic Quest for Oil, Money and Power,* PBS, 1993.

Captain William Marsden, *The Oldest Living Confederate Widow Tells All,* CBS, 1994.

Adam Czerniakow, *Uprising,* NBC, 2001.

Narrator, *Queen Victoria's Empire,* PBS, 2001.

Richard Straker, *Salem's Lot* (also known as *Stephen King's "Salem's Lot"*), TNT, 2003.

Captain Walton, *Frankenstein,* 2004.

Bartholomew, *The Pillars of the Earth,* Starz!, 2009.

Television Appearances; Movies:

Terry–Thomas, 1963.

Fortinbras, *Hamlet* (also known as *Hamlet at Elsinore*), BBC, 1964.

The American Civil War, 1965.

Charles Givens, *Play of the Month: Lee Oswald Assassin,* 1966.

Benedeck, *The Sunshine Patriot,* NBC, 1968.

Ethan Hawley, *The Winter of Our Discontent* (also known as *John Steinbeck's "The Winter of Our Discontent"*), CBS, 1983.

Dr. Norman Bethune, *Dr. Bethune* (also known as *Bethune: The Making of a Hero*), 1989.

(Uncredited) *Long Road Home,* 1991.

Doc Murdoch, *Quicksand: No Escape,* USA Network, 1992.

Roger Hawthorne, *The Railway Station Man,* TNT, 1992.

Dr. "Mac" Maclean, *The Lifeforce Experiment* (also known as *The Breakthrough, Dead Men Talk,* and *Le silence de la liberte*), syndicated, 1994.

Citizen Fetisov, *Citizen X,* HBO, 1995.

Garrett Lawton, *Hollow Point* (also known as *Rysk Roulette*), HBO, 1995.

Ted Robards, *Natural Enemy,* HBO, 1997.

Judge Rolf Rausenberg, *Free Money,* Starz!, 1998.

Dr. Bob Shushan, *Behind the Mask,* CBS, 1999.

General Pierre G. T. Beauregard, *C.S.S. Hunley* (also known as *The Hunley*), TNT, 1999.

Jimmy "The Gent" Burke, *The Big Heist,* Arts and Entertainment, 2001.

Clark Clifford, *Path to War,* HBO, 2002.

Customs Agent Bill Meehan, *Human Trafficking,* 2005.

Dr. Charles Eastman, *The Eastmans,* 2009.

Television Appearances; Specials:

The Death of Bessie Smith, [England], 1965.

Lee Harvey Oswald, "Assassin," *Play of the Month,* BBC, 1966.

The Diahann Carroll Show, NBC, 1971.

Bertolucci secondo il cinema, 1976.

Night of 100 Stars (also known as *Night of One Hundred Stars*), ABC, 1982.

Matthew Bennell, *Terror in the Aisles,* 1984.

Narrator, *People of the Forest: The Chimps of Gombe,* 1988.

Voice of Paul Gauguin, *Paul Gauguin: The Savage Dream,* PBS, 1989.

Narrator, *The Poky Little Puppy's First Christmas,* Showtime, 1992.

Narrator, *The Art of War,* The Learning Channel, 1993.

Narrator, *War of the Worlds,* The Learning Channel, 1993.

Narrator, *Le Morte D'Arthur: The Legend of Arthur,* The Learning Channel, 1993.

Narrator, *Frankenstein—The Making of a Monster,* The Learning Channel, 1993.

Narrator, *Beyond Genesis—The Origin of Species,* The Learning Channel, 1993.

Narrator, *Alice in Wonderland,* The Learning Channel, 1993.

Narrator, *Huck Fin,* The Learning Channel, 1994.

Roger Moore: A Matter of Class, 1995.

Host and narrator of *Don Quixote,* The Learning Channel, 1996.

Narrator, *The Scarlet Letter,* The Learning Channel, 1996.

Narrator, *The Prince,* The Learning Channel, 1996.
Narrator, *The Odyssey,* The Learning Channel, 1996.
Narrator, *Plato's Republic,* The Learning Channel, 1996.
Narrator, *Native Son,* The Learning Channel, 1996.
Narrator, *Moby Dick,* The Learning Channel, 1996.
Narrator, *Gulliver's Travels,* The Learning Channel, 1996.
Narrator, *Great Expectations,* The Learning Channel, 1996.
Narrator, *Freud's Interpretation of Dreams,* The Learning Channel, 1996.
Narrator, *Catch–22,* The Learning Channel, 1996.
Narrator, *Walden,* The Learning Channel, 1997.
Narrator, *The Great Gatsby,* The Learning Channel, 1997.
Narrator, *Galileo,* The Learning Channel, 1997.
Narrator, *Bhutan, the Last Shangri-La,* PBS, 1998.
Narrator, *The Naked and the Dead,* The Learning Channel, 1998.
Narrator, *Red Badge of Courage,* The Learning Channel, 1998.
Narrator, *One Flew Over the Cuckoo's Nest,* The Learning Channel, 1998.
Narrator, *Lord of the Flies,* The Learning Channel, 1998.
Narrator, *Heart of Darkness,* The Learning Channel, 1998.
Narrator, *Dracula,* The Learning Channel, 1998.
Narrator, *All Quiet on the Western Front,* The Learning Channel, 1998.
Narrator, *Mind Control,* TBS, 1998.
Narrator, *Alone on the Ice,* PBS, 1999.
Narrator, *Napoleon's Lost Fleet,* The Discovery Channel, 1999.
Narrator, *Pride and Prejudice,* The Learning Channel, 1999.
The AFI's 100 Years ... 100 Stars: America's Greatest Stars, CBS, 1999.
Narrator, *Malcolm X,* The Learning Channel, 1999.
Narrator, *Madame Bovary,* The Learning Channel, 1999.
Narrator, *Crime and Punishment,* The Learning Channel, 1999.
Narrator, *The Grapes of Wrath,* The Learning Channel, 2000.
Narrator, *Queen Victoria's Empire,* PBS, 2000.
Narrator, *1984,* The Learning Channel, 2000.
"Clint Eastwood: Out of the Shadows," *American Masters,* PBS, 2000.
Captain Benjamin Franklin "Hawkeye" Pierce, *Twentieth Century Fox: The Blockbuster Years,* 2000.
The Making of "Space Cowboys," 2000.
AFI's 100 Years, 100 Thrills: America's Most Heart-Pounding Movies, CBS, 2001.
History vs. Hollywood, History Channel, 2001.
The Magic of Fellini, 2002.
Making the Movie: "The Italian Job," MTV, 2003.
The Life and Times of Arthur Erickson, 2004.
Mr. Bennet, *Pride and Prejudice Revisited,* BBC, 2005.

Cannes, 60 ans d'histoires, France 3, 2007.
Nathan Templeton, *President Hollywood,* BBC4, 2008.
Narrator, *Stonehenge Decoded,* National Geographic Channel, 2008.
For Love of Liberty: The Story of America's Black Patriots, Elkins Entertainment, 2010.

Also appeared in *Give Me Your Answer True* and *Hallmark Hall of Fame;* appeared on British television in *Marching to the Sea* and *The Rose Tattoo.*

Television Appearances; Awards Presentations:
The ... Annual Academy Awards, 1972, ABC, 1989.
Presenter, *The ... Annual Academy Awards,* 1977, ABC, 1994.
Presenter, *The American Movie Awards,* 1980.
The Kennedy Center Honors: A Celebration of the Performing Arts, 1981.
The ... Annual Golden Globe Awards, 1981, TBS, 1992, NBC, 2003.
The American Film Institute Salute to Frank Capra, CBS, 1982.
Presenter, *The 47th Annual Primetime Emmy Awards,* Fox, 1995.
The American Film Institute Salute to Clint Eastwood, 1996.
The Kennedy Center Honors: A Celebration of the Performing Arts, CBS, 2000.
2000 Blockbuster Entertainment Awards, 2000.
Announcer, *The 74th Annual Academy Awards,* ABC, 2002.
Presenter, *18th Annual American Cinematheque Award,* AMC, 2003.
The 32nd Annual People's Choice Awards, CBS, 2006.
The 17th Annual Screen Actors Guild Awards, 2011.

Television Appearances; Episodic:
"Flight into Danger," *Studio 4,* BBC, 1962.
Dr. Hal Seaton, "The Troubled Heart," *Suspense,* 1963.
Mitch Scott, "A Pattern of Little Silver Devils," *The Sentimental Agent,* 1963.
Canadian, "For King and Country #1: Out There," *ITV Play of the Week,* ITV, 1963.
James McCleary, "The Happy Suicide," *The Saint,* Associated Television, 1965.
Philip, "Millionaire's Daughter," *Gideon's Way,* Incorporated Television, 1965.
John Wood, "Escape Route," *The Saint,* Associated Television, 1966.
"All Is a Dream to Me," *Court Martial,* ABC, 1966.
Priest, "Focus," *Theatre 625,* 1966.
Union captain, "On the March to the Sea," *Theatre 625,* 1966.
Earle, "Which Way Did He Go, McGill?," *Man in a Suitcase,* Incorporated Television, 1967.
Jessel, "The Superlative Seven," *The Avengers,* Associated British Picture Corporation, 1967.

David Crayley, "Shadow of the Panther," *The Champions,* Incorporated Television, 1968.

Willard, "Day of Execution," *Man in a Suitcase,* Incorporated Television, 1968.

"The Suntan Mob," *The Name of the Game,* NBC, 1969.

The Dick Cavett Show, 1970.

"The First Big Try," *Norman Corwin Presents,* 1972.

Front Page Challenge, 1977.

Good Morning America (also known as *G.M.A.*), 1978.

La edad de oro, 1984.

The Last Resort with Jonathan Ross (also known as *The Last Resort*), Channel 4, 1987.

"Mary Tyler Moore: All American–Girl," *Biography,* 1995.

Voice of Hollis Hurlbut, "Lisa the Iconoclast," *The Simpsons* (animated), Fox, 1996.

Showbiz Today, 1997.

Inside the Actors Studio, Bravo, 1998.

Late Night with Conan O'Brien, 2000.

"Clint Eastwood: Out of the Shadows," *American Masters,* 2000.

"M*A*S*H," *Backstory* (also known as *Hollywood Backstories*), AMC, 2000.

"M*A*S*H: Comedy Under Fire," *History vs. Hollywood* (also known as *History Through the Lens*), 2001.

The Rosie O'Donnell Show, syndicated, 2001.

"A Man for All Stages: The Life and Times of Christopher Plummer," *Life and Times,* 2002.

Cinema mil, Televisio de Catalunya, 2005.

"Donald Sutherland," *HARDtalk Extra,* BBC, 2005.

GMTV, ITV, 2005.

"'Pride & Prejudice': A Classic in the Making," *HBO First Look,* HBO, 2005.

Live with Regis and Kelly, syndicated, 2005.

Corazon de ..., 2006.

MADtv, Fox, 2006.

Narrator, "1966 Green Bay Packers," *America's Game: The Superbowl Champions,* NFL, 2007.

Entertainment Tonight (also known as *E.T.* and *This Week in Entertainment*), syndicated, 2007 and 2009.

The O'Reilly Factor, Fox News, 2008.

Up Close with Carrie Keagan, 2008.

Friday Night with Jonathan Ross, BBC, 2008.

Also appeared in episodes of *Backstory* (also known as *AMC Backstory* and *Hollywood Backstories*), AMC; and *Parkinson,* BBC.

Stage Appearances:

Wally, *The Male Animal,* Hart House Theatre, Toronto, Ontario, Canada, 1952.

August for the People, Royal Court Theatre, London, 1963.

Black man, *Buck White,* George Abbott Theatre, New York City, 1969.

Humbert Humbert, *Lolita,* Brooks Atkinson Theatre, New York City, 1981.

Night of 100 Stars (also known as *Night of One Hundred Stars*), Radio City Music Hall, New York City, 1982.

Enigma Variations, Mark Taper Forum, Los Angeles, 2000, then Royal Alexandra Theatre, Toronto, Ontario, Canada, later Savoy Theatre, London.

Malcolm Raphelson, *Ten Unknowns,* Mitzi E. Newhouse Theatre, New York City, 2001.

Appeared in *Gimmick,* London; and *The Tempest,* Hart House Theatre, Toronto, Ontario, Canada; also appeared in productions of *On a Clear Day You Can See Canterbury, The Shewing Up of Blanco Posnet,* and *Spoon River Anthology.*

Radio Appearances:

This Morning, CBC, 2000.

Performed voice of Scrooge for a radio broadcast of *A Christmas Carol.*

RECORDINGS

Videos:

Narrator, *The War of the Worlds: Great Books,* 1994.

Virus: Ghost in the Machine, 1999.

Hawkeye, *Enlisted: The Story of "M*A*S*H,"* 2000.

Breaking Down the Walls: The Road to Recreating the Warsaw Ghetto Uprising, 2001.

The Making of "Final Fantasy: The Spirits Within," 2001.

Armed and Deadly: The Making of "The Dirty Dozen," Warner Home Video, 2006.

The Bennets, Universal Studios, 2006.

On Set Diaries, Universal Studios, 2006.

Appeared in the video game *Conspiracy;* appeared in the music video "Cloudbusting" by Kate Bush, 1986.

WRITINGS

Screenplays:

(With others) *F.T.A.* (also known as *Foxtrot Tango Alpha, Free the Army,* and *The FTA Show*), American International Pictures, 1972.

OTHER SOURCES

Books:

International Dictionary of Films and Filmmakers, Volume 3: *Actors and Actresses,* St. James Press, 1996.

Periodicals:
Empire, Issue 73, 1995, pp. 64–65.
Premiere, September, 1998, p. 34.

SYAL, Meera 1961(?)–
    (Feroza Syal)

PERSONAL

Original name, Feroza Syal; born June 27, 1961 (some sources say 1962 or 1964), in Wolverhampton, Staffordshire, England; married Chandra Shekhar Bhatia (a journalist), 1989 (divorced, 2002); married Sanjeev Bhaskar (an actor), January 21, 2005; children: (first marriage) Chameli; (second marriage) Sanjeev. *Education:* Studied drama and English at Manchester University.

Addresses: *Agent*—United Agents, 12–26 Lexington St., London W1F 0LE, England.

Career: Actress, writer, and producer. Appeared in television commercials, including Lloyds banking, 2001.

Awards, Honors: Betty Trask Award, 1996, for *Anita and Me;* decorated Member of the Order of the British Empire, 1997; Race in the Media Personality of the Year Award, Commission for Racial Equality, 2000; EMMA (BT Ethnic and Multicultural Media Award), media personality of the year, 2001; Television Award nomination, best entertainment performance, British Academy of Film and Television Arts, 2003, for *The Kumars at No. 42;* National Student Drama Award.

CREDITS

Film Appearances:
Rehana, *Majdhar,* Video Collective, 1983.
Rani, *Sammy and Rosie Get Laid* (also known as *Sammy and Rosie*), Cinecom Pictures, 1987.
Sita, *A Nice Arrangement* (short film), 1994.
It's Not Unusual (short film), 1995.
Miss Chauhan, *Beautiful Thing,* Sony Pictures Classics, 1996.
Breathing generator, *Sixth Happiness,* Regent Releasing, 1997.
Carmen, *Girls' Night,* K2 Entertainment, 1998.
Auntie Shalia, *Anita and Me,* Icon Film Distribution, 2002.
The King of Bollywood, 2004.
Joe's co–passenger, *Scoop,* Focus Features, 2006.

Satvinder's mother, *Jhoom Barabar Jhoom* (also known as *Dance Baby Dance* and *J.B.J.*), 2007.
Rashmi, *Mad Sad & Bad,* Soda Pictures, 2009.
Pushpa Patel, *Desert Flower,* National Geographic Entertainment, 2009.
Lopa Dutt, *Rafta Rafta,* Optimum Releasing, 2010.
Dia's parent, *You Will Meet a Tall Dark Stranger,* Sony Pictures Classics, 2010.

Film Work:
Coproducer, *Anita and Me,* 2002.

Television Appearances; Series:
Val, *Kinsey,* 1990.
Various, *The Real McCoy,* BBC, 1991.
Tina Beare, *Keeping Mum,* BBC, 1997–98.
Aysha Kapoor, *Fat Friends,* ITV and BBC America, 2000.
Ruby, *Bedtime,* 2001.
Sushil "Ummi" Kumar aka Granny Sushila, *The Kumars at No. 42,* BBC2 and BBC America, 2001–2006.
Rupinder, *All About Me,* BBC, 2002.
DCI Anita Wishart, *Murder Investigation Team* (also known as *M.I.T.: Murder Investigation Team*), ITV, 2003, and Arts and Entertainment, 2004.
Narrator, *Drama Connections,* BBC, 2005.
Sunita, *Life Isn't All Ha Ha Hee Hee,* 2005.
Narrator, *The Cult of ...,* BBC, 2008.
Aunty Hayley, *Beautiful People,* ABC Family, 2008–2009.
Storyteller, *Horrible Histories,* 2009.
Tara Sodi, *Holby City,* BBC, 2009.

Television Appearances; Miniseries:
Anna, *A Little Princess,* PBS, 1986.
Anne Denver, *Band of Gold* (also known as *Gold*), ITV and HBO, 1995.
Zita, *Holding On,* BBC and BBC America, 1997.
Madam Marlene, "The Rising of the Moon," *The Mrs. Bradley Mysteries,* BBC America, 1999.
Liz Shannon, *The Amazing Mrs Pritchard,* BBC, 2006, PBS, 2007.
Miranda, *Jekyll,* BBC1 and BBC America, 2007.

Television Appearances; Movies:
Devi Kumar, *Bureaucracy of Love,* 1987.
Mira (Erratic Dramatic), *Gummed Labels,* Channel 4, 1992.
Tasleema, *Flight,* 1995.
Various, *Jack and Jeremy's Police 4,* 1995.
Reporter, *Crossing the Floor,* BBC, 1996.
Judith Adams, *Forgive and Forget,* 2000.
Joyti De–Laurey, *The Secretary Who Stole £4 Million,* BBC, 2005.
Mary (The BFG), *The Children's Part at the Palace,* BBC, 2006.

Television Appearances; Specials:

The Great Book Quiz, 1998.

2000 Today, BBC, 1999.

100 Greatest TV Moments from Hell, Channel 4, 2000.

Various, *Goodness Gracious Me: Back Where They Came From,* 2001.

Party at the Palace: The Queen's Concerts, Buckingham Palace, BBC, 2002.

Narrator, *Bitches & Beauty Queens: The Making of Miss India* (documentary), Channel 4, 2002.

Sushil "Ummi" Kumar aka Granny Sushila Kumar, *The Kumars at No. 42,* BBC2 and BBC America, 2002.

The Big Read (documentary), BBC, 2003.

Dale's Wedding (documentary), 2003.

Sushil "Ummi" Kumar, *Children in Need,* BBC, 2003.

Sushil "Ummi" Kumar, *Christmas Night with the Stars,* BBC, 2003.

Sushil "Ummi" Kumar, *Comic Relief 2003: The Big Hair Do,* BBC, 2003.

Various, *The All Star Comedy Show,* ITV, 2004.

Narrator, *A Place in France: An Indian Summer,* 2004.

2003 TV Moments, BBC, 2004.

(Uncredited) *The Comedians' Comedian,* Channel 4, 2005.

Britain's 50 Greatest Comedy Sketches, Channel 4, 2005.

100 Greatest Funny Moments, Channel 4, 2006.

Happy Birthday BAFTA, ITV1, 2007.

Narrator, *What's Eating Victoria Beckham?,* BBC America, 2007.

Television Appearances; Episodic:

(As Feroza Syal) Woman in street, "A Friend in Need," *The Bill,* ITV1, 1984.

Mrs. Singh, *The Secret Diary of Adrian Mole Aged 13 3/4,* ITV and PBS, 1985.

(As Feroza Syal) "Undesirable Activities," *Black Silk,* BBC, 1985.

Matron, "No Crying He Makes," *Ruth Rendell,* PBS, 1988.

Council supervisor, "Trouble in the Fields," *Boon,* ITV, 1990.

Solicitor, "Machines," *The Bill,* ITV1, 1991.

Linda, "Reputations," *The Bill,* ITV1, 1991.

Sharon Lal, "Double Exposure," *Taggart,* 1992.

Farah Khan, "My Sister–Wife," *Screen Two,* BBC, 1992.

Have I Got News for You, BBC, 1992, 1993, 1999.

The Brain Drain, BBC, 1993.

Ranting woman, "O Mary This London," *Screen Two,* BBC, 1994.

Suzy, "New Best Friend," *Absolutely Fabulous,* BBC1, 1994.

Miss Choudry, "Knowing the Score," *The Bill,* ITV1, 1995.

Dr. Jean Lowell, *Degrees of Error,* BBC, 1995.

Sangita Sharma, "The Army Game," *Soldier Soldier,* ITV, 1995.

Sangita Sharma, "Love and War," *Soldier Soldier,* ITV, 1995.

Sangita Sharma, "Stick Together," *Soldier Soldier,* ITV, 1995.

Barmaid, "Sex 'n Death," *Drop the Dead Donkey,* Channel 4, 1996.

Ruby, BBC, 1997.

"Goodness Gracious What a Great Show," *Light Lunch,* Channel 4, 1998.

Melinda's Big Night In, 1998.

Various, *Goodness Gracious Me,* BBC2, 1998.

Late Lunch, Channel 4, 1999.

Room 101, BBC, 1999.

Comedy Cafe, 1999.

Volunteer, "Angels," *The Strangers,* Sky Television, 2000.

It's Only TV ... But I Like It, 2000.

Late Review, 2000, 2005.

Loose Women, ITV, 2000, 2005, 2006, 2008.

Marta Drusic, "Blue on Blue: Part 2," *In Deep,* 2001.

Marta Drusic, "Ghost Squad: Part 1," *In Deep,* 2001.

"Meera Syal," *The South Bank Show,* ITV, 2002.

"Spotlights & Saris: Making Bombay Dreams," *Omnibus,* BBC, 2002.

The Buzz, YTV, 2002.

Sukie, "New England," *Linda Green,* BBC1 and Showtime, 2002.

Sushil "Ummi" Kumar, *Top of the Pops,* BBC, 2003.

V Graham Norton, Channel 4, 2003.

"Aquatic Animals," *QI,* BBC, 2003.

This Morning, ITV, 2003, 2006.

Janan Hamad, *Bad Girls,* 2004.

The Terry and Gaby Show, Channel 5, 2004.

"Meera Syal," *Star Portraits with Rolf Harris,* BBC, 2004.

Richard & Judy, Channel 4, 2004.

From Bard to Verse, 2004.

"Meera Syal," *Who Do You Think You Are?,* NBC, 2004.

GMTV, ITV, 2004.

Breakfast, BBC, 2004, 2005.

"Goodness Gracious Me," *Comedy Connections,* BBC, 2005.

Parkinson, 2005, 2007.

The Paul O'Grady Show, ITV, 2005, 2009.

8 Out of 10 Cats, Channel 4, 2006.

Girls Who Do: Comedy, BBC, 2006.

The F Word, Channel 4 and BBC America, 2007.

School's Out, BBC, 2007.

Headteacher, *Kingdom,* ITV, 2007.

"Meera Syal," *A Taste of My Life,* BBC, 2008.

Snooty neighbor, "Uncle Max Builds a Shed," *Uncle Max,* 2008.

Jess Robinson, "In Vino Veritas," *Minder,* 2009.

Who Wants to Be a Millionaire, syndicated, 2009.

Nasreen Chaudhry, "The Hungry Earth," *Doctor Who,* BBC1 and Syfy, 2010.

Nasreen Chaudhry, "Cold Blood," *Doctor Who,* BBC1 and Syfy, 2010.

"After Effects," *Doctor Who Confidential,* BBC, 2010.

The 5 O'Clock Show, 2010.

The ONE Show, BBC, 2010.

Also appeared as herself, *Nigella;* voice, *Bob and Margaret* (animated), Comedy Central.

Television Work; Series:
Associate producer, *Life Isn't All Ha Ha Hee Hee,* 2005.
Script consultant, *Mumbai Calling,* 2008.

Stage Appearances:
Bibi, *The Great Celestial Cow,* Royal Court Theatre, London, 1984.
Shaheen, *Minor Complications,* Royal Court Theatre, 1984.
Ursula, *Byrthrite,* Royal Court Theatre, 1986.
Film Film Film, Shaw Theatre, London, 1986.
All the Fun of the Fair, Half Moon Theatre, London, 1986.
Jacinta, *Serious Money,* Royal Court Theatre, then Joseph Papp Public Theatre, New York City, both 1987.
Anita, *My Girl,* Theatre Royal Stratford East, London, 1989.
Anitra, Ase, and cowgirl, *Peer Gynt,* National Theatre, London, 1990.
The Oppressed Minorities Big Fun Show, Edinburgh Festival and Shaw Theatre, London, 1992.
The Vagina Monologues, New Ambassador's Theatre, London, 2001.
Spike Mulligan: I Told You I Was Ill, Guildhall Theatre, London, 2002.
Lopa, *Rafta Rafta,* National Theatre, 2007.
Title role, *Shirley Valentine* (one–woman play), Chocolate Factory Theatre, London, 2010.

Also appeared as Leonardo's wife, *Blood Wedding,* Half Moon Theatre, London; Sona, *Kirti Dona and Ba,* Haymarket Theatre, London; Babbli, *Kissing God,* Hampstead Theatre, London; Mrs. Candour, *School for Scandal,* Bristol Old Vic, Bristol, England.

Major Tours:
Bibi, *The Great Celestial Cow,* U.K. cities, 1984.

RECORDINGS

Music Videos:
Appeared in "Spirit in the Sky" by Gareth Gates.

WRITINGS

Screenplays:
Bhaji on the Beach, First Look Pictures, 1993.
A Nice Arrangement, 1994.
Anita and Me, 2002.

Screenplay Stories:
Bhaji on the Beach, First Look Pictures, 1993.

Television Movies:
Goodness Gracious Me: Back Where They Came From, 2001.

Television Episodes:
Tandoori Nights, 1985.
(As Feroza Syal) "Undesirable Activities," *Black Silk,* BBC, 1985.
The Real McCoy, BBC, 1991.
"My Sister–Wife," *Screen Two,* BBC, 1992.
Goodness Gracious Me, BBC2, 1998.
Life Isn't All Ha Ha Hee Hee, 2006.

Television Music; Episodic:
Goodness Gracious Me, BBC2, 1998.

Stage Plays:
The Oppressed Minorities Big Fun Show, Edinburgh Festival and Shaw Theatre, London, 1992.

Stage Musical Books:
Bombay Dreams, Apollo Victoria Theatre, London, 2002, then Broadway Theatre, New York City, 2004.

Novels:
Anita and Me, Flamingo, 1996, New Press, 1997.
Life Isn't All Ha Ha Hee Hee, 1999, New Press, 2000.

OTHER SOURCES

Books:
Contemporary Authors Online, Gale, 2004.

Periodicals:
Daily Mail (London), April 7, 2010, p. 35.

T

TAKESHI, Kosugi Kane
     See KOSUGI, Kane

TAYLOR, Buck 1938–

PERSONAL

Original name, Walter Clarence Taylor III; born May 13, 1938, in Hollywood, CA; son of Dub Taylor (an actor); married Judy Nugent, March 18, 1961 (divorced, 1983); married Goldie (a flight attendant); children: (first marriage) Tiffany, Adam C. (an actor and director; deceased), Matthew (a stunt performer), Cooper (an actor). *Education:* Attended Chouinard Art Institute, Los Angeles.

Addresses: *Agent*—Twentieth Century Artists, 4605 Lankershim Blvd., Suite 305, North Hollywood, CA 91602; Linda McAlister Talent, 100 Oak Lane, Waxahachie, TX 95167.

Career: Actor and artist.

Awards, Honors: Golden Boot Award, Motion Picture and Television Fund, 1993; inducted into Cowboy Hall of Fame, 1981; Cowboy Spirit Award, Festival of the West, 1998; Bronze Wrangler Award (with others), outstanding theatrical motion picture, Western Heritage Awards, 2007, for *Truce.*

CREDITS

Film Appearances:
Mannion, *Ensign Pulver,* 1964.

Dear John, *The Wild Angels,* American International Pictures, 1966.

Gabriel, *And Now Miguel,* Universal, 1966.

Gage, *Devil's Angels,* American International Pictures, 1967.

Poolside interviewer number two, *The St. Valentine's Day Massacre,* 1967.

Mike Lassiter, *Doc Hooker's Bunch,* 1976.

Bovey, *Pony Express Rider,* Doty/Dayton, 1976.

Beartooth (also known as *The Adventures of Beartooth*), 1978.

Dynamite Dick, *Cattle Annie and Little Britches,* Universal, 1981.

Robert Edward Gattlin, *The Legend of the Lone Ranger,* Universal, 1981.

Sergeant Bridges, *Triumphs of a Man Called Horse* (also known as *El triunfo de un hombre llamado Caballo*), Jensen Farley, 1982.

The Slim Dusty Movie, 1984.

Charlie, *Dark Before Dawn,* 1988.

Bob, *Big Bad John,* Magnum Entertainment, 1990.

Nick, *Payback,* Republic, 1991.

Colonel William Gamble, *Gettysburg* (also known as *The Killer Angels*), New Line Cinema, 1993.

Turkey Creek Jack Johnson, *Tombstone,* Buena Vista, 1993.

Eye–crossed reb, *Wild Wild West,* Warner Bros., 1999.

Captain Myles Keogh, *Comanche,* 2000.

Pap Doolin, *Jericho,* Black Knight Productions, 2000.

Big Texas Show judge, *Grand Champion,* 2002.

General Maxcy Gregg, *Gods and Generals,* Warner Bros., 2003.

Old man Nickels, *Screen Door Jesus,* FCM Productions, 2003.

Settler, *The Alamo,* Buena Vista, 2004.

Bob Draper, *The Wendell Baker Story,* RCV, 2005.

Harry Dodds, *Truce,* Anthem Pictures, 2005.

Dr. Adam Galen, *Hell to Pay,* Echo Bridge, 2005.

Buckskin Charlie, *Miracle at Sage Creek* (also known as *Christmas Miracle at Sage Creek*), Universal, 2005.

Wagner, *Flicka,* Twentieth Century–Fox, 2006.

Ambrose Cornell, *The Mist* (also known as *Stephen King's "The Mist"*), Metro–Goldwyn–Mayer, 2007.

Narrator, *Bloody Dawn: The Lawrence Massacre*, Lone Chimney Films, 2007.

W. H. "Pete" Snyder, *The Legend of Hell's Gate: An American Conspiracy*, Silver Sail Entertainment, 2010.

Frank Taylor, *Palominas*, Desert Moon, 2010.

Bent, *The Last Horseman*, Hometown Studio, 2010.

Television Appearances; Series:

John "Brad" Bradford, *The Monroes*, ABC, 1966–67.

Newly O'Brien, *Gunsmoke* (also known as *Gun Law* and *Marshal Dillon*), CBS, 1967–75.

Detective Bussey, a recurring role, *Dallas*, CBS, 1990–91.

Television Appearances; Miniseries:

Reed Carney, *Louis L'Amour's "The Sacketts"* (also known as *The Daybreakers* and *The Sacketts*), NBC, 1979.

Joe McBride, *Wild Times*, syndicated, 1980.

John Steinbeck's "East of Eden" (also known as *East of Eden*), ABC, 1982.

Egloffstein, *Dream West*, CBS, 1986.

Television Appearances; Movies:

George Fewster, *Standing Tall*, NBC, 1978.

Joe, *Kate Bliss and the Ticker Tape Kid*, ABC, 1978.

Petrie, *Dangerous Company*, CBS, 1982.

Feeny, *No Man's Land*, 1984.

Cowboy, *Wild Horses*, CBS, 1985.

Grey, *Louis L'Amour's "Down the Long Hills"* (also known as *Down the Long Hills*), ABC, 1986.

Homer, *Proud Men*, ABC, 1987.

John Colorado "Buck" Smith, *The Alamo: Thirteen Days to Glory*, NBC, 1987.

Newly O'Brien, *Gunsmoke: Return to Dodge*, CBS, 1987.

Shaving cowboy, *Timestalkers*, CBS, 1987.

Porter, *Desperado: The Outlaw Wars*, NBC, 1989.

Tile Coker, *Louis L'Amour's "Conagher"* (also known as *Conagher*), TNT, 1991.

Steve Grisham, *Dallas: J. R. Returns*, CBS, 1996.

George Neville, *Rough Riders* (also known as *Teddy Roosevelt & the Rough Riders*), TNT, 1997.

Captain Adam Gunther, *Hard Time*, TNT, 1998.

Charlie, *The Soul Collector*, CBS, 1999.

Parson Brown, *The Trail to Hope Rose*, 2004.

Television Appearances; Episodic:

Gunman, "Mission—Varina," *The Rebel*, 1961.

Eddie, "The Treasure," *Have Gun Will Travel*, CBS, 1962.

Mickey Vecchione, "My Son the Social Worker," *Going My Way*, 1963.

Joe, "Don't Look Down, Don't Look Back," *The Greatest Show on Earth*, 1963.

Jamie, "Terror at High Point," *The Fugitive*, ABC, 1963.

"Gold–Plated Maverick," *Stoney Burke*, ABC, 1963.

"Kincaid," *Stoney Burke*, ABC, 1963.

Josh, "Johnny Shiloh: Part 1 & 2," *Disneyland* (also known as *Disney's Wonderful World*, *The Disney Sunday Movie*, *The Magical World of Disney*, *The Wonderful World of Disney*, *Walt Disney*, *Walt Disney Presents*, and *Walt Disney's Wonderful World of Color*), 1963.

Bruce Baker, "The Disastro–Nauts," *My Favorite Martian*, CBS, 1964.

Corporal Moody, "Decision," *Twelve O'Clock High*, ABC, 1964.

Deputy Plumb, "Smile of a Dragon," *The Virginian*, NBC, 1964.

Gard Hayden, "Don't Open Till Doomsday," *The Outer Limits*, ABC, 1964.

Howard Sears, "Divorce, Bryant Park Style," *My Three Sons*, ABC, 1964.

Scott Briscoe, "A Gallows for Sam Horn," *The Virginian*, NBC, 1964.

"A Bird in the Solitude Singing," *Ben Casey*, ABC, 1964.

"The Hostage," *Bonanza*, NBC, 1964.

Tony, "The Night the Monkey Died," *The Greatest Show on Earth*, 1964.

Carlisle, "Rick, the Law Clerk," *The Adventures of Ozzie & Harriet*, 1964.

Jim Fraser, "Home, James," *Karen*, 1964.

Corporal Moody, "Decision," *12 O'Clock High*, 1964.

"Little Girl Lost," *Mr. Novak*, 1964.

"The Silent Dissuaders," *Mr. Novak*, 1964.

"Honor—and All That," *Mr. Novak*, 1965.

Dancer, "Death Scene," *The Alfred Hitchcock Hour*, NBC, 1965.

Howard Sears, "All the Weddings," *My Three Sons*, ABC, 1965.

John Bedford, "The Dead Man's Hand," *The Legend of Jesse James*, ABC, 1965.

Skeeter Ames, "The Chottsie Gubenheimer Story," *Wagon Train*, ABC, 1965.

Tobin, "The First Day," *Combat!*, ABC, 1965.

Turk, "The Young Marauders," *The Big Valley*, ABC, 1965.

Corporal, "A Destiny Which Made Us Brothers," *Branded*, NBC, 1966.

Ed Rule, "The Cave–In," *The F.B.I.*, ABC, 1966.

Jonathan Warren, "The Lost Colony," *Daniel Boone*, NBC, 1966.

Lem Bliss, "Men with Guns," *The Virginian*, NBC, 1966.

Jeetleman, "The Bankroll," *Combat!*, ABC, 1967.

Leonard Parker, "Vengeance: Parts 1 & 2," *Gunsmoke*, CBS, 1967.

"The Taming of Trudy Bell," *Death Valley Days*, syndicated, 1969.

"Ken Curtis," *This Is Your Life*, 1972.

Foster, "Shadow of Fear," *Barnaby Jones*, CBS, 1977.

Laird, "The Cherokee Trail," *Disneyland* (also known as *Disney's Wonderful World, The Disney Sunday Movie, The Magical World of Disney, The Wonderful World of Disney, Walt Disney, Walt Disney Presents,* and *Walt Disney's Wonderful World of Color*), 1981.
Clyde, "Child's Play," *The Fall Guy,* ABC, 1982.
Renfield, "The Woman in White," *Matt Houston,* ABC, 1983.
Buddy, "Bloodlines," *Simon & Simon,* CBS, 1984.
Sam Rand, "Psychic Terror," *T. J. Hooker,* ABC, 1984.
"Minneapolis: Six Months Down," *Lottery$,* ABC, 1984.
Captain Angus Flint, "Buffalo Who?," *Wildside,* ABC, 1985.
Ralph Russell, *General Hospital,* ABC, 1985.
Officer Phillips, "Blood Sport: Parts 1 & 2," *T. J. Hooker,* CBS, 1986.
Driver, "Appearances," *Starman,* ABC, 1987.
Stan, "The Test," *Starman,* ABC, 1987.
"Squaring Off," *Paradise* (also known as *Guns of Paradise*), CBS, 1989.
Fred Morgan, "Eye of the Beholder," *Knots Landing,* CBS, 1991.
Fred Morgan, "The Gun Also Rises," *Knots Landing,* CBS, 1991.
Fred Morgan, "The Question Game," *Knots Landing,* CBS, 1991.
Slatter, "The Women," *Paradise* (also known as *Guns of Paradise*), CBS, 1991.
"The Presence of Mine Enemies," *The Young Riders,* ABC, 1991.
Logan Reno, "War Zone," *Walker, Texas Ranger,* CBS, 1995.
Sheriff Jack Lynch, "Miracle at Middle Creek," *Walker, Texas Ranger,* CBS, 1996.
Ben Lily, *Comanche Moon,* 2008.

Television Appearances; Pilots:
Billy Burnett, *The Busters,* CBS, 1978.
Laird, *The Cherokee Trail* (also known as *Louis L'Amour's "The Cherokee Train"*), CBS, 1981.

Television Appearances; Specials:
All American Cowboy, 1985.
We Stand Alone Together: The Men of Easy Company, HBO, 2001.
TV Road Trip: Los Angeles, Travel Channel, 2002.

RECORDINGS

Videos:
The Making of "Miracle at Sage Creek," Universal, 2005.
When Darkness Came: The Making of "The Mist," 2008.

TEED, Jill

PERSONAL

Children: one daughter.

Career: Actress.

CREDITS

Television Appearances; Series:
Laura, *Cold Squad* (also known as *Files from the Past*), 2000–2002.
Peggy Tanner, a recurring role, *Falcon Beach,* ABC Family, 2006–2007.
Mrs. Gordon, *Flash Gordon,* Sci–Fi Channel, 2007–2008.

Television Appearances; Movies:
Ellen, *Seasons of the Heart,* NBC, 1994.
Barbara Thomas, *Roommates,* NBC, 1994.
News anchor, *Nowhere to Hide,* ABC, 1994.
Webster, *Dangerous Indiscretion,* 1994, ABC, 1997.
Sandi, *She Stood Alone: The Tailhook Scandal,* ABC, 1995.
Christina Beckett, *Deceived by Trust: A Moment of Truth Movie,* NBC, 1995.
Daniels, *The Final Cut,* HBO, 1996.
Jolene, *When Friendship Kills* (also known as *A Secret Between Friends: A Moment of Truth Movie*), NBC, 1996.
FBI Special Agent Karen Carter, *Abduction of Innocence* (also known as *Abduction of Innocence: A Moment of Truth Movie*), NBC, 1996.
Kit, *Fear of Flying* (also known as *Turbulence 2: Fear of Flying*), Cinemax, 2000.
Michele, *First Shot* (also known as *Cross Line*), TBS, 2002.
Lisa Rudolph, *Damaged Care,* 2002.
Clair, *A Peek Inside,* 2004.

Television Appearances; Pilots:
(Uncredited) Joanna, *Party of Five,* Fox, 1994.
Mrs. Gordon, *Flash Gordon,* Sci–Fi Channel, 2007.

Television Appearances; Episodic:
Officer Rice, "Partner in Crime," *Street Justice,* 1992.
Glenna, "The Jersey Devil," *The X–Files,* Fox, 1993.
Detective Shelly Stein, *Traps,* CBS, c. 1993.
Marshal Lisa Van Horn, *The Marshal,* ABC, c. 1994, 1995.
"The Furlough," *Hawkeye,* syndicated, 1994.
Serena Braxton, "The Weaker Sex," *Sliders,* Fox, 1995.

Kayla Brooks, "Reluctant Heroes," *Highlander* (also known as *Highlander: The Series*), syndicated, 1995.

Mystery woman, "Brothers Grim," *Strange Luck,* Fox, 1995.

September Rehne, "Blinded by the Son," *Strange Luck,* Fox, 1996.

Trent, "Cold Storage," *Viper,* syndicated, 1997.

Carolyn, "Criminal Nature," *The Outer Limits* (also known as *The New Outer Limits*), Showtime, 1998.

Nora, "Options," *Welcome to Paradox,* Sci–Fi Channel, 1998.

Talia, "The Undesirables," *First Wave,* Sci–Fi Channel, 1998.

Sister, "Spellbound," *Night Man,* The Disney Channel, 1999.

Jane Farraday, "Zero," *The Net,* USA Network, 1999.

Jane Farraday, "Last Man Standing," *The Net,* USA Network, 1999.

Tory Beth Walters, "What Will the Neighbors Think?," *The Outer Limits* (also known as *The New Outer Limits*), Showtime, 1999.

Marika Layton, "The Real Deal," *The Sentinel,* UPN, 1999.

Gwen Hutchinson, "Abaddon," *The Outer Limits* (also known as *The New Outer Limits*), Showtime, 2000.

Dr. Packard, "Lonewolf," *Freedom,* UPN, 2000.

Yolanda Reese as Stacy Monroe, "Wormhole X–Treme!," *Stargate SG–1,* Showtime, 2001.

Valerie Simms, "Moonstruck," *Beyond Belief: Fact or Fiction* (also known as *Beyond Belief*), 2002.

Colonel Larsh, "Code of Silence," *Just Cause,* PAX, 2002.

Captain Maggie Sawyer, "Insurgence," *Smallville* (also known as *Smallville Beginnings*), The WB, 2003.

Captain Maggie Sawyer, "Exile," *Smallville* (also known as *Smallville Beginnings*), The WB, 2003.

Judge Marjorie Rustin, "Family Man," *John Doe,* Fox, 2003.

Young Blades, PAX, 2004.

Suzie Colter, "Day 1,370: Part 1," *The Days,* ABC, 2004.

Sergeant Hadrian, "Act of Contrition," *Battlestar Galactica* (also known as *BSG*), Sci–Fi Channel, 2004.

Sergeant Hadrian, "Litmus," *Battlestar Galactica* (also known as *BSG*), Sci–Fi Channel, 2004.

Janice, "Welcome to the Funhouse," *Zixx: Level Two,* YTV, 2005.

Janice, "Trust No One," *Zixx: Level Two,* YTV, 2005.

Janice, "Pet Project," *Zixx: Level Two,* YTV, 2005.

Janice, "Dwayne's World," *Zixx: Level Two,* YTV, 2005.

(In archive footage) Yolanda Reese as Stacy Monroe, "Citizen Joe," *Stargate SG–1,* Sci–Fi Channel, 2005.

Detective Maggie Sawyer, "Exposed," *Smallville* (also known as *Smallville Beginnings*), The WB, 2005.

Teri, "Labia Majora," *The L Word,* Showtime, 2006.

Teri, "Lost Weekend," *The L Word,* Showtime, 2006.

Yolanda Reese as Stacy Monroe, "200," *Stargate SG–1,* Sci–Fi Channel, 2006.

Mrs. Prendergast, "What about Blob," *Reaper,* The CW, 2007.

Mrs. Prendergast, "Love, Bullets, and Blacktop," *Reaper,* The CW, 2007.

Detective Maggie Sawyer, "Descent," *Smallville* (also known as *Smallville Beginnings*), The WB, 2008.

Colonel Sasha Patel, "End of Line," *Caprica,* Syfy, 2010.

Television Appearances; Other:

SEAL team member, *Creature* (miniseries; also known as *Peter Benchley's "Creature"*), ABC, 1998.

X–Pose: X2 Mutants Uncovered (special), Fox, 2003.

Film Appearances:

Beth, *Impolite,* Asylum, 1992.

Jane, *Bad Company,* 1995.

Renee Cote, *Mission to Mars* (also known as *M2M*), Buena Vista, 2000.

Tracie, *Along Came a Spider,* Paramount, 2001.

Madeline Drake, *X2* (also known as *X–Men 2, X–Men 2: X–Men United,* and *X2: X–Men United*), Twentieth Century–Fox, 2003.

Claire, *Going the Distance* (also known as *National Lampoon's "Going the Distance"*), Seville Pictures, 2004.

Bartender, *An Unfinished Life,* Miramax, 2005.

News reporter, *Black Christmas* (also known as *Black X–Mas*), Metro–Goldwyn–Mayer/Dimension Films, 2006.

Miss Johnson, *American Pie Presents: The Book of Love,* Universal Studios Home Entertainment, 2009.

Grace Carroll, *Charlie St. Cloud,* Universal, 2010.

WRITINGS

Television Songwriter; Episodic:

"What a Day," in "Voices Carry: Part 1," *Degrassi: The Next Generation,* The N, 2004.

THOMPSON, Sarah 1979–

PERSONAL

Born October 25, 1979, in Los Angeles, CA; married Brad Kane. *Education:* Attended Barnard College, Columbia University; studied acting with Deborah Aquila, and at Lesly Kahn and Company, HB Studio, Moscow Art Theatre, Circle in the Square, and the Juilliard School.

Addresses: *Agent*—Silver, Massetti, and Szatmary, 8730 West Sunset Blvd., Suite 440, West Hollywood, CA 90069.

Career: Actress.

CREDITS

Film Appearances:
Beth, *The Ice Storm,* Twentieth Century–Fox, 1997.
Erica, *A Wake in Providence,* Mister P. Productions, 1999.
My Gardener, 2003.
Krista the Barista, *Malibu's Most Wanted,* Warner Bros., 2003.
Cindy, *L.A. Twister,* Indican Pictures, 2004.
Herself, *"Angel": The Final Season* (documentary), 2005.
Zoe Adams, *Brutal,* Barnholtz Entertainment, 2007.
Katie, *The Pink Conspiracy,* Cinema Epoch, 2007.
Samantha Billows, *Dear Me,* 2008.
The woman, *Break,* Cinema Epoch, 2008.
Angie Albright, *Babysitter Wanted,* Big Screen Entertainment Group, 2008.
Katie, *Broken Windows,* Vanguard Cinema, 2008.
Bertha Cronje, *Hansie,* Global Creative Studios, 2008.
Reagan, *A Christmas Proposal,* Peace Arch Home Entertainment, 2008.
Herself, *Saravia* (documentary), 2008.
Sarie, *Brooklyn's Finest* (also known as *Crossing*), Overture Films, 2009.
Herself, *"Babysitter Wanted": Behind the Scenes* (short documentary), Lions Gate Films Home Entertainment, 2009.
Sarah, *Raajneeti,* 2010.
Tina, *A Nanny for Christmas,* Feifer Worldwide, 2010.

Television Appearances; Series:
Dana Poole, *Boston Public,* Fox, 2000–2002.
Eve, *Angel,* The WB, 2003–2004.
Bambi, *Line of Fire,* ABC, 2003–2004.
Rose, *7th Heaven* (also known as *Seventh Heaven*), The WB, 2005–2006.

Television Appearances; Movies:
Danielle Sherman, *Cruel Intentions 2* (also known as *Cruel Intentions 2: Manchester Prep* and *Manchester Prep*), Fox, 2000.
Annie, *Taking Chance,* HBO, 2009.

Television Appearances; Pilots:
Daria, *Madigan Men,* ABC, 2000.
Bambi, *Line of Fire,* ABC, 2004.

Television Appearances; Episodic:
Bobbi, "The Lost Sheep Squadron," *Soul Man,* ABC, 1997.
Bobbi, "Public Embarrassment and Todd's First Sermon," *Soul Man,* ABC, 1997.
Lucienda, "College," *The Sopranos,* HBO, 1999.

Brittany, "Old Habits–New Beginnings," *Strangers with Candy,* Comedy Central, 1999.
Young Deena Silva, *As the World Turns,* CBS, 1999.
Delaney Park, "Subject: Three Thirteen" (also known as "Subject: Homecoming"), *Freaky Links,* Fox, 2000.
Christina, "Rules of the Road," *Going to California,* Showtime, 2001.
Kristie, "Two Sides to Every Angel," *Touched by an Angel,* Fox, 2002.
Madeleine Bainbridge, "Body Double," *The Division,* Lifetime, 2003.
Lilly Dolan, "Crash and Burn," *Without a Trace* (also known as *W.A.T.*), CBS, 2007.
Nikki, "Last Resort," *House M.D.* (also known as *House* and *Dr. House*), Fox, 2008.
The John Kerwin Show, syndicated, 2008.
Cynthia, *All My Children,* ABC, 2010.

RECORDINGS

Music Videos:
Appeared in music video for Pete Munday, 2002.

TOLAN, Peter 1958–

PERSONAL

Full name, Peter James Tolan III; born July 5, 1958, in Scituate, MA; married; wife's name, Leslie (a producer and editor); children: (previous marriage) a son; (with Leslie) Beatrice, one other son. *Education:* Attended University of Massachusetts at Amherst.

Addresses: *Agent*—Creative Artists Agency, 2000 Avenue of the Stars, Los Angeles, CA 90067.

Career: Writer, producer, director, and actor. With Linda Wallem, formed comedy–theatrical team "Wallem & Tolan."

Awards, Honors: Emmy Award, 1992, and Emmy Award nomination, 1993, both outstanding comedy series (with others), for *Murphy Brown;* Emmy Award nomination (with others), outstanding writing in a comedy series, 1993, for "The Spider Episode," *The Larry Sanders Show;* Annual CableACE Awards (with others), best comedy series, National Cable Television Association, 1993, 1994, 1995, and Emmy Award nominations (with others), outstanding comedy series, 1993, 1994, 1995, all for *The Larry Sanders Show;* two Emmy Award nominations (with Garry Shandling), outstanding writing for a comedy series, 1995, for episodes "Hank's Night in the Sun" and "The Mr. Sharon

Stone Show," *The Larry Sanders Show;* Emmy Award nomination, outstanding writing for a comedy series, and Writers Guild of America Television Award, best episodic comedy, both 1996, for "Arthur after Hours," *The Larry Sanders Show;* Emmy Award nomination, 1997, for "My Name Is Asher Kingsley," *The Larry Sanders Show;* Writers Guild of America Television Award nomination, best episodic comedy, 1997, for "Eight," *The Larry Sanders Show;* Emmy Award nomination (with Shandling), outstanding writing for a comedy series, 1998, for the episode "Flip," for *The Larry Sanders Show;* Emmy Award nominations (with Denis Leary), outstanding writing for a drama series and outstanding directing for a drama series, both 2005, for pilot episode, *Rescue Me;* honorary doctorate, University of Massachusetts at Amherst, 2008; Emmy Award nomination (with Brad Hatfield), outstanding original music and lyrics, 2010, for song "How Lovely to Be a Vegetable," in episode "Disease," *Rescue Me.*

CREDITS

Television Work; Series:
Coproducer, *Home Improvement,* ABC, 1991.
Coproducer, *Murphy Brown,* CBS, 1991–93.
Executive story editor, *Murphy Brown,* CBS, 1991–92.
Supervising producer, *The Larry Sanders Show,* HBO, 1992.
Co–executive producer, *The Larry Sanders Show,* HBO, 1992–93.
Executive producer, *The Larry Sanders Show,* HBO, 1994.
Coproducer, *Good Advice,* CBS, 1994.
Creator and executive producer, *The George Wendt Show,* CBS, 1995.
Creator, *Buddies,* ABC, 1996.
Creator and executive producer, *Style and Substance,* CBS, 1998.
Executive producer, *America's Sweethearts* (also known as *American Sweetheart*), 2001.
Creator and executive producer, *The Job,* ABC, 2001–2002.
Creator and executive producer, *Wednesday 9:30 (8:30 Central)* (also known as *My Adventures in Television*), ABC, 2002.
Creator and executive producer, *Rescue Me,* FX Network, 2004–2006.
Director, *Rescue Me,* FX Network, between 2004 and 2010.
Executive producer, *The Unusuals,* ABC, 2009.

Television Executive Producer; Pilots:
Dave Chappelle, Fox, 1998.
HMO, ABC, 2001.
(And creator) *The Job,* ABC, 2001.
(And creator) *Phil at the Gate,* NBC, 2003.
(And creator and director) *Rescue Me,* FX Network, 2004.

(And creator and director) *Fort Pit,* NBC, 2007.
(And creator and director) *The End of Steve,* Showtime, 2008.
Brave New World, NBC, 2011.

Television Director; Episodic:
Sessions, HBO, 1991.
"Vacation," *The Job,* ABC, 2002.
"Sacrilege," *The Job,* ABC, 2002.
"Chinese Baby," *Wednesday 9:30 (8:30 Central),* ABC, 2002.

Television Appearances; Episodic:
Piano player, *Love and War,* CBS, 1992.
Adam Loderman, "Off Camera," *The Larry Sanders Show,* HBO, 1993.
Mr. Taylor, "Two Times Twenty," *Good Advice,* CBS, 1994.
Carl, "Chelsea Gets an Opinion," *Style and Substance,* CBS, 1998.
Dr. Devon, "The Greatest Story Ever Toad," *Maggie,* CBS, 1998.
Sean, "Sacrilege," *The Job,* ABC, 2002.
Chief Pecher, "Beached," *Rescue Me,* FX Network, 2006.
Charlie Rose (also known as *The Charlie Rose Show*), PBS, 2005.

According to some sources, appeared as a piano player in an episode of *Love & War,* CBS.

Film Director:
Finding Amanda, HDNet Films/Magnolia Pictures, 2008.

Film Appearances:
Jeremy, *Home,* 1989.
Dorothy's Christmas party guest, *Alice,* Orion, 1990.

Stage Appearances:
Laughing Matters, Arts Common at St. Peter's Church, New York City, 1989.

RECORDINGS

Videos:
The Making of "The Larry Sanders Show," Sony Pictures Home Entertainment, 2007.
The Dialogue: An Interview with Screenwriter Peter Tolan, 2007.

WRITINGS

Television Series:
Murphy Brown, CBS, 1991–93.
The Larry Sanders Show, HBO, 1992–98.

Buddies, ABC, 1996.
The Job, ABC, beginning 2001.
Rescue Me, FX Network, beginning 2004.

Television Episodes:
Premiere episode, *Wish You Were Here,* CBS, 1990.
"Teacher, Teacher," *Carol & Company,* 1990.
"Adventures in Fine Dining," *Home Improvement,* ABC, 1991.
"Nothing More than Feelings," *Home Improvement,* ABC, 1991.
Sessions, HBO, 1991.
"Two Times Twenty," *Good Advice,* CBS, 1994.
The George Wendt Show, CBS, 1995.
"Secrets & Ellen," *Ellen* (also known as *These Friends of Mine*), ABC, 1997.
"The Boss and Other Disasters," *Style and Substance,* CBS, 1998.

Television Pilots:
Buddies, 1996.
Style and Substance, CBS, 1998.
Dave Chapelle, Fox, 1998.
HMO, ABC, 2001.
The Job, ABC, 2001.
Wednesday 9:30 (8:30 Central) (also known as *My Adventures in Television*), ABC, 2002.
Phil at the Gate, NBC, 2003.
Rescue Me, FX Network, 2004.
Fort Pit, NBC, 2007.
The End of Steve, Showtime, 2008.
Brave New World, NBC, 2011.

Television Movies:
Name, ABC, 1999.

Television Specials:
Dave Chappelle (also known as *The Dave Chappelle Project*), 1998.

Television Music; Series:
Theme song, *Wednesday 9:30 (8:30 Central)* (also known as *My Adventures in Television*), ABC, 2002.

Television Music; Episodic:
Lyricist, "How Lovely to Be a Vegetable," in episode "Disease," *Rescue Me,* FX Network, 2009.

Screenplays:
My Fellow Americans, Warner Bros., 1996.
(With Harold Ramis and Kenneth Lonergan) *Analyze This* (also known as *Analyze Me;* also based on story by Tolan), Warner Bros., 1999.

What Planet Are You From?, Sony Pictures Entertainment, 2000.
Bedazzled, Twentieth Century–Fox, 2000.
America's Sweethearts (also known as *American Sweetheart*), Sony Pictures Entertainment, 2001.
Stealing Harvard (also known as *Campus Crazy;* also based on story by Tolan), Sony Pictures Entertainment, 2002.
(Contributor) *Analyze That* (also known as *Analyze You*), Warner Bros., 2002.
Guess Who, Columbia, 2005.
Just Like Heaven, DreamWorks, 2005.
The Smoker, Paramount, 2005.
Finding Amanda, HDNet Films/Magnolia Pictures, 2008.

Also uncredited rewriter of scripts by other screenwriters.

Stage Plays:
"Best Half Foot Forward," Program B, *Festival of One Act Plays,* Manhattan Punch Line Theatre, New York City, 1988.
(With Linda Wallem; and musical composer and lyricist) *Laughing Matters,* Arts Common at St. Peter's Church, New York City, 1989.
"Pillow Talk," Evening B, *Festival of One Act Comedies,* Judith Anderson Theatre, New York City, 1989.
"Stay Carl Stay," Evening A, *The 7th Annual Festival of One Act Comedies,* Judith Anderson Theatre, 1991.

TOMEI, Concetta 1945–

PERSONAL

Born December 30, 1945, in Kenosha, WI; married; husband an attorney and in business. *Education:* University of Wisconsin at Madison, B.S., education; Goodman School of Drama (now part of DePaul University), B.F.A., theatre arts. *Avocational Interests:* Reading, travel, walking, yoga.

Addresses: *Agent*—Tim Curtis, William Morris Agency, 151 El Camino Dr., Beverly Hills, CA 90212; Steve La-Manna, Innovative Artists, 1505 Tenth St., Santa Monica, CA 90401.

Career: Actress. Alley Theatre Company, Houston, TX, member of company for two years. Also worked as a junior high school teacher in Milwaukee, WI, for four years.

Awards, Honors: St. Clair Baysfield Shakespeare Award, c. 1983, for *Richard III.*

CREDITS

Television Appearances; Series:

Dr. Estelle Kramer, a recurring role, *Falcon Crest,* CBS, 1986.

Blank Dominique, *Max Headroom* (also known as *Max Headroom: 20 Minutes into the Future*), ABC, 1987.

Major Lila Garreau, *China Beach,* ABC, 1988–91.

Delia Buckner, *Madman of the People,* NBC, 1994–95.

Ann Hines–Davis–Wilson–Jefferson–Ali, *Lush Life,* Fox, 1996.

Lynda Hansen, *Providence,* NBC, 1999–2002.

Television Appearances; Miniseries:

Hazel Carter, *Doubletake,* CBS, 1985.

Clara Stern, *The Burden of Proof* (also known as *Scott Turow's "The Burden of Proof"*), ABC, 1992.

Television Appearances; Movies:

Janet Crisp/Martin Bloodall, *Agatha Christie's "Murder in Three Acts"* (also known as *Murder in Three Acts*), CBS, 1986.

Doyen Salsig, *In Love and War,* NBC, 1987.

Jan Thompson, *The Betty Ford Story,* ABC, 1987.

Abigail Samuels, *One Special Victory,* NBC, 1991.

Marina Preston, *Sin & Redemption,* CBS, 1994.

Mrs. Wyatt, *The Wyatts,* Fox, 1994.

Rita, *Gone But Not Forgotten* (also known as *Phillip Margolin's "Gone But Not Forgotten"*), 2004.

Ms. Fitch, *The List,* ABC, 2006.

Television Appearances; Specials:

Mrs. Mixner, "Amy and the Angel," *ABC Afterschool Specials,* ABC, 1982.

Elizabeth Henderson, *American Eyes,* CBS, 1990.

Different Worlds: An Interracial Love, CBS, 1992.

More True Stories from Touched by an Angel, CBS, 1999.

Television Appearances; Awards Presentations:

Presenter, *The 14th Annual Genesis Awards,* Animal Planet, 2000.

The 16th Annual Soap Opera Awards, NBC, 2000.

Television Appearances; Episodic:

Ilene Robson, "The Warning," *Dynasty,* ABC, 1986.

Mrs. Trager, "Teacher's Pet," *My Sister Sam,* 1986.

Elise Praeger, "Final Cut," *St. Elsewhere,* NBC, 1988.

Susan Hauber, "God Rest Ye Little Gentleman," *L.A. Law,* NBC, 1990.

Susan Hauber, "Watts a Matter?," *L.A. Law,* NBC, 1990.

Susan Hauber, "Spleen It to Me, Lucy," *L.A. Law,* NBC, 1991.

Sylvia, "The Late Mrs. Biggins," *Wings,* NBC, 1991.

Ellen McGrath, "The Contenders," *Picket Fences,* CBS, 1992.

Susan Hauber, "Diet, Diet My Darling," *L.A. Law,* NBC, 1992.

Diana Gottfried, "Crimes and Ms. Demeanors," *Sisters,* NBC, 1993.

Ellen McGrath, "Fetal Attraction," *Picket Fences,* CBS, 1993.

Helen Gould, "Alien Aided Affection," *Civil Wars,* ABC, 1993.

Elizabeth Keegan, "Lower Than the Angels," *Birdland,* ABC, 1994.

Ellen McGrath, "Divine Recall," *Picket Fences,* CBS, 1994.

Ellen McGrath, "Howard's End," *Picket Fences,* CBS, 1994.

Sister Regina, "Sister Michael Wants You," *Diagnosis Murder,* CBS, 1994.

Susan Hauber, "The Green, Green Grass of Home," *L.A. Law,* NBC, 1994.

Sylvia, "Roy Crazy," *Wings,* NBC, 1994.

Honey Dupree, "The Prodigal Father," *John Grisham's "The Client"* (also known as *The Client*), CBS, 1995.

Sabrina, "Educating Kirk," *Kirk,* The WB, 1995.

Jeanette Rennick, "Chapter Eighteen," *Murder One,* ABC, 1996.

Kate Carpenter, "'Til We Meet Again," *Touched by an Angel,* CBS, 1996.

Professor Bass, "Witness," *Ellen,* ABC, 1996.

Doris Dial, "I Hear a Symphony," *Murphy Brown,* CBS, 1997.

Minister Odala, "Distant Origin," *Star Trek: Voyager* (also known as *Voyager*), UPN, 1997.

Doris Dial, "Wee Small Hours," *Murphy Brown,* CBS, 1998.

Hollywood Squares (also known as *H2: Hollywood Squares*), 2000.

Joanne (some sources cite DeeDee) Collins, "CSO: Hartford," *Judging Amy,* CBS, 2003.

Joanne (some sources cite DeeDee) Collins, "Kilt Trip," *Judging Amy,* CBS, 2003.

Mrs. Hampton, "Major League," *7th Heaven* (also known as *7th Heaven: Beginnings*), The WB, 2004.

Christia, Ryan's mother, "The Dinner Party," *Second Time Around,* UPN, 2005.

Joyce, "Catching Hell," *The King of Queens,* CBS, 2005.

Celia's mother, "Higher Education," *Weeds,* Showtime, 2005.

Dr. Sarah Kemple, "Protest," *Numb3rs* (also known as *Num3ers*), CBS, 2006.

Grace, "An Affair to Remember," *Kitchen Confidential,* Fox, 2006.

Mrs. Rawley, "The Other Woman," *The Closer,* TNT, 2006.

Roxane's Duenna, "Cyrano de Bergerac," *Great Performances,* PBS, 2008.

Violet Golding in 1998, "Wednesday's Women," *Cold Case,* CBS, 2008.

Margaret, "Imaginary Friends and Enemies," *Ghost Whisperer,* CBS, 2008.

Maureen Ayers, "Christian Troy II," *Nip/Tuck,* 2010.

Television Appearances; Pilots:
Major Lila Garreau, *China Beach,* ABC, 1988.

Film Appearances:
Mrs. Crandell, *Don't Tell Mom the Babysitter's Dead,* Warner Bros., 1991.

Sam's mother, *Twenty Bucks,* Triton Pictures, 1993.

Victoria Van Borins (Doris the bird lady), *The Goodbye Bird,* 1993.

Madge, *Out to Sea,* Twentieth Century–Fox, 1997.

Patricia Ruiz, *Deep Impact,* DreamWorks, 1998.

Nurse Rennert, *The Muse,* USA Films/October Films, 1999.

Lily Elias, *Purpose,* Lakeshore Entertainment, 2002.

Mrs. Stewart, *View from the Top,* Miramax, 2003.

Ms. Fitch, *The List,* 2007.

Mama, *Marino's* (short film), 2009.

The Master, *Four Steps,* Myrina Films, 2009.

Stage Appearances:
The Runner Stumbles, Alley Theatre, Houston, TX, 1976–77.

Blithe Spirit, Marriott's Lincolnshire Theatre, Lincolnshire, IL, 1977–78.

Pericles Prince of Tyre, Globe Playhouse, 1978–79.

Pinhead, Miss Sandwich, Countess, and Princess Alexandra, *The Elephant Man,* Booth Theatre, New York City, 1979.

Rita, *Little Eyolf,* Roundabout Theatre, New York City, 1979.

Elena, *Goodbye Fidel,* New Ambassador Theatre, New York City, 1980.

Mrs. Kendal and Pinhead, *The Elephant Man,* Booth Theatre, 1980–81.

Edward/Victoria, *Cloud 9,* Theatre De Lys (now Lucille Lortel Theatre), New York City, 1981–82.

Berthe, *Lumiere,* Ark Theatre, 1982.

Queen Elizabeth, *Richard III,* New York Shakespeare Festival, Delacorte Theatre, Public Theatre, New York City, 1983.

Vera, *A Private View,* New York Shakespeare Festival, Martinson Hall, Public Theatre, New York City, 1983–84.

Belinda Blair, *Noises Off,* Brooks Atkinson Theatre, New York City, c. 1983–85.

Japanese businessman, Nell, May, and Mavis, *Fen,* New York Shakespeare Festival, Estelle R. Newman Theatre, Public Theatre, New York City, 1984.

Dr. Emma Brookner (some sources cite Dr. Emma Bruckner), *The Normal Heart,* New York Shakespeare Festival, LuEsther Hall, Public Theatre, New York City, 1985.

Charlotte Cushman, *Romance Language,* Mark Taper Forum, Los Angeles, 1985–86.

Matilde's mother/Ana, *The Clean House,* Mitzi E. Newhouse Theatre, New York City, 2006–2007.

Roxane's Duenna, Sister Marthe, *Cyrano de bergerac,* Richard Rodger's Theatre, New York City, 2007–2008.

In the Daylight, Mcginn–Cazale Theatre, New York City, 2009.

Also appeared in productions with the Alley Theatre Company, including *A Christmas Carol, The Cocktail Party, The Front Page, Indians, Juno and the Paycock, The Last Meeting of the Knights of the White Magnolia, Old Times,* and *The Show–Off.*

Major Tours:
Toured in a production of *The Elephant Man,* U.S. cities.

TURNER, Ted 1938–
　　(R. E. Turner)

PERSONAL

Full name, Robert Edward Turner III; born November 19, 1938, in Cincinnati, OH; son of Robert Edward (a billboard advertising mogul) and Florence (maiden name, Rooney) Turner; married Judy Nye Hallisey, 1960 (divorced, 1964); married Jane Shirley Smith (a flight attendant), 1965 (divorced, 1988); married Jane Fonda (an actress), December 21, 1991 (divorced, 2001); children: (first marriage) Robert Edward IV, Laura Lee; (second marriage) Beauregard, Rhett, Jennie. *Education:* Attended Brown University, 1957–60. *Avocational Interests:* Sailing, fishing, spectator sports.

Addresses: *Office*—Turner Enterprises, 133 Luckie St. NW, 7th Floor, Atlanta, GA 30303.

Career: Broadcasting executive and producer. WTBS (independent television station), Atlanta, GA, president and board chair, 1970–96; Turner Broadcasting System (also known as TBS), Atlanta, president and board chair, 1979–96; Time Warner, Inc., vice chair, 1996–2000, member of board of directors, 1996–2006; retired from broadcasting, c. 2006. AOL Time Warner, vice chair and member of board of directors, 2001–03; Turner Enterprises, Atlanta, chair, beginning 2003. Creator of several broadcasting services, including Cable News Network, 1980, CNN–Radio and Headline News (television channel), 1982, Turner Network Television (TNT), c. 1988, Turner Classic Movies (TCM), 1994, Cartoon Network, Cable News Network Radio, and Cable Music Channel; acquired Satellite News Channel, 1983, Omni International (also known as CNN

Center), c. 1986, MGM/UA Entertainment Co., (brief affiliation) 1985, New Line Cinema and Castle Rock Entertainment, 1993, and World Championship Wrestling (affiliation ended, 2001). Turner Outdoor Advertising, began as account executive, 1961–63, became president and chief operating officer, 1963–70; Ted's Montana Grill, founder of restaurant chain; DT Solar, partner, 2007. Former professional sports executive; Atlanta Braves (baseball team), became owner and president, 1976; Atlanta Hawks (basketball team), became part–owner and board chair, 1977; Goodwill Games, organizer, 1985. Martin Luther King Center for Nonviolent Change, Atlanta, member of the board of directors; Better World Society (promoter of "socially conscious" television programming), founder and executive, 1985–91; Turner Foundation (philanthropic organization), founder and chair, beginning 1991; Nuclear Threat Initiative, cofounder and cochair, beginning 2001; United Nations Foundation, served as chair; appeared in public service announcement for RepowerAmerica.org.

Member: National Cable Television Association, National Association for the Advancement of Colored People (life member; board of directors, Atlanta chapter), National Audubon Society, Cousteau Society, Bay Area Cable Club (honorary member).

Awards, Honors: Broadcasting and business awards include Regional Employer of the Year Award, National Association for the Advancement of Colored People, 1976; named outstanding entrepreneur of the year, *Sales Marketing and Management Magazine,* 1979; President's Awards, National Cable Television Association, 1979, 1989; inducted into Promotions and Marketing Association Hall of Fame, 1980; named salesman of the year, Sales and Marketing Executives, 1980; Private Enterprise Exemplar medal, Freedoms Foundation at Valley Forge, 1980; CableACE Special Recognition Award, National Cable Television Association, 1980; named communicator of the year by Public Relations Society of America, and New York Broadcasters, 1981; named international communicator of the year, Sales and Marketing Executives, 1981; National News Media Award, Veterans of Foreign Wars, 1981; Vanguard Award for Associates, National Cable Television Association, 1981; Distinguished Service in Telecommunications Award, College of Communications, Ohio University, 1982; Carr Van Anda Award, E. W. Scripps School of Journalism, Ohio University, 1982; Special Award, Edinburgh International Television Festival, 1982; Board of Governors Award, Atlanta chapter, Academy of Television Arts and Sciences, 1982; Media Awareness Award, United Vietnam Veterans Organization, 1983; World Telecommunications Pioneer Award, New York State Broadcasters Association, 1984; Silver Satellite Award, American Women in Radio and Television, 1984; Lifetime Achievement Award, New York International Film and Television Festival, 1984; named business executive of the year, Georgia Security Dealers Association, 1985; Golden CableACE Award, National Cable Television Association, 1987; Sol Taishoff Award for Excellence in Broadcast Journalism, National Press Foundation, 1988; Chairman's Award, Cable Advertising Bureau, 1988; Directorate Award, Academy of Television Arts and Sciences, 1989; Paul White Award, Radio and Television News Directors Association, 1989; Business Marketer of the Year Award, American Marketing Association, 1989; Edward Weintal Prize for Diplomatic Reporting, Institute for the Study of Diplomacy, Georgetown University, 1990; Vanguard Award for Programmers, National Cable Television Association, 1990; Global Television Outstanding Achievement Award, Banff Television Festival, 1991; inducted into Television Hall of Fame, Academy of Television Arts and Sciences, 1992; Special Award, National Board of Review, 1992; Governor's Award, Emmy Awards, Academy of Television Arts and Sciences, 1992; Golden Boot Award, Motion Picture and Television Fund, 1993; career achievement awards, Television Critics Association, 1995, and International Documentary Association, 1996; David Susskind Lifetime Achievement Award, Golden Laurel Awards, Producers Guild of America, 1995; Personal Award, George Foster Peabody Broadcasting Awards, Henry W. Grady School of Journalism and Mass Communication, University of Georgia, 1998; Humanitarian Award, Crystal Awards, Women in Film, 1999; CINE Lifetime Achievement Award, Committee on International Nontheatrical Events, 2002; received star on Hollywood Walk of Fame, 2004; inducted into Advertising Hall of Fame, 2004; Bower Award for Business Leadership, Franklin Institute, 2006; Silver Satellite Award, American Women in Radio and Television. Other awards include winner of America's Cup yacht race as captain of the *Courageous,* 1977, Fastnet Trophy, 1979, and several other honors as yachtsman of the year; Special Olympics Award, Special Olympics Committee, 1983; Dinner of Champions Award, Georgia chapter, Multiple Sclerosis Society, 1983; Praca Special Merit Award, New York Puerto Rican Association for Community Affairs, 1983; Corporate Star of the Year Award, National Leukemia Society, 1985; Distinguished Achievement Award, University of Georgia, 1985; Tree of Life Award, Jewish National Fund, 1985; Lifetime Achievement Award, Popular Culture Association, 1986; George Washington Distinguished Patriot Award, Sons of the American Revolution, 1986; inducted into National Association for Sport and Physical Education Hall of Fame, 1986; Missouri Honor Medal, School of Journalism, University of Missouri, 1987; Lowell Thomas Award, International Platform Association, 1987; Citizen Diplomat Award, Center for Soviet–American Dialogue, 1988; Distinguished Service Award, Simon Wiesenthal Center, 1990; Glastnost Award, Volunteers of America and *Soviet Life* Magazine, 1990; named *Time* Magazine Man of the Year, 1991; Carnegie Medal of Philanthropy, 2001; Captain of Innovation Award, Technology Association of Georgia, 2006; inducted into Junior Achievement

Business Hall of Fame, 2007. Honorary degrees include S.Dc., Drexel University, and LL.D., Stamford University, both 1982; D. Entrepreneurial Science, Central New England College of Technology, 1983, LL.D., Atlanta University, honorary doctorate, Massachusetts Maritime Academy, and D. Public Administration, all 1984; D.B.A., University of Charleston, 1985; B.A., Brown University, 1989, followed by L.H.D., 1993; honorary degrees from Emerson College, 2000, and Trinity College, Hartford, CT, 2001.

CREDITS

Television Appearances; Specials:
Hope News Network (also known as *Bob Hope's News Network*), NBC, 1988.
CNN Special Report: A Conversation with Carl Sagan, Cable News Network, 1989.
A Conversation with Castro, Cable News Network, 1990.
Ted Turner Talking with David Frost, PBS, 1991.
First Person with Maria Shriver, NBC, 1992.
Clash of the Champions XX: 20th Anniversary, 1992.
November 22, 1963: Where Were You? A Larry King Special Live from Washington, TNT, 1993.
First Person with Maria Shriver, NBC, 1993.
The 10th Annual Television Academy Hall of Fame, The Disney Channel, 1994.
Barbara Walters Presents The 10 Most Fascinating People of 1995, ABC, 1995.
Panelist, *An American Family and Television: A National Town Hall Meeting,* multiple cable networks, 1997.
The Goodwill Games Opening Ceremonies, TBS, 1998.
AFI's 100 Years ... 100 Movies: America's Greatest Movies, CBS, 1998.
(In archive footage) *Hulk Hogan: The E! True Hollywood Story,* E! Entertainment Television, 1999.
Jane Fonda: The E! True Hollywood Story, E! Entertainment Television, 2000.
(In archive footage) *THS Investigates: Hazing,* E! Entertainment Television, 2007.

Television Appearances; Miniseries:
Cosmos, 1980.
MGM: When the Lion Roars (also known as *The MGM Story*), TNT, 1992.
Naked News, Arts and Entertainment, 1995.
Feeding the Beast: The 24–Hour News Revolution, Trio, 2004.
The 100 Most Memorable TV Moments, TV Land, 2004.
Stephen Fry in America, BBC, 2008.

Television Appearances; Episodic:
The Tonight Show Starring Johnny Carson, NBC, 1986.

(As R. E. Turner) Voice of Fred Lerner, "Who's Running the Show?," *Captain Planet and the Planeteers* (animated; also known as *The New Adventures of Captain Planet*), 1995.
Himself, "How to be a Good Listener," *Arli$$,* HBO, 1997.
Mundo VIP, 1997.
Late Show with David Letterman (also known as *The Last Show* and *Letterman*), CBS, 2005, 2008.
(In archive footage) *Hannity & Colmes,* 2005.
(In archive footage) *Countdown w/ Keith Olbermann,* MSNBC, 2006.
Meet the Press (also known as *Meet the Press with Tim Russert*), NBC, 2008.
Tavis Smiley, PBS, 2008.
(In archive footage) *The O'Reilly Factor,* Fox News Channel, 2008.
"Ted Turner," *Pozner,* 2009.
"Haiti Crisis!," *Larry King Live,* Cable News Network, 2010.

Television Appearances; Awards Presentations:
The 11th Annual ACE Awards, multiple cable networks, 1990.
Fourth Annual Environmental Media Awards, TBS, 1994.
2001 World Awards, 2001.

Television Executive Producer; Series:
Portrait of America (occasional series), TBS, beginning 1983.
WCW Worldwide Wrestling (also known as *WCW Worldwide* and *World Wide Wrestling*), 1991.
WCW Saturday Night (also known as *WCW Saturday Morning*), 1991.
WCW Monday Nitro (also known as *World Championship Wrestling Monday Nitro*), 1995.
WCW Thunder, TNT, 1998.

Television Creator; Series:
Captain Planet and the Planeteers (animated; also known as *The New Adventures of Captain Planet*), 1990.

Television Work; Specials:
Creator, *Portrait of the World USSR,* 1987.
Creator, *Without Borders,* TBS, 1989.
Executive producer, *WCW Superbrawl VIII,* 1998.
(As R. E. Turner) Creator, "The Cold War" (also known as "Cold War: A Television History"), *CNN Perspectives,* Cable News Network, 1998.

Film Appearances:
Himself, *Southern Voices, American Dreams,* 1985.
(Uncredited) Darryl Fan, *The Slugger's Wife* (also known as *Neil Simon's "The Slugger's Wife"*), 1985.

(Uncredited) Lieutenant Colonel W. T. Patton, *Gettysburg,* New Line Cinema, 1993.

Himself, *The Race to Save 100 Years,* 1997.

Rooted in Peace, Blue Water Entertainment, 1999.

Fidel (documentary; also known as *Fidel: The Untold Story*), First Run Features, 2001.

(As R. E. Turner) Colonel Tazewell, *Gods and Generals,* Warner Bros., 2003.

Himself, *Global Eugenics: Using Medicine to Kill* (documentary), 2009.

Himself, *President* (documentary), Georgia Pictures, 2009.

(In archive footage) *Nuclear Tipping Point* (documentary), Nuclear Security Project, 2010.

Film Executive Producer:

Gods and Generals, Warner Bros., 2003.

RECORDINGS

Video Appearances; In Archive Footage:

The Monday Night War: WWE Raw vs. WCW Nitro, WWE Home Video, 2004.

The American Dream: The Dusty Rhodes Story, World Wrestling Entertainment, 2006.

WWE: McMahon, WWE Home Video, 2006.

Endgame: Blueprint for Global Enslavement, Disinformation Co., 2007.

Nature Boy Ric Flair: The Definitive Collection, World Wrestling Entertainment, 2008.

Starrcade: The Essential Collection, World Wrestling Entertainment, 2009.

WWE: The Rise and Fall of WCW, World Wrestling Entertainment, 2010.

Video Executive Producer:

Starrcade (also known as *NWA Starrcade* and *WCW Starrcade*), annually, 1985–2000.

NWA Halloween Havoc (also known as *Halloween Havoc* and *WCW Halloween Havoc*), annually, 1989–98.

WCW/NWA Capital Combat (also known as *Capital Combat '90: Return of RoboCop* and *WCW Capitol Combat*), 1990.

WCW Beach Blast, 1992.

WCW Uncensored, 1996.

WCW Bash at the Beach, 1996.

WCW World War III, 1997 and 1998.

WCW Fall Brawl, 1998.

WCW/NOW Superstar Series: Diamond Dallas Page—Feel the Bang!, 1998.

WCW Souled Out, 1999.

WCW Road Wild '99, 1999.

Video Producer:

WCW New Blood Rising, 2000.

WRITINGS

Nonfiction:

(With Gary Jobson) *The Racing Edge,* Simon & Schuster, 1979.

(With Janet Lowe) *Ted Turner Speaks: Insights from the World's Greatest Maverick,* Wiley & Sons, 1999.

(With Bill Burke) *Call Me Ted* (memoir), Grand Central Publishing, 2008.

OTHER SOURCES

Books:

Auletta, Ken, *Media Man: Ted Turner's Improbable Empire,* W. W. Norton, 2004.

Bibb, Porter, *It Ain't as Easy as It Looks: Ted Turner's Amazing Story,* Crown Publishers, 1993.

Business Leader Profiles for Students, Volume 2, 2002.

Goldberg, Robert, and Gerald Jay Goldberg, *Citizen Turner: The Wild Rise of an American Tycoon,* Harcourt Brace, 1995.

Schonfeld, Reese, *Me and Ted Against the World: The Unauthorized Story of the Founding of CNN,* Cliff Street Books, 2001.

Turner, Ted, and Bill Burke, *Call Me Ted,* Grand Central Publishing, 2008.

Periodicals:

Atlanta Journal–Constitution, June 2, 2005.

Cosmopolitan, September, 1995, p. 262.

Current Biography, June, 1998, p. 52.

Esquire, March, 2003, p. 66.

Fortune, March 3, 2003, p. 56; May 26, 2003, p. 124.

Harper's, December, 1997, p. 10.

Inc., April, 1997, p. 11.

Maclean's, February 17, 2003, p. 36.

People Weekly, December 25, 1995, p. 87.

Reader's' Digest, December, 2008, pp. 26–27.

USA Today, December 8, 2008, p. 7B.

U.S. News & World Report, October 28, 2002, p. 38.

Variety, February 24, 2003, p. 6.

V

VALANCE, Holly 1983–

PERSONAL

Original name, Holly Rachel Vukadinovic; born May 11, 1983, in Melbourne, Victoria, Australia (some sources say New Zealand); daughter of Rajko (a singer, model, and clothing store owner) and Rachel (a model) Vukadinovic. *Avocational Interests:* Swimming, going for walks, watching kickboxing, cars, and watching films.

Addresses: *Agent*—International Creative Management, 10250 Constellation Blvd., 9th Floor, Los Angeles, CA 90067.

Career: Actress. Previously worked as a model; appeared in K–Mart catalogs; appeared in ads for "Wave" drinks; appeared in television commercials, including 0800 Reverse calling service; face of Schwarzkopf (a hair coloring product), 2004. Also a pop singer.

Awards, Honors: Logie Award nomination, most popular new talent—female, 2000, for *Neighbours.*

CREDITS

Film Appearances:
Christie Allen, *DOA: Dead or Alive* (also known as *DOA*), Weinstein Company, 2006.
Jessica, *Pledge This!* (also known as *National Lampoon's "Pledge This!"*), Vivendi Entertainment, 2006.
Sheerah, *Taken*, Twentieth Century–Fox, 2008.
Sammy Walters, *X Returns* (short film), Shorts International, 2009.

Herself, *Kambakkht Ishq* (also known as *Incredible Love*), Eros International, 2009.
Rose, *Surviving Georgia,* 2010.
Sally, *Luster,* Epic Pictures Group, 2010.
Angela, *Red Herring,* Rat Rod Films, 2010.
Katie, *Big Mamma's Boy,* 2010.
Tess, *Mercy,* IFC Films, 2010.

Television Appearances; Series:
Felicity Scully, *Neighbours,* Ten Network, 1999–2002, 2005.
Nika Volek, *Prison Break,* Fox, 2005–2006.

Television Appearances; Movies:
Kanga, *Marple: The Pale Horse,* ITV, 2010.

Television Appearances; Specials:
Presenter, *The 2002 Top of the Pops Awards,* 2002.
It Shouldn't Happen to a ... Soapstar, ITV, 2002.
Wella Hot Look, *The ELLE Style Awards,* 2002.
The 16th Annual ARIA Awards, Ten Network, 2002.
Performer, *Smash Hits Poll Winners Party 2002,* Channel 4, 2002.
Herself (greetings for the show), *Junior Eurovision Song Contest* (also known as *Junior ESC 2003* and *Junior Eurovision Song Contest 2003*), 2003.
Children in Need, BBC, 2003.
Presenter, *The National Music Awards 2003,* ITV, 2003.
Avid Merrion's XXXmas Special, 2005.

Television Appearances; Episodic:
"Neighours" Revealed, 2000.
Joonas Hytonen Show, 2001.
The Big Breakfast, Channel 4, 2001.
The Saturday Show, BBC, 2001, 2002.
SM:TV Live, ITV1, 2002.
Blue Peter, BBC, 2002.
Performer, *Quelli che ... il calcio,* 2002.
Johnny Vaughn Tonight, BBC, 2002.
Richard & Judy, Channel 4, 2002.

Patrick Kielty ... Almost Live!, BBC, 2002.
V Graham Norton, Channel 4, 2002.
RI:SE, Channel 4, 2002.
CD:UK, ITV, 2002.
Popworld, 2002.
Top of the Pops, BBC, 2002.
GMTV, ITV, 2002.
Oblivious, The Nashville Network, 2003.
Performer, *Musica si,* 2003.
Top of the Pops Saturday, BBC, 2003.
Today with Des and Mel, ITV, 2003.
Kay Coleman, "Addiction," *CSI: Miami,* CBS, 2004.
Leanna, "My Maserati Does 185," *Entourage,* HBO, 2005.
Lydia, "YoungBlood," *CSI: NY* (also known as *CSI: New York*), CBS, 2005.
Lola, "B.C.," *Moonlight,* 2007.
Christina Shaw, "Every Breath You Take," *Shark,* CBS, 2007.
Vivi Langdon, "Act Naturally," *Valentine,* The CW, 2008.
"Australia," *Keith Lemon's Very Brilliant World Tour,* 2008.

RECORDINGS

Video Games:
Brenda Snow, *Command & Conquer: Red Alert 3—Uprising,* Electronic Arts, 2009.

Albums:
Footprints, WP, 2002.
State of Mind, Warner Music, 2004.

Music Videos:
Appeared in "He Don't Love You" by Human Nature.

VANOVER, Jilon Ghai
   See GHAI, Jilon

Van SANT, Gus 1952(?)–
(Gus Van Sant, Jr.)

PERSONAL

Full name, Gus Green Van Sant, Jr.; born July 24, 1952 (some sources cite 1953) in Louisville, KY; son of Gus Green (a clothing manufacturer and salesman) and Betty (maiden name, Seay) Van Sant. *Education:* Rhode Island School of Design, B.F.A., 1975. *Avocational Interests:* Playing guitar.

Addresses: *Office*—Meno Film Co., 1300 NW Northrup St., 3rd Floor, Portland, OR 97209. *Agent*—WME Entertainment, 9601 Wilshire Blvd., 3rd Floor, Beverly Hills, CA 90210.

Career: Director, writer, producer, and film editor. Assistant to director Ken Shapiro, 1975; producer of commercials for an advertising agency, 1981–83; Northwest Film Center, Portland, OR, teacher of film production skills, c. 1983; Meno Film Co., Portland, principal; member of the band Kill All Blondes; also works occasionally as sound recordist and re–recording mixer for his own films. Sundance Film Festival, member of dramatic jury, 1991. Previously worked as a press attache, painter, and photographer.

Awards, Honors: Los Angeles Film Critics Award, best independent or experimental film or video, 1987, and Festival Plate, Turin International Gay and Lesbian Film Festival, 1988, both for *Mala Noche;* Teddy Award, best short film, Berlin International Film Festival, 1987, for *Five Ways to Kill* and *My New Friend;* Los Angeles Film Critics Association Award (with Daniel Yost), best screenplay, 1989, Independent Spirit Award (with Yost), best screenplay, and Independent Spirit Award nomination, best director, both Independent Features Project/West, National Society of Film Critics Awards, best film, best director, and best screenplay (with Yost), and New York Film Critics Circle Award (with Yost), best screenplay, all 1989, CICAE Award, forum of new cinema, Berlin International Film Festival, 1990, Literary Award (with Yost), best screenplay adaptation, International PEN, and Critics Award, Deauville Film Festival, 1991, all for *Drugstore Cowboy;* International Critics (FIPRESCI) Award, Toronto International Film Festival, and nomination for Golden Lion, Venice Film Festival, both 1991, Independent Spirit Award, best screenplay, and Independent Spirit Award nomination, best director, 1992, all for *My Private Idaho;* Freedom of Expression Award, Oregon American Civil Liberties Union, 1992; nomination for Golden Palm, Cannes Film Festival, 1995, for *To Die For;* Golden Space Needle Award, best short film, Seattle International Film Festival, 1997, and honorable mention for FICC Prize, Oberhausen International Short Film Festival, 1998, both for *Ballad of the Skeletons;* Academy Award nomination, Directors Guild of America Award nomination, and Golden Satellite Award nomination, International Press Academy, all best director of a motion picture, and nomination for Golden Berlin Bear, Berlin International Film Festival, all 1998, for *Good Will Hunting;* Outfest Achievement Award, L.A. Outfest, 1999; Prize of the Guild of German Art House Cinemas and nomination for Golden Berlin Bear, both Berlin International Film Festival, and Heartland Award of Excellence, Heartland Film Festival, all 2001, for *Finding Forrester;* Filmmaker on the Edge Award, Provincetown International Film Festival, 2002; special citation, Visions Awards, Toronto International Film Festival, and nomination for Golden Leopard, Locarno International Film Festival, both 2002, and Independent Spirit Award nomination, best director, 2003, all for *Gerry;* nomination for Golden Palm, Best Director Award, and Cinema Prize of the French National Education System, all Cannes Film Festival, 2003, Independent Spirit Award nomination, best director, Cesar Award nomination, best foreign film, Academie des Arts et Techniques du Cinema, and Critics Award, French Syndicate of Cinema Critics, all 2004, and Bodil Award nomination, best American film, 2005, all for *Elephant;* nomination for Golden Palm, Cannes Film Festival, 2005, for *Last Days;* 60th Anniversary Prize and nomination for Golden Palm, Cannes Film Festival, 2007, Independent Spirit Award nomination, best director, 2008, and Bodil Award nomination, best American film, 2008, all for *Paranoid Park;* Boston Society of Film Critics Award, San Francisco Film Critics Circle Award, Chicago Film Critics Association Award nomination, and Satellite Award nomination, all best director, 2008, Academy Award nomination, Directors Guild of America Award nomination, London Critics Circle Film Award nomination, and Critics Choice Award nomination, Broadcast Film Critics Association, all best director, David di Donatello Award nomination and nomination for Award of the Argentinean Academy, Academy of Motion Picture Arts and Sciences of Argentina, both best foreign film, all 2009, Cesar Award nomination, best foreign film, Robert Festival Award nomination, best American film, and Bodil Award nomination, best American film, 2010, all for *Milk;* Sonny Bono Visionary Award, Palm Springs International Film Festival, 2009.

CREDITS

Film Director:
(And producer and film editor) *The Discipline of D.E.* (short film), 1978.
My Friend, 1983.
My New Friend, Frameline Distribution, 1985.
(And producer and film editor; also song performer, "To Die for Your Love") *Mala Noche* (also known as *Bad Night*), Northern Film, 1986.
(As Gus Van Sant, Jr.; and producer) *Ken Death Gets Out of Jail,* 1987.
Five Ways to Kill Yourself (short film), 1987.
Junior, 1988.
(As Gus Van Sant, Jr.) *Drugstore Cowboy,* Avenue Pictures, 1989.
(And executive producer) *My Own Private Idaho,* Fine Line, 1991.
(As Gus Van Sant, Jr.; and executive producer and film editor) *Even Cowgirls Get The Blues,* New Line Cinema, 1993.
To Die For, Alma–Kino–Filmverleih, 1995.
Ballad of the Skeletons, 1996.
Good Will Hunting, Buena Vista, 1997.
(And producer) *Psycho,* Universal, 1998.
Finding Forrester, Sony Pictures Entertainment, 2000.
(And film editor) *Gerry,* THINKFilm, 2002.
(And film editor) *Elephant,* Fine Line, 2003.

(And film editor) *Last Days,* Fine Line, 2005.
"Le Marais" segment, *Paris, je t'aime* (also known as *Paris, I Love You*), First Look International, 2007.
(And film editor) *Paranoid Park,* IFC Films, 2007.
Milk, Focus Features, 2008.
"First Kiss" segment, *To Each His Own Cinema* (also known as *Chacun son cinema ou ce petit coup au coeur quand la lumiere s'eteint et que le film commence*), Cannes Film Festival, 2008.
(And film editor) "Mansion on the Hill" segment, *8,* LDM Productions, 2008.
Restless, Columbia, 2011.

Also directed *Alice in Hollywood* and the four–minute film *Four Boys in a Volvo,* 1996.

Film Work; Executive Producer Only:
Kids, Miramax, 1995.
Speedway Junky, Regent Entertainment, 1999.
Tarnation (documentary), Wellspring Media, 2004.
Lightfield's Home Videos, 2006, Big Screen Entertainment Group, 2008.
Wild Tigers I Have Known, IFC First Take, 2007.
Howl (animated), Oscilloscope Pictures, 2010.
What's Wrong with Virginia, Killer Films/TicTock Studios, 2010.

Feature Film Appearances:
(Uncredited) Man behind hotel counter, *My Own Private Idaho,* Fine Line, 1991.
(Uncredited) Man talking to man in cowboy hat, *Psycho,* Universal, 1998.
(Uncredited) Library assistant, *Finding Forrester,* Sony Pictures Entertainment, 2000.
Himself, *Jay and Silent Bob Strike Back,* Dimension Films, 2001.
Phone voice, *Last Days,* Fine Line, 2005.

Documentary Film Appearances:
Guns on the Clackamas, PlympCorp Productions, 1995.
Strange Parallel, 1998.
Orientations—Christopher Doyle: Stirred Not Shaken, 2000.
Larry Clark, Great American Rebel, 2003.
Here's Looking at You, Boy (also known as *Here's Looking at You, Boy—The Coming Out of Queer Cinema* and *Schau mir in die augen, kleiner*), SND Films, 2007.
Critico, FiGa Films, 2008.
Searching for Elliott Smith, 2009.
The Advocate for Fagdom, Le Chant Qui Fume, 2010.

Television Work; Specials:
Producer, director and film editor, "Thanksgiving Prayer," *American Flash Cards,* PBS, 1992.

Television Appearances; Specials:
(In archive footage) *The 70th Annual Academy Awards,* ABC, 1998.

The Director's Vision: Hollywood's Best Discuss Their Craft, Sundance Channel, 1998.

(In archive footage) *101 Biggest Celebrity Oops,* E! Entertainment Television, 2004.

Fabulous! The Story of Queer Cinema, Independent Film Channel, 2006.

Wanderlust, Independent Film Channel, 2006.

In the Mood for Doyle, 2007.

The 81st Annual Academy Awards, ABC, 2009.

William S. Burroughs: A Man Within, PBS, 2010.

Television Appearances; Episodic:

Dias de cine, 1992.

Nyhetsmorgon, 1998.

"Finding Forrester," *HBO First Look,* HBO, 2000.

Campus, le magazine de l'ecrit, 2003.

The American Avant Garde, 2004.

Comme au cinema, 2005.

(In archive footage) *Cinema mil,* Televisio de Catalunya, 2005.

Himself, "Return to Queens Blvd," *Entourage,* HBO, 2008.

Charlie Rose (also known as *The Charlie Rose Show*), PBS, 2008.

Appeared in episodes of *Champlin on Film,* Bravo; and *Hi–Octane* (also known as *High Octane*), Comedy Central.

RECORDINGS

Albums:

(With William S. Burroughs) *The Elvis of Letters* (spoken–word album), Tim Kerr, 1985.

Gus Van Sant, PopTones, 1997.

18 Songs about Golf, 1983, PopTones, 1998.

Singles include (with Burroughs) "The Hipster Bebop Junkie."

Video Appearances:

Red Hot Chili Peppers: Funky Monks, 1991.

"*Psycho*" *Path,* 1999.

Rescued from the Closet, Columbia TriStar Home Video, 2001.

Video Director:

Bowie: The Video Collection, 1993.

(And executive producer) "Fame '90," *The Best of Bowie,* 2002.

"Under the Bridge" *Red Hot Chili Peppers: Greatest Videos,* 2003.

On the Set of "Elephant:" Rolling through Time, HBO Films, 2004.

Cinema16: American Short Films, Warp Films, 2006.

"San Francisco Days," *Best of Chris Isaak,* Reprise, 2006.

Director of the music videos "Bang Bang Bang" by Tracy Chapman, 1992; "The Last Song" by Elton John, 1992; "Creep" by Stone Temple Pilots, 1993; "Just Keep Me Moving" by k. d. lang, 1993; "Understanding" by Candlebox, 1996; "Weird" by Hanson, 1998; "Fame '90" by David Bowie; and "Thanksgiving Prayer" by William S. Burroughs.

WRITINGS

Screenplays:

The Discipline of D.E. (short film), 1978.

Mala Noche (also known as *Bad Night*), Northern Film, 1986.

(As Gus Van Sant, Jr.; with Daniel Yost), *Drugstore Cowboy,* Avenue Pictures, 1989.

My Own Private Idaho, Fine Line, 1991.

Even Cowgirls Get the Blues, New Line Cinema, 1993.

Ballad of the Skeletons, 1996.

Gerry, THINKFilms, 2002.

Elephant, Fine Line, 2003.

Last Days, Fine Line, 2005.

"Le Marais" segment, *Paris, je t'aime* (also known as *Paris, I Love You*), First Look International, 2007.

Paranoid Park, IFC Films, 2007.

Television Specials:

"Thanksgiving Prayer," *American Flash Cards,* PBS, 1992.

Books:

108 Portraits (photographs by the author), 1992.

Pink (novel), Nan A. Talese, 1997.

Also photographer for cover and booklet to accompany the album *Blood Sugar Sex Magic* by the Red Hot Chili Peppers.

OTHER SOURCES

Books:

International Dictionary of Films and Filmmakers, Volume 2: Directors, St. James Press, 1996.

Paris, James Robert, *Gus Van Sant: An Unauthorized Biography,* Thunder's Mouth Press, 2001.

Periodicals:

Advocate, March 31, 1998, p. 46; April 22, 2008, p. S42.

Entertainment Weekly, January 30, 2009, p. 62.

Esquire, August, 2005, p. 36; January, 2009, p. 87.

Film Comment, September, 1991, p. 35; September, 2003, pp. 26–27, 29, 31–33; July, 2005, p. 16.

Interview, March, 1991, p. 126; January, 1998, p. 42; December, 1998, p. 32.

Newsweek, April 15, 1991, p. 68; December 7, 1998, p. 70; December 15, 2008, p. 14.

New York Times, July 17, 2005; March 2, 2008, pp. AR15, AR18.

Rolling Stone, October 31, 1991, p. 61.

VICKARYOUS, Scott 1975–

PERSONAL

Full name, Scott E. Vickaryous; born September 13, 1975, in Port Alberne, British Columbia, Canada; son of Rom and Donna Vickaryous. *Education:* Attended high school in Sherwood Park, Alberta, Canada.

Addresses: *Agent*—Lucas Talent, Sun Tower, 100 West Pender St., 7th Floor, Vancouver, British Columbia V6B 1R8, Canada. *Manager*—Insomnia Media Group, Rock Hudson Building, Suite G, 100 Universal City Plaza, Universal City, CA 91608.

Career: Actor and singer. Worked as a model in Toronto, Ontario, Canada.

CREDITS

Television Appearances; Movies:
Cold diver, *Breaking the Surface: The Greg Louganis Story,* USA Network, 1997.
Eric Landau, *The Right Connections,* Showtime, 1997.
Ben Palmer, *The Accident: A Moment of Truth Movie,* NBC, 1997.
Luke Muldenhower, *A Champion's Fight* (also known as *A Champion's Fight: A Moment of Truth Movie* and *Shattered Hearts*), NBC, 1998.
Brad Meyers, *Race Against Fear* (also known as *Race Against Fear: A Moment of Truth Movie*), NBC, 1998.
Paul Archer, *Our Guys: Outrage in Glen Ridge* (also known as *Outrage in Glen Ridge*), ABC, 1999.
Scott Sparkman, *Final Run* (also known as *Ground Panic 90 Seconds*), CBS, 1999.
Taylor Bradley, *Romy and Michele: In the Beginning,* ABC Family, 2005.

Television Appearances; Series:
Clay Forman, a recurring role, *Get Real,* Fox, 1999–2000.

Television Appearances; Pilots:
Hayden Loring, *Safe Harbor,* The WB, 1999.

Television Appearances; Episodic:
Sebastian Maddox, "Whistle Blower," *Viper,* syndicated, 1997.
Bobby Warner, "The Devil's Lighthouse," *Poltergeist: The Legacy,* Showtime and syndicated, 1997.
Max Ballard, "Sun Ahso Rises," *Breaker High,* UPN, 1997.
Young Sinclair, "Last Supper," *The Outer Limits* (also known as *The New Outer Limits*), Showtime, 1998.
Daniel Evans, "Chapter Nineteen," *Boston Public,* Fox, 2001.
Daniel Evans, "Chapter Twenty," *Boston Public,* Fox, 2001.
Daniel Evans, "Chapter Twenty–One," *Boston Public,* Fox, 2001.
Daniel Evans, "Chapter Twenty–Two," *Boston Public,* Fox, 2001.
Lance Montague, "The Romeo & Juliet Episode," *Maybe It's Me,* The WB, 2002.
David, "Now I Lay Me Down to Sleep," *The Division,* Lifetime, 2004.
David, "Acts of Desperation," *The Division,* Lifetime, 2004.
John Doe in 1980, "One Night," *Cold Case,* CBS, 2006.
Tim Sexton, "Truly, Madly, Deeply," *Close to Home,* CBS, 2006.

Film Appearances:
Eli, *A Time for Dancing,* Eagle Pictures/East of Doheny, 2000.
Stu, *Whatever It Takes,* Columbia, 2000.
Mark, *Silent Scream* (also known as *The Retreat*), Lions Gate Films Home Entertainment, 2006.
Jacob Buchanan, *Eating Out 2: Sloppy Seconds* (also known as *Eating Out 2: Different Rocks*), Ariztical Entertainment, 2006.
Mitch, *TV Face,* Panamapros, 2007.

RECORDINGS

Albums:
Backup vocalist, *No One Does It Better,* by Souldecision, 1999.

VICKERY, John 1950–

PERSONAL

Born November 4, 1950, in Alameda, CA. *Education:* Attended University of California, Berkeley, and University of California, Davis.

Addresses: *Agent*—TalentWorks, 3500 West Olive Ave., Suite 1400, Burbank, CA 91505.

Career: Actor. California Actors Theatre, Los Gatos, actor, 1976.

Awards, Honors: Joseph Jefferson Award, best actor in a principal role in a play, 1996, for *I Hate Hamlet.*

CREDITS

Stage Appearances:
Malcolm, *Macbeth,* Vivian Beaumont Theatre, Lincoln Center, New York City, 1981.
Reverend Rushbrooke, *A Call from the East,* Manhattan Theatre Club, New York City, 1981.
Henry, Prince of Wales, *Henry IV, Part I,* New York Shakespeare Festival, Delacorte Theatre, Public Theatre, New York City, 1981.
Edward "Ned" Sheldon, *Ned and Jack,* Little Theatre, New York City, 1981.
Victor Salt, *Eminent Domain,* Circle in the Square, New York City, 1982.
Charles Lutwidge Dodgson/Lewis Carroll, *Looking–Glass,* Entermedia Theatre, New York City, 1982.
Manfred von Richthofen, the Red Dragon, *The Death of von Richthofen as Witnessed from Earth,* New York Shakespeare Festival, Estelle R. Newman Theatre, Public Theatre, New York City, 1982.
Richard II, Yale Repertory Theatre, New Haven, CT, 1984.
Ian, *The Vampires,* Astor Place Theatre, New York City, 1984.
Henry, *The Real Thing,* Plymouth Theatre, New York City, 1984.
Henry David Thoreau and George Armstrong Custer, *Romance Language,* Mark Taper Forum, Los Angeles, 1986.
Marcus Brutus, *Julius Caesar,* National Shakespeare Festival, Old Globe Theatre, San Diego, CA, 1987.
Stephen Britter, *Made in Bangkok,* Mark Taper Forum, 1988.
Geoffrey Duncan, *The Sisters Rosenweig,* Mitzi E. Newhouse Theatre, New York City, then Ethel Barrymore Theatre, New York City, 1993.
Harry Lime, *The Third Man,* L.A. TheatreWorks (also recorded for future radio broadcasts), Los Angeles, 1995.
I Hate Hamlet, Jujamcyn Theatre, Chicago, IL, 1996.
Scar, *The Lion King* (musical), Orpheum Theatre, Minneapolis, MN, 1997, then New Amsterdam Theatre, New York City, 1997–98, then Los Angeles, 2000.
Estragon, *Waiting for Godot,* Matrix Theatre, Los Angeles, 2000.
Steven, Sam, and P. J., *Princess Marjorie,* Julianne Argyros Stage, South Coast Repertory, Costa Mesa, CA, 2005.

David Manning, *Stuff Happens,* Mark Taper Forum, 2005.
Old Uncle, *The Black Rider* (musical), Ahmanson Theatre, Los Angeles, 2006.

Television Appearances; Series:
Constantine/Richard Scanlon, *The Edge of Night,* ABC, 1983.
Jesse Wilde, *One Life to Live,* ABC, 1984–85.
(English–language version) Voice of Dagger/Gunnar, *Teknoman* (animated; also known as *Starknight Tekkaman Blade;* Japanese version released as *Uchu no kishi tekkaman bureido*), UPN, 1994.
Alit Neroon, a recurring role, *Babylon 5* (also known as *B5*), The WB, between 1994 and 1997.

Television Appearances; Miniseries:
Bourrienne, *Napoleon and Josephine: A Love Story,* ABC, 1987.
George McLure, *I Know My First Name Is Steven* (also known as *The Missing Years*), NBC, 1989.
Anthony Alistair Wilmot "Tony" Longbridge, *Till We Meet Again* (also known as *Judith Krantz's "Till We Meet Again"*), CBS, 1989.

Television Appearances; Movies:
Pastor Evans, *Promised a Miracle,* CBS, 1988.
Dr. Simon, *The Boys* (also known as *The Guys*), ABC, 1991.
Swanson, *Deconstructing Sarah,* USA Network, 1994.
Brack, *The Big Time,* TNT, 2002.

Television Appearances; Specials:
Malcolm, *Macbeth,* 1982.

Television Appearances; Pilots:
Stephen, *Ask Rita,* CBS, 1994.

Television Appearances; Episodic:
Everett Steele, "Strange Bedfellows," *Crime Story,* NBC, 1986.
Everett Steele, "Fatal Crossroads," *Crime Story,* NBC, 1987.
Everett Steele, "Torello on Trial," *Crime Story,* NBC, 1987.
Everett Steele, "Ground Zero," *Crime Story,* NBC, 1987.
Lawyer Kenneth Clipner, "Armand's Hammer," *L.A. Law,* NBC, 1990.
Lawyer Kenneth Clipner, "Rest in Pieces," *L.A. Law,* NBC, 1991.
Al, "Plane Nine from Nantucket," *Wings,* NBC, 1991.
Counselor Andrus Hagan, "Night Terrors," *Star Trek: The Next Generation* (also known as *Star Trek: TNG*), syndicated, 1991.
"Playing the Part: Characters and Actors in Drama," *Literary Visions,* 1992.

"A Frame for Meaning: Theme in Drama," *Literary Visions*, 1992.

Chet Mitford, "His Honor's Offer," *Civil Wars*, ABC, 1992.

Mr. Welles, "The Fall of the Night," *Babylon 5* (also known as *B5*), The WB, 1995.

Seth, "Davy Jones," *The Single Guy*, NBC, 1996.

Gul Rusot, "The Changing Face of Evil," *Star Trek: Deep Space Nine* (also known as *Deep Space Nine, DS9,* and *Star Trek: DS9*), syndicated, 1999.

Gul Rusot, "When It Rains ...," *Star Trek: Deep Space Nine* (also known as *Deep Space Nine, DS9,* and *Star Trek: DS9*), syndicated, 1999.

Gul Rusot, "Tacking into the Wind," *Star Trek: Deep Space Nine* (also known as *Deep Space Nine, DS9,* and *Star Trek: DS9*), syndicated, 1999.

Mr. Welles, "Appearances and Other Deceits," *Crusade*, TNT, 1999.

Forrest St. James, "Sometimes a Fritter Is Just a Fritter," *Stark Raving Mad*, NBC, 1999.

Dwayne Cochrane, "Culture Clash," *Judging Amy*, CBS, 2000.

Jack the Ripper, "Don't Dream It's Over," *The Others*, NBC, 2000.

Reggie, "The Play's the Thing," *Early Edition*, CBS, 2000.

Cory Beacham, "Puppy Love," *NYPD Blue* (also known as *N.Y.P.D.*), ABC, 2001.

Voice of townsperson, "Eli Whitney's Flesh Eating Mistake," *Time Squad* (animated), Cartoon Network, 2001.

Cory Beacham, "Here Comes the Son," *NYPD Blue* (also known as *N.Y.P.D.*), ABC, 2002.

Cory Beacham, "Humpty Dumped," *NYPD Blue* (also known as *N.Y.P.D.*), ABC, 2002.

"Prodigy," *Without a Trace* (also known as *W.A.T.*), CBS, 2003.

Petyr, "Roe to Perdition," *Frasier*, NBC, 2003.

Prosecutor Orak, "Judgment," *Star Trek: Enterprise* (also known as *Enterprise*), UPN, 2003.

Matt St. John, "The Last Action Queero," *I'm with Her*, ABC, 2003.

Interpol Inspector Hugh Benson, "Leap of Faith," *NCIS: Naval Criminal Investigative Service* (also known as *Navy NCIS: Naval Criminal Investigative Service* and *NCIS*), CBS, 2007.

Gerald Prosser, "Will the Real Fred Rovick Please Stand Up?," *Medium*, CBS, 2010.

Film Appearances:

Dr. Caius, *The Merry Wives of Windsor*, 1980.

First detective, *Out of Bounds*, Columbia, 1986.

(English–language version) Voice of Ken, *Fist of the North Star* (Japanese–language version released as *Hokuto no ken*), Streamline Pictures, 1986.

Hotel manager, *Big Business*, Buena Vista, 1988.

Detective, *Rapid Fire*, Twentieth Century–Fox, 1992.

Dr. Chamberlain, *Dr. Giggles*, Universal, 1992.

Dad, *Son for Sail*, 1995.

The priest, *Shooting LA*, 2001.

Restaurant manager, *Murder by Numbers* (also known as *Murd3r 8y Num8ers*), Warner Bros., 2002.

Mr. Woodruff, *Debating Robert Lee*, 2004, Radio London Films, 2006.

RECORDINGS

Video Games:

Voice, *Vampire: The Masquerade—Redemption*, 2000.

Voice of Lucifer, *Dante's Inferno*, Electronic Arts, 2010.

W–Y

WADE, Geoffrey

PERSONAL

American. *Education:* Attended Amherst College, 1973, and Central School of Speech and Drama, London, 1976.

Addresses: *Agent*—Eric Stevens, Rainbow High Entertainment, 10 Universal City Plaza, Suite 2000, Universal City, CA 91608.

Career: Actor. Appeared in industrial films and commercials; also radio actor.

Member: American Federation of Television and Radio Artists, Actors' Equity Association, Screen Actors Guild, British Actors' Equity Association.

CREDITS

Stage Appearances:
Captain Lancy, *Translations,* Plymouth Theatre, New York City, 1995.
Jimmy and understudy for the roles of Walter and Timber, *An American Daughter,* Cort Theatre, New York City, 1997.
Sailor, *The Mask of Moriarty,* Paper Mill Playhouse, Millburn, NJ, 1998.
Colin, *Private Jokes Public Places,* Theatre at Center for Architecture, New York City, 2003–2004.

Appeared in *And a Nightingale Sang,* Geva Theatre, Rochester, NY; *Bedroom Farce,* Center Stage, Baltimore, MD; *Champagne Charlie Stakes,* New Play Festival, Philadelphia, PA; *A Life in the Theatre; Much Ado about Nothing; The Music Man,* Weston Playhouse; *On the Verge,* Cincinnati, OH; *The Rocky Horror Show; Six Degrees of Separation,* Repertory Theatre of St. Louis, St. Louis, MO; *Sylvia,* Cincinnati Playhouse, Cincinnati, OH; also appeared as an understudy, *The Middle Ages* and *Twelve Dreams,* Lincoln Center Theatre, New York City. Appeared in productions at Caldwell Theatre; Denver Theatre Center, Denver, CO; Old Globe Theatre, San Diego, CA; Pennsylvania Stage; and Philadelphia Drama Guild.

Major Tours:
Appeared in touring productions of *Crazy for You* and *Dancing at Lughnasa,* Oxford Playhouse, Oxford, England.

Film Appearances:
Butler at Gracie Mansion, *City Hall,* Columbia, 1996.
Dr. Filts, *August* (short film), University of Southern California, 2007.
Romeu, Viagem, *Tres* (short film), Wild Card Productions, 2007.
Frank, *TV Face,* Panamapros, 2007.
Dad, *Running* (short film), 2009.

Television Appearances; Episodic:
Mitchell, Weisbrod, "Savior," *Law & Order,* NBC, 1996.
Dr. Frederick Austin, "Ritual," *Law & Order,* NBC, 1997.
Peter Hammermesh, "Ramparts," *Law & Order,* NBC, 1999.
Dr. Kipperman, "Turning Thirty," *Ally McBeal* (also known as *Ally My Love*), Fox, 2000.
Alan Sweet, "Spoil the Child," *Judging Amy,* CBS, 2000.
Brandan Robb, "Quid Pro Quo," *Profiler,* NBC, 2000.
Drummond, "City Hall," *Law & Order,* NBC, 2004.
Dr. Bailey, "My Jiggly Ball," *Scrubs* (also known as *Scrubs: Med School*), NBC, 2006.
Marcus, "Gambling m' Diction," *The King of Queens,* CBS, 2006.
First old juror, "Prior Convictions," *Justice,* Fox, 2006.

Mandy's lawyer, "Mr. Monk and the Leper," *Monk,* USA Network, 2006.

The doctor, "George's House Has Two Empty Wombs," *George Lopez,* ABC, 2007.

Judge Hudson, *Saints and Sinners,* MyNetworkTV, 2007.

Mediator, *The Young and the Restless* (also known as *Y&R*), CBS, 2008.

Darrell Amos, "Life after Death," *ER,* NBC, 2008.

Third board member, "You Get What You Need," *Brothers & Sisters,* ABC, 2008.

Defense attorney, "Guilt Trip," *Numb3rs* (also known as *Num3ers*), CBS, 2009.

Reverend Haskell, *The Bold and the Beautiful* (also known as *Belleza y poder*), CBS, 2009.

Television Appearances; Other:

Malcolm Christopher, *The City* (series; sequel to *Loving*), ABC, 1995.

Eugene, "Crazy for You" (special), *Great Performances,* PBS, 1999.

WALKER, Albertina 1929–2010

PERSONAL

Born August 29, 1929, in Chicago, IL; died of respiratory complications, October 8, 2010, in Chicago, IL. Singer. Grammy Award-winning contralto gospel singer Walker was famous worldwide as the Queen of Gospel. For more than six decades, she toured, performed, and recorded and helped launch the careers of many young gospel soloists. A protge of Mihalia Jackson, she was prominent in the Chicago gospel scene in her youth and began touring Midwest churches with the Willie Webb singers, recording her first single, Hell Be There. She joined Robert Anderson and His Gospel Caravan, taking charge of the group when Anderson retired in 1951. Renamed the Caravans, it became the eras most popular womens gospel group in the United States. During the 1950s and 1960s, the group recorded numerous hits, including Lord Keep Me Day by Day, Walkers signature song. She released her solo album debut, *Put a Little Love in Your Heart,* in 1975, followed by dozens of others, including *Spirit* in 1987 and *I'm Still Here* in 1997. In 1979 she received her first Grammy nomination when she teamed with James Cleveland on *Please Be Patient With Me.* Her cameo in the 1992 film *Leap of Faith* brought her talents to a movie audience. She was presented with the Grammy for Best Traditional Soul Gospel Album for her 1994 recording *Songs of the Church: Live in Memphis.* Her many honors include her 2001 induction into the Gospel Music Hall of Fame, a 2002 White House ceremony in which President George W. Bush honored her contribution to gospel music, and a 2005 Heritage

Fellowship from the National Endowment for the Arts. In June 2010 Walker performed for the last time in a Caravans reunion at the Chicago Gospel Music Festival.

PERIODICALS

Los Angeles Times, October 9, 2010.
New York Times, October 9, 2010.
Washington Post, October 8, 2010.

WALTERS, Barbara 1929–

PERSONAL

Full name, Barbara Jill Walters; born September 25, 1929, in Boston, MA; daughter of Lou (a nightclub operator and theatrical producer) and Dena (maiden name, Selett) Walters; married Robert Henry Katz (a business executive), June 20, 1955 (marriage annulled); married Lee Guber (a theatrical producer), December 8, 1963 (divorced, December, 1976); married Merv Adelson (a television production executive), May 10, 1986 (divorced, 1992); children: (second marriage) Jacqueline Dena. *Education:* Sarah Lawrence College, B.A., 1953.

Addresses: *Agent*—Harry Walker Agency, 355 Lexington Ave., 21st Floor, New York, NY 10017; (literary) Morton L. Janklow, Janklow and Nesbit Associates, 445 Park Ave., New York, NY 10022. *Publicist*—Cindi Berger, PMK/BNC New York, 650 Fifth Ave., 33rd Floor, New York, NY 10019.

Career: Broadcast journalist, producer, and writer. Began career as a writer and producer for local television stations, including WNBC–TV, WPIX, and CBS–TV; Barwall Productions, New York City, founder and president, 1976. Also worked in advertising and public relations.

Member: National Association for Help for Mentally Retarded Children (honorary chair, 1970).

Awards, Honors: Daytime Emmy Award nomination, best host of a talk, service, or variety series, 1974, for *Not for Women Only;* named Woman of the Year in Communications, 1974; honorary L.H.D., Ohio State University and Marymount College, Tarrytown, NY, both 1975; Award of the Year, National Association of Television Program Executives, 1975; Daytime Emmy Award, best host of a talk, service, or variety series, 1975, for *The Today Show;* Mass Media Award, Institute for Human Relations, American Jewish Committee, 1975; Illinois Broadcasters Association established the Barbara Walters College Scholarship in Broadcast Journalism, 1975; named Woman of the Year, Theta Sigma Phi, and Broadcaster of the Year, International Radio and Television Society, 1975; Gold Medal, National Institute of Social Sciences, 1976; Matrix Award, New York Women in Communications, 1977; Lowell Thomas Award, International Platform Association, 1977; Hubert H. Humphrey Freedom Prize, Anti–Defamation League, B'nai B'rith, 1978; Emmy Award, best news program segment, and Emmy Award, best news and documentary programs and program segments (with others), both 1980, for *ABC News Nightline;* Emmy Awards, best interviewer, 1982 and 1983, Emmy Award (with others), outstanding informational series, 1983, and Emmy Award nominations (with others), best informational series, 1984–94, all for *The Barbara Walters Special;* honorary L.H.D., Wheaton College, 1983; Emmy Award, best interviewer, 1983, Emmy Award nomination, best interview segment, 1984, Emmy Award nomination, best background/analysis of a single current story, 1987, and Emmy Award, best interview segment, 1988, all for *20/20;* President's Award, Overseas Press Club of America, 1988; Lowell Thomas Award, Marist College, 1990; elected to Academy of Television Arts and Sciences Hall of Fame, 1990; Lifetime Achievement Award, International Women's Media Foundation, 1992; honored by the American Museum of the Moving Image, 1992; Lifetime Achievement Award, Women's Project and Productions, 1993; honored by Museum of Television and Radio, 1996; Excellence in Media Award, GLAAD Media Awards, Gay and Lesbian Alliance Against Defamation, 1996; Distinguished Service Award, National Association of Broadcasters, 1997; Muse Award, New York Women in Film and Television, 1997; Lucy Award, Women in Film, 1998; Daytime Emmy Award nominations, outstanding talk show, annually 1998–2003, 2004–08, outstanding talk show host, annually, 1999–2009, and Daytime Emmy Award, 2003, all (with others) for *The View;* News and Documentary Emmy Award (with others), outstanding program or segment of a news or documentary program, 2000, for *ABC 2000: The Millennium;* Daytime Emmy Award, lifetime achievement, 2000; Lifetime Achievement Award, Academy of Television Arts and Sciences, 2000; received star on Hollywood Walk of Fame, 2007; News and Documentary Emmy award, lifetime achievement, 2009; additional honorary degrees from Ben–Gurion University of the Negev, Hofstra University, and Temple University.

CREDITS

Television Appearances; Series:
Regular correspondent for "The Rise and Shine Review" segment, *Today Show* (also known as *NBC News Today* and *The Today Show*), NBC, c. 1963–74.

Coanchor, *Today Show* (also known as *NBC News Today* and *The Today Show*), NBC, 1974–76.
Moderator, *Not for Women Only*, syndicated, 1974–76.
Coanchor, *The ABC Evening News* (also known as *World News Tonight*), ABC, 1976–78.
Host, *The Barbara Walters Special* (series of occasional specials; also known as *Barbara Walters: Interviews of a Lifetime* and *The Barbara Walters Summer Special*), ABC, between 1976 and 1993.
Correspondent, *20/20* (also known as *ABC News 20/20*), ABC, 1981–84.
Coanchor, *20/20* (also known as *ABC News 20/20*), ABC, 1984–2004.
Substitute anchor, *Nightline* (also known as *ABC News Nightline*), ABC, 1991–2004.
Host, *Barbara Walters Presents the 10 Most Fascinating People of [the Year]*, ABC, annually, 1993—.
Cohost, *The View*, ABC, 1997—.
ABC News Saturday Night, ABC, 1998.
Anchor, *America.01*, ABC, 2001.

Television Appearances; Specials:
Host, *The Barbara Walters Special* (series of occasional specials; also known as *Barbara Walters: Interviews of a Lifetime* and *The Barbara Walters Summer Special*), ABC, beginning 1976.
Moderator, *1976 Presidential Debate*, 1976.
"Mickey's 50," *The Wonderful World of Disney*, NBC, 1978.
Host, *Homage for the Duke*, 1979.
The Television Annual: 1978/1979, 1979.
Olympic Gala, 1984.
All–Star Celebration Honoring Martin Luther King, Jr., NBC, 1986.
Host and commentator, *Liberty Weekend Preview*, ABC, 1986.
Commentator, *Liberty Weekend*, ABC, 1986.
Host, *Life: Fifty Years* (also known as *The 50th Anniversary of Life Magazine*), ABC, 1986.
Today at 35, NBC, 1987.
A Star–Spangled Celebration, ABC, 1987.
Sesame Street, Special (also known as *Put Down the Duckie: A Sesame Street Special* and *Sesame Street: Put Down the Duckie—An All–Star Musical Special*), PBS, 1988.
Host, *The 50th Barbara Walters Special*, ABC, 1988.
Anchor, *America's Kids: Why They Flunk* (also known as *Burning Questions*), ABC, 1988.
Regis & Kathie Lee: Special Edition, 1988.
Fifty Years of Television: A Golden Celebration, CBS, 1989.
Reporter, *Presidential Inauguration*, ABC, 1989.
Anchor, *Survival Stories: Growing Up Down and Out* (also known as *Kids in Trouble: Fighting Back*), ABC, 1989.
America's Kids: Teaching Them to Think (also known as *Burning Questions*), ABC, 1989.
Night of 100 Stars III, NBC, 1990.
Fifteen Years of MacNeil/Lehrer, PBS, 1990.

Anchor, *The Perfect Baby,* ABC, 1990.

"Edward R. Murrow: This Reporter," *American Masters,* PBS, 1990.

The Best of Disney: 50 Years of Magic, ABC, 1991.

(In archive footage) *The Wayne and Shuster Years,* 1991.

Host, *The Best of Barbara Walters: Legend—The New Generation,* ABC, 1992.

Donahue: The 25th Anniversary, NBC, 1992.

Host, *Twentysomething: What Happened to the American Dream?,* ABC, 1992.

Today at 40, NBC, 1992.

Narrator, *In a New Light: A Call to Action in the War against AIDS,* 1992.

Legend to Legend Night, NBC, 1993.

Kathie Lee Gifford's Celebration of Motherhood, ABC, 1993.

The 12 Most Fascinating People of 1993, ABC, 1993.

Narrator, *In a New Light '93,* ABC, 1993.

Host, *What Is This Thing Called Love? The Barbara Walters Special,* ABC, 1993.

Host, *One on One: Classic Television Interviews,* CBS, 1993.

Host, *Great Television Moments: What We Watched,* ABC, 1993.

Host, *20/20 15th Anniversary Special,* ABC, 1993.

Host, *Switched at Birth: Kimberly's Story* (special presentation of *Turning Point*), ABC, 1993.

(In archive footage) *Fallen Champ: The Untold Story of Mike Tyson,* 1993.

(In archive footage) *One on One: Classic Television Interviews,* 1993.

Segment host, "Watching History Happen," *ABC's 40th Anniversary Special,* ABC, 1994.

Host, "25/25," *Sesame Street's All–Star 25th Birthday: Stars and Street Forever!* (also known as *All–Star 25th Birthday: Stars and Street Forever!*), ABC, 1994.

Host, *In a New Light '94,* ABC, 1994.

Host, *The Barbara Walters Special: Happy Hour,* ABC, 1994.

Host, *The Barbara Walters Special: The Price of Fame,* ABC, c. 1994.

Anchor, *Whiz Kids,* ABC, 1995.

Host, *Princess Diana: The Interview,* ABC, 1995.

Into the Jury's Hands, ABC, 1995.

Inside the Hate Conspiracy: America's Terrorists, ABC, 1995.

Presenter of introduction, *In a New Light: Sex Unplugged,* ABC, 1995.

Narrator, *Happily Ever After?,* The Discovery Channel, 1995.

Sex, Drugs and Consequences, ABC, 1996.

Host, *Race for a Miracle: The Brad and Vicki Margus Story,* ABC, 1996.

Host, *The Kennedy Center 25th Anniversary Celebration,* PBS, 1996.

Barbara Walters: 20 Years at ABC, ABC, 1996.

Mike Wallace Remembers, CBS, 1997.

(In archive footage) "Judy Garland: Beyond the Rainbow," *Biography,* Arts and Entertainment, 1997.

Host, *Men Are from Mars, Women are from Venus—But We Have to Live on Earth,* ABC, 1997.

Hollywood and the News, AMC, 1997.

(In archive footage) *Gloria Swanson: The Greatest Star,* 1997.

Host, *Barbara Walters Presents 6 to Watch,* ABC, 1997, 1998.

Academy of Television Arts a& Sciences 13th Annual Hall of Fame, Showtime, 1998.

Monica: The Untold Story, E! Entertainment Television, 1999.

Intimate Portrait: Star Jones, Lifetime, 1999.

Host, *A Celebration: 100 Years of Great Women with Barbara Walters,* ABC, 1999.

"Ann Landers: America's Confidante," *Biography,* Arts and Entertainment, 1999.

ABC 2000: The Millennium, ABC, 1999.

Super Bowl XXXIV, ABC, 2000.

"Barbara Walters: A Driving Force," *Biography,* Arts and Entertainment, 2000.

The Nightclub Years, Arts and Entertainment, 2001.

Intimate Portrait: Liz Smith, Lifetime, 2001.

The I Love Lucy 50th Anniversary Special (also known as *I Love Lucy's 50th Anniversary Special*), CBS, 2001.

Breaking the News, CBS, 2001.

Host, *Born in My Heart: A Love Story,* ABC, 2001.

NBC 75th Anniversary Special (also known as *NBC 75th Anniversary Celebration*), NBC, 2002.

Gilda Radner's Greatest Moments, ABC, 2002.

Host, *After Party at "The View",* ABC, 2002.

Intimate Portrait: Paula Zahn, Lifetime, 2002.

Host, *20/20: Living with Michael Jackson,* ABC, 2003.

100 Years of Hope and Humor, NBC, 2003.

Host, *The View: His & Her Body Test,* ABC, 2003.

Intimate Portrait: Christiane Amanpour, Lifetime, 2003.

Host, *Hillary Clinton's Journey: Public, Private, Personal with Barbara Walters,* ABC, 2003.

Presenter, *ABC 50th Anniversary Celebration,* ABC, 2003.

Cristina: El 15 aniversario, 2004.

(In archive footage) *101 Biggest Celebrity Oops,* E! Entertainment Television, 2004.

(In archive footage) "Fidel Castro," *The American Experience,* PBS, 2005.

Correspondent, *In the Path of Katrina,* ABC, 2005.

Host, *A Barbara Walters Special: Heaven; Where Is It? How Do We Get There?,* ABC, 2005.

Peter Jennings: Reporter, ABC, 2005.

Legends Ball, ABC, 2006.

"Walter Cronkite: Witness to History," *American Masters,* PBS, 2006.

Michael J. Fox: The E! True Hollywood Story, E! Entertainment Television, 2006.

The View: The E! True Hollywood Story, E! Entertainment Television, 2007.

(From archive sound footage) *Brando,* TCM, 2007.

Host, *In Performance at the White House: Thelonious Monk Institute of Jazz,* PBS, 2007.

That's the Way It Is: Celebrating Cronkite at 90, CBS, 2007.

Mark Twain Prize: Billy Crystal, PBS, 2007.

(In archive footage) "Bo Derek: The Perfect 10," *Biography,* Arts and Entertainment, 2007.

Host, *Barbara Walters Oscar Special,* ABC, annually, 2007–2009.

Host, *Live to 150, Can You Do It?,* ABC, 2008.

Audition: Barbara Walters' Journey, ABC, 2008.

Anchor, *20/20: The Royal Family,* ABC, 2008.

Big Night of Stars (also known as *Jimmy Kimmel's Big Night of Stars*), ABC, 2008.

Remembering Tim Russert, NBC, 2008.

Anchor, *20/20: The Life and Death of Michael Jackson,* ABC, 2009.

Anchor, *20/20: Farrah Fawcett; Her Life, Her Loves, Her Legacy,* ABC, 2009.

Television Appearances; Pilots:
Anchor, *Turning Point* (also known as *20/20 Wednesday*), ABC, 1994.

Television Appearances; Episodic:
Today Show (also known as *NBC News Today* and *The Today Show*), NBC, 1989.

Entertainment Tonight (also known as *E.T.* and *This Week in Entertainment*), syndicated, more than sixty appearances, beginning 2003.

Extra (also known as *Extra: The Entertainment Magazine*), syndicated, 2003.

This Hour Has 22 Minutes (also known as *22 Minutes*), CBC, 2003.

"Heavy Burden," *48 Hours* (also known as *48 Hours Investigates* and *48 Hours Mystery*), CBS, 2003.

Inside the Actors Studio (also known as *Actors Interview* and *Inside the Actors Studio: The Craft of Theatre and Film*), Bravo, 2005.

"Elizabeth Hasselbeck's Baby Shower," *Party Planner with David Tutera,* The Discovery Channel, 2005.

"Sexiest Men," *TV Land's Top Ten,* TV Land, 2005.

"I'll Take Manhattan," *The Girls Next Door,* E! Entertainment Television, 2005.

Anchor, *Primetime Live,* ABC, c. 2005–2006.

American Morning, 2006.

(Uncredited; in archive footage) "The Tank Man," *Frontline,* PBS, 2006.

The Hour (also known as *CBC News: The Hour*), CBC, 2008.

(In archive footage) *Just In with Laura Ingraham,* Fox News Channel, 2008.

20/20 (also known as *ABC News 20/20*), ABC, 2009.

(In archive footage) *WWE Smackdown!,* The CW, 2009.

(In archive footage) *The Tonight Show with Conan O'Brien,* NBC, 2009.

(In archive footage) *Live from Studio Five,* Channel 5, 2009, 2010.

This Week, BBC, 2010.

Also appeared in episodes of *Issues and Answers,* ABC.

Television Talk Show Guest Appearances; Episodic:
Girl Talk, 1967.

The Mike Douglas Show, 1968.

The Dick Cavett Show, 1970.

The David Frost Show, 1970, 1971.

The Tonight Show Starring Johnny Carson, CBS, 1970, 1972.

Dinah!, 1977.

Good Morning America (also known as *G.M.A.*), ABC, multiple appearances including some as guest host, between 1978 and 2006.

Live with Regis and Kathie Lee, syndicated, 1989.

The Howard Stern Show (also known as *The Howard Stern Summer Show*), 1992.

Late Show with David Letterman (also known as *The Late Show* and *Letterman*), CBS, multiple appearances, beginning 1993.

Howard Stern, 1995.

The Rosie O'Donnell Show, syndicated, between 1996 and 2002, guest host, 2001.

Late Night with Conan O'Brien, NBC, multiple appearances, between 1998 and 2008.

The Tonight Show with Jay Leno, NBC, 2003, 2004.

The Tony Danza Show, syndicated, 2004, 2005.

The Oprah Winfrey Show (also known as *Oprah*), syndicated, 2004, 2008.

The O'Reilly Factor, Fox News Channel, 2004, 2005, 2008.

Live with Regis and Kelly, syndicated, 2005.

Larry King Live, Cable News Network, multiple appearances, between 2005 and 2009.

Howard Stern on Demand (also known as *Howard TV on Demand*), 2007.

Ellen: The Ellen DeGeneres Show, syndicated, 2007, 2008.

Tavis Smiley, PBS, 2008.

The Daily Show with Jon Stewart (also known as *The Daily Show* and *The Daily Show with Jon Stewart Global Edition*), Comedy Central, 2008.

The Colbert Report, Comedy Central, 2008.

Rachael Ray, syndicated, 2009.

Late Night with Jimmy Fallon, NBC, 2010.

Television Appearances; Awards Presentations:
Presenter, *The 1st Academy TV Hall of Fame,* 1984.

The ... Annual Television Academy Hall of Fame, Fox, 1990, ABC, 1994.

Presenter, *The 48th Alfred I. Dupont—Columbia University Awards,* PBS, 1990.

Presenter, *The Essence Awards,* Fox, 1994.

Presenter, *The ... Annual Daytime Emmy Awards,* NBC, 1998, CBS, 1999, ABC, 2001, CBS, 2002, ABC, 2003, NBC, 2004, ABC, 2008, The CW, 2009.

The ... Annual Daytime Emmy Awards, ABC, 2000.

Presenter, *The 57th Annual Tony Awards,* CBS, 2003.

Presenter, *The 56th Annual Primetime Emmy Awards,* ABC, 2004.

New York 360 Degrees Presents: The 2007 Matrix Awards, 2007.

The ... Annual Academy Awards, ABC, 2010.

Television Executive Producer; Series:
The Barbara Walters Special (series of occasional specials; also known as *Barbara Walters: Interviews of a Lifetime* and *The Barbara Walters Summer Special*), ABC, between 1992 and 2009.

Barbara Walters Presents the 10 Most Fascinating People of [the Year], ABC, between 1993 and 2008.

Co–executive producer, *The View,* ABC, 1997–2000.

Television Executive Producer; Specials:
Born In My Heart: A Love Story, ABC, 2001.

The View: His & Her Body Test, 2003.

Barbara Walters Oscar Special, ABC, 2008, 2009.

Television Work; Episodic:
Executive producer, "America's Most Eligible and Overlooked Bachelors," *Iyanla,* syndicated, 2001.

Film Appearances:
The Line King: Al Hirschfeld (also known as *The Line King*), 1996.

(In archive footage) Interviewer, *Transformation: The Life and Legacy of Werner Erhard,* Screen Media Ventures, 2006.

(Uncredited; in archive footage) *Tyson,* Sony Pictures Classics, 2008.

Radio Appearances:
Presenter, *Barbara Live,* Sirius, 2007.

Moderator of the radio programs *Emphasis* and *Monitor;* host of the popular series *Not for Women Only,* NBC; (in archive footage) appeared in the series *Barbara Walters' Best of the Very Best,* Sirius.

Stage Appearances:
Night of 100 Stars III, Radio City Music Hall, New York City, 1990.

WRITINGS

Television Series:
"The Rise and Shine Review" segment, *Today Show* (also known as *NBC News Today* and *The Today Show*), NBC, 1961–63.

The Barbara Walters Special (series of occasional specials; also known as *Barbara Walters: Interviews of a Lifetime* and *The Barbara Walters Summer Special*), ABC, between 1992 and 2009.

Television Specials:
The Perfect Baby, ABC, 1990.

The Best of Barbara Walters: Legend—The New Generation, ABC, 1992.

What Is This Thing Called Love? The Barbara Walters Special, ABC, 1993.

20/20 15th Anniversary Special, ABC, 1993.

The Barbara Walters Special: Happy Hour, ABC, 1994.

Barbara Walters: 20 Years at ABC, ABC, 1996.

Barbara Walters Presents: 6 to Watch, ABC, 1997.

Hillary Clinton's Journey: Public, Private, Personal with Barbara Walters, ABC, 2003.

A Barbara Walters Special: Heaven; Where Is It? How Do We Get There?, ABC, 2005.

Barbara Walters Oscar Special, ABC, annually, 2007–2009.

Live to 150, Can You Do It?, ABC, 2008.

Writer for *Issues and Answers,* ABC.

Books:
Barbara Walters Best Interviews, Meredith Corp., 1994.

How to Talk with Practically Anybody about Practically Anything, Doubleday, 1970.

Audition: A Memoir, Alfred A. Knopf, 2008.

Contributor to periodicals, including *Family Weekly, Good Housekeeping,* and *Reader's Digest.*

OTHER SOURCES

Books:
Walters, Barbara, *Audition: A Memoir,* Alfred A. Knopf, 2008.

Periodicals:
AARP, March, 2008, p. 22.

Broadcasting and Cable, June 21, 2004, p. 3A.

Entertainment Weekly, March 19, 1999, pp. 81–82.

George, November, 1997, pp. 108–13, 142, 144.

Ladies' Home Journal, April, 1996, p. 128.

Life, February 18, 1966, pp. 49–50, 52; November 18, 1997, p. 36.

Los Angeles Times, March 9, 2009.

Nation, December 15, 1997, p. 36.

Newsweek, May 6, 1974; May 3, 1976; October 11, 1976.

New York Daily News, May 1, 2008; May 6, 2008.

New York Post, May 7, 2008.

New York Times, May 2, 1976; August 23, 1992; May 5, 2008, pp. E1, E4; March 4, 2010, p. C1.

Orlando Sentinel, May 5, 2008.

People Weekly, June 21, 1982; May 26, 1986.

Time, May 3, 1976; October 18, 1976.

TV Guide, January 2, 1999, pp. 12–19; December 19, 2005; December 3, 2007, p. 67; May 5, 2008, p. 16.
USA Today, September 17, 2004, p. 16E.
Washington Star, April 23, 1976.

Other:
"Barbara Walters: A Driving Force" (television special), *Biography,* Arts and Entertainment, 2000.

WERNER, Tom 1950–

PERSONAL

Full name, Thomas Werner; born April 12, 1950, in New York, NY (some sources cite NJ); brother of Peter Werner (a director); married; wife's name, Jill (in business), 1972 (separated, 2000); children: Teddy, Carolyn, Amanda. *Education:* Harvard University, B.A. (cum laude), 1971.

Addresses: *Office*—Carsey–Werner Distribution, 4024 Radford Ave., Building 3, Studio City, CA 91604; Good Humor Television, 9255 Sunset Blvd., Suite 1040, Los Angeles, CA 90069. *Agent*—Martin Lesak, Creative Artists Agency, 2000 Avenue of the Stars, Los Angeles, CA 90067.

Career: Producer and executive. ABC–TV, began as researcher, became programming executive, 1972–81; Carsey–Werner Distribution (and predecessor companies), Studio City, CA, partner of Marcy Carsey and producer, c. 1981—; Good Humor Television (also known as Werner Entertainment), Los Angeles, principal. Worked as a documentary filmmaker and consultant. Co–owner of professional baseball teams, including San Diego Padres, 1991–94, and Boston Red Sox, beginning 2002. Member of board of directors, Old Globe Theatre, San Diego, CA, and Sharp Hospital.

Awards, Honors: Emmy Award, 1985, and Emmy Award nominations, 1986, 1987, all outstanding comedy series (with Marcy Carsey and others), and Hall of Fame Award for television programs (with Carsey), Producers Guild of America, 2000, all for *The Cosby Show;* Image Award (with Carsey), best episode of a comedy series or special, National Association for the Advancement of Colored People, 1989, for an episode of *A Different World;* nomination for Wise Owl Award (with Carsey and others), Retirement Research Foundation, 1993, for "Ladies' Choice," *Roseanne;* inducted into Broadcasting and Cable Hall of Fame, 1996; Emmy Award nominations (with others), outstanding comedy series, 1997, 1998, both for *3rd Rock from the Sun;*

David Susskind Lifetime Achievement Award in Television (with others), Golden Laurel Awards, Producers Guild of America, 2002.

CREDITS

Television Executive Producer; Series:
Co–executive producer, *Oh, Madeline,* ABC, 1983–84.
The Cosby Show, NBC, 1985–92.
Roseanne, ABC, 1988–97.
Co–executive producer, *Chicken Soup,* ABC, 1989–90.
Co–executive producer, *Grand,* NBC, 1990.
Co–executive producer, *Davis Rules,* ABC, 1991, CBS, 1991–92.
Co–executive producer, *Frannie's Turn,* CBS, 1992.
Co–executive producer, *You Bet Your Life,* syndicated, 1992.
Co–executive producer, *Grace Under Fire* (also known as *Grace Under Pressure*), ABC, 1993–98.
Cybill, CBS, 1995–98.
Townies, ABC, 1996.
Men Behaving Badly, NBC, 1996–98.
3rd Rock from the Sun (also known as *Encounters of the Personal Kind* and *3rd Rock*), NBC, 1996–2001.
Damon, Fox, 1998–99.
That '70s Show (also known as *Feelin' All Right, The Kids Are Alright, Reeling in the Years,* and *Teenage Wasteland*), Fox, 1998–2006.
Days like These, 1999.
God, the Devil and Bob, NBC, 2000.
Normal, Ohio, Fox, 2000.
Dot Comedy, ABC, 2000.
Grounded for Life, Fox, 2001–2003, then The WB, 2003–2005.
You Don't Know Jack, ABC, 2001.
The Downer Channel, NBC, 2001.
That '80s Show, Fox, 2002.
Whoopi, NBC, 2003.
The Tracy Morgan Show, NBC, 2003–2004.
Happy Hour, Fox, 2006.
Hank, ABC, 2009.
The Life & Times of Tim (animated), HBO, 2008–10.

Television Producer; Series:
She TV, ABC, 1994.
Cosby, CBS, between 1996 and 2002.

Television Executive Producer; Pilots:
Callahan, ABC, 1982.
I Do, I Don't, ABC, 1983.
Co–executive producer, *Grace Under Fire* (also known as *Grace Under Pressure*), ABC, 1993.
Dirty Rotten Scoundrels, ABC, 1997.
That '70s Show (also known as *Feelin' All Right, The Kids Are Alright, Reeling in the Years,* and *Teenage Wasteland*), Fox, 1998.
Earth Scum, ABC, 1998.

The Binikers, NBC, 2000.
Speak, ABC, 2001.
The Mayor of Oyster Bay, ABC, 2002.
That '80s Show, Fox, 2002.
How to Be a Man, Fox, 2003.
Are We There Yet?, The WB, 2003.
These Guys, ABC, 2003.
The Tracy Morgan Show, NBC, 2003.
My Roommate Is a Big Fat Slut, Oxygen, 2003.
Blue Aloha (animated), Fox, 2004.
Game Over (animated), UPN, 2004.
Peep Show, Fox, 2005.
Grand Union, NBC, 2006.
Happy Hour, Fox, 2006.
Twenty Good Years, NBC, 2006.
Playing Chicken, Fox, 2007.
Pit Crew, Fox, 2008.
Hank, ABC, 2009.
Good Vibes (animated), Fox, 2009.

Television Executive Producer; Specials:

A Carol Burnett Special … Carol, Carl, Whoopi, and Robin (also known as *Carol, Carl, Whoopi and Robin*), ABC, 1987.
Brett Butler: The Child Ain't Right, HBO, 1993.

Television Work; Episodic:

Co–executive producer, "Pride and Prejudice," *A Different World,* NBC, 1990.
Executive producer, "Oh, Brother," *Good Girls Don't …,* Oxygen, 2004.

Television Executive Producer; Other:

Single Bars, Single Women (movie), ABC, 1984.
Richard Dawson and You Bet Your Life (game show; also known as *You Bet Your Life*), 1988.
The Scholar (miniseries), ABC, 2005.

Television Appearances; Miniseries:

TV Land Moguls, TV Land, 2004.

Television Appearances; Specials:

The Cosby Show: A Look Back, NBC, 2002.

Film Work:

Producer, *Hidden and Seeking,* 1971.
Executive producer, *Let's Go to Prison,* Universal, 2006.
Producer, *The Brothers Solomon,* Screen Gems, 2007.

RECORDINGS

Videos:

Faith Rewarded: The Historic Season of the 2004 Boston Red Sox, Hart Sharp Video, 2004.

Still We Believe: The Boston Red Sox Movie (also known as *We Still Believe: The Boston Red Sox Story*), Hart Sharp Video, 2004.
History Rings True: Red Sox Opening Day Ring Ceremony (also known as *History Rings True*), Hart Sharp Video, 2005.

OTHER SOURCES

Periodicals:

Broadcasting & Cable, November 18, 1996, pp. 28–30; January 19, 2004, p. 8A; July 26, 2004, p. 12.
People Weekly, July 1, 2002, p. 46.
Time, September 23, 1996, pp. 68–70.

WHITEHEAD, Cassandra
    See JEAN, Cassandra

WILLIAMS, Bradley Leland
    See LELAND, Brad

WILLIS, Michael 1949–
    (Michael S. Willis)

PERSONAL

Full name, Michael Stephan Willis; born October 4, 1949, in Lancaster, PA; son of Charles Hampton and Barbara Alice (maiden name, Rosenthal) Willis; married Lori Jo Alderton, January 15, 1983 (some sources cite 1984); children: Michael Stephan, Jr., Amy Alderton, Rebecca. *Education:* Attended University of Maryland.

Addresses: *Agent*—Hartig–Hilepo Agency Ltd., 54 West 21st Street, Suite 610, New York, NY 10010.

Career: Actor and writer. Woolly Mammoth Theatre Company, Washington, DC, member of resident company. Worked as a freelance writer and columnist for *Backstage. Military service:* U.S. Air Force, 1969–75; served in Vietnam and Korea; became sergeant.

Member: American Federation of Television and Radio Artists, Screen Actors Guild (member of board of directors, 1986–87), Actors' Equity Association.

Contemporary Theatre, Film and Television • Volume 111

Awards, Honors: Named best actor, Washington Theatre Festival, 1986; Helen Hayes Award nomination, outstanding lead actor, Washington Theatre Awards Society, 1986, for *NY Mets;* Helen Hayes Award, outstanding lead actor, 1989, for *The Boys Next Door;* Helen Hayes Award nomination, outstanding supporting actor, 1992, for *Mud People;* Helen Hayes Award nomination, outstanding supporting actor, 2004, for *Patience;* Helen Hayes Award nomination, outstanding supporting actor, 2006, for *The Faculty Room.*

CREDITS

Stage Appearances:
Bill, *America Hurrah,* Woolly Mammoth Theatre Company, Washington, DC, 1984–85.

Granfa, *And Things that Go Bump in the Night,* Woolly Mammoth Theatre Company, 1985–86.

Phil, *NY Mets,* Woolly Mammoth Theatre Company, 1985–86.

Consul, *To Clothe the Naked,* Woolly Mammoth Theatre Company, 1986–87.

Ed, *The Vampires,* Woolly Mammoth Theatre Company, 1987–88.

Wally, *National Defense,* Woolly Mammoth Theatre Company, 1988.

Walter, *Luna Vista,* Woolly Mammoth Theatre Company, 1988–89.

Norman, *The Boys Next Door,* Round House Theatre, 1989.

Dad, *Sharon and Billy,* Woolly Mammoth Theatre Company, 1989.

Jerry, *Tales of the Lost Formicans,* Woolly Mammoth Theatre Company, 1989–90.

Emerald City, 1990.

Heinrich, *Life During Wartime,* Woolly Mammoth Theatre Company, 1991–92.

Buzzy, *Mud People,* Woolly Mammoth Theatre Company, 1992–93.

Otis, *Strindberg in Hollywood,* Woolly Mammoth Theatre Company, 1992–93.

Mr. Astro, *Half Off,* Woolly Mammoth Theatre Company, 1993–94.

Rabbi Falker, *Patience,* Woolly Mammoth Theatre Company, 2002–2003.

Jerry, *Big Death and Little Death,* Woolly Mammoth Theatre Company, 2004–2005.

Karl, *Grace,* Woolly Mammoth Theatre Company, 2004–2005.

Roderick, *After Ashley,* Woolly Mammoth Theatre Company, 2005–2006.

Bill, *The Faculty Room,* Woolly Mammoth Theatre Company, 2005–2006.

Bill the doorman, *Current Nobody,* Woolly Mammoth Theatre Company, 2007.

Fred Clotaldo, *Fever/Dream,* Woolly Mammoth Theatre Company, 2009.

Appeared as a member of the chorus, *Antigone,* Round House Theatre; Lindy, *Melissa Arctic,* Folger Shakespeare Theatre, Washington, DC; Gross, *The Water Engine,* Round House Theatre; a beggar, *Tartuffe,* Arena Stage, Washington, DC; and Orus, *Two–Bit Taj Mahal,* Theatre of the First Amendment; also appeared in presentations of New Playwrights, and Burn Brae and Kings Jester dinner theatres.

Film Appearances:
Teller service person, *Prime Risk,* Almi, 1985.

(As Michael S. Willis) Mr. Shubner, *Tin Men,* Buena Vista, 1987.

News person at governor's mansion, *Hairspray,* New Line Cinema, 1988.

Jocko, *On the Block,* Vidmark Entertainment, 1990.

Samson, *Elliot Fauman, Ph.D.,* Taurus Entertainment, 1990.

Airport photographer, *Major League II,* Warner Bros., 1994.

Foreman, *Someone Else's America,* October Films, 1996.

Sid, *Rescuing Desire,* 1996.

Cop in morgue, *Men in Black* (also known as *MIB*), Columbia, 1997.

Television customer, *Just the Ticket,* United Artists, 1999.

Pat Feeney, *Pushing Tin,* Twentieth Century–Fox, 1999.

Teamster, *Cecil B. DeMented* (also known as *Cecil B. the Cinema Wars*), Artisan Entertainment, 2000.

Tony the Tickler, *A Dirty Shame,* New Line Cinema/Fine Line, 2004.

Counselor, *Coming Up Roses,* Bullet Pictures, 2010.

Also appeared in the film *The Jackal, Protocol,* and *That Night.*

Television Appearances; Series:
Darin Russom, a recurring role, *Homicide: Life on the Street* (also known as *H.L.O.T.S.* and *Homicide*), NBC, between 1993 and 1999.

Andy Krawczyk, *The Wire,* HBO, 2003–2008.

Television Appearances; Episodic:
"A Time and a Place," *A Man Called Hawk,* ABC, 1989.

Joe Williams, "House Counsel," *Law & Order,* NBC, 1995.

Father Carney, "Angel," *Law & Order,* NBC, 1995.

Richard Peterson, "Survivor," *Law & Order,* NBC, 1996.

"Mob Street," *New York Undercover,* Fox, 1998.

Mr. Declan, "Darkness," *Law & Order,* NBC, 2008.

Dale, "I Hate a Date," *Mercy,* NBC, 2010.

Mr. Fletcher, "Wannabe," *Law & Order: Special Victims Unit* (also known as *Law & Order: SVU* and *Special Victims Unit*), NBC, 2010.

Also appeared in the series *All My Children,* ABC, and *Loving,* ABC.

Television Appearances; Other:
Second heavy–set man, *The Bronx Is Burning* (mini-series), ESPN, 2007.

Appeared in the pilot *Living Today,* syndicated.

RECORDINGS

Videos:
Voices of merchant, dead dwarf, and tracker, *Death Gate* (video game), 1994.

Appeared as T. R. Roosterman in *Fashions for Living,* a safety training video.

WILSON, Michael G. 1942–
(Michael Wilson)

PERSONAL

Full name, Michael Gregg Wilson; born January 21, 1942, in New York, NY; son of Lewis Gilbert and Dana (maiden name, Natol) Wilson; stepson of Albert R. Broccoli (a producer); stepsister of Barbara Broccoli (a producer and executive); married Coila Jane Hurley; children: David G., Gregg, Ryan Michael. *Education:* Harvey Mudd College, B.S., 1963; Stanford University, J.D., 1966. *Avocational Interests:* Collecting nineteenth– and twentieth–century photographs, taking still photographs.

Addresses: *Office*—Danjaq Productions, 2401 Colorado Ave., Suite 330, Santa Monica, CA 90404; Eon Productions, Eon House, 138 Piccadilly, London W1V 9FH, England.

Career: Producer, writer, executive, and actor. Eon Productions, London, staff member, 1972–74, legal advisor, 1974–78, producer and managing director, beginning 1978; Danjaq Productions, Santa Monica, CA, president. Also worked as an attorney; member of the Bar of California, New York, and District of Columbia; Federal Aviation Administration and Department of Transportation, Washington, DC, legal advisor, 1966–67; Surrey, Karasik, Gould, Green (law firm), Washington, DC, associate, 1967–71; Surrey and Morse, partner, 1971–74.

Awards, Honors: WGA Screen Award nomination (with Richard Maibaum), best comedy adapted from another medium, Writers Guild of America, 1982, for *For Your Eyes Only;* Edgar Allan Poe Award nomination (with Maibaum), best motion picture, Mystery Writers of America, 1990, for *Licence to Kill;* Special Award (with Barbara Broccoli), *Evening Standard* British Film Awards, 2003; Alexander Korda Award nomination (with others), best British film, British Academy of Film and Televison Arts, 2007, for *Casino Royale;* decorated officer, Order of the British Empire, 2008.

CREDITS

Film Executive Producer:
Moonraker (also known as *Ian Fleming's "Moonraker"*), United Artists, 1979.
For Your Eyes Only, United Artists, 1981.
Octopussy (also known as *Ian Fleming's "Octopussy"*), Metro–Goldwyn–Mayer, 1983.

Film Producer:
(With Albert R. Broccoli) *A View to a Kill* (also known as *The Beautiful Prey* and *Ian Fleming's "A View to a Kill"*), United Artists, 1985.
(With A. R. Broccoli) *The Living Daylights* (also known as *Ian Fleming's "The Living Daylights"*), United Artists, 1987.
(With A. R. Broccoli) *Licence to Kill* (also known as *Albert R. Broccoli's "Licence to Kill"* and *License to Kill*), United Artists, 1989.
(With Barbara Broccoli) *GoldenEye,* United Artists, 1995.
(With B. Broccoli) *Tomorrow Never Dies* (also known as *TND*), United Artists, 1997.
(With B. Broccoli) *The World Is Not Enough* (also known as *Pressure Point* and *T.W.I.N.E.*), Metro–Goldwyn–Mayer, 1999.
(With others) *Die Another Day* (also known as *D.A.D.*), Metro–Goldwyn–Mayer, 2002.
Casino Royale (also known as *007 Casino Royale*), Columbia, 2006.
Quantum of Solace (also known as *Evening Prayer*), Sony Pictures Releasing, 2008.

Film Appearances:
(Uncredited) Soldier, *Goldfinger* (also known as *Ian Fleming's "Goldfinger"*), United Artists, 1964.
(Uncredited) Man in audience at Pyramid Theatre, *The Spy Who Loved Me,* United Artists, 1977.
Narrator, *007 Stage Dedication* (also known as *007 Stage Dedication: An Original 1977 Featurette*), 1977.
(Uncredited) NASA technician, man in St. Mark's Square, and Captain Scott's copilot, *Moonraker* (also known as *Ian Fleming's "Moonraker"*), United Artists, 1979.
(Uncredited) Greek priest, *For Your Eyes Only,* United Artists, 1981.
(Uncredited) Member of Soviet Security Council and man on tour boat, *Octopussy* (also known as *Ian Fleming's "Octopussy"*), Metro–Goldwyn–Mayer, 1983.

(Uncredited) Man heard over loudspeaker at San Francisco City Hall, *A View to a Kill* (also known as *The Beautiful Prey* and *Ian Fleming's "A View to a Kill"*), United Artists, 1985.

(Uncredited) Opera patron, *The Living Daylights* (also known as *Ian Fleming's "The Living Daylights"*), United Artists, 1987.

(Uncredited) Voice of DEA agent, *Licence to Kill* (also known as *Albert R. Broccoli's "Licence to Kill"* and *License to Kill*), United Artists, 1989.

(Uncredited) Member of Russian Security Council, *GoldenEye*, United Artists, 1995.

(Uncredited) Tom Wallace, *Tomorrow Never Dies* (also known as *TND*), United Artists, 1997.

(Uncredited) Man in casino, *The World Is Not Enough* (also known as *Pressure Point* and *T.W.I.N.E.*), Metro–Goldwyn–Mayer, 1999.

General Chandler, *Die Another Day* (also known as *D.A.D.*), Metro–Goldwyn–Mayer, 2002.

Chief of police, *Casino Royale* (also known as *007 Casino Royale*), Columbia, 2006.

(Uncredited) Man sitting in chair in Haitian hotel lobby, *Quantum of Solace* (also known as *Evening Prayer*), Sony Pictures Releasing, 2008.

Marc Forster—Der Weg zu 007 (documentary), First Hand Films, 2009.

Television Appearances; Specials:

Roger Moore: A Matter of Class, 1995.
GoldenEye: The Secret Files, 1995.
James Bond: Shaken and Stirred, 1997.
Nobody Does It Better: The Music of James Bond, 1998.
The Bond Cocktail, 1999.
And the Word Was Bond (also known as *And Then There Was Bond*, *The Word Is Bond*, and *The Word Was Bond*), 1999.
The James Bond Story (also known as *007: The James Bond Story*), AMC, 2000.
Cubby Broccoli: The Man behind Bond, 2000.
Now Pay Attention 007! (also known as *Now Pay Attention 007! A Tribute to Desmond Llewelyn*), 2000.
James Bond Down River (also known as *Bond Down River*), 2000.
Fading Images, 2001.
Premiere Bond: Die Another Day, ITV, 2002.
Best Ever Bond, ITV1, 2002.
James Bond: A BAFTA Tribute, BBC, 2002.
MTV Movie Special: Die Another Day, MTV, 2002.
Happy Anniversary Mr. Bond, 2002.
The Ultimate Film, Channel 4, 2004.
(As Michael Wilson) *Greatest Ever Screen Chases*, Sky Television, 2005.
Just Another Day, 2006.
Becoming Bond, ITV, 2006.
The National Movie Awards, 2007.
Bond on Location, ITV, 2008.

Quantum of Solace: Royal World Premiere Special, ITV, 2008.
Bond Girl Diaries, 2008.

Television Appearances; Miniseries:
British Film Forever, BBC, 2007.

Television Appearances; Movies:
(As Michael Wilson) Jim–Wilson Follet, *All the Way Home*, 1971.

Television Appearances; Episodic:
"Producing," *Making of James Bond* (also known as *The Making of James Bond—007* and *The Making of "The Spy Who Loved Me"*), 1977.
Breakfast with Frost, 2002.
Film '72, BBC, 2006.
The South Bank Show, ITV, 2008.

Stage Producer:
A Steady Rain, Gerald Schoenfeld Theatre, New York City, 2009.

Also producer of *Chitty Chitty Bang Bang*, Foxwoods Theatre.

RECORDINGS

Videos:
James Bond in India, 1983.
Kenworth Truck Stunt Featurette, 1989.
Highly Classified: The World of 007, Metro–Goldwyn–Mayer Home Entertainment, 1997.
(In archive footage) *The Secrets of 007: The James Bond Files*, 1997.
Terence Young: Bond Vivant, 1999.
Inside "Licence to Kill," 1999.
(In archive footage) *The Making of "GoldenEye": A Video Journal*, 1999.
Inside "On Her Majesty's Secret Service," 2000.
Inside "For Your Eyes Only," 2000.
The Music of James Bond, 2000.
(As Michael Wilson) *Ken Adam: Designing Bond*, 2000.
(As Michael Wilson) *Inside "The Spy Who Loved Me,"* 2000.
Inside "The Man with the Golden Gun," 2000.
Inside "The Living Daylights," 2000.
Inside "Octopussy," 2000.
Inside "Moonraker," 2000.
Inside "A View to a Kill," 2000.
Designing Bond: Peter Lamont, 2000.
Silhouettes: The James Bond Titles, 2000.
Inside "Dr. No," 2000.
Die Another Day: From Script to Screen, 2002.
Shaken and Stirred on Ice, 2002.

Inside "Die Another Day," Metro–Goldwyn–Mayer Home Entertainment, 2003.

(As Michael Wilson) Narrator, *Escape from Atlantis Storyboard Sequence* (also known as *Escape from Atlantis*), Metro–Goldwyn–Mayer Home Entertainment, 2006.

(As Michael Wilson) Narrator, *Whicker's World: Highlights from the 1967 BBC Documentary,* Metro–Goldwyn–Mayer Home Entertainment, 2006.

(As Michael Wilson) Narrator, *Animated Storyboard Sequence: The Boat Chase,* Metro–Goldwyn–Mayer Home Entertainment, 2006.

(As Michael Wilson) Narrator, *Cable Car Alternative: Storyboard 1,* Metro–Goldwyn–Mayer Home Entertainment, 2006.

(As Michael Wilson) Narrator, *Girls Fighting,* Metro–Goldwyn–Mayer Home Entertainment, 2006.

(As Michael Wilson) Narrator, *Cable Car Alternative: Storyboard 2,* Metro–Goldwyn–Mayer Home Entertainment, 2006.

(As Michael Wilson) Narrator, *Ian Fleming on Desert Island Discs,* Metro–Goldwyn–Mayer Home Entertainment, 2006.

(As Michael Wilson) Narrator, *Neptune's Journey,* Metro–Goldwyn–Mayer Home Entertainment, 2006.

(As Michael Wilson) Narrator, *Location Scouting with Peter Lamont: Die Another Day,* Metro–Goldwyn–Mayer Home Entertainment, 2006.

(As Michael Wilson) Narrator, *Thunderball Boat Show Promo* (also known as *Thunderball Boat Show Reel*), Metro–Goldwyn–Mayer Home Entertainment, 2006.

(As Michael Wilson) Narrator, *Satellite Test Reel,* Metro–Goldwyn–Mayer Home Entertainment/Sony Pictures Home Entertainment, 2006.

(As Michael Wilson) Narrator, *Oil Rig Attack,* Metro–Goldwyn–Mayer Home Entertainment/Sony Pictures Home Entertainment, 2006.

(As Michael Wilson) Narrator, *Explosion Tests,* Metro–Goldwyn–Mayer Home Entertainment/Sony Pictures Home Entertainment, 2006.

Narrator, *Bond '79,* Metro–Goldwyn–Mayer Home Entertainment, 2006.

Narrator, *George Lazenby: In His Own Words,* Metro–Goldwyn–Mayer Home Entertainment, 2006.

(As Michael Wilson) Narrator, *Skydiving Test Footage* (also known as *Learning to Freefall* and *Learning to Freefall—Skydiving Test Footage*), Metro–Goldwyn–Mayer Home Entertainment, 2006.

Directing Bond: The Martin Chronicles (also known as *The Martin Chronicles*), Metro–Goldwyn–Mayer Home Entertainment, 2006.

Narrator, *Bond in Cortina,* Metro–Goldwyn–Mayer Home Entertainment, 2006.

Narrator, *Bond '89,* Metro–Goldwyn–Mayer Home Entertainment, 2006.

Narrator, *GoldenEye: Building a Better Bond* (also known as *Building a Better Bond*), Metro–Goldwyn–Mayer Home Entertainment, 2006.

Narrator, *Casting on "Her Majesty's Secret Service,"* Metro–Goldwyn–Mayer Home Entertainment, 2006.

Narrator, *Bond in Greece,* Metro–Goldwyn–Mayer Home Entertainment, 2006.

Ken Adam's Production Films: Moonraker, Metro–Goldwyn–Mayer Home Entertainment, 2006.

(As Michael Wilsons) Narrator, *Circus Footage,* Metro–Goldwyn–Mayer Home Entertainment, 2006.

James Bond: For Real, Sony Pictures Home Entertainment, 2006.

(In archive footage) *Ken Burns On–set Movie,* Metro–Goldwyn–Mayer Home Entertainment, 2006.

(In archive footage) *Premiere Bond: Opening Nights,* Metro–Goldwyn–Mayer Home Entertainment, 2006.

(In archive footage) Narrator, *On Location with "The Man with the Golden Gun,"* Metro–Goldwyn–Mayer Home Entertainment, 2006.

Death in Venice: The Sinking Palazzo (also known as *Death in Venice*), Sony Pictures Home Entertainment, 2008.

The Road to Casino Royale, Sony Pictures Home Entertainment, 2008.

WRITINGS

Screenplays:

(With Richard Maibaum) *For Your Eyes Only,* United Artists, 1981.

Octopussy (also known as *Ian Fleming's "Octopussy,"* also based on a story developed by Wilson), Metro–Goldwyn–Mayer, 1983.

A View to a Kill (also known as *The Beautiful Prey* and *Ian Fleming's "A View to a Kill"*), United Artists, 1985.

The Living Daylights (also known as *Ian Fleming's "The Living Daylights"*), United Artists, 1987.

(With Maibaum) *Licence to Kill* (also known as *Albert R. Broccoli's "Licence to Kill"* and *License to Kill;* also based on a story by Wilson), United Artists, 1989.

Books:

Pictorialism in California, Getty Museum, 1994.

OTHER SOURCES

Periodicals:

Starlog, December, 2008, pp. 17–21.

WILSON KING, Robb
(Rob Wilson King, Robb King)

PERSONAL

Born in Hollywood, CA; parents a theme park designer and a jazz pianist. *Education:* Trained as an architect.

Addresses: *Agent*—Montana Artists Agency, 9150 Wilshire Blvd., Suite 100, Beverly Hills, CA 90212.

Career: Production designer, art director, set designer, producer, and consultant. Designer of music videos for Mariah Carey, No Doubt, Puff Daddy, Will Smith, and recording artists.

Member: Art Directors Guild.

Awards, Honors: Art Directors Guild Award nomination (with others), excellence in production design for a television movie or miniseries, 2009, for *The Librarian: The Curse of the Judas Chalice.*

CREDITS

Film Production Designer:
(And set designer) *Swamp Thing,* Embassy, 1982.
Friday the 13th Part III, Paramount, 1982.
The Osterman Weekend (also known as *Mission CIA*), Twentieth Century–Fox, 1983.
Losin' It, Embassy, 1983.
The New Kids (also known as *Striking Back*), Columbia, 1985.
Savage Dawn, Media Home Entertainment, 1986.
Iron Eagle, TriStar, 1986.
Where Are the Children?, Columbia, 1986.
Retribution, Taurus Entertainment, 1987.
Iron Eagle II (also known as *Metal Blue*), TriStar, 1988.
The Return of the Swamp Thing, Millimeter Films, 1989.
Hard to Kill, Warner Bros., 1990.
Courage Mountain (also known as *Courage Mountain: Heidi's New Adventure*), Triumph Releasing, 1990.
Pump Up the Volume, New Line Cinema, 1990.
Marked for Death, Twentieth Century–Fox, 1990.
Aces: Iron Eagle III, Seven Arts/New Line Cinema, 1992.
Ladybugs, Paramount, 1992.
Christopher Columbus: The Discovery, Warner Bros., 1992.
Rudy, TriStar, 1993.
A Low Down Dirty Shame, Buena Vista, 1994.
Moonlight and Valentino, Gramercy, 1995.
Set It Off, New Line Cinema, 1996.
Money Talks (also known as *Runaway*), New Line Cinema, 1997.
Rush Hour, New Line Cinema, 1998.
Price of Glory, New Line Cinema, 2000.
(And associate producer) *Scary Movie,* Dimension Films, 2000.
Tomcats, Columbia, 2001.
Run Ronnie Run, New Line Cinema, 2002.
Barbershop 2: Back in Business, Metro–Goldwyn–Mayer, 2004.
Paparazzi, Twentieth Century–Fox, 2004.

Just Friends, New Line Cinema, 2005.
Trapped Ashes (also known as *Death Room*), Lions Gate Films, 2006.
Behind the Smile, THINKFilm, 2007.
(And producer) *The Wind Fisherman* (short film), American Film Institute, 2007.
Hostel: Part II, Lions Gate Films, 2007.
MacGruber, Universal, 2010.

Film Appearances:
Son, *The Monkey's Paw* (short film), 1978.

Television Production Designer; Series:
Breaking Bad, AMC, 2008–2009.

Television Production Designer; Movies:
Special Bulletin, NBC, 1983.
The Sky's No Limit, CBS, 1984.
(As Robb King) *Longshot* (also known as *Long Shot Kids*), CBS, 1985.
Dreams of Gold: The Mel Fisher Story, CBS, 1986.
A Different Affair, CBS, 1987.
Bates Motel, NBC, 1987.
Follow Your Heart, NBC, 1990.
Opposites Attract, NBC, 1990.
In the Company of Darkness, CBS, 1993.
Marked for Murder, NBC, 1993.
Jack Reed: Badge of Honor, NBC, 1993.
Knight Rider 2010, UPN, 1994.
(As Rob Wilson King) *Another Woman's Husband,* Lifetime, 2000.
Running Mates, TNT, 2000.
The Librarian: Return to King Solomon's Mines (also known as *The Librarian 2: Return to King Solomon's Mines*), TNT, 2006.
The Librarian: The Curse of the Judas Chalice (also known as *The Librarian 3*), TNT, 2008.
Secrets in the Walls, Lifetime, 2010.

Also production designer for *Special Bulletin,* NBC.

Television Production Designer; Pilots:
Doorways, 1993.
The Monroes, ABC, 1995.
Breaking Bad, AMC, 2008.
Chaos, CBS, 2010.

Also production designer for the pilots *Bad Cop, Bad Cop,* Fox; *H.M.O.,* ABC; and *Hollywood Tales,* Fox.

Television Production Designer; Specials:
Treasure Island: The Adventure Begins, NBC, 1994.

Television Production Designer; Episodic:
"You're Not Alone," *Medical Investigation,* NBC, 2004.

Also production designer for *Downtown,* CBS; *The Pretender,* NBC; and *Wind on Water,* NBC.

RECORDINGS

Videos:
Production designer, *Ground Zero Texas* (video game), Sony Imagesoft, 1993.

OTHER SOURCES

Electronic:
Robb Wilson King Official Site, http://www. robbwilsonking.com, September 22, 2010.

WINTON, Colleen

PERSONAL

Raised in New Westminster, British Columbia, Canada; married Russell Roberts (an actor); children: Sayer, Gowan. *Education:* Studied acting at University of British Columbia.

Career: Actress. Vagabonds (acting company), actress; Burr Theatre, task force member. Also a producer of children's theatrical productions, an art projects advisor, and a task force member for high school arts programs.

Member: Massey Theatre Society (vice chair of board of directors).

Awards, Honors: Jessie Richardson Theatre Award nomination, outstanding performance in a musical in a supporting role, Vancouver Professional Theatre Alliance, 1985, for *A Chorus Line;* Bernie Legge Cultural Award, New Westminster Chamber of Commerce, 2002; a Jessie Richardson Theatre Award and additional Jessie Richardson Theatre Award nominations; Dora Mavor Moore Award, Toronto Theatre Alliance.

CREDITS

Television Appearances; Series:
Constance Gracen, *Profit,* Fox, 1996.
Judy McDougal, *Cold Squad,* CTV, beginning 2000.

Television Appearances; Movies:
Dana, *Deadly Deception,* CBS, 1987.

Andrea Borland, *Yes, Virginia, There Is a Santa Claus,* ABC, 1991.
Karen, *Shadow of a Stranger,* NBC, 1992.
Donna Fusco, *Relentless: Mind of a Killer,* NBC, 1993.
Gail Betts, *Miracle on Interstate 880* (also known as *Miracle on I–880*), NBC, 1993.
Senator Binsfeld, *Moment of Truth: A Child Too Many,* NBC, 1993.
Dr. Ellen Kelly, *Heart of a Child,* Lifetime, 1994.
Elaine Warren, *Green Dolphin Beat* (also known as *Green Dolphin Street*), Fox, 1994.
Jocelyn Samuels, *Betrayal of Trust* (also known as *Under the Influence*), NBC, 1994.
Torie Brainard, *Don't Talk to Strangers* (also known as *Dangerous Pursuit*), USA Network, 1994.
Assistant district attorney Larsen, *Deceived by Trust: A Moment of Truth Movie,* NBC, 1995.
Toni, *The Other Mother: A Moment of Truth Movie,* Lifetime, 1995.
Doctor, *She Woke Up Pregnant* (also known as *Crimes of Silence*), ABC, 1996.
Pamela Harnsberger, *When Friendship Kills* (also known as *A Secret Between Friends: A Moment of Truth Movie*), NBC, 1996.
Eleanor Bradley, *Badge of Betrayal,* ABC, 1997.
Gayle Sharpel, *Dad's Week Off* (also known as *National Lampoon's "Dad's Week Off"*), Showtime, 1997.
Suzanne Preston, *Daughters* (also known as *Our Mother's Murder*), USA Network, 1997.
Committee chair, *Big and Hairy,* Showtime, 1998.
Mrs. Krouse, *Every Mother's Worst Fear,* USA Network, 1998.
Veterinarian, *In the Doghouse,* Showtime, 1998.
Army spokesperson, *Fatal Error* (also known as *Reaper*), TBS, 1999.
Mrs. Hotchkiss, *The Wedding Dress,* CBS, 2001.

Television Appearances; Episodic:
Television reporter, "The Vigilantes," *Danger Bay,* 1986.
Barbara, "Cabin Fever," *The Hitchhiker,* HBO, 1987.
Natalia Velskaja, "Gold Rush," *MacGyver,* ABC, 1989.
"And They Swam Right over the Dam," *Unsub,* NBC, 1989.
"Duck Flambe," *Mom P.I.,* CBC, 1990.
Sarah's mother, "Providence," *Neon Rider,* syndicated, 1991.
Dr. Marcy Wright, "Back from the Dead Again," *Street Justice,* syndicated, 1992.
Gwenn, "An Innocent Man," *Highlander* (also known as *Highlander: The Series*), syndicated, 1992.
Lie detector technician, "Squeeze," *The X–Files,* Fox, 1993.
Mrs. Hodges, "Family Business," *The Commish,* ABC, 1993.
Ms. Brim, *Birdland,* ABC, 1994.
Patricia Fowler, "Blood Brothers," *The Outer Limits,* Showtime and syndicated, 1995.
Patricia Fowler, "If These Walls Could Talk," *The Outer Limits,* Showtime and syndicated, 1995.

Bride, "Black Widow," *Dead Man's Gun,* Showtime, 1997.

Mrs. Dolores Garry, "Covenant," *Millennium,* Fox, 1997.

Spokeswoman Adrian Wheeler, "A Special Edition," *The Outer Limits,* Showtime and syndicated, 1997.

Mrs. Foley, "The Reckoning," *Two,* 1997.

Dr. Greene, "Prisoners," *Stargate SG–1,* Showtime and syndicated, 1998.

Dr. Peyton, "Breakout," *Viper,* syndicated, 1998.

Mrs. Lewis, "Known to the Ministry," *Da Vinci's Inquest,* CBC, 1998.

Therapist, "Kitsunegari," *The X–Files,* Fox, 1998.

Wendy Coombs, "Fireball," *The Net,* USA Network, 1998.

Fay Kelly, "Last Resort," *Mercy Point,* UPN, 1998.

Jean Sheldon (some sources cite role as Jean Sanderson), "Saturn Dreaming of Mercury," *Millennium,* Fox, 1999.

Joyce Williams, "Spirit Falls," *Strange World,* ABC, 1999.

Mrs. Kelly, *Mercy Point,* UPN, 1999.

Oakley, "Eat Flaming Death," *Level 9,* UPN, 2000.

Dr. Wood, "I–24gate," *Breaking News,* Bravo, 2002.

Mrs. Mattucci, "Can Bend, But I Won't Break," *Da Vinci's Inquest,* CBC, 2004.

National Security Advisor, "Lost City: Part 2," *Stargate SG–1,* Sci–Fi Channel, 2004.

Ruth, "Lockdown," *The 4400,* USA Network, 2005.

Ruth, "The Fifth Page," *The 4400,* USA Network, 2005.

Dr. Weaver, "Post Partum," *Blood Ties,* Lifetime, 2007.

Appeared as Jane Thomas, *The Commish,* ABC.

Television Appearances; Pilots:
Sally, *Wiseguy,* CBS, 1987.

Television Appearances; Miniseries:
Beth Keys, *Taken* (also known as *Steven Spielberg Presents Taken*), Sci–Fi Channel, 2002.

First woman Royal Canadian Mounted Police, *Human Cargo,* CBC, 2004.

Film Appearances:
The Skip Tracer, 1977.
Deputy porter, *Watchers,* Universal, 1988.
Anchorwoman, *Stay Tuned,* Warner Bros., 1992.

Stage Appearances:
A Chorus Line (musical), Vancouver Playhouse, Vancouver, British Columbia, Canada, c. 1985.

Appeared as Curtizan, *The Comedie of Errors;* as Katherine, *The Taming of the Shrew,* Bastion Theatre; as Lady Constance, *The Life and Death of King John;* as Mariana, *Measure for Measure;* and as Mistress Page,

The Merry Wives of Windsor. Also appeared in *Amo, Amas, Amat,* Christ Church Cathedral; *The Heiress,* Chemainus Theatre; *King Lear,* Stratford Festival, Stratford, Ontario, Canada; *A Midsummer Nights Dream,* Citadel Theatre; and in *South Pacific* (musical). Also performed at Shaw Festival, Niagara–on–the–Lake, Ontario, Canada.

Major Tours:
Joan, *Dames at Sea,* Arts Club Theatre Company, Canadian cities, 2003.

Stage Director:
Directed a production of *The Merry Wives of Windsor,* Graffiti Theatre, Saltspring Island, British Columbia, Canada.

WOODLEY, Denise
    See CRONENBERG, Denise

YATES, Janty 1950–

PERSONAL

Born 1950; daughter of Denys Ainsworth (a military officer) and Margaret (maiden name, Tyrer) Yates. *Education:* Attended Katinka College of Dress Design, London. *Avocational Interests:* Gardening, art, film, theatre, riding, swimming, walking, reading, travel, scuba diving.

Addresses: *Agent*—Paul Hook, International Creative Management, 10250 Constellation Way, 9th Floor, Los Angeles, CA 90067.

Career: Costume designer. Also worked as costume and wardrobe assistant, wardrobe supervisor, and assistant costume designer.

Member: Academy of Motion Picture Arts and Sciences.

Awards, Honors: Sierra Award, best costume design, Las Vegas Film Critics Society Awards, 2000, Academy Award, Film Award nomination, British Academy of Film and Television Arts, Saturn Award nomination, Academy of Science Fiction, Fantasy, and Horror Films, Golden Satellite Award nomination, International Press Academy, and Phoenix Film Critics Society Award nomination, all best costume design, 2001, all for *Gladiator;* Costume Designers Guild Award nomination, excellence in costume design for a period or fantasy film, and Golden Satellite Award nomination, best costume design, both 2005, for *De–Lovely;* Satellite Award nomination, 2005, and Goya Award nomination, Academia de las Artes y las Ciencias Cinematograficas de Espana, 2006, both outstanding costume design, for *Kingdom of Heaven.*

CREDITS

Film Costume Designer:
Bad Behaviour, October Films, 1993.
The Englishman Who Went up a Hill but Came down a Mountain, Miramax, 1995.
Jude, Gramercy, 1996.
Welcome to Sarajevo, Miramax, 1997.
The Man Who Knew Too Little, Warner Bros., 1997.
Plunkett & Macleane, Gramercy/USA Films, 1999.
With or Without You, Miramax, 1999.
Gladiator, DreamWorks, 2000.
Enemy at the Gates (also known as *Stalingrad*), Paramount, 2001.
Hannibal, Metro–Goldwyn–Mayer, 2001.
Charlotte Gray, Warner Bros., 2001.
De–Lovely, Metro–Goldwyn–Mayer, 2004.
Kingdom of Heaven, Twentieth Century–Fox, 2005.
Miami Vice, Universal, 2006.
American Gangster, Universal, 2007.
Body of Lies (also known as *World of Lies*), Warner Bros., 2008.
Robin Hood, Universal, 2010.

Television Costume Designer; Series:
Yellowthread Street, YTV, 1990.
The Comic Strip Presents, BBC2, 1990–93, Channel 4, 1998.
Full Stretch, 1993.

Television Costume Designer; Miniseries:
Karaoke, Bravo, 1996.

Television Costume Designer; Movies:
The Endless Game, Showtime, 1990.
An Evening with Gary Lineker, 1994.

Television Costume Designer; Episodic:
"The Mad Woman in the Attic: Part 1," *Cracker,* Granada, 1993, then broadcast as a movie by Arts and Entertainment, 1994.
"To Say I Love You: Part 1," *Cracker,* Granada, 1993, then broadcast as a movie by Arts and Entertainment, 1994.
"One Day a Lemming Will Fly," *Cracker* (also broadcast as a movie by Arts and Entertainment), Granada Television, 1994.
"Splat," *Glam Metal Detectives,* BBC, 1995.

Television Appearances; Specials:
The 73rd Annual Academy Awards, ABC, 2001.
Kingdom of Hope: The Making of "Kingdom of Heaven," 2005.

Television Appearances; Episodic:
"Kingdom of Heaven," *HBO First Look,* HBO, 2005.

RECORDINGS

Videos:
"Kingdom of Heaven": Interactive Production Grid, Twentieth Century–Fox Home Entertainment, 2005.
Strength and Honor: Creating the World of "Gladiator," DreamWorks Home Entertainment, 2005.
The Path to Redemption, Twentieth Century–Fox Home Entertainment, 2006.
Colors of the Crusade, Twentieth Century–Fox Home Entertainment, 2006.
Fallen Empire: Making "American Gangster," MCA/Universal Home Entertainment, 2008.

ADAPTATIONS

The costumes designed by Yates for the television miniseries *Karaoke* in 1996 were also featured in the miniseries *Cold Lazarus,* broadcast by Bravo in 1996.

YOUNG, America 1984–
(Danielle Young, Danielle America Young)

PERSONAL

Born December 6, 1984, in Santa Fe, NM. *Avocational Interests:* Martial arts.

Career: Actress, producer, director, casting director, and stunt coordinator.

CREDITS

Film Appearances:
(As Danielle Young) Betty Cooper, *The Archies in Jugman* (animated), Teletoon, 2003.
Cindy, *Toi and Poochie,* Illuminare Entertainment, 2004.
Jess, *Great Lengths* (short film), University of Southern California, 2004.
(As Danielle Young) Office worker, *Thomas Grey's Rainy Day* (short film), 2004.
Barbara Fugate, *Starkweather,* THINKFilm, 2004.

Stacy, *Promtroversey* (short film), Power Up Films, 2005.

(As Danielle America Young) Misty, *Evil's City* (also known as *Demon Town* and *Evil City*), Genius Entertainment, 2005.

Mia, *Danos del amor* (short film), 2006.

Sara, *Point of Contact* (also known as *Ghost Hunters: Point of Contact*), Singa Home Entertainment, 2006.

Lisa, *The Long Way Back* (short film), 2007.

Serena Parnet, *Ultimate Weapon* (short film), 2007.

Georgeann Hawkins, *Bundy: An American Icon* (also known as *Bundy: A Legacy of Evil*), Lions Gate Films, 2008.

Voice of Wendy Darling, *Tinker Bell* (animated; also known as *Tincker Bell*), Walt Disney Studios Home Entertainment, 2008.

Carey, *Freshmyn* (short film), 2009.

Third reporter, *April Showers*, Pure Motive, 2009.

Helena, *Mugging* (short film), 2009.

Fantasy girl, *The Streamroom*, 2010.

Erin O'Dowell, *Dreamkiller*, Delaware Pictures, 2010.

Shelly, *The Dead Undead*, 2010.

Jocelyn, Joyanne's daughter, *The Binds That Tie Us* (short film), 2010.

Title role, *Mia* (short film), 2010.

Amanda, *Abandoned*, Anchor Bay Entertainment, 2010.

The Aftermath: A 2012 Story (short film), 2010.

Film Work:

Coproducer, *Danos del amor* (short film), 2006.

Producer, *The Long Way Back* (short film), 2007.

Producer and casting director, *The Don of Virgil Jr. High* (short film), 2007.

Stunt coordinator, *Jar* (short film), 2007.

(Uncredited) Stunts, *Alien Agent*, Allumination Filmworks, 2007.

Stunt double, *Ninja Cheerleaders*, Peace Arch Entertainment Group, 2008.

Coproducer and casting director, *Killing Ariel*, MTI Home Video, 2008.

Stunt coordinator, *April Showers*, Pure Motive, 2009.

Director, *Intrepid Nothing* (short film), Dances with Films, 2009.

Producer, *Volvo* (short film), 2009.

Producer, *Mugging* (short film), 2009.

Director and executive producer, *Fairly Criminal*, 2010.

Coproducer, *The Aftermath: A 2012 Story* (short film), 2010.

Producer, *Mia* (short film), 2010.

Television Appearances; Series:

The monster, *Damsels and Dragons*, 2009.

Lori Banks, *First Edition*, 2010—.

Television Appearances; Movies:

(As Danielle Young) Lira, *Time Kid*, 2003.

Maria, *Catherine & Annie*, 2009.

Television Appearances; Pilots:

Kate, *Hackett*, Fox, 2008.

Television Appearances; Episodic:

Shale, "The Great Race," *Trollz*, Toon Disney, 2006.

Also appeared as voice of Betty Cooper, "Archie and the Riverdale Vampires," *Archie's Weird Mysteries*, PAX; Shale, "Troll Fast, Troll Furious," *Trollz* (animated), Toon Disney.

Television Work; Movies:

Director and executive producer, *Groupidity*, 2008.

Director and executive producer, *Catherine & Annie*, 2009.

Television Work; Episodic:

Director and producer, "Reunited," *Damsels and Dragons*, 2009.

Featurette director and producer, "Sex Party," *The Romantic Foibles of Esteban*, 2009.

Producer, "Lush," *The Romantic Foibles of Esteban*, 2009.

Producer, "Yoke," *The Romantic Foibles of Esteban*, 2009.

RECORDINGS

Video Games:

(As Danielle Young) Dagger, *Marvel: Ultimate Alliance 2*, 2009.

Video Games; as Motion Capture Actress:

Tony Hawk's Project 8, Activision, 2006.

Spider–Man 3, Activision, 2007.

Conan, THQ, 2007.

Guitar Hero II: Legends of Rock, Neversoft Entertainment, 2007.

Spider–Man: Web of Shadows, Activision, 2008.

Quantum of Solace (also known as *007: Quantum of Solace*, *James Bond: Quantum of Solace*, *QOS*, *Quantum of Solace: The Game*, and *Quantum of Solace: The Video Game*), Activision, 2008.

Marvel: Ultimate Alliance 2, 2009.

Uncharted 2: Among Thieves, 2009.

YOUNG, Danielle
    See YOUNG, America

YUSTMAN, Odette 1985–

PERSONAL

Full name, Odette Juliette Yustman; born May 10, 1985, in Los Angeles, CA; daughter of Victor and Lydia Yustman; married Dave Annable (an actor), October 10, 2010. *Education:* Attended Riverside Community College. *Avocational Interests:* Sports and fashion.

Addresses: *Agent*—International Creative Management, 10250 Constellation Blvd., 9th Floor, Los Angeles, CA 90067. *Manager*—Evolution Entertainment, 901 North Highland Ave., Los Angeles, CA 90038. *Publicist*—Viewpoint, Inc., 8820 Wilshire Blvd., Beverly Hills, CA 90211.

Career: Actress. Also worked as a model.

Awards, Honors: Teen Choice Award nomination, choice movie actress—horror/thriller, 2008, for *Cloverfield.*

CREDITS

Film Appearances:
Rosa, *Kindergarten Cop,* Universal, 1990.
Angela, *Dear God,* Paramount, 1996.
Kissing couple, *The Holiday,* Universal, 2006.
Socialite, *Transformers* (also known as *Transformers: The IMAX Experience*), Paramount, 2007.
Reefer girl, *Walk Hard: The Dewey Cox Story* (also known as *Walk Hard* and *Walk Hard: American Cox, The Unbearably Long, Self–Indulgent Director's Cut*), Columbia, 2007.
Beth McIntyre, *Cloverfield* (also known as *1–18–08, Monstrous,* and *Cloverfield: Hakaisha*), Paramount, 2008.
The VFX of "Cloverfield" (short documentary), Paramount Home Entertainment, 2008.
Casey Beldon, *The Unborn,* Rogue Pictures, 2009.
Temperence, *Operation: Endgame* (also known as *Rogues Gallery*), Anchor Bay Films, 2010.
Ellie, *And Soon the Darkness,* Anchor Bay Films, 2010.
Joanna, *You Again,* 2010.
Vanessa, *Group Sex,* 2010.
Beverly Hills Chihuahua 2, Walt Disney Studios, 2010.

Television Appearances; Series:
Arielle Casta, *South Beach,* UPN, 2006.
Aubrey, *October Road,* ABC, 2007–2008.

Television Appearances; Movies:
Charlotte, *Remembrance* (also known as *Danielle Steel's "Remembrance"*), NBC, 1996.
Emma Norman, *Reckless Behavior: Caught on Tape,* Lifetime, 2007.

Television Appearances; Pilots:
Melanie Green, *Breaking In,* Fox, 2010.

Television Appearances; Episodic:
Kelly Helberg, "(Disdainfully) the Helbergs," *Quintuplets,* Fox, 2004.
Courtney, "Mr. Monk, Private Eye," *Monk,* USA Network, 2006.
Adrienne, "Have You Seen Your Mother, Baby, Standing in the Shadows?," *Life on Mars,* ABC, 2008.
Up Close with Carrie Keagan, 2009.
Herself, "Kia," *Free Radio,* VH1, 2009.

RECORDINGS

Video Games:
Voice of Amata Almodovar, *Fallout 3,* Bethesda Softworks, 2008.

Music Videos:
Appeared in "Emergency" by The Perfect Victim, 2008; also appeared in "(If You're Wondering If I Want You To) I Want You To" by Weezer.

Cumulative Index

To provide continuity with *Who's Who in the Theatre*, this index interfiles references to *Who's Who in the Theatre*, 1st–17th Editions, and *Who Was Who in the Theatre* (Gale, 1978) with references to *Contemporary Theatre, Film and Television*, Volumes 1–111.

References in the index are identified as follows:

CTFT and volume number—*Contemporary Theatre, Film and Television*, Volumes 1–111
WWT and edition number—*Who's Who in the Theatre*, 1st–17th Editions
WWasWT—*Who Was Who in the Theatre*

B

BARBER

C

M

S

Cumulative Index

Cumulative Index

Cumulative Index

W

517

Cumulative Index